THE SECRET OF BRYN ESTYN

THE MAKING OF A
MODERN WITCH HUNT

Richard Webster

The Orwell Press

Published in 2005

2 4 6 8 10 9 7 5 3 1

www.richardwebster.net

Published by
The Orwell Press
61 Hayfield Road
Oxford OX2 6TX
www.orwellpress.co.uk

The Isis-Orwell Press Limited
Reg No 5196817

A CIP catalogue record for this book is available
from the British Library.

ISBN 0 9515922 4 6

Set in Bembo by
Avocet Typeset
Chilton, Aylesbury
www.typesettinguk.com

Printed, sewn and bound in Great Britain
by Biddles Ltd, King's Lynn
www.biddles.co.uk

Contents

Outline chronology   viii
Maps   ix
Names, pronunciation and notes   xiii
Preface   xv

INTRODUCTION: the story of the story   I

I ALISON TAYLOR AND GWYNEDD
(1976–90)

I   The newspaper   15
2   The freelance   20
3   The whistleblower   27
4   An invaluable placement   36
5   A bump and a bruise   40
6   Black and blue   43
7   Aide-memoire   48
8   Two cans of shandy   53
9   A mysterious caller   56
10   Over the goalposts   60
11   A righteous zeal?   64
12   Illicit relationships   71
13   Eye witness   76

II THE BRYN ESTYN INVESTIGATION
(1991–93)

14   From California to Clwyd   83
15   Hard evidence   95
16   Prime witness   104
17   The loner   114
18   The crowbar   118
19   Lying for love   128
20   The art teacher   135
21   Knights, masons and MI5   141
22   To Bangor   146
23   The dossier   153
24   The classic symptoms   156
25   Pornography   161

Contents

26   Outward bound   166
27   The minibus   175
28   Glue sniffing   179
29   A missing transcript   182
30   A superintendent calls   189

III   LIES AND LIBELS
(1992–94)

31   The bogey man   197
32   The article   201
33   Dog walking   208
34   The chandelier   214
35   Unblocking the past   221
36   Operation Antelope   234
37   Jackanory stuff   239
38   The grey-haired man   246
39   The second man   250
40   The photograph   254
41   Pestered by the press   265
42   A memory prompt   275
43   Lies and libels   281
44   *Private Eye* and the Kincora legacy   289
45   More coals to Cardiff   296

IV   THE TRIALS
(1994)

46   Waiting   301
47   The trial   309
48   Judge and jury   326
49   Majority verdicts   339
50   Brides in the bath   342
51   At the Monmouth Assizes   348
52   'A particular perverted lust'   354
53   Striking similarities   360
54   Incest and injustice   363
55   Paying a witness   372
56   Court 13: the libel trial   379
57   The death of a witness   400
58   From Jillings to Waterhouse   406

Contents

V WATERHOUSE: ERRORS OF JUDGMENT
(1996–2000)

59   Care goes on trial   419
60   No stone unturned   427
61   A mason-free zone   436
62   Trial by ambush   443
63   Lost in care   448

VI FRAGMENTS OF A WITCH-HUNT
(1994–2004)

64   The photograph album   463
65   Operation Bugle   476
66   Unused evidence   483
67   Policing in reverse   490
68   Going to jail with a clear conscience   499
69   The football manager   508
70   The net widens   512
71   Artists in dishonesty   520
72   The long march to freedom   529
73   Fragments of a witch-hunt   536

VII REFLECTIONS ON CULTURAL HISTORY

74   'Attacking the devil'   555
75   Patriarchalism and the new puritanism   567

AFTERWORD: Return to North Wales   577
APPENDIX I: Democracy, justice and
              legitimate violence   581
APPENDIX II: Bryn Estyn: my *alma mater*   593
APPENDIX III: North Wales: a chronology   597
APPENDIX IV: People and places   603

Notes and references   621
Index   693

ILLUSTRATIONS

The illustrations will be found between pages 204–5, 414–5, 512–13 and 558–9.

North Wales: outline chronology

For a more detailed chronology see Appendix III, p. 597

1973	November	• Peter Howarth appointed to Bryn Estyn
1976	September	• Alison Taylor deputy officer-in-charge, Tŷ'r Felin
1977	November	• Nefyn Dodd (ex-Bryn Estyn) to Tŷ'r Felin
1980	September	• Taylor leaves for CQSW course in Wrexham
1982	March/June	• Taylor on 10-week placement at Bryn Estyn
	August	• Taylor officer-in-charge at Tŷ Newydd, Bangor
1984	September	• Taylor reports boy's bump and bruise to police
1986	February	• Taylor calls police again. DCS Owen investigates
1987	January	• After new 2nd-hand complaints, Owen reinvestigates
	3 November	• Taylor dismissed by Gwynedd County Council
1990	5 October	• Norris (ex-Bryn Estyn) pleads guilty to abuse
1991	May/June	• Taylor takes her allegations to Cllr Dennis Parry
	2 August	• Police launch trawling operation re Clwyd homes
	12 October	• Dean Nelson meets Taylor at her home in Bangor
	1 December	• *Independent on Sunday* prints Nelson's article
1992	February	• Nelson returns to seek evidence against Anglesea
	15 March	• 16 former Bryn Estyn staff arrested in dawn raid
1994	13 June	• Trial of Howarth and Wilson on sexual charges
	14 November	• Anglesea libel trial begins in London
1996	17 June	• Government announces Waterhouse Tribunal
1997	21 January	• The Tribunal opens in Ewloe, Flintshire
2000	15 February	• Tribunal report published as 'Lost in Care'

Wales: county boundaries 1974–1996

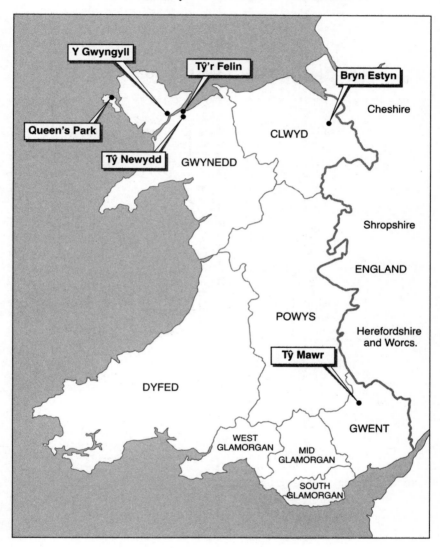

Map 1: Wales, showing the county boundaries as they were redrawn in 1974. In April 1996 the counties were reorganised once again. At that point Clwyd ceased to exist and was replaced by Wrexham, Flintshire, Denbighshire and part of Conwy.

The North Wales investigation, 1991–2

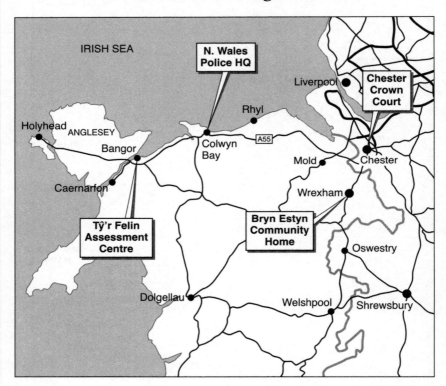

Map 2: The major 1991–2 investigation was launched by the North Wales Police in August 1991. It originally focused on Bryn Estyn but eventually included children's homes throughout Clwyd and Gwynedd.

North Wales, Cheshire and Merseyside: trawling operations, 1991–2000

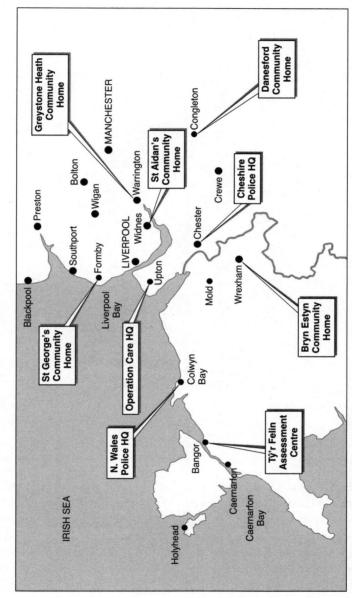

Map 3: The North Wales investigation spread first to Cheshire (where police operations were based mostly in Widnes and Warrington), and then to Merseyside, where Operation Care, based at Upton on the Wirral, investigated more than 90 children's homes.

Police trawling operations in England and Wales, 2001

Map 4: In this map, based on one published in the *Independent* in 2001, the shaded areas indicate police authorities with active trawling operations at the time the map was compiled. The black dots represent the number of different investigations which were in progress. They do not represent either their size or their exact site. Because the North Wales Police and the Merseyside Police consolidated their investigations into single operations (which were nearly over by this time), they do not feature on the map as prominently as they otherwise would. The police authorities which are not shaded did not report any 'historic abuse' investigations at the time. This does not necessarily mean that there were none.

Names, pronunciation and notes

Names

The names of all former residents of care homes who are still living (and of some other people) have been changed. A guide to People and Places will be found at the end of the book on page 603. A full Chronology of the main events in the North Wales story will be found on page 597.

Pronunciation

The pronunciation of some Welsh names will not be obvious to non–Welsh speakers. The most important are these:

Clwyd: klooid
Gwynedd: gwinneth (hard 'th' as in 'the')

Bryn Estyn: brin estin
Cartrefle: kartrevleh
Tŷ'r Felin: teervellin
Tŷ Newydd: tee nehwith
Y Gwyngyll: uh gwingith
Tŷ Mawr: tee mauer (rhymes with 'hour')

A single Welsh 'f' is usually pronounced as a 'v' eg Nefyn Dodd = Nevin Dodd

A note on notes

There are two kinds of notes in this book: footnotes and endnotes. The former should be treated as part of the text. The endnotes, however, are placed at the back of the book in order to prevent them distracting the reader from the narrative. During a first reading of the book they should be treated like condiments at a good dinner table and used rarely, if at all.

Preface

THIS BOOK, WHICH RELATES one of the most extraordinary stories in recent British history, deals with many subjects. But it is, in the first place, a book about allegations of sexual abuse, and about the consequences for individuals and for society when a large number of false allegations are taken to be true and ratified by the courts.

One of the questions I am frequently asked is why I have taken such an interest in the problem of false allegations. There are many answers to this question but one of them is relatively simple. Thirty-five years ago, when I was an undergraduate reading English literature at the University of East Anglia, I stumbled upon a book by the historian Norman Cohn, *The Pursuit of the Millennium*. This was Professor Cohn's widely acclaimed study of the role played in mediaeval European history by millenarian fantasies – by the belief that there would come a time when all those who were unbelievers or 'impure' would be vanquished, and the 'pure' who remained would reign with Christ over a utopian kingdom which would last for a thousand years.

The extraordinary range and power of Cohn's book led me to read his other work – his book about conspiracy theories and modern anti-semitism, *Warrant for Genocide*, and, when it appeared in 1975, *Europe's Inner Demons*, his study of the great European witch-hunt of the sixteenth and seventeenth centuries. All three books seek to establish the role played in history by collective fantasies and all three are concerned with 'the urge to purify the world through the annihilation of some category of human beings imagined as agents of corruption and incarnations of evil' (*Europe's Inner Demons*, p xiv).

The topic which fascinated Professor Cohn, and continued to do so throughout his scholarly career, came to fascinate me as well – not least because it seemed to me that without studying the role of collective delusions in history we could scarcely begin to understand our own nature and our own culture. But this interest also had a more practical and more worldly aspect. The Paladin paperback edition of *Europe's Inner Demons*, which appeared in 1976, bore on its cover these words of Anthony Storr: 'This is a book of real stature which I hope will have wide impact. Only if we begin to understand the horrifying recesses of the human imagination can we prevent the recurrence of those dreadful, irrational persecutions which have so disfigured human history.' Without my fully realising it at the time, these words influenced me deeply and I have since taken it for granted that the principal reason why we should study the witch-hunts of the past is to enable us the better to recognise and oppose the witch-hunts of the present and the future.

This book is the product of that belief. In some respects it came about by accident. When, after having published a large book about Freud in 1995, I felt it was time to get down to writing my next book, I decided to procrastinate by spending a few weeks looking into a topic which had arisen from my work on psychoanalysis – sexual abuse 'scares' and the false allegations which tend to go with them. I then wrote a small (unpublished) booklet which gave an account of the Cleveland sexual abuse crisis of 1988, the Nottingham satanic abuse scare of 1989 and a number of other cases, in some of which innocent people were sent to prison. This was in the spring of 1996, at a time when the *Independent* was giving extensive, almost daily, coverage to the allegations about sexual abuse in children's homes in North Wales. At this point I had a conversation with my literary agent, David Godwin, during which I attempted to explain what I meant by sexual abuse 'scares'. 'You mean all these allegations about North Wales children's homes?' he said.

'No,' I replied, 'It looks as though what is happening in North Wales is exactly the opposite. I'm writing about cases where people who are innocent are put in prison when they shouldn't be. In North Wales it would seem that there are a lot of guilty people who aren't in prison but should be.' One of the reasons I said this was because the *Independent*, which had at that point always shared the same news desk and the same reporting staff as the *Independent on Sunday*, had a good track-record for exposing sexual abuse scares. It had been the *Independent on Sunday*, for example, that had published two articles by Rosie Waterhouse which played a decisive role in undermining the belief in satanic ritual abuse then spreading among social workers (see below, p. 88). This newspaper, I felt, was one of the few whose reporting on such issues could be trusted.

What led me to reconsider this view was an almost chance encounter with some former members of staff from Bryn Estyn, the community home for adolescent boys in Wrexham which was at the centre of the scandal. That spring, soon after my conversation with David Godwin in April 1996, I attended the annual general meeting of the British False Memory Society – a society of which I have never been a member but whose immensely valuable work on false allegations of sexual abuse I have often admired. The afternoon session of the meeting included a surprise contribution by a speaker who had not been announced in advance. He was John Rayfield, a retired residential child care officer who had once worked at Bryn Estyn. I recall that the eloquence and apparent respectability of this 71-year-old Methodist lay preacher sat oddly with the horrific reports of the Bryn Estyn 'hell' which had been appearing day after day, week after week, in the *Independent*.

The gist of Rayfield's brief address was that, because of acts of sexual abuse which had been committed at Bryn Estyn by one colleague (who had subsequently pleaded guilty and was still serving a prison sentence) the entire staff at Bryn Estyn had been damned by association and now found themselves the object of a bizarre witch-hunt. They had, Rayfield said, been caught up in something which was far greater than most people could grasp and they simply did not understand what had happened or how it had come about.

Sceptical of, but fascinated by, this unexpected claim, I sought Rayfield out after the meeting and was introduced by him to Gwen Hurst. This former Bryn Estyn teacher, who was also now retired, had travelled to London with Rayfield so that, for the first time, they could put their case in public. I spoke to them briefly and found what they had to say both disturbing and intriguing. They said that if I wanted to find out more about Bryn Estyn I should come Wrexham. I said that I would think about it.

One of the factors which led me to consider this proposal seriously was my concern about whether the British False Memory Society had been right to invite a group of the most notorious care workers in the country to address a meeting concerned with *false* allegations of sexual abuse. If not, I needed to find out rapidly if only to protect my own reputation. Another factor was that the story which Rayfield had briefly related was a strangely familiar one, in that it appeared to have many of the ingredients of a 'real' historical witch-hunt. Could this really be a recurrence of the very kind of irrational persecution which, as Anthony Storr had written, had 'so disfigured human history'?

A few days after the meeting in London I telephoned John Rayfield and Gwen Hurst to arrange to interview them in Wrexham and to inquire about other people I might talk to. I then bought a small battery-powered tape-recorder and half a dozen blank tapes, booked a hotel, and set off for North Wales. I thought that I would spend a week or so gathering the evidence I needed and might write a brief article about what I had discovered. With that out of the way I could then get down to work on the book about human nature and human nurture which I had always had in mind as the sequel to my Freud book. I did not for one moment realise then that it would take me not nine days but almost nine years to complete the assignment I had set myself.

One of the many reasons why it has taken so long to produce this book is that, a matter of weeks after I began to inquire into what had happened in North Wales, the campaign which had been launched by the *Independent* in April 1996 had borne fruit, and the government had announced that the North Wales allegations would be investigated by a full Tribunal of Inquiry. Almost four years would pass before the report of the Tribunal was published in February 2000.

Although the Tribunal delayed my progress, I owe a considerable debt to the witnesses who gave evidence to it and to the barristers who cross-examined them. During the 18 months of Tribunal hearings, the transcript of which runs to 30,000 pages, a massive amount of evidence was placed in the public domain for the first time. In addition, thousands of documents were disclosed to Tribunal witnesses and their legal teams. Much of the most important evidence which emerged, however, disappeared without trace from the Tribunal report. I have tried to rescue some of that discarded evidence and to point to its significance in the pages that follow.

These pages, however, are not based solely on documents and transcripts. In the course of my research I have travelled thousands of miles and interviewed hundreds of people, sometimes having to queue at prison gates in order to do so. To name all those who have spoken to me or helped me in other ways would take up many pages and this book is long enough already. But they know who they are and I would like to thank them all.

The result of all this research is not simply a book about residential care, about allegations of sexual abuse, about dangerous techniques of police investigation, or wrongful convictions, although it is about all of these things. It is, as I hope will be recognised, a book about human nature. But it is a very different book from the one I had in mind to write before that fateful encounter in London.

The Secret of Bryn Estyn, then, has taken a long time to complete and I am grateful to all those who have encouraged me along the way. To

Gwen Hurst and her husband, John, (who has become, in his retirement, the unofficial archivist of Bryn Estyn), my special thanks are due for the immense patience with which they have dealt with endless queries and requests.

There are some other people I must thank by name because they have read this book (or sections of it) in draft form and commented on it. I am grateful to Michael Barnes, Tania Hunter, Rory O'Brien, David Rose, Chris Saltrese, Gail Saunders, Ruth Whittaker and Bob Woffinden, all of whom made extremely helpful comments, corrections or editorial suggestions. Another reader, Tony Burke, proof-read a version of the book in his prison cell. I am particularly grateful to him and, for different reasons, to Jane Carey, who wrote, over the final page of the draft version she had just finished reading, 'They should make a film of this!' Of course, they almost certainly won't, but her response lifted my spirits at a time when they needed lifting.

John Jevons, the former director of social services for Clwyd (and later Cardiff), also read this book in draft form and made extensive comments on it, some of which were justly critical. Without his well-informed criticisms, this book would be a much less accurate record of events than it now is. This is not to say that he agrees with the views which are expressed in it. But, although we do not see eye to eye about some matters, I remain grateful to him for his very helpful comments.

I did not know when I started writing this book that my friend and neighbour, Jane Roberts, was a copy editor and proof-reader of genius. Neither, perhaps, did she. But I have told her so many times now that I think she is beginning to believe it. Coming to the manuscript at a fairly late stage, she has worked tirelessly and has improved the text immeasurably by providing an unceasing flow of suggestions, corrections and queries. I cannot thank her enough. Simply because she did enter the project so late it may well be the case that some errors remain. For these the responsibility is mine alone.

Since it would be unwise to publish any book of this nature without consulting lawyers, I must also record my gratitude to two libel lawyers I came to know well during the many months we worked together (after an investigation I had undertaken with Bob Woffinden) before and during the Shieldfield libel trial. This trial took place in the high court over a period of six months in the first half of 2002 and it succeeded in restoring the reputations of two Newcastle nursery nurses, Dawn Reed and Christopher Lillie, who had been falsely accused of belonging to a paedophile ring and driven into hiding because they feared they would be murdered. Without the deep understanding and tireless advocacy which Adrienne Page QC and Adam Speker brought to the case, it would never have reached a successful conclusion. I am therefore doubly grateful to them, both for achieving this result and for giving me legal advice on the contents of this book

It only remains to say that one late change to the design of this book was contributed by Suzy Harrison and Jason Hayes of Fine Print as we were proofing the jacket here in Oxford. It was they who suggested that I should produce two different designs for the endpapers rather than using the same design for the front and the back as I had intended. As a result, I produced one newspaper collage consisting of stories or headlines which appeared *before* the North Wales Tribunal and another, for the back of the book, which was taken entirely from newspapers which appeared during the Tribunal itself or after the publication of its report in February 2000. These endpapers are not intended to be merely decorative. They are an integral part of the story. What I had not anticipated was how graphically they would illustrate an important feature of it. The front endpaper, which charts the rise of a moral panic that soon extended far beyond North Wales, consists almost entirely of cuttings taken from broadsheet newspapers. It is only after the Tribunal that the story is picked up and given massive coverage by *tabloid* papers. This progression represents the opposite of what most people would expect. The obvious conclusion to draw is that this witch-hunt was the creation of the relatively well-educated and that only afterwards did it become a popular or populist cause. Although this pattern may surprise many observers, it is precisely what most students of the history of witch-hunts would expect. One of the purposes of this book is to attempt to explain why this is so.

Oxford, January 2005

Introduction: the story of the story

THERE IS A VIEW OF HISTORY which suggests that, as we progress towards civilised rationality, we are less and less likely to fall prey to unreason, or to be gripped by those episodes of collective insanity which have scarred European history. The demonological anti-semitism of the Christian middle ages or the great European witch-hunt of the sixteenth and seventeenth centuries were, according to this perspective, terrible aberrations from the path of progress; they belong to the childhood of humankind rather than to the state of rational maturity we have now reached. Witch-hunts are things that happen in other countries or other eras than our own. We have passed beyond them.

This book is written in the belief that such a view of human progress is not only mistaken but dangerous. The history of twentieth-century Europe certainly offers no evidence to support it. Both modern European anti-semitism and Stalin's purges were marked by collective fantasies in which people identifying themselves as the 'pure' sought to persecute or even destroy entire groups of human beings imagined as 'evil' or 'unclean'. These are not the only modern examples of our susceptibility to large-scale delusions in which, through a terrible process of psychological projection, we attribute to minorities we have defined as evil or unclean, our own unacknowledged desires and darkest impulses.[1]

The widespread belief that, belonging as we do to a rational scientific age, we are no longer vulnerable to such fantasies, is itself one of the most dangerous of all our delusions. For it is precisely because of our rationalism, and the difficulty we have in acknowledging our own violence and the full depth and complexity of our sexual imagination, that we are probably more susceptible to dangerous projections than we ever have been.

If we briefly survey the role which has been played in medieval and modern history by collective fantasies, one fact which will almost immediately become apparent is that many of the most powerful historical fantasies involve children and the need to protect them. For although we sometimes assume that our own anxieties about the vulnerability of innocent children are distinctively modern, this is very far from the case. The notion that there exists an evil conspiracy given to preying on children and causing them harm is an ancient one. One of the many forms it has taken was the accusation of ritual murder traditionally levelled against Jews by Christians during the days leading up to Good Friday. First made in Norwich in 1144, the accusation usually consisted in a baseless claim that a group of Jews had kidnapped a Christian child and tortured or murdered it for ritual purposes. This 'blood libel' circled the globe and travelled down the centuries to the time of Hitler, establishing itself as one of the main motifs of Christian and post-Christian anti-semitism. The sinister conspiracy of child-murdering Jews which it conjured up existed only in the imagination, but this did not prevent countless innocent Jewish people from being hunted down and killed in the name of Christian virtue. The notion that Jews were actually in league with the Devil, and that they had designs on Christian children, lay at the very heart of medieval demonological anti-semitism – which is one of the most important but least acknowledged elements in the cultural heritage of Christian Europe.[2]

A comparable fantasy, which was to prove just as compelling to the Christian imagination, would eventually emerge. This maintained the existence of a society of witches who flew through the air astride rams, pigs or broomsticks, and gathered together to engage in the orgiastic worship of their master Satan. The members of this evil conspiracy supposedly took particular delight in besmirching that which was holy and destroying innocence. They were sometimes imagined killing and eating young children or babies in sacrificial rituals.

Such fantasies as these do not belong, as we like to believe, to some primitive, archaic mode of thought which we long ago transcended. The more we feel impelled, in our pursuit of civilised rationality, to exclude from our own self-image violent, destructive or sexually perverse impulses, the more we tend to define such feelings as irredeemably external or alien. Projecting feelings we experience as alien onto those whom we define as alien is one of the ways in which we attempt to get rid of them. The process of demonising cultural enemies is, in this sense, entirely normal.

It is also dangerous. Whenever we allow any group of human beings to be demonised, the anxieties associated with our dreams of purity throughout history will almost inevitably be brought into play; we will begin to imagine the group in question in the same terms which are found in other demonological fantasies. They will be seen as members of an evil, highly organised conspiracy intent on infiltrating our national life and harming the very people towards whom our own feelings are most complex and most ambivalent – our children.[3]

Over the last fifteen years one particular group of people has been demonised in this way: residential care workers. From about 1990 onwards a new idea began to gain currency in Britain among social workers, child protection workers and journalists. This was the belief that residential care homes for young people had been infiltrated by paedophile rings. Many people remained sceptical about the idea. But in a small circle it became accepted almost as an orthodoxy. In Britain, during the spring and early summer of 1996, the idea was given much wider currency in the press and the broadcasting media. So rarely was it challenged that, in the minds of some observers, almost all care workers became paedophiles, or potential paedophiles, or silent abetters of evil crimes which they were presumed to have witnessed or suspected. In June 1996 a presenter on the BBC radio programme *The World at One* suggested that we might have to face up to the possibility that abuse in children's homes was 'the norm' rather than the exception. A few days later, speaking in the House of Commons, the Labour Welsh affairs spokesman, Rhodri Morgan, said that although children's homes were meant to provide care, 'they had dished out a diet of sadism by day and sodomy by night'. In 1997, in an article in the *Guardian* which was not even about residential care, the respected feminist journalist, Linda Grant, referred almost casually to children's homes as being run by 'a bureaucracy of paedophiles'.[4]

It was just such a belief that was held by those who triggered the massive police inquiry into alleged abuse in North Wales which was launched in August 1991. Largely as a result of this investigation and the extraordinary stories of wholesale abuse which emerged from it, the approach used by the North Wales Police was adopted by other police forces in neighbouring areas.

Similar concerns about paedophile rings were entertained by the social workers and police officers who, in 1994, launched an even larger investigation in Cheshire, just over the English border. This investigation in turn spread to Merseyside. Instead of waiting for allegations to be made spontaneously, the police began actively to look for them. They did so through massive trawling operations in which they deliberately sought out former residents of care homes and invited them to make complaints – sometimes against specific workers. Thousands of young men and women were contacted. Many of them were damaged and highly suggestible, and a significant proportion had criminal records which included offences of dishonesty and deception. Although the vast majority had never made any complaint about their time in care, hundreds now made allegations of serious physical or sexual abuse, describing incidents which they said took place ten, twenty or even thirty years beforehand.

By 1998 trawling operations had been launched not only in North Wales, in Cheshire, and on Merseyside, but also in South Wales, in Manchester, in north-east England and in a number of other regions. By the end of 2000 these investigations had spread from police force to police force until almost a hundred were in progress and practically the whole of Britain was covered by a trawling net. As a result, an entirely new form of police inquiry was beginning to be regarded as a normal method of investigation.

Three of the largest trawling operations, those conducted in North Wales, South Wales and on Merseyside, have between them collected allegations against some 1500 people. At least thirty other police forces have conducted major trawling operations, although most of these are on a smaller scale. By now allegations have been made against thousands of care workers and former care workers. Many of these have been arrested and questioned. The majority have been released, but a significant proportion have been charged and convicted. Hundreds of millions of pounds of public money has been spent on these investigations and the civil and criminal processes associated with them. Several thousand former residents of care homes have made claims for compensation and some have already received sums approaching £100,000.[5]

Any suggestion that all the care workers convicted in this way are innocent would be wholly misleading. It requires only a little knowledge of human nature to recognise that wherever adults and young people are placed together in residential settings – whether in boarding schools, in religious institutions or in families – sexual abuse will sometimes take place. Care homes are no exception to this and some of those who are now in prison are there for no other reason than that they are guilty of the crimes alleged against them. But many of those who have direct knowledge of these investigations, including a significant number of solicitors and barristers, have become more and more disturbed by what is happening. They are concerned above all about the manner in which allegations have been obtained and about the soundness of some of the convictions they have led to. Some defence lawyers have expressed the view that false allegations are now being made on a massive scale, and that the majority of the most serious allegations made against care workers are false.

That many innocent people have been caught up in these investigations is now beyond question. In December 2000, after a nightmare which lasted more than two years, the former Southampton football manager, David Jones, was acquitted in Liverpool Crown Court after his trial collapsed. At one point he was facing 21 counts of child abuse including a number of counts of buggery. The collapse of his trial meant that the jury was unable to hear compelling evidence that all these allegations were false, with the prospect of compensation as one possible motive.

David Jones is by no means alone. Earlier in the same year the distinguished child psychotherapist Robin Reeves, once head of a residential school for disturbed children, faced a similar ordeal. Largely because of the excellent work done by his defence team, evidence was adduced which suggested that all 34 counts against him were untrue. The judge directed the jury to acquit. Reeves subsequently said that he did not believe that compensation was a major factor in the emergence of these false allegations. He did take the view, however, that those who had accused him were highly suggestible and had responded to leading questions in a manner which could have been predicted.

Meanwhile, in the same year, one Merseyside defendant, the father of a BBC journalist, had his case dismissed by the judge. He had pleaded not guilty to 63 allegations of abuse, having originally faced more than 90 counts, all of which, in the view of his solicitor, were untrue.

In these three cases alone, it would seem that trawling operations were responsible for producing almost 150 false allegations. In January 2001, in Swansea Crown Court, another case collapsed. This had originally involved four care workers who supposedly belonged to a paedophile ring operating in a home for difficult adolescents. When originally charged, they had faced between them more than 250 counts of sexual abuse. The trial collapsed when, after a prosecution which had lasted three years and cost hundreds of thousands of pounds, it became clear that the original complainant was a fantasist who had made a number of sexual allegations against people who did not exist. The allegations of the subsequent complainants were so riven with inconsistencies and untruths that the prosecution could not rely on them.

Yet in spite of evidence which points to the proliferation of false allegations of abuse, the belief persists that young people who were in care in the last decades of the twentieth century were subjected to systematic physical and sexual abuse on a massive and horrifying scale.

This belief is not only found in Britain. Partly for cultural reasons, and partly because their legal systems offer protection against long-delayed prosecutions, the United States and most European countries – with the notable exception of Portugal – have not as yet been seriously affected by what I have called, in an earlier brief book, 'the great children's home panic'.[6] But a process in which care workers have been progressively demonised has taken place in some Commonwealth countries, especially Canada. As this book goes to press there are signs of a similar development in Australia and New Zealand. For cultural and geographical reasons the problem has also assumed significant proportions in the Irish Republic where a massive compensation programme has so far led to more than four thousand people making allegations about their time in care. In 2004 an Irish government report estimated that the potential final number of claimants could be around 8,900, at a cost of €828 million in compensation payments.[7]

The case of Canada is particularly significant. There, as in Britain and Ireland, many thousands of allegations of abuse have been made by former residents of care homes and thousands of 'counsellors' and other members of staff have had complaints made against them. So widespread are the accusations that the bill for compensation amounts to hundreds of millions of dollars and, until it was rescued by the government, the Anglican Church of Canada faced bankruptcy because of the huge claims made against it.[8]

In Canada, as in Britain and Ireland, residence in a care home during the latter half of the twentieth century has come to be regarded by some as almost synonymous with being a victim of abuse, and in every Canadian province there have been long-delayed complaints which have resulted in large compensation claims. One of the most instructive examples is that of Nova Scotia. Here, a large number of allegations have been made against former members of staff from the Shelburne Youth Centre, a home for difficult or delinquent teenage boys, and the Nova Scotia Residential Centre, an equivalent institution for girls.

The complaints about the Shelburne Youth Centre go back to 1992 when police conducted an investigation into allegations of abuse against a former counsellor at the home. Although he was convicted, a thorough police investigation made at the time concluded that there was no widespread problem of abuse. Indeed, no allegation had been made against any current member of staff. In 1995, however, the Nova

Scotia Minister of Justice publicly announced that the province would pay compensation in respect of allegations made. By the end of 1997 no fewer than 1,457 adults from this single province had made complaints that they had been abused either in the two main homes or in three other institutions administered by the province. The allegations implicated more than 300 current or former members of staff, almost all of whom were accused of some form of sexual abuse. Former residents who complained suggested that sexual and physical abuse had taken place on a massive scale, that it was systematic and blatant, and that the Shelburne Youth Centre was so rife with abuse that it was essentially a 'war zone' or 'house of horrors'.

In response to the earliest complaints, which were of physical abuse only, the Nova Scotia Department of Justice had already, by the end of 1995, set up an Internal Investigation Unit staffed by experienced police officers. Their task was to examine the allegations in order to provide for the safety of the various young offenders held at the institutions in question, and to make recommendations about the kind of action which should be taken against members of staff who had been accused. As the volume and seriousness of the allegations grew, so too did the task of the investigators. During a three-year investigation they scanned almost 2 million documents into a computer system, interviewed hundreds of former residents and staff members, conducted polygraph tests, and analysed the complaints in detail.

The conclusion reached by this team, who between them had more than 700 years of police investigative experience, was remarkable. In their view, the idea that abuse had been systematic or carried out on the scale claimed by the complainants was without foundation. There was, however, a close correlation between the various promises of compensation which had been made by the Minister of Justice, involving a budget of $56 million, and the progressively mounting volume and seriousness of the complaints which were made. Having expressed the view that many of the allegations levelled against employees of the juvenile detention centres in question 'appear to be concocted [and] contain blatant falsehoods and gross exaggerations', the inquiry team reported as follows:

> Based on our investigation over the last four years, we have advanced the overall conclusion that former residents of the institutions for youths have not been subjected to widespread or systemic abuses by staff or employees and that, insofar as such incidents are corroborated,

they were likely of an aberrational or sporadic nature. We have reached this conclusion according to the weight of the objective evidence and by reasonable and realistic deductions and inferences made from the materials available to us, as well as a review of a cross-section of what we believe are reliable and credible statements by knowledgeable individuals.

We firmly believe that a thorough scrutiny of most of the allegations about institutional abuse will raise questions as to their legitimacy. Allegations made recently by former residents in the circumstances of the *Compensation Program* are, in our view, mostly unreliable and inconsistent with the facts as we have been able to discover them.

We are mindful of the controversial and highly politicised mandate of this investigation. It would seem that, in many quarters – both inside and outside of government – there is a real inclination to believe unquestionably that wide-scale or systemic institutional abuses took place. This report will likely do little to assuage those particular beliefs. However, we believe that our report will withstand scrutiny over time.[9]

Although the Nova Scotia report would appear to be directly relevant to events in Britain, there is a clear difference between the two situations. As the Canadian investigators stress, the vast majority of the complaints in Nova Scotia have never been tested in criminal trials or public inquiries, with the result that those making them have never been subjected to cross-examination.[10]

In Britain the situation is different. The belief that physical and sexual abuse took place on a massive scale in children's homes seems to be a great deal more securely based. It rests on the conclusions reached at the end of a three-year public inquiry presided over by a retired high court judge: Sir Ronald Waterhouse's North Wales Tribunal. In this £15 million inquiry, during which scores of complainants were cross-examined by leading barristers, the horrific allegations of physical and sexual abuse which began to emerge in North Wales in 1991 were publicly tested. When the report of the Tribunal was published in February 2000, the veracity of these complaints (or of the vast majority of them) was officially endorsed.[11]

Of all the allegations of abuse which have been made in the recent history of child care in Britain, there can be little doubt that those made in North Wales are among the most serious. They have certainly been the most influential in bringing about the climate of suspicion in which every care worker or former care worker is now compelled to live. Most disturbing of all are the complaints which concern the home which has been described as 'the Colditz of care' and 'the children's hell' – Bryn Estyn.

Housed in a spacious mock–Tudor mansion on the edge of the town of Wrexham, Bryn Estyn had originally been an approved school and as such had maintained a strict, authoritarian regime. In 1974, however, it had become a community home presided over by a progressive headmaster, Matt Arnold. Arnold, who at one point was highly regarded within his profession, had begun to transform the old approved school regime into one which was more relaxed and more caring. This transformation was never successfully completed, however. For both political and economic reasons there was a move away from large-scale residential establishments, and Bryn Estyn was closed down in 1984.

There was never any suggestion at the time of any sexual impropriety at the home. Yet, according to reports which began to appear in the quality press in 1991, there was evidence to suggest that Bryn Estyn had lain at the centre of a network of evil which had spread from care home to care home in North Wales, in a conspiracy of corruption on a scale undreamed of only a few years previously. Not only was it suggested that this conspiracy might involve the extensive homosexual abuse of young boys by a paedophile ring, but there was also supposed to have been widespread physical abuse.

Not every element in this story was accepted by the Tribunal. But it did find that the horrific allegations of physical and sexual abuse were substantially true. Ever since the allegations were first made, however, a group of former Bryn Estyn care workers has maintained that the truth about Bryn Estyn is almost the exact opposite of the received view. It is their contention that what took place in North Wales during the main police investigation of 1991-3 was not the revelation of abuse on an unprecedented scale, but the collection of an unprecedented number of false allegations. They argue that, because these allegations have been officially endorsed rather than repudiated, they have become the basis of a national witch-hunt.[12]

How, it might be asked, given the findings of the Tribunal, can the facts of what happened in North Wales still be in dispute? How could an inquiry presided over by a judge ever be held responsible for helping to lay the foundations of a modern witch-hunt?

One way of answering these questions is to point out that, of all the misconceptions about historical witch-hunts, perhaps the most important is the notion that they were driven forward by the common people – that they were based on the untutored instincts of the mob. This is the very opposite of the truth. In historical reality the witch-hunts of the sixteenth and seventeenth centuries were the creation of the learned. They were set in motion not by ordinary people but by an educated elite consisting of bishops, ministers, magistrates and judges. These zealous agents of Christian purity pursued those they deemed witches not out of whims or fantasies but on the basis of what they sincerely believed to be solemnly attested facts. Historically, indeed, witch-hunts have always relied on judges and magistrates, and on official inquiries, in order to maintain their power and authority.

By turns fascinated and horrified by its vivid sexual content, many of those who were called upon, some three centuries ago, to scrutinise evidence of witchcraft, suspended their critical judgment. They unsceptically accepted accounts of crimes which were unlikely or impossible and came to believe unreservedly that they had discovered solid evidence for an evil conspiracy which did not in fact exist. As a result, countless innocent men and women were convicted of offences they had not committed and many were executed or burned alive.

Whenever we allow demonological fantasies to develop in our midst, as we have in relation to the paedophile ring theory of children's homes, there is always a danger that the same process of self-delusion may take place over again. For, when small, zealous groups become seized by this kind of fantasy, they may well, as has happened repeatedly throughout history, construct a narrative so powerful that they cannot escape from its grip. There is then a very great danger that they – or the agents of the church or state they succeed in mobilising – may begin unwittingly to 'create' the very evidence they need to intensify this fantasy.

Because fantasies of this kind are immensely powerful, and because we are all susceptible to them, it is more than likely that we will fail to recognise what has happened. This danger is particularly acute when a delusion is based upon a palpable reality. For, when fantasy is mixed with fact in unequal proportions, the fantasy can sometimes become even more dangerous and even more destructive.

In dealing with the modern witch-hunt that is the subject of this book, we are certainly not confronted all the time by unquestioning zealots driven by unbridled fantasies. Many of the men and women who have taken part in it are outwardly moderate, rational and sceptical. They are concerned sincerely to combat a problem – child sexual abuse – of whose reality there can, or should, be no doubt. The lesson of history, however, is that the existence of real enemies does not stop the tendency of people to battle against imaginary ones. And sometimes it is just those who are most zealous to crusade against real social ills who are most susceptible to imagining themselves pitted against dark conspiracies which do not in fact exist.

The received version of the story of North Wales invokes many such conspiracies. The story is, without doubt, extremely powerful. But, because the role which has been played by fantasy in its construction is all but invisible, it is also dangerous. Whenever we allow ourselves to be in thrall to a story of this kind, there is only one way to undo its influence. This is to document how the narrative which has achieved such power was actually created in the first place. In short, it is to tell another story — the story of the story.

In the pages which follow, this is what I have tried to do. The tale which they contain is one of the most extraordinary that has ever been told. If I have related it at times as though it were fiction it is because, in some respects, this is exactly what it is. What renders it dangerous is that, until now, it has generally been taken to be fact.

I

ALISON TAYLOR
AND GWYNEDD
(1976–90)

1 The newspaper

AT FIVE O'CLOCK IN THE AFTERNOON of Saturday 30 November 1991, Ian Jack was sitting at the editor's desk in the offices of the *Independent on Sunday*. The paper's deadline – the time it had to be sent electronically to its various print sites – was 5.30pm, though often this was stretched to 6pm. Most of the paper had already been cleared for publication but just after 5pm a proof of the front page was brought to Jack's office.

The page included stories about Aids, about Winston Silcott, who had successfully appealed after being wrongly convicted of the murder of PC Keith Blakelock, and about a man who intended to walk into his local supermarket on Sunday morning and steal the cheapest item he could find. According to the man, who was seeking to launch a mass-protest against Sunday trading, 'it was no crime to take goods from a shop that should not be open'.

But on this particular Saturday it was another story which had provided the paper with its main lead. And it was this that caused Jack most concern. The story was spread across all eight columns of the front page beneath the headline 'NEW CHILD ABUSE SCANDAL'. It continued inside the paper where it occupied the whole of page three.

As an experienced journalist who had consolidated his already excellent reputation by his work on the 'Death on the Rock' scandal, and who had subsequently become editor of the *Independent on Sunday,* Jack was used to handling powerful stories. But the claims contained in the edition of the paper which was just about to go to press were among the most disturbing he had ever published.

He had already checked the main story as it appeared on page three and passed it for publication. The outline was clear. As a result of a tip-off and an investigation carried out mostly by a young freelance journalist, Dean Nelson, the paper had uncovered an extraordinary saga of sexual and physical abuse in children's homes in North Wales. The new revelations, coming as they did a mere forty-eight hours after the Leicestershire care worker, Frank Beck, had been given five life sentences for sexually abusing those in his care, could scarcely have been better timed. The Beck case had itself been described as Britain's biggest-ever child abuse case. But, according to the front-page story whose proofs Jack was now checking, those with intimate knowledge of the allegations in North Wales believed that an even bigger scandal was waiting to be uncovered.

At the heart of this new scandal lay events which were alleged to have taken place at Bryn Estyn, a former approved school situated just outside Wrexham which had been closed on financial grounds in 1984. The story revealed that in October 1990 a senior care worker, Stephen Norris, had pleaded guilty to sexually abusing boys in another Clwyd children's home. Norris had once worked at Bryn Estyn. Two other former members of staff had also been convicted of sexual offences. Although neither of these offences related to the home, and although one related to adolescent girls, the fear had been expressed that Bryn Estyn might have been the centre of a paedophile ring. As a result the social services department had called in the police who, in August 1991, launched a major investigation into the home.

At this point the police inquiry was still in its early stages. What gave the paper's story its edge was the fact that the journalist, Dean Nelson, appeared to be much further advanced with his investigation than the police were with theirs. Indeed, the front-page report, which Jack was now checking, opened with a fierce attack on the police for allegedly failing to interview key witnesses, and deterring others from making complaints through their heavy-handed methods. Particular prominence was given to the views of Dennis Parry, the Labour leader of Clwyd County Council, who said 'we are fighting a machine trying to cover things up'. Parry went on to accuse the North Wales Police explicitly 'of mounting a cover-up to conceal the failure of senior officers and social services executives to reveal the extent of abuse in the children's homes'.

In view of the fact that the story focused not only on a sexual abuse scandal but also on an apparent cover-up by the police, the picture which was printed in the centre of the front page was perhaps not as remarkable as it might otherwise have seemed. It was a snatched photograph of the deputy head of Bryn Estyn, which appeared over a one-line caption: 'Peter Howarth, who is alleged to have sexually assaulted boys'.

It was unusual for any newspaper to print a photograph of an innocent man who had not even been interviewed by the police, while simultaneously alleging that he was a paedophile. But Jack appears to have been confident that his journalists had produced enough evidence to enable the paper to defend a libel action, in the unlikely event of one being brought. Inside the paper, on page three, Howarth was not even referred to as an 'alleged' sex offender. The story began with a simple and straightforward claim that he was a paedophile:

> The police arrived nine years too late to save Steven* from the pae-dophile who is still wrecking his life. They were also many years too late to help Paul, who now suffers from depression and has attempted suicide.
>
> The paedophile in question is Peter Howarth, the former deputy head of Bryn Estyn children's home in Wrexham. He retired in 1984 shortly before the home was closed down. He has not yet been arrested. Steven and Paul know where he lives, and often think of revenge. To them his assault seems like only yesterday, despite their best efforts to forget. ...
>
> Our investigation has found evidence that Peter Howarth made sex-ual assaults on young people in his care at Bryn Estyn while he enter-tained them with beer and games at his flat and house in the grounds.

The story went on to present what seemed to Jack irrefutable evidence of Howarth's guilt. In the first place Steven and Paul, who were both now grown men with children, each made explicit allegations that Peter Howarth had indecently assaulted them. What was perhaps even more impressive, however, was that their allegations were supported by a former care worker who claimed that she had herself received com-plaints of sexual abuse during the time she had worked at Bryn Estyn:

> Alison Taylor, a former senior residential social worker in Gwynedd, was working on a training placement at Bryn Estyn when she was told of abuse being committed by Howarth. She said one boy told her Howarth had buggered him and forced him to have oral sex.
>
> Taylor said she reported the incident to her supervisor, but was told the boy should not be believed. Two other boys told her they had been molested by Howarth. One of them was nick-named 'Vaseline' by boys and staff, because he spent so much time in Howarth's flat.

The article then made a series of general allegations against Bryn Estyn, which was implicitly portrayed as a den of sexual iniquity where staff

---

* The names are as given in the original newspaper article where they had been changed at the request of the men concerned.

regularly and openly showed pornographic videos to the boys. It went on to make a clutch of further allegations against the Tŷ'r Felin Assessment Centre in Bangor, Gwynedd – and in particular against its officer-in-charge, Nefyn Dodd.

Dodd had himself worked at Bryn Estyn as a housemaster until 1978 and was described in the article as 'a protégé of Peter Howarth'. Like Howarth, Dodd was an innocent man who had not been charged with any offence. He too, however, was now portrayed in the article as a child abuser. Although some of the complaints cited in the article had a sexual dimension, implying that Dodd was a voyeur who kept hard-core pornography, most concerned physical abuse. Ryan Tanner*, for example, who, as a boy, had been in care both at Tŷ'r Felin and at Bryn Estyn, claimed that he had been physically assaulted by Dodd, who had used his stomach to pin him against the wall. Once again what was impressive about these allegations, and what seemed to place them beyond question, was that they were backed up by the same care worker who said she had received the early allegations against Peter Howarth – Alison Taylor.

Taylor had worked as Nefyn Dodd's deputy. In 1980, according to the main page-three article, she had rescued a young boy from a savage beating in an office at Tŷ'r Felin: 'The boy, Lewis Harper, now settled with children, was dragged into the office because he had run away to his mother's. "I managed to drag Lewis away and throw him out of the office. But Dodd was screaming at him to get down on his knees and lick his shoes and kiss his feet," she said.'

The allegations against Dodd were by no means as serious as those against Howarth, but they were clearly sufficient to destroy his entire career. From the evidence which was actually presented in the article, moreover, it appeared that these allegations were well-founded. What troubled Ian Jack as he read through the front-page story was not the treatment of these two principal characters. It was a new allegation which did not appear anywhere in the main report: 'According to former residents at Bryn Estyn, Supt Gordon Anglesea, a former senior North Wales Police officer, was a regular visitor there. He recently retired suddenly without explanation. Another serving officer has been accused of assaulting a child at Tŷ'r Felin.'

Ian Jack recalls that when he read this part of the article 'I don't exag-

---

* This name, like the names of all former residents of care homes who are still living, has been changed.

gerate when I say that the sentence naming Anglesea flashed a warning like a beacon. Its implication was clearly libellous. Did we have evidence to substantiate it?' Jack now talked to the senior staff journalist under whose aegis the story had been written. '[He] said that I was not to worry, because "we've got tons of gear on this guy", or a phrase like this, and the story had been "squared" (or a word like this) with the lawyer. In other words, the paper had in its possession information (statements, documents, whatever) which would substantiate the implication.'[13]

Jack was not the only senior journalist who was concerned about this part of the story. His deputy editor, Peter Wilby, also had anxieties about the reference to Anglesea. Since the police officer, who had supposedly retired suddenly and in mysterious circumstances, played such a minor role, Wilby could not accept that it was wise to name him. To do so, he felt, was to take an unnecessary risk.[14]

In the event, however, the enthusiasm of those who had worked on the story triumphed over the caution of their editors. Ian Jack accepted the assurances he was given and, as the clock ticked on towards six, he gave the go-ahead for the paper's copy to be sent electronically to its print sites. At the various printers the electronic data would rapidly be transferred to film, and from film the printing plates would be made. Some two hours after Jack had taken his fateful decision, the presses would begin to roll. They would continue until more than a quarter of a million copies of the paper had been printed. A bleak and disturbing story, which ended by noting that Clwyd County Council 'will look sympathetically on claims for compensation from those who suffered abuse', was about to find its way from a newspaper office in London into the larger world.

At eight o'clock that Saturday evening one thing seemed certain. By the end of the next day the reputation of three men, and of the two care homes in North Wales with which they had been associated, would be utterly and irretrievably destroyed.

2 The freelance

DEAN NELSON, THE FREELANCE JOURNALIST who had been entrusted with the North Wales story, had started his career as a television news reporter. He had worked for *New Society* and Channel 4 and had already done some work for the *Independent*. One of the stories on which he had built his reputation as a crusading investigator also involved a care home in Wales. It was referred to in passing in the front-page article which Ian Jack had passed for publication. The new scandal in North Wales, it was noted, 'comes only … five months after the *Independent* uncovered a catalogue of abuse at Tŷ Mawr children's home in Abergavenny, Gwent — now the subject of an official inquiry.'

The earlier story had appeared in the *Independent* in May 1991 as part of a campaign to highlight allegations of abuse in care homes in the days leading up to the publication of the Staffordshire 'Pindown' report. The outcome of the inquiry into this harsh children's home regime was featured under the front-page headline 'PINDOWN VICTIMS TO SEEK DAMAGES'.[15]

Days earlier, the Tŷ Mawr story had itself provided the paper with its front-page headline, spread over six columns: 'SCANDAL OVER SUICIDE TEENAGER'. The story revealed that a 15-year-old former resident of Tŷ Mawr, Phillip Knight, had hanged himself in Swansea Prison. Only a month earlier the same boy had, according to the paper, made a bloody suicide attempt while locked in a secure unit at the home. The implication was that Tŷ Mawr was to blame for the boy's suicide. Indeed, Nelson reported that Phillip Knight's social workers 'felt staff at the home had not taken the incidents seriously and that they were "more interested in damage to property than damage to life and limb".' The story went on to claim that three other children had also attempted suicide at Tŷ Mawr.

Inside the paper, on page three, was a much longer piece. Headlined 'BOY TELLS OF TORMENT AND SUICIDE ATTEMPTS', it was illustrated by a picture of Tŷ Mawr in which the home resembled a prison, or even a concentration camp. Approached by a metal gate, it was surrounded by what appeared from the photograph to be a high wire perimeter fence.

In the story Nelson introduced another former resident of Tŷ Mawr, a boy of sixteen, who was referred to as 'Lawrence'. Lawrence said that he had been sent to Tŷ Mawr when he was thirteen and complained that he had been constantly ridiculed by members of staff and told that he was a failure. He was desperate to leave but 'it took five suicide attempts before staff acknowledged that he needed help they could not provide':

> Lawrence said he slashed his wrists, took tablets, drank, and crashed cars. After five attempts at suicide he was finally moved to a psychiatric unit last year, where he has struggled to overcome depression. But he is still bitter about the school: 'All I want to do is get the facts about Tŷ Mawr out because there could be kids there being treated exactly the same as I was. I do not want that. If I'd never been to Tŷ Mawr, I wouldn't have tried to kill myself.'

The article closed by quoting a spokesman for NAYPIC (the National Association of Young People in Care) who called for the school to be closed down.

These stories by Nelson, with their implication that teenagers were being driven to suicide by a brutal regime, were disturbing. They also had a sequel. In June 1991, a confrontation between Tŷ Mawr residents and an inexperienced member of staff turned into a violent protest reminiscent of the recent riot at Strangeways Prison. Seven boys climbed onto the roof, tore up slates and hurled them down, aiming them at parked cars and breaking windows. They also shouted obscenities at the staff below. By the time the police arrived, the boys had done a great deal of damage. Even though four boys were arrested, the violence and abuse continued in the police van and at the police station.

Partly because of the press coverage given to this disturbance and partly because of renewed pressure from NAYPIC, the secretary of state for Wales almost immediately set up an inquiry into Tŷ Mawr. It was undertaken by Gareth Williams QC (later, as Lord Williams of Mostyn, to become Attorney General under Tony Blair), and John McCreadie, a specialist in residential care.[16]

Early in August, a few days after they began to take evidence in Gwent, a local boy, who had just turned seventeen, was found dead. He had shut the doors of the garage where he worked, and killed himself by inhaling the fumes from a car exhaust. He was Leslie Clements, who had on a number of occasions been placed in care at Tŷ Mawr. Although he had no contact with the inquiry team, he had been in touch with

NAYPIC and Dean Nelson. Indeed, Leslie was none other than 'Lawrence', whose earlier attempts at suicide Nelson had featured in his article, and for which Tŷ Mawr had already been publicly blamed.

An inquiry into allegations which were already grave now became even more serious. Chief among its many tasks was to determine whether Tŷ Mawr had indeed been responsible for driving young men to self-harm and suicide as Dean Nelson had suggested.

The conclusions reached by the Tŷ Mawr inquiry might also bear indirectly on some of the allegations made subsequently in relation to homes in North Wales. Here too it would be widely suggested that the brutal regimes allegedly operated in some of the homes had led to self-harm and suicide. At one point it would be claimed that no fewer than twelve young men had killed themselves as a result of being abused in North Wales homes.

The full and extremely sensitive inquiry report on Tŷ Mawr did not appear until some months after Dean Nelson had embarked on his second Welsh investigation – this time into Bryn Estyn. But it did throw an interesting light on his reliability as a reporter.

The overall conclusion was, in one sense at least, negative. The report recommended the closure of Tŷ Mawr on the grounds that it had developed the defects of 'an institution which is under-funded, under-resourced and to an extent overwhelmed by its own history'. It found that 'there was a degree of low level physical violence (slapping, cuffing, knuckling, that is striking on the head with the knuckles) by certain members of staff'. Although many residents who were interviewed accepted this as the norm, and although there were understandable reasons why this rough and physical culture had grown up, the report made it clear that it regarded such behaviour as unacceptable. However, it went out of its way to reject many of the charges which had been made against Tŷ Mawr staff in the media.[17]

It stressed that 'a very considerable amount of good was done by Tŷ Mawr, as many boys testified to us with a degree of affection and gratitude that we had not expected'. Some examples of the views of former residents were contained in letters written to members of staff by boys who had taken part in the rooftop disturbance, and who had been sent to Onley Young Offenders' Institute as a result. A typical letter was addressed to Christopher Phelan, the principal:

Hi there Mr Phelan,

How are you Sir. Sorry about waht I done OK. And I hope you will forgive me for it. Like most of the boys say that used to be there. Tŷ Mawr was the best days of my life I wish I was there now oh I really do. This letter is only short because I have all ready wrote two befor this one tell all the boys in there to stay out of prison because it's a bad place to be. I heard that you are having a meeting there about were I can go hope I can come back I know it sounds cheeky after what I done but I would love to come back there. By the way I was not the ring leader know one was we just all edged each other on. Anyway I am very very sorry for what I done and I would like you to tell all the staff that. You can come and visit me if you want Sir I am not arslicking you Sir I would love to come back so see you can get me back there OK. Goodbye for now see you soon.

P.S. – If I cannot come back I will still come and visit OK. Goodbye.
P.P.S. – Don't forget to tell the boy's and staff what I said.[18]

The report did make criticisms of the unhappiness caused by the regime 'for the sensitive, weaker boy'. These criticisms, however, were peripheral. 'The central question which we are called upon to address is "whether allegations of a regime which encouraged, permitted or acquiesced in brutal or emotionally cruel treatment of children and young persons are well founded". **In our opinion the answer is no'** [original stress].[19]

Williams and McCreadie went on to consider the suicides of Phillip Knight and Leslie Clements together with a number of other attempted suicides which journalists, including Dean Nelson, had sought to associate with the regime at Tŷ Mawr. They related how, during a brief placement at Tŷ Mawr, Phillip Knight had barricaded himself into a room and ripped the wash-basin from the wall. He was found lying on a bed covered in blood with a deep gash on the back of his right hand. After treatment in hospital he was placed in secure accommodation for his own safety. In spite of being checked every fifteen minutes he managed to remove the stitches from his first wound and was found bleeding heavily again. The next day it was decided that Tŷ Mawr was an inappropriate placement for him and he was moved.

Phillip had arrived at Tŷ Mawr in June 1990, but had almost immediately run away. He was returned a few days later and when he finally left the home on 12 June he had spent no more than four days there. A month later, having been remanded at Swansea Prison, he killed himself while awaiting sentence.

In their report the inquiry team noted that 'A connection was … made by some between Phillip's time in Tŷ Mawr and his suicide.' After what was clearly a reference to the article by Nelson, they presented their own, very different assessment of Phillip Knight's suicide:

> In our judgment, having reviewed the files carefully and taken a good deal of evidence, no proper criticism can be made of Tŷ Mawr, or any member of Tŷ Mawr's staff. ... we conclude that there is no fair basis upon which staff at Tŷ Mawr or employed by Gwent County Council could reasonably be criticised in respect of either Phillip's treatment at Tŷ Mawr or his ultimate suicide in Swansea Prison.[20]

The report also criticised Nelson's treatment of the case of Leslie Clements, whose suicide attempts and allegations against Tŷ Mawr were at the heart of Nelson's article inside the paper. Nelson had conducted a lengthy interview with Clements, but later the young man regretted what he had said and asked his foster brother to intervene. As a result some of his allegations were not published.

The inquiry documented this incident. To Nelson's credit it recorded the brother's opinion that 'Mr Nelson had behaved honourably' when he was approached as a result of Leslie's second thoughts. But the report continued with an implied criticism of Nelson for treating Leslie as a reliable source. The common description of Leslie, it noted, was that he was 'articulate, well spoken, well mannered and well turned out. He was plainly deeply unhappy. *He was not always truthful. On occasion he fantasised or exaggerated* [italics added].'[21]

In 1990 Leslie had made an allegation of sexual abuse against another boy at Tŷ Mawr. In the Autumn of 1990 a case conference was held about these allegations. According to the report, 'The decision was made that, bearing in mind his frail emotional state, *it would not be right to interview Leslie at any length with a view to the complaint being pursued.*' The report added: 'We have carefully reviewed all the material available in respect of this decision and have concluded that it was a decision properly and responsibly made on appropriate professional advice.'[22]

During the early part of 1991 Leslie increasingly came under pressure as discussions continued about whether he should be moved from his long-term foster parents who were very attached to him. 'It was at this time of difficulty and stress (April 1991) that Leslie had his interview with Mr Dean Nelson,' the report said.[23]

The implicit criticism here is serious: that Nelson had interviewed a vulnerable and damaged young man at a time of great stress, with the intention of publishing a newspaper story which might actually increase that stress.

Nelson's suggestion that Leslie Clements had committed suicide because of his experiences at Tŷ Mawr was rejected. The report concluded that his foster mother loved Leslie deeply and quoted her view of the home: '[She] spoke of the care given at Tŷ Mawr in the highest terms. She felt that the staff offered help to Leslie and to her family at a time when they were unable to cope with him.' Having considered the circumstances of Leslie's suicide, the authors concluded: 'Neither Tŷ Mawr nor its staff could be fairly blamed for Leslie's death.' Moreover, while Tŷ Mawr lacked relevant psychiatric expertise, 'within the limits of what was available, the staff at Tŷ Mawr did their best'.

The section of the report dealing with cases of suicide and self-harm is particularly instructive and demonstrates how dangerous it can be to make causal inferences from sets of facts (or alleged facts) which may not in reality be causally related. 'In many ways,' the authors wrote, '... Tŷ Mawr unfortunately became the whipping boy in respect of incidents, many of which could not sensibly be connected to Tŷ Mawr and certain of which Tŷ Mawr was not to blame for.'[24]

A further implicit criticism of Nelson and other journalists who had covered the story is contained in one of the report's conclusions:

> Every journalist should, we believe, pause carefully before publishing allegations so as to ensure that young persons' interests are not sacrificed in favour of short-term sensation. ... There are many opportunities for mischievous allegations against institutions like Tŷ Mawr. Such allegations can cause great damage and ought to be verified with care before being published.[25]

Earlier in their report the authors issued a general warning to journalists and others:

> We would ... issue a word of caution. Anyone interested in the welfare of young people should be extremely circumspect in dealing with those who may be vulnerable or suggestible. Irresponsible allegations without careful verification can be extremely damaging.[26]

However, while the Tŷ Mawr report was commendably full in many respects, two points were omitted from it. Perhaps the most important was its failure to make clear how the allegations against Tŷ Mawr had come to prominence in the first place. According to a former teacher at the home, the publicity had its origins in a personality clash between two members of staff and the principal.

In pursuing a grudge against the principal, these members of staff had involved the organisation NAYPIC, and a concerted attempt had then been made to ensure that the school was given bad publicity. According to the same teacher, a number of the boys involved in the rooftop riot in June had met up the evening before the demonstration with somebody from outside the home in what amounted to 'a council-of-war'. 'When the riot actually took place,' recalls the teacher, 'I'll never forget watching the press running across the fields – because they'd all been forewarned. So these kids, most of them very, very, very disturbed, were being used really just to pursue salaciousness. And I think that was the thing that really upset me more than anything about it.'[27]

In becoming involved uncritically in a campaign to discredit an entire institution, Dean Nelson had shown questionable judgment. In presenting sensational and tendentious links between acts of suicide or self-harm and the regime at Tŷ Mawr, he was effectively accepting a script which others had written. Almost as disturbing was the manner in which the entire story had been presented.

Although the photograph of Tŷ Mawr published in the *Independent* on 27 May appeared to show a prison-like building surrounded by a high wire perimeter fence, Tŷ Mawr did not have a perimeter fence. Outside the confines of the small secure unit, boys were free to come and go as they pleased. How, then, had the *Independent* managed to take a photograph of the home which gave a quite different impression?

A teacher at the school has given his account of the photographer's visit: 'He came on the site one day and opened the tennis court, took a photograph of our cell block through the mesh of the gates of the tennis court and then through the wire mesh to make it look as though we were some sort of prison camp. It was the most disgraceful bit of journalism I've ever come across in my life.'[28]

It is conceivable that the photographer in question was not deliberately setting out to misrepresent the nature of the home. However, as the journalist responsible for investigating the entire story, Dean Nelson must have become aware at some point, whether before or after its publication, that the photograph was misleading. Yet there is no indication that he ever voiced disquiet about it.

It was this same journalist, practically every aspect of whose investigation into Tŷ Mawr was open to question, who had now been entrusted by the *Independent on Sunday* with the task of investigating the story of Bryn Estyn.

3 The whistleblower

IN THE AUTUMN OF 1991, as Dean Nelson embarked on his second investigation into care homes in Wales, the Tŷ Mawr inquiry had only recently begun to hear evidence. The inquiry was still in session when his article about Bryn Estyn and Tŷ'r Felin appeared on 1 December 1991. Had the Tŷ Mawr report already appeared, the editor of the *Independent on Sunday* might well have reached a different conclusion about the paragraph on Gordon Anglesea which he decided to publish.

When, just over a week after the appearance of Nelson's articles, the offices of the *Independent on Sunday* received a letter from Anglesea's solicitor, it became a matter of urgency to assemble the evidence on which the passage about him, with its libellous implication that he was involved in the abuse of children at Bryn Estyn, had been based. As the hunt for evidence began, one thing rapidly became clear. There was none.

In relation to the two principal figures in the story – Peter Howarth and Nefyn Dodd – there was some material which might be produced. Its quality was open to question, but at least it existed. In the case of Anglesea, as Ian Jack would later candidly admit to me, the newspaper had published one of the gravest possible libels without having 'a shred of evidence' to support it. At this point there was not even an allegation against him.[29]

It was certainly true that Anglesea *had* resigned from the police. And although it would not be accurate to describe him as a regular visitor to Bryn Estyn, his ordinary police duties had taken him there on a number of occasions. But, so far as the libellous implication of the paragraph was concerned, there was nothing at all to suggest that this was based on anything other than an error, or a malicious invention.

Once it had been established that the evidence which would have been required to justify the libel did not exist, the simplest course for the paper to take would have been to back down, agree damages and print an apology. However, it would seem that the journalists who were most closely associated with the story had themselves become convinced that Anglesea's sudden resignation and his visits to Bryn Estyn concealed a sensational scandal. In their view, the responsible course for the paper to take was to investigate this part of the story further. Perhaps because of the very seriousness of the allegations, Ian Jack allowed himself to be persuaded on this point.

Dean Nelson was in due course despatched to North Wales again. Ideally his role would have been to dig deeper into the story to establish whether Anglesea was indeed involved in sexual abuse at Bryn Estyn, or whether he was an innocent man who had been libelled. In practice, however, it would seem that Nelson saw his task as a simple one: it was to discover evidence which would substantiate the libel and vindicate his story.

The decision to send Dean Nelson back to North Wales as part of an attempt to defend a libel action was intrinsically hazardous. In due course it would vastly complicate a story which was already complicated enough and add immeasurably to the sum of human anguish associated with it.

But, even without the story of Anglesea, the saga which had begun to unfold was sensational enough, involving as it did some of the most serious allegations about care homes which had ever been made. It would be quite wrong, however, to hold Nelson himself entirely responsible for this saga. For if it had a main author, then this was not the freelance journalist who had brought it to the attention of the public. It was the woman on whom he had relied as his principal witness throughout the period in which he had researched his article – the former residential social worker, Alison Taylor.

By now the name of Alison Taylor is reasonably well known to many people. Even at the time Dean Nelson's article appeared in the *Independent on Sunday*, in December 1991, she had already played a central role in a television programme about Tŷ'r Felin made by HTV. Since 1991 she has been the subject of countless newspaper interviews and features, and has appeared in innumerable radio and television programmes. The publicity given to her increased considerably with the setting up of the North Wales Tribunal. On a number of occasions she was portrayed in the media (quite accurately in many respects) as the single individual without whom one of the most powerful government tribunals in modern history would not have come into being.

Alison Taylor, however, does not only have a claim on public attention through her involvement in the North Wales Tribunal. She is also a writer. In 1995 her first crime novel, *Simeon's Bride,* was published. Marcel Berlins in *The Times* described it as 'a dark, densely woven tale of passion'. It was, he wrote, 'a disturbingly good debut'. In 1996, on the strength of this debut, she received a substantial advance from Penguin Books in a two-book deal. In 1998 Heinemann brought out her novel *The House of Women*, and compared their new author directly to Ruth Rendell and P. D. James.

As one of the principal witnesses to the abuse which allegedly took place at Tŷ'r Felin, where she worked as the deputy to Nefyn Dodd, and at Bryn Estyn, where she completed a three-month placement in 1982, Taylor's credentials have often seemed to be beyond question. This was certainly the case in 1991 and there can be no doubt at all that the story which Dean Nelson heard from her lips was a compelling one. A story which skilfully wove together a senior police officer who had retired in mysterious circumstances, a deputy head of a community home who was a bachelor and a secret child abuser, and the head of an assessment centre who had a reputation for kindliness but who was in reality a sadist and a voyeur, might very well turn out to be true. And a larger plot, linking all these characters by the device of a paedophile ring which had infiltrated children's homes throughout North Wales, and bought the silence of an entire police force by paying senior offi-cers in the currency of children – even such an improbable plot as this might have a basis in fact. But it might also turn out to be a fiction, cre-ated (in part at least) by an author who was indeed a worthy successor to Ruth Rendell and P. D. James.

Ultimately it is only by considering carefully the events which led to the creation of the story of North Wales that we can discover whether this story is based on fact or whether, in some respects at least, it is a work of the imagination. Before we follow the thread of the narrative forwards by relating what took place when Dean Nelson returned to North Wales, it is therefore necessary first to follow it backwards to the very centre of the labyrinth from which it originally emerged. For that thread leads to Alison Taylor herself and to a series of allegations which were mysteriously made in an order quite different from the chronol-ogy of the events they claimed to record.

The woman who would eventually side with those she saw as the vic-tims of authority in North Wales had herself had a troubled life, both as a child and as a young adult.

Alison Taylor was born on 20 April 1944. The daughter of Welsh par-ents, she was brought up in England. When she was eight her parents separated 'or rather,' as she herself has vividly put it, 'ripped apart the family like wild animals fighting over a carcase'. The searing pain conveyed by these words is something she seems still to feel, and in 2004 she recalled this period in her life in the column she writes for the social work magazine *Community Care*:

> As a child I was bullied for being plump, clever, foreign (Welsh) and from a broken home, suffering for my differences through no fault of my own. Miserable but angry, I eventually took the war into the enemy's camp and, in front of a full class and a teacher, floored the ringleader.
>
> However, the broken home issue, when an eight-year-old girl slung the barb 'your father doesn't love you enough to live with you', before admitting that she was only repeating her mother's words, proved how often adults make the bullets that children fire.[30]

From primary school, where she had clearly at times been deeply unhappy, Taylor went to her local grammar school in Glossop, Derbyshire. She was a gifted pupil who took A levels in French, pure and applied mathematics and the history of art and architecture. She then embarked on a course in architecture at Manchester University.

After two years of study, however, she gave up her course at around the time that her first child – a girl – was born. Suffering, it seems reasonable to infer, from the stigma which still attached to being an unmarried mother during the 1960s, she appears to have had considerable difficulty in establishing a career.[31]

It was at this point that she turned her sights towards social work. Over the next twelve years, between 1964 and 1976, she mixed voluntary work with a series of short-term jobs which included spells working in a psychiatric clinic, a rehabilitation unit in Stockport and a probation hostel in Sheffield.

It was during this difficult period in her life that her mother suddenly died. As she would write in a newspaper article, 'Thirty years ago, an allergic reaction to medication killed my mother very quickly and without any warning.' Her reaction was interesting and perhaps significant. She imagined that her mother's ghost was present in the house: 'Unprepared and obviously unwilling to leave us, she roamed house and garden for the following three days. I saw her leaning over my daughter's bed; my daughter saw her everywhere; on the eve of her funeral a neighbour and myself watched her walk downstairs then heard the front door open and slam shut.'[32]

In 1974, at the age of 30, Taylor married a 19-year-old man, Geoffrey

Taylor, whom she had met during her work some two years earlier. By the time she married this bright but emotionally troubled young man, her daughter was eight or nine years old. Soon after she had married she gave birth to a second child, a boy. She and her husband then decided to move from inner-city Sheffield to a more rural environment. Taylor at this point applied for the post of deputy-officer-in-charge at the Tŷ'r Felin Assessment Centre in Bangor. She was successful in her application and took up her post in September 1976. Untrained and unqualified, like many residential social workers in the 1970s, she now began an extremely difficult job at a time when she had a six-month-old baby who was cared for by her husband while she was at work.

Although Alison Taylor had never completed her university course, she was regarded by some of those who worked with her at this time as something of an intellectual. She appears to have been familiar with some progressive writings about institutional care – in particular the work of Erving Goffman – and there seems little doubt that she was motivated by a genuine idealism. From the very beginning of her career as a residential social worker she set herself against the pressures towards conformity which were much in evidence in residential care homes in the 1970s. She had an ability to establish relationships with some of the most difficult and damaged adolescents she encountered, and to take their part against authorities which were sometimes seen as oppressive or tyrannical. Her own experience of being the victim of bullying as a child seems to have played a significant role in shaping her subsequent life. She readily identified with anyone she felt might be a fellow victim, and she seems never to have forgotten that moment of childhood triumph when she says she floored her main oppressor in front of a full classroom. Precisely because she had such a ready sympathy with victims, and because she was also intelligent, resolute and determined, she appeared to have many of the qualities required of a good residential social worker.

Tŷ'r Felin, the home she joined at the beginning of her new career, had been opened in 1975 as a centre to assess the needs of almost all the children – or young adolescents – who were taken into care in the county of Gwynedd. Children might become the subject of care orders made by the courts for a number of reasons. It might be because of family violence or breakdown or it might be because of persistent criminal offences. A care order in effect meant that control of the child passed from parents to social workers. From the point it was made it would be for the social services to decide on a child's future – whether the child would be fostered, sent to a small children's home, returned to its own family, or sent to a community home with education on the premises (CHE). This latter was generally regarded a tougher option, reserved for more difficult children, many of whom would previously have been sent to approved schools.

The assessment process at Tŷ'r Felin, which soon began to focus on more difficult children who were considered unsuitable for fostering, normally lasted for twelve weeks. It was carried out by a team which included a visiting educational psychologist, child guidance staff, the child's social worker and the staff of the home itself. One of the duties of the officer-in-charge was to organise the whole process and to chair the case conferences and reviews which were held in relation to almost every young person who passed through the home.

The first head of Tŷ'r Felin, a well-qualified and experienced man, was Haydn Jones. Jones appeared to be coping well with a difficult task. However, soon after Alison Taylor was appointed, there were signs of conflict. Rightly or wrongly he came to the conclusion that Taylor was seeking to undermine his authority. He felt that his inexperienced but talented deputy was ignoring instructions and trying to replace the regime he had established with one of her own. Taylor for her part gives a quite different account in which she portrays Tŷ'r Felin as an institution which was without direction or proper management. Her view was that Jones was impervious to change and that, whenever she suggested necessary changes in the regime, she would be brushed aside.[33]

Wherever the truth may lie there can be no doubt that relations between Jones and his deputy became progressively worse. The failure to establish a good working relationship placed Jones under immense stress and on a number of occasions he came close to breaking-point. In January 1977, four months after Alison Taylor had started work, there was a dramatic development. D. A. Parry, the deputy director of Gwynedd Social Services, who was in charge of residential care, received a phone call from Haydn Jones, asking him to visit Tŷ'r Felin urgently. When he arrived he discovered Jones in a state of emotional distress. He told Parry that he had been reduced to this state by the behaviour of his deputy, that 'she had undone everything again' and that he couldn't take any more. So great was Jones's distress that Parry recalls having to 'cuddle him like a child'.[34]

Simply because he was in a state where he appeared close to a nervous breakdown, Haydn Jones was sent home. He began a long period of sick leave from which he would never return.

In his absence, Alison Taylor took over as acting officer-in-charge and was faced with the challenging task of running Tŷ'r Felin on her own. In spite of her many talents she did not succeed in winning the approval of her immediate line manager, D. A. Parry. He felt that she did not discharge her new role effectively and that her style of management left a great deal to be desired.

In 1977, a few months after she had taken on the duties of Haydn Jones, and while he was still on sick leave, Taylor applied for the position of third-in-charge at a care home in Glamorganshire. In the reference he wrote, Parry made positive mention of 'her immediate link with the children'. This was prefaced, however, by a more negative appraisal: 'It is my view that she is a person unsuited to the post which she currently occupies. She is not happy working with the total responsibility of the establishment devolving upon her. … Her professional experience especially of residential care is limited and the truth is that in many respects she is "learning on the job".'

Taylor did not succeed in the application but, when the post of officer-in-charge at Tŷ'r Felin was advertised, later in 1977, she applied. Although she was interviewed, she was unsuccessful again. The candidate appointed was Nefyn Dodd, who came to Gwynedd with glowing references – which included a recommendation by Matt Arnold, then the head of Bryn Estyn where Dodd had worked.

Dodd, however, did not only come with good references; he had considerable experience of residential care, a professional qualification, and a reputation for being both firm and fair towards the children in his care. On his appointment in November 1977 he was immediately sent on an induction course. He finally took up his post at Tŷ'r Felin in January 1978. At this point Alison Taylor was notified by letter that she had been relieved of her temporary responsibilities and that her salary would be reduced to its former, lower level.

The relationship between the new officer-in-charge and his deputy had not got off to a good start. Their first contact had taken place in August 1977 shortly after the post had been advertised. After making a prior arrangement with Gwynedd County Council, Nefyn Dodd and his wife, June, arrived at Tŷ'r Felin to look over the home. They recall that they were turned away by Taylor who declined to show them over Tŷ'r Felin on the grounds that she was off-duty at the time.[35]

Taylor's abilities to form links with children were still very much in evidence. But her managers regarded her attitude to work as a matter of continuing concern. On 1 February 1978, she received a letter signed by the director and initialled by D.A. Parry, who clearly bore the major responsibility for its contents. The letter was an official reprimand relating back to Taylor's performance as acting officer-in-charge. It noted that she had received an exceptional amount of support and guidance but that, 'it remains a matter of deep concern that much of that guidance was responded to inadequately or ignored'.

The letter acknowledged that her work with the children was satisfactory, but it gave examples of what it called Taylor's 'unsatisfactory fulfilment of administrative and managerial responsibilities', noting that 'these have been detailed to you verbally *ad nauseam* by Mr D.A. Parry'. Further complaints referred to slip-shod book-keeping and to the 'indefensible condition' of case records. The emphasis of the letter, however, fell on 'the problems of co-operation between yourself and the original officer-in-charge as well as with your recent deputy'. The purpose of the letter was to make clear that the attitudes Taylor was said to have shown were unacceptable.[36]

How fair these strictures were is now impossible to say. Taylor may very well have felt that, as a progressive-minded and ambitious woman who was in some ways more talented than her immediate line managers, she was being victimised and even bullied by her male superiors. Her managers may have seemed to her more concerned with form-filling than with the inner welfare of the children in their care. The letter she received, however, did end on a more positive note: 'I am certain that you will find in Mr J.N. Dodd a senior officer capable of enabling you to feel that your contribution to the progress of Tŷ'r Felin is given full support and encouragement.'

Almost as soon as Dodd took up his post, however, Taylor took extended sick-leave after falling ill with an allergy. In her absence Dodd introduced sweeping changes both to the regime of the home and to its fabric. When he arrived at Tŷ'r Felin he felt strongly that it was run-down and lacked any feeling of comfort or homeliness. As it was increasingly being used for longer term residents, and not simply as an assessment centre, he decided on a programme of refurbishment. The premises were decorated, the gardens tidied and pictures hung on the walls. The regime itself was subject to a process of 'tightening-up' and Taylor's attitudes towards child care, which might be described as 'libertarian', were replaced by attitudes which were much more structured and which in some respects might fairly be characterised as authoritarian, or even regimented.

Although the new regime was much stricter than the old, for many who visited the home at this time there seemed to be a palpable improvement both in its physical appearance and in its atmosphere. It would appear, however, that Taylor resented these changes and that she also resented the way in which her own position of authority had been usurped. Larry King, a principal officer who socialised with Nefyn Dodd and with Alison Taylor, and who had a high regard for the abilities of both, recalls a social evening he spent with Taylor. She told him of her unhappiness at having to work with Mr Dodd and referred to his introduction of a 'school uniform' for the young people in care at Tŷ'r Felin. 'As I listened to her,' King would tell the North Wales Tribunal, 'I realised that her dislike was more to do with not being in charge. Her dominant character was much the same as that of Mr Dodd and here I was, being invited to take sides.'[37]

Taylor now claims that she was a reluctant applicant for the post of officer-in-charge, and had put herself forward only after pressure from Parry. However, this scarcely squares with the low estimate of her abilities Parry held at the time. Nor was it the impression gained by Larry King. 'She wasn't very reluctant. I don't believe she was reluctant to take charge. She would have taken charge immediately if Dodd had disappeared.' In King's view she was disappointed not to have been offered the post herself.[38]

Although the relationship between Taylor and Dodd had not broken down at this point, considerable tensions were in evidence. So acute did these sometimes become that Dodd may well have felt relief when, after two years, Alison Taylor was seconded to undertake professional training.

In September 1980, she left Tŷ'r Felin to attend the Cartrefle branch of Wrexham College, where she embarked on a two-year course with the aim of gaining her first professional qualification – a Certificate of Qualification in Social Work. During this course she would undertake a placement in a community home which then enjoyed a mixed reputation, but which has subsequently become the most reviled and notorious 'children's home' in modern British history – Bryn Estyn.

In view of the various dark pictures of Bryn Estyn which have been drawn in recent years, many of them endorsed by Taylor herself, it is particularly illuminating to study the small cache of evidence which survives from the period of her first contact with the home.

4 An invaluable placement

ALISON TAYLOR BEGAN HER PLACEMENT at Bryn Estyn on 15 March 1982. As a mature student with five years' experience of residential care, she was given a wide variety of duties. This meant that she had every opportunity to observe the workings of the home both through the eyes of the staff and of the sixty or so boys who were resident there at the time.

One of Taylor's duties was to organise activities involving shopping, budgeting and clothing, which had already been introduced by permanent members of staff. Another task led her deeper into the home's workings, for she undertook a survey on perceptions of care, using the high figure of 50% of Bryn Estyn boys as her sample.

As might be expected of any institution in which a large proportion of the residents had actually been sent by the courts, and therefore had criminal records, the views of Bryn Estyn which this survey revealed were far from being wholly positive. When asked about their level of trust in the staff, 70% of boys said that they trusted some staff. But 20% said they trusted no staff. On the question of punishment 80% of the boys thought that the system of punishment at Bryn Estyn was fair. At the same time, however, 50% of the boys questioned felt that the system was inconsistently applied.

The survey which Alison Taylor conducted certainly did not indicate universal content. But, to those who approach the results of this survey by way of the home's more recently acquired reputation, the portrait which it paints is unexpected. Commenting on the results of this survey in June 1982, Taylor herself wrote that: 'In general, there seemed to be a very low level of negative comment about Bryn Estyn itself.' She added that 'a high proportion of the sample also felt that positive changes were occurring in their own level of functioning since admission and they attribute much of this to the establishment itself'.[39]

The significance of the survey, however, went far beyond its tabulated results. For, by the very act of giving her questionnaire to the boys, Taylor was obliquely advertising the presence of a sympathetic outsider – one who, as the content of the questionnaire proclaimed, was prepared

to listen to negative comments. Yet, in the documentation which survives from the period of her placement, there is no record of any specific complaint made to Taylor, let alone any complaint of physical or
sexual abuse.

Far more eloquent than the lack of any such record are the words
which Taylor wrote in the Bryn Estyn log book after she had completed her placement in June 1982:

MR ARNOLD AND ALL STAFF

I would like to express my sincere gratitude and appreciation to yourself and your staff for the support, guidance, warmth and interest
extended to me during the past three months. I have found the placement to be invaluable on a professional level, and exceedingly satisfactory on a personal level and am sorry that the time has passed so
quickly. I shall take many very pleasant memories, and a great deal of
valuable experience, back to Gwynedd with me. My very best wishes
for the future, and many thanks for all you have offered. I hope we shall
have further contact in the future, and that you will all be able to continue to offer what I feel is a fine service to the boys here.[40]

These words convey the impression that Mrs Taylor's view of Bryn
Estyn was positive, that she felt the staff generally performed their
duties competently and caringly, and that in some respects at least, boys
were benefiting from their stay there.

It was also the case that, while she was at the home, Alison Taylor
demonstrated her ability to make relationships with exceptionally troubled young people. One of the boys whom she got to know at this time,
Ryan Tanner, was considered difficult even by Bryn Estyn standards.

Tanner, like Taylor, had been at Tŷ'r Felin before coming to Bryn
Estyn. In a number of respects his experience as a child in care exem-
plified many of the shortcomings of the system. According to the
account which he gave to the police in 1991, his parents had split up
when he was only one and his stepfather had moved into the family
home when he was three. Although his mother and stepfather had tried
hard to control him, he says that he became a 'tearaway' at a very young
age. When he was eight he began stealing money from the electricity
meters which were housed in the coal sheds of a nearby estate. He himself said that because he was getting away with it he soon became
obsessed with stealing. 'I was a compulsive thief, but then I started getting caught for my wrong-doing. As far as I can remember, I would say
that between the ages of eight and ten, I would be at a police station

two or three times every month as a result of stealing.'[41]

At this stage in his life Ryan and his mother might be thought to be in need of help and guidance. However, then as now, the age of criminal responsibility was ten and, at the extraordinarily young age of 10½, the boy was actually taken away from his family and remanded into the care of the local authority. After spending the 21-day remand period at Tŷ'r Felin, he was taken to court at Holyhead where he was made the subject of a care order and placed in another Gwynedd home. The care order was imposed for 'burglary and theft from a meter'. The court took 23 other offences into consideration.[42] Although the initial care order was for a relatively brief period, Ryan found that it was difficult to return home. He had, in short, been effectively 'sentenced' to spend the rest of his childhood in care. The first report on him, signed by Nefyn Dodd, captures both the vulnerability and the sensitivity of the young boy at the beginning of his long separation from his family:

> Ryan was admitted to Tŷ'r Felin accompanied by his social worker. He was visibly shocked and tearful but quickly settled after his social worker's departure. In fact, considering he had never been in care before, his adjustment to his new environment was made with relative ease.
>
> ... Ryan is a bright, pleasant boy who outwardly presents a cheeky couldn't-care-less attitude. He is, however, quite sensitive and unsure of himself ... His behaviour, as such, has not given cause for concern. He appears very open and honest. For the most part he has behaved sensibly, but has on a number of occasions needed to be reminded of his behaviour. ... He is a likeable boy.[43]

After his brief spell of remand at Tŷ'r Felin, Ryan spent several months at two other homes in Gwynedd, returning in between the two placements to his family. Then, in September 1981, at the age of fourteen, he was sent to Bryn Estyn.

It was perhaps not entirely surprising that this highly intelligent but unruly child, finding himself surrounded by other boys, and by an almost entirely male staff, appears rapidly to have arrived at the conclusion that toughness was a virtue and that might was right.

Effectively schooled in a culture of bullying – the kind of culture which almost inevitably grows up among boys in male-dominated boarding schools (which in effect Bryn Estyn was), Ryan Tanner soon emerged as one of the shrewdest and toughest of all Bryn Estyn residents. In a note written during the period of Taylor's placement, Matt

Arnold recorded his impressions of the boy. 'Tanner,' he wrote, 'certainly is becoming one of the most unpopular children in Bryn Estyn both amongst his peers and staff. This unpopularity is centred largely around his verbal abuse of all, coupled with threatening and belligerent attitudes to younger children and to such staff as he feels he can comfortably threaten.' To this assessment he added a single, seemingly gratuitous observation. 'Alison Taylor has a working relationship with Ryan Tanner.'

Seven years were to pass before Taylor would renew her relationship with Tanner. When this happened he would become one of the principal figures in the North Wales story. Partly as a result of his actions and of the manner in which he came to believe – apparently quite sincerely – in a version of his past which Taylor had helped him to construct, Bryn Estyn would be presented in a very different light from that in which it appeared in Taylor's farewell note.

Before meeting up again with Tanner, however, Taylor would single-handedly trigger two police investigations in Gwynedd. The first, in 1984, involved one allegation against a single teacher. The second, in 1986, involved a number of allegations. This second investigation, though still relatively small, was carried out by two police officers, one of whom was the head of the North Wales CID. The investigation which he led had a disturbing outcome and the report he submitted to the Crown Prosecution Service was both forceful and unusual.

Fortunately, as a result of the North Wales Tribunal, most of the elements of a police investigation which would normally remain hidden, including a report to the Crown Prosecution Service, have been brought into the public domain. For the first time it is possible to tell the full story of what actually happened in the 1986 investigation.

Before that, however, it is necessary to relate the events that took place in 1984. The inquiry mounted by the North Wales Police on this occasion would be regarded by most people as a minor one. But, just as a mighty river has small beginnings, the consequences that ultimately flowed from it would be momentous indeed.

5 A bump and a bruise

WHEN ALISON TAYLOR HAD completed her placement at Bryn Estyn and her CQSW course at Cartrefle College, she returned to the authority which had seconded her – Gwynedd County Council. In August 1982, she took up a post at Tŷ Newydd, a small care home on the outskirts of Bangor, where she became non-resident officer-in-charge.

She now had a degree of autonomy which she clearly and under-standably welcomed. Her working relationship with Nefyn Dodd, however, which had become so vexed in the period leading up to her secondment, continued. This was because, as principal officer-in-charge of residential care for children, he remained effectively her manager.

There is some evidence that Dodd made efforts to repair his rela-tionship with Taylor and to bestow praise on her where he thought it was due. But the relationship remained strained. So too did Taylor's relationship with other senior officers. One sign of this came some two years into her new job when she received a letter from the deputy director, Gethin Evans. The letter asked her to explain why, on the pre-vious day, when a group of six magistrates had paid a pre-arranged visit to Tŷ Newydd, she had declined to welcome them or meet them, and had stayed in her office throughout their visit.

Taylor replied claiming that she was ill and suggesting that 'certain members of the Department are seeking for every opportunity to level criticisms about me, whether these are warranted or not'. The deputy director did not accept Taylor's explanation and, on 23 May 1984, asked her to attend a formal disciplinary hearing relating to 'an unacceptable standard of performance by an employee'.[44]

Three days after this request had been made, Taylor typed a memo to the deputy director and to Dodd. It related to a 14-year-old resident at Tŷ Newydd, John Mason, who was then attending school at Tŷ'r Felin. Taylor wrote that she had been informed on the previous night by John and another boy 'that John had received a blow on the head on Thurs-day, and that he had a painful swelling and bruising'. He had been taken to hospital on Saturday from Tŷ Newydd and an X-ray had revealed no serious injuries. Taylor closed her memo by noting that the injury had apparently been sustained in the schoolroom at Tŷ'r Felin and that John had prepared written details of how it occurred.

In this memo no indication was given that Mason's injury was anything other than accidental. Three days later, however, Taylor wrote a letter to the director, Lucille Hughes. In this letter the incident had become an allegation and she reported for the first time that Mason wished to make a complaint. She enclosed a copy of the boy's own statement in which he claimed that, during one of the lessons, the teacher, John Roberts, had smacked his face and knocked his head against a desk. The boy said this had resulted in a swelling on his temple.

The letter was acted on at once and the social services department served a copy of the complaint on Roberts. He then supplied a statement giving his account of what had happened on the day in question. Either as a result of this statement, or as a result of a further internal investigation, the allegation was deemed to be without substance.

Four months later, however, in September 1984, Alison Taylor contacted the police and informed them that Mason wished to make a complaint of assault against a member of staff at Tŷ'r Felin. As was noted in a police report compiled by Woman Detective Constable Joanne Bott, the complaint concerned 'a bump and a bruise which later faded'. But Taylor was also complaining about her employers and sought to bring the matter forward without her own identity being revealed: 'Mrs Taylor claims that she has not been informed of the action taken, if any, in response to her report, and took it upon herself to report the matter, in confidence, to the police. She is obviously fearful that a "cover-up" has taken place ... and she is therefore reluctant that the police reveal the source of their information.'[45]

The investigation into this complaint was undertaken by Detective Inspector Roy Gregson and WDC Bott. They interviewed the main protagonists including John Mason, Nick Embury (another boy), John Roberts and Alison Taylor. Roberts, they said, had been described as 'a sincere, dedicated teacher with a completely unblemished career record'. When interviewed, he freely admitted that, after Mason had repeatedly misbehaved on the day in question, he had given him 'a tap' on the top of his head with an open hand. But he had not hit him on the side of his head. 'There is no way he hit his head on the desk', he said, 'it's too low. He only got a tap on the head and a row.'

Both officers questioned the motivation of Taylor in contacting the police. In her report WDC Bott noted that the relationship between Mrs Taylor and the social services department had 'become strained' as a result of persistent absconding by children in her charge 'for which she was admonished by her department'.

In his report DI Gregson wrote that 'This incident has been blown up out of all proportions.' He felt that both Mason and Embury were unreliable witnesses and, having drawn attention to the delay in reporting the alleged incident, he continued in the following terms:

> I am given to understand that Mrs Taylor has been reprimanded by her employers (Social Services) in relation to her duties, and I have no doubt whatsoever that she started the wheels in motion purely to 'get one back' on her employers, because of her mistaken belief of a 'cover-up' by them. … It might well be that Mason did sustain a swelling to his temple but it might equally be that he sustained it outside school hours.

What Gregson did not know when he wrote these words was that the Tŷ'r Felin log book for the relevant period contained entries which lent weight to his suggestion. These came to light thirteen years later when the incident was examined by the North Wales Tribunal. As was pointed out by the barrister representing Roberts, the delay in reporting Mason's injury meant that it could have had a quite different origin, such as a fight. The barrister then cited a series of entries in the log book in the days immediately preceding the complaint. These entries suggested that Mason had indeed been involved in fights with another boy. Since Taylor had made these entries herself it was remarkable, to say the least, that she had not brought this evidence to the attention of the investigating officers in 1984.[46]

If Taylor's approach to the North Wales Police on behalf of John Mason was intended to embarrass the senior officers who had given her a formal disciplinary warning, it was not, on this occasion, successful. However, as would gradually become clear over the next decade, Taylor's approach to the police in 1984 about a bump and a bruise was but a preliminary skirmish. Her next attempt would take place two years later, in 1986. It too would, in the short-term at least, prove to be unsuccessful. But it would have much larger repercussions which would be felt far beyond Gwynedd. It would lead not only to sensational coverage in the national press but to concerns being expressed by a member of parliament and to the intervention of the Attorney General himself. Indeed the 1986 investigation would ultimately lead, by way of Clwyd and the involvement of two Conservative prime ministers, to the setting-up of the North Wales Tribunal.

6 Black and blue

THE DISCIPLINARY WARNING which Taylor was given about the magistrates' visit was not the only rebuke she received. Some idea of the range of complaints made against her during this period is conveyed in a letter sent to her in July 1985 from the county personnel officer. It had been written in response to complaints she had made about the attitude taken by management and senior colleagues towards her. In particular she had objected to being told that she was 'never in work', that she 'owed time to the department', and that she was 'lying'. The personnel officer expressed his view that these were 'matters which could be ironed out in a "round the table" discussion and any misunderstandings cleared up'. Taylor contested all these charges, arguing that the allegations against her were unfounded: 'I am advised that these allegations are very serious, and tantamount to an accusation of fraudulent practice, and must therefore insist on the matters being investigated properly, particularly the allegation that I owe time to the department.'[47]

Whatever the rights and wrongs of the various contested issues (and the fault may not have been all on one side) it is clear that there was considerable friction between Taylor and her managers. One of the factors which almost certainly speeded the development of the events which were soon to unfold was that Alison Taylor's position now became even more precarious. This was because plans were mooted to close Tŷ Newydd. In November 1985 a memo from the director, Lucille Hughes, referred to the closure of Tŷ Newydd as 'imminent'. Were this to happen there was a strong possibility that Alison Taylor might be made redundant. As her husband was unemployed and she was the sole breadwinner, this was something she could ill afford.[48]

By this time the relationship between Dodd and Taylor had deteriorated further. In November 1985 Dodd prepared a hand-written memo to his superiors opposing a request by Taylor for an increase in salary:

In terms of progress/development it is sincerely felt that this worker remains the victim of her own folly, in that she fails miserably to exploit her own potential, and persists with her insatiable appetite for mayhem and conflict with management ... whilst less experienced Officers-in-Charge, potentially less capable, use their personal talents and attributes to the full, for the benefit of client children and the department.[49]

Until this point Taylor had made no allegations against Mr Dodd. However, in the year which had elapsed since she had unsuccessfully triggered the investigation into John Roberts, she had accumulated a number of further complaints, some of which did concern Dodd.

At the beginning of 1986 Taylor approached a local Liberal councillor, Keith Marshall, and told him that she was aware of a number of allegations of physical abuse which had been made by young people in care against employees of Gwynedd County Council. She claimed that some of these complaints had already been brought to the attention of senior management and that no appropriate action had been taken. The complaint which Taylor made to Marshall was therefore a serious one which suggested not only that young people were being abused, but that the very social services department responsible for their care was failing to investigate complaints properly. It might even have been inferred from Mrs Taylor's words that the management was actively engaging in a cover-up whose purpose was to conceal the abuse which was being alleged.

Councillor Marshall now contacted the police in order to relay these complaints to them. Because of their political sensitivity, they were immediately brought to the attention of the assistant chief constable. It was then decided at the very highest level of the North Wales Police that, in view of the seriousness of the allegations, a senior officer, Detective Chief Superintendent Gwynne Owen, would be instructed to take charge of the investigation in person.

Owen had joined the North Wales Police in 1956. He had risen steadily through the force, had been promoted to detective superintendent after 18 years and to detective chief superintendent after 24 years. In his role, first as the deputy head, and then as the head of the CID, he had taken part directly or indirectly in the investigation of all major crimes in North Wales over a twelve year period. By 1986 he had already dealt with almost fifty cases of murder and during his long career he had received a number of commendations and awards.

His investigation into complaints about residential care in Gwynedd began in February 1986 when he visited Councillor Keith Marshall at his home in Bangor. Alison Taylor was also present at this meeting and it was immediately clear she was the person who was bringing forward the complaints – complaints which she suggested others had made.[50]

As well as describing these complaints in detail, Taylor referred to allegations of abuse which she said had been investigated by Nefyn Dodd and Larry King. She claimed, in effect, that allegations had been swept under the carpet.[51]

Owen was concerned both about the age of the allegations which Taylor had brought forward and about the lack of first-hand evidence. Some of the allegations she relayed also struck him as highly coloured; she described one young person as having been 'beaten black and blue', in spite of the fact that she had not witnessed the alleged assault or seen the victim's injuries.[52]

Partly because of his own misgivings, and partly because he had noted the views expressed by Detective Inspector Gregson in his report on the earlier investigation, Owen approached Taylor's new complaints with a degree of caution. But he acknowledged that the allegations were serious and recommended that they be investigated.[53] After the chief constable instructed Owen to conduct the investigation himself he took a full statement from Taylor on 26 March 1986. Her statement did not contain any evidence that she had witnessed abuse herself. But it did supply information about seven alleged offences of physical assault. These offences were said to have been committed by various care workers, including the teacher John Roberts, an untrained care worker Robert Sussams*, and Nefyn Dodd, together with his wife June Dodd, who also worked at Tŷ'r Felin.

Since Alison Taylor's allegations hinted at the existence of an organised cover-up stretching into the uppermost reaches of the social services department, Owen decided that, in order to avoid any further suggestion of cover-up or collusion, he would begin his investigation without approaching any of Taylor's superiors.

When he began to investigate, however, it soon became clear that there were difficulties with the evidence. Jennifer Dunlop, the first young person referred to by Mrs Taylor, had supposedly been beaten severely by Mr Dodd. As a result she was badly bruised on her body; it was she who had been, in Taylor's words, 'beaten black and blue'. Other members of staff who were there at the time were said to have been aware of this incident, as were the other young people in residence.

* Not his real name.

But when Jennifer was interviewed by WDC Joanne Bott in the presence of her foster mother, she made it clear that no such incident had happened. In the statement compiled by the officer she says, 'It is fair to say that whilst I stayed at Tŷ'r Felin at no time was I treated in an unreasonable or unfair manner. Never was I smacked by any member of staff for any reason. I heard the boys got smacked when they were naughty but the girls were never smacked. On no occasion did Mr Dodd lift a finger towards me, or even threaten to do so.'[54]

The freshest of the seven allegations concerned a boy, Michael Thomas, who was said to have complained in February 1986 directly to Alison Taylor that Mrs Dodd had assaulted him. The incident had taken place after Michael and two other boys had caused trouble at the home and then run away. The alleged assault took place when they were returned to the home later that night. According to a memo written by Taylor at the time, the next day Michael 'stated without any prompting to myself, Mrs Ashton and a police officer that Mrs Dodd had hit him the previous night. He said that she thumped him on the shoulder and knocked him into a chair when he refused to apologise for his part in the trouble.'

Taylor added that this version of events had 'essentially been confirmed separately by two of the children who witnessed the incident'. She then asked that this complaint should be investigated by her managers.[55]

This allegation was in fact investigated, after a delay, by Gethin Evans, the head of children's services. On 12 March he spoke to Michael Thomas and to the two other boys who had been present. None of them said that he had been hit by Mrs Dodd, still less 'thumped'. All three suggested that she had pushed him when he had been cheeky to her and had refused to apologise. He had then fallen into an easy-chair.

Subsequently Gwynne Owen interviewed the boy, who demonstrated what had happened. Mrs Dodd had placed the flat of her hand on his shoulder and pushed him down into a chair behind him. This version of events was confirmed by Mrs Gillian Roberts, who had been present:

> Mrs Dodd asked them to apologise to Mrs Jandrell for the trouble caused. The three other boys apologised, Michael Thomas did not. He smiled defiantly and would not apologise. Mrs Dodd had Michael by the shoulder of his clothing and pushed him into a soft easy-chair and told him off for his cheek. That's all the so-called assault amounted to. It was nothing more than what I would apply to my own child. It was

not an assault by any stretch of the imagination. I would like to point out that Mrs Dodd was very fair, but firm with all the boys.[56]

In her statement Taylor said that Michael Thomas had not only informed her 'that he had been assaulted by Mrs June Dodd' but that he had made the same complaint to PC Evans. In his report, however, Evans said that no such complaint had ever been made to him.[57]

Another allegation was actually brought forward after the investigation was underway. A boy, Sam Doherty, had told Beryl Condra, the officer-in-charge at Queen's Park in Holyhead, that his friend, Barry Doughty, had complained of 'being battered' by Nefyn Dodd. Mrs Condra then relayed this to Taylor. Taylor, instead of ascertaining the strength of the complaint, telephoned DCS Owen. Although described in the North Wales Tribunal as 'third-hand information', this complaint was, if true, fourth-hand. Yet when Barry Doughty was interviewed about his time at Tŷ'r Felin, he said that no assault had taken place. Described by Owen as an 'alert, sharp, courteous boy', he made a statement which included the following words:

> During the whole of my time there – one year and eleven months – no member of staff there ever hit me, beat me or did anything wrong to me in any way. If anyone says that I was beaten he or she would be saying lies. I have been told that Sam Doherty says I told him that Mr Dodd had battered me; this is not true – Sam is saying lies. I know Sam doesn't like Mr Dodd. I have never been beaten by Mr Dodd.[58]

Alison Taylor had also sought to revive the complaint concerning the bump and bruise sustained by John Mason, even though this had already been investigated by the police. At the same time she had brought forward a new complaint behind which there lay a disturbing story. Because of the serious form which this complaint would take, and because of the particular role which Taylor would play in recording its details, it was one of the most important in the entire 1986 investigation.

7 Aide-memoire

IN THE STATEMENT she made to DCS Owen on 26 March 1986, Alison Taylor reported an allegation she said had been made by a 16-year-old boy, Peter Harbour. Then a resident of Y Gwyngyll, a small children's home at Llanfairpwll in Anglesey, he had previously spent a year at Tŷ'r Felin. During this time he had supposedly been subjected to persistent assaults by Nefyn Dodd and John Roberts. In her statement Taylor made an even more disturbing claim: 'The assaults occurred not only after Peter had misbehaved, but it would seem on a regular basis as "entertainment" for others. It is alleged he was punched, slapped, kicked.'

Understandably, given the seriousness of the complaints, Owen chose to interview Peter Harbour himself, with the assistance of Joanne Bott. They conducted their first interview with him on 10 June 1986 at Y Gwyngyll.[59] The boy was adamant that he had not been abused in any way by either Dodd or Roberts:

> Whilst at Tŷ'r Felin and Tŷ Newydd, I got to know the members of staff quite well and it would be fair to say that I was treated in a decent manner and on no occasion was I improperly treated. Never during my stays at Tŷ'r Felin and Tŷ Newydd was I assaulted or publicly humiliated by any member of staff.[60]

However, during the afternoon of 10 June, Peter asked to speak privately to Detective Chief Superintendent Owen. He now said that he *had* been assaulted on a number of occasions by Dodd and Roberts. He described one incident where he claimed he had been punched in the mouth by Dodd, and another where he said that Roberts had kicked him in his 'private'. Owen asked him if he would make a signed statement to this effect. He said that he would if this could be done in the presence of his social worker. This meeting was duly arranged and took place a week later. On this occasion Peter declined once again to make any statement. He did, however, make his allegations orally, though in a revised form. He described how he and two other boys had been overheard planning to run away from Tŷ'r Felin. This information had been relayed to Dodd, he claimed, and the three boys had been called to his office. Here, he said, in the presence of June Dodd and another care officer (the alleged informer), Dodd had punched him in the mouth, cutting his lip with the ring which he wore.

Harbour went on to revise his allegation about John Roberts. Whereas he had previously claimed that Roberts had kicked him 'in the private' he now said he had been '*elbowed* in the balls' as entertainment for the class. He also said that Roberts had caused a revolving blackboard to strike him on the head. He further claimed that he had reported these incidents to Alison Taylor two and a half to three years previously (which would have been while he was still at Tŷ'r Felin).[61]

If the latter claim was true Taylor would have been aware of Harbour's allegations when she first brought forward the complaint about John Mason in 1984. The fact that she made no mention of any such allegations at the time strongly suggests that this particular claim was an invention. What makes Harbour's entire complaint even more doubtful is the fact that he had already made an allegation against another care worker which is now known to have been fabricated.

The care worker was Gerry Norman, a former marine, who had only recently begun working at Y Gwyngyll. The false allegation had been made shortly after a tragic incident. One evening, only a week before Taylor made her statement to DCS Owen, one of the girls at Y Gwyngyll, Tracy Partington, received a phone call from her sister. She had telephoned to tell her that a boy called John, whose girlfriend, Sue Carter, was in care at Y Gwyngyll, had committed suicide. Tracy rushed to tell Sue, who became hysterical and had to be calmed down by members of staff.

Gerry Norman, who was on duty, rang another care officer and discovered that the boy had in fact died from an overdose and that suicide was not suspected. By this time, however, Peter Harbour was running along the corridor shouting about suicide and Sue had become convinced that she was to blame for her boyfriend's death.

Later that day Sue, Tracy and Peter insisted on going to the hospital to see the body. They returned in the evening, deeply distressed. Norman, who had opposed their visit, now alienated them further by sending them to bed without any supper. The following day, according to Norman, Peter kept 'winding Sue up' by saying that nobody could stop her going to see the dead boy or going to the funeral. When the cook, Mrs Worrall, arrived she spent some time comforting Sue. But, as she recalled, this had a bad effect on Peter: 'Because of this Peter became, in a word, jealous of the attention that Sue was receiving. I knew Peter quite well and I had grown to know his ways. He's the type of person who enjoys the 'limelight' – an attention-seeking individual.'[62]

Peter then retired to his room, apparently sulking, while Norman stayed in the kitchen with Mrs Worrall. A little later Peter abruptly came downstairs and walked out of the home. Later that afternoon two police officers arrived and told Norman that Peter had accused him of assaulting him. Norman thought this was a joke and asked where Peter was. He was told that he was on the way to Tŷ'r Felin with another police officer in order to see Mr Dodd. Dodd, however, was not available and Peter was later brought back to Y Gwyngyll. He was, as Mrs Worrall put it, 'sporting a very swollen left cheekbone'. Peter had told the police that he had been sitting in his room listening to the radio when Norman had burst in and started 'beating the shit out of me'. He had, he said, been punched repeatedly in the face. Mrs Worrall, who had been with Norman most of the time, did not believe the allegation: 'There was no indication that any harm had befallen him ... if Gerry Norman ... had assaulted him, he would have told me about it.'[63]

Having returned to the home, Peter was determined to take matters further. He now left again and went to the telephone box at the railway station. He spoke to Lucille Hughes, the director of social services, and told her of his complaint. She immediately arranged for a car to pick the boy up. He was then taken to Caernarfon where he was interviewed by her. On his return to Y Gwyngyll he made it clear that he did not wish the police to take further action.

The police officer who investigated the complaint wrote in his report that it was his personal feeling 'that this is a malicious allegation made by Harbour in order to cause distress to this person [Norman]. Thus the reason why he does not want to pursue the matter with the police. It would not be hard to believe that the injury to Harbour was self-inflicted.'[64]

Five years later, during the main 1991–2 police investigation, this view received striking confirmation when officers took a statement from Sue Carter. She described how Peter had been arguing with a member of staff whose description matched that of Norman:

> Following the argument Harbour came to join us by the steps to the loft. He had a bruise on his face from an earlier incident on his left cheek. We were talking about it and Peter decided to start hitting himself to his face by this bruise to cause a more serious injury. He then said he would make a false allegation against the ex-army member of

staff to get him dismissed. He was not liked because he was very strict. … We all agreed to go along with his story, although we all knew Peter had not been assaulted at all. Peter rang Lucille Hughes or somebody similar to make the complaint. The police were involved and this man was suspended and never came back to work at Y Gwyngyll.

This statement renders inescapable the conclusion towards which the evidence already pointed: Peter Harbour's allegation against Norman had been deliberately fabricated and his injury had been self-inflicted.[65]

There is nothing to suggest that Alison Taylor had any involvement in this allegation, but it seems almost certain she would have been aware of it. It may well have been a factor in her decision to bring forward the entirely new set of allegations she attributed to the boy. The fact that Harbour refused to make a police statement about this second complaint, and also refused to make a statement in the presence of his social worker, only underlines the parallel between the two allegations.

However, this was not the end of the matter. It so happened that at this particular point in time Y Gwyngyll was closed and the boy was transferred to Tŷ Newydd where Taylor was officer-in-charge. The next month, Gwynne Owen received a telephone call from Taylor. She said that Harbour now wished to make a statement of complaint to the police 'as he doesn't want the same thing to happen to other children'. Joanne Bott was sent to Tŷ Newydd in order to interview the boy. When she arrived she was presented with a typed statement which Taylor had prepared for Harbour as an aide-memoire.

Although Harbour had learning difficulties, and although Taylor herself had described him as 'somewhat slow-witted', the statement which she had prepared was fluent and articulate. In language which was clearly not his own, Harbour said that he had changed his mind about making a statement: 'I have now had time to think about things and I know that I have an obligation to make a statement because other children could suffer if they are treated the same way.'

The statement which Taylor had compiled on his behalf also contained a series of allegations about Nefyn Dodd and John Roberts. Some of the allegations had already been made orally to Owen. In his 'statement', however, Harbour now claimed not only that he had been elbowed in the testicles by Roberts, but that 'Mr Dodd also kicked and kneed me in the testicles on several occasions'. After two of these occasions, Harbour claimed, in what was a novel complaint, and, in part at least, a medical *non sequitur*, 'I was in great pain when I passed water and also coughed up thick blood.'

In a progressive intensification of the atrocities previously proclaimed, the statement goes on to describe the punishment allegedly
meted out to him after he had been overheard plotting to abscond. He
claims that Dodd, while wearing heavy rings on his hand, punched him
'really hard in the mouth':

> Blood started pouring out of my mouth. My bottom lip was cut right
> across. My clothes were taken off me so that I could not go out and I
> was not allowed to see a doctor. ... My face was swollen for about five
> days. I was kept in my pyjamas all the time and not allowed out, and
> was not allowed to contact my parents or my social worker.[66]

In a significant change of testimony, the two witnesses previously
referred to, June Dodd and the other care officer, now disappeared.
There were also aspects of Peter's recent allegation against Norman
which made the new story outlined by Taylor all but impossible to
uphold. In the first place, the person to whom he had initially wanted
to relate his complaint about Norman was Nefyn Dodd. In the statement taken from him on 10 June, Harbour said 'I wanted to see him
specifically because he is Principal Officer in charge of homes in this
area and I regard him as a fair trustworthy man.' Owen noted that Harbour also told him 'that Mr Dodd was kind to him and would help him'.
This view would appear to be wholly incompatible with the story of
Harbour's having been systematically bullied and humiliated by Dodd.

In the second place the fact that Harbour had, again on his own initiative, successfully contacted the director of social services and been
interviewed by her, made the complaints about Dodd and Roberts
even more unlikely. The idea that Harbour, while being interviewed by
the director about Y Gwyngyll, had omitted to bring to her attention
a series of allegations about much more brutal forms of bullying at Tŷ'r
Felin, is almost wholly implausible.

Although Harbour made a statement to DC Bott whose terms closely
followed the aide-memoire, it is reasonably clear from all the circumstances that the testimony he gave as a direct result of Taylor's intervention was unreliable and, in all probability, untrue in every particular.

However, although Harbour provided what might be described as a
spectacular example of unsound testimony, the common thread which
ran through a whole series of unreliable allegations was Taylor herself.

8 Two cans of shandy

MOST OF THE COMPLAINTS brought forward by Mrs Taylor at this time were of physical abuse. But there were also some hints of sexual impropriety. These, relating principally to a former resident of Bryn Estyn, would gradually develop into serious allegations. In a number of respects, they prefigured what was to come.

The allegations emerged during the course of Taylor's attempt to revive complaints which had been made against Robert Sussams, a part-time care worker who at one point had complained to Nefyn Dodd about Taylor's frequent absences from work.[67]

In the statement which Taylor gave to Owen on 26 March 1986 she repeated one complaint which had originally been made in 1985. This particular allegation – that Sussams had slapped a girl called Helen Jones – appeared to be well-founded in that the incident had actually been witnessed and reported by another care worker. The matter had been dealt with at the time by senior officers and Sussams had been warned about his conduct. However Taylor now claimed, for the first time, that Helen had made several previous reports to her of 'physical chastisement' by Sussams: 'Helen claimed that Mr Sussams used to hit her around her head – usually when she was upstairs – going to bed or at bathtime.'

Owen saw these words as hinting at a sexual irregularity. For this reason Helen was questioned closely by Joanne Bott. However, she made it clear that Sussams never visited her in her bedroom when she was on her own, and that he had never been in the bathroom at the same time as her. Helen, indeed, seemed shocked by the very suggestion. Perhaps more importantly there was no evidence to support Taylor's claim that Helen had made 'several previous reports' to her of physical chastisement. Helen said that she had been slapped by Sussams on only one occasion. Taylor herself had made no reference to any earlier complaints made by Helen when she had originally brought the matter to the attention of her senior officers in July 1985.

The reference to Helen Jones, however, was not the only allegation against Sussams that Taylor sought to revive. She had already, in 1985, brought forward another complaint – namely that on one occasion he had taken a boy called Simon Birley to a pub and allowed him to drink a number of cans of shandy. Birley, who had previously been at Bryn Estyn, was nearly seventeen at the time.

When Dodd and King had investigated this complaint, Sussams had freely admitted that, while supervising Simon Birley for a decorating project, he had, as a treat, taken the boy to the Douglas Arms at Bethesda. He said that this pub had a full-size snooker table, that Simon had said he would like to play on one and that it 'had all been quite normal, public and socially instructive. He had purchased two tins of shandy – they had certainly not been drinking all afternoon – distances alone would preclude this and he resented the inference that he might perhaps be trying to corrupt this youth. He [Birley] is not a little child, but nearly a man, who had been to Detention Centre and Approved School [i.e. Bryn Estyn] …. He felt no harm was done.'[68]

The complaint about the visit to the pub was discussed by Nefyn Dodd who suggested to Sussams that the problem was 'not so much what was done – as what can be read … into it by anyone who wishes to twist the facts – not forgetting the dangers inherent should the youth later make allegations'.

It is not clear whether Taylor was aware of these words at the time. If she was, they may have planted an idea in her mind. For during the original meeting with Councillor Marshall and Gwynne Owen she had referred to Birley. Moreover the suggestion which she now made was that, to use Owen's words, 'there had been a homosexual relationship' between Robert Sussams and two former residents of Tŷ Newydd – Simon Birley and another boy, Sean Herbert.

In Owen's view it was significant that when Taylor made a signed statement some days later she did not repeat what he describes as 'this allegation'. Nevertheless, given the grave implications of what she had said in the initial meeting, Owen felt he had a duty to investigate. Although he was, at first at least, unsuccessful in tracing Herbert, he managed to trace Birley to an address near Wrexham. Birley told him that no sexual advances had ever been made to him while he had been in the care of Gwynedd County Council. He made a statement in which he confirmed this: 'During my time at these homes I was never assaulted, ill-treated or humiliated in any way by members of the staff. Most of the staff were fair and firm. I have no knowledge of any cases of assault or ill-treatment of children, and there were, as far as I am aware, no homosexual practices among inmates and staff. No homosexual advances were ever made towards me.'[69]

It might be thought that the statement given by Birley to Owen in July 1986 would signal the end of any suggestion by Taylor that he might have been sexually abused. However, perhaps because she was never made aware of the outcome of Owen's inquiries in this respect, the opposite was the case. Birley would eventually be contacted by Taylor herself and would play a key role in the allegations which she brought forward against former members of staff at Bryn Estyn.

However, Birley would not reappear in the story until five full years had elapsed. For the time being at least Taylor would remain almost entirely concerned with events which had taken place – or which had not taken place – in Gwynedd. The principal reason why her predicament in Gwynedd now became so serious was that Detective Chief Superintendent Owen, despite conducting extensive inquiries, had failed to find any evidence which might conceivably lead to a successful prosecution. More disturbingly still he had discovered a significant amount of evidence which suggested that, in some cases at least, Taylor was bringing forward allegations whose unreliability she must at least have suspected. In some instances, as in the case of Peter Harbour, there were indications that the situation was even more serious.

The time was drawing near when Owen would have to express his own conclusions about such matters both to his senior colleagues and to the prosecuting authorities.

9 A mysterious caller

OWEN'S SCEPTICISM ABOUT TAYLOR'S MOTIVES was not dispelled by the long interview he now conducted with Nefyn Dodd. He expressed this scepticism, with considerable force, in the report which he sent to the newly-formed Crown Prosecution Service.

By the time Owen submitted his report to the CPS, he and his colleague, Joanne Bott, had interviewed dozens of witnesses, including a number of Taylor's colleagues. Having set out in detail the results of these investigations and the deficiencies in the evidence which they revealed, Owen gave his own view of the woman who had triggered the investigations:

> Mrs Alison Gwyneth Taylor's role in the whole episode is questionable. She is an intelligent, articulate and strong-minded woman who appears to exert a strong influence over colleagues. Her attitude towards the management of the social services in Gwynedd can properly be described as subversive. ... Her relentless pursuit of every opportunity to discredit her colleagues is unfortunate. ... It is the investigating officer's opinion that many of the allegations were not spontaneous complaints made by child residents, but rather the result of deliberate trawls and subtle interrogation of children facilitated by some form of reward, e.g. cigarettes.[70]

On 14 October 1986 the Crown Prosecution Service decided, in the light of this report, that there would be no prosecution. This decision was then relayed by letter on 20 October to Councillor Marshall and Mrs Taylor.

Taylor would later claim that, when the letter addressed to her (and marked 'confidential') arrived, she was not at Tŷ Newydd. She said that, in her absence, the letter was opened by another member of staff and that this led to recriminations against her. Whether this claim is true or not, it was undoubtedly the case that many of her colleagues felt they had been betrayed by her and subjected to an orchestrated campaign of false allegations.

These feelings of betrayal were all the more acute because of the manner in which the investigation had been reported. Initially there had been no publicity. But on 11 September 1986 a prominent story appeared in the *Daily Mail* under the headline 'POLICE NEAR VERDICT ON CHILDREN'S HOME PROBE'. According to this story a six-month police investigation into 'allegations of brutality at a council children's home' was nearing completion. Various details of the allegations were given. These included the entirely false claim that 'a 12-year-old girl has told police that she was beaten black and blue after being overheard to say she did not like the home'. In a clear reference to the allegations made by Harbour, the report told of a 16-year-old boy who claimed he had been persistently assaulted: 'He claims on one occasion his lip was split by a punch in the mouth and he was then kept in his pyjamas for five days without medical attention until the swelling went down.'

From the details which were given it was reasonably clear that, although the story may have come to the *Daily Mail* by an indirect route, it had originated with Taylor herself. Not surprisingly it was immediately taken up by the local press, with the *Bangor Mail* giving prominence to a photograph of Tŷ'r Felin above a story headlined 'HOME UNDER A CLOUD'.

Around the time these stories were appearing, in September 1986, copies of an anonymous hand-written statement were sent to a number of individuals and local organisations. These included the chairman of the social services committee, the clerk to Gwynedd County Council, the director of social services and the police. Alison Taylor also claimed that she had received a copy.

The statement, purporting to be made on behalf of '**Concerned parents and Residents in Gwynedd**', referred to the allegations which were being investigated by the police and suggested that there was malpractice and corruption on the part of officers of Gwynedd Social Services. It went on to demand a public inquiry.

In October 1986 a copy of this statement was sent anonymously to a local councillor. Enclosed with it were two documents he subsequently produced to the police. The first was a copy of the statement taken from Peter Harbour by Alison Taylor. The second was a statement taken by Taylor's colleague, Beryl Condra, making an allegation of sexual abuse against a woman care worker.*

The only possible sources for these documents were the two care workers who had prepared them and the police officers to whom they

---

* This was an allegation made by Graham Ennis, see below, pp. 71–4

had been given during the investigation. However, the copy of the second document in the possession of the police bore Beryl Condra's signature and the words 'This was written in my presence'. The copy received by the councillor did not have this endorsement. The circumstantial evidence strongly suggested that the 'confidential' statements had been put into circulation by Taylor herself.[71]

By this time Taylor had been informed of the fact that the police and the CPS had decided not to prosecute. This decision, taken in mid-October, was reported prominently in the local press under such headlines as 'CLOUD LIFTED FROM CHILDREN'S HOME' and 'HOMES CLEARED OF CHILD ASSAULT'. Claims that staff at these homes had been 'cleared' and 'entirely vindicated' were now vigorously contested by a correspondent in the *Bangor Mail* who signed himself 'James Browne', and whose address was withheld. In a series of letters he implied that children in care in Gwynedd were still at risk. Two local councillors took issue with his comments. Councillors Frank Woodcock and Jill Knight wrote to the paper to say that they had visited Tŷ'r Felin on a number of occasions, often unannounced, and were confident that the staff were doing good work: 'If your correspondent, Mr James Browne, is so positive that abuse has occurred at the Tŷ'r Felin Children's Home, why does he not give his evidence to the proper authorities and allow his address to be published in your paper?'[72]

The identity of 'James Browne' remained a mystery. It emerged, however, that during September, shortly before the appearance of the story in the *Daily Mail,* some local councillors, including Keith Marshall, had received telephone inquiries from a man who called himself 'Geoffrey Brown' and described himself as a 'freelance journalist'. Although inquiries were made by the police, no such journalist could be traced. One lead, however, was provided by a former reporter on the *Bangor and Anglesey News.* She did have a contact called Geoffrey who, she said, made a habit of bringing her stories, and who had provided her with information about Tŷ'r Felin. The name of this contact was Geoffrey Taylor.

One evening in February 1987 Councillor Jill Knight received a phone call from a man who identified himself as 'James Browne'. He claimed that there were fresh allegations and asked if this would make her change her mind about Tŷ'r Felin. Knight immediately recognised the distinctive voice of her mysterious caller as that of a man who, in her capacity as chair of the local Citizens Advice Bureau, she had recently interviewed for a vacancy as a voluntary worker. She could not remember the name of this man but she did recall him saying that he did not have a job and looked after his son while his wife worked full-time.

This phone call was brought to the attention of the director of social services, Lucille Hughes, who was herself the chair of the Caernarfon Citizens Advice Bureau. Recognising the circumstances of the applicant described by Councillor Knight, and knowing the woman who was the organiser of the Bangor CAB, Hughes inquired of her whether she knew a Mr Geoffrey Taylor and whether she and Councillor Knight had ever interviewed him. The organiser confirmed that a Geoffrey Taylor had applied to be a CAB interviewer in the summer, that he had been interviewed and, though not accepted, was now helping with office work.

From these various clues the identity of the mysterious caller was clear. He was none other than Geoffrey Osbourne Taylor, who looked after his young son during the day while his wife, Alison Taylor, worked full-time as officer-in-charge at Tŷ Newydd.

There is, of course, nothing to suggest that Alison Taylor's husband was attempting to mislead anyone about where the truth actually lay. On the contrary he may have sincerely believed his wife's reports of alleged abuse and may have considered that he had a citizen's duty to support her allegations. If so, he would be by no means the last person to take such a view.

10 Over the goalposts

WHATEVER THE MOTIVATIONS of 'James Browne' may have been, the message conveyed by his actions was that a campaign was now being conducted against Gwynedd Social Services. This campaign was not going to cease merely because of a decision taken by the Crown Prosecution Service. This was confirmed when, on 12 November 1986, the *Bangor Chronicle* published a story under the headline 'SHOCK MOVE AFTER HOME CLEARED'. This reported that the Lancashire MP Geoffrey Dickens, who was described as 'a leading campaigner for child protection', had been contacted by 'local people' who were dissatisfied with the outcome of the police investigation.

Dickens, who in 1988 would speak in parliament about the alleged prevalence of satanic abuse in Britain, said he had been sent 'a pile of evidence' about Tŷ'r Felin. This consisted of a 15 to 20-page file containing correspondence from 'concerned people', including statements from some of the children who were formerly at the home. He said he was deeply concerned: 'I am not at all satisfied and feel that not all the evidence was revealed during the police investigation.' He forwarded the file to the Attorney General, Sir Michael Havers, who agreed to look into the decision not to prosecute. Before this review could be completed, however, there were two further developments.[73]

Having discovered that Taylor had been responsible for calling in the police, a number of colleagues expressed their unwillingness to work with her. On 1 December 1986 the director of social services wrote to her, asking her not to come into work while the breakdown of working relationships was being investigated. The director interviewed members of staff at Tŷ'r Felin and Tŷ Newydd and a catalogue of complaints emerged. Some colleagues felt that communication between the two homes had become impossible because of Taylor's reluctance to entrust any information, however trivial, to any member of staff she deemed 'junior'. Taylor's compliance with the duty rota was also a problem. According to a document produced by a senior officer, 'Staff of Tŷ Newydd … referred to the constant need to make excuses and lie when someone telephoned from Tŷ'r Felin wishing to speak to Mrs

Taylor in person. Also they referred to Mrs Taylor's ... habitually being unwell ... and having missed the bus and wishing staff to come and collect her by car. ... Mrs Taylor's lateness, I understand, became the subject of bets!'[74]

More seriously, in the view of one of her colleagues, Taylor had sacrificed the welfare of children in order to pursue her own campaign: 'If a person is suspicious of a child being ill-treated there is a procedure to take that is for the benefit of the child. The procedure which Mrs Taylor has taken, I feel, was not for the benefit of any child, especially the children with whom we work.'[75]

Even as these criticisms were being made, and in spite of the fact that she had been reprimanded and formally disciplined, Taylor was quoted in the local press as saying that her work had never been criticised. 'The longer I am away from work,' she said, 'the more damage will be done to my professional reputation, which until now has never been subject to criticism.' Six days later, on 13 January 1987, Taylor was officially suspended because of 'the breakdown of professional working relationships between yourself and other staff of the children's section'.[76]

There was also another development. In February 1987 the social work magazine, *Community Care*, reported that there was to be a second abuse inquiry in Gwynedd. At the end of December 1986 a Police constable had been contacted by a Mrs Hannah Thomas, who had been in care at Tŷ'r Felin during the time Taylor had been deputy to Dodd. Hannah Thomas now claimed that four young people had been physically assaulted during this period.

The first assault which she described had supposedly been carried out by Dodd at Tŷ'r Felin on a 12-year-old boy, Sean Smith. Thomas gave a graphic description of how Dodd had allegedly attacked the boy for failing to clean his shoes properly: 'Mr Dodd grabbed hold of Sean and kicked him, as if he was kicking a football, he struck Sean in the stomach. The kick winded Sean who just fell onto the floor and curled up, he lay groaning on the floor, curled into a ball. ... From memory the kick was to the solar plexus with the toe of his right foot and at the time he wore shoes.'[77]

Sean Smith was traced and numerous attempts were made to interview him. On every occasion, however, he declined to co-operate with the police. It was subsequently discovered that he had never been at Tŷ'r Felin.[78]

Hannah Thomas's second allegation concerned Tony Harris, who was about fifteen at the time of the alleged incident. She said that Harris had been mowing the grass when Dodd had become angry with him: 'All of a sudden he picked him up like a bag of spuds [and], using both hands, he threw him over the top bars of the football posts. ... Tony landed with a loud thud the other side of the goalpost and lay there. He was helped up to his feet by a care staff member whom I think was named Mr Martin.'

When interviewed, Harris said that he had indeed been thrown over the goalposts in the manner described. He also alleged a number of other assaults. He said that one of these, which he described in graphic terms, had been witnessed by one of the Tŷ'r Felin domestic staff, Mrs Florence Williams. When interviewed, Mrs Williams said that she had no knowledge of the incident and had not witnessed it.[79]

Mr Martin was then interviewed about the goalpost incident and said he had not witnessed any such assault. Another former member of staff *had* heard Dodd rebuking Harris for trying to mow the grass when it was wet. This witness said she thought that Dodd's attitude was unreasonable but she did not see him physically punish the boy in any way.

Gwynne Owen established that, at the time in question, Harris had weighed about nine-and-a-half stone. Even though the Tŷ'r Felin goalposts were considerably lower than the regulation height of eight feet, Harris's claim merited scepticism. When it was set in the context of the three negative witness statements, the only conclusion that could reasonably be drawn was that the allegation was false. The two other allegations proved, on investigation, to be no more substantial.[80]

Partly because of the timing of Hannah Thomas's approach, Gwynne Owen suspected the involvement of Taylor. This was vehemently denied at the time by Thomas. During the North Wales Tribunal, Taylor's own denials that she had prompted Thomas to complain were prominently reported by *Private Eye*.

In the course of the 1991–2 police investigation, however, Hannah Thomas was interviewed again by the police. She was given a copy of the statement which she had made in 1987 and said that she stood by all her allegations. But she went on to give an account of how she had come to make the statement. 'About two to three weeks prior to my making this initial statement I had a letter from Mrs Alison Taylor. ... This letter asked me to get in touch with her as she wanted to discuss Tŷ'r Felin with me. I telephoned her and she asked if I would give a statement to the police regarding my stay and treatment at Tŷ'r Felin.'[81]

Alison Taylor has disputed this version of events and claims that the only contact she had with Hannah Thomas took place after Thomas had approached the police at the end of 1986. Whether or not this was the case, nothing Gwynne Owen learned during his second investigation disposed him to change his mind about Taylor. When he submitted another report to the CPS he concluded it with the following words:

> The officer's view regarding Taylor remains unchanged and there is every likelihood that she will manipulate others in the future to make similar complaints, in an effort to keep the matter in the public domain, and in the belief that if sufficient mud is thrown some will stick.[82]

For the next ten years these prescient words would remain in the files of the CPS and the police with very few people aware that they had ever been written.

DCS Owen's words, like the details of his investigation, raise serious questions about Taylor's integrity. As the North Wales story developed over the next few years, their relevance would become progressively greater. However, in assessing the unusual course on which Alison Taylor had embarked it would be the easiest thing in the world to vilify her for consequences which came about as the result of the conduct of others. To do this would be quite wrong. It was not the fault of Alison Taylor if some of the fictions which she appears so artfully to have created were eventually treated by others as true. It is not she who should be held responsible for the fact that a story which she put into circulation, whose falsity should have been clear (and the falsity of whose prologue was certainly evident to Owen), would be treated by politicians, investigative journalists and even a retired high court judge, as a reality.

The question of why Alison Taylor acted in the way she did is a very significant one. Even more important, however, is the question of why, in Britain in the late twentieth century, an entire series of individuals, groups and organisations would respond to her allegations so positively.

11 A righteous zeal?

AFTER FAILING TO ATTEND two disciplinary hearings in front of local councillors, Taylor was finally dismissed on 3 November 1987. When she later took Gwynedd County Council to an industrial tribunal, the council chose to settle out of court rather than fight the action, but it is reasonably clear that this move was a pragmatic compromise rather than a principled reversal of their original position.

The outcome of the industrial tribunal notwithstanding, Taylor had suffered a disastrous setback. If, as the evidence suggests, she had launched the original 1984 police investigation partly in an attempt to shore up a precarious position and keep her job with Gwynedd Social Services, she appeared now to have overreached herself. She had destroyed both her career and her family's livelihood. As a direct result of her actions she was now distrusted by many of her colleagues and regarded with wariness by her former employers and the police.

Faced by such an outcome, most campaigners would give up the fight and rebuild their lives elsewhere. Taylor, however, did not give up. In part this was because she was an exceptionally determined woman who was also unusually resilient. However, there was perhaps another reason. For, in choosing the role of a campaigner against child abuse, Alison Taylor had, almost inevitably, bestowed upon herself a quite extraordinary degree of power.

The role of the moral crusader is well established in our culture. Those who find themselves playing this role most naturally are usually motivated by an idealism which is entirely genuine. Moral crusaders are often seized by the conviction that the world in which they find themselves is deeply corrupt and that the only course open to them is to oppose the tyrannical regime to which they believe they are subject.

Although some observers might feel that the kind of righteousness described here is at odds with the indifference to the truth which Taylor appears sometimes to have shown, to think in this manner is to fail to understand what might be called 'the psychology of righteousness'.

For throughout human history the pattern of conduct displayed by those people who seem to be motivated by a burning conviction in the rightness of a particular cause has been disturbing. Again and again it becomes apparent that those whose consciousness is dominated by feelings of righteousness appear to be psychologically incapable of weighing the moral significance of individual acts according to any calculus other than one derived from their own most passionate beliefs. Indeed, feelings of righteousness sometimes play such a role in an individual's self-image that they overpower ordinary moral sensitivity. Such feelings make it psychologically difficult to acknowledge even the possibility that any action taken in pursuit of an aim which is considered right could conceivably be bad or immoral.

The pattern of conduct described here does not belong to any aberrant or deviant cultural tradition. It is implicit in much of the Bible and was made explicit by Puritan writers in the sixteenth and seventeenth centuries. The Puritan officer in Cromwell's army who saw in the words of Psalm 137 — 'Happy shall he be, that taketh and dasheth thy little ones against the rock' — a licence to murder the infants of Irish Catholics, was merely taking to its logical terminus a doctrine which was openly formulated by some of his Christian contemporaries. 'God is an absolute God,' wrote William Perkins, a pious academic and a fellow at Christ's College, Cambridge, 'and so above the law; and may therefore command that which the law forbids.' Under such doctrines, deception could very easily become legitimate, as is recognised by the historian Michael Walzer:

> Joshua's stratagem in the battle for Ai, Abraham's failure to avow his wife before Pharaoh, Rahab's lie to the king's messengers: all this might be justified by God's command. Rahab hid the spies, Perkins argues, 'not in treachery but in faith'. As God's instruments men may sometimes act in ways to all outward appearances unjust. ... Alexander Leighton allowed considerable latitude to the saintly spy: 'he may conceal the truth, or some part of the truth, change his habit, make show of what he meaneth not to do. In all of which he must take heed that [his lies] be not in matter of religion.'[83]

Although we might like to think that this attitude towards deception is remote from the realities of modern secular society, there is no convincing evidence that this is the case. In business, in international relations, and in party politics there are many examples of the manner in which righteous duplicity, as sanctioned by Puritan divines, still plays a significant role in our public life. Indeed habits of righteous deception have become in some quarters almost second nature. In many cases the person who is in fact practising duplicity may barely perceive the fundamental dishonesty of their own actions and may, because of the very intensity of their righteous zeal, sincerely believe in their own moral probity.

To say this is not to suggest that Alison Taylor stands simply and transparently in the tradition of righteous crusading which is described here. For one of the enduring temptations for almost anyone who is brought up in a Puritan culture is to borrow the robes of righteousness. These robes can then be used to clothe motives which may sometimes have a great deal more to do with self-interest than altruism, or with the opportunistic acquiring of power than its renunciation.

Because 'pure' righteousness is itself, almost inevitably, stained with some form of self-interest, and because it may go hand in hand with an element of dishonesty, it may be extremely difficult to distinguish it from dissembled righteousness; indeed often these two forms are inextricably woven together. But it is perhaps only if we locate Alison Taylor's conduct somewhere in this wide spectrum of behaviour that we can begin to understand the nature of her crusade, and the extent to which an entire society has come very close to entering into complicity with it.

What seems clear is that whenever a cause is regarded as holy and righteous, as the pursuit of alleged abusers now undoubtedly is, it follows that any society which remains essentially Puritan in its outlook will tend to look with a degree of sympathy on any conduct apparently devoted to that cause, however doubtful or devious that conduct may seem. It is also sometimes the case that those who begin by dissembling righteousness for their own ends may actually succeed in deceiving themselves about their true motives. They may end by believing in their own righteous vocation and may actually find it difficult to acknowledge the extent of their own dishonesty in the cause to which they have devoted themselves.

Indeed there are many indications that a course of conduct which may originally be developed through conscious acts of 'justified' deception may gradually come to be seen by the person who follows it in very different terms. Claims which appear to be consciously false, and which may originally have been so, can all too easily become delusions or partial delusions – components in a distorted belief-system which is maintained with at least a degree of what would ordinarily be termed 'sincerity'.[84]

Whether or not this perspective on Taylor's conduct is accepted, it is important to recognise the extent to which Nefyn Dodd remained in many respects vulnerable to criticism. Knowing what she did about his regime at Tŷ'r Felin, Taylor may well have felt that a victory for her own particular kind of righteousness was still possible.

To many who knew him professionally at this time, the idea that Nefyn Dodd was vulnerable might seem surprising. Dodd himself was highly regarded by many senior officers in the social services department and he had also impressed many others who had come into contact with him, from police officers to head teachers. He held firmly to the view that difficult and disturbed young people needed a strong structure imposed upon their lives before they would feel secure, and the force of his own personality, coupled with his sheer physical size (during his time at Tŷ'r Felin he weighed eighteen stone) made him more effective at imposing such a structure than many. Some of those who spoke well of the regime he maintained at Tŷ'r Felin would readily admit that he was 'rough-tongued' and that he would chastise young people verbally. But reliable evidence that he punished young people physically is much more difficult to come by. Many former residents have spoken well of him in this respect. Even Hannah Thomas appeared almost reluctant to believe her own allegations when she reaffirmed them in 1991. In her police statement she made it clear that 'My times at Tŷ'r Felin were happy times. That is as happy as you could be whilst in care. I was allowed a lot of freedom and was never struck by any member of staff. In fact I still felt some allegiance to Mr Dodd.'

Others have been less qualified in their praise. In 1992, for example, after publicity about the latest allegations against Tŷ'r Felin, the Dodds received a letter from former resident Peter Millett which expressed what many others almost certainly felt about their time at Tŷ'r Felin. The letter, which ends by sending a greeting to the Dodds' daughter, Sian, is reproduced here as it was written:

Dear Mr and Mrs Dodd,

Just a few lines to see how you are keeping. Im sorry to hear about the troubles you two have been having. I my self have been interviewed by the NORTH Wales cid. and let me asure you i told them if anything you helped me with my Problem's and in no way did you Absued me in any way what so ever and if need be i would stand in court and say my part for you. Mr and Mrs Dodd if anything this sounds like some little shit is trying to Get his own back on you. Mr and Mrs Dodd if anything i owe you a big favour because if it wasent for you and youre staff putting up with my tantrum's and violent outburst's i would shouley be in H.M. Prison

As you know im in the Welsh Guards at the moment serving in Northern Irland About 15 miles away from Londonderry Well the both of you i WISH YOU the very best in the future and all the best on the troubles youre having Again i thank you for having me.

Good luck
Peter Millett x

P.S. Please say hello to sian

In a number of respects, Peter Millett's letter is a powerful testimony both to the value of the regime at Tŷ'r Felin and to the fact that, at the heart of it, was a strong and determined impulse to care for exceptionally difficult and disturbed young people. However, it would be wrong to suggest that Dodd's approach to childcare was beyond reproach.

The major criticism of his regime, which was outlined by some observers at the time, is that it depended too much on an ethos of control and regimentation. Writing in January 1978, Dodd himself had expressed the desire to achieve a balance between control and permissiveness: 'Our setting should not demand conformity, but there should be an *underlying sense* of control. A moderate amount of permissiveness, space and a sense of freedom are essential so that our children have an opportunity to behave in a characteristic way, and *within limits* give vent to their anxieties and feelings, otherwise observation of their behaviour would not be meaningful.'[85]

Some visitors to the home came away feeling that these aims had been achieved. A Welsh Office inspector in 1978 expressed the view that there seemed to be 'a warm relationship' between Dodd and the children. Much later, in 1989, inspectors noted that 'the general atmosphere was relaxed and friendly'.[86] However, others have since expressed different views. Dewi Evans, the director of social services for Carmarthen, visited the home in 1981. He told the North Wales Tribunal in 1997 that Tŷ'r Felin had the atmosphere of an army camp: 'the kerbstones were all painted white, the youngsters were in uniform and were required to wear a tie with Tŷ'r Felin written on it, and every time they went to the shop for sweets they had to bring back a receipt.' Under cross-examination, however, Evans admitted that the report he had written at the time, while mentioning the use of uniforms and expressing non-specific reservations about Dodd's management style, had made none of the criticisms he now expressed sixteen years later.[87]

Whatever disputes there may be about the degree of Dodd's authoritarianism, there can be no doubt at all that the regime at Tŷ'r Felin was informed by it. It is clear that this affected not only Dodd's relationships with children, but also the way in which he treated his staff. Like many people with powerful personalities he appears to have been unaware of the extent to which he could intimidate people almost by his mere presence. Massively confident in his own approach to child-care, and touchily intolerant of criticism, he tended to drive dissent underground.

One feature of Dodd's regime was his habit of communicating with his staff in writing. Partly because he was frequently absent from Tŷ'r Felin while engaged on his other duties, and partly because his staff worked staggered hours, he rarely held staff meetings. Instead he relied on what might be called 'management by memo', writing opinionated and sometimes abrasive messages for his staff in the Tŷ'r Felin log book. 'My systems are based on several years in the work with more formidable colleagues,' ran one entry, 'so don't doubt my ability, question your own.'[88] Perhaps because he was himself aware of the negative effects of his frequent criticisms, another entry, written in January 1980, ran as follows: 'There is a true saying "To be continually admonished, is to be continually discouraged" so for God's sake and the children's give me an opportunity to express satisfaction of your work.'[89]

Although he frequently rebuked his staff for criticising him behind his back, the vigorous and sometimes bullying nature of his log book entries would almost inevitably tend to encourage the very tendency they ostensibly opposed. All members of staff, except June Dodd, were subjected to criticism. As the Waterhouse report noted, however, Alison Taylor, as deputy officer-in-charge 'fared rather better than the others'. In the entry Dodd wrote on 29 March 1980 there seems even to be a note of regret at her imminent departure to her social work course in Wrexham: 'AGT has responded by doing that bit "EXTRA" which separates the professional from the wage earner. I am sure she will be missed when she goes on CQSW ...'[90]

Like many insecure leaders in all walks of life, Dodd sometimes ran the institution over which he presided as a kind of fiefdom and was vigilant about any attempts to challenge his authority. 'Do not be tempted to usurp my position,' he wrote in the log book, 'or you might have to take on something no one else at this time can cope with.'[91]

It would be quite wrong to stress this side of Dodd's character to the exclusion of all else, but it was an important dimension in the way that Tŷ'r Felin was run. This was reflected in the view of Dodd's regime that was contained in Gwynne Owen's report to the Crown Prosecution Service:

> In the opinion of the investigating officer, Joseph Nefyn Dodd is a strict disciplinarian, jealously protective to maintain and be seen to maintain a well run establishment. He displays varying attitudes of rigidity and flexibility and sternness and kindness, he is somewhat vain and immature in some respects, but he seems anxious to provide a secure and loving environment for unfortunate children.[92]

Whereas some members of staff appear to have accepted the regime he imposed uncomplainingly, other staff members – not only Taylor – reacted to his leadership with resentment. The situation which appears to have resulted was one where some would have liked to criticise Dodd and his regime but were intimidated into silence. This at least was the view of Owen, who wrote in his 1986 report that there was an atmosphere within the residential care sector of Gwynedd County Council where a number of members of staff were 'anxious to wound but afraid to strike'.[93]

This atmosphere was one of which Taylor herself would undoubtedly have been aware, and this can only have strengthened her determination to press on with her campaign against the council in general and Nefyn Dodd in particular. In the first place it meant that she could wage her campaign in the knowledge that at least some elements of the resentment she harboured against Dodd were soundly based. Insofar as she really did experience Dodd's regime as rigid and oppressive she could the more easily justify to herself bringing forward allegations against him whose reliability she was in no position to guarantee. In the second place the resentment harboured by some of her colleagues (and by some social workers) towards Dodd meant that there was a significant pool of people who were ready and even keen to think the worst of him.[94]

What was perhaps even more important was that there were some occasions on which Nefyn Dodd's behaviour had provided even clearer grounds for the kind of righteous criticism that Alison Taylor was intent on bringing forward. It is to the most important of these that we must now turn.

12 Illicit relationships

THE MOST CONTROVERSIAL INCIDENT during the period Taylor was still working for Gwynedd took place at Queen's Park, a small community home at Holyhead in Anglesey. It took place shortly before Taylor made her 1986 statement to the police and concerns a claim made by a resident that he had sex with a young female member of staff at Queen's Park. Shortly afterwards he was moved from the home abruptly in order, he has said, 'to keep my mouth shut about the fact I was sleeping with [her]'.[95]

What happened was that in November 1985, at a time when the officer-in-charge, Beryl Condra, was away on extended sick leave, rumours began to circulate among the residents of Queen's Park. According to these rumours a care officer, Jane Harkness*, was having sex with one of the boys at the home, 15-year-old Graham Ennis.

At the time no formal complaint was made but, in the evening of 20 November, Harkness, who was on duty, told one of her colleagues that she had just received a phone-call from Nefyn Dodd. She said that Ennis was going to be moved out of the home, and a taxi was on its way to collect him. Ennis was half way through eating his tea in the dining room when he was told to pack his belongings.[96]

Without being told where he was going or why, the boy was bundled into a waiting taxi and driven off into the gathering darkness. One of the two men in the taxi eventually told the boy that they were going to Abergavenny and at about 10.30pm they deposited him at the door of Tŷ Mawr – the home which had been the subject of Dean Nelson's first investigation. Explaining to the staff that they were taxi-drivers, they handed over a large envelope containing social services documents and left.[97]

No social worker accompanied Ennis and he had clearly not been prepared for the very different regime he would find at Tŷ Mawr. He had arrived dressed in punk fashion with a lavatory chain and a studded dog collar around his neck, two studded belts around his waist,

---

* Not her real name.

obscene badges on his jacket and similar graffiti covering his jeans. In the view of the staff his punk garb, together with his Mohican hairstyle, would make him into an object of ridicule for Tŷ Mawr residents. To protect him from this he was placed in the secure unit overnight. In the morning he was held in a chair while his hair was cut off. Only then was he allowed to mix with the other residents. The principal of Tŷ Mawr, Christopher Phelan, subsequently complained about the manner of his transfer. As already noted, Ennis himself has said he believed he was moved in order to stop him talking about his claim that he had slept with a member of staff.[98]

When Beryl Condra, the officer-in-charge, returned from sick-leave at the beginning of February, she learned about the sudden transfer. She was then told by a girl resident, and by the brother of another resident, that Jane Harkness had been having sex with Ennis. The brother, who was eighteen, told Condra he had also had sex with Harkness at the home on New Year's Eve. He then made a written statement to this effect.[99]

Condra immediately reported these claims to Dodd. On the following day, Jane Harkness was interviewed by Dodd and his fellow principal officer, Larry King. She denied that there had been any impropriety, saying that the allegations were 'all lies'. Beryl Condra was also interviewed. In her evidence to the Tribunal, Condra said that she was given the impression by Dodd that somebody would be going to Tŷ Mawr the next day (4 February) in order to interview Ennis.[100]

The following afternoon, according to Condra, Nefyn Dodd arrived at Queen's Park and showed her a document which he claimed was a statement from Ennis in which he said nothing had happened between him and Harkness.[101] Condra says that Dodd would not allow her to hold this document and told her that he would deny ever showing it to her. Later that same day a letter was sent to Harkness by Gwynedd County Council informing her that she was 'completely exonerated'.[102]

Subsequently, however, it became clear that no one had visited Ennis in Tŷ Mawr, and no statement had been taken from him. Instead, Dodd had himself compiled a two-page hand-written document, which he claimed was a report of an 'inquiry' he had conducted on the morning of 4 February 1986. The report said that early in the morning of 4 February, 'a telephone request was made ... to Tŷ Mawr that Graham Ennis be interviewed regarding the allegations that he had had sexual intercourse with Miss Harkness within the confines of his bedroom when he was a resident of Queen's Park.' According to the report this telephone request was acted on swiftly and a response was received at a time which was recorded very precisely:

> Following the early morning request by Mr King and Mr Dodd to Tŷ Mawr, at 11.38 of the same date, Mr Dodd received a telephone call from a man well-known to him over the years, that is Mr Phelan, Deputy Headmaster of Tŷ Mawr. Mr Phelan claimed to have thoroughly investigated the allegation with Graham over a protracted period of time and surrendered the following information:
>
> (1) The youth completely 'REFUTES' the allegation, and disclaims any knowledge of any illicit staff/client relationships whilst in residence at the Holyhead Community Home.
>
> (2) Graham admits to a relationship with another client girl, but again he denies any sexual involvement with her, despite at one time absconding to London with her. ...
>
> (3) Mr Phelan then informed the boy 'if you're still feeling bitter about the staff having had you sent to Tŷ Mawr here is a good chance to right an injustice if you want to'. Graham replied 'I got on with all the staff ... and anyway, unlike Tŷ Mawr, 5 Queens Park Close is only a couple of rooms and everyone would know if there was anything going on.'
>
> ...
>
> (5) Mr Phelan stated 'I am thoroughly convinced that Graham is telling the truth and that the whole affair is pure fabrication'. The Deputy Officer then went on to relate to Mr Dodd, as to the very 'Positive' levels of functioning presented by Graham to date at Tŷ Mawr, and the very sound relationship that the boy had formed with himself.
>
> (6) Mr Phelan was thanked on behalf of the Director for his 'punctilious' action on behalf of the Gwynedd Social Services Department.[103]

It is reasonably clear, however, that the telephone call Dodd recorded in such detail did not take place in the manner he described. When Phelan himself gave evidence to the Tribunal, he said he could not recall conducting any investigation into the allegations about Ennis and did not remember making any phone-call to Dodd. When Phelan was asked if it was true that he was well-known to Dodd over the years, he replied: 'Whether Mr Dodd got to know of me by second-hand information, I cannot make any comment, but I was not well-known to Mr Dodd and he was not well-known to me.'[104]

Early in 1986 Ennis himself apparently told the police that the claim about his having had sex with Harkness was true. He also made this claim to a senior social worker. When Harkness was interviewed by the police, however, she again denied the allegations and no action was taken against her. Ennis repeated his allegation to the Tribunal:

> I used to stay up like most nights with whatever member of staff was on the sleep-in and sit in the office and have a brew and a chat and that, and it was one night that [Jane Harkness] was doing the sleep-in, I'd been in the office with her till about three-ish, half-three, something like that, and then I had gone off to my room and then she followed me into my room, and one thing led to another, do you know what I mean?'[105]

When he gave evidence to the Tribunal, Ennis insisted that he had at no time, whether at Tŷ Mawr or elsewhere, attempted to withdraw the allegation.[106] Although this might seem to indicate that Dodd's account of his phone call to Tŷ Mawr was a complete fabrication, there appears to have been at least an element of truth in it. For when Ennis had been interviewed by a television researcher in 1989, he told her that he 'was called into the office of the O in C at Tŷ Mawr and asked if he had slept with any staff. He said no (feeling vulnerable) but did not sign any statement – "absolutely positive about that".'[107]

Given this evidence, and given the fact that Phelan, when questioned at the Tribunal, could remember neither the telephone conversation with Dodd nor calling Ennis into his office, the most likely explanation of what happened is that Dodd had fabricated not the fact of the telephone call, but the details which he recorded. It seems possible, indeed, that the inquiry he made was deliberately cursory, and that Phelan had failed to remember his interview with Ennis precisely because the questions he had been asked to put to the boy had been of a general and vague nature. If this was so then one possible reason for conducting an inquiry in this manner was that its instigator – Dodd – might himself have been seeking a negative result.

This version of events must remain speculative. But if, as I have suggested, Dodd deliberately conducted a 'weak' inquiry into the allegations, the apparent purpose of his action was to persuade his senior officers to exonerate Jane Harkness and allow her to keep her job. Although Dodd denied it at the Tribunal, the evidence suggests that he had himself originally given the order for Ennis to be moved from Queen's Park and that he had done so in a deliberate attempt to protect Harkness from an allegation which, whether true or false, would have been damaging to her.[108]

Whether or not this explanation is correct, Dodd's conduct in relation to this matter was not straightforward. It seems reasonably clear, however, that the motives for his apparent dishonesty were not sinister in the sense that he was attempting to conceal known or suspected paedophile activity. Both Nefyn Dodd and his wife had got to know Jane Harkness well. Dodd was evidently fond of her, and he may genuinely have come to the conclusion that she was facing a false allegation. Alternatively he may have sought to prevent her from becoming the victim of a witch-hunt because of a sexual misdemeanour which he regarded as a mere youthful indiscretion. In either case he may have allowed his judgment to be influenced by his own acquaintance with Harkness or by the fact that one of her relatives was directly connected to the county council.

But, however it is viewed, Dodd's conduct remains questionable. And, from the point of view of Alison Taylor, the episode could only strengthen her own apparent conviction that she was fighting on the side of righteousness against a corrupt and dishonest regime. On this evidence at least, it might be argued that the regime in question really was organising a cover-up of abuse which had taken place within homes run by Gwynedd County Council.

In her subsequent campaign against Dodd, Taylor frequently referred to the Graham Ennis episode. It is almost certainly not a coincidence that she chose to trigger the 1986 police investigation only a matter of weeks after the incident had been referred to the police, and at a time when, because of the recent events, she felt she could be confident of the support of at least some of her colleagues.

The tragedy for Nefyn Dodd was that, even as he became the chief prey of the campaign which would be waged against Gwynedd County Council over the next ten years, he had seriously undermined his own credibility.

13 Eye witness

AFTER THE DECISION NOT TO PROSECUTE Nefyn Dodd had been made known (and after it had been confirmed by the Attorney General), Alison Taylor had another target in addition to Gwynedd Social Services – the North Wales Police. She wrote a number of letters to senior police officers, to Sir Philip Myers, Her Majesty's Inspector of Constabulary, to the clerk of the North Wales Police Authority and to the Police Complaints Authority. While on the one hand she sought to remonstrate with the police for allegedly failing to keep secret her own role in the 1986 investigation, on the other hand she began to make the suggestion that the 1986 and 1987 investigations had not been carried out with sufficient thoroughness. In a letter written to the clerk of the North Wales Police Authority on 26 January 1989, she wrote that 'Children who wished to give statements were not allowed to do so by the police, the evidence of others was not recorded, crucial witnesses were either not interviewed at all, or only seen *after* the investigation had been closed.'[109] It is now evident that almost all of these claims were untrue.

During the same period Taylor wrote a series of letters to politicians setting out her own view of what had happened in Gwynedd. These letters were addressed to the prime minister, Margaret Thatcher, to John Major who was then a home office minister, to Douglas Hurd, the home secretary, to health minister, Tony Newton, to a number of Labour shadow ministers and to her local MP, Wyn Roberts. She also wrote to the Director of Public Prosecutions, the local office of the Crown Prosecution Service, the National Union of Public Employees and a number of other bodies.

These letters are significant since, although they were written at a time when Taylor was no longer working for Gwynedd, and was therefore in no position to witness abuse, they show the gradual emergence of an entirely new allegation.

When Alison Taylor had first approached the police in 1984 over the case of John Mason, she had not, according to her own account, witnessed any abuse herself. The situation remained exactly the same when she triggered the second and larger police investigation in 1986. On this occasion, as we have seen, and as Owen noted at the time, all the allegations she brought forward were second- or third-hand. Yet when Taylor wrote to Margaret Thatcher on 17 January 1987, four days after her suspension, to 'ask most earnestly' for her intervention, she had suddenly become a first-hand witness.

In her letter she explained that she had worked at Tŷ'r Felin from 1976 to 1980 and that, because she had lived on the premises, she had the opportunity to observe what was happening there:

> For the whole of my period of work at Tŷ'r Felin, I and my family had to be resident. My daughter was then 12, and my son a few months old. My husband, due to ill health, has been unemployed since 1975.
>
> Our living quarters at Tŷ'r Felin were integral with the main building and it was inevitable that my family saw and knew a great deal of what happened although they made every effort not to [illegible] on the children's privacy. On several occasions they [illegible] children being [illegible] and abused.
>
> My husband also witnessed children being assaulted by Mr Dodd as well as the teacher at the unit. I regret to admit that at the time I prevented my husband from taking any action on these issues because I was afraid for our security: we had no other source of income apart from mine, and nowhere else to live. *After several instances of seeing children abused myself,* I informed Mr Dodd that I would take action myself if it did not cease [italics added].[110]

A year later, in January 1988, in a letter addressed to the Director of Public Prosecutions, Taylor made a claim which was even more significant. She said that in 1986 she had given the police 'a substantial written statement, detailing those assaults of which I had been informed by children, *and those I had witnessed* [italics added].[111] The second part of this claim was plainly untrue.

Two weeks later, she developed the claim. In a letter to the health minister, Tony Newton, she began, as she had done to Mrs Thatcher, by making a non-specific reference to a number of incidents of abuse she claimed to have witnessed:

> I held the post of deputy in charge at Tŷ'r Felin from September 1976 to September 1980, when I left to undertake professional training. *On a number of occasions, I directly witnessed ill-treatment and abuse of children by Mr Dodd,* and eventually, challenged him directly on the matter, informing him that I would take my own steps to deal with the abuse unless it ceased [italics added].

On this occasion, however, Taylor immediately went on to give a specific example:

> A particularly brutal incident occurred with a boy named Lewis
> Harper, who was at the time about 15 years old. Lewis had absconded
> from Tŷ'r Felin to see his family, as his contact with them was severely
> restricted by Mr Dodd. On the boy's return, he was called into the
> office, at which point Mr Dodd started to beat him about the head and
> body with his fists and with a cane which was kept in the office. The
> boy was knocked to the floor, after which Mr Dodd stood over him,
> and told him to crawl towards him and lick his feet. Mr Dodd contin-
> ued beating Lewis until he complied. I witnessed this incident from
> start to end.[112]

Although she referred, both in her letter to Margaret Thatcher and in
her letter to Tony Newton, to a number of *different* instances of abuse,
this claim would subsequently disappear. By 1991 she would be claiming that the incident which she proffered to Tony Newton as 'a particularly brutal' example of Dodd's abuse was in fact the only incident she
ever witnessed in which Dodd himself assaulted a child.

It was the same incident which Dean Nelson reported in the *Independent on Sunday* in December 1991. But in the years which had
elapsed since the original account given in the letter to Tony Newton,
a number of details had changed.

The manner in which an allegation referring to the year 1980
appeared mysteriously in 1988 and then subsequently developed, with
crucial details changing at practically every stage, would eventually
provide a telling insight into Taylor's campaign. For the time being,
however, it became by far the most potent of all the weapons in her
armoury. For now she could say what she had never previously
claimed in any of her various encounters with journalists, local politicians and police officers. She could present herself not simply as a concerned residential social worker, but as the eye-witness of a horrific
and perverted assault carried out by a senior officer on a defenceless
boy (who would have been thirteen at the time). It was not long
before an opportunity to deploy this weapon presented itself.

One of the organisations which Taylor had contacted in the course
of her campaign to secure the prosecution of Dodd was the Children's
Legal Centre, an independent charity offering advice on all aspects of
the law in relation to children. In 1989 James Cutler, a producer from
the Yorkshire Television documentary series *First Tuesday*, approached

Taylor through the Children's Legal Centre and expressed interest in making a programme about Tŷ'r Felin.

Cutler and his researcher, Mandy Wragg, began to try to piece together the Tŷ'r Felin story and Taylor now related to them how she had opened the door of the office and seen Dodd assaulting a 15-year-old boy. At the time they were impressed by her story and made efforts to contact more witnesses who might be in a position to give first-hand accounts of abuse. For six months, frequently accompanied by Taylor, Wragg drove around North Wales interviewing former residents of Tŷ'r Felin, most of whose names had been supplied by Taylor herself.

One former resident was contacted by Taylor and Wragg in a warehouse near Wrexham where he was working. He was Ryan Tanner, the boy who had been remanded into care at the age of ten for stealing from electricity meters, and whom Taylor had subsequently got to know during her Bryn Estyn placement.[113]

Wragg first met Tanner, who was now 22, on 15 August 1989. She talked to him in detail about Tŷ'r Felin and rapidly came to regard him, after Taylor, as the most important of all the witnesses she had discovered. He was interviewed at length on film on 12 September, the same day that Taylor herself was interviewed at her home at Bangor. A number of other former residents also gave filmed interviews. However, Cutler and Wragg did not complete their project and the programme was never made. In the first place Cutler felt that, since Nefyn Dodd had by this point effectively retired, he could not pose any further threat to children, even if the allegations were well-founded. In the second place the complaints that Taylor was bringing forward concerned mainly physical abuse, and although there were suggestions of sexual abuse, the evidence in this respect was not extensive. For these and other reasons, including the many legal difficulties, Cutler decided to drop the story and turn his attention elsewhere.[114]

However the appearance of Yorkshire Television on the scene, and the interest they showed in Taylor's story, would make a significant contribution to the way in which this story developed. Perhaps the most important factor was the reappearance of Ryan Tanner. Until the point that she made contact with Tanner again, Taylor had been concerned solely with residential care in the sparsely populated county of Gwynedd. But, soon after Tanner's reappearance, she began to turn her attention to Clwyd as well, where she would paint a portrait of Bryn Estyn very different from the one she had drawn eight years previously, at the time she had met Tanner there as a 14-year-old boy. Largely because he had been both at Tŷ'r Felin and at Bryn Estyn, Tanner proved to be an ideal contact. Because his help came at a critical time, when the climate of opinion about residential care was changing, Alison Taylor now found that she was able to transform her entire campaign, giving it a scope and effectiveness which it had never previously possessed.

Before she could do this, however, she needed a larger repertoire of allegations. Until this point almost all her allegations had concerned physical abuse. She would now increasingly turn her attention to the possibility of sexual abuse – both in Gwynedd and in Clwyd.

II

THE BRYN ESTYN
INVESTIGATION
(1991–93)

14 From California to Clwyd

THE MANNER IN WHICH ALISON TAYLOR'S campaign now developed, and the reasons it changed in the way that it did, are perhaps best understood by pointing to the direction taken by the Yorkshire Television documentary team after it left North Wales. For when James Cutler decided not to pursue the project it was not out of any aversion to the general subject-matter.

If anything the reverse was true. For in the years which had elapsed between the time Taylor had approached the police in 1986, and the time she was contacted by Yorkshire Television, an entire climate of opinion had begun to change. For a variety of reasons both social workers and journalists were now much more receptive towards allegations of abuse in general and towards allegations which concerned care homes in particular.

When Cutler and his team decided to abandon their North Wales project in the early part of 1990 it was partly because they had already uncovered another story with a similar theme. The documentary which they now set about making in earnest took as its subject another care home – Castle Hill in Ludlow, Shropshire. In this case the complaints at the heart of the story were of sexual abuse. After an allegation had been made by a boy in 1989, the police began systematically to interview former residents of the privately run home. As a result they collected a large number of complaints of sexual abuse and the principal of the home, Ralph Morris, was arrested and charged. Although he continued to protest his innocence throughout his trial, Morris's past behaviour (which included acts of fraud and dishonesty) discredited his testimony and he was convicted.

The documentary made by Cutler was entitled *The Secret of Castle Hill* and it was broadcast on 7 May 1991, about a month after the trial had ended. It contained disturbing footage in which former residents of the home made detailed allegations of sexual abuse against the man in whose care they had once been. The very fact that this film was made and broadcast was a sign of the profound shift in attitudes towards child sexual abuse and residential care which had been taking place over a period of some ten years.

The Castle Hill investigation was one of the most significant mile-stones in this gradual transformation of public consciousness. During his summing-up at the end of Morris's trial on 12 April 1991, Mr Justice Fennell said: 'I am happy that [Shropshire Social Services and West Mercia Police] will make available the experience and wisdom that has been accumulated over this trial … and hopefully now be much more alert to these situations.' In response to these remarks, Shropshire County Council published *The Castle Hill Report*, which was offered as a guide to good practice in such investigations. The report contained the following advice about sexual abuse in residential establishments:

> The importance of the powerful culture within such establishments cannot be overstated when attempting to understand the inability of young men to disclose their experiences …The identification and awareness of organised institutional abuse is still in the early stages and a significant feature of our investigation was the disbelief of other pro-fessionals and their initial inability to accept and comprehend the sheer volume and extent of the abuse. Within this setting the 'disbelief fac-tor' exacerbated the disempowerment, vulnerability and isolation of the individual victims. It is essential, therefore, that professionals involved in this area of work be conversant with these issues, for only then can they be in a position to accept new 'systems' and take forward their practice in relation to organised abuse. *An open mind and a pre-paredness to accept and objectively analyse improbable and sometimes unbe-lievable scenarios are essential* [italics added].

Although *The Castle Hill Report* was not published until some time after the trial, the ideas which informed it were in circulation among social workers from about 1990 onwards. These ideas included belief in wide-spread 'organised institutional abuse' even though the Castle Hill inves-tigation itself involved only a single care worker and provided no evidence of any organised abuse.

The origins of this interest in organised abuse in institutional settings went back many years to the new culture of child protection which had emerged in the United States – above all in California – during the 1970s. At the heart of what many regarded as a revolutionary change in consciousness was a retreat from practically all forms of scepticism. Believing, correctly in many cases, that allegations of sexual abuse had too often been disbelieved in the past, many feminists, therapists and social workers began a concerted and necessary fight against such dis-belief.

One of the factors which helped to shape this new attitude was the work of a group of paediatricians in Denver, Colorado led by C. Henry Kempe. They used X-rays to document cases of 'hidden' physical abuse, involving children with healed fractures in their legs or arms and other signs of unreported injury. In 1961 Kempe conducted a symposium at the American Academy of Paediatrics in Chicago and proposed that 'unrecognised trauma', inflicted in many cases by parents, 'was a frequent cause of permanent injury or death'. He and his colleagues coined the phrase 'the battered child syndrome' and when their paper was published under this title in 1962 it received massive publicity throughout the United States and beyond.[115]

Kempe's medical background had a significant influence on the approach of the new child protection profession which now began to emerge. One of the assumptions which guided this approach was the belief that child abuse was a medical problem, and that, like more conventional diseases, it could be identified, treated and cured. As early as 1973 this assumption was translated into legislation in Walter Mondale's CAPTA – the Child Abuse Prevention and Treatment Act. This promoted the view that those who inflicted physical abuse on their children were suffering from a psychological malady which could strike any parent.[116]

So long as the abuse inflicted on children had been viewed principally as a criminal matter, the investigation of allegations had remained for the most part in the hands of the police and the courts. However imperfectly, their approach was informed at least by some residues of the traditional presumption of innocence and by a recognition that allegations should not be relied on unless they were backed up by solid evidence.

But, as Debbie Nathan and Michael Snedeker have pointed out in their outstanding study of ritual abuse allegations in America, the progressive medicalisation of the problem of child abuse transformed this approach. Increasingly, abuse investigations were placed in the hands of therapists, social workers, psychologists and clinicians. This was particularly so in California where a new therapeutic approach to accusations of incest was developed throughout the 1970s.[117]

The problem with this development was that in some cases an attitude of disbelief was replaced not by an open-minded willingness to investigate, but by a kind of systematic credulity. In the new Californian model of child protection it thus gradually became an article of faith among social workers and therapists that children did not make false allegations of sexual abuse. As early as 1978 this new view was noted approvingly by Roland Summit, the Los Angeles county mental health consultant who rapidly came to regard himself, and to be regarded by his fellow professionals, as one of the leading authorities on child sexual abuse. 'It has become a maxim among child sexual abuse intervention counsellors and investigators,' wrote Summit, 'that children never fabricate the kinds of explicit sexual manipulations they divulge in complaints and interrogations.' His own view was that children should always be believed, no matter how unlikely their accusations. 'The more illogical and incredible the initiation scene might seem to adults,' he wrote, 'the more likely it is that the child's description is valid.' This kind of faith in the accuracy of children's allegations was, in Summit's view, a necessary doctrine for all who worked in the field of child-care, and only if it was embraced unreservedly could society be cured of one of its most dangerous ills.[118]

Neither Summit nor any of the other leading child protection experts at the time, appears to have suspected that the main reason why children's testimony should sometimes be viewed with caution was not because of their own intrinsic untruthfulness, but because of the mis-placed zeal of the adults who were seeking evidence of sexual abuse. It was only years later, as a result of research carried out by a number of child psychologists, including Stephen Ceci in the United States and Maggie Bruck in Canada, that the extent of children's susceptibility to adult influence in this respect began to be recognised. The particular danger – that suggestive questioning by therapists, counsellors and investigators, could very easily lead young children to 'adopt' and then relate as facts, speculative narratives constructed by adults – was simply not recognised by those who were the pioneers of the most influential new approaches to child sexual abuse.[119]

In 1979 the Californian model of child protection to which Roland Summit's views belonged was officially adopted by the American National Council for Child Abuse and Neglect, and used as the basis for a national training programme. As the Californian model and derivatives of it began to be adopted throughout America, the phrase which was most frequently to be heard on the lips of social workers and therapists was 'Believe the children!' These words, indeed, became the informal and immensely powerful slogan of the entire exercise in consciousness-raising which was undertaken by campaigning feminists and child protection workers throughout the 1970s and 1980s. It was this Cali-fornian approach which would profoundly influence child protection work not only in America but throughout the English-speaking world.

By the mid 1980s the Californian model, with its ideological taboo against disbelieving any allegation of child sexual abuse, had already achieved considerable currency among British social workers and child protection professionals. That this approach had already reached North Wales, and was familiar to Alison Taylor herself, is suggested by a letter written by 'James Browne' in the *Bangor Mail* on 12 November 1986, immediately after the results of the 1986 police investigation had been made public. This letter noted that 'all the social work literature on child abuse, and more recent press coverage nationally of the subject, urges that the first principle in dealing with abuse must be to believe the child who claims he is being abused, unless and until it can be proved conclusively to the contrary.'

Over the next five years the prescription to 'believe the children' was gradually reapplied to all allegations of child sexual abuse, whether made contemporaneously by young children or retrospectively by adults. It was these developments within the realm of social work, reflected as they were in media coverage of child abuse stories, which effectively transformed an entire climate of opinion.

Once child sexual abuse had been redefined not simply as a social ill, which it undoubtedly was and is, but as the supreme evil of our age, and once the obligation to believe any allegation had become almost mandatory, it was perhaps inevitable that ancient demonological fantasies would be mobilised once again.

Throughout the early 1980s a particular fantasy began to grip the imagination of an influential grouping of child protection workers who had been trained in the new climate of credulity. This fantasy, which initially gained currency in California in 1983, maintained that small children, usually in pre-school nurseries, were being systematically preyed on by an organised conspiracy of adults who belonged to a satanic sexual cult. By 1987 these beliefs had crossed the Atlantic, and the first investigation into satanic abuse in Britain was made in Congleton, Cheshire. This was followed in 1988 by better known cases in Nottingham, Rochdale and the Orkneys and by a series of more than 80 others.[120]

For some child protection workers, belief in this new and powerful fantasy became almost a form of religious faith. So complete was their dedication to the crusade against the forces of evil, they could not even consider the possibility that the evil conspiracies they had come to believe in might not, in fact, exist at all. They certainly never suspected that in some cases they had themselves created the 'disclosures' which they attributed to children, or that their fight against 'evil' might lead to the conviction of innocent people. Yet, in countless tragic cases, in the United States and elsewhere, this is what happened. The members of a movement which had set out to combat child sexual abuse had become so consumed by a crusade against what they regarded as the supreme evil that they sometimes ended by abusing innocent children and innocent parents themselves.*

By the late 1980s the crisis produced by the spread of false allegations began to grow to acute proportions particularly in America. In the McMartin case of 1983, to cite but the best known of all the American scandals, a number of day care workers were accused of sexually abusing hundreds of very young children. The allegations emerged after the anxieties of a mother, subsequently diagnosed as schizophrenic, had been spread to 200 other parents at a public meeting. Eventually all charges against the accused in the McMartin case would be either rejected by a jury or dismissed, and sceptical investigators produced evidence which clearly showed that the entire episode was the product of a moral panic. The trials, however, took seven years and, in the words of Superior Court Judge William Pounders, the case 'poisoned everyone who had contact with it.'[121]

So grave were the concerns caused by McMartin in America, and in Britain by satanic scares such as those in Nottingham, Rochdale and the Orkneys, that the first concerted opposition began to emerge. In Britain scepticism first emerged during the Nottingham case where police officers who investigated allegations of satanic abuse could find no supporting evidence. A more general scepticism about satanic abuse was expressed by the journalist Rosie Waterhouse in the *Independent on Sunday* and taken up by other newspapers, including *Private Eye*. When journalists ridiculed the belief in organised satanic cults as a delusion and pointed out that 'investigations have produced no bodies, no bones, no bloodstains, nothing' some believers resisted fiercely. Even today,

---

* It is commonly believed that the various satanic scares in Britain did not lead to any convictions. This is not the case. In June 1994 in Pembroke, west Wales, in the largest trial of organised child sexual abuse ever to have taken place in Britain, six men received prison sentences totalling 53 years. Although the investigation produced allegations against as many as 200 people, and although these allegations included many of the usual features of satanic scares, social workers and police were careful to downplay both the size of the supposed conspiracy and the satanic elements. By eliminating the more implausible claims, this undoubtedly helped to secure the convictions.

some fifteen years after belief in satanic abuse was discredited, a surprising number of social workers and therapists find it difficult to accept that it was a delusion. Many cling resolutely to their belief that organised satanic abuse is a real phenomenon.[122]

Yet, largely because of the hostility shown by police forces and journalists towards such allegations, those who continued to believe in satanic abuse were rendered effectively powerless. Without the support of journalists they could not maintain the support of the public and without the support of the police they could never hope to secure convictions.

For this reason, from 1990 onwards, some believers in satanic abuse began to adapt to the climate of scepticism which had grown up around their wilder claims. From a pragmatic point of view such willingness to adapt was a necessity if they were to retain credibility within the larger community of social workers and therapists, many of whom did not share their extremism. The problem for conspiracy theorists was, in a sense, one of evolutionary survival; the task was to find the theory which possessed the greatest fitness to survive in an environment of scepticism.

One crucial stage in this evolutionary process was the gradual rejection of the term 'satanic abuse' in favour of the more sober 'organised abuse'. This label emerged as a diplomatic compromise which could be applied *both* to real or imaginary paedophile rings *and* to cases where satanic abuse by organised cults was alleged. Its use was supported by the British Association of Social Workers, and by the Department of Health in the guidelines for child protection workers, *Working Together*, which it issued in 1991 in relation to the Children Act. 'By using a neutral term,' Jean La Fontaine has written, 'both organisations hoped to avoid a damaging split in their ranks between those who believed the allegations of "satanic" or "ritual abuse" and those who did not.'[123]

Another factor was the attitude of the police. Until this point police forces in Britain had tended to meet the more extreme claims of child protection workers with a great deal of scepticism. This had been the case in the Cleveland crisis of 1988, when paediatricians used an untried medical technique to help diagnose more than a hundred cases of alleged buggery or indecent assault of young children. Similar scepticism was shown by the police in the Nottingham satanic abuse case of 1989. Here, after ten members of an extended family had been convicted of sexual abuse, a team of social workers became convinced that they were uncovering evidence of a satanic conspiracy.

The scepticism of the police officers involved in Cleveland and Nottingham arose not out of purely ideological factors, but out of a belief that social workers and other professionals were driving forward cases without sound evidence, and that innocent people were suffering, or were in danger of suffering, in consequence.

In both cases the empirically based scepticism of the police was subsequently vindicated. With regard to Cleveland this happened when medical research, in Britain and the United States, revealed that the 'anal dilatation test' at the centre of the scandal, was entirely without clinical foundation, and could not be relied on as an indicator of sexual abuse.[124] In Nottingham it happened when a Joint Enquiry Team, set up by the director of social services and the chief constable, came to the conclusion that the allegations of satanic abuse, though ostensibly made independently by children, had actually been engendered by the social workers investigating the case. In the view of the Joint Enquiry Team, the entire case demonstrated 'how evidence can, for want of a better term, be "created". This is to say you start with nothing except your own beliefs and end up with the story that you expected and wanted to hear before you started.'[125]

The vindication of the positions adopted by the police forces in Cleveland and Nottingham, however, received virtually no publicity. The findings made by researchers about the anal dilatation test came too late to influence the Butler-Sloss report of 1988, and remain largely unknown to this day. The Nottingham JET report, completed in 1990, was never published and its findings were effectively suppressed by civil servants and politicians who were anxious to avoid a public outcry.

Instead of receiving the public praise which was their due, the police forces in question were subjected to extensive criticism by the child protection movement. For the general tenor of such criticism we have only to consult Beatrix Campbell's influential book *Unofficial Secrets: Child Sexual Abuse – the Cleveland Case*. Published by Virago in 1988, this rapidly became a classic of feminist polemics and a key text for child protection courses in universities throughout Britain. In a book which is fiercely critical of the police who investigated Cleveland, Campbell characterises police forces generally as the institutional guardians of the oppressive (and abusive) values of patriarchy:

> Sexual abuse, whether revealed by children's testimonies or by the signs on their bodies, stands as an accusation against adults in general and men in particular. For the police there is a particular problem; as a

praetorian guard of masculinity, sexual abuse faces them with an accusation against their own gender. Police and judicial mastery over evidence has for over a century enabled them to banish the sexual experiences of women and children. Was that mastery threatened in Cleveland?[126]

By 1991 such sentiments had become part of the credo of many social workers and child protection professionals throughout the country. Similar ideas were taken up by some journalists and social commentators.

The effect of such fierce criticisms on the attitude of the police was amplified by the response of the authorities. Although all the most responsible research had upheld the cautious approach of the police, this was ignored by government agencies and the British Association of Social Workers, who effectively turned these findings upside down.

The guidelines issued by the Department of Health, *Working Together* (which took into account the experience of Cleveland), were evidently benign and constructive in intent. But, by insisting that different agencies – above all social workers and the police – should co-operate at all times, and by failing to warn against the dangers of the Californian approach, the government effectively destroyed the informal safeguards which had previously been in place. For in these circumstances there was almost bound to be some kind of accommodation between the empirical approach of the police and the revivalist culture of social work.

In practice what happened was that the extremely valuable, but intellectually unsophisticated, evidence-based ethos of the police found itself in conflict with a powerful ideology which appeared to be based on scholarly research, whose flawed methodology and premises were extremely difficult to contest. In an effort to equip themselves for the new work they were being called upon to do, many police forces set up child protection units of their own. The officers in these units were required to steep themselves in the emerging culture of child protection. They found themselves participating in training sessions whose powerful sexual content sometimes served to mask the unsoundness of the ideas which were imparted in them. In these circumstances some police officers began to absorb elements of the Californian model and to employ the vocabulary of child protection professionals. In some cases they too began to be influenced by the approach which regarded complaints of sexual abuse not as allegations to be investigated but as 'disclosures' to be accepted. Many police officers, perhaps the majority, continued to resist such views. But they did begin to gain at least a degree of acceptance.

This was the complex environment in which new ideas about 'organised abuse' evolved. Perhaps because Britain had not developed day care facilities for young children to the same extent as the United States, the new concerns were focused principally on residential homes for older children and adolescents. Claims began to appear in the social work press that sexual abuse was occurring in 75% or even 100% of the nation's children's homes. It was against the background of such unfounded speculation and the discredited notion of satanic conspiracies, that there grew up the belief that some children's homes had been virtually taken over by paedophile rings.

In the years which immediately preceded the 1991 investigation in North Wales, the notion that paedophile rings had infiltrated some children's homes began to grip the imagination of some social workers and child protection professionals in much the same way as satanic abuse fantasies had done previously. This new secularised and 'desatanised' conspiracy theory rapidly became established within the culture of social work.

Unlike the bizarre and implausible claims made about satanic conspiracies, this new idea was a beguiling one for some police officers. There could, after all, be no doubt that sexual abuse in children's homes did sometimes take place and that it was a real and serious problem. Investigations which set out to discover such abuse retrospectively appealed to police officers' concern about vulnerable children while allowing them to work with adults rather than children. Since adults could be interviewed without social workers being present, male police officers could reassure themselves that, although they were dealing with allegations of abuse against children, they were really doing 'a man's job'. The idea was also beguiling in another way. Since the early care home investigations mostly concerned sexual acts allegedly committed by men against boys, they accommodated existing prejudices. For any police officer given to homophobia of the kind which tends to be particularly strong in male-dominated, authoritarian institutions, care home investigations provided an arena in which such prejudices could be expressed quite legitimately.

One crucial implication of the new stress on inter-agency co-operation was that it could easily hide from police officers the possibility that the evidence they were collecting might be contaminated. In

Nottingham the conflict between police and social workers had sharpened the critical faculties of the police, and led them to examine social workers' methods with more than ordinary care. In his Gwynedd investigation DCS Owen remained acutely aware of the problem of contamination. But, as police forces absorbed the culture of child protection, there was a danger that they might begin to contaminate their own evidence in the same way that social workers had in Nottingham.

One of the early cases in which this may have happened was the Beck investigation. Frank Beck was a Liberal Democrat councillor and a prominent local figure who was perhaps the most highly regarded residential social worker employed by Leicestershire Social Services. In 1989, however, a few well-placed people became convinced that a paedophile ring was being operated in the county's children's homes, and that this might involve not only sexual abuse, but also murder and the production of pornography and 'snuff' films. No evidence for such a ring was ever found, and at first it proved impossible, in spite of a massive investment of resources, to build a case against Beck. But, after some months, Leicestershire police did collect a series of allegations against him. Although some of these allegations were shown to be false, and although Beck's defence team became convinced that the police, in their anxiety to gain a conviction, had inadvertently suggested allegations to the witnesses they were interviewing, Beck was convicted of a number of offences in November 1991.

Beck never ceased to protest his innocence and his lawyers began work on his appeal. In 1994, however, Beck died of a heart attack in prison. His solicitor asked leave from the home secretary to continue his appeal posthumously, but legal aid was not granted. The key members of Beck's defence team continued to believe that he was innocent of the sexual allegations. However, because the appeal was never submitted, the strength or weakness of Beck's case will perhaps never be established.[127]

The doubts which surrounded Beck's conviction barely entered the public domain at the time. But the case did receive massive publicity as an instance of proven depravity. During the same period similar publicity was also given to the Castle Hill investigation, the report of which called, as has been noted, for 'a preparedness to accept and objectively analyse improbable and sometimes unbelievable scenarios'.

Back in 1986, when Alison Taylor had triggered the investigation into Tŷ'r Felin, none of these developments had taken place. While police officers and social workers were not wholly resistant to the kind of alle-

gations she brought forward, they treated them with appropriate caution. Five years later the situation at the national level had been transformed. Social workers who wanted to be in the vanguard of their
profession were not simply receptive to allegations of abuse against care
workers; some were almost eager to receive them. As the Beck investigation indicated, this changed climate had already begun to affect
police forces.

It could not but affect Alison Taylor as well and the campaign she was
still seeking to wage against Gwynedd County Council and Dodd. For
while the new climate had made it much easier to bring forward genuine allegations of abuse, it also created the ideal conditions for making
false allegations. With the breaking of the Staffordshire Pindown scandal during the same period, the climate became even more favourable,
with newspapers carrying stories about the large amounts of compensation which might be paid to victims of abuse in care homes. On 31
May 1991, for example, the *Independent* carried the front-page headline
'PINDOWN VICTIMS TO SEEK DAMAGES'. The sequel to this story, 'PIN-
DOWN VICTIMS GET 2 MILLION COMPENSATION', appeared on 12 August,
ten days after the launch of the North Wales investigation.[127a]

In addition to this change of climate, there was a local factor which
would perhaps prove, in the long run, even more important. In October 1990, after a police investigation, Stephen Norris, who was the officer-in-charge of the Cartrefle community home in Clwyd, pleaded
guilty to five specimen charges of indecent assault against boys in his
care. He was sentenced to three and a half years' imprisonment.

For anyone concerned with standards of care in residential homes in
North Wales, this development was significant. It demonstrated beyond
doubt that the problem of sexual abuse in care homes was a real one
and that at least one home in Clwyd had been affected by it. The news
had a particular significance for Alison Taylor. For before Norris moved
to Cartrefle he had worked at Bryn Estyn. Taylor had actually met him
during her three month placement there in 1982. Norris's wife, who
also worked there, had been her placement supervisor.

Norris's conviction in the autumn of 1990, taken together with other
developments, helped to focus suspicion on Bryn Estyn in a manner
which brought an unprecedented opportunity for Alison Taylor. Perhaps because she had by now become convinced of the rightness of her
cause, it was an opportunity she did not hesitate to take. The care home
whose staff she had congratulated for 'the excellent service' they provided would soon be presented in a very different light.

15 Hard evidence

AT SOME POINT DURING THE LATE SPRING of 1991, six months after the conviction of Stephen Norris, and around the time when stories about Tŷ Mawr and Pindown were making front-page headlines, Alison Taylor made a telephone call which would change the course of her entire campaign. It would also help to bring about, indirectly at least, the arrest of Nefyn Dodd, June Dodd, and John Roberts, the arrest of fifteen former members of staff of Bryn Estyn, the trial and conviction of Peter Howarth, the libelling of Gordon Anglesea and, in the long term, the setting up of the North Wales Tribunal.

Taylor's own role was but one factor in a complex chain of causality. One of the reasons her telephone call proved so significant lay in the identity of the man who received it. He was Dennis Parry, a retired steelworker who had himself been brought up in a care home and who, as a well known left-wing councillor, had recently become the leader of Clwyd County Council. Parry was also a member of the police authority and even before he heard from Taylor he had taken a critical stance towards the North Wales Police. In particular he had taken an interest in the cause of a former police officer, Harry Templeton, who, after losing his job, had made allegations of malpractice against the chief constable and the deputy chief constable. It was Parry's close involvement with police matters, according to his own recollection, that had prompted Alison Taylor to contact him in the first place: 'She said that … it was in my capacity as a member of the police authority that she rang me … and she felt that she had some complaints and grievances against the North Wales Police and would I meet her on them. She didn't want to speak on the phone.'[128]

Parry immediately arranged to meet her at her home in Bangor. A significant part of this meeting, which took place at some time prior to 10 June 1991, involved a discussion of Taylor's grievances against the police in relation to the 1986-7 investigation.

By this stage in her campaign Taylor had developed a more detailed version of her complaints. In particular, since the visit of the team from Yorkshire Television, she had begun to compile a dossier giving details of former residents of homes in Gwynedd and Clwyd, of their alleged complaints, and of the care workers against whom they were made. By November of 1991 this dossier would run to 129 pages. In its finished form it reiterated some of the claims she had already made, accusing the police of failing to investigate her allegations thoroughly, of refusing to interview key witnesses and of interviewing others in front of Dodd. But it also contained new material. Her claim to have witnessed a brutal assault on Lewis Harper, for example, was set out in detail and accompanied by the suggestion that his name had been given to the police in 1986 and that they had failed to interview him. More significantly still it suggested the existence of a 'vice ring' which stretched from Gwynedd to Clwyd and linked the activities of a number of supposed abusers.[129]

The copy she gave to Parry was an early draft which did not include some of the material contained in the final version. However, it is clear that during her meeting with Parry several new elements entered her story. Instead of restricting her complaints to Gwynedd, Taylor now invoked Nefyn Dodd as a link to Clwyd, and in particular to Bryn Estyn. In his evidence to the Tribunal, Parry recalled their conversation:

> The part that then came to interest me was when she mentioned that she had also spent some time at Bryn Estyn and she talked about a character called Nefyn Dodd who was head of a home, Tŷ'r Felin, and then said that he had worked at Bryn Estyn and also she started to talk about other characters that had worked at Bryn Estyn, saying that they had committed abuse or she had heard something about them or knew something about them. So by the end of my meeting I had scratched some notes down of some names of different people that she had mentioned, and that was virtually the beginning of the investigation which is now known as Bryn Estyn, which has ended up here.[130]

No record is available of the exact information which Alison Taylor imparted but, according to Parry and others who later became party to this information, one of the names which Parry 'scratched down' was that of Peter Howarth. It may well have been at this point that Taylor first outlined the idea which would later be disseminated to police officers and journalists – namely that there was in existence a 'vice ring' which involved Stephen Norris, Nefyn Dodd, Peter Howarth and other former Bryn Estyn workers.

What seems beyond doubt is that Parry came away from that meeting with the idea that organised abuse might be taking place in children's homes in North Wales, that Bryn Estyn was a particular focus of this abuse, and that the police were in some way involved in it, or had a vested interest in covering it up.

The impact of these various allegations on an excitable councillor who had recently been elevated to the position of leader, and who already appeared to be hostile to the North Wales Police, may be judged by his subsequent actions. These in turn are perhaps best conveyed through the words of the man who was, in effect, his deputy – Malcolm King. A charismatic local politician with a gift for phrase-making, King had himself once worked for Clwyd County Council as a social worker involved in 'Intermediate Treatment' – an approach which aimed to keep juvenile offenders out of care or prison. After some friction with his senior officers, which may have come about through no fault of his own, he resigned. He then became the manager of a charitable organisation called 'The Venture' – a combined adventure playground and youth club based on the Queen's Park Estate in Wrexham; later he also became a Labour county councillor and chair of social services.

For Malcolm King the entire saga of the Bryn Estyn investigation began on the day he returned from holiday in June 1991:

> I remember it very clearly, a very dramatic start to it all was Barbara Roberts, who was vice chair of social services, extremely loyal and incorruptible. ... And Barbara phoned me up at home the night I got back, and said that she and Dennis had got some awful information about abuse, though I can't remember exactly what she said. Either way it was dramatic, we need to meet immediately, like tomorrow, so we met the next day. What had happened was that Dennis had met Alison Taylor and she'd given him a list of people who seemed to make sense, that there was a smell coming out of Bryn Estyn, and that there were links with the Cartrefle home and Norris and various other people there, and it wasn't just, it definitely wasn't just Cartrefle. So there was a whole smell coming from Bryn Estyn, and that coincided with John [Jevons] also saying well yeh well Banham is – we've seen his report – and he's saying there's a smell coming from Bryn Estyn.[131]

The meeting to which King refers actually took place in Dennis Parry's Clwyd County Council office in Shire Hall, Mold, on 10 June 1991. In addition to Parry and King, two other men were present – Andrew Loveridge, the county solicitor, and John Jevons, Clwyd's recently appointed director of social services.

During this meeting one factor emerged which, as King intimates, seemed to lend credibility to Alison Taylor's claims. In the aftermath of the conviction of Stephen Norris, Jevons had appointed a senior social worker from Cheshire, John Banham, to conduct an internal investigation. Banham had been indirectly involved in the Congleton satanic abuse case, and, as a Cheshire social worker, would almost inevitably have been well-schooled in the theories of organised abuse which had played a part in this case. But he was also a professional who enjoyed a good reputation in the field of child protection, and whose judgments Jevons felt there was no cause to doubt.

Banham had noted that two other care workers against whom allegations had been made had also worked at Bryn Estyn. One of these was Fred Rutter, a former policeman who had recently been arrested, after a teenage girl at a hostel for unemployed young people where he was working had made an allegation of improper sexual behaviour against him. The initial allegation was eventually discredited but it had led to a police trawling operation during which new allegations were collected. The quality of this evidence was open to question. A number of features of the allegations suggested they had been fabricated and that Rutter had himself become the victim of a police trawling operation.[132]

John Banham, however, linked Rutter to another former member of staff at Bryn Estyn, David Gillison. Gillison was suspended from Bryn Estyn on full pay in 1979 not because of any alleged impropriety, but because he had 'come out' as a homosexual. Six years later Gillison had a brief sexual relationship with a young Wrexham resident who, it subsequently emerged, was both under age at the time (he was sixteen) and in care. Gillison pleaded guilty to indecent assault and was sentenced to 3½ years imprisonment.

Banham now began to entertain the idea that Norris, Rutter, and Gillison might have been engaged in organised abuse. He was later said by Dean Nelson to have expressed the fear that they were part of a paedophile ring.[133] This idea was highly implausible, not only because the three men had different sexual orientations, but because Gillison had never met Rutter (who arrived at Bryn Estyn three years after Gillison had left).

In the particular atmosphere which had been generated at the meeting at Shire Hall, however, it would seem the spark of Taylor's allegations was sufficient to ignite the dry tinder of John Banham's suggestion. By the time the meeting had ended, late in the evening,

Malcolm King in particular, and to some degree Dennis Parry as well, had both embraced a conspiracy theory about widespread abuse in North Wales and about why the police had failed to uncover this abuse.

Perhaps more importantly still, the two senior council officials who were also present at the meeting, though more cautious in their approach, were evidently ready to treat the conspiracy theories elaborated by the two councillors as representing a serious possibility.[134]

Looking back on that fateful meeting five years later, Malcolm King recalled its outcome in the following terms:

> So we came to the conclusion that there was evidence that there could have been widespread paedophile activity within Clwyd Social Services, that it could have involved the police, so we decided that we were not going to tell the police straight away, that the next morning we would seize as many files as possible ... because if people get wind of it we could have files going missing, we don't know how far, we don't know who we can trust in the department, we don't know who we can trust in the county council, we must assume that we can't trust anyone in the police at the moment – if we gave it to them straight away, they could, well we don't know what they could do.
>
> So we made, in effect, the four of us made a pact that night, that evening in Dennis's office, that we all firmly believed that something dreadful had gone wrong, and that we would need to take drastic and, to start off with, covert action.[135]

King's recollection of what happened at the meeting is clearly highly coloured. John Jevons certainly does not accept it as an accurate account of his own reactions. He accords a much less important role to the information which came from Alison Taylor and sees the input from the Banham report as having been far more significant.

This point of view notwithstanding, both Dennis Parry and Malcolm King have made it clear that they regard Alison Taylor as the main instigator of the investigation which followed. King in particular, during a long taped interview I conducted with him in November 1996, embraced the paedophile ring theory of abuse with great fervour. He credited Taylor with seeing links which remained invisible to others:

> Well, she'd made the connections, which no one else had, or at least no one that I know of had. I'm sure Howarth and other people already knew about the connections. ... So she brought that light to it really, of making those connections, that things were not isolated incidents that happened, and that's the key thing throughout. And that's what of

course is part of the damage-limitation stuff which the police still constantly pump out, that, you know, they were all isolated incidents, and
no one knew each other. Now I've been doing interviews standing
next to, you know, five yards away from [Detective Superintendent]
Ackerley [of the North Wales Police], where he's been saying that there
is nothing, that there are no connections between them and I'm saying, you know, anyone who thinks there are no connections between
all this stuff, you know, would win the world record in naivety. You
only have to draw a map of where all these people work and where
they trained together and all the rest of it. You know, a five-year-old, if
you showed a map to them and explained it to them, they would say
'Oh well, they must all know each other, this is a cooked up job isn't
it.' I mean you'd have to be seriously brain-damaged not to know – to
know – as much as you can know anything, it is all a question of definition, unless you can measure it in a test-tube, you know, can you
empirically know anything, but in terms of it being fucking obvious
to anybody, you know they're all, you know, a good number of them
are all mixed together. All the history of paedophilia and all the rest of
it is that it's a very common factor, people network and share victims
together, you know it's hard not to come to that conclusion.[136]

For both Parry and King it is clear that by far the most disturbing consideration at this point was the one which Alison Taylor had imparted
– that in 1986 the North Wales Police had effectively covered up abuse
which she had attempted to expose, and that they had been engaged in
a continual cover-up ever since.

If the police could not be trusted it was essential, in the view of the
two councillors, that they should not immediately inform them, for fear
that the allegations made by Alison Taylor and the suspicions voiced by
John Banham would be snuffed out. Instead they took the view that
they should conduct their own preliminary investigation with a view
to putting flesh on the allegations.

This investigation was referred to in the North Wales Tribunal during the cross-examination of Dennis Parry by Gerard Elias QC, counsel
for the Tribunal:

ELIAS: So this preliminary investigation, if you like, was designed to
produce hard evidence?
PARRY: Yes.
ELIAS: Which would be handed on to the police for their investigation?
PARRY: That's right.[137]

In fact there were two aspects of the investigation. In the first place it was agreed at the meeting that Jevons should instigate a piece of desk research within the social service department's own files – looking particularly at personnel files, records of disciplinary matters and Bryn Estyn log books. 'The aim,' Jevons has said, 'was to test out the suspicion that historically Clwyd Social Services department had pulled its punches when responding to allegations and disciplinary matters and to see if there was any other information resting in archived files which might either support or refute suspicions that allegations of abuse were more widespread.'[138]

Another aspect of the 'investigation', however, was revealed by Malcolm King. When I interviewed him in 1996, he described how he took his suspicions to Colin Powell, his deputy at The Venture, and to Alan Taylor (nicknamed 'Bounce'), who used to work there, and instructed them to conduct their own informal investigation:

> I didn't know many people in Bryn Estyn, I couldn't think of anyone there, so I – Colin is my deputy here – knows Queen's Park very well, better than I do and Bounce who used to work here. ... So we got Bounce in and Colin and said 'Well look I think there are things that have gone wrong in Bryn Estyn, kids being sexually abused, you've got to keep this very tight and calm without the police getting to know. Who do you know that's been to Bryn Estyn who we can ask?' I can't be seen to be doing it directly as chairman of social services and Colin and Bounce were the people I could trust the most to be able to do it without there being any comeback. So they, so they approached two or three people, and the first one they approached was Brendan Jones [not his real name] – 'Brendan can we talk to you? – Because you were in Bryn Estyn weren't you, we gather there was abuse there?' And his face just fell and they said that *they both knew at that instant that what we were talking about was true* [italics added].
>
> So they both knew then. Whatever happened he just said 'I don't want to talk, I'm going', and went. And I remember them saying that they looked at each other and said 'Yeah, it happened. It definitely happened to him.' Well, Colin and Bounce come back saying 'everybody it happened to'. Well not exactly everybody but it was just commonplace, it was just considered to be normal. ... Shit. So in those two or three weeks, four weeks or something before we put it in the hands of police, I was reporting back to John and Dennis and Andy that, yeah, my finding amongst the people who'd been at Bryn Estyn, it was definitely happening.

One telling perspective on the 'investigation' mounted by King was provided when Brendan Jones was interviewed by the police in 1992. Although he would appear as a prosecution witness in the trial of Peter Howarth, he gave evidence only about the Bryn Estyn routine and made no allegation of sexual or physical abuse. In the statement he made to the police on March 4 1992 he said: 'Looking back on my time at Bryn Estyn I have to say that I thoroughly enjoyed myself.'

Although the 'evidence' gathered by his assistants impressed King, it was received less enthusiastically by the two council officers who had been present at the meeting. They had not agreed to any such private detective work. Jevons now says that 'Andrew Loveridge and I were horrified when we learned that Malcolm King had … set in train these additional investigations using staff from The Venture.'[139]

However, the four men who had met in Parry's office on the evening of 10 June 1991 decided that they must take matters further. While King and Parry wished to appoint an independent investigator (a distinguished senior barrister, or a retired policeman such as John Stalker), Jevons and Loveridge were in favour of calling in the police.[140] It was the latter view which triumphed, partly it would seem, because of the impracticability of the course favoured by the two councillors. On 17 July Andrew Loveridge drafted a letter to the chief constable of North Wales asking him to investigate the possibility of widespread abuse of children in care in Clwyd.[141] Attached to the letter was an appendix containing the names of employees of Clwyd Social Services who were deemed to be suspect. Perhaps the most remarkable feature of the letter was that it endorsed, as a real possibility, the theory which was being championed with great fervour by Malcolm King:

> From the lists that I have enclosed you will observe that there is, in my view, an unusually high level of convictions and admissions and the level of suspicion and query is such that the county council cannot but be gravely concerned as to any possible explanation for those suspicions and queries. I understand when your officers investigated the case against Mr Rutter they were at one stage concerned as to the question of the existence of a paedophile ring in North Wales.
>
> This question exercises my mind greatly and I believe it would be a matter of equal concern to you. A perusal of the contents of the list of individuals will immediately demonstrate that there are an overwhelming number of links back to … Bryn Estyn which has now closed. It may, of course, be nothing more than coincidence but if it is coincidence then it appears to be an extremely high level of coincidence.[142]

It is quite clear that, at the time this letter was written, there was no reliable evidence for the existence of any paedophile ring. Even the conclusion that there was in Clwyd 'an unusually high level of convictions' was ambiguous. For while this might indeed have been a sign of depravity, it might also have indicated a culture of vigilance.

We should recall, however, that the fateful meeting in Shire Hall took place only a month after Yorkshire Television had transmitted its report on Castle Hill. Given that a climate of incipient moral panic already existed, it is perhaps understandable that two senior officers of Clwyd County Council decided to lend their sober authority to the theory of two zealous councillors that a paedophile ring might be at work. Significantly, they did so in a letter which did not itself identify Taylor as the source of any of their concerns.[143]

Having helped to trigger a massive police investigation by the very force who had examined and rejected her complaints in the past, Alison Taylor would naturally be concerned that this new investigation would not be snuffed out in the same way that the 1986 investigation had been. To the extent that she genuinely believed that there had been widespread abuse in both Gwynedd and Clwyd, it was now vital that she should 'help' the police to reach the same conclusion.

16 Prime witness

THE LETTER WHICH CLWYD COUNTY COUNCIL sent to the chief constable was posted on 17 July 1991. On 30 July, the trial of Fred Rutter, who had worked briefly at Bryn Estyn during the period immediately after Alison Taylor's placement there, came to an end. In spite of a great deal of evidence which cast doubt on the truthfulness of the allegations which had been trawled against him, and of the motivation of those who had complained, Rutter was found guilty and sentenced to twelve years. Supported by his wife and his two grown-up daughters, he immediately began to protest his innocence and his case was taken up at one point by a researcher from the BBC TV documentary programme *Rough Justice*. His guilt, however, had apparently been assumed by some even before his conviction, and on 2 August 1991, three days after he had been sentenced, the North Wales Police officially launched their investigation into Bryn Estyn.[144]

This investigation would become the largest police inquiry into organised sexual abuse, or indeed into any form of child abuse, in the whole of the British Isles.[145] By the time it had been completed police officers had taken more than three thousand statements from over two thousand different witnesses.

In any massive police investigation of this kind, some of the most important statements are often those which are taken in the early stages. Sometimes such statements can influence the entire shape of the inquiry and can actually determine the selection of witnesses the police go on to approach.

In this respect it is a matter of some interest that the first person to make a statement to the police was Ryan Tanner. On 8 August 1991, six days after the launch of the investigation, Tanner presented himself at Mold police station (12 miles from Wrexham where he was then living) and gave a long statement in which he made a number of allegations he had never voiced before. The statement was duly marked in the top right-hand corner 'ST 1', signifying that Tanner had become, nominally at least, the police's prime witness.

Tanner began by explaining that he was now twenty-four and lived with his fiancée to whom he had been engaged for the last six years. He then gave a brief account of how his parents had split up when he was one and how he had come to the attention of police after he had repeatedly stolen money from electricity meters. He says that soon after his tenth birthday he went to court and was sent to Tŷ'r Felin. Tanner says that he was frightened and upset and claims that when the officer-in-charge, Nefyn Dodd, came into the office, the following conversation took place:

DODD: Siarad cymraeg? (*Do you speak Welsh?*)
TANNER: No.
DODD: Nac oes, dim in siarad yn Tŷ'r Felin, bastard Holyhead? (*This is your first lesson, then, do you understand, you Holyhead bastard?*)
TANNER: Yes sir.
DODD: Oes, fucking oes [the italicised translations are those given in the original statement and do not entirely correspond to the Welsh].

He then claims that, although his own family was English-speaking, everything from then on was conducted in Welsh. 'My first impression of Mr Dodd was that he was a massive, angry Welshman – a monster. No one had ever spoken to me in that manner before.'

Tanner then goes on to say that his recollection of Tŷ'r Felin was that it was an extremely strict regime 'with no happy memories whatsoever'. He claims that nobody from outside Tŷ'r Felin ever came into the home to see him, 'so I was unable to tell anyone how upset and unsettled I was'. He says that he was slapped daily both by Mr and Mrs Dodd and by the teacher John Roberts for such trivial offences as looking out of the window. His only vivid memory of violence more extreme than a slap was when Mr Dodd caught him smoking:

Mr Dodd took me into the 'boot room', a small cloak room where we cleaned our shoes. Mr Dodd worked himself up into a frenzy – he was in a rage and shouting like a mad man. He took hold of my ears and pulled my face into his stomach. He was a huge man and he held my face buried into his stomach whilst he was shouting. I literally could not breathe. I was suffocating. I truly believed Dodd was trying to kill me. The next thing I recall was him letting me go and I fell to my knees. I began to scream at him – 'You're mental, you tried to kill me,' and tried to run towards the door. As I did Dodd caught hold of me and pushed me away from the door. I can recall that at this time he was so furious, he was frothing at the mouth.

There were no other persons in the room and I was so frightened because Dodd seemed out of control. He then 'charged' at me and butted me away with his stomach. This caused me to fall against the wall and hit the back of my head on a coat hook, which caused a large lump on the back of my head. Mr Dodd then told me to remain in this room until I could behave myself.

I did not report this incident to anyone because there was no person higher (in authority) than Mr Dodd.

Having portrayed Tŷ'r Felin as a tyrannical and bullying regime, cut off from the outside world and presided over by a Welsh 'monster', Tanner goes on to describe the rest of his time in care. He says that he left Tŷ'r Felin after seven or eight weeks and went to a home called Eryl Wen where he stayed for a year. Then, after six or seven weeks in Y Gwyngyll, he was transferred, in 1981, to Bryn Estyn.

He then offers sketches of a number of members of Bryn Estyn staff. Some are said to be bullies who would punch, kick or knee the boys in their care. Others are portrayed as possible sexual abusers. His principal target in this latter regard is Peter Howarth. According to Tanner:

Mr Howarth was known as 'Vaseline' because it was believed by myself and others that he was queer (homosexual). The reasons for believing this were that there were three boys namely Andrew Singer from Wrexham, James Shaldon from mid Wales and John Evans from South Wales, who individually went to Howarth's flat in Bryn Estyn every night after 9pm … The boys I have named admitted going to his flat, but they would never say why they had gone or what had happened whilst there. I used to see James Shaldon regularly walking over from Clwyd House where he was resident, to the main school and to Howarth's flat.

Howarth was a single man and not particularly friendly with any member of staff. It was because the above named boys never offered any explanations for their visits to Howarth's flat, that we assumed something indecent must have been taking place. In addition to this Evans, Singer and Shaldon always had more money than the rest of us and were regularly taken by Howarth to play golf. Andrew Singer was a very effeminate boy.

Mr Howarth would always stand and stare at us when we were showering. No other member of staff would do this, they would merely supervise.

A boy named Carl Holden was another regular visitor to Mr Howarth's flat. Carl was 14 or 15 years. Although I didn't actually see it happen, the other boys in the dormitory told me that Stan Fletcher, the night care officer, would wake Holden up for him to go to Howarth's flat.

Although Tanner, by his own account, had been stealing since he was eight, his statement claims that it was Bryn Estyn which had introduced him to crime:

> My overall impression of my time in Bryn Estyn is that it introduced me to juvenile delinquency. I met boys who taught me to commit crime – burglaries, car thefts etc. I also believed you could get anything you wanted if you bullied people and hit them enough. I became an awful bully when I was there. I believe I picked up this side of my character from the staff and the system I was in.

He went on to describe the time he spent at Y Gwyngyll on Anglesey, after he left Bryn Estyn, and to allege (in graphic detail) that he had been seduced by a female care worker who came into his bedroom late at night.

The statement which Ryan Tanner gave to the police on 8 August 1991 had a number of unusual features. In the first place, although he made a whole string of serious allegations, some of them dating back more than ten years, none of these complaints had ever been made before. In retrospective investigations, this kind of delay is usually explained by the embarrassment and shame involved in making allegations of sexual abuse. Most of the complaints which Tanner made, however, did not involve any sexual element. And, with one exception, those that did concerned third parties and not Tanner himself. In most cases there was no plausible reason why the complaints could not have been made either at the time or at least many years earlier.

Another feature of the statement was that it contained a number of motifs which had already appeared in the allegations brought forward by Alison Taylor in 1984 and 1986. Like John Mason, Tanner complained of a lump caused when an assault had made him hit his head against a hard object. Like Peter Harbour, he complained of being hit 'daily' by Nefyn Dodd and John Roberts for no apparent reason. And like Graham Ennis he alleged he had been seduced by a young female care worker who came into his room late at night.

Tanner ended his statement by professing his own altruistic motives: 'I feel so strongly about my time in the care of the social services that I wish to make a formal complaint as I would do anything within my power to prevent another child going through the same terrifying experiences which I endured.'

The sentiment here is very similar to that attributed to Peter Harbour in the statement prepared for him by Alison Taylor: 'I have now had time to think about things and I know that I have an obligation to make a statement because other children could suffer if they are treated the same way.'[146]

These various similarities might, of course, be dismissed as coincidences. At the same time, however, the very fact that Tanner made a statement so soon after the inquiry had been launched suggests that he may have been prompted to do so. Indeed the circumstantial evidence points towards the possibility that Alison Taylor may have played some part in Tanner's decision to give a statement to the police, rather as she had done previously in the case of Peter Harbour. In this respect one of the most revealing pieces of evidence to emerge during the Tribunal came when Tanner was cross-examined by David Knifton, counsel for Nefyn Dodd and for a number of Bryn Estyn care workers. Having established that Alison Taylor and Ryan Tanner had renewed contact after he had left Bryn Estyn, Knifton pursued the point:

> KNIFTON: Did she have any involvement in your approaching the police to make your first statement to them in 1991?
> TANNER: She accompanied me, if I'm right.
> KNIFTON: How did that come about?
> TANNER: Over the telephone. Me and my ex-girlfriend arranged to meet Alison in Bangor because I felt I needed someone with experience, shall we say.
> KNIFTON: Did Alison Taylor contact you to arrange that or did you contact her?
> TANNER: I think she contacted my mam and my mam contacted me.[147]

Tanner here appears to suggest that the initial contact about making the statement had come from Taylor and not from him. In fact the visit to the police station he refers to here took place four days before the occasion when he actually gave his statement at Mold police station. It was on 4 August, a mere two days after the start of the investigation, that he had first tried to make a statement at Bangor police station. It was on this occasion that Alison Taylor had accompanied him. He had apparently made the 60 mile journey from Wrexham in order to enable her to do so. At the Tribunal he admitted that he had discussed with her some of the 'events' of his life in care which he subsequently described in his statement.[148]

On this first occasion in Bangor, the police refused to take a statement from Tanner on the grounds that he had come to the wrong place. It was as a result of Taylor's intervention that an arrangement was made for him to make his statement at Mold four days later. Tanner's evident haste to contact the police at the earliest possible point in the inquiry stood in curious contrast to his tardiness in bringing to their attention events which he said had happened up to thirteen years previously.

Neither Tanner's delay in making these allegations, nor the fact that he was apparently encouraged to do so by Taylor, automatically discredits them. Nor should any aspect of Tanner's statement lead to the conclusion that any of his claims were made either maliciously or insincerely. But, like all allegations of this kind, his claims need to be examined with more than ordinary care. One of the most significant features in this respect is the complaint Tanner makes against the teacher John Roberts.

According to his statement Roberts was one of three people – the others being Nefyn and June Dodd – who slapped him 'daily'. In the course of time Tanner would dramatically enlarge the scope of the allegations he made against John Roberts, claiming that he was not only slapped, but also punched, kicked and caned by him.[149] However a scrutiny of the Tŷ'r Felin records reveals a significant inconsistency in this claim.

The records show that the account of his time in care given in his statement bears only a tenuous relationship to the actual chronology of his placements. Tanner had apparently deduced the date of his being sent to Tŷ'r Felin from the time he was placed under a care order – 22 February 1978. Having found this date on his criminal record, he assumed that it marked the beginning of his stay at Tŷ'r Felin. In fact it marked the end. He was sent to Tŷ'r Felin for a 21-day period of remand on 1 February 1978.[150] On 22 February he appeared in court at Holyhead where he was placed under a care order and transferred to Eryl Wen. He therefore spent a mere three weeks at Tŷ'r Felin at this point instead of the eight or nine weeks he claimed in his statement. Much more remarkable than this is the fact that John Roberts did not begin working in Tŷ'r Felin until September 1979, 18 months after Tanner had left. The only time at which the paths of Roberts and Tanner might conceivably have crossed was during the period between 1 June and 10 June 1981 when Tanner had been returned briefly to Tŷ'r Felin pending his transfer to Bryn Estyn. Yet, since Tanner himself remains adamant that the assaults he alleged took place during his first spell at Tŷ'r Felin (and refuses to accept that he ever returned there), his story is at odds with the facts.[151]

The only conclusion we can reasonably draw is that the allegations Tanner made against John Roberts in 1991, allegations which would become progressively more serious with the years, were completely untrue.[152]

Tanner's further claim that he could not convey his unhappiness about Tŷ'r Felin because nobody came into the home from outside is also contradicted by the records. On 20 February 1978, shortly before his remand period ended, a visiting psychiatrist met Tanner and wrote a report on him. On the same date Nefyn Dodd himself wrote the report on the boy which has already been quoted in which he described him as 'sensitive and unsure of himself' (see above, p. 38).

Confronted by this report at the North Wales Tribunal, Tanner was unable to offer any persuasive response. His only reaction was to attempt to deny that the report, clearly signed by Dodd, had been written by him: 'It couldn't have been written by Nefyn Dodd. ... I don't believe for one minute Nefyn Dodd has written that report. I know Nefyn Dodd. I knew Nefyn Dodd.'[153]

The content of Dodd's report and the existence of the psychiatrist's report do not in themselves negate Tanner's claims. But they do cast doubt on his credibility. The doubts are multiplied if we compare the complaints he made to the police about Dodd in August 1991 with what he said on other occasions. One of the most interesting perspectives is provided by the verbatim records of what Tanner told Yorkshire Television almost exactly two years before he made his police statement.

Most striking of all is that these records, which were not seen by the Tribunal, document what appears to be an earlier version of Tanner's central allegation. As we have seen, in 1991, Tanner described how, after having been caught smoking, he was taken into the boot-room where Dodd supposedly tried to 'kill' him with his stomach. Two years earlier, however, he had made a different claim about what had happened when he was caught smoking: 'He made me clean the boots in the boot-room. Once he caught me smoking, took me to the showers, took my trousers down and smacked my bare bottom.'[154]

In Tanner's 1991 statement, as already noted, the 'smoking incident' was presented as his only vivid memory of violence 'more extreme than slapping'. In 1989 it was a relatively minor complaint overshadowed by other allegations: 'I would never go to the Salvation Army on a Sunday, and one day he kicked me at the back of my neck, I didn't know he could get his foot so high. ... He would hit us with table-tennis bats, anything he could lay his hands on. One of his favourite tricks was to hit your head against the wall if you were standing near one. He was a monster.'[155]

When Tanner was interviewed by HTV, either in late August or September 1991, his complaints changed again. Instead of claiming that he was 'slapped daily' he said that 'every other day I was belted by Mr Dodd' and went on to say that he was 'caned regularly', an allegation which was clearly incompatible with what he had said in his statement only a few weeks earlier.[156]

Taken together with the facts about John Roberts, what all this evidence suggests is that Tanner's portrait of Dodd as a 'Welsh monster' is a product of his imagination rather than his memory.

When Dodd's counsel, David Knifton, suggested to Ryan Tanner that he might be mistaken about the date he was sent to Tŷ'r Felin, Tanner replied succinctly, and in some respects impressively: 'You would remember the day you went to hell, Mr Knifton'.[157] In practice, however, the proposition that any man is likely to remember the date of an event, however significant, which took place almost twenty years earlier, when he was ten, is far from self-evident. It is certainly the case, however, that Tanner's portrait of the home was in keeping with the answer he gave to Knifton. Tŷ'r Felin was indeed presented as a kind of hell: a diabolical and repressive regime run by a vicious tyrant. In this respect, however, one item of documentary evidence is particularly interesting.

In one of the reports prepared by Ryan Tanner's social worker it is recorded that, in 1984, after Tanner had left Y Gwyngyll and gone into approved lodgings, he became involved in a dispute with his landlady. At this point he contacted Nefyn Dodd directly and asked whether he could be readmitted into residential care. Although this request was refused, the very fact that it was made at all suggests that Tanner's attitude at the time bore no resemblance to that which he later claimed. At the time he apparently regarded Dodd not as a vicious monster, but as somebody whom he could – and did – approach for help.[158]

There is, indeed, no evidence at all that Tanner ever held the view of Dodd which he expounded in 1991 during the period he was actually in care. The circumstantial evidence suggests that he made the various complaints contained in his statement partly in response to the prompting of Alison Taylor and partly because of his own ability to 'create' vivid memories.

To say this is not necessarily to accuse Ryan Tanner of bad faith or to claim that he habitually concocted stories about his past which he knew to be untrue. The pattern of Tanner's conduct in the years since Taylor met up with him again in 1989 does not suggest that he either is or was simply a malicious fabricator. It suggests that, perhaps as a result of meeting up with Taylor, and of frequent conversations with her, he gradually came to believe in a version of his past which she had helped him to 'retrieve'. Many of the changes in his story which have been noted, although they sometimes suggest conscious fabrication, are compatible with this alternative explanation. The case may not be a simple one and some of Tanner's claims may, originally at least, have been deliberately invented. But many of the beliefs he now holds about his past appear to be sincere. And one thing we do know, from numerous psychological studies, is that human memory is often both malleable and highly unreliable.[159]

In this respect, one small detail of the evidence which Tanner gave to the Tribunal is perhaps significant. During his cross-examination by barrister Barrie Searle, Tanner was asked why there had been no mention in his 1991 police statement of a number of allegations he had made, years later, during his Tribunal evidence. 'You see,' said Searle, 'there is no mention, is there … in the police statement, of Mr Roberts being uncontrollable, a man who shook you violently, put a pencil in your ear, your back or your arm, or allowed the revolving blackboard to come on your head, there is no mention of that at all is there, in the statement?' Pressed on why these matters had not been mentioned in his 1991 statement, Tanner replied simply: 'They weren't in my memory at that time.'[160] Although these words are certainly not conclusive, when taken together with the surrounding evidence they do suggest that Tanner may, on some occasions at least, have quite genuinely recovered 'memories' of incidents which had not in fact taken place at all.

The deceptively realistic quality of such reconstructed 'memories' should also make us wary of assuming that Taylor was herself necessarily engaged in the conscious and deliberate manipulation of the memories of those young people from whom she succeeded in eliciting allegations. There is by now a substantial body of evidence to show that those who successfully elicit from others 'memories' which are subsequently shown to be false, are usually themselves either convinced of their veracity, or willing to suspend their disbelief.[161]

What can be said with confidence is that, now Taylor's own version of Nefyn Dodd appeared to have been confirmed by Tanner's portrait of him as a Welsh monster, her own position was rendered a great deal stronger.

Far more significant than Tanner's complaints about Dodd, however, were the various comments he made about Bryn Estyn – and about Peter Howarth in particular. The importance of these would be difficult to overstate. As police officers began to explore the various paths which Tanner had indicated, they were inevitably influenced by the anxieties about vice rings which had already been communicated, via Councillor Parry, by Alison Taylor herself. When the North Wales Police, invisibly guided by both Tanner and Taylor, began to look for evidence of a paedophile conspiracy centred on Bryn Estyn, the results were surprising indeed.

17 The loner

PETER HOWARTH, THE MAN WHO, through his trial and conviction on charges of sexual abuse, would become the most important figure in the entire North Wales investigation, was born in Doncaster in 1931. His father was a borough treasurer and his mother a housewife. Because his education had been interrupted by a long illness, he left Doncaster Grammar School at the age of fifteen without qualifications. He worked at first as an accounts clerk and, while employed by the Cementation Company, began doing welfare work for them – running children's parties and visiting sick employees. He found this kind of work fulfilling and, when the firm moved to London, he did not move with it but went to work at a school for maladjusted children in Surrey. After taking various care posts he was appointed as housemaster to an approved school and subsequently took a one-year residential course in childcare at Ruskin College, Oxford.

In 1966, soon after finishing at Ruskin, Howarth received a telegram from Matt Arnold, who had been a part-time tutor on his course. Arnold had recently taken up a headship at Axwell Park, an approved school in the north east, and wrote inviting Howarth to apply for a job there. Subsequently he followed Arnold from Axwell to Bryn Estyn, a former approved school which had been reconstituted as a Community Home with Education on the Premises (CHE).

Howarth joined the Bryn Estyn staff in November 1973 as third-in-charge and became deputy head three years later. During his time at the school he was responsible for much of its day-to-day running, for the management of staff and for the discipline of the boys. A gruff Yorkshireman, he had a gift for 'reading' difficult adolescents and he was particularly keen on bringing out any hidden potential he divined in them. A fundamentally lonely man, who lacked social skills and was insecure about his own abilities, he had felt that the best way to maintain his authority over his staff was to distance himself from them. This in turn seems to have led him to socialise more with the boys in his care. He spent a great deal of time with boys who struck him as promising or in need of guidance, and groups of boys used regularly to visit his flat during the evening.

Although not universally popular with his colleagues, and disliked by some officials and social workers in County Hall, Howarth was remembered fondly by a number of Bryn Estyn's former residents. Some saw him as a friend or even a father-figure who had helped to make their time at the home bearable, and in some cases even enjoyable. One of many former residents who looks back on the time he spent at Bryn Estyn with gratitude is David Noakes:

> After an initial settling down period I settled into the ways of Bryn Estyn and I would describe Bryn Estyn as the happiest days of my childhood. I got to know Peter Howarth who was the deputy head. I would describe him as grumpy but basically a nice fellow. I recollect him with a pipe in his mouth. I would spend a lot of time with him. He used to have a flat on the first floor in the main building and later he moved to Clwyd House. I used to spend a lot of time going to see him in the flat and in Clwyd House. I usually went with Eddie Hale but sometimes I went on my own. He used to talk to me to get me to sort myself out. I also used to spend some time with Mr Norman Green who used to give me the same advice. Apart from motoring offences I have not committed any offences since leaving Bryn Estyn. ... I look back on Bryn Estyn as the time when my life became more organised and I sorted myself out.[162]

Another former resident who looked back to his days at Bryn Estyn with the same kind of gratitude was James Innes who, after leaving the home, married and gained a place at university. Innes had been sent to Bryn Estyn under a care order after committing a number of offences and coming before the juvenile court. He became very close to Howarth while he was at Bryn Estyn. After he had left to start work, he had problems finding accommodation and, for a brief period, he actually lived in Howarth's flat, treating it as a half-way house. He later spoke of how Howarth had taken him and another boy 'under his wing':

> I regard Peter Howarth with a deal of affection in the proper sense of the word. He did a lot for me, he was like a substitute father. Other members of staff were equally helpful, I particularly remember Robert Jones, Dave Cheeseborough and Gwen Hurst. Peter was a bachelor and there was never any suggestion that he had homosexual tendencies. In fact I remember him having a dalliance with one of the female members of staff, I think her name was Jean but I don't think he was successful in that respect. I also seem to recall that he had an interest

in another lady but I cannot remember any details. ... I cannot remember any incident involving Peter Howarth which had any sexual connotation. I did have a close relationship with him. I can remember when he was ill in bed, he had a problem with his ankle and he had a badly cricked neck and he could hardly move. I remember Rob Jones and I going to his bed, he was naked in bed, and helping him move. The other occasions when I went into his bedroom was when I took him his early morning cup of tea but on none of these occasions was there any sexual involvement or abuse.[163]

It is perhaps significant that, even though Howarth often placed himself in a position where he was vulnerable to false allegations, not a single allegation was ever made during his time at Bryn Estyn. What undoubtedly did happen was that the invisibility of Howarth's sex life served to fuel speculation that he might be homosexual. Such speculation is frequent in institutions like Bryn Estyn. Boys who have become the favourites of a particular member of staff may find themselves teased by others whose envy frequently takes the form of imputations of homosexuality. Those who spent time with Howarth were often referred to as 'spongers' or 'bum boys' and Howarth himself was aware of this. In the 1970s and early 1980s, however, it was much easier to disregard such name-calling than it would be today. Such gossip notwithstanding, there was, in the view of those who worked at the school, no reason to believe that Howarth was guilty of such abuse.

According to Dennis Parry it was only when Alison Taylor approached him in June 1991 that Howarth became a suspect. And it was only when Tanner approached the police in August 1991 and presented them with his statement that he became the *principal* suspect.

The claims about Howarth which were actually contained in Tanner's statement were a mixture of truth and falsehood. It certainly was true that some boys did visit Howarth's flat, and both John Evans and Andrew Singer did so at the time in question. James Shaldon, however, has said he did not visit the flat and during the Tribunal he specifically rejected Tanner's suggestion that he did.

Perhaps the most significant part of Tanner's statement, however, concerned the way he described the boys' attitude towards Howarth. Occasional light-hearted or malicious banter about the possibility of Howarth being homosexual was now represented as a serious and well-founded suspicion. This suspicion was linked very specifically to a number of former residents whom Tanner named. Unless the police were to risk being accused of a lack of conscientiousness, they had little alternative but to interview these men – Andrew Singer, Carl Holden, James Shaldon and John Evans.

In the new climate of anxiety which followed the conviction of Stephen Norris, the fact that Tanner should ascribe a sinister significance to the gossip there had been about Howarth was not surprising. Given that he was in close contact with Alison Taylor shortly before he made his statement, it seems possible that she may have encouraged his suspicions. But there is no reason to suggest that there was anything resembling a conspiracy to mislead the police. By this point Tanner appeared to have convinced himself that Dodd had indeed been a monster and that Bryn Estyn had been a place of hidden depravity.

By making a statement to the police before they had interviewed any witnesses, and by naming a number of potential witnesses, he had effectively determined the direction of the investigation. What he almost certainly did not realise was that, in doing this, he was advancing the cause of a woman who had misled the police in the past, and who was likely to do so again in the future.

18 The crowbar

WHEN THE POLICE EMBARKED upon the investigation whose initial stages had been mapped out for them in Ryan Tanner's statement, the first witness they visited was Andrew Singer.

On 19 August 1991, eleven days after Tanner had made his statement, they traced Singer to an address in Cardiff. That evening two police officers knocked on his door. Singer did not make any allegation but the officers told him that they would call again the following morning. The next morning Singer briefly discussed their visit with a young woman he worked with, who happened to be a trainee counsellor. He told her that he had been in two children's homes and that he had been physically and sexually abused. He said that the police were coming back to see him shortly, but that he didn't know what to say to them. Then the police arrived and he went off with them.[164]

Later that day, Singer made a statement whose central allegation was a complaint that he had been sexually abused by Howarth. Specifically he claimed that, some time after midnight, about three weeks after he had arrived at Bryn Estyn, Howarth had come into the room he shared with Carl Holden and woken him up. Howarth, he said, then told him to follow him and went back to his flat, passing on the way the night care officer, who appeared to be asleep. Singer went on to allege that an act of oral sex took place.

He said that he returned to his room, that he saw no one on his way back, that Holden was still asleep, and that he had never before, until the police came to see him ten years later, told anyone about what had happened that night.

This was not the only sexual incident which Singer alleged in his statement. He went on to claim that the same thing happened three or four times a week for the following four weeks. By this time, he said, he was expected to go to Howarth's flat on his own. 'I would know when to go as he would tell me during the day something like "Tonight."'

After three or four weeks of visits that, according to Singer's statement, involved either oral sex or masturbation, he said that Howarth buggered him. He then said that for the next twelve months until he left Bryn Estyn he continued to have either anal or oral sex with Howarth about three or four times a week. He added that on occasions 'Mr Howarth would push things like cucumbers, bananas and vibrators into my bottom'.

Singer went on to make a claim about a young care worker who, throughout his time at Bryn Estyn, had been visibly and actively heterosexual. Singer claimed that he had, of his own accord, entered willingly into a homosexual relationship with this care worker. He also alluded to incidents involving another member of staff, Paul Wilson: 'There are certain events that took place that involve Paul Wilson that I do not think I can bring myself to talk of at this time.'

The two visits which police officers made to Singer in August 1991 proved, in one respect, extremely successful. For if the investigation had been given a remarkable start by Tanner's initial statement, it now had an equally remarkable sequel. The very first person they had contacted in order to check up on Tanner's suspicions about Howarth appeared to have confirmed them.

What was perhaps even more striking was that, a mere three weeks later, when the police managed to trace Carl Holden, he too made an allegation of sexual abuse against Howarth. Holden was also living in Cardiff. He was interviewed at a community drugs centre in the presence of his key worker, and began by claiming that a care worker in South Wales had threatened him with an unruly order and then sexually abused him. He then went on to make almost exactly the same claim about Howarth. He said that, while discussing an unruly order with him, Howarth had put his arm around him and, without warning 'he grabbed my private parts with his hand and said "Do you really want to go to Borstal?"'

Holden said Howarth had done the same on two subsequent occasions and that each time he pushed him away or protested. On the last occasion he said that he was so upset that he ran away: 'I went to a railway bridge and jumped off it onto a coal train and eventually ended up in Cardiff.' He said that he told Derek Brushett, the head of his former care home in South Wales, that he did not want to go back to Bryn Estyn but that he was taken back there. 'When I returned,' he said, 'Mr Howarth had moved his flat to a flat in Clwyd House. I don't know why this was.' He went on to say that Howarth never made any sexual advances towards him after that.

The statements made by Andrew Singer and Carl Holden might

appear to support one another. Yet, had the details of these statements been examined closely at the time, a rather different conclusion might have been reached. One anomaly was that Singer had made a specific claim about Howarth's alleged sexual habits. Although he said he had visited Howarth's flat to be sexually abused on some two hundred occasions, he said that 'on all the occasions I went to Mr Howarth's room he never once touched my penis'. Yet the sexual behaviour Carl Holden described was the precise opposite of this. The *only* sexual behaviour he attributed to Howarth was that he had touched his penis. The divergence of the two statements was significant. At the very least it raised the possibility that either Holden or Singer (or both of them) might not be telling the truth.

Holden's statement contained a number of claims which need to be examined. One was that, when he returned to Bryn Estyn after his dramatic journey in a railway truck, Howarth had moved his flat to Clwyd House. This was not true. In fact Howarth did not move until May 1983, ten months after Holden had left Bryn Estyn. The only reason he knew about this move was that he *had* returned to visit Peter Howarth in 1984, almost a year after leaving. He had gone with Derek Brushett, a man for whom he had a very high regard, and who was godfather to one of his children. They had gone to discuss an impending criminal case against Holden which involved drugs, and they had met in Howarth's new flat in Clwyd House. The fact that he made this visit at all suggests that at this point Holden felt neither animosity nor hatred towards Howarth, but that he was happy to seek his help. His claim that 'I have not made contact with Mr Howarth since I left Bryn Estyn' was not true.[165]

It is possible that Holden had simply become confused about such details; there were a number of factors which might have contributed to this kind of confusion. When he was interviewed he was under treatment for drug dependency and alcoholism. He often drank about fifteen pints of beer a day and told the Tribunal in 1997 that he had regularly taken speed, ganja [marijuana], benzodiazepines, morphine, and 'the fair majority of all the drugs', and that he often suffered from the shakes, and sometimes experienced blackouts.[166]

Some elements of Holden's statement, however, cannot be explained so easily. One of these is his claim that, following one of Howarth's alleged sexual advances, he ran away from Bryn Estyn by jumping on a coal train which ended up in Cardiff. The first problem with this is that jumping from a bridge onto a moving train would be very dangerous.

Since the minimum drop from railway bridges in the Wrexham area onto a loaded truck is approximately 12 feet, it might lead to injuries or even death.

This point, however, is merely academic. While it is a matter of proverbial wisdom that coals are not generally carried to Newcastle, it is a matter of fact that, at this time, there were no trains which carried coal from the Wrexham area to Cardiff.

It is true that Holden did return to Cardiff at about this time, and that he did talk to Derek Brushett. But he had not run away at all. Early in 1982 Matt Arnold, the head of Bryn Estyn, had contacted Brushett to ask for his help in seeking to rehabilitate Carl Holden in South Wales. In subsequent months Holden made a number of officially sanctioned visits to South Wales during which he stayed at a children's home in Cardiff. Brushett recalls that one of these visits took place in May and involved a charity cycle ride; there was no question of Holden having run away from Bryn Estyn. But Derek Brushett does remember quite clearly that Carl said he did not want to return to Bryn Estyn. He pleaded to be allowed to stay in Cardiff, saying that he had enjoyed the weekend very much, that he didn't like the regime at Bryn Estyn and that some of his property had been stolen there.[167]

Holden's claim that he had run away to Cardiff by jumping on a coal train was clearly untrue. The only conceivable reason for fabricating this dramatic and improbable journey was to lend credibility to his allegation that he had been groped by Peter Howarth. The most understandable reason for wanting to do this was that the allegation was not true. If so, he had made his complaint, it would seem, only because the idea had actually been put into his head by the police officers who interviewed him.

One of the most alarming features of the investigation into Bryn Estyn was that the elementary inquiries required to discredit Holden's allegation appear not to have been made. Although the police officers concerned may well have been privately sceptical about Holden's unusual journey to Cardiff, no formal evidence on this point was ever gathered. More importantly, the police did not interview Derek Brushett until January 1993, nearly eighteen months after the original allegation.* Although Holden's allegation would be dropped by the Crown Prosecution Service before Howarth's trial, the initial failure to

---

* Derek Brushett was interviewed only after Holden had made another allegation of sexual abuse, this time relating to retired police superintendent Gordon Anglesea.

investigate it properly meant that it played a role in shaping, and even fuelling, the investigation on which the North Wales Police had only recently embarked.

Something similar can be said about the statement which Andrew Singer made to the police on 20 August. The various allegations made in this statement were superficially plausible, partly because details of sexual activity almost inevitably distract attention from other aspects of a complaint which may be less plausible.

One of the most striking aspects of Singer's statement is the number of occasions on which he claims to have visited Howarth's room during the middle of the night without his visits ever being noticed by the night care officer – who was specifically employed in order to monitor and control just such irregularities. Singer himself implicitly recognises this difficulty when he claims that, on the first occasion he went to Howarth's room, the night officer was asleep. While this claim in itself may be believable, the idea that different night care officers were always asleep on the *two hundred* or so occasions on which Singer says he visited Howarth's flat in the middle of the night is simply not credible.

Singer's further claim that he was buggered by Howarth needs to be considered just as carefully. Singer said in his statement that the first act of buggery led to bleeding which stopped only after three or four days. He says that he never told anyone about this and implies that this horrific injury was not noticed by any member of the staff. Given the domestic regime at Bryn Estyn, this would have been unlikely. As a matter of routine boys would hand their dirty underpants over to the housekeeping staff each evening. Repeated bloodstaining would almost certainly have been noticed. Singer, moreover, was enuretic so his sheets were always examined with particular care by the housekeeping staff, who were supervised by the matron. To claim, as Singer does, that he had bled for four days without any member of staff noticing, merely adds to the overall implausibility of his allegations.

One claim made by Singer was plainly untrue, and the police were in a position to establish this. He claimed that, four years previously, he and his girlfriend, with whom he had two young children, had a number of domestic problems. 'During this time,' he said, 'the two children were assaulted. I don't know if it was me or my girlfriend but I said it was me and I ended up in Walton Prison in Liverpool. I served 10 months and I was released in February 1989.'

Singer's implicit claim that he served a prison sentence for assaults on children which he may not have committed, but for which he took the blame, was false. In 1988 it came to the attention of social workers that the two children of Singer and his partner had sustained non-accidental injuries. When this had been reported, the children's mother had gone to the police station and given a statement saying that she had physically assaulted her children. Only when this statement was investigated did it become clear that it had been made under pressure from Singer. He had fabricated a story which made her responsible for the children's injuries and then pressurised her into signing a statement to this effect. As a result Singer was convicted at Mold County Court for causing actual bodily harm to the two children and for attempting to pervert the course of justice.[168]

Another claim Singer made to a former member of staff during the summer of 1992, was that he had spoken to his social worker Bonnie Shore, and told her about the supposed abuse soon after it had taken place. He said she had laughed at him. This information was relayed to the police in a statement given by the member of staff in February 1993.[169] Singer himself subsequently repeated this claim in his statement to the Tribunal: 'I had a social worker called Bonnie Shaw [sic] ... I told her about what was happening; she told me I was imagining it.'

When I got in touch with Bonnie Shore in 1999, eight years after Singer had made his original allegations, she said she had not been contacted at any point either by the police or the Tribunal. She was not even aware that Andrew had been involved in a police investigation. She said he had never made any claim to her about abuse at Bryn Estyn. She also said that, during his time there, he had always been a fantasist, and that he had on several occasions fabricated incidents which had never happened.

Because no attempt was made to investigate properly either the complaints made by Singer, or the allegations contained in Carl Holden's statement, there was a danger that the two complaints might be seen as corroborating one another. The investigating officers may well have been more sceptical than this. But, perhaps because of changes in the climate of opinion which had recently taken place, the approach adopted by DCS Owen in his Gwynedd investigation, in which he tested every allegation, seems no longer to have been open to them.

When the two officers who had originally interviewed Singer returned to interview him again on 24 September 1991, nine days after Carl Holden had been interviewed, any private scepticism they already felt is likely to have been strengthened. This is because the new claims made by Singer were unusual. In the first place he described an incident which he said took place during a canoeing trip on the canal near Llangollen. He said that a group of boys had been taken there in a minibus by a member of staff, Paul Wilson. He then said that he found himself alone with Wilson and two other boys and that Wilson told him to engage in oral sex, saying 'Come and suck these two off and then me'. He said that when he refused, Wilson hit him and then fetched a crowbar from the minibus. Wilson then supposedly struck him with the crowbar and tore his shorts and T-shirt off, leaving him standing naked: 'The next thing I knew was that Mr Wilson was pushing the end of the crowbar, the end with the hook and the nail extractor, up my back passage. I knew that the end had actually entered my back passage because I felt pressure in my stomach. He was moving the crowbar about and then he pushed me into the water, the crowbar remained stuck in my back passage.'

Singer went on to claim that Wilson repeatedly pushed him under the water with the canoe paddle. He said that the two boys then intervened and he was able to climb out of the canal: 'When I removed the crowbar from my back passage I noticed that I was bleeding. I saw a lot of blood running down my leg.'

In his second police statement Singer made another allegation. He claimed that, several months after the incident with the crowbar, he was summoned to see Mr Howarth in his flat. He said he found both Howarth and Wilson sitting at a table covered with pornographic magazines. He was ordered to strip and Howarth then fetched a small shoe box. He took three pairs of handcuffs from this box and used two pairs to handcuff Singer's ankles and hands: 'Mr Howarth then produced a flesh coloured "dildo" (artificial penis) from the box, he then produced a black object, it was slightly shorter than the dildo and had spikes on [and] ... pushed the black object with spikes up my back passage. As he was doing this both were laughing.'

Singer described an act of oral sex which supposedly now took place with Wilson. He said that he had no memory of what happened next and implied that he must have blacked out.

Once again the horrific and pornographic nature of these allegations may have had the effect of giving them a degree of plausibility, since it is psychologically difficult to bring ordinary scepticism to bear on such claims. If the alleged assaults are considered purely from a medical point of view, however, it should be clear that they would have very severe consequences. One example of the kind of injuries which can result from being penetrated with a hard implement was provided by an incident which took place in a New York police station in August 1997. In this case a Haitian immigrant, Abner Louima, was arrested by police on suspicion of assault. He was then attacked by police officers in the bathroom of a New York police station and sodomised with the handle of a bathroom plunger. After another officer intervened he was taken to hospital and reported to be in a critical condition, suffering from a torn intestine and a ruptured bladder.[170] The New York assault was carried out with a smooth, wooden handle of relatively small dimensions. Any assault carried out with the hooked, four-inch-wide end of a standard steel crowbar would have had much more serious consequences. Even to attempt to insert a crowbar into the anus of a fifteen-year-old boy would cause damage. To succeed in inserting it in the way Singer claimed, and then subsequently to withdraw it, would tear and rupture the bowel and bladder in ways which, if left untreated, would probably result in death. Yet Singer said he travelled home in the minibus without even revealing what had happened to the boys who had not seen the incident. There was, in short, every indication that the allegation was false.

Exactly the same conclusion must be reached about the second allegation. To have driven a spiked object into a boy's anus in the manner described would have caused grave injuries. Once this had been done it would be virtually impossible to remove the object without performing surgery.

Yet although, from a common sense perspective, there can be no doubt at all that the bizarre incidents which Singer described did not take place, the police appear to have felt obliged to treat his claims as potentially credible accounts of real events. In doing so it would seem that they enacted the suspension of common sense which is found in many sexual abuse inquiries involving false but horrific allegations. They may also have been influenced by the climate of opinion which was beginning to develop among child protection professionals, who were being advised that they had a professional duty to believe the unbelievable and to imagine the unimaginable.

The allegations contained in Singer's second statement were taken seriously not only by the police, but also by the Crown Prosecution Service, who recommended that they should form the basis of criminal charges against both Howarth and Wilson. This was in spite of the fact that the police had failed to find either of the two alleged eye-witnesses of the crowbar incident, and that a number of Bryn Estyn boys who had been on the only documented canoeing trip to Llangollen with Singer and Paul Wilson testified that no such incident had taken place.

The attitude taken to Singer's allegations was all the more difficult to understand in view of his psychological profile. While he was at Bryn Estyn, he had been regarded as a 'Billy Liar' character who frequently invented stories which he sometimes came to half-believe himself. That this tendency to confabulate continued after his time in care was suggested by the third statement he gave to the police. In this he claimed to have received a series of anonymous phone calls in February 1992 from a man whose voice he recognised as Howarth's. In his statement Singer claimed that Howarth had said: 'We know where you are. If you don't retract your statements we're going to blow you away.' Since Howarth at this point had not been arrested and was not aware that Singer had made any statements to the police, these claims clearly belonged to the realm of fantasy.

It is only in the light of all these circumstances that Singer's claims can be properly assessed. The most likely explanation of the elaborate and implausible stories of sexual abuse which Singer imparted to the police in August 1991 is that, like the equally elaborate and medically impossible stories he told a month later, they were fabrications which bore no relationship at all to any real events.

Had the allegations made by Singer and Holden been seen in this light, the investigation which had been launched into Bryn Estyn in general, and Peter Howarth in particular, might have developed in a quite different way. But, perhaps because the entire inquiry, including the focus on Howarth, had been underwritten by the director of social services and the council, the police seemed reluctant to interrogate the crowbar allegation too closely. Although the inquiries they made about the scene of the alleged crime, and about possible witnesses, demonstrated some scepticism, and although this may have been their underlying attitude, they appear to have made no formal attempt to assess the medical plausibility of the allegation. Nor, as has been noted, was any proper inquiry mounted into the various claims made by Holden.

Thus it was that two sets of allegations which were mutually contradictory in one respect, and which bore all the marks of fantasy and fabrication, became keystones in the architecture of what would become the largest investigation ever mounted into allegations of sexual abuse in Britain.

One question which inevitably arises is whether either Holden or

Singer (or both) had been contacted by Tanner and made aware of their role in his statement before they were interviewed by the police. One piece of evidence which suggests that this was not the case is that Singer actually claimed in his first statement that while he had been at Bryn Estyn he had been gang-raped by a number of residents among whom was Tanner.

Confronted with this allegation by the police, Tanner said that it was not true. Asked if he had anything more to say, he said that Singer was evidently not well and that he felt sorry for him.

There is no evidence whatsoever to suggest that Singer's allegation against Tanner was anything other than a fabrication. In any case, the question of whether there was any contact between Tanner and the two other witnesses is little more than academic. For the nature of the investigation which was now being conducted made it almost certain that Tanner's suggestion about the kind of relationship which existed between Singer and Holden and Peter Howarth would be conveyed to the two potential complainants in any case. It would be conveyed, almost inevitably, by the very police officers who were given the task of interviewing them.

19 Lying for love

IN MOST ORDINARY POLICE INVESTIGATIONS it might seem unusual if two witnesses, who were apparently independent, made allegations against the same man which turned out to be false. It was perhaps because of this that the police appear to have treated the testimony of Singer and Holden as significant.

Most ordinary police investigations, however, are quite different from the one in which the North Wales Police had now become involved. The vast majority of police inquiries have as their starting point the fact that a crime has been committed. In North Wales a massive investigation had been set in motion even though there was no factual evidence of any crime.

Although the investigation had precursors, such as the Frank Beck inquiry in Leicestershire, and the Castle Hill investigation in Shropshire, nothing like it had ever happened before in the North Wales force – or indeed in most of the police forces in Britain. For this reason it was very difficult for the police officers involved to escape from habits of mind developed in relation to traditional police operations. Since crimes are normally reported spontaneously by members of the public, and since there is usually no incentive to report fictitious crimes, the allegations of abuse made during the North Wales investigation were very often treated as though they too were spontaneous, and as though they therefore corroborated one another.

However, since in practice one of the purposes of the police operation was to seek out allegations of sexual abuse, and since certain individuals were under suspicion from the outset, the allegations collected were, almost by definition, not spontaneous. The danger that any evidence obtained would be the product of contamination was acute. For even when police officers are carefully briefed to avoid leading questions, they have inevitably to explain the purpose of their investigation to the witnesses they contact. The exact manner in which they do this is never formally recorded, but in the case of the visits made to Andrew Singer and Carl Holden it is clear that the police officers had a quite specific purpose. This was to check whether Tanner's suggestion that they had been sexually abused by Howarth was true. If, as seems likely, the police officers in question explained their mission – however obliquely – they were in effect offering their witnesses a template for the very allegation they were seeking.

This approach poses particular dangers if the group of witnesses being contacted contains a high proportion who are practised in the art of fabrication. Through no fault of their own, the former residents of care homes tend to be just such a group.

In order to place the problem in perspective, we should recognise that making up stories in order to impress, shock or horrify others is something which almost all children do at some stage in their development. In most families, however, the habit of presenting such stories as the truth will be strongly discouraged and children will be taught to understand the difference between telling the truth and telling lies. More often than not the distinction will be enforced through the ultimate emotional sanction – the threat that parental love and affection will be withdrawn if the ideal of truthfulness is not respected.

Precisely because taboos against dishonesty are so powerful among most adults from secure emotional backgrounds, it is difficult for them to understand families where such taboos are weak or absent. Yet those who come from emotionally troubled backgrounds, or who find their way as children into a relatively lawless youth culture, sometimes learn that the art of deception is necessary to survival. Such children can become skilled confabulators. Taboos against untruthfulness are either barely encountered or are never internalised. This is partly because children who have no stable family support cannot be subjected to the ultimate sanction – the threat of losing parental love.

The perilous emotional situation of such virtual 'orphans' may actually increase their psychological dependence on confabulation and dishonesty. For children who are not given the kind of attention they need in order to gain a sense of their own self-worth, sometimes discover that it is only by making up stories that they can incite and sustain the kind of emotional attention which they crave. Such children may very easily acquire the habit of 'lying for love'.

Throughout most of the last twenty or thirty years the majority of the boys who were placed in community homes such as Bryn Estyn were sent there either because they were beyond the control of their parents or because they had become involved in youthful criminality – some of it petty and some of it serious. By the time they were admitted they usually had a long history of failed placements and rebellion

against authority.* Often many of these boys were streetwise and had
become skilled and habitual confabulators even before they arrived.
Some did respond favourably to the regime they found. But many
remained almost compulsively given to making up stories about their
lives. While some developed the art of deception to avoid detection or
arrest, a significant minority were unable to relinquish the habit they
had acquired as children – of 'lying for love'. For this reason, the former residents of care homes constitute a very unusual pool of witnesses
who are much more likely than most others to make up stories, and to
do so for emotional or financial gain – or both.

There can be no doubt that in the past the perception that many
young people in care are dishonest or untruthful has led to a significant
number of quite genuine allegations of physical or sexual abuse being
dismissed as fabrications. But the remedy for such dangerous disbelief
is not to abandon the accurate perception that former residents of care
homes are sometimes liable to engage in deception. It is to take allegations of abuse more seriously and to investigate them thoroughly and
with an open mind.

The great mistake which appears to have been made at the outset of
the North Wales investigation was that some police officers, schooled in
a new and powerful ethos of child protection, allowed the traditional
(and predominantly negative) stereotype of former residents of care
homes to be challenged in the wrong way. Instead of replacing the
stereotype of the 'congenital liar' with a more subtle and sympathetic
analysis, they sometimes adopted an attitude which led to the acceptance of almost all allegations.

The ordinary empirically-based scepticism of police officers did not,
of course, vanish overnight. But, on some occasions at least, investigating officers appear either to have become blind to the suggestibility of
witnesses or to have deliberately turned a blind eye towards it. Too
often they seem to have remained unaware of the possibility that they
themselves (or the publicity given to their investigation) might be sow-
ing the seeds of the allegations they were harvesting.

Police trawling operations are dangerous in any circumstances. The
special dangers of trawling for allegations among witnesses who sometimes have long records of dishonesty should have been painfully obvi-

---

* During this period, girls were much less likely to be placed on care orders for criminal behaviour, and in most cases were regarded as 'welfare' cases, in care for their own
protection.

ous. Yet at the outset of the North Wales investigation these dangers appear never to have been realistically assessed. Above all there appears to have been a failure to recognise the powerful and complex motives which can impel people from all kinds of backgrounds to make false allegations of abuse. Most young adults, even those brought up in stable families, carry within them a feeling that, as children, they have sometimes been belittled, intimidated or misunderstood by parents, teachers or other adults. This perception may well be quite accurate. Yet, simply because the wounds they feel have been inflicted on them are invisible, their feeling that they have been ill-treated is sometimes extremely difficult to express. Most children will succeed in coming to terms with these complex feelings during their adolescence. In some cases they may only do so by going through a stage of rebellion in which they themselves inflict hurt, and even anguish, on their parents. Adolescents may well imagine such phases of rebellion as part of a campaign of emotional 'reprisals', through which they intuitively seek to reverse the power relationships of their childhood by 'punishing' adults who were once perceived as all-powerful.

Some adolescents, however, may never succeed in giving adequate expression to resentments which they nevertheless feel intensely. In a culture which is acutely conscious of child abuse they may well, in certain circumstances, find themselves tempted to transmute the 'normal' hurts of childhood and adolescence into the abnormal hurts of child abuse. They may do this by deliberately fabricating an allegation of abuse which they know to be untrue. Alternatively, they may persuade themselves that an incident they have begun by imagining is actually true. Or they may, as adults, allow themselves to be persuaded, by well-intentioned but misguided therapists or counsellors, that they have actually repressed memories of sexual or physical abuse. They may then be led to believe that they will regain a feeling of psychological wholeness only by recovering these 'memories'.[171]

What is not generally understood is that the act of making a false allegation of abuse can and often does bring a feeling of psychological satisfaction. In the first place, the power of accusation is itself immense. People who have previously felt overlooked and insignificant may suddenly find themselves the centre of attention, concern and sympathy. At the same time the idea that they are now engaged in a battle against evil, in which many other people, including counsellors and social workers, are fighting alongside them, can be a source of great emotional energy. It may give people both a *raison d'être* and a feeling of strength and solidarity which they did not previously have.

The complex motivations which may impel adolescents or young adults from 'normal' supposedly 'secure' backgrounds to make false allegations of abuse are sometimes felt even more acutely by those who have spent their childhood in care. They are even more likely than most children to feel that a series of invisible emotional wounds have been inflicted on them by their own families – or, indeed, by teachers or care workers. Their flight into criminality may be a part of their rebellion – an attempt to replace a sense of powerlessness with feelings of transgression and control. They will almost certainly experience care orders, and the institutions they are sent to, as an attempt to thwart this rebellion. A significant number may respond positively to their new regime. But one of the most difficult dimensions of being in care is the feeling of powerlessness which it can promote. While rebellious adolescents in 'secure' families are very often successful in their attempts to reverse the power-relationships of their childhood, the complexity, the resilience and the sheer scale of community homes and similar institutions, mean that would-be rebels in such institutions find that their rebellion is often thwarted.

When they leave residential care many, perhaps most, will continue to be in trouble with the law. This may be in part because crime has become a way of life. But it may also be an attempt to continue a form of adolescent rebellion. Simply because of the immense institutional power of police forces and of prisons, however, it is likely that this attempt to rebel will be thwarted once again.

It is from this perspective that we should attempt to understand the impact on a former care home resident that a visit from police officers who are investigating the possibility of 'historic abuse' might well have. Most of the young adults who receive such visits, particularly in the case of men, will have had many dealings with the police before. They will almost always have been in situations where the police have treated them with suspicion and hostility and in which they have felt controlled and overpowered. The experience of being treated sympathetically by police officers is likely to seem very unusual. Those who have actually been physically or sexually abused will almost certainly respond with a mixture of embarrassment and genuine gratitude. When those who have not been abused, however, realise that they are being offered the opportunity to make an allegation of abuse, this opportunity may well prove attractive. In the first place to make such an allegation is to find a way of expressing in a dramatic and potent form the general resentment they feel against 'the system' or against particular adults. It also offers an opportunity to reverse entirely the power relationship they have had with the police in the past, while simultaneously exacting a kind of vengeance on them. The power of accusation is in itself seductive.

An allegation of abuse may also furnish a beguiling explanation for aspects of their lives which may previously have induced feelings of guilt. Broken relationships, sexual confusion, emotional difficulties, alcoholism, drug addiction and criminality can all be 'explained' by invoking a history of abuse. Whether or not that history is true may be all but irrelevant to its explanatory power and psychological potency.

When all this is placed alongside the possibility of gaining thousands of pounds in compensation from the Criminal Injuries Compensation Authority (or a sum approaching a hundred thousand pounds through a civil action against the local authority) the temptation to make an allegation may be difficult to resist. If the former resident is in prison, or if criminal proceedings are pending, there is an added incentive to co-operate with the police in order to earn remission or have charges dropped.

The proportion in which these various motives are mixed in the minds of those who do make false allegations will differ from one individual to another. Some false allegations may be motivated almost entirely by the possibility of financial gain and have relatively little emotional content. Some may, on the contrary, be impelled predominantly by psychological rather than financial factors. Indeed in some cases it seems probable that false allegations emerge directly out of the suggestibility of those who make them and are believed by the complainant from the start. In many other cases allegations which are initially made as part of a conscious strategy of deception, may, as has already been suggested, be transmuted into genuine delusions so that what begins as a lie ends up being perceived as a memory.

It seems reasonable to suggest, however, that in trawling operations involving care homes, the factor which makes false allegations more likely to be made is the facility for confabulation which is possessed by many of the potential witnesses. The failure of the police to give sufficient recognition to this danger was extremely serious. So too was their evident failure to assess the threat of contamination posed by both Taylor and Tanner. In these respects and others they were – quite understandably – unprepared for the events which would shortly begin to unfold.

The final factor which complicated the police's task was the simple fact that the sexual and physical abuse of young people who are in care *does* take place and, in that Stephen Norris would eventually plead guilty to offences he committed there, undoubtedly had taken place at Bryn Estyn itself.

Any police force confronted by these difficulties would be likely to make serious mistakes. At the same time they would almost certainly make a series of discoveries relating to incidents which until now had been forgotten. As a result their trawling net, when it was finally hauled in, would contain both true and false allegations. The problem for the North Wales Police was that they had virtually no way of telling the one from the other.

20 The art teacher

WHENEVER A CRIME ATTRACTS massive publicity and the suspect is explicitly characterised as 'evil' or 'a monster', one of the effects can be to galvanise both police forces and potential witnesses in such a way that the criminal is tracked down. But this kind of publicity can also have a quite different, unintended result. It can help to create a frame of mind among investigating officers where bringing a suspect to justice becomes almost a psychological necessity. In such circumstances, as illustrated by the murder of PC Keith Blakelock, the murder of the Staffordshire newspaper boy Carl Bridgewater, or the IRA bombings in Guildford, it is all too easy for serious miscarriages of justice to take place. In some cases police officers become psychologically incapable of assessing the evidence objectively, so that they will drive a case on against a particular suspect by disregarding evidence which actually points to their innocence.

The barrister Michael Mansfield has described this approach as 'targeting':

> Put shortly this is where an investigation operates upon preconceived notions of who is believed to be guilty. Such preconceptions may derive from criminal intelligence accumulated over a number of years or from prejudices about the kind of people who commit the kind of crime under investigation or from individual bits of information from local sources. The risk is that a hypothesis or hunch becomes a fact. It leads to the exclusion of material that is seen to be inconsistent or inconvenient and a concentration upon avenues thought to confirm or corroborate the thesis being pursued.[172]

In cases of this kind the compulsion to gain convictions has sometimes led police officers to apply pressure to suspects, and to force innocent men to confess to crimes they have not committed.

If these dangers are relevant to many murder investigations, they are also relevant to practically any investigation into alleged sexual abuse. Because of the particular characteristics of trawling operations, however, the main danger was not that *suspects* would be pressurised into making false confessions but that *witnesses* might be pressurised into making false statements. This applied to the former residents of care homes who were potential complainants. But it also applied to others who were approached by the police.

One of the most striking statements gathered by the North Wales Police during the course of their 1991–2 inquiry was given to them by former Bryn Estyn art teacher, Justin Soper, on 30 September 1991. Soper had in fact already given one statement to the police four days earlier in which he had made a number of allegations relating to Stephen Norris and also related rumours and gossip which appeared to incriminate Peter Howarth. This first statement had therefore corresponded almost exactly to the narrative of Bryn Estyn which Ryan Tanner had helped to create at the outset of the investigation. Soper, however, had evidently made his statement against the clock for it ended with these words: 'I have got other incidents to relate but due to other commitments I must stop this statement at this time.'

Four days later Soper made his second statement which, like the previous one, closely followed the narrative which had been outlined by Tanner. This time, the most shocking feature of his statement was the allegation he made against Connie Bew, who had lived with her husband (also a care worker) in a flat attached to Cedar House, a unit for the younger boys. According to Soper: 'Mrs Bew would openly encourage boys to visit the flat, I don't think Mr Bew was keen. On several occasions I witnessed boys from Clwyd House sitting on Mrs Bew's lap, the boy would have Mrs Bew's blouse open and have his hand inside Mrs Bew's bra fondling her breasts.'

Even more disturbing was Soper's claim that Mrs Bew was quite open about such behaviour and that it was a matter of general knowledge among the staff:

> I discussed these incidents with Mrs Bew and she didn't see anything wrong in her behaviour, in fact it was her opinion that it was part of her job as a house mother to provide the boys with some form of sex education, if a boy wanted to fondle her breasts or private parts then she would allow them to do so. This would take place in Clwyd House, that's where I witnessed it, or in their flat. ... The boys who I can recall having seen fondling Mrs Bew were Ian Mayfield, Ed Turton, Barry Hempnall and James Shaldon.
>
> Mrs Bew would make no effort to hide the fact that she would permit the boys to fondle her. Most of the staff were aware of this. Mrs Bew would quite readily discuss her reasons for this behaviour with members of staff.

Soper's story is indeed a striking one. In normal circumstances the idea that such behaviour was common knowledge among members of staff, and yet none had expressed concern, or reported it, would render his claims completely implausible. But in the particular circumstances of this investigation, in which Bryn Estyn was suspected of harbouring not simply isolated sexual abusers, but an entire paedophile ring, even Soper's claims did not seem too far-fetched.

But were they true?

The answer was supplied by Justin Soper himself when, in January 1997, he rang a solicitor to ask whether he would represent him at the Tribunal. The solicitor, Chris Saltrese, told Soper that he could not do so since he had made a very serious allegation against one of his clients – Mrs Bew. Soper immediately began to plead the very special circumstances under which he had made his statement. He explained that, at the time, he had only just begun a new job, that he was insecure and had felt under huge pressure. He had then been phoned by the police at work. They had told him to go to a nearby car park during his lunch break and to get into the back of an unmarked police car. This he did. The two statements which he gave to the police, he now intimated, contained a number of serious allegations which were false and which he had deliberately fabricated to satisfy the police officers and to consolidate his position with his new employer by distancing himself from Bryn Estyn.

Saltrese immediately invited Soper to make a fresh statement, confirming what he had said on the telephone. Soper, however, declined to discuss the matter further. After contacting the police he told the Tribunal that he wished to stand by his original statements.

When Soper eventually came to give evidence it emerged that, although all four of the boys he named had been interviewed by the police, none had made any complaint about Mrs Bew and two had exonerated her. Barry Hempnall, for example, in his police statement, specifically rebutted the suggestion that Mrs Bew had allowed him to fondle her breasts: 'I can categorically state that I have never done this and never witnessed anybody else doing it either.'[173] In his Tribunal evidence he observed that one former resident 'put a statement in against an innocent man'. Asked if there were any other instances of this, he said:

Yes, what has been said in one of them statements I was reading yesterday, saying that I was sitting on Connie Bew's lap and fondling her breasts. I don't know where he got that from because that's not even true. From the day I went to Bryn Estyn they brought me up as if I was their own, they was like mother and father to me and they had their own daughter and we grew up like brother and sister. So I don't know where you get all that from.[174]

When Soper appeared at the Tribunal as a witness, his evidence differed markedly from that given in his police statement. He now claimed that the fondling allegation referred only to Mrs Bew's breasts and that it applied to only one (unidentified) boy, not four named ones.[175]

Under cross-examination he explained that he had been interviewed by the police in the Kwik Save car park near where he worked because 'I had been in the job four days when the police made ... contact with me and I didn't want to jeopardise my employment by having police turn up at a ... school asking questions about alleged child abuse.' He said that he had been interviewed by the police three times at his own home before he agreed to meet them in the car park. If this was true, the police had interviewed him no fewer than five times. He said that they had given him the names of several former members of staff and asked for comments.

He was asked by David Knifton, counsel for Mrs Bew, whether he in fact had witnessed any incident involving her:

KNIFTON: Can you now say, please, having thought about the matter, what is your recollection? Do you say that you witnessed an incident or incidents involving Mrs Bew or that you simply recalled a conversation about Mrs Bew?
SOPER: I feel it was a conversation.
KNIFTON: You don't recall witnessing any incident?
SOPER: No.[176]

Soper was then cross-examined by counsel for a former Bryn Estyn teacher against whom he had made a serious allegation of physical abuse. In his police statement he said that on one occasion he had heard a loud crash coming from the teacher's room:

This caused me to leave my classroom to investigate the noise. As I left my classroom I saw a boy, whose name I don't recall, suddenly fly backwards through double doors leading to [the teacher's] classroom. The boy landed on the floor on his back. The boy was followed immediately by [the teacher] who landed on top of the boy. [The teacher], who was screaming, ranting and raving, grabbed the boy around the throat with both his hands and shook the boy.[177]

It was pointed out to Soper that, although he had kept a diary through-out his time at Bryn Estyn, no mention had been made of the incident of the flying boy. Indeed, asked about this incident again, he appeared to withdraw his allegation entirely, saying that the teacher in question had been 'doing his best'. He was then cross-examined further by Bar-rie Searle, counsel for the teacher:

SEARLE: Now I take the same approach as my learned friend ... which is right, the answer that you gave to me in cross-examination that Mr Ilton was doing his best, or the statement that you gave to the police?
SOPER: The reply I gave to you, that he was doing his best.
SEARLE: Thank you.

In order to clarify this, the chairman of the Tribunal put his own ques-tion: 'Just so we understand, does that mean your statement to the police was incorrect?' Soper replied: 'Yes.'[178]

The credibility of Justin Soper as a witness was further undermined when he was cross-examined by counsel for the Welsh Office. He was asked about a particular inspection of Bryn Estyn in 1980, during which he had been criticised by the two inspectors. In the Tribunal he was reminded that he had become 'a little overwrought' and had told the inspectors that he was unable to teach properly because he hadn't had any paint for twelve months. As soon as this claim was made, the inspectors went to the head of education, Mr Matthews. He showed them the storeroom, which was well-stocked with paint. When they pointed this out to Soper he slammed his desk, saying 'I've had enough of this'. He then left the classroom and later failed to attend a staff meeting at which the inspectors were present. Asked by the chairman of the Tribunal what had been the point of the complaint about the paint, Soper replied 'I honestly don't know. I don't know.'[179]

It was clear that no reliance could be placed on Soper's evidence. As he was cross-examined by a succession of barristers he emerged as a witness who habitually made up stories in order to escape difficulties. Indeed, he appeared to be so suggestible that he found it difficult to sustain any position. When barristers pressed him to admit that claims made in his police statement were untrue, he almost always did so either explicitly or implicitly. Pressed by other barristers to retract his retractions and maintain his original story, he did this as well.

It was easy to see that, subjected even to reasonable pressure by police officers, who may genuinely have believed the narrative of Bryn Estyn which had emerged in the early stages of the investigation, Soper would have been ready, and even eager, to accept this narrative and elaborate upon it.

One of the striking things about his police statements was the extent to which they repeated specific claims which had already been made, but which were later shown to be false. To take but the most significant example, the allegation made by Soper against Connie Bew corresponded to, and seemed to substantiate, a claim which had been made by Ryan Tanner in his statement of 8 August 1991. Tanner had said that 'Mrs Bew was over-friendly with the boys. It was rumoured that she was always trying to seduce the good-looking lads.' Although the hundreds of witness statements subsequently taken by the police from former residents contained no allegations against Mrs Bew, it is striking that, less than two months after Tanner had made this claim, the police had managed to obtain what seemed to be confirmation of it. By far the most plausible explanation is that the officers who interviewed Soper had actually put to him (quite legitimately) specific claims made by Tanner and that Soper had used these claims as a basis on which to elaborate his own allegations.

For Mrs Bew herself the effects of Soper's allegation were traumatic and long-lasting. It would lead directly to her arrest in March 1992 and may well have led, indirectly, to a heart-attack she suffered during the Tribunal hearings five years later.

But Justin Soper's statements appear also to have played a critical role in the evolution of the North Wales story. The view of Bryn Estyn which had emerged from Alison Taylor's intervention, from Tanner's statement, and from the allegations made by Singer and Holden, was that it was so rife with sexual and physical abuse that all who worked there must have known about it. When that picture was apparently confirmed by a witness who had himself been a member of staff there, it was only to be expected that the efforts of the North Wales Police to bring the alleged abusers to justice would be redoubled.

Already the narrative which had been created by Taylor and Tanner had become extremely powerful. Even if they had played no further role in the investigation their effect on it would have been considerable. However, by the time Justin Soper had given his statements to the police there had been a new development in the story. This would eventually lead to Taylor and Tanner playing an even more significant role in shaping the course of the investigation.

21 Knights, masons and MI5

THE PERSON WHO, AT THIS POINT in the story, did most to drive the plot onwards, sometimes in unexpected directions, was Councillor Dennis Parry. Although he and Malcolm King had not prevailed when they had argued that the Bryn Estyn investigation should not be placed in the hands of the North Wales Police, their distrust of the police remained. Parry in particular was unhappy. Since he evidently found Taylor a credible witness, the fact that the Clwyd investigation was being undertaken by the very police force who, according to her, had been responsible for failing to uncover extensive abuse in Gwynedd, was disturbing. 'I was concerned,' he said, in a statement to the Tribunal, 'that the North Wales Police would not take this matter seriously, as A. Taylor had difficulty in persuading them on her evidence.'[180]

Parry was not content to express his misgivings privately and, early in September 1991, he contacted David Connett, a reporter who then worked for the *Independent*. He passed on to Connett 'a tip that there was a police investigation and that there were various issues surrounding their inquiry'.[181] Connett had in the past worked with the freelance journalist Dean Nelson and knew that he had carried out the investigation into Tŷ Mawr. He therefore gave the story to Nelson who immediately telephoned Parry. A week later Parry travelled to London where he met Nelson at a hotel in Kensington.

When Parry gave evidence to the North Wales Tribunal in 1998 he claimed that he could not remember travelling to London to meet Nelson, though he said he had met him once. Fortunately, however, Nelson's notes of the interview had been preserved, and some of these were produced for the Tribunal. They suggested that Parry's meeting with Nelson had been a great deal more interesting than the councillor's evidence now implied.

Parry had begun by outlining the allegations about Bryn Estyn. He suggested that it was the centre of a paedophile ring, and that there were links between it and Tŷ'r Felin, where two police investigations had failed to discover serious abuse which was taking place. According to Nelson, Parry had pointed him towards 'Alison Taylor who, I believe, was the source of what he knew at that time'.[182] But Parry had also imparted more sensitive material. As the councillor eventually admitted, 'There was a mountain of stuff that was discussed that day'.[183]

The most interesting part of this 'mountain' was the explanation Parry had suggested for the alleged failure of the police investigations which had already been carried out. Parry mentioned Gordon Anglesea and linked his name to two other senior officers in the North Wales Police against whom, he said, allegations had been made. Some of these allegations were already, according to Parry, in the public domain and were related to the campaign being waged by the 'ex-copper', Harry Templeton. But one of them was not part of Templeton's complaint. This was an allegation that a senior officer in the North Wales Police had been involved in an illicit sexual relationship, supposedly with a girl in care. Although this allegation proved to be entirely without foundation, Parry claimed that the same senior officer had supervised Gwynne Owen's investigation in 1986, and that it was he (not Owen) who had said that there was no case to answer. Parry linked this cover-up to the fact that Anglesea had 'by coincidence' been promoted to superintendent.[184]

He then discussed the manner in which Anglesea had suddenly left the force. Anglesea's own account of what had happened, given during the 1994 libel trial and then again to the Tribunal in January 1998, was mundane and unsalacious. At a time when he was contemplating retirement he had been called to the deputy chief constable's office and told that there was to be an investigation into an apparent discrepancy in one of his expense claims. The sum involved was in the region of eight or nine pounds. Anglesea, who says that there was no irregularity, was told that to complete the investigation it would be necessary to suspend him. Dismayed that he should be treated in this way after 33 years' service, he immediately tendered his resignation, thus avoiding the ignominy of being suspended.[185]

Anglesea's retirement took effect on 1 April 1991, a mere two months before Alison Taylor had approached Parry with her concerns about Tŷ'r Felin and Bryn Estyn. It was, apparently, this coincidence of timing, coupled with the fact that Anglesea had once been connected with Bryn Estyn, that led to his story becoming intertwined with the allegations against Dodd and Howarth. It is not clear who was originally responsible for weaving him into the story but, by the time Parry met Nelson in London, the suggestion of a conspiracy had already emerged.

Nelson's note of what Parry told him read:

Gordon Anglesea by coincidence the chief inspector of Bryn Estyn then became chief superintendent, he resigned from the police about 12 months ago [sic]. Gordon Anglesea, no one could find out why he left the force. ... Some say his hand in the till, others say it was young kids.

The coincidence is that when he was in Wrexham he was part of the team which dealt with Bryn Estyn. Anglesea was friends with Dodd, Dodd used to threaten the kids that if they did not behave he would get Anglesea to come and see them.[186]

Parry told the Tribunal that the particular claim about there being a relationship between Anglesea and Dodd had come from Taylor: 'Alison Taylor said to me and the exact words to me was that: "Nefyn Dodd used the name of Gordon Anglesea to frighten the children there, and that Nefyn Dodd had worked at Bryn Estyn and that's where he had met Gordon Anglesea."'[187]

Parry, however, was not content to link Anglesea to the senior police officer wrongly alleged to be sexually involved with a child in care. He went on to cite a completely different case involving a local politician who had supposedly been facing charges involving pornography and child abuse when those charges were suddenly dropped – allegedly because the North Wales Police had deliberately lost an incriminating pornographic video. This politician was in turn supposed to be linked to Anglesea's senior colleague through a circle of friends, some of whom were related to the police officer and were involved in a 'pornographic video network' which was in turn linked to the sexual abuse of children in care.

Behind what Parry described to Nelson as this 'huge mass of connections' there loomed an even more mysterious international conspiracy. For one of Parry's informants, who professed to be an MI5 agent, had apparently imparted to him her own understanding of 'Operation Gladio'. This was the name given to the Italian branch of a CIA-funded intelligence service reportedly set up in Europe after the Second World War to organise resistance against communism. In the latter part of 1990 Gladio had been the subject of much comment in newspapers such as the *Guardian* and the *Independent*.[188]

However, according to Parry's 'MI5' informant – Tara Davidson – Gladio was no longer controlled by the CIA or by NATO. It had been taken over by freemasons and the Knights of Columbus (a Roman Catholic fraternal aid organisation formed in Connecticut in 1881). Each country's organisation had a code number, and 'P2', which was

Britain, was 'exposed'. No less a person than the chief constable of North Wales was said to be involved, and one of his roles had been to infiltrate the Sons of Glyndwr, an extreme Welsh nationalist group. One of these organisations (it is not clear which) 'used ritual abuse to keep a hold over people'.[189]

Confronted at the North Wales Tribunal by photocopies of Nelson's notes, Parry was defensive. He said he had related the story only as an example of an 'incredible tale' somebody once told him. At this point Andrew Moran QC, counsel to the North Wales Police, pointed out that Parry had treated Tara Davidson as a reliable witness in at least one respect. She had been the source of a serious allegation made by Parry against the North Wales Police, that a detective inspector based in Gwynedd had halted an investigation into child sexual abuse because of pressure by freemasons. Although this claim was unfounded, Parry had apparently relayed it to colleagues, including the county solicitor Andrew Loveridge. This had, almost inevitably, undermined confidence in the North Wales Police and called into question their suitability to investigate the allegations brought forward by Alison Taylor.[190]

Although claims about masonic influence on the North Wales Police would play a crucial role in the development of the scandal, it is only fair to Nelson to say that they played no part in the story which he wrote. The overall story related by Parry, however, was a striking one even without these ingredients. The idea that children in North Wales care homes had fallen prey to an extensive paedophile ring and that senior police officers might be a part of this ring, and were systematically interfering with any investigations designed to expose it, was a compelling one. The proposition that such a conspiracy of evil had been accidentally uncovered by a lone residential social worker, who had been sacked for trying to expose it, was almost as intriguing.

Nelson was certainly impressed enough to want to investigate further. Five days after the meeting in the Kensington hotel, he wrote a letter to Taylor. He introduced himself as a Channel 4 journalist who had also written articles for the *Independent* about Tŷ Mawr. He explained that Dennis Parry had suggested he should contact her and asked her to telephone him with a view to arranging a meeting.[191]

It might well be thought the arrival of this letter from Dean Nelson marked the first sign of the North Wales allegations being given major publicity. This, however, would be to underestimate Alison Taylor's own powers of persuasion, and the effectiveness of Parry in carrying her story to the media. Nelson's letter to Taylor was written on 24 September

1991. On the day it was received its significance may have been over-shadowed by another journalistic project which was much further advanced. For one of Parry's first actions on meeting Taylor had been to put her in touch with an HTV documentary producer, David Williams, who then embarked on making a programme which focused on Taylor's allegations about Nefyn Dodd and Tŷ'r Felin. This programme was shown on 26 September, two days after Nelson's letter had been posted.

The programme, which was in effect the documentary which York-shire Television had decided not to make, featured Taylor, together with a number of former residents of Tŷ'r Felin, including Ryan Tanner and Lewis Harper. Almost all the witnesses whose testimony was now shown on film made allegations of physical abuse either against Nefyn Dodd or John Roberts or both.

The screening of this programme proved to be one of the most important developments in Taylor's entire campaign. Up to this point, although she had, with the help of Parry, played a crucial role in trig-gering the Bryn Estyn investigation, she had not succeeded in bringing about any new police investigation into her original Gwynedd com-plaints. The sensational allegations broadcast throughout Wales on 26 September, however, placed Gwynedd Social Services in a position where they had no alternative but to follow the example of Clwyd. On 30 September, the director, Lucille Hughes, wrote a letter to the chief constable in which she invited the North Wales Police to investigate the allegations made in the programme. The Gwynedd investigation, ini-tially supervised by Acting Detective Superintendent Eric Jones, was duly launched.[192]

What this meant was that, even before Nelson met her, Alison Tay-lor, who had been directly or indirectly responsible for triggering inves-tigations into Tŷ'r Felin in 1984, 1986 and 1987, had successfully revived her campaign against Dodd and Gwynedd Social Services, by initiating a fourth investigation. The difference between this investigation and the earlier ones was that, at the heart of the television programme, there had been an allegation made by Taylor herself. On HTV she had made in public, for the first time, the complaint against Nefyn Dodd which had first emerged in the letter she had written to health minister Tony Newton three years earlier. What this meant was that although Nelson's research into the story would end by focusing on Bryn Estyn, the alle-gations against Nefyn Dodd were, once again, live issues. Of all these the most important was Taylor's claim that she had herself witnessed a sadistic assault on a defenceless boy – Lewis Harper.

22 To Bangor

ON 12 OCTOBER 1991, a month after meeting Parry in London, Nelson had his first meeting with Alison Taylor at her home in Bangor.[193] No record exists of this meeting, but a few days later Taylor wrote to Nelson supplying him with documents relating to a recent complaint to the police. At this point Nelson secured a commission to write the story for the *Independent on Sunday*. He was engaged by David Felton, the home affairs editor, on 7 November 1991.[194]

This meant that Nelson had just three weeks to complete his investigation before the story appeared on 1 December. During this period he relied heavily on information given to him by Alison Taylor in Bangor, and by Ryan Tanner sixty miles away in Wrexham. Nelson described Tanner as 'a regular contact' and would tell the Tribunal that he met Tanner 'endlessly' throughout the course of the investigation.[195]

Although the focus of this investigation would ultimately shift to Wrexham and Bryn Estyn, it began with Taylor's allegations about Tŷ'r Felin. What was most striking about these, although Nelson was not in a position to recognise this, was that the claims she now made were quite different from the ones she had made in 1986, even though they referred back to exactly the same period. Moreover, one of her more recent claims – the allegation about Lewis Harper – was itself now cast in a different form.

In her letter to the Health Minister, Tony Newton, she had described only one assailant – Nefyn Dodd. He had supposedly used his fists and a cane to hit the boy. Taylor claimed he had asked the boy to lick his feet and continued beating him until he complied. Taylor herself apparently played an entirely passive role, raising no protest at all against the savage and perverted beating she claimed to have witnessed (see above, pp. 18, 78).

But when, 3½ years later, Nelson interviewed her, practically every element in the story had changed. Although the participation of John Roberts was not mentioned in the article which was published, it is described vividly in Nelson's transcript of his interview. The time when the assault supposedly took place is also carefully specified:

TAYLOR: The first assault I witnessed was on Lewis Harper, some time in 1980, some two weeks after he had been admitted. He had been promised weekend [leave] at the end of his first week at Tŷ'r Felin, and it was then refused by Dodd. So Lewis stuck it out and then went on the run to go home on the Saturday. I was on duty at the weekend, I recovered him from home on the Sunday. When Dodd came back on the Monday morning, he had him brought into the office. June Dodd was present, John Roberts the teacher, I was present and a child care officer called Peter Jones was present. Dodd started abusing Lewis, screaming at him and then started hitting him.

NELSON: How was he hitting him?

TAYLOR: With his fists, his forearm, he was lashing out wildly and hitting Lewis anywhere he could land a blow. ... I told him to stop, but he took no notice of me. He was out of control. John Roberts had got in on the act, sort of held Lewis, so that Lewis could not escape, and so that Dodd could hit him. In the end I managed to drag Lewis away from them and throw him out of the office. But Dodd was screaming at him to get down on his knees and lick his shoes and kiss his feet.

An incident which in 1988 was supposedly witnessed only by Taylor herself, now has two more witnesses: June Dodd and Peter Jones. And Dodd is now assisted by the teacher John Roberts; six people are involved instead of three.

Taylor's own role is quite different. Whereas in her letter to the health minister she had merely looked on, watching Dodd beat Harper until he complied with his command to lick his feet, she now intervenes physically before this has happened. There can be no question but that the descriptions refer to the same incident, as she has repeatedly said that she witnessed only one such attack.

If we examine the pattern of her responses in her interview with Nelson, some interesting features emerge:

NELSON: [Did Dodd land] blows on his face?

TAYLOR: He was landing blows wherever he could.

NELSON: Did he draw blood?

TAYLOR: I think he split Lewis's lip. I mean, his face was all colours.

NELSON: Black eyes, bruises?

TAYLOR: He had bruises.

...

NELSON: How did Dodd react to you taking [Lewis] out?

TAYLOR: He just screamed.

NELSON: What did he say?

TAYLOR: 'Mind your so-and-so business'. I had no right to interfere...

Although Taylor does not initially mention any specific injury sustained by Harper, a leading question about whether Dodd had drawn blood immediately elicits the response 'I think he split Lewis's lip'. (Three months later she contradicted this when she told the police 'I didn't see any injury on the day of the assault.')[196] When Nelson, in another leading question, asks whether Harper had a black eye or bruises, she answers that he had bruises, apparently forgetting that bruises take time to form. When Nelson asks how Dodd reacted, she says he 'just screamed' with the implication that he did not say anything at all. Yet when Nelson asks what he said, she immediately supplies a spoken utterance – 'Mind your so-and-so business.' The pattern of these responses suggests that Taylor is actually making up details as she goes along, in response to Nelson's questions.

If we examine the allegation more closely, and set it against the records which were kept at the time, inconsistencies become apparent. Taylor told the Tribunal that she thought Lewis had absconded 'either the first or second weekend'.[197] This detail at least corresponds to the documentary evidence since, according to the log book, Lewis ran away on his first weekend. Having been admitted to the home on 1 May 1980, he absconded on the evening of Sunday 4 May. He was recovered that same evening by Alison Taylor from the village where he lived.

There is, however, a significant discrepancy between Taylor's account and the contemporary records. For although the later versions of Taylor's allegation allotted a prominent role to John Roberts, Monday 5 May was a bank holiday. John Roberts, as a teacher, would not have been at Tŷ'r Felin on that day, something which was inadvertently confirmed to the Tribunal by Taylor herself.

In one of the most bizarre of many bizarre episodes which took place during the Tribunal, a close and revealing cross-examination of Taylor on this point by Dodd's counsel, David Knifton, was effectively discarded by Sir Ronald Waterhouse, the chairman. After Knifton had carefully elicited a detailed account of the events and log book entries surrounding Lewis's absconding on 5 May, the Chairman inquired: 'Does the fact that Monday was a bank holiday have any relevance to the dating of the incident?' To this Taylor immediately responded that 'in that case it couldn't possibly have been that Monday because Mr Roberts was involved in that incident *and he would not have been in the building on a bank holiday*' [italics added]. The Chairman then observed that 'we are probably barking up the wrong tree' and Knifton, in deference to him, immediately abandoned an extremely promising line of cross-examination. Sir Ronald was evidently assuming the truthfulness of Taylor's testimony. A more perceptive chairman might have concluded that Taylor's comment about bank holidays fatally undermined her own evidence and confirmed that the incident had indeed been fabricated.[198]

The records disclose yet more inconsistencies. According to the interview with Nelson, 'when Dodd came back on Monday morning, he had [Lewis] brought into the office.' It was at this point that the assault supposedly took place, early in the morning. Yet during that same Monday, Taylor made an entry in the log book which read 'Children generally happy and relaxed and there has been a noticeable absence of squabbling and moods this week. Reprimands have met with apologies and attempts at recompense excluding Lewis.'[199] While Lewis is specifically excluded from Alison Taylor's positive comments, this does not appear to be written by a woman who has just witnessed a vicious assault on the boy.

Even more telling is an entry by Taylor in Harper's personal file for the same day. 'Lewis is saying,' she wrote, 'that either myself or CW hit him last night. As I have no intention of being alone with him, I have informed Lewis that matters will be discussed on Thursday with JND.'[200] This entry is then referred to in another entry in the log book, which was apparently written by Taylor late in the day on Monday 5 May: 'Would advise all staff to be very circumspect in their handling of Lewis. He is apparently prone to making accusations of assault, so do not take any risks, i.e. make sure that you are not in a position where he can allege assault.'[201] Taylor presumably would not have written these words directly after having witnessed a vicious attack on Harper by Dodd.

One of the central mysteries surrounding the only direct allegation which Alison Taylor has made against Nefyn Dodd, is the question of why she failed to bring it forward in 1986 when she had every opportunity to do so. A further mystery is that almost every significant element in the allegation changed between the time it was first made in 1988, and the time it was brought to the attention of the police in 1991.

As has been noted, Taylor's allegation was first made public in September 1991 in the HTV documentary. The programme claimed that Taylor 'named Lewis Harper to the police during their initial investigation in 1986 and she put herself forward as a witness to the assault'. If she had indeed witnessed such an assault in 1980, this is undoubtedly what she would have done. In fact, however, the claim was not true. She had not at any point during the 1986 investigation named Harper to the police as a possible victim of Dodd, and she had not put herself forward as a witness.

When these inconsistencies are placed alongside the entries in Lewis's personal file and in the log book, and the fact that John Roberts was not even working at Tŷ'r Felin on the day in question, only one conclusion is feasible. This is that the incident which Alison Taylor described never took place. It appears to have been a deliberate fabrication which Taylor gradually elaborated between the time she wrote to Margaret Thatcher in January 1987 and the time she imparted it, in 1991, first to HTV, then to Dean Nelson.

If the most important allegation which Alison Taylor has made against Nefyn Dodd was indeed fabricated, we might well ask how it was that a false allegation would come to be endorsed – or appear to be endorsed – by Lewis Harper.

One answer to this question is that the allegation made by Taylor has never been endorsed in detail by Harper. He has, however, made a number of allegations about his time at Tŷ'r Felin some of which vaguely resemble hers. A clue to the origin of these allegations was provided by Taylor in the log book entry she had made in 1980 and whose existence, by 1991, she might well have forgotten. What she made clear there was that Lewis Harper was prone to making false complaints. His most celebrated achievement in this respect was to have made a hoax 999 call in which he said that a man had jumped off the Menai Strait bridge into the sea. This had resulted in an RAF helicopter being scrambled, and Tŷ'r Felin being presented with a bill for several thousand pounds.[202]

If Taylor decided to invent an allegation against Nefyn Dodd in 1988 in order to rectify what she saw as the incorrect decision not to prosecute him, Lewis Harper would have been a good choice as a 'victim' since he had a record of making false complaints. It would further follow that Taylor, having decided on the nature of her allegation, might make some attempt to contact Harper so that she could outline the imaginary incident to him in the hope that he would respond to her suggestions. Harper, in the statement which he made to the police in November 1991, indicated that Taylor had indeed tried to contact him but he had been in prison at the time. On his release from prison in August 1990 he claims he was told that Taylor had contacted his mother. Harper subsequently visited her and, according to his Tribunal evidence, 'she assured me that she was going to put in her statement that she had witnessed a couple of assaults on me, like'.[203]

However, one significant piece of evidence which never emerged during the Tribunal is that Harper's statement is not accurate. Although it is true that he was in prison when Taylor first contacted him, it is not the case, as his statement implies, that their meeting was delayed until after his release. Taylor actually made a special journey to Wymott Prison in order to speak to Harper. She went with Mandy Wragg, the Yorkshire television researcher. No record exists of what communication took place between Taylor and Harper before this visit. But it may be because their first meeting was in the company of a television journalist that the allegations which he eventually made never quite corresponded to the incidents which Taylor said she had witnessed.

The meeting took place on 17 November 1989. In her notes, Wragg records Harper as saying that Dodd had punished him for running away. However, the assault he described was quite different from that alleged by Taylor. Wragg's note reads: 'Assaulted by Dodd for absconding, Lewis was eating his breakfast and was hit across the face by Dodd. No warning, nothing said.'[204]

In the HTV programme two years later, Harper does claim that he was given a beating by Dodd in his office. Although he gives few details, his allegation as broadcast was at least compatible with the description of an alleged assault given in the same programme by Taylor. By the time he gave his police statement in November 1991, however, his evidence had changed. He did describe an assault which he said took place about two weeks after he had started at the home. Like the assault described by Taylor, this incident supposedly took place on a Monday immediately after he had absconded and been fetched by Taylor. However, the assault Harper describes was completely different. He located it in the dining room at breakfast time, saying that he was slapped from behind by Mr Dodd in front of a number of other children. He went on to say that he was then slapped five or six times on his face or body. No reference was made to a cane, to Mr Roberts, to Taylor, or to his being told to lick Dodd's boots.

Later on in his statement, Harper did refer to a boot-licking incident. But this supposedly took place on a different occasion: 'One day I was told by Mr Dodd to lick his boots, but I refused, whereupon I was assaulted by him. He slapped me about the head and body. Whilst I was being assaulted by Mr Dodd, Mrs Alison Taylor came into the room. She saw what was going on and she told me to go. I left the room.' Here it will be noted that the sequence of events is different and that no mention is made of any of the other parties – June Dodd, John Roberts or Peter Jones.

In another of the clutch of allegations Harper made to the police, he recalled the hoax call and claimed that when he returned he was assaulted by Dodd in the presence of Taylor. The hoax call, however, was made in October 1980. This new allegation was clearly untrue since Taylor had left Tŷ'r Felin the previous month to begin her CQSW course.[205]

The loose and unconvincing fit between the boot-licking incident as described by Taylor and the complaints made by Lewis Harper strongly suggests that Taylor had fabricated the incident, and that Harper had become understandably confused when asked to recall accurately a brutal assault which had not in fact taken place at all.

23 The dossier

DURING THE BRIEF PERIOD OF RESEARCH Nelson conducted before writing his article, he visited Taylor at her home on at least two occasions. On one of these occasions she handed over to him a copy of the dossier which she called her 'Gwynedd County Council Analysis'. The early version of this apparently focused exclusively on allegations made in relation to Tŷ'r Felin and other Gwynedd homes. According to evidence given to the Tribunal, this version had been handed to Parry during Taylor's first meeting with him in the spring of 1991 and he in turn had passed it on to John Jevons, the director of social services.[206]

Later versions of the dossier, which would ultimately run to 129 pages, were broader in their scope and contained much material about Bryn Estyn. It was one of these later versions that Nelson received. In his Tribunal evidence he offered a description of the document: 'She had something called an analysis, which was a summary of various allegations. It was a list of names and contact telephone numbers; it was a kind of cast for everybody who had ever been mentioned in the context of these children's homes, which was very useful.'[207]

Of all the many thousands of documents associated with the North Wales investigation this is perhaps the most important. It contained details of scores of former residents who had supposedly been abused or maltreated. It also contained sections on suspected abusers including teachers, care workers and a number of police officers.

One significant feature of the dossier was that, although it repeated many of Taylor's 1986 complaints, it contained a number of startling claims also referring to the period before 1986, which were entirely new. Some of these complaints were of physical abuse. These included a brief reference to the supposed assault on Lewis Harper. This, however, was not the only incident of physical abuse Taylor now claimed to have witnessed first-hand.

Among the entries on various Gwynedd personnel was a paragraph about Paul Gwynfor Johnson*, a teacher in a school which had links

---

* Not his real name.

with Tŷ'r Felin and Tŷ Newydd and which educated some of their residents. The entry referred to an assault which had supposedly taken place during a visit by Johnson to Tŷ Newydd. He had at this time been the teacher responsible for liaising with Tŷ Newydd where Taylor was the officer-in-charge. She wrote: 'I witnessed one incident where Johnson assaulted a boy in residence at Tŷ Newydd, with J. N. Dodd encouraging the assault.'[208]

At this stage no name was given to the alleged victim. On December 5 1991, however, in a police statement, Taylor named the boy as Steven Parfitt:

> In December 1981 in the hallway outside the front room I found Mr Johnson and Steven. Mr Dodd was standing in the open doorway of the front room. Steven was wearing his school uniform at the time. This included a tie. Mr Johnson had hold of Steven's tie quite close to his collar and was twisting the tie around in his hand. As I approached, I saw Mr Johnson bring his knee ... up into the groin of Steven Parfitt. Steven was continually shouting. Mr Dodd appeared to be verbally encouraging Mr Johnson.

When the police investigated this claim both Dodd and Johnson denied that any assault had taken place. The statement given by Mr Johnson, however, gave an illuminating account of the context of the complaint. He said that whereas the school's relationship with Tŷ'r Felin and Mr Dodd had been excellent, the same was not true of Tŷ Newydd, where Mrs Taylor had been in charge:

> We felt that Tŷ'r Felin actively displayed a far greater interest in co-operating with [us] than did Tŷ Newydd. We felt that Tŷ'r Felin laid great emphasis on partnership with the school and the staff there went out of their way to co-operate on issues which were important to the school; it appeared to us that Tŷ Newydd did not share the same values. ...
>
> Unlike Tŷ'r Felin, Tŷ Newydd had no pictures of children in evidence, no prominent display of personal effects or ornaments, no little items that transformed a building into a home. There was no atmosphere of warmth and caring. The staff at Tŷ'r Felin went to great lengths to welcome and assist visitors from [our school] whereas it was felt that Taylor and Tŷ Newydd were not particularly welcoming.

In the end the school severed its direct relationship with Tŷ Newydd and dealt with all matters relating to the homes through Dodd. Johnson then said:

I knew then and I can fully appreciate with hindsight that I alienated and deeply offended Taylor at this particular time.

Because I know for certain that the allegations made against me in Taylor's statement are absolutely without foundation I have to consider whether they arise from the fact that I offended Taylor more deeply than I ever imagined.[209]

Even more significant was the fact that, when the North Wales Police interviewed Steven Parfitt, he said quite explicitly that he had never been hit or otherwise ill-treated by any of the staff at the school in question.[210]

The Parfitt allegation, like the alleged assault on Lewis Harper, was not mentioned in the statement Taylor gave to DCS Gwynne Owen in 1986 even though it had supposedly already happened. Once again there is only one plausible explanation for this omission. As this assault was denied by its alleged perpetrators and by its alleged victim, there is no reason to suppose that it ever took place.

24 The classic symptoms

ALTHOUGH TAYLOR'S DOSSIER contained more new allegations, these, like her original 1986 complaints, were in many cases second- or third-hand. In a very small number of cases they appear to have had some substance. In the vast majority of cases, however, the evidence suggests that the allegations Taylor relayed were false. Sometimes these false allegations were repeated by the alleged victims. Frequently, however, those whose names had been cited by Taylor made it clear that they had not been victims of any assault.[211]

During the Tribunal Andrew Moran QC, counsel to the North Wales Police, said that he had been able to find at least 32 complaints in Taylor's dossier which, when investigated, had proved to be without substance. Even this figure, however, does not convey the scale on which Taylor's document misleads its readers.[212] By far the most important reader at this time was, of course, Dean Nelson, who was now urgently completing his assignment for the *Independent on Sunday*.

The limited time he had left was undoubtedly one of the reasons why, as he told the Tribunal, he found that Taylor's dossier was 'very useful'. For it appeared that she had already done much of the research. It should not be imagined, however, that Nelson was merely a passive actor in this investigation, an inert receiver of the information which was given to him. His own enthusiasm for the story and his own willingness to believe even Taylor's more extreme claims were almost palpable. This seems to have had a powerful effect on allegations which had been lying dormant for many months. It was as if Nelson's interest and the promise of public attention acted on Taylor's imagination like the warmth of spring. In a number of cases the bare boughs of the complaints contained in her dossier now began to blossom in a detail which would previously have been inconceivable.

This process can actually be observed in the transcript of the key interview which Nelson conducted with Taylor.[213] In one instance an entirely new allegation suddenly and visibly grows in the course of the interview itself. The interview begins with Nelson asking Taylor about the first incident she had witnessed: 'Can you tell me when you first saw anything untoward?' It is this question which leads to the detailed exchange about the alleged assault on Lewis Harper which has already been cited. But no sooner has Taylor concluded her account of this 'first physical assault' than she goes on to describe another assault which supposedly happened even earlier. The claim involves Dodd's predecessor at Tŷ'r Felin, Haydn Jones:

> You see the previous officer-in-charge had left because after I had been there three months … I'd been on duty one weekend, and three girls ran off. … They weren't away long, I got them back, and I didn't think any more of it. Children running away is part of the job. Haydn Roberts [sic] came back on the Monday morning, called all the girls down to his staff house, I went down with them, he lined them up, and said why did you run away. So they started laughing. He just walked down the row and slapped each one across the face. Then walked out of the room and disappeared.[214]

If this allegation is stripped down to its essential features, it closely resembles the one about Lewis Harper. In both cases young people abscond during the weekend while Taylor is on duty, are recovered by her, and are physically chastised on the Monday when the officer-in-charge returns.

The other respect in which this alleged assault resembles the boot-licking incident is that there is no evidence that it ever took place. Taylor has said that she reported the assault to D. A. Parry, who established the facts of what had happened by asking her and the girls. 'And then he had a sort of discussion with Haydn Roberts [sic], after which he went off sick from that moment.' Parry, however, has said that he knew of no such incident, that no complaint was ever made to him, and that Haydn Jones took sick-leave purely because of stress and nervous exhaustion.[215]

In this case the allegation has no discernible origin. It is not referred to in Taylor's dossier, nor was it featured in the HTV programme which had so recently been broadcast. The circumstances in which the complaint did emerge suggest that it may well have been brought into existence either by the process or the prospect of being interviewed.

The same factors seem to be in play in a number of cases where Nelson's interview leads Taylor to elaborate, and sometimes modify, allegations which are made in the dossier in a somewhat bare form, devoid of circumstantial detail. One of Taylor's recurrent claims, clearly originating from the Graham Ennis case (see chapter 12), was that Dodd had blocked the investigation of complaints of sexual abuse. A particularly interesting example of this claim, on which she laid great emphasis, concerned a 14-year-old girl, Tricia Everett, who had been in residence at Tŷ'r Felin while Taylor was working there. According to Taylor, Tricia had complained at the time of being sexually abused by a senior care officer, Edward Compton*:

> A 14 year-old girl made persistent allegations that E. Compton was abusing her; she was transferred to Silverbrook [a Treatment Centre in Pontypridd with a secure unit for 'difficult' girls], where she continued with the allegation, which was reported back to GCC by Gwent. No action was taken apart from GCC's informing Gwent that Tricia would not be readmitted to a GCC home under any circumstance.[216]

Even with the complaint in this form, in which the officer who supposedly transferred the girl is not identified by name, Taylor's claim is seriously misleading. While Tricia Everett was a disturbed young woman who fantasised a lot and engaged in violence and self-harm, she had made no allegations of sexual abuse during her stay at Tŷ'r Felin. It was because of her disturbed and violent behaviour that she was transferred to Silverbrook. After her arrival there she began to talk about Edward Compton as her 'husband' and did make an allegation of sexual abuse against him, claiming that they did have intercourse and that she had become pregnant as a result. This allegation was fully investigated at the time by senior officers of Gwynedd Social Services. It transpired that Tricia Everett had previously made a similar allegation against another person which had proved to be false. The investigation concluded that the allegation was without substance and Compton, who had been interviewed during the course of the investigation, was informed accordingly.[217]

It is noticeable that, in her brief dossier entry, Taylor makes no claim that Tricia Everett had made any allegations to her personally. Nor does she make any complaint against Nefyn Dodd, or even mention his name. She merely makes the untrue assertion that there were 'persistent allegations' while she was still at Tŷ'r Felin.

However, during the course of his main interview with Taylor, Nelson asks a specific question: 'Were there ever any allegations of sexual abuse while you were at Tŷ'r Felin? Were any disclosures ever made to

---

* Not his real name.

you by the children?' In response to this question Taylor greatly elaborates the story of Tricia Everett. She says that Tricia 'did in fact exhibit all the classic symptoms of sexual abuse'. Asked by Nelson to say what these were, Taylor is unable to give any specific answer: 'Look at some sort of child care document on sexual abuse of children,' she says. 'The classic symptoms, the behavioural symptoms these children exhibit.' Nelson then repeats his question: 'What symptoms?' Taylor is once again unable to give any specific answer. 'An increased pattern of disturbed behaviour,' she says. Then, as if recognising that this is inadequate, she goes on to say: 'With anything like that you have to eliminate certain things, like mental disorder, or circumstances under which the child is living, day to day circumstances. Partly a process of elimination, and I think Tricia saw more than one psychiatrist and they actually didn't find anything wrong with her.' Far from exhibiting the 'classic symptoms of sexual abuse', it would appear from this account that the girl was not exhibiting any symptoms which were recognised as such by the psychiatrists she saw.[218]

Taylor goes on to give examples of Tricia's behaviour. She claims that Tricia had told her that Edward Compton was sexually abusing her:

NELSON: So what did you do about it?
TAYLOR: I reported it to Dodd. He was the officer-in-charge. I wanted to get Tricia moved and I did badger Dodd about it. He said that he had reported it to D A Parry and that they would investigate it. Then Tricia came and told me that it was still going on, so I had a set to with Dodd and Parry about it.

Asked how Dodd reacted, she says: 'It was shock horror, I'll do something about it right away.' She says that he certainly appeared to take it seriously: 'the upshot of the incident was ... that it had been investigated, Dodd told me this, and Edward Compton denied anything of the kind ...'[219]

In the statement which Taylor gave to the police a month later, however, Taylor appears to have forgotten what she had told Nelson, and gave a different account of what had happened. In this version of events, far from taking the allegation seriously, Dodd had immediately discounted it:

I immediately told Mr Nefyn Dodd and his response was that he disbelieved Tricia. I again spoke with Tricia, she again told me that Edward Compton had been having sexual intercourse with her. I again

told Mr Nefyn Dodd and he told me to let the matter drop. There
were veiled threats that life may be made difficult for me if I persisted
with the matter. About six weeks or so later, Tricia repeated her allegations to me and, I believe, Nefyn Dodd and a short time later she
was transferred to the Silverbrook Secure Unit, Abergavenny, South
Wales.[220]

In the first version of events it is Taylor who seeks to have Tricia moved
and Dodd who does not respond immediately. In the second version
this has been reversed and it is Dodd who moves the girl to get rid of
her; as Taylor would later put it in her evidence to the Tribunal, 'Tricia
was shifted to keep her quiet'.[221] The two accounts are contradictory.
More significantly still, neither is true.

Tricia Everett was in fact transferred to the Silverbrook secure unit
in South Wales on 14 February 1977, 11 months before Dodd took up
his duties at Tŷ'r Felin. At the time of the transfer Dodd was still a senior housemaster at Bryn Estyn sixty miles away. Nor could Taylor have
confused him with any other officer-in-charge. For at the time Tricia
Everett was transferred, the officer-in-charge was none other than Taylor herself.[222]

Taylor had made a grave allegation against Nefyn Dodd which could
not possibly be true.

25 Pornography

AS NELSON INTERVIEWED ALISON TAYLOR at her Bangor home, the trial of Frank Beck was taking place in Leicester Crown Court. This added an even greater urgency to his investigation. For the prospect of trumping the reports of Beck's conviction with news of an even greater and more horrific scandal was one that few news editors could resist. What made the new story even more compelling was that Taylor, perhaps influenced by the stories of paedophile rings which had surfaced in the Beck case, added a new element to the claims she had made five years earlier. She now suggested that the abuse in North Wales had been organised.

By recording a number of shadowy and frequently unattributed allegations, Taylor implied that Nefyn Dodd was very far from being an isolated offender. She hinted that he was part of a 'vice ring' which stretched across North Wales from Gwynedd to Clwyd and through which 'boys were supplied to senior staff and outsiders'.[223] The centre of this ring was apparently to be found at Bryn Estyn, where Dodd himself had once worked, and where Taylor had completed a three-month placement without mentioning the widespread abuse and the climate of fear she now described. Although the 'vice ring' referred to by Taylor involved physical abuse, its principal concerns were sexual. The allegations made against Dodd changed accordingly. Presented in 1986 as a bully and a tyrant, he was now portrayed additionally as a voyeur and a pervert.

One of the claims which Taylor made concerned pornography. Mr Dodd, she wrote in her dossier, 'had a large collection of very hard core pornographic magazines, mostly foreign in origin, which would be given to female staff, or left in the duty office, and which he looked at regularly'.[224] This claim is, once again, made in a bare form in the space of the single sentence cited here. No details are given of the kind of pornographic material supposed to be involved and there is no hint that it might involve children. Dean Nelson, however, apparently saw in this single sentence a claim which was potentially significant.

NELSON: What was it? How did you know it belonged to Dodd?
TAYLOR: I'll tell you how I knew, because he used to give it to me. He used to leave it in my office. That was his way of expressing that he was interested in me sexually. ...
NELSON: What kind of pornography was it?
TAYLOR: It was really hard core pornography. He used to have some in his desk, because I once saw it when I was looking for something. He used to keep his desk locked and he was off for a weekend on holiday and I was looking for some documents.

There follows a discussion about the content of the pornography, in the course of which Nelson is clearly anxious to elicit from Taylor a clear statement that the pornography involved young children:

NELSON: What do you call hard core? Did it show erect male genitalia? Was that the sort of thing you're talking about? I'm just trying to find out what your idea of hard core pornography is ... what did it show?
TAYLOR: It showed people having sex with each other, and having sex with youngsters.
NELSON: How young?
TAYLOR: It's difficult ... what I called children's bodies. It's hard to tell by a child's face how old it is, certainly undeveloped bodies. There was one, I don't know where he got it from, which was full of one female having three men at a time.
NELSON: It was pornography across the spectrum, from heterosexual to homosexual and animals, and child pornography?
TAYLOR: Yes.
NELSON: Were they clearly children?
TAYLOR: Bodies yes. You know what an undeveloped child's body looks like.
NELSON: What did you say to him?
TAYLOR: Bugger off and take it away with you. He actually said one time that you get used to it, you get to like it after a while. (Men with pigs, dogs. Women with dogs and pigs. Women with snakes. Scandinavian.)

The last answer seems to suggest that Taylor did not report the behaviour she claimed to have seen. It was this version of events she would relate to the Tribunal in 1997. Asked whether she had made any complaint to her employers about this, she said 'I don't know, probably not.'[225] In his interview with her in 1991, however, Dean Nelson was quick to point out the seriousness of her claims. In response to his remarks, Taylor had given a different version of events:

NELSON: Did you report this? Child pornography is photographic evi-
dence of child abuse. And it's illegal.
TAYLOR: I can't remember whether it was D. A. Parry or Gethin Evans
I reported it to. I think it was Gethin Evans.
NELSON: What was his title.
TAYLOR: I think it was principal assistant director. ...
NELSON: Would the complaint have been recorded?
TAYLOR: It should have been. ....

In fact there was no record of any such complaint and Parry and Evans
have said quite clearly that no complaint about pornography was ever
made to them.

Although her replies to Nelson suggest that she looked at the
pornography closely enough to see its contents, she told the Tribunal
that she had only seen the covers of the magazines 'so I don't know
what was actually inside'. When it was pointed out to her that, both in
the police statement she made in December 1991 and in her Tribunal
statement, she had said clearly that the magazines contained pictures of
children, she replied by claiming she only knew about the magazines'
contents because 'other people' had told her.[226]

One of the claims made by Alison Taylor, however, was unequivocal.
In her 1991 'GCC Analysis' she wrote as follows:

DCS Gwyn [sic] Owen had information in my formal statement about
the extent and nature of the pornographic literature in J. N. Dodd's
possession but does not appear to have acted. ... It is my understanding that certain types of evidence are usually seized as soon as possible,
to prevent their destruction or disposal.

On this matter, information to the police that a senior Social Services employee in almost total control of a large number of children in
care is known to be in possession of extensive hard core pornographic
material should prompt immediate action.[227]

In view of the fact that her allegations referred to the period before 1982
– some nine years earlier – it might be asked why Taylor had not herself
taken immediate action. Much more important, however, is the fact that
Taylor's signed statement of March 1986, in which she detailed the complaints she was bringing forward, made no reference to pornography. Her
claim that it did is simply false. Owen himself is clear that this matter was
never raised and there is no reference to it in any of Alison Taylor's volu-
minous correspondence in the wake of the 1986 investigation. All the
available evidence, in short, supports the claim made by barrister David

Knifton during the Tribunal that 'the suggestion that Mr Dodd was in possession of pornographic literature' was 'entirely fabricated'.[228]

Taylor's references to pornography were part of a series of complaints in which she questioned the integrity and effectiveness of the 1986 investigation. Her principal contention was that there had been a failure to interview key witnesses: 'From information I have received from children since 1986, it would seem that many children with crucial information about assaults they had suffered, others of which they had knowledge, and with information about other matters of interest to the police, were never interviewed, despite the fact that their names had been given to DCS Owen in 1986.'[229]

Once again the claim made by Taylor was not true. All those whom she had named to DCS Owen in 1986 had been traced and interviewed. One person who had not been interviewed was Lewis Harper. The reason for this is simple. At that point Taylor had not made any complaint in relation to Harper. The first time she mentioned Dodd's alleged assault on him was in February 1988. Yet in her dossier she wrote this: 'Although his name was given to NWP in 1986 and 1991, Lewis has never been interviewed.' Once again we are confronted by a claim which, in relation to 1986 at least, is completely untrue.

However, when Alison Taylor met Dean Nelson in the autumn of 1991, he did not see her 1986 statement. He did not interview DCS Owen and had no access to any of the police documents relating to the investigation. He was, in short, not in a position to check any of the claims which Taylor made about the conduct of the investigation.

Nelson tried hard to find first-hand witnesses of the regimes of abuse which Taylor alleged both at Bryn Estyn and Tŷ'r Felin. But he was researching against the clock. It is perhaps not surprising, therefore, that in a number of cases, he allowed others to select his witnesses for him.

What must have seemed at the time an advantage was that one of his principal guides was Taylor herself. She had pointed him towards a number of former residents of Tŷ'r Felin and of Bryn Estyn, who supposedly had allegations of abuse they wished to make. But she had also mentioned the names of some members of staff whose testimony might carry even more weight.

By far the most important of these was a former Bryn Estyn care officer by the name of Paul Wilson. During her interview with Nelson, Taylor implied that Wilson could give evidence which might be vital to the case against Dodd and which might also reveal what the regime at Bryn Estyn was really like.

In the light of what Taylor told him, it was clear that Nelson would be well advised to begin his researches into Bryn Estyn by interviewing Paul Wilson.

As Nelson left Bangor to undertake his investigation into Bryn Estyn, he continued to rely on the many leads which Taylor had already given him. But as the story he was pursuing came to focus on Bryn Estyn, he began to depend more and more on the second of his two main guides. This was the former resident whom Taylor had originally met during her 1982 placement at Bryn Estyn – Ryan Tanner.

26 Outward bound

ONE EVENING IN NOVEMBER 1991, soon after Dean Nelson had embarked upon his investigation, former care worker Paul Wilson answered the telephone at his home outside Wrexham. According to Wilson the conversation went like this:

> TANNER: Hello, is that Paddy Wilson?
> WILSON: Yes.
> TANNER: Hello Paddy, it's Ryan here, Ryan Tanner. How are you doing?
> WILSON: Fine thanks. Long time no see, Ryan, what can I do for you?
> TANNER: Well, it's like this Paul, we've got a journalist who's come up from London and he's doing a story about abuse at Bryn Estyn. We're out to get Howarth and Doddy and I wondered whether you would help us Paul? Would you come and meet us for a drink.

Tanner went on to mention the names both of Dean Nelson and Alison Taylor.[230]

That a conversation along these lines took place has been confirmed by Tanner. Under cross-examination during the Tribunal, Tanner admitted that he had telephoned Wilson:

> MR LEVER [counsel to Wilson]: Is it not the case that ... you contacted Mr Wilson by telephone?
> TANNER: I did, yes.
> LEVER: ... The gist of that conversation was to ask him if he would meet with a reporter ... and yourself for a pint.
> TANNER: That's right.
> LEVER: That you wanted his help to really provide information against Howarth and, as you called him, Doddy?
> TANNER: You can imagine how naive I was doing that.
> LEVER: So we agree on that.
> TANNER: We do.[231]

Tanner went on to say that Wilson had said he would think about it, but that he phoned back and refused: 'He told me to piss off'. The implication of Tanner's Tribunal evidence was that his phone call had been in vain. Indeed, Tanner specifically confirmed the suggestion made by Wilson's counsel that Wilson had 'refused to attend'. In fact, however, Wilson did agree to meet Dean Nelson and, on 12 November, the journalist recorded an interview with him.

There were a number of reasons why Wilson might have felt it wise to meet Nelson. Of all members of staff at Bryn Estyn, Paul Wilson was the most likely to find himself under investigation by the police. Tanner himself had made allegations against him during his first police statement and these included the claim that he had witnessed Wilson filling the boot of his car with equipment he had stolen from Bryn Estyn. Similar claims were also made by some members of staff. It was in any case a fact that Wilson had a criminal record. Shortly before he took up his post at Bryn Estyn he was convicted of stealing property from a house. For this relatively minor offence he had received a conditional discharge in the magistrates' court.[232] Arnold had been aware of the conviction at the time he employed Wilson and appears to have believed that Wilson's criminal record might give him more sympathy with the many Bryn Estyn residents who themselves had criminal records.

'Paddy' Wilson was born in Ireland. He was 24 when he took up his post at Bryn Estyn in 1974. He proved to be extremely talented as an organiser of outdoor activities for the boys. An outstanding hockey player who had played for the Irish under-21 team and, later, for North Wales, he was physically fit and active. He rapidly made himself indispensable at Bryn Estyn because of his knowledge of camping, canoeing and hill-walking, his physical toughness, and his enthusiasm for 'outward bound' activities. However, there were a number of documented occasions when he allegedly used physical violence. Sometimes he had punched boys and, on at least six separate occasions, complaints were made. These complaints appear to have been dealt with unsatisfactorily by Howarth and Arnold. As a result a man who was temperamentally unsuited to working with children continued to be employed as a residential social worker.

Since Wilson would almost certainly find himself facing criminal charges as a result of the police investigation, there was a powerful motive for him to co-operate with a journalist and a former resident who seemed intent on pursuing much graver allegations against two of his former colleagues. When he met Nelson on 12 November, he had agreed in advance that although his words could be quoted, his name should not be used in any article which was published. The transcript of the interview which Nelson made is therefore headed 'non attributable'.

In order to assess the picture of Bryn Estyn which Wilson drew, it is necessary to place it in perspective. In the accounts given by the many former residents who speak positively of their time at the home Paul Wilson is, on a number of occasions, singled out for criticism.

One statement was made by former resident, Keith Martell, in response to an inquiry from Chris Saltrese, a solicitor representing Bryn Estyn staff at the Tribunal:

Dear Mr Saltrese,

Thank you for your letter dated the 6th of March 1997, about Bryn Estyn school in Wrexham. I was there from 1975 to 1977. I found it to be a good school, good caring staff, I have fond memories of Bryn Estyn School.

I remember in 1976 my grandfather died and I wasn't allowed to go home for Christmas 1976 In them days I was football mad, so on Boxing Day the school payed for me and two other kids who also have to stay behind for Christmas, to go and see Liverpool play at Anfield against Stoke and the staff members who took us David Massey and Mrs Nibbit, Mrs Nibbit took us back her house for a meal, afterwards at her home in Wrexham

Mr Saltrese the staff at Bryn Estyn school were good honest people and good to me. What happened after 1977, when I left I can't comment on because I wasn't there. But one staff member Paul Wilson was a bully in which I told the police, I seen him hit a boy called Jim Nolan. He used to bully people, he knew he could get away with it The project in which he took was camping which ... never really interested me.

... ...

Mr Saltrese Bryn Estyn school was a good school when I was there and good staff members David Massey, Gwen Hurst, John Hilton [Ilton], Nevin Dodd, Len Strich, David Cheeseborough, Graham Roberts, Mrs Nibbitt, Mr Green, Mr Hughie Roberts, Mrs Jones, Mr Jones, Mr Leighton All good honest people, who would go out of their way to help you not hurt you. These people should of been praised for the work they done

Another former resident, now a social worker himself, wrote an assessment of the home in which he recognised a number of shortcomings. But his overall view of the school was favourable. 'Bryn Estyn', he wrote,

provided both 'a real sense of warmth, security and care', and 'an undeniable sense of being wanted' by members of staff who 'really did care'.
However, he too singled out Wilson as an exception and described him
as 'quite capable' of physical abuse. 'In this day,' he wrote, 'I do not believe
he would have made it through his probationary period.'[233]

Many similar examples could be cited. One of these emerged in the
Tribunal. On the sixth day of the hearings Norman Young, who had
two spells at Bryn Estyn, the first beginning in 1978 and the second in
1981, was cross-examined by Anna Pauffley QC. Like Keith Martell, he
too remembered the way in which he had been treated at Christmas.
He began by paying tribute in particular to two care workers:

> YOUNG: Well, so far as Rob Jones is concerned, him and Liz [Evans]
> actually lived together, but they both worked there, and they used to
> do a lot with me like when we stayed over Christmas and this, that and
> the other, there was only two of us stopping there so, basically, they
> took us out for Christmas dinner and this, that and the other and basi-
> cally I had a good relationship with Rob and with Liz Evans.
> PAUFFLEY: Were they kind to you?
> YOUNG: Yes they were, yes.
> PAUFFLEY: Did they treat you well at all times?
> YOUNG: Yes ...
> PAUFFLEY: What, if anything, would you like to add about Liz Evans
> and the way in which she treated you at Bryn Estyn?
> YOUNG: Basically, I take my hat off to her.
> PAUFFLEY: Sorry?
> YOUNG: I take my hat off to her, because she was very good, her and
> Rob.
> PAUFFLEY: Was that a remark that just applied to you or applied to oth-
> ers who were at Bryn Estyn and who you saw being cared for by Liz
> Evans?
> YOUNG: Yes, I would say the same throughout.[234]

In response to questioning from barrister David Knifton, Young went
on to broaden his tributes:

> KNIFTON: I presume ... there were others who you would say were
> kind to you and helped you?
> YOUNG: Yes ... there was a Dave Cheeseborough, John Hilton [Ilton],
> Mr Arnold was okay. Mr Roberts, the gardener, Mr Matthews and Mr
> Jones who actually took the woodwork. There was quite a few of
> them.[235]

Once again, however, there was an exception:

> KNIFTON: I think the only member of staff you had any complaint
> about was Mr Wilson?
> YOUNG: Yes, that's correct.[236]

Yet another example of this characteristic view of Bryn Estyn was provided by former resident Derek Oliver, in a written statement set
before the Tribunal:

> My recollection [of Bryn Estyn] is that it was alright. I would not say
> that they were good times but they were not bad. I remember John
> Ilton. I regard him as one of life's gentleman and a good teacher. He
> was bright and cheerful and I would be happy when he came and
> woke us up in the morning. I was taught at Bryn Estyn for about 8
> months before I went to an outside school. I was taken by a number
> of teachers. Mr Ilton was easy going but when teaching he would not
> let you muck about. He kept discipline in the classroom by using his
> voice. He was a good teacher. Dave Cheeseborough was also a teacher.
> He was a nice bloke. People were frightened of his sheer size but he
> never used it. He used to take me weight-training. Mr Ilton never took
> me for weights. I do not remember him throwing anything in the
> classroom.
>   The teachers treated me well. They did more than I am sure they
> were expected to do. They would take [us] off to the Rugby Club
> disco on Fridays. Sometimes I would sit with Liz Evans and talk, but
> normally teachers sat together and let us go to the disco. They did not
> have to do it.
>   There were other good times. For example, on Saturdays we used to
> have form teams to clean the school. There were prizes for the team
> who were judged to have done the best job. It sounds stupid but I
> enjoyed that. There was a machine for polishing and buffing the floor.
> I loved using it …
>   It was a disciplined environment and because there were so many
> boys together there were of course scuffles. We played games like kick-
> the-can, and sometimes boys [would] get over-excited and a fight
> would start. If the staff saw anything, they stepped straight in to stop it.
> The only trouble was with Wilson. Paddy Wilson was hated. A horri-
> ble man who we tried to avoid. …
>   Gwen Hurst took me for something. I recall her as being a nice
> woman. No problems at all with her. The teachers were generally good
> except Paddy Wilson. He was a nasty vindictive man who should never
> have been working with children.

Such views of Bryn Estyn were held and have been expressed by many former residents. In his interview with Dean Nelson, however, Wilson inverts this picture. Instead of his own attitude to physical violence being seen as the exception, it is portrayed as if it were the norm.

Wilson's revised view of Bryn Estyn emerges only gradually. Nelson begins by asking him directly 'Did you ever see any physical abuse there?' He answers by describing a regime in which discipline was not enforced by physical sanctions. This answer does not satisfy Nelson who asks 'What about physical punishment?' Wilson gives an answer which seems to contradict what he has already said and portrays a culture of covert violence:

> WILSON: If you're asking me if young people were thumped by members of staff ... I'd be lying if I said some kids didn't receive physical punishment. But this was always something which was talked about in a quiet subdued manner. No one boasted that a kid had been knocked about. There were occasions when certain young people were hard to control and certain members of staff would be asked to sort it out.
> NELSON: What do you mean 'sort it out'?
> WILSON: It could have meant go and deal with him as you need to deal with him. Use your own initiative. ... There was no guideline to say if a child steps out of line you must go and batter that child. Certain members of staff who felt threatened by a group of young people, would possibly sort out the trouble maker and deal with him privately away from any form of supervision, or where they could be seen. ... Out of twenty staff who were at Bryn Estyn I would say nineteen or twenty of them were investigated because of allegations that children had made.

This last claim was doubly untrue. Because of the turnover of staff, the total number of Wilson's colleagues over the ten-year period he was at Bryn Estyn was probably in excess of 50. Of these only three or four were ever investigated as a result of allegations made against them, and nobody had been subjected to multiple investigations as Wilson himself had. On every count the picture of Bryn Estyn he was painting was a gross distortion.

Months later, after Wilson had been arrested, he said this to the police: 'I found it strange that you took so long to come and interview me but it was suggested to me that you were building a case and I might be one of the people you were building a case against.' When the police asked him who had suggested this, he replied 'a newspaper'.

During the Tribunal, David Knifton put it to Wilson that, at the time of his interview with Nelson, he knew that he had used excessive violence on boys and that there were members of staff who would be prepared to bear witness to this. 'So you decided, didn't you Mr Wilson, to make a pre-emptive strike ... to make allegations against others in the hope of diverting attention or shifting blame from yourself.'[237]

Although Wilson denied this suggestion there is no other plausible explanation for the distorted view of Bryn Estyn he imparted. Indeed, he appears to have treated the interview as the opportunity for a trade-off. If Nelson would accept a version of his time at Bryn Estyn which relieved him of blame, he would supply him with the material which, as he knew from Tanner's phone call, he was seeking – material which could be used against Howarth and Dodd. After Wilson has described an incident in the shower in which an unnamed care worker loses his temper and rains blows down on an unidentified boy (who remains mysteriously uninjured), Nelson prompts him:

> NELSON: Was the incident in the shower the worst you saw?
> WILSON: It was the worst outburst of physical violence I saw. And the person I'm talking about is Nefyn Dodd who lost his rag one day. I think one of the kids told him his wife was a motherfucker or something.

After Wilson has given, at some length, a negative assessment of Dodd's character, Nelson asks him if there were ever any sexual allegations. When Wilson says that there were not, he persists in this line of questioning:

> NELSON: I've heard an allegation that he was selecting boys for other people there.
> WILSON: Other people? In connection with what?
> NELSON: Howarth.
> WILSON: You're talking about the flat list now, aren't you?
> NELSON: I think so. I've heard Dodd used to select boys and send them up to Howarth's room. And make sure they didn't have their pants on, to be buggered by Howarth.

Since Nelson does not say who made this sensational allegation, its provenance remains uncertain. However, in that it links Dodd and Howarth together as part of a vice ring, it is clearly compatible with the narrative already created by Taylor.

The 'flat list' to which Wilson refers would become a key part of the North Wales story. The list in question contained the names of boys who would visit Howarth's flat as a group in the evening. These visits took place with the full knowledge of the head and the staff. They had their origin in policies introduced by Matt Arnold whilst he had been the head of Axwell Park, the approved school to which Howarth had been appointed housemaster in 1966. Arnold's thinking has been described by another former housemaster at Axwell:

> Mr Arnold was at that time considered by many people to be one of the leading authorities on reforms in residential care of children and I was very pleased to be working under him. One of the systems Mr Arnold was beginning to reform was the older view that the children should be sent to bed in the large dormitories quite early at night thus causing problems with the older boys. Mr Arnold's view was that certain groups of boys should be removed from the dormitories during the early evening. They would be taken to the rooms of the housemasters to watch the television. This was to combat the rowdyism and bullying that had previously been going on.[238]

Howarth continued this practice after he moved to Bryn Estyn. He did so with the approval of Matt Arnold, who himself sometimes used to invite groups of boys to watch television with his family. One senior member of staff at Bryn Estyn has described how Howarth would make a list of boys who would be allowed to come to his flat at around 9.30 pm. The number of boys varied from 2 to 12 and 'they were allowed to stay until around midnight before returning to their dormitories. ... I certainly never heard of any strange occurrences taking place at the flat, and the boys in small ways seemed to respond positively to being allowed such a privilege.' As these words imply, the flat list was not regarded by the boys as sinister. It was almost always seen as a treat and inclusion on it was something which they sought eagerly. To find that you were not on the list was almost always a disappointment.[239]

Since, in order to reduce absconding, all boys were required to change out of their day clothes at 9.30pm, the boys who visited Howarth's flat wore pyjamas as a matter of course. These pyjamas were specially adapted; the flies were sewn up half-way to make them more suitable for wearing around the home before the boys went to bed. It was a Bryn Estyn house rule that underpants (which were changed daily) were not to be worn beneath pyjamas. Although this would be considered entirely normal in most ordinary homes, Wilson placed a sinister interpretation on it. He implied to Nelson that the rule was Howarth's own and claimed, falsely, that members of staff used to make sexually loaded comments to boys who were going up to Howarth's flat:

> WILSON: At night kids used to walk towards the flight [flat?], past the members of staff, and jokes would be said like 'Have you got your knickers the right way round?' 'Have you got the hole opened up right?'
> NELSON: Kids used to joke about this?
> WILSON: The staff used to joke about this.

Although the flat list had never given rise to any allegation while Bryn Estyn was open, or during the police investigation which was still in progress, Wilson expressed the view that sexual abuse may have been taking place all the time. Although he knew that the list was compiled by Howarth, he told Nelson that Dodd 'could have had some say in who might have gone to the flat.' In answer to a leading question from Nelson, he said that boys sometimes came out of the flat looking upset. He then claimed that a boy called Simon Birley 'had feminine ways about him' and that 'he was a favourite of Howarth's and Nefyn Dodd's'. Like much of what Wilson told Nelson, this was not true. Birley did not start at Bryn Estyn until October 1982. Dodd had left in 1977.

Wilson also said that Tanner had fallen from favour with Howarth because he did not relate to Nefyn Dodd. 'There was a lot of ill feeling between Dodd and Tanner'. In fact Tanner did not start at Bryn Estyn until 1981, four years after Dodd had left. If Wilson knew that 'there was a lot of ill feeling between Dodd and Tanner', it was because Tanner had recently told him about the allegations he had made, and not because he had observed it at Bryn Estyn.[240]

In all these respects, and in others, it is clear that Paul Wilson deliberately misled Dean Nelson. However, he misled him in a way which powerfully confirmed the story Nelson had already heard from Alison Taylor.[241] Now that her version of events had seemingly been corroborated by an independent witness, it was almost inevitable that Nelson would place more and more reliance on what she told him.

27 The minibus

THE DELIBERATELY DISTORTED VIEW of Bryn Estyn which Paul Wilson gave to Nelson was important for three main reasons. In the first place, it seemed to lend weight to the allegations Taylor had been making about Dodd ever since 1986. Secondly, it suggested that there might indeed have been a regime of physical brutality at Bryn Estyn. But, most importantly, Wilson's testimony, and in particular the misleading account he gave of Howarth's flat list, suggested something altogether more serious. It seemed to confirm what Taylor had suggested (and what Tanner had implied in his police statement) – that the deputy head of Bryn Estyn was a paedophile.

One of the reasons why Nelson must have found this suggestion so persuasive was that Taylor herself claimed that she had actually found out about Howarth's supposed sexual activities from boys who had been abused by him. One of the claims contained in Taylor's dossier referred back to her 1982 placement at Bryn Estyn. Like the allegations of physical abuse involving Lewis Harper and Steven Parfitt, this was a new claim which mysteriously made its appearance nine years after the incident it purported to describe. In its original form it was both simple and brief: 'John Evans ... was alleged to be repeatedly and regularly sexually assaulted by Peter Howarth, and possibly by others. He has very recently been interviewed by the police in connection with the Clwyd investigation. ... Was thought to be in care for non-school attendance only.'[242]

It is perhaps significant that this paragraph is worded in a way which implies that Taylor did not know Evans herself and had had no contact with him. However, when Nelson asks her directly which boys had disclosed sexual abuse to her, Taylor's response is curious:

NELSON: Which [boys] disclosed sexual abuse to you?
TAYLOR: Andrew Singer was one of those who gravitated towards me. ... I knew [John Evans] was very unhappy, *but he never said anything directly to me.* Except things like I'll be out of here soon. It won't last for ever. I'd say what won't last for ever? He'd say just being here [italics added].

Although these words seem to convey quite clearly that Evans had said nothing to Taylor explicitly, she almost immediately changes tack, and begins to relate, perhaps for the first time, a quite different story:

> TAYLOR: The day I finished the placement at Bryn Estyn, John was actually discharged and I travelled into Wrexham with him and with Andrew Singer in the van. We were living in Wrexham and John was being taken to the station. I can't remember who was driving. I was leaning over the seat talking to them. John actually told me that day I was leaving and he was leaving, that Howarth had been sexually abusing him throughout most of his placement.
> NELSON: What did he actually say?
> TAYLOR: Pretty nearly that. That's what he said. I can't remember his exact words. I said why in God's name didn't you tell me? He said what could you have done? He said what can you do now? It's over, he said. And this ... actually happened with a lot of children.
> NELSON: Did you report that?
> TAYLOR: No. Because he didn't want anything done about it. ...
> NELSON: Did he say in detail what Howarth was doing?
> TAYLOR: He said he had done everything to him that he possibly could. He didn't specify blow by blow. ...
> NELSON: What about Singer?
> TAYLOR: Singer told me after John got out of the van that Howarth had had a go at him as well. ... He just said that Mr Howarth had been abusing him as well and that they weren't the only ones.[243]

Because of the circumstantial detail it contains, Taylor's story has at least a degree of plausibility. But it is precisely the detail which, when examined carefully, calls it into question. Her claim that the minibus was actually being driven by someone else and that the two boys had made their allegations to her while she was leaning back over the seat is an odd one. That such confessions should be made in the presence of another unidentified adult seems improbable. The suggestion was certainly in conflict with the claim Taylor was later to make at the Tribunal, that the matter remained known to her, and to her alone.[244]

No sooner was this point raised during the Tribunal by Andrew Moran QC than the story changed:

> MORAN: Was this other person in the minibus, that you refer to, present when these allegations were being made?
> TAYLOR: I have a vague idea that it was Paddy Wilson driving but I can't, you know I just can't be sure.

MORAN: Were the allegations made whilst Wilson was in the vehicle?
TAYLOR: No, the allegations were made as we got out of the vehicle.
MORAN: At the station?
TAYLOR: I don't remember whether they were actually at the station or not, or sort of towards the station.[245]

The fact that the story should suddenly be changed under the pressure of cross-examination strongly suggests that it was not true.

But there is another much more important fact which casts doubt on Taylor's story, and which indeed shows it to be false. Although she says that her last day at Bryn Estyn coincided with Evans's, this was not the case. On the day Taylor's placement formally ended – 4 June 1982 – John Evans was not even at Bryn Estyn. He was on extended home leave in the north of England from which he did not come back until 7 June 1982. He was, in other words, returning to Bryn Estyn at the very time Taylor claims he was leaving for good. Evans was actually discharged from Bryn Estyn on 25 June 1982, more than two weeks after Taylor had left. He returned not to South Wales, as Taylor claimed in her police statement, but to a city in the north of England to which his parents had moved.[246]

When I interviewed John Evans in 1996 he said that he had never made any allegation of sexual abuse to Taylor, whom he did not remember and whose photograph he did not recognise. He said that Peter Howarth had never sexually abused him, that he was 'a good bloke' and that 'he treated me right'.

If Taylor's story about the minibus had been true, the most improbable part of it would have been her implicit claim that she had received a grave allegation of sexual abuse from a 16-year-old boy without taking any action at all. This would have been particularly reprehensible in view of the fact that Howarth was still responsible for the care of many other adolescent boys. The idea that Taylor had remained silent about such a serious matter for nine whole years, in spite of the fact that she had already been involved in two police investigations of abuse, and had already met with senior police officers during the course of the 1991 investigation, was simply not credible.

There is, of course, nothing to indicate that Taylor ever withheld any allegation in this manner. All the evidence points to one conclusion: the minibus incident did not happen.

Once again Taylor had relayed a grave allegation which she said had been made by a former resident of a care-home, but which, according to all the evidence which is available, appears to have been entirely her own creation. The problem for Dean Nelson was that he had no access to the documents needed to check Taylor's claim. Nor, at this stage, was he able to contact either Evans or Singer.[247]

Since Nelson's most pressing journalistic need at this point was to locate witnesses who said that they had been sexually abused at Bryn Estyn, and to interview them in person, he had no practical alternative but to rely on the two potential witnesses he *was* now able to contact. Both these young men were former Bryn Estyn residents who lived in Wrexham. Both had been at Bryn Estyn at the same time as Ryan Tanner and both had been specifically mentioned to Nelson by Taylor as possible victims of abuse. It was now time for Nelson to put the reliability of Taylor's testimony to the test by visiting these men.

28 Glue sniffing

THE FIRST OF THE TWO MEN Nelson visited was a 23-year-old former resident of Bryn Estyn, Peter Wynne. Wynne had arrived at Bryn Estyn in September 1980 after a deeply troubled childhood. His parents had split up when he was young in a manner which meant that Peter was effectively homeless. At the age of eight he was taken into care by the social services department and was sent to a children's home in Colwyn Bay for assessment. After six months he had gone to live with foster parents but was unable to settle, with the result that, after only four weeks, he was moved to the Little Acton Assessment Centre in Wrexham where he remained for over a year.

He was then briefly allowed to return home to his mother. Feeling that he was not wanted, he was once again placed in the care of social services. He was sent to Gatewen Hall where he was treated kindly and where he says he felt 'quite happy'. However, his mother decided that she wanted him back, and he returned home for another six months before it became clear that his relationship with his mother had broken down beyond repair.

On this occasion he was sent to Park House in Prestatyn. However, he proved to be an exceptionally difficult child and, because of his unruly behaviour, he was sent to Bryn Estyn. He was twelve when he arrived and would normally have joined boys of his own age in Clwyd House, the junior section of the home. However, because he was so difficult, he was initially placed in the main school. Physically small for his age, Peter now found himself surrounded by much bigger boys who were also considerably older than he was.

Only when it became clear that he was being persistently bullied by some of the older boys was he moved to Clwyd House. He returned to the main school when he was fourteen. He remained a deeply insecure child, prone to outbursts of violence, and given to glue-sniffing, which was a serious problem at Bryn Estyn, as it was in practically every institution of its kind at this period.

In her dossier Taylor makes only a brief reference to Wynne, whom she describes as 'a very disturbed boy', and of whom she says, as if by way of explanation of his disturbed state, 'it is very likely that Peter was assaulted at Bryn Estyn'. No indication is given that he had made any such claim to her. However, when Taylor had been interviewed by Nelson in Bangor, she told him a different story. It would appear that she had originally related this story before the tape-recorder was switched on, for in the transcript of the interview, as soon as she has finished the minibus story, Nelson makes a specific request: 'Tell me about Peter Wynne.' She replies by saying that during her Bryn Estyn placement in 1982 Peter Wynne went missing one day. She says she searched the grounds and found him lying on a bank where he had been glue-sniffing:

> I found him down there with the remains of a can of evostick, plastic bags, he was completely out of it. I couldn't get him to move or anything. I was getting quite panicky that he needed hospital treatment, and I wondered what to do. One of the other boys was around there. I told whoever it was to go back to the main school to get help.

Nelson then asks 'How did he tell you he was sexually abused?'

> TAYLOR: He was mumbling and I was trying to get him to sit up and stand up so I could move him and deal with it. He was rambling on about all these things, saying 'you don't know why I do this. Do you want to know why I do this?' I was talking to him, and he then told me he did it because Howarth was …
> NELSON: Was what?
> TAYLOR: Fucking his arse was what he said.
> NELSON: Is that what he actually said?
> TAYLOR: Yes. He said 'he makes me suck his cock.' interspersed with 'bastards', 'fuckers,' which seemed to be what he was saying about staff.

Taylor went on to claim that she had relayed Wynne's complaint to her placement supervisor, Margaret Norris, but had been told that she should not believe Peter Wynne.

This claim conflicts with the entry for Peter Wyn [sic] which Taylor had already made in her dossier. For here there is no mention at all of the story she told Nelson. If this story had been true it seems inconceivable that Taylor would not have included it in a document whose central purpose was to disseminate just such claims.

The story is also at odds with the evidence Wynne had already given to the police. On 12 September 1991 he had been interviewed at his home in Wrexham. The statement he signed included references to John Evans and Andrew Singer which resembled those already made by Ryan Tanner. He described one incident in which he witnessed a boy being hit and another in which he was himself roughly handled by Paul Wilson. Although the details of these incidents are disputed, there is no doubt that both of them took place. In his statement Wynne also made it clear that he thought Bryn Estyn 'was the best home I was in' and he concluded by repeating this sentiment:

> Apart from the incidents I have outlined, I enjoyed my time at Bryn Estyn. There were some very caring staff there, one of whom was Liz Evans and another was Cath Colbert. Tony Curran was another very good member of staff. I have not encountered any incidents of sexual abuse at Bryn Estyn or any other home at which I was resident.

The circumstantial evidence, when assessed in the light of Wynne's own statement, and Taylor's general unreliability, suggests that, although something resembling the glue-sniffing incident may have taken place, Wynne's 'allegations' were an embellishment of her own.

When Nelson visited Peter Wynne at his home in Wrexham a great deal turned on what Wynne himself would tell him. The outcome of the interview was apparently unequivocal. Wynne said that nothing had happened to him and that he had no knowledge of any sexual abuse during his time in care. Nelson duly recorded this in his notebook: 'On Friday 15 November I went to see Peter Wynne who denied knowledge of any abuse at Bryn Estyn.'

The implications of this were potentially catastrophic. If Wynne was telling the truth, it would be necessary for Nelson to confront the possibility that Alison Taylor was deliberately fabricating allegations in order to incriminate particular care workers. If that was so, he would have no option but to abandon his entire investigation and forsake the most important story he had ever worked on or was ever likely to. Perhaps because he found this possibility too difficult to contemplate, Nelson added a single sentence to his note on what Wynne had said:

> I did not believe him.

29 A missing transcript

FRIDAY 15 NOVEMBER 1991 was a busy day for Dean Nelson. In addition to seeing Peter Wynne, he had conducted an interview with the former police officer Harry Templeton. He then met former staff member David Gillison. And, at some point in the day, he met up again with Ryan Tanner. Finally, he interviewed another former resident of Bryn Estyn – Simon Birley.[248]

Birley was, like Wynne, 23 years old. Like Wynne he had been mentioned by Alison Taylor as a possible victim of sexual abuse. Indeed, in her interview with Nelson, Taylor had referred to somebody called Simon in passing, in terms which suggested that he had already made an allegation of sexual abuse to her. Having told Nelson that she had not reported John Evans's supposed allegation on the grounds that 'he didn't want anything done about it', she says: 'It's the same with Simon now. If the child tells you and he doesn't want anything done, what do you do? The child has already had enough misery and abuse. You're sort of compounding it in a way.'[249]

Birley was the first person Alison Taylor had ever pointed to as a possible victim of sexual abuse. In 1986, as we have seen, she had told DCS Owen that there were 'rumours' about his relationship with a male member of staff. Birley, who was seventeen at the time, was interviewed by Owen and made a statement saying that he had never been physically or sexually abused by any member of staff (see above, pp. 54–5). Before being sent to Tŷ Newydd, however, Birley had been at Bryn Estyn. It was in this connection that Taylor had now put his name forward again as a possible victim – this time to Dean Nelson.

Birley had arrived at Bryn Estyn in October 1982, four months after Alison Taylor had completed her placement. Pale, lightly built and very intelligent, he had been placed under a care order at the age of 14 after being found guilty of a number of thefts and burglaries. At Bryn Estyn he had been seen as a promising pupil who, academically, was on a much higher level than most of the other boys there. He seemed at one point to be destined for university. However, about a year after his arrival, he had fallen under the influence of another boy who had introduced him to glue-sniffing and he had become addicted. As a young man he declined further into addiction, becoming a heavy user of drugs and glue. During the Tribunal he was recalled by one former member of staff as 'a pitiable sight of a boy. … I remember seeing him round Wrexham in the same condition and thinking the poor – well he wasn't a poor little boy then – poor person, because he was still on glue then and half out of his mind half the time when I saw him in Wrexham.'[250]

Like Wynne, Birley had been interviewed by the police at an early stage of the Bryn Estyn investigation. He had been visited at home by two police officers in October 1991. He told them that he had never been sexually or physically abused and, because he had made it clear that he had no complaints about his time at Bryn Estyn, they took no statement from him.[251]

Alison Taylor, however, had made an entry on Birley in her dossier. She had noted that, on his transfer from Bryn Estyn to Tŷ Newydd, he was 'very disturbed and addicted to glue and alcohol'. Although she had not previously, in 1986, voiced any suspicions about what had happened at Bryn Estyn, she now speculated that he 'was possibly assaulted' while he was there.[252]

Thus it came about that, some hours after he conducted his interview with Peter Wynne, Nelson followed up Taylor's lead and visited Birley at home. Although he had told police officers a month previously that he had not been abused at Bryn Estyn, Birley now told Nelson that Howarth had sexually abused him.

The precise details of what Birley said to Nelson are not clear. This is because, whereas Nelson supplied the Tribunal with a complete transcript of the formal parts of most of his key interviews, he did not provide any transcript of this one. Fortunately, there is a record of a crucial part of what Birley told Nelson. It can be found in no other place than the article which appeared, two weeks later, in the *Independent on Sunday*. In the article Simon Birley is referred to as 'Steven'. Nelson introduces the relevant passage by claiming that what nobody knew when the police inquiry into Bryn Estyn was launched was that the deputy head, Peter Howarth, 'was himself a paedophile'. He goes on to present the evidence gathered from Birley:

> Our investigation has found evidence that Peter Howarth made sexual assaults on young people in his care at Bryn Estyn while he entertained them with beer and games at his flat and house in the grounds.

One former boy, Steven, now married with children, said Howarth sexually assaulted him after inviting him to his house for a drink. 'I started feeling a bit uncomfortable. He started rubbing my leg. I wanted to just get up and go but I just sat there.

The article goes on to quote Birley as claiming that Howarth had undone his trousers and started to masturbate him. Far more important is Nelson's account of what happened next:

After the incident, Steven had sex on two occasions with boys at the home during glue-sniffing sessions. One of the boys, Paul, was disturbed by this and confided in his housemaster, Stephen Norris. Within days of confiding in Norris, Paul had also been sexually abused by Howarth.

This passage contains a number of striking claims. If true, these would furnish clear evidence of exactly the kind of conspiracy between care workers one would expect if a paedophile ring was in operation at Bryn Estyn. What is perhaps most surprising, however, is that 'Paul', the boy with whom Birley allegedly had sex and who was then supposedly abused by Howarth, is none other than Peter Wynne. The article, indeed, implies that Wynne accepted this version of events.

The reason that Nelson was able to make this suggestion is that, on Saturday 16 November, the day after his interview with Birley, he had gone back to see Peter Wynne for a second time. In the light of what Birley had said the day before, and of what Alison Taylor had told him about Wynne's alleged 'disclosure', Nelson had apparently convinced himself that Peter Wynne had indeed been sexually abused, and that it might be possible to persuade him to reveal what had happened. As he told the Tribunal: 'When I met Peter Wynne [for the first time] his manner was such that it gave me reason to believe that there may well be some things that he wanted to tell me about which he didn't feel quite ready to tell me about.'[253]

It may very well have been that Dean Nelson, whose wife worked for a child protection charity, was sincere about Wynne's presumed need to 'disclose'. The journalist, as much as anyone involved in the story, appears to have accepted the Californian model of child protection and to have believed that victims of abuse sometimes needed to be helped or prompted before they would disclose. To what extent Nelson did prompt those he interviewed, however, is not always clear. At this point we encounter another gap in the records. For, in spite of the fact that

Wynne had told him the previous day that he had *not* been sexually abused, the transcript of Nelson's second interview begins, with scarcely any preamble, with what amounts to a specific request for a sexual allegation:

> WYNNE: My name is Peter Wynne, I'm doing this interview on the understanding that my name will not be used in the newspaper or articles.
> NELSON: When were you at Bryn Estyn?
> WYNNE: 1979 to 1984.
> NELSON: Can you tell me about any sexual incidents involving any of the staff at Bryn Estyn?

Given the contents of the interview the day before, it is quite clear that something has happened between the two interviews, and that Nelson had already elicited a different version of events before the tape-recorder had been switched on. No record appears to exist, however, of this preliminary conversation.

What we do know is that, on the tape, Wynne immediately responds to Nelson's blunt question by giving an entirely new version of his time at Bryn Estyn. The story he tells corresponds in some of its external details to that related by Alison Taylor. It involves glue-sniffing on the bank and a complaint of sexual assault against Peter Howarth. However, where Taylor had recounted allegations both of buggery and of oral sex, Wynne describes an act of masturbation: 'One minute I was on the bank sniffing it [glue] and the next I was in his flat … with him giving me a wank.'[254]

Wynne claims that as soon as he realised what was happening he ran out of Howarth's flat back to the bank. If Taylor's story were true it would have been at this point that Wynne encountered her. According to Nelson's transcript of his interview, however, Wynne clearly says that he did not tell anyone about what had happened: 'I ran out the back way and down the bank. I didn't tell no one. It wasn't worth telling no one. No one would have believed me.' He tells Nelson that 'I fully understood what had happened, like. Because that sobered me up from the glue. Sobered me up fully.' The interview continues:

> NELSON: Were you emotional afterwards?
> WYNNE: How do you mean, emotional?
> NELSON: Did you cry?
> WYNNE: Yeah, cried my fucking eyes out.

NELSON: Where were you when you were crying?
WYNNE: Down the bank. Near the rugby club.

Nelson at this point, as though in an attempt to confirm Taylor's version of the story, puts a specific question to Wynne: 'Did anyone see you
crying?' Wynne replies: 'No, I had good hiding places down the bank.'

The lack of fit between Taylor's version of the story and Wynne's casts
doubt once again on Taylor's veracity. Equally significant, however, is the
fact that the story Nelson succeeds in eliciting from Wynne at this stage
does fit remarkably well with what Birley had told him the previous day.

After Wynne has described the alleged assault by Howarth, Nelson
says: 'You told me about another incident with another boy, do you
think that may have been related to the incident with Howarth?' Nelson's question is in one respect mysterious, in that, in the transcript of
the earlier part of the interview, Wynne has not described any incident
involving a boy. Nelson is evidently referring to the conversation he has
had with Wynne before switching the tape-recorder on. From the section of the interview which is recorded, however, it is possible to recon-
struct part of this conversation. Nelson had evidently elicited from
Wynne the claim that, while he was at Bryn Estyn, he had had sex with
another boy (of whose identity he appears to have remained unaware),
and that this had happened while both were under the influence of
glue. Nelson now goes on to coax Wynne into relating the story of how
he had told his housemaster, Stephen Norris, about the incident with
the boy: 'He was alright about it, like. Because I was upset about that as
well. Because I was hallucinating at the time, and like I thought it was
a woman. That's what my hallucination was. I thought it [the other boy]
was a woman. But when I started to come off my dream, like, I realised
that it was a man. And that fucking shocked me.'

Questioned by Nelson, Wynne says that about two weeks after he
had told Norris about having had sex with a boy while under the influence of glue, Howarth had taken advantage of one of his glue-sniffing
sessions to sexually assault him.

Once again, as in the suggestion made to Paul Wilson that Dodd had
supplied boys to Howarth, the story which Nelson elicited from Wynne
matched one of Taylor's main suggestions: that Bryn Estyn lay at the
centre of a vice ring in which boys (or information about boys) were
passed from one sexual predator to another. Wynne's story thus
appeared to offer a striking and extremely disturbing confirmation of
one of Taylor's least plausible claims.

Wynne's role would prove to be a particularly important one. From making a statement to the police in September 1991 in which he said that he had enjoyed his time at Bryn Estyn, that it been the best home he had been in, and that he had not encountered any incident of sexual abuse, he had, by the middle of November, developed a totally different version of events. In this revised version he had been sexually abused and physically bullied by members of staff.

It was apparently not a coincidence that Wynne's revised account of Bryn Estyn closely resembled that which had been developed (over a much longer period) by Alison Taylor. The community home she had parted from happily at the end of her placement in 1982, from which she said she would take 'many very pleasant memories', was now portrayed as a haven for abuse.

Yet a number of aspects of Nelson's interview with Wynne give rise to doubts. One of these is his failure to elicit from Wynne any confirmation of Taylor's account of how she had found him lying on the bank after Howarth's alleged assault. Another is the manner in which he did manage to get from Wynne a story which matched Birley's. At one point on the tape, as we have seen, he says to Wynne: 'You told me about another incident with another boy.' These words are, however, potentially misleading. For, given the particular circumstances, it seems rather more likely that, initially at least, it was not Wynne who had told Nelson about this alleged incident, but Nelson who had told Wynne: that Nelson had, while preserving Birley's anonymity, carried his version of events to Wynne and invited him to confirm it.

Nine years after the event, Dean Nelson wrote a letter which appears to confirm this reading of events:

> My first witness, Simon Birley, was married with two children and a steady job when I met him. His first sexual experience, at the age of 14, had been a sexual assault by Howarth, which had left him questioning his sexuality. He told me that, after that assault, he had had sex with another boy, Peter Wynn [sic]. I had already interviewed Peter, who'd told me he had been physically, but not sexually, abused. ... *When I returned to ask him about his encounter with Simon*, he told me he had in fact been abused by Howarth [italics added].[255]

Nelson himself may well have believed that, by reminding Peter Wynne about the incident related by Birley, he was simply enabling him to recover genuine memories which had been repressed or 'blocked'. What the journalist seems not to have understood was the possibility that, by asking leading questions, he might himself plant in the mind of a suggestible young man the very story he was anxiously seeking to confirm.

In the light of these two possibilities there is one question above all which needs to be answered. The question is a simple one: could the version of events relayed by Birley, and subsequently endorsed by Wynne, conceivably be true?

30 A superintendent calls

ONE OF THE MOST INTRIGUING facts about Birley and Wynne's unwitting collaboration is that part of their story disappeared completely after its brief airing in the *Independent on Sunday* on 1 December. This was the very part which Nelson had gone to such lengths to confirm: namely the 'chain' linking Birley, Wynne, Norris and Howarth.

The first sign that this part of the story had gone missing was the statement Wynne made to the police in January 1992, five weeks after Nelson's article appeared. The beginning of his statement corresponds closely with what he had told the journalist. However, the second part tells a different story and Taylor now plays a central role:

> As soon as I realised what he had done I jumped up and ran off and back down to the bank where I stayed crying for about two hours. I don't know if it was on the same day or a few days later I spoke to one of the staff at the home. It was a female and her name was Alison Taylor. I told her everything that had happened the day I ended up in Mr Howarth's room. I said that I woke up and found him with his hands down my underpants. Having told her about this incident I don't remember if she said she would do anything about it but from my recollection nothing was ever done. I think that when I spoke to Mrs Taylor I had again been glue-sniffing and I think I started to cry.

In Wynne's police statement there appears to have been a deliberate attempt to bring his story into conformity with the account which had been given by Taylor to Dean Nelson. Even here, however, the sexual allegation which Wynne made was quite different from that relayed by Taylor: a complaint of buggery was replaced by an allegation of indecent assault. Even more important is that Wynne's police statement made no reference at all to his having had sex with another boy while under the influence of glue. Just as mysteriously as this story made its appearance in the transcript of Nelson's interview, so it disappeared entirely from Wynne's police statement.

Simon Birley, who had originally imparted this story to Nelson, did not make any statement to the police at this point. In an addendum to her dossier, written in the same week that Nelson had conducted his interviews in Wrexham, Taylor makes a comment which appears to explain this omission:

> He [Simon] states now that he does not wish the fact of his abuse at Bryn Estyn to become known because of the repercussions this would doubtless have for his family, especially for his two young children. It is therefore absolutely essential that those who now know of the abuse respect Simon's wishes in this matter.
>
> He appears still to be very much affected by what happened to him: since disclosing the abuse to us and his wife, he appears to have become extremely disturbed, and it is hoped that he will accept support and counselling if necessary. I feel that he is entitled to be assured that his confidences will be respected.

It was perhaps because of these cautionary words that, although Taylor handed a copy of her dossier to the police on 9 December 1991, they did not obtain any statement from Birley. A statement was only taken three months later when Birley himself contacted the police. This was about four months after Nelson had interviewed him. According to the evidence Birley gave at Howarth's trial, the contact was made because he had approached a solicitor about the possibility of obtaining compensation. The fact that Birley took this initiative himself casts doubt on Taylor's appraisal of his psychological state. The solicitor advised him that before they instituted proceedings Birley should first get in touch with the police.

When he made a statement to two police officers in March 1992, Birley described the sexual assault Howarth had allegedly made on him. He did so in terms similar to those reported by Nelson in his article. But Birley made no reference whatsoever to the sexual encounter with Peter Wynne which had supposedly ensued.

It is clear why this story, which had already disappeared from Wynne's version of events, now disappeared altogether. This is because it could not possibly be true. According to the story as told by Birley and Wynne, the sequence of events was unambiguous. First Howarth sexually abused Birley. Then Birley had sex with Wynne. Then, after several weeks had passed, Wynne told Stephen Norris about Birley (or about sex with an unidentified boy). Then, after two more weeks, Peter Howarth sexually abused Wynne. At some point after this, Alison Taylor discovered Wynne on the bank and he told her what had happened.

If all this had happened, the sequence of events would have taken about six weeks to unfold and it would have required the presence of both boys throughout most of Taylor's placement at Bryn Estyn. But Simon Birley did not arrive at the home until 26 October 1982, five months after Taylor had left. By this time she was actually back working in Gwynedd at the other end of North Wales.

The statement Birley gave to the police made matters even clearer. He claimed that he had been at Bryn Estyn 'for just over a year' when the incident with Howarth took place. In other words, by the time the conversation between Wynne and Taylor supposedly occured in the grounds of Bryn Estyn, almost eighteen months had passed since Taylor had left.

Given the impossibility of the combined testimony, and the fact that this would soon have become apparent to Alison Taylor, it is not surprising that she should have tried so hard to dissuade others from approaching Birley. Nor is it surprising that the transcript of Nelson's interview with Birley seems to have gone missing. For if what Wynne told the police in January 1992 about confiding in Taylor was true, what Birley told Nelson in November 1991 was false. Indeed Birley's testimony, if confirmed to the police in its original form, would undermine Nelson's entire investigation by suggesting that the only two allegations of sexual abuse he had collected against Howarth were both false.

Perhaps the most important question which needs to be answered, however, is how it was that Birley came to make his allegation against Howarth in the first place, only a matter of weeks after he had told the North Wales Police that he had no complaints to make.

The first factor which should be pointed out is that, although we might assume that when Nelson arrived to interview Birley, he was on his own, this appears not to have been the case. If we are to rely on the evidence which Birley gave during the trial of Peter Howarth, Dean Nelson did not come on his own. Asked by Howarth's counsel, John Rogers QC, whether he had been contacted in the autumn of 1991 by a reporter, he replied 'And an ex-resident of Bryn Estyn, yes'. The following exchange then took place:

ROGERS: Well, let us take them one by one. Were you contacted by a man called Dean Nelson?
BIRLEY: At the same time as a resident, yes.
ROGERS: And were you contacted by someone called – well, let us take it bit by bit. Who was the resident of Bryn Estyn who contacted you?
BIRLEY: He arrived at the same time as the reporter, Ryan Tanner.
ROGERS: Ryan Tanner; thank you.[256]

It is by no means clear, however, that Tanner, if he did indeed accompany Nelson, was his only companion. For a passage included in the addendum to Taylor's 'GCC Analysis' reads as follows: 'Simon was interviewed by NWP some weeks ago, and has stated that they were "not sympathetic". He did not make any complaint, *but has this week (w/e 16 November) informed myself and another adult* that he was sexually abused by Peter Howarth whilst resident at Bryn Estyn' [italics added].

This passage suggests either that Taylor had seen Birley on a different occasion that week or that she had actually been present during Nelson's interview. The latter possibility should not be ruled out, partly because Taylor has frequently pointed out that she does not drive (and therefore could not easily have made the journey from Bangor to Wrexham to see Birley on her own), and partly because, on a subsequent occasion, she accompanied Dean Nelson when his specific aim had been to conduct another interview with Birley (see below, chapter 42). If Taylor was present during the original interview and contributed to it, this might itself account for the fact that no tape-recording or transcript of the interview has ever been disclosed.

In a statement made to the police in May 1992, Birley himself confirmed that he had been in contact with Taylor at the relevant time:

> Some time last year, I think it was October 1991, two police officers visited my home to see if I wished to make any complaints. I told them at that stage I did not wish to make a complaint. Following that interview I spoke to Alison Taylor, but I can't remember when, about the officers visiting me. A man called Dean Nelson, who is a reporter for the Independent newspaper, also spoke to me about the same thing.[257]

Taylor's close involvement with Birley at the time his allegation suddenly emerged is consistent with her conduct in a number of other cases. In this particular instance the circumstantial evidence strongly suggests that, as in the case of Lewis Harper, she provided the 'template' for the allegations Birley went on to make. This template appears then to have been conveyed to Wynne by Nelson. This would explain why the story which emerged went to extraordinary (and chronologically impossible) lengths to implicate Norris and Howarth in just the kind of conspiracy Taylor herself claimed to have detected.

It is also conceivable that Taylor may have been in direct touch with Wynne at some point before his second interview with Nelson. But although she may have been in contact with Birley and Wynne in Wrexham on the Friday or Saturday (15/16 November), or at some time before this, it would appear that no such contact took place on the Thursday. For, on Thursday 14 November, Alison Taylor was safely at home in Bangor. We know this because at some point that day there was a knock at her front door. Her visitor was none other than Detective Superintendent Peter Ackerley, the officer in charge of the Bryn Estyn investigation.

The reason for Ackerley's call was to follow up suggestions from Councillor Dennis Parry that the North Wales Police were intent on covering up allegations of child sexual abuse. Since Parry had named Taylor as one of his sources for this claim, Ackerley had come to ask her whether she was in a position to supply any evidence to substantiate it. It transpired that she had no evidence of any kind to offer.[258]

During his conversation with Taylor, however, Ackerley learned something which caused him disquiet: 'I formed the view that she was actively involving herself with witnesses and potential witnesses, and I was concerned in the context of any subsequent criminal proceedings that allegations of witness management could be levelled against her, and that it could impact upon the integrity of any witnesses that were used in the prosecution.'[259]

Having warned her verbally against such involvement, Ackerley followed up his visit with a letter, the final paragraph of which read as follows:

> I take this opportunity to remind you of my words of caution regarding possible dangers of you maintaining close contact with witnesses or potential witnesses in the inquiry, in the event that at some stage criminal proceedings are commenced. Indeed, I would ask that you desist from any close involvement with other witnesses or potential witnesses in order to avoid any possible suggestion of any coaching or other improper practice which could result in their evidence being discounted or carrying less weight.[260]

This letter was delivered to Taylor by hand. It would appear, however, that she either ignored the warning or that it was already too late.

As the journalist, Dean Nelson, continued to conduct interviews in and around Wrexham, the threads of a disturbing narrative were gradually being drawn together. However, before this narrative could assume its final form, one more strand remained to be woven into it. This related to the role supposedly played in the alleged abuse by the very people who were now in the process of investigating it – the North Wales Police.

III

LIES AND LIBELS
(1992–94)

31 The bogey man

WHEN, IN 1986, ALISON TAYLOR had taken her complaints to the North Wales Police, she had clearly hoped that they would result in charges being brought against Nefyn Dodd. This was in spite of the fact that she had not witnessed any incident of abuse herself and was, at this point, not even claiming that she had. As soon as the decision was taken not to prosecute, she began, as we have seen, a letter-writing campaign directed against the North Wales Police.

By the autumn of 1991, however, Taylor's campaign had developed further and she began, in parallel to Councillor Dennis Parry, to make allegations against, or cast doubt on the integrity of, individual officers. In her dossier Taylor included the names of a number of officers from the North Wales force in contexts which called their conduct into question. Some of her comments were directed against DCS Owen who had led the 1986 investigation. At one point she wrote:

> In August 1991, I had a meeting with the team of officers from the Serious Crimes Squad NWP, headed by Detective Inspector Rowlands, which was investigating allegations on behalf of Clwyd CC. The meeting was at the urgent request of NWP, and appeared to be concerned in the main with eliciting how much information I possess. No statement was taken. Under pressure from me on the subject of the 1986 investigation, and the fact that these same allegations were again surfacing, despite claims by GCC that there was no substance, and despite the absence of any prosecution, DI Rowlands admitted that there had been 'shortcomings at least' in the 1986 investigation.[261]

During the Tribunal, however, it emerged that the North Wales Police had not made any urgent request for a meeting with Taylor. It was Taylor who had sought an interview with Inspector Rowlands. A meeting had indeed taken place in August, but Rowlands has said that he made no comment about the conduct of the 1986 investigation, of which he had no knowledge.[262]

Taylor's dossier also contained comments about other officers. Some of these concerned Y Gwyngyll:

Former residents of Y Gwyngyll have stated that regular visits were made to Edward Compton and the home by two officers ... and by a third officer ... who was ... completely out of any operational area responsible for Y Gwyngyll. [This officer] is stated to have taken boys swimming and for weight training, but at a later stage took only Mark Hall out alone with the full consent of E Compton.

The implication of these remarks, made in the context of a document which contained allegations of sexual impropriety against Compton, was that the officer was himself engaged in an improper sexual relationship with a boy in care. However, when he was interviewed by the North Wales Police in June 1992, Hall made it clear that the officer had become friendly with his mother, and that he had originally met him while on home leave. He described the officer as 'a good bloke', and said that he used to visit him at Y Gwyngyll and that on one occasion he took a group of boys mountaineering: 'I have no complaint whatsoever to make against [him]. As I've said he was a good bloke and great to get on with.'[263]

Some of the claims made by Taylor, however, were more explicit. In discussing a senior officer in the North Wales force, she wrote 'It has been stated to me by a civilian that there is an allegation that [name of officer] was involved in a sexual relationship with a girl in care.' In reality, as we have already seen, no such allegation had ever been made (see above, p. 142).[264]

There were many other critical references to police officers, some of which were, in themselves, much less serious. One of these concerned retired Superintendent Anglesea, who had been an inspector during the time he was associated with Bryn Estyn. In the same document in which she claimed that Nefyn Dodd was 'a key figure in a vice ring that was in operation at Bryn Estyn, where boys were supplied to senior staff and outsiders', Taylor wrote this about Anglesea:

J. N. Dodd claimed on many occasions to be a close friend of Inspector Anglesey [sic] and used to tell children at Tŷ'r Felin that Insp. Anglesey would send them to prison for misbehaving. Children were told that they would be 'sent down' by Insp. Anglesey if they made any complaint about ill-treatment or any other matter. J. N. Dodd also claimed that Insp. Anglesey would do anything J. N. Dodd requested of him. He was also used by J. N. Dodd as a threat to children who stated that they would report J. N. Dodd for having assaulted them.[265]

Taylor repeated this claim in her interview with Dean Nelson:

> ... on many occasions I used to hear Dodd telling children that if they
> didn't behave themselves Inspector Anglesea, who was a big friend,
> would come and take them away. He used Gordon Anglesea's name
> with great frequency. ... He was presented as a high-up police officer
> who was big mates with Dodd and would do whatever Dodd wanted
> him to do.[266]

The claim that Dodd had invoked Anglesea as a bogey man in order to
frighten children, or intimidate them into silence about 'ill-treatment',
clearly referred back to the period before 1980 when Taylor had
worked alongside Dodd at Tŷ'r Felin. Yet, like many other allegations
which referred to that period, it had never been made during the 1986
investigation.

The main reason why it is unlikely to be true is that the careers of
Anglesea and Dodd have never overlapped. Anglesea was first posted to
Wrexham in July 1976, and it was not until 1979 that his role in running an Attendance Centre brought him into contact with Bryn Estyn
boys. It was not until 1980 that he began to visit Bryn Estyn in the
course of his duties. By this time Dodd had left Bryn Estyn and had
been running Tŷ'r Felin in Bangor for three years. There is no reason
to suppose that Dodd and Anglesea had ever met.

One of the most obvious implications of Taylor's claim was that, if it
were true, Anglesea's name would have been well known to most former residents of Tŷ'r Felin and to those who had worked alongside
Dodd. During the Tribunal, Andrew Moran QC raised this point during
his cross-examination of Detective Superintendent Ackerley:

MORAN: One matter that has been raised [is] as to whether there was
ever evidence of some link between Nefyn Dodd and Gordon Angle-
sea?
ACKERLEY: Yes, sir.
MORAN: The only evidence that the Tribunal has heard in relation to
that is a suggestion, from Mrs Alison Taylor, that Nefyn Dodd used to
use the name of Anglesea, as it were, to threaten children?
ACKERLEY: That is correct.
MORAN: In all of the hundreds of witnesses that you interviewed from
Bryn Estyn and Tŷ'r Felin, indeed all over the inquiry, did anyone else
anywhere ever suggest a link between Nefyn Dodd and Gordon
Anglesea?
ACKERLEY: No one ever did, sir, no.[267]

Once again the evidence suggests that a claim made by Alison Taylor was without any foundation in fact and that it was, indeed, her own invention.

The implication of her dossier was that the North Wales Police was a haven for corrupt, dishonest or sexually perverted officers, and that this was one reason why they had failed to detect the abuse she alleged in 1986. Another reason, as she had suggested in a letter to the home secretary, Kenneth Clarke, was that the force was being manipulated by masons: 'There have been persistent suggestions in North Wales,' she wrote, 'that pressures and influences have been brought to bear on North Wales Police officers in the matter of allegations of abuse through masonic lodges.'[268] In this respect, as in others, Taylor's document echoed the criticisms of the North Wales Police which were being put forward at the same time by Dennis Parry.

So extensive were the criticisms of police officers contained in Taylor's dossier that, on 17 December 1991, she was interviewed about them at length by Ackerley. A statement she gave to him included the names of about thirty officers she had specifically mentioned in her dossier. Although she had relayed complaints against many of these, she was now obliged to admit that she did not have evidence to substantiate any of them. She said that, as far as she was aware, she had never met Superintendent Gordon Anglesea and she had no complaints to make against him.[269]

By the time Taylor made this statement, however, the innuendoes against the North Wales Police which had been present in her dossier had already been taken one stage further. For by this point Dean Nelson's article had appeared in the *Independent on Sunday*. Its suggestion that Gordon Anglesea might actually be part of a paedophile ring based at Bryn Estyn went beyond anything Taylor had written, and was now conveyed to a much larger audience than her dossier would ever reach.

32 The article

THE STORY WHICH WAS PUBLISHED in the *Independent on Sunday* on 1 December 1991 appeared under the name of Dean Nelson. The other names given in the by-line were Rachel Borrill and David Connett. In his statement to the Tribunal Nelson wrote:

> On December 1 the *Independent on Sunday* published the results of my investigation, which was assisted by Rachel Borrill and David Connett. It revealed systematic abuse of children in North Wales homes over two decades and provoked a national outcry. Of all my investigations it is the one which has had most impact and of which I am most proud. I wrote and stand by every word of it.

In claiming that his story led to a national outcry Nelson was perhaps exaggerating. It would be more accurate to say that the story continued and intensified the sense of public outrage which had already been provoked by the Pindown scandal and the Frank Beck case. Nelson's article, like the earlier articles he had written about Tŷ Mawr, was in this respect a piece of reactive journalism. It did not create its own agenda but fitted in with an agenda already created by others.

Even the idea of a police cover-up was not new. This idea had already surfaced in a number of satanic abuse cases in America. When attempts to track down putative satanic cults failed, as they invariably did, it was always possible to explain away the failure by suggesting that police officers might themselves be involved in the cult. As Jean La Fontaine notes, 'one account of the supposed satanic cult states categorically that those high up in the cult "frequently" include members of the police'.[270]

The belief that police forces might actively seek to conceal abuse had also been strengthened by the reporting of the trial of Frank Beck. During this trial a number of prosecution witnesses claimed that they had been sexually abused by Beck, that they had reported this to police officers at the time, but that they had been disbelieved or turned away. Although there was never any evidence to substantiate such claims, they were widely believed, with the result that the role of the police in investigating allegations of abuse was already in question.

The manner in which Dean Nelson's article was presented by the *Independent on Sunday* was clearly shaped by these factors. The full headline was 'New Child Abuse Scandal: After Leicester, homes in Wales – Victims say they asked in vain for the police to help them'. In fact the story which followed contained no reference to any occasion on which police officers were supposed to have rejected children's pleas for help. It is quite clear that the North Wales scandal was being poured into a pre-existing narrative mould, and that this mould was actually determining, to some extent, the shape of the story itself.

The story's opening did, however, stress the alleged failures of the North Wales Police:

> Dozens of children in North Wales children's homes were subjected to sexual and physical abuse for over a decade, an investigation by the *Independent on Sunday* has revealed.
>
> At least two police investigations and numerous complaints to senior social services officials failed to uncover a catalogue of sexual abuse, physical assaults and humiliating rituals.

Having hinted at a cover-up, Nelson went on to claim quite explicitly that the police had 'failed to interview key witnesses', and that they had 'failed to persuade key sex abuse witnesses to co-operate because they had used heavy-handed methods'. As we have already seen, the first of these claims, which had originated with Alison Taylor, was false. The second clearly related to Simon Birley and Peter Wynne who had only become 'key sex abuse witnesses' after Taylor's intervention.

What made Nelson's story seem authoritative was the manner in which these opening claims appeared to be confirmed by others: 'Denis [sic] Parry, the leader of Clwyd County Council, has accused the police of mounting a cover-up to conceal the failure of senior officers and social services executives to reveal the extent of abuse in the children's homes.' Having named Gordon Anglesea and described him as a retired police superintendent, who used to be a regular visitor to Bryn Estyn, the article went on to quote Parry's views on the original Gwynedd investigation: 'I'm disturbed about the way these young people are being interviewed. We are fighting a machine trying to cover things up.' After a reference to the sacking of Alison Taylor, Nelson quoted Parry again:

> Mr Parry said: 'The 1985-86 investigation was suddenly, abruptly halted. The young people were interviewed in front of Nefyn Dodd.

Children ran away because of it. You have to pose the question, what led the police to that sort of investigation? Was it because senior police people had links with social services and the police complaints authority?

'If the police were to be trusted on this, I could go to the chief constable and say we've got a young person who wants to give evidence and make allegations but does not want his life disrupted. But I'm frightened to death because I do not know who I can trust' he added.

The scarcely veiled implication was that Anglesea might himself be one of the 'senior police people' who had links with social services and who might have been responsible for halting the earlier investigation. What readers of these words were not to know was that the county councillor who appeared to confirm Nelson's story had himself gleaned his information from the same source as Nelson had done – Alison Taylor. And the claim that young people had been interviewed by the police in the presence of Nefyn Dodd was untrue.

It was only after the story had been introduced on the front page as one which was concerned above all with a police cover-up, that the allegations against Dodd and Howarth were outlined.

In the front-page story, the idea that a conspiracy might be operating at Bryn Estyn was obliquely present. Inside the paper this suggestion was made explicit. John Banham, the Cheshire social worker who had conducted the inquiry into the conviction of Stephen Norris, was said to have expressed concern 'that a paedophile ring was operating at Bryn Estyn'. This concern was based on the seemingly unrelated convictions of Stephen Norris, Fred Rutter and David Gillison, none of whom had been convicted in relation to Bryn Estyn, but all of whom had worked there.

Nelson's article was implicitly presented as the confirmation of the fears which Banham had expressed. The sensational 'discovery' which it announced concerned the role supposedly played by Peter Howarth. 'What neither Mr Banham nor the police knew,' wrote Nelson, 'was that the "line-manager" at Bryn Estyn of all three sex offenders – Peter Howarth – was himself a paedophile.'

The story of how 'Steven' [Simon Birley] and 'Paul' [Peter Wynne] had supposedly been sexually assaulted by Howarth was now given in detail. A crucial feature of this story, which seemed to prove beyond doubt the existence of a 'ring', was the implicit claim that Norris had passed information about a potential victim to Howarth (see above, pp. 184, 186).

As we have seen, one of the many problems with this story, quite apart from the chronological impossibility of Alison Taylor's involvement, was that Wynne's version of events was at odds with Taylor's. Taylor claimed Wynne had told her about being sexually abused whereas Wynne, at this stage, said he had not. At the same time Taylor and Wynne had referred to quite different kinds of sexual assault. In his article Nelson navigated a way through these difficulties by reporting Wynne's version of events: 'Paul [Peter Wynne] said: "I didn't tell anyone. No one would have believed me. Who could I turn to, to say something like that? I'd have been called a queer and everything wouldn't I? He was deputy head as well; he was in a big position. I felt ashamed, angry and embarrassed all in one."'

From this it might appear that Nelson had decided to discount entirely the story proffered by Alison Taylor. However, no sooner has he reported Paul's story, than he writes the following introductory paragraph to a new section of the article:

> Alison Taylor, a former residential social worker in Gwynedd, was working on a training placement at Bryn Estyn, when she was told of abuse being committed by Howarth. She said one boy told her Howarth had buggered him and forced him to have oral sex. Taylor said she reported the incident to her supervisor, but was told the boy should not be believed.

The implication here is that it was not Paul [Peter Wynne] but a different boy who reported buggery and oral sex to Taylor. Nelson, in other words, has inverted the true significance of Taylor's claim and a piece of evidence which casts doubt on the credibility of Wynne and Taylor is presented as though it actually reinforces their testimony. In a clear instance of dishonest journalism, two alleged victims, Birley and Wynne, have been transformed into three.

In a reference to Taylor's story about the boys in the minibus, Nelson also writes that 'two other boys also told her they had been molested by Howarth'. His article thus adduces – or appears to adduce – no fewer than five victims of indecent assault by Howarth, and Bryn Estyn is presented as a veritable hive of sexual abuse. The direct or indirect source of all these claims was, of course, Alison Taylor.

In a section of his article which was to have a decisive influence on the development of the case against Howarth, Nelson went on to give a description of Howarth's 'flat list'. It should be noted that none of the allegations which had at this point been made against Howarth had

| PEARL HARBOR Fifty years on, the loser takes all *Review, page 6* | BOOKS OF THE YEAR Personal favourites and Christmas choices *Review, page 28* | FINE DETAILS This year, style resides in the accessories *Review, page 54* | A COMMON DESTINY Neal Ascherson describes how he became a European *Page 25* | FAR FAIRER FOWL Turkey if necessary, but not necessarily turkey *Review, page 59* |

New child abuse scandal

By Dean Nelson, Rachel Borrill and David Connett

DOZENS of children in North Wales children's homes were subjected to sexual and physical abuse for over a decade, an investigation by *The Independent on Sunday* has revealed.

Peter Howarth, who is alleged to have sexually assaulted boys

Anthony Dowell and Marguerite Porter rehearse for *Dance for Life*, a gala for World Aids Day, to be performed today in Her Majesty's Theatre in the presence of the Princess of Wales. Tickets are priced £35 to £250. All funds go to Aids charity Crusaid

Aids: we fear it but carry on as before

By Judith Jones and Liz Hunt

THE GOVERNMENT was urged by Aids campaigners today to mount an education campaign after a poll by NOP for *The Independent on Sunday* showed an alarming complacency about the risks of HIV infection among the British public.

Hope of hostage release

BEIRUT (Agencies) — Events in the Middle East pointed last night to the release within days of one or more US hostages in Lebanon.

On the seventh day thou shalt steal?

By Adam Sage

SOMETIME between 10am and 4pm today, Roy Edey will carry out an "independent direct action" in protest at the failure to prosecute Sunday traders.

Detective to face charges

By David Connett

THE SENIOR Scotland Yard detective who led the murder inquiry into the death of PC Keith Blakelock during the riots on the Broadwater Farm Estate, north London, in 1985, will face charges.

CONTENTS

NEWS
Home news .... 2 - 11
Foreign news .... 12 - 18
Sport .... 26 - 32
Weather 8

BUSINESS

SUNDAY REVIEW
TV ..... Review, Back Page
Crosswords ..... 38, Review, 92

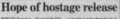

9 770958 172173

PEARL HARBOR
Fifty years on, the loser takes all
Review, page 6

BOOKS OF THE YEAR
Personal favourites and Christmas choices
Review, page 28

FINE DETAILS
This year, style resides in the accessories
Review, page 54

A COMMON DESTINY
Neal Ascherson describes how he became a European
Page 25

FAR FAIRER FOWL
Turkey if necessary, but not necessarily turkey
Review, page 59

New child abuse scandal

After Leicester, homes in Wales: victims say they asked in vain for the police to help them

By Dean Nelson,
Rachel Borrill
and David Connett

DOZENS of children in North Wales children's homes were subjected to sexual and physical abuse for over a decade, an investigation by *The Independent on Sunday* has revealed.

At least two police investigations and numerous complaints to senior social services officials failed to uncover a catalogue of sexual abuse, physical assaults and humiliating rituals. In two homes children were shown hardcore pornography by staff.

The scandal raises vital questions about the way children's homes are run in Britain. It comes only 48 hours after Frank Beck, the former head of three Leicestershire children's homes, was given five life sentences for sexually abusing children in care, and five months after *The Independent* revealed continuing abuse at Ty Mawr children's home in Abergavenny, Gwent – now the subject of an official inquiry. The

Beck case, described as Britain's biggest-ever child abuse case, prompted the Secretary of State for Health, William Waldegrave, to order a national inquiry into the recruitment and monitoring of staff at children's homes. Those with intimate knowledge of the allegations in North Wales believe that an even bigger scandal is waiting to be uncovered.

Our investigation there has revealed allegations that the police:
■ failed to interview key witnesses
■ failed to realise that three social workers jailed for sex offences had all worked together at a children's home where sexual assaults were reported
■ failed to investigate allegations involve at least four children's homes
■ failed to persuade key sex abuse witnesses to co-operate because they used heavy-handed methods

accused witnesses of being paid by a television station to make allegations of abuse.

The Crown Prosecution Service decided not to press charges following the police investigations, and the Welsh Office minister, Sir Wyn Roberts, said in July that the matter had already been "properly investigated". But two new police investigations into allegations in Clwyd and Gwynedd are now under way.

Denis Parry, the leader of Clwyd County Council, has accused the police of mounting a cover-up to conceal the failure of senior officers and social services executives to reveal the extent of abuse in the children's homes. "I want to know why the police didn't uncover all the staff that is coming out now," he said.

Peter Howarth, who is alleged to have sexually assaulted boys

care and by former staff – focus on two homes, Bryn Estyn in Wrexham, Clwyd, and Ty'r Felyn in Bangor, Gwynedd.

According to former residents at Bryn Estyn, Mr Howarth, a former senior North Wales police officer, was a regular visitor there. He recently retired suddenly without explanation.

Another serving officer has been accused of assaulting a child at Ty'r Felyn.

Police in Clwyd began a fresh investigation into Bryn Estyn an inquiry after the central allegations in an independent review of conditions at the Cartrefle children's home in nearby Broughton. This review followed the jailing of the head at

Cartrefle on sex charges involving young boys. The expert who carried out the review told the council that he was one of three social workers jailed for rape, buggery and other sexual offences against children in care. All three had once worked at Bryn Estyn under the deputy head, Peter Howarth.

The Independent on Sunday has been told that Howarth sexually assaulted and buggered boys in his flat at the home while entertaining them with beer and TV. Mr Howarth has not been arrested by police. He said he "emphatically denied" the allegations.

A separate police team in Gwynedd began yet another investigation into cruelty allegations against the county's former head of children's homes, Nefyn Dodd, after its has broadcast victims' claims in a documentary in September.

Mr Dodd, a former Bryn Estyn housemaster, is now being investi-

gated in connection with allegations of physical assaults against dozens of children in his care at Ty'r Felyn Assessment Centre in Bangor. Mr Dodd retired recently and his wife June took over the management of the home. She once worked at Bryn Estyn under the deputy head, Peter Howarth.

Mr Dodd has been investigated several times before, but grave concerns have been raised about police methods in both past and present investigations. Mr Parry said he had received complaints that young people were interviewed in front of those accused of abuse, and he is unhappy about reports of police handling of the present investigation.

"I'm disturbed about the way these young people are being interviewed. We are getting a machine trying to cover things up," he said in September.

One senior Gwynedd social worker who witnessed abuse was sacked after a letter from the dep-

uty chief constable, thanking her for her co-operation, was sent to her workplace, where it was opened by colleagues accused of assaults.

Mr Parry said: "The 1985-86 investigation was suddenly, abruptly halted. The young people were interviewed in front of Nefyn Dodd. Children ran away because of it. You have to pose the question, what led the police to that sort of investigation? Was it because senior police people had links with social services and the police complaints authority?

"If the police were to be trusted on this, I could go to the chief constable and say we've got a young person who wants to give evidence and make allegations but does not want his file disrupted. But I'm frightened to death because I do not know who I can trust," he added.

North Wales police declined to comment on the allegations.

Independent on Sunday, 1 December 1991: front-page story.

Police are uncovering a decade of alleged sexual and physical assaults in North Wales children's homes

The victims — █████, who says he was made to chew carbolic soap at Ty'r Felyn; █████ — 'physically assaulted' at Bryn Estyn and █████ — 'dragged down stairs' at Ty'r Felyn

Lives wrecked by years of abuse

THE POLICE arrived nine years too late to save Steven* from the paedophile who is still wrecking his life. They were nine years too late to help Paul*, who he suffers from depression and an attempted suicide.

The paedophile in question is Peter Howarth, the former deputy head of Bryn Estyn children's home in Wrexham. He retired in 1984 shortly before the home was closed down. He has not yet been arrested. Steven and Paul knew about his life there, and often think of revenge. To them his sexual assaults like only yesterday, despite their best efforts to forget.

As they interview former Bryn Estyn boys throughout Britain, North Wales police are now learning just how many others they failed to save. But their investigation goes far beyond the Wrexham home — to allegations of sexual assaults, physical abuse and ritual humiliation at children's homes throughout North Wales during the past decade.

[The remainder of the article body consists of multiple columns of small print that continue the report on abuse at North Wales children's homes, including testimony relating to Peter Howarth, Bryn Estyn, Ty'r Felyn and other homes.]

Report by Dean Nelson, David Connett and Rachel Borrill. Photographs by David Rose

Inmates of the Ty Mawr home have complained often about their treatment. **Dean Nelson** reports

Boy tells of torment and suicide attempts

Ty Mawr school at Abergavenny in Gwent. According to a former pupil, 'the harshness of the regime "turned his life upside down" and drove him to repeated suicide attempts' Photograph: Glenn Edwards

Charities unite to help victims of abuse in care

Philip Knight, who tried to commit suicide at Ty Mawr before he died in jail

Co-operative that speaks from experience

Welfare system failing to meet the needs of vulnerable adolescents

Jack O'Sullivan argues that children's homes are caught in a crisis caused by under-investment, poor staff training, low morale and a lack of direction

Independent, 27 May 1991, Tŷ Mawr and the tennis court (see p. 26).

involved the flat list, or even registered its existence. Ryan Tanner had not referred to it in his initial statement to the North Wales Police and neither Singer nor Holden had mentioned it in their statements. Nor had it played any part in the allegations made by Birley and Wynne. Nelson, however, now used quotations from an interview to describe the flat-list visits in terms which made them seem like calculated opportunities for sexual abuse.

> One former member of staff, who asked not to be named, said boys sometimes went to Howarth's flat unaccompanied and that he insisted boys be dressed in pyjamas without underpants underneath. 'At night,' he said, 'kids used to walk towards the flat past members of staff and jokes would be said like "have you got your underpants on? … Have you got your Vaseline with you?"'

The unnamed member of staff quoted here was Paul Wilson. Yet, according to the transcript of Nelson's interview with him, the quotation given does not correspond to what he said. The transcript of the relevant portion of Nelson's interview has already been cited. It reads as follows:

> WILSON: … At night kids used to walk towards the flight [flat], past the members of staff, and jokes would be said like 'Have you got your knickers the right way round?' 'Have you got the hole opened up right?'
> NELSON: Kids used to joke about this?
> WILSON: The staff used to joke about this.

According to the transcript Wilson had contradicted himself. For having said (quite correctly) that the boys who went to the flat were *not* wearing underpants, he claimed that staff were in the habit of making suggestive jokes which assumed that they were. This inconsistency is important because it is precisely the kind of mistake likely to be found in evidence which is being made up on the spur of the moment. In the article, however, Nelson has invisibly removed the contradiction and seamlessly joined the first half of one of Wilson's replies to some words he did in fact utter, but at a different point in the interview. In another example of unscrupulous journalism, he has once again converted a piece of evidence which undermines the credibility of his source into a detail which appears to support the allegations against Howarth.

Having made an apparently damning case against Howarth, the arti-

cle goes on to make allegations of physical abuse and cruelty against
Nefyn Dodd, who is described as 'a protégé of Peter Howarth'. Alison
Taylor is said to have rescued a boy from a savage beating at Dodd's
hands. Predictably enough the two main witnesses who are cited are
the boy who was supposedly rescued, Lewis Harper, and Ryan Tanner.
Photographs of Harper and Tanner appear at the head of the page.

Nelson goes on to write that there were 'further allegations that
Dodd kept hard-core pornography', and that he 'masturbated while
peeping into the girls' bathroom'. What he does not make clear is that
these are not additional allegations made by independent witnesses, but
claims made by the same people who have already been quoted. The
first originated with Alison Taylor, and the second was a complaint she
attributed in her dossier to Lewis Harper.

Having related Taylor's own version of how she came to be dismissed
from her Gwynedd post, the article concludes with the following paragraphs:

> Clwyd County Council will look sympathetically on claims for com-
> pensation from those who suffered abuse, but the council leader, Den-
> nis Parry, said no amount of money could make good the damage
> caused.
>
> 'Lives have been ruined by this. God help us, how many young peo-
> ple with drugs and sexual problems have come from these kinds of
> establishments? It's frightening because it's a microcosm of what's
> going on around the country.'

The two ideas with which Dean Nelson's article closed – that compensation could be claimed by those who made allegations of abuse,
and that the North Wales scandal might be a microcosm of what was
happening in the country – would play a crucial role in the way the
North Wales story developed. But the overriding idea that there had
been an unprecedented cover-up would ultimately prove even more
important.

The story would maintain that Bryn Estyn had lain at the centre of
a massive conspiracy of evil, which had remained undiscovered for so
long because its tentacles stretched deep into the very body which had
been charged with the task of investigating it – the North Wales Police.

All the ingredients of this idea were present in Dean Nelson's article. What rendered the story so potent, conferring on it the status,
almost, of a modern myth, was that it was effectively self-confirming. If
the police investigation which had been launched in August 1991 did

not result in an unprecedented number of convictions, this would merely demonstrate how pervasive and successful the cover-up had been. If it did not uncover abuse on a massive scale and produce conclusive evidence that a paedophile ring existed, then this would show how deeply the North Wales Police were themselves implicated in the conspiracy.

The publication of Nelson's article was to have many consequences. The most immediate was that it placed the North Wales Police under massive pressure to re-double their efforts, and to hunt down the members of the network of evil whose existence Nelson, with the help of Alison Taylor, seemed to have proved beyond all reasonable doubt.

33 Dog walking

AT THE HEADQUARTERS OF THE North Wales Police in Colwyn Bay, high above the coastal stretch of the A55 which links Bangor and Wrexham, reaction to the publication of the sensational *Independent on Sunday* article was swift and decisive.

Until this point the police investigation of Bryn Estyn and other residential establishments in Clwyd had been kept separate from the inquiry into homes in Gwynedd, which had been launched on 1 October in the wake of the HTV documentary. On Monday 2 December, however, the day after the appearance of Dean Nelson's article, the two inquiries were amalgamated and supported by a HOLMES* computerised major incident room. Detective Superintendent Peter Ackerley, who was leading the Clwyd investigation, was placed in overall charge of the combined operation.

By Tuesday 3 December, Ackerley had prepared a document which reviewed the progress of the investigation so far and outlined the course which should be adopted in the future. This document was discussed at a policy meeting held at police headquarters next day. It was agreed that the investigation of Tŷ'r Felin and Bryn Estyn should be given priority, with other homes in Gwynedd and Clwyd being investigated afterwards.[271]

Whenever any crime or alleged crime attracts major national publicity the pressure on the police to achieve convictions inevitably increases. In this case, the unfounded allegations in the *Independent on Sunday* article about the competence and integrity of the North Wales Police rendered the pressure even more acute. Because the newspaper had lent its considerable authority to the notion that Bryn Estyn might be the centre of a paedophile ring, this idea seems to have become the main engine of the investigation.

It was given even more impetus by the introduction of a telephone advice service. Set up jointly by the North Wales Police and Clwyd Social Services, 'the Bryn Estyn helpline' was introduced on 4 Decem-

---

* HOLMES: Home Office Large Major Enquiry System.

ber 1991. It was run independently by NSPCC child protection workers headed by Viv Hector. He and his team offered information, help and counselling to former residents, especially if they wanted to make an allegation of abuse. The opening of the helpline was announced in the local press. Days later a local newspaper reported that it had received 'a flood' of calls.

One former resident of Bryn Estyn who became aware of the general publicity surrounding the Bryn Estyn investigation at the time, was Martin West. West, who was 24, was serving a three-year prison sentence for a number of offences involving dishonesty. On 10 December the police visited him in prison. This visit took place nine days after the publication of the *Independent on Sunday* article, which had included two photographs of Peter Howarth, captioned by the statement that he was a paedophile.

West made an allegation which involved the claim that he had regularly taken Peter Howarth's dog for a walk. He claimed he had gradually got to know Howarth who had then taken advantage of the relationship which had been established. He said that Howarth had made him have oral sex on a number of occasions in his flat and that he had then attempted to rape him. He claimed that he managed to avoid this, grabbed his things and, apparently while he was still completely naked, ran out of the room. A few days afterwards, West said he returned to the flat and that Howarth then pinned him to the floor and raped him. He offered no explanation of why he voluntarily returned to the flat of a man who had already tried to rape him.

Soon after this he said he had to stay in bed in his dormitory with a throat infection and, hearing shouting, had looked through the window into the living room of Howarth's flat and had seen Howarth having oral sex with a boy. During Howarth's trial it was pointed out that it was not possible to see into Howarth's living room from the dormitory in the manner he described.

It was also pointed out that his claim about walking Howarth's dog was implausible. As many former residents and members of staff had testified to Howarth's legal team, his dog was well known by everyone to be of the self-exercising variety; it wandered freely without a collar around the Bryn Estyn grounds and appears never to have been taken for a walk by anyone. As Howarth would tell the jury at his trial, 'You couldn't take that dog for a walk. It wasn't a walkable dog.'

Six weeks later another 24-year-old man who had once been at Bryn Estyn made a similar claim. John Duke told the North Wales Police that he too had got to know Howarth through his dog and that Howarth had 'allowed' him to take this dog for regular walks. Duke, like West, claimed that Howarth had taken advantage of the relationship, that he had indecently assaulted him and then raped him.

If Duke did not know West their remarkably similar stories might be mutually corroborative. However, the second paragraph of Duke's statement read as follows:

> Sometime around June 1981 I was taken into care because I had been in trouble with the police. As a result I was admitted to Bryn Estyn, Wrexham, where I was allocated a bed in a three-bed dormitory. I can recall that one of the staff, Mr Birch, was responsible for our side of the landing. The only person I can remember from my dormitory was a lad from South Wales. I think his surname was West.

As well as sharing a dormitory with West, Duke had also seen him much more recently. Both during the trial of Howarth and during the Tribunal, Duke admitted that he had seen West in Swansea Prison during a period he was on remand there. He said he could not say when this was. West had in fact started his most recent sentence in June 1991.[272]

Even more significant was the fact that, when West was asked during Howarth's trial if he remembered Duke, he said that he did not. When Duke was brought into court West admitted that his face was familiar but he was adamant that he had not seen him since leaving Bryn Estyn. One of them was apparently not telling the truth.

The details of Duke's own complaint in themselves cast doubt on its veracity. He claimed that immediately after Howarth had raped him he had looked for a member of staff to tell. He had found David Birch and says he told him, in explicit terms, what had happened.

Birch was widely regarded as an enthusiastic care worker who had natural authority and who was also very fair. Indeed he was one of the most popular of all members of staff. One of the house mothers worked alongside him for almost ten years, first at Bryn Estyn and then at Chevet Hey. She recalls how boys would ask her towards the end of a shift who was coming on next: 'Is it Birchy? Is it Birchy? If you said "yes" their eyes would light up. If you said "no" they would be disappointed. The kids used to wait for him to come on duty. They loved him.'[273] Liz Evans, another colleague, confirmed this view during her evidence to the Tribunal. 'I have very good memories of him,' she said. 'I thought he was excellent with the boys. He was like an older brother to them. He seemed to be very, very popular at the time.'[274] As these words imply, Birch was very much on the side of the boys he cared for.

In his statement to the police, however, Duke painted a completely different picture. He claimed that Birch had responded to his complaint about Howarth by punching him on his 'arms and ribs', slapping him across the head, and pushing him into a nearby pond. 'As I was trying to get out he kicked my hands off the bank, saying that I wouldn't be allowed out until I'd learnt my lesson. He kept me in the pond for about five minutes before I was allowed out. He kept saying "You should never tell lies about members of staff, we're your last chance."'

Duke went on to claim that, later that evening, he had sought out 'the nurse' and told her that he had stomach pains and was bleeding from his anus. She had supposedly given him milk of magnesia and sent him to bed. He said that in the morning he was 'still bleeding' so he returned to the nurse. 'She said something about piles but didn't examine me. She sent me back to bed and told me not to eat anything for a day or so. I was not referred to a doctor at all.'

Both David Birch, and the matron Isabel Williams, a respected member of staff who was also a magistrate, have said that these events never happened. In her Tribunal statement Mrs Williams made the following comments:

I note that [John Duke] makes serious allegations of sexual abuse against Mr Howarth, of which I have no knowledge. I can only comment, however, that the suggestion that Mr Birch responded to the complaint of buggery by assaulting John Duke would, in my view, have been completely out of character. I remember Mr Birch as an extremely popular member of staff, who was regarded as something of a hero by many of the boys. As regards the allegation that 'the Nurse' (whom I presume to be me) failed to examine John Duke despite his complaints of stomach pains and bleeding from the back passage, I consider that this is a complete fabrication. Had any boy made a complaint of such bleeding to me, I would have contacted the doctor immediately. I would also have examined the boy's anus or asked to see his underpants. Likewise, had he made a further complaint about anal bleeding the following morning I would have examined his pyjamas and bedding, detained him in sick-bay and summoned immediate medical assistance from the doctor. Once again, I am sure that no such complaint was made by John Duke. The only medical record of which I have been made aware concerning John Duke is an entry in the main school log dated 6 July 1981 (9.30 a.m.) where I have recorded that John Duke complained of tummy pains and was sent to lie down in the dormitory, with an indication that he should consume liquids only for 24 hours. Although I have no specific recollection of this incident, it is consistent with a simple complaint of stomach upset, for which the treatment prescribed was appropriate. ... I do not consider that this written entry is in any way consistent with the allegations made by John Duke.[275]

Although Duke said in his police statement that he had gone to 'the nurse' in the evening, the log book entry produced at the Tribunal recorded that he had made a report about stomach pains at 9.30 in the morning. Remarkably, after having supposedly been brutally raped by Howarth, Duke says he voluntarily went to Howarth's flat again and that a sexual act took place which involved Howarth's dog. He had then supposedly returned once more and the same thing had happened.

In the statement he made in 1992, Duke went on to claim that some weeks after he had been assaulted by Howarth he was sitting near the pond feeling homesick when he was approached by Mr Norris. He says that Norris patted him on the back and then began to sexually assault him. He claims that this encounter led to an act of buggery in which Norris 'entered me a little bit', causing pain in his anus. He further claims that some two weeks later a second sexual encounter took place in a tool shed in the grounds, just after he had put a lawn mower away there. This had supposedly been an act of buggery in which he was fully penetrated.

It is a matter of considerable interest that Stephen Norris, who *was* guilty of sexually abusing boys at Bryn Estyn, and who pleaded guilty to a number of sexual assaults including some of buggery, emphatically denied that he had ever sexually abused Duke, a boy who was not resident in Norris's section of the school, Clwyd House, and of whom he said he had no recollection. As a result the allegations were allowed to lie on file and Duke never had to repeat them for the purpose of a trial.

When, in 1997, Duke gave evidence to the Tribunal, the allegations he made against Peter Howarth, which he had repeated at Howarth's trial in 1994, corresponded closely to what he had said in his original statement in 1992. When it came to recounting the story about Norris, however, he had considerable difficulty. In spite of heavy prompting by one of the Tribunal barristers, he said quite explicitly that Norris had not buggered him on the first occasion. In relation to the second alleged incident of buggery he was again heavily prompted but was unable to recall his allegation. Pressed to give details of what had happened, he said that his mind had gone blank. A man who had made two allegations of buggery against Norris in January 1992, thus made no such allegations against him in at the North Wales Tribunal in 1997. When Duke was cross-examined by counsel to Stephen Norris it became clear that his original allegations were highly implausible and that the acts he alleged almost certainly never took place.[276]

Taken cumulatively, the circumstantial evidence surrounding the grave allegations made by West and Duke strongly suggests that they had been fabricated. When the many inconsistencies and implausibilities in their allegations are placed alongside the striking similarities, questions are inevitably raised about how the allegations came to be made. These questions are underlined by the fact that Duke admitted meeting West in prison but that West denied it (and at first claimed he did not remember Duke). The most likely explanation of their allegations is that Duke fabricated his complaint against Howarth either in concert with West or in imitation of the false allegation West had already made.

The fact that the first of these allegations emerged within days of the publication of the *Independent on Sunday* article, and that both West and Duke admitted during Howarth's trial that they had seen television coverage of the Bryn Estyn investigation before being visited by the police, suggests that such publicity was already contaminating the investigation and would inevitably continue to do so.

If the allegations made by West and Duke were indeed false, a question inevitably arises about their motives. One possible answer was provided by the inquiries made by Howarth's legal team before he stood trial. Even before the case had come to court, Duke had consulted a solicitor and launched a civil action against Clwyd County Council for the abuse he claimed to have suffered. In view of the gravity of the allegations he made, and the fact that two different assailants were supposedly involved, such a claim might have been expected to result in a payment in excess of £50,000.

34 The chandelier

JOHN DUKE WAS NOT THE FIRST former Bryn Estyn resident to seek compensation from Clwyd County Council for abuse he had allegedly suffered. On 11 December 1991, less than two weeks after the *Independent on Sunday* article (and the day after the police had paid their first visit to Martin West in prison), a story appeared in the Wrexham *Evening Leader* under the headline 'Men Sue Over Abuse Claims'. The story was one of at least four similar pieces which appeared in the local press around this time. One of the other stories featured a prominent photograph of Ryan Tanner. The story which appeared on 11 December, however, was printed alongside a picture of Peter Wynne:

MEN SUE OVER ABUSE CLAIMS

Two men who say they were abused as youngsters in children's homes are suing Clwyd's social services department.

Mr Peter Wynne and Mr Ryan Tanner, both 24, claim they were victims of physical abuse and ritual humiliation at the Bryn Estyn Home in Wrexham.

They decided to act after widespread media publicity of an alleged police cover-up of abuse at the home.

They have contacted Wrexham solicitor Gwylim Hughes, who has confirmed he will be representing them.

Mr Wynne of Gwenfro, Wrexham, was a resident at Bryn Estyn between 1979 and 1984. He said he was suing the social services for alleged neglect, alleging a series of incidents involving physical abuse. He said: 'I was put in the home to avoid that sort of thing but I ended up being subjected to it by members of staff themselves.'

Mr Tanner ... says he was physically abused at both Bryn Estyn and another children's home in Gwynedd.

Mr Wynne, a machine operator with Brake Engineering, on the Redwither Industrial Estate, Wrexham, said life for many residents at the home was 'hell'. He alleges a catalogue of incidents, including:

- Having his face rubbed in splintered glass as a punishment for breaking a chandelier.
- Having a tattoo transfer on his arm rubbed off with a matchbox.

• Being picked up by the throat.

Mr Wynne, who now has four young daughters, said he is acting to prevent another Bryn Estyn. He said: 'I went through five years of hell and I don't want anyone else to suffer the same thing.'

This story suggests that Peter Wynne and Ryan Tanner were now co-operating and were both being represented by the same solicitor. To those who knew them this was surprising.

During the time that they were at Bryn Estyn, Tanner frequently bullied Wynne, verbally tormenting him because he had no family and because of his supposed sexual underdevelopment. Tanner would call him names such as 'homeless', 'orphan' and 'pubeless'. When I met Ryan Tanner in August 2004 and asked him about Peter Wynne, he immediately admitted that he and the other boys at Bryn Estyn used to bully him partly because it was easy to provoke Peter into a spectacular frenzy, which they found amusing. 'Dinky Wynne,' Ryan recalled, 'was our play station.'[277]

Because Wynne was one the youngest residents of the main school, and because he was effectively without any family to care for him, one member of staff, Liz Evans, took him under her wing. She persuaded Matt Arnold to allow Wynne certain privileges to compensate for his emotional deprivation. In particular he was allowed to keep a budgerigar, which became his beloved companion. One day, however, he found that the cage had been opened and the budgerigar was nowhere to be found. It is a measure of the way in which Wynne regarded Tanner, that he always believed, rightly or wrongly, that it was Tanner who had opened the cage to torment him with the bird's loss.

Ryan now says that he does not remember Wynne's budgerigar. However, he did recall another incident involving a bird at Bryn Estyn. When he was about fourteen, he found a baby jay which had fallen out of its nest. He took it back to his dormitory and carefully fed it; 'I loved that bird.' But after a week or so, as he put it, 'it croaked on me'. Ryan recalls that he was heart-broken. When he had composed himself he summoned his gang: 'Come on lads, get down the fucking bank; my bird's died and there's going to be a funeral.' He led the boys down to the grassy bank in the grounds, and had them gather in a circle around him. As some twenty boys stood with their hands together and, in some cases, presumably, their eyes shut, Ryan Tanner said the Lord's Prayer: 'Our father, which art in heaven, hallowed be thy name. Thy kingdom come … '

'That was my bird,' he recalled twenty years later, 'it meant a lot to me.'

The stories of Wynne, Tanner and their two birds are significant, not least because they indicate the sensitivity and vulnerability of two boys who have sometimes been regarded simply as violent 'thugs'. Tanner himself now recognises that he bullied Wynne and others in a manner which was 'completely out of order' and seems to accept that, while they were at Bryn Estyn, Peter Wynne hated him.

When Tanner left Bryn Estyn in June 1983 he was transferred to Y Gwyngyll in Anglesey. After 18 months he went into lodgings and was finally discharged from care in 1985, aged 18. Soon after this he was sent to a detention centre for three months. 'When I came out I went to live in Wrexham and met a girl whose mother turned out to be a drugs dealer. I went to prison for 10 months for drug dealing and came out a reprobate – drinking, fighting and taking drugs.'[278] After his time in prison Tanner went into alcohol counselling. It was at the beginning of his long struggle to lead a normal life, in about December 1989, that his relationship with Wynne flared into violence. There are different accounts of why this happened, which apportion responsibility in different ways. Wherever the truth may lie, however, it would seem that Wynne resolved to turn the tables against the person who had repeatedly bullied him in the past.

The first Tanner knew of this was when there was a knock at the door of his Wrexham flat. When he opened it he found Peter Wynne standing in front of him brandishing a twelve-inch bayonet. Wynne said 'Time for it, Tanner!' and raised the bayonet upwards to stab him in the neck or face. Tanner, who now claims he believed that Wynne had come to murder him, managed to deflect the blow with the result that, although he sustained injuries to his face, he remained standing. Tanner alleges that at this point one of Wynne's friends advanced on him, wielding a meat cleaver. Tanner says he managed to get back inside the flat and barricaded himself in with a wardrobe. He then called the police. Wynne was subsequently convicted for this attack and served a short prison sentence.

When Wynne came out of prison, Tanner met up with him again in circumstances and for reasons which have never been satisfactorily explained. As the Bryn Estyn investigation gathered pace in the autumn of 1991 in the wake of Nelson's article, Wynne and Tanner appear to have buried their differences and were frequently seen together.

It was during this period that Wynne's portrayal of Bryn Estyn underwent its dramatic change. His original verdict on Bryn Estyn, that it was the best home he had been in, and that he had enjoyed his time there, was communicated to the police on 12 September 1991. By the time he gave his second statement, on 6 January 1992, the account he gave of his time at the home had been utterly transformed. He now gave a vivid description of an incident which had not even been mentioned in the first statement. This incident, in which Ryan Tanner had supposedly played a key role, involved a horrific punishment which Wynne said had been inflicted on him by David Birch:

On another occasion I was involved in an argument with one of the other lads called Ryan Tanner. I remember we were in the dining room and Tanner called me names, and because he was a lot bigger than me I decided to hit him with a chair. I took hold of a chair and as I was swinging it over my head I hit a chandelier above my head and it shattered all three bulbs in it. The glass from the broken bulbs landed on the floor behind me and the next thing I remember was David Birch grabbing hold of the chair and he took it off me. When the chair had gone he still had hold of me and he told me to clean up the glass from the floor. I was in a temper so I refused to do it, saying that Tanner had started it so he should clean up the mess. Anyway he told me about four times to clean the glass and I kept on refusing so he took hold of my legs and lifted them up in the air and held me face-down towards the floor. He then got me in such a position where he was holding both my arms and both my legs so that I could not move.

He then pushed my head towards the floor until my face was right up against the broken glass with my legs pointing towards the ceiling. He pushed my face into the glass on the floor which caused me to receive about 10 small cuts on my forehead. Two of these were quite deep and the others were only scratches. When he was doing this I kept on struggling and he kept saying 'Are you going to pick it up?' I think he held me there for some five or ten minutes although I can't be specific about the time. When he did let me go he just dropped me to the floor away from the glass, I got up, ran off in a craze and into the entrance to the dining room where, in a temper at what he had done to me, I smashed about six or eight small panes of glass in the sliding doors at the entrance to the dining rooms. I broke all these with my fists. I am not quite sure but I think I may have cut my hands doing this and I believe I had both my head cuts as well as the cuts on my hand treated by the matron, Mrs Williams.

When this incident occurred I believe that Ryan Tanner was present and saw what happened but I don't know if anyone else was.

Although Wynne refers to a 'chandelier', it is clear from his reference to 'three bulbs' that what he had in mind was a simple light fitting. This aside, there are a number of features of the statement which raise questions. In the first place, it is barely credible that the incident Wynne describes would, if the account is accurate, have been omitted from his initial statement. It is also curious that, at a time when both were making claims for compensation, Wynne should identify Tanner as the sole witness to what happened. Tanner would later tell the police that he had indeed witnessed the incident which Wynne described. More than five years later he repeated this claim in his evidence to the Tribunal, and gave a vivid account of what had supposedly happened. This corresponded closely to Wynne's statement.[279]

This account, however, was never properly tested because the Tribunal had failed to find the entry in the Bryn Estyn log book which referred to the incident. As the Tribunal report would later note, this entry was discovered only after the hearings had been completed. The entry is dated 22 March 1984:

> [Peter Wynne] refused to wash his hands for Mr Birch at tea time. He was told he'd have his tea as soon as he did, but he still refused. Peter said he didn't want any tea and went out of D/room. I found him later in the kitchen waiting for Cook to make him some toast. When he was told he couldn't have any he stormed back into the D/room and smashed a light bulb, which he refused to sweep up.[280]

The failure of the Tribunal team to locate this entry is difficult to understand, not least because the police had already discovered it during their 1992 investigation. In August 1992 they checked with Wynne, who confirmed that he could only recall one incident that involved breaking a light-bulb. They then interviewed the house mother who wrote the entry. She said that she did not recall Birch having to restrain Peter Wynne on that occasion and added 'I do not recall Peter having any injuries at all on that day.'[281]

Judging by the statement they took from Wynne in August 1992, which discussed the date Tanner had left Bryn Estyn, the police had noticed a significant anomaly in the evidence before them. For Ryan Tanner had not been present in the dining room on the occasion recorded in the log book. Indeed he had not been at Bryn Estyn at all. He had left the home on 6 June 1983, a full nine months before the dining room incident took place.

From other statements taken shortly after Wynne made his allegation, it would appear that there probably was a physical confrontation between him and Birch. But the log book entry which records the incident makes no reference to any injury. Given that the house mother on duty, whose integrity and reliability have never been questioned, would have been the first to know about any significant cuts or bleeding, and given that Wynne himself had not mentioned the incident at all in his first statement, it seems likely that the injuries which he claimed to have sustained were a product of his imagination.

One thing which is certain is that the relationship between Birch and Wynne was exceptionally good, that it remained so after the incident in the dining-room, and, indeed, after Wynne left Bryn Estyn. Liz Evans has confirmed this: 'Peter Wynne loved David Birch,' she told me. 'He used to look up to him like a Dad.'[282]

Wherever the truth about the incident may lie, there can be no doubt at all that the version of events which Wynne gave to the police in January 1992 was untrue. Wynne's claim that the incident had its origins in a clash between him and Tanner was clearly false. In this respect perhaps the most telling piece of evidence comes from another former resident, Christopher Hands.

While being cross-examined at the Tribunal, Hands was referred to a statement he had made in August 1992 in which he had offered his version of events (which did suggest that Wynne had sustained some minor injuries). In this statement he had specifically said 'I do not believe Ryan Tanner was there'. Hands now confirmed this: 'I do say that and that's true. ... I thought he'd left.'[283]

Hands's evidence on this point removes all doubt about the status of the testimony given by Wynne and Tanner. All the evidence indicates that they had arrived jointly at the version of the incident which Wynne related to the police in January 1992. Whether Tanner had by this time become so highly suggestible, and so prone to imagining incidents of abuse, that he quite genuinely believed he had witnessed this one seems possible. It was also the case, though, that Wynne and Tanner were both using the same solicitor to make a claim for compensation. The untrue story which they both now told would make a successful outcome much more likely.

The fact that both Wynne and Tanner appeared to have a financial motive for making up stories, however, should not be taken to indicate that this was their only motivation. Tanner in particular appears to have been driven by the kind of zeal which is sometimes shown by those who have a disadvantaged, or, indeed, criminal background. He frequently acted in the manner of a campaigner – or even as a born-again evangelist, convinced of the need to do battle with all that is evil.

If Ryan Tanner had by this point embarked upon a crusade, it would seem that he had succeeded in enlisting the services of Peter Wynne to help him. In her evidence to the Tribunal, Liz Evans said that she had kept in touch with a number of former residents after Bryn Estyn closed in 1984. While she was being cross-examined by David Knifton, the following exchange took place:

KNIFTON: Did you ever from your dealings with any of those boys obtain an understanding that any of them were collecting allegations, if you understand what I mean by that, going round other boys bringing forward further allegations?

EVANS: Yes ... Liam Hempnall told me that a couple of boys had gone to his house to ... encourage him to make allegations.

CHAIRMAN: This is a rather serious allegation. What exactly did he say?

EVANS: He told me that a couple of boys had gone to his house.

CHAIRMAN: Did he name the boys?

EVANS: He did, yes.

CHAIRMAN: Who were they?

EVANS: Ryan Tanner and Peter Wynne.[284]

During this period Tanner and Wynne spent a great deal of time together and frequently talked to other former residents about their time at Bryn Estyn. In one particular case, which involved a former resident of Bryn Estyn, the part played by Ryan Tanner would, as we will eventually see, have very serious consequences.

It is not clear to what extent the North Wales Police were aware that their evidence was being contaminated in this way. In relation to some allegations they continued to show a degree of scepticism. But their principal concern at this stage of their inquiry seems to have been less with investigating the complaints they were collecting, than with attempting to confirm them. The easiest route to such apparent confirmation was to go out and collect more allegations. This approach was a novel one. But they were now taking part in one of the most unusual operations in the history of British policing. This operation would have a decisive influence on the methods adopted during the next decade by practically every police force in Britain.

35 Unblocking the past

THE FLURRY OF ACTIVITY which took place at the North Wales Police HQ in the days following the publication of Dean Nelson's article continued into the new year. The appearance of the story seems to have had the effect of galvanising the force in relation to an operation they had always recognised as particularly sensitive and difficult.

The process of re-organising the investigation and revising its objectives culminated, on 2 January 1992, in a training and briefing meeting for the officers involved. According to the evidence which Detective Superintendent Ackerley gave to the Tribunal, its object was 'to educate … those who were to be engaged on the inquiry, and those who had been engaged on the inquiry since its inception, to brief them fully … and to provide training as to how they should approach the investigation and the tasks that they were to be set'.[285]

This description of the meeting's aims implies that the investigation had originally been launched without a comprehensive briefing having been held. There were undoubtedly many difficulties at the outset of the investigation which had led to this state of affairs. But what it meant in practice was that the first four months of the inquiry, which had inevitably influenced its entire course, had already been completed before the training-day was held.

During these four months there had been a number of developments which, had they been more closely monitored, might well have given rise to disquiet. One of these concerned the manner in which one of the key witnesses had been interviewed by the police. The witness in question was the young man who had been identified at the outset, along with Singer and Holden, as a possible victim of Peter Howarth – John Evans.

One factor which clearly affected the police's approach to Evans was a prior interview with another former resident. On 8 October 1991, about a month after they had interviewed Holden, the North Wales Police had visited Nigel Curtis, who had been a friend of Tanner at Bryn Estyn. Curtis claimed that he had once walked into Peter Howarth's flat to take him his lunch and had seen Evans with his head between Howarth's legs, apparently engaged in oral sex with him. Surprisingly, he said that both the flat door and the living room door had been left open, and that he had simply left Howarth's lunch on the floor and gone back to the main school. Even more surprisingly, he said he had not told anyone at the time about what he had seen. Indeed, he had not told anyone at all until the police came to see him nine years later.

After Curtis had made his statement, two officers from the North Wales Police visited John Evans at his home in the north of England. According to Evans, instead of asking him whether he had been sexually abused by Howarth, they told him that they knew he had. As evidence for this they cited Curtis's statement. Evans says he told them that the incident was a fabrication, that he was never abused by Peter Howarth and never had any sexual relationship with him.

In a statement he gave to a solicitor during the Tribunal, Evans says the police officers told him that 'some of the former Bryn Estyn boys stood to make money from compensation from abuse claims. ... I denied again that I had been abused. They then called me a liar. I became angry and I asked them to leave my house. It is my impression that the police officers were not interested in listening to me but were only interested in confirming that I had been abused by Mr Howarth.'[286]

Evans's account of the police's visit suggests that, even before the publication of Nelson's article, they had felt under pressure to obtain complaints against Howarth which would substantiate the two allegations they had already collected. He quite clearly says that the police themselves raised the subject of compensation. In this respect his experience appears to have been similar to that of Tanner, who would go on record as saying that the police had told him that he would 'get loads of money' as a result of a particular allegation he had made against Paul Wilson.[287]

During the Tribunal another former Bryn Estyn resident, Mark Hinton, who appeared as a complainant alleging physical abuse, was asked whether, when he had been visited by the North Wales Police during the 1991–2 investigation, he had been questioned about Peter Howarth:

MR JENNINGS (counsel to Howarth): Did they ask you about Mr Howarth specifically?
HINTON: They mentioned his name, yes.
JENNINGS: Did they ask as to whether you had anything to say about

activities by Mr Howarth whilst you were at Bryn Estyn?

HINTON: And I said I didn't know.

JENNINGS: Did they ask you generally whether you could provide any information that reflected on the role of Mr Howarth as deputy head?

HINTON: No, no, no. Had I witnessed any sexual abuse from Mr Howarth, had I been abused, did I know anyone that was being abused; them sort of questions.

JENNINGS: They were interested in any abuse by Mr Howarth that you were aware of, yes?

HINTON: Yes, I figured serious abuse, yes.

JENNINGS: You mean that they were not interested in minor abuse?

HINTON: No, not at all, no, not at the time, no. Everything was up in the air and everyone was looking for convictions, yes, and they was getting them as well, yes, because they was guilty.[288]

Later on, cross-examined by Andrew Moran QC, counsel to the North Wales Police, Hinton indicated that the questions he had been asked about Howarth had been explicit and detailed: 'Your officers told me about apparent vibrators and apparent sex rooms that Howarth had, your officers told me this. I haven't spoken to anyone in 15 years, do you know what I mean. I wasn't abused, I haven't had no vibrators, I hadn't seen no sex room, do you know what I mean?'[289]

Here there would appear to be clear evidence of how the details of one allegation could be 'carried' by police officers from one witness to another; for the unusual idea that boys might have been sexually abused with vibrators was, as we have seen, contained in the statement given by the very first witness to make an allegation against Howarth, Andrew Singer (see above, p. 119).

To cite one more example, Peter Wynne, during his first tape-recorded interview with Dean Nelson, claimed that the police had encouraged him to make a statement to them by suggesting that, if he did, they would not bring charges against him in relation to a motoring offence: 'I got chased by the police and he said, not in so many words like, but if I co-operated he would drop the charges. ... They said if you co-operate with the coppers like, I won't push it any further. I co-operated with them like and never heard anything else about it.'[290]

Another key issue here was the subject of compensation. During the Tribunal, Ackerley was asked by Gerard Elias, counsel to the Tribunal, whether police officers involved in the investigation were advised how they should handle this issue:

ACKERLEY: Yes, sir, I'd drawn on the experience of the Leicestershire Constabulary, and in particular those officers who had dealt with the Beck investigation. One of the issues during the course of the trial, I was led to understand, was the issue of collusion and compensation being a motivator for false complaints. I was therefore keen to ensure that any victims who were used as prosecution witnesses in North Wales were not in the position where they would have a forceful cross-examination, albeit a proper cross-examination, in terms of the issue of compensation.

ELIAS: So that would not be raised by any police officer at the interviews relating or taking witness statements?

ACKERLEY: That is correct, sir, for the reasons I outlined.[291]

The official advice given to police officers was clearly proper. The reasons advanced for giving such advice, however, are worthy of note. It would seem from his Tribunal evidence that the officer in charge of the investigation was not principally concerned that the lure of compensation might lead to false allegations. His main concern was to protect complainants, whom he refers to as 'victims', from facing 'a forceful cross-examination' on the issue of compensation.

The further assumption made in Detective Superintendent Ackerley's evidence, that official guidance given to officers would necessarily be heeded on all occasions by police officers on the ground, is optimistic. One witness who was visited early in 1992 was Keith Martell. In the same letter to Chris Saltrese in which he paid tribute to Bryn Estyn staff (see above, p. 168), he related his own experience of being interviewed:

> Well Mr Saltrese as to the child abuse case in Bryn Estyn School, when the police from North Wales took a statement at my address, they told me, if I was abused, I would get money in compensation, I was just dumbfounded when he came out with it, I feel Mr Saltrese that most people thought they would get compensation just saying it, that's why most people have come forward, trying to make a quick buck out of the system. I feel Mr Saltrese the police putting pressure on people to come forward saying you get compensation.
>
> Some people [think] money's the be end of everything. I am willing to bet my life on it that when I went there in 1975 to 1977 no person was abused by staff at Bryn Estyn school.

The specific issue of compensation aside, it might be thought that the general question of false allegations would be dealt with in depth at the

January training session. Above all it might be expected that senior officers would have addressed the question of the suggestibility of witnesses and the danger that police interviews might, if not carefully
conducted, have the effect of encouraging false allegations.

However, to make this assumption would be to misunderstand the
extraordinarily difficult climate in which the investigation was being
conducted and the immense, and at times intolerable pressure which
was being put on the North Wales Police. At this point no coherent
criticisms had ever been made of police trawling operations. The term
'trawling' itself had no currency, and the idea that false allegations of
sexual abuse might actually be made as an unintended consequence of
such investigations would have been considered so offensive that it
would have been difficult to canvass it in public. There was still, as part
of the legacy of the Cleveland crisis and the Nottingham satanic abuse
case, massive criticism of police forces in general for their supposed
reluctance to take the problem of child sexual abuse seriously.

This was the context in which the particular criticisms of the North
Wales Police made by Councillor Parry and Alison Taylor, and amplified in the *Independent on Sunday*, were made. In the circumstances, it
should not be surprising that the North Wales Police, accused as they
were of attempting to cover up child sexual abuse and of dealing with
witnesses in a heavy-handed manner, appear to have given little or no
attention to the possibility of false allegations. They focused instead on
the question of how they might actually make it easier for witnesses to
make complaints without unnecessary embarrassment or anxiety.

In this respect perhaps the most important participant in the briefing was Chief Inspector Lorraine Johnson, who specialised in child
protection and family work, and who had been drafted in by Ackerley
to help with the main training session. In her evidence to the Tribunal
she made it clear that among the assumptions which informed the
investigation was the idea that witnesses might initially deny that abuse
had occurred because they had suppressed painful memories:

> ANDREW MORAN QC: Let's deal with the special type of this case. Here
> we had adults who may have had abusive sexual experiences many
> years previously who were blocking out memories?
> JOHNSON: Right.
> MORAN: And who were psychologically damaged?
> JOHNSON: They may have been.
> MORAN: And who required a particular kind of approach, an informed
> approach, when it came to interviewing them?

JOHNSON: That's correct ... we were going to deal with people that may be very damaged, but there is a huge difference between interviewing what we would term as a therapeutic interview and one which is an investigative interview.

MORAN: All the more important in an investigative interview to understand the psychiatric goings on ... to understand how a person who is damaged may respond and may be blocking.

JOHNSON: I believe the officers were aware of that.[292]

As well as accepting the notion of 'blocking', Johnson also said that, while it was important to distinguish between investigative and therapeutic interviews, if the person being interviewed was able to tell police officers 'what, if anything, had happened, in my opinion that would be the first stage of therapy'.[293]

The suggestion that a police interview, if it elicited an allegation of abuse, might actually be part of a therapeutic process, illustrates the extent to which some senior officers had already adopted an approach to 'disclosure' previously associated with social work and therapy. A similar view was expressed by Detective Superintendent Ackerley when he told me that the officers involved in the investigation saw their task as being not simply to receive allegations but to overcome what he described as 'the problem in terms of disclosure', by creating 'the climate to facilitate people to tell us what went on'.[294] It was also the case, he told the Tribunal, that police officers 'were to judge if any of the persons interviewed required counselling'.*[295]

The habitual use by some senior officers of the term 'disclosure' is perhaps best viewed in the perspective of the Butler-Sloss report on the Cleveland crisis, which gave some attention to the role played by ideas recently imported from America. Many of these ideas had been introduced into Britain by a team based at Great Ormond Street Hospital, led by child psychiatrist Arnon Bentovim. Bentovim had started off by favouring the Freudian view that accounts of child sexual abuse were sometimes the result of fantasy. In 1979, however, he appears to have undergone an experience akin to conversion, at a London conference

---

* A striking omission in the proceedings of the Tribunal was the failure to investigate the extent to which counselling was provided to those interviewed by the police, the nature and content of such counselling, and the question of whether it might have contaminated the allegations which were made. There is clearly a possibility that some allegations were inadvertently 'created' by counselling and that some fabricated allegations were effectively 'naturalised' and converted into false memories. See the comments on Mark Humphreys in chapter 40.

addressed by Henry Kempe.[296] He subsequently became an assiduous searcher for evidence of child sexual abuse. A proselytiser of the idea that children who might have been sexually abused needed help to overcome the tendency to 'denial', he ran workshops for child protection professionals. In these he taught 'disclosure work', including the use of anatomically correct dolls and leading questions designed to elicit 'disclosures' from children 'who could not, or would not, talk about possible abusive experiences spontaneously'.[297]

The comments made in the Butler–Sloss report about this approach are significant. While the report did not pass any overall judgment on the ideas which lie behind the approach, and while it did not directly criticise the work of Dr Bentovim and his team, it did express considerable scepticism about the use of the term 'disclosure'. The report quoted the views of the child psychiatrist Dr David Jones:

> A fundamental problem of the 'disclosure' approach is that it is inherent in the concept that there is something to disclose. The problem is highlighted by those professionals who consider that the child is either disclosing or 'in denial', The third, and crucial, alternative possibility, namely that the child has no sexual abuse to disclose, is not considered as a viable option. ... The premise that abuse has occurred, yet is hidden and shrouded from discovery, is inherent in the very term 'disclosure work'.[298]

In her own comments on the 'disclosure interviews' carried out in Cleveland during 1987, Dame Elizabeth Butler-Sloss makes it clear that some of these interviews were deeply unsatisfactory:

> It was apparent that various feelings came together at the time of interviewing some at least of these children – anxiety, the need for a solution, beliefs about 'denial' and the therapeutic benefits for children of talking about abuse, the perceived need to believe the child. ... There was in many instances a presumption that abuse had occurred, and the child was either not disclosing or denying that abuse. There was insufficient expertise, over-enthusiasm, and those conducting the interviews seemed unaware of the extent of pressure, even coercion in their approach.[299]

It would be quite wrong to suggest that the North Wales Police consciously engaged in any form of 'disclosure work'. It would also be misleading to suggest that they abandoned all scepticism about the allegations being made to them. A number of improbable allegations against members of social services staff who were held in high regard, were investigated thoroughly and in some instances rejected. John Jevons has said that he had several meetings with Peter Ackerley over the course of the investigation and that 'for the whole of the investigation [the police] conveyed the impression … that they were sceptical about a great many of the allegations, but that they had to investigate and be seen to be investigating each and every one.'[300]

However, it would also be wrong not to recognise that some of the senior police officers involved in the investigation had been significantly swayed by the less sceptical attitudes adopted by many social workers. Some officers seemed influenced by the assumption that a negative response to an initial police interview might actually be a mask for memories of abuse which, with sufficient coaxing, might yet be revealed.

Asked how officers would approach the task of 'interviewing damaged adults and unblocking the past', Lorraine Johnson replied:

> My feeling very much is that we were there to investigate and to listen, to actively listen, to whatever anybody had to say to us, and we were going to leave our details with the person in the event that they wanted to come back and tell us anything, and our experience is – and certainly I when I have spoken to psychiatrists and psychologists *it's very much that it's very unlikely that the unblocking, as you term it, will occur at the first meeting*, and it's very important that the door is left open for them to make contact at a later stage; and, in fact, the officers were told to leave their name, telephone number, and to diplomatically say that if there was anything they wanted to say further, if there was anything [sic] they wanted to contact, etc, then they would be able to [italics added].[301]

When Andrew Moran suggested to her that 'It might take several visits for the interviewee to be able to unburden themselves about what they had experienced?' she agreed. 'That was my experience,' she said, 'as opposed to academic research.'[302]

In another example of the extent to which the 'gradual disclosure model' had been adopted by some police officers, Detective Inspector Cronin, who led the original investigation into Stephen Norris, ventured an explanation of why witnesses who had made no allegation of sexual abuse when interviewed during his investigation, subsequently did make allegations when interviewed by Detective Superintendent Ackerley's team: 'It would be speculation but there is now a lot of knowledge and information about victims and how they disclose and frequently they do not disclose immediately and it takes a lot of time to disclose; it's quite a thing for them to disclose.'[303]

The suggestion that genuine allegations of abuse are sometimes made only after a considerable delay (which may be years) is, of course, quite true. It is a matter of observable fact. What is significant in the evidence given by Chief Inspector Johnson and Detective Inspector Cronin, however, is that they appear not to have considered, or at least not allowed themselves to express, the idea that some allegations are made after a long delay for no other reason than that they are false. The evidence which clearly indicates that this has sometimes happened is simply disregarded. Indeed the use of the term 'disclosure' implicitly forecloses that possibility, since the choice of this term actually implies that an allegation is true; you cannot 'disclose' something which hasn't happened.

The central flaw in the gradual disclosure model, as the psychiatrist Dr David Jones implies, is the assumption that those who have been sexually abused are not simply reticent or embarrassed about revealing this fact, but that they are actually in denial to the point where they may have 'blocked' their own memories of abuse. According to this model, the 'natural' response of any adult who was sexually abused as a child will be to deny this fact and to repress any memory of the incident. A further assumption is that it may subsequently be possible to 'unblock' memories of the past and that this process will tend to happen progressively. In other words the 'survivor' of abuse will probably not retrieve his or her memories on the first occasion, but will need several attempts. Typically, victims will 'disclose' by gradually peeling off layer after layer of amnesia, uncovering at each stage new memories of abuse in a sequence where the most serious or most horrific details of an assault are the last to be revealed. It therefore follows that the final account of abuse is likely to be different from, and may actually flatly contradict, the initial account.

The problem with this model of disclosure, which is still upheld by many therapists, psychologists and social workers, is that there is no credible empirical evidence for its validity. Indeed, a study conducted by two American psychologists in 1995 specifically looked for evidence of a pattern of gradual disclosure among genuine victims of child sexual abuse and failed to find it. Of 234 cases examined, the majority of subjects made full or partial 'disclosures' in the initial investigative interview.[304]

Perhaps more importantly still the provenance of the model can be shown quite clearly. Deriving originally from unvalidated Freudian theories of repression, it was applied to the disclosure of child sexual abuse by the same group of therapists and counsellors who created what I have called 'the Californian model'. One of the main testing-grounds for this theory was the series of American day-care cases which emerged, initially in California itself, during the 1980s. In these cases, as has already been noted, counsellors and social workers successfully elicited from nursery-age children horrific sexual allegations against their carers and teachers, which often included allegations of animal sacrifice and satanic sexual abuse.[305]

The manner in which these allegations emerged conformed almost exactly to the gradual disclosure model. At first, many children would say quite clearly that nothing had happened to them at all. But gradually, over a number of intensive sessions, counsellors would elicit from them a series of increasingly disturbing scenarios which suggested that they had indeed been sexually abused in a quite horrific manner. It was this experience that provided American psychologists and child protection workers with a fund of data which seemed to offer confirmation of the model which had been derived from psychoanalysis.

What was not understood, either at the time this model was first promulgated, or when it was imported into Britain, is that the majority of the 'disclosures' gathered in this way were not in fact disclosures at all. They were not even allegations. They were fanciful constructions – stories – which children had made up in response to deeply suggestive interviewing techniques. In many cases what had happened was that, through leading questions and other forms of influence, adult interviewers had inadvertently led children to reproduce just the scenarios of abuse they were anxiously seeking.

The fact that these children's 'disclosures' appeared to be progressive was not because therapists and counsellors had successfully uncovered layer after layer of hidden memories. It was because the children were faithfully reflecting the beliefs held by their interviewers and their conviction that behind every memory of abuse there lay another, yet more horrific memory waiting to be revealed.

The effective dissolution of the data which had been treated as confirming the model of progressive disclosure took place in the United States only gradually. Its principal manifestation was the collapse, over a period of some ten years, of practically every one of the most celebrated day-care cases. In the McMartin pre-school case of 1983, and in many similar cases, psychologists and well-informed defence attorneys were able to overturn convictions and to document the pressures which had been brought to bear on the children making the allegations.[306]

However, by the time this evidence began to emerge, the Californian model of sexual abuse, and the theory of progressive disclosure associated with it, had already been invested with great authority, and had been proselytised with the kind of fervour normally associated with religious faith. Because psychologists, therapists and social workers in Britain were remote from the visibly disintegrating data which had once seemed to offer confirmation of the theory, the Californian model was able to establish itself here even more securely than it had in America itself. In 1988 the Butler-Sloss report registered the power of the new belief-system when it quoted from a paper in the *Lancet* in which the child psychiatrist, Dr Harry Zeitlin, cautioned against the dangers of over-enthusiasm and spoke of 'disclosure' having taken on 'almost the character of a crusade'. In the report, these words are placed alongside an extract from a submission by the Official Solicitor, who said: 'The topic has acquired a mystique; and good sense is not always to be seen amongst the skills which are put to work.' The mystique of 'disclosure' was not only evident in the approach of therapists and social workers. Both Dr Marietta Higgs and Dr Geoffrey Wyatt, the paediatricians at the centre of the Cleveland controversy, were quoted in the report as saying that 'disclosure work' was the 'gold standard' in the detection of sexual abuse.[307]

However, partly because the Butler-Sloss inquiry was conducted before the full extent of the dangers of the orthodox disclosure model had become apparent, many of the errors of Cleveland were actually preserved and enlarged in subsequent sexual abuse inquiries (see above, chapter 14).

Four years after Cleveland, when the North Wales Police held their briefing session in Colwyn Bay, the Californian model of sexual abuse was no longer part of an alien belief system being imposed on the police from without by social workers. To a surprising degree, senior officers had begun to embrace the idea that the denial that sexual abuse had occurred was a normal part of the process of disclosure. Some of them at least seemed to accept the view implicit in the Californian model, that memories of sexual abuse were essentially hidden, that they were therefore unlikely to be brought to the attention of the police through spontaneous complaints, and that 'victims' might need help or support before they could make allegations. From this it seemed to follow that police officers had a right – and perhaps even a duty – actively to seek out victims and invite, or even encourage, them to make complaints.

This transformation in the attitude of senior police officers was crucial, and without it the North Wales investigation could never have progressed in the way that it did. Without for one moment being aware of what had happened, police officers such as Lorraine Johnson now began to employ, as a touchstone by which the veracity of complaints of sexual abuse was to be judged, a model of progressive disclosure which actually reflected the manner in which *false* allegations tend to develop. This meant that the more inconsistencies and contradictions a series of allegations contained, and the more inherently implausible it was from a common sense point of view, the more credible it became when viewed through the distorting lens of the Californian model.

The lengths to which some of the investigating officers evidently went in order to create 'the climate to facilitate people to tell us what went on', to use Ackerley's words, undoubtedly did make it easier for those who genuinely had been abused to tell their story. But, at the same time, it could not but have an effect on those who were highly suggestible, and liable to make false allegations – whether or not there was any conscious attempt to deceive. As Jean La Fontaine has observed, 'It is likely that situations in which belief is ensured from the outset are more conducive to such allegations being made than others where there is no such atmosphere.'[308]

La Fontaine also notes that when interviewers or counsellors hold the belief that disclosing sexual abuse is therapeutic, this puts pressure on those who are making allegations to produce more and more stories:

> Sympathetic acceptance of a story slides easily into a curiosity to learn more. When the listener is eager to hear more, gratitude for support may impel the young person to … find ever more dramatic memories to recount. This approach to abuse gives no indication of how to tell when the account has ended; the victim's claim to have no more to tell may not be accepted but be interpreted as a refusal to tell something even worse than what has already been recounted.[309]

There can be no doubt that, when officers in the North Wales Police adopted some of the main tenets of the Californian model, and when they launched a telephone helpline and counselling service staffed by

NSPCC child protection workers, they had the very best intentions. They were clearly trying to make it easier for those who genuinely had been abused to overcome their embarrassment and to relate what had happened to them. What they appear not to have understood was that they were simultaneously creating the ideal climate in which those who had not been abused could claim that they had.

Psychological pressures were, in this instance, compounded by financial pressures. As we have already seen, national and local publicity had already been given to the question of compensation. In these circumstances it seems almost inevitable that the word on the street, among some of those who had been in care in North Wales, was that a great deal of money might suddenly become available. The prospect of gaining £10,000 or even £100,000 could now be talked about as a real possibility. All in all, if a deliberate attempt had been made to encourage false allegations, it would have been difficult to better the conditions which had been created. Large numbers of young men, many of whom belonged to a culture in which financial gain goes hand in hand with some form of crime or dishonesty, were now presented with a hitherto undreamed-of opportunity. They found themselves in a position where allegations against their former carers were being actively solicited by police officers. Because of the model of disclosure which the police were increasingly using, (and which, we may presume, some potential complainants rapidly 'sussed'), it was not always the case that false allegations would be challenged by those to whom they were initially made. Although police officers undoubtedly remained sceptical in the face of some of the allegations, there is very little evidence of such scepticism in relation to the main suspects – in particular Peter Howarth.

By the time the January training meeting was held, it must have been apparent to the officers who were present that they were taking part in the largest investigation into child abuse there had ever been in Britain. What they remained unaware of, as they were briefed by Chief Inspector Lorraine Johnson and Detective Superintendent Peter Ackerley, was that it was also the most dangerous.

36 Operation Antelope

AS THE VARIOUS POLICE OFFICERS engaged in the investigation left Colwyn Bay police station early in January 1992, the major part of their inquiry, which targeted Bryn Estyn, was well-advanced. The North Wales force had already collected three complaints of sexual abuse against Howarth. These were the original allegations made by Singer and Holden, and the 'dog-walking' allegation made by Martin West in the days immediately following the publication of Nelson's article. In addition to these, it was clear that at least two more allegations had already been made against Howarth by the witnesses quoted in the article.

Four days after the briefing session, one of these 'unofficial' complaints was made formally, when Peter Wynne made his second statement to the police. Soon after this the police visited John Duke and collected the second dog-walking allegation.

The fact that so many complaints against Peter Howarth had suddenly emerged, almost twenty years after he had taken up his post at Bryn Estyn, might, in any ordinary circumstances, have given rise to serious doubts about their veracity. These doubts would only have been heightened by the many inconsistencies and implausibilities in the stories that had been told, and, in the case of Wynne, by the fact he had completely contradicted in his second statement the account he had given in his first.

Partly because of the immense potency of the gradual disclosure model, however, ordinary scepticism seems to have been suspended. In the period following the horrific coverage of Frank Beck's conviction, a climate had rapidly been established in which allegations of sexual abuse, particularly when made by former residents of care homes, had begun to assume almost a sacred character. To express scepticism about such allegations, or in any way to withhold belief from them, was, in some quarters at least, the equivalent of a form of heresy which might lead to subtle forms of social ostracism. That such sanctions might very well be applied to an entire police force was made quite clear by the article in the *Independent on Sunday*.

Given the huge and wholly unjustified pressure to which they were now being subjected, it was not surprising that the North Wales Police appear to have been unable to assess the evidence before them objectively. In the atmosphere of moral panic which Nelson's article helped to create, they now redoubled their efforts and intensively interviewed witness after witness about their time at Bryn Estyn.

Although the majority of former residents who were contacted had no complaints about their time at Bryn Estyn, and although many gave an account of the home which flatly contradicted the view of it as 'a children's hell', positive views of the home were not always recorded. In the early stages of the investigation they were actually categorised by the police as 'negative statements' and not recorded.[310]

By the beginning of March 1992, the North Wales Police had already collected enough allegations to warrant arrests, and plans for a raid on the homes of a number of former members of Bryn Estyn staff began to be made. At this stage there was another significant development.[311]

On 5 March, police visited former Bryn Estyn resident Ian Surtees. Surtees, who had made no previous complaint, now said that on two occasions he had visited Howarth's flat on his own, and that on the second occasion he had been indecently assaulted by Howarth and made to engage in oral sex with him. Surtees went on to claim that he had run away wearing his pyjamas, and that members of staff had chased him across the fields. Although he gave no account of what would have been, had it taken place, a most unusual and memorable journey, he claimed that he had managed to reach the home of a friend at Deeside, fourteen miles away, that he had still been wearing his pyjamas and that his friend had given him proper clothes to wear, after which he had gone to see his mother. He said that his friend was called Jenkins but that 'I don't want to say his first name as I don't want anyone to know what Mr Howarth has done to me.' He ended his statement with the following words: 'I have never ever told anyone before what Howarth did to me.'[312]

This allegation against Howarth was not the only complaint Surtees made. Six days after they had taken Surtees's first statement, the police returned. On this occasion he described a number of incidents which he had apparently been unable to recall on the previous occasion. He began by saying that he had been punched by Paul Wilson as a punishment for looking at the breasts of a female member of staff, went on to claim that he had been beaten up by David Birch and Stephen Norris, said that he had been punched on the back of the head by another member of staff and also claimed that another, whose name and appearance he could not remember, had forced him to lie on the floor and had then ordered a number of boys 'to piss and shit on me'. Surtees went on to become the first person to make an allegation against Matt Arnold, the headmaster. He claimed that Arnold had taken him for a ride in his car and then touched his thigh and his groin. He added that he had told his social worker about what Mr Arnold had done 'but I don't think he believed me'.[313]

By the time of Howarth's trial, more than two years later, it would appear that Surtees had forgotten some of the details of his story. When he gave evidence, he actually transposed onto the allegation against Howarth the claim, originally made in relation to Arnold, that he had told his social worker about what had allegedly happened. Indeed, he went further and said that he had told *three* social workers in all about what Howarth had done to him, that he had also told his friend Jenkins, that he had 'partly' told his mother and that he thought he had told the matron as well. Pressed by Howarth's counsel on this last point, he immediately began to elaborate. He gave details of the conversation he claimed to have had with the matron, saying that she had promised to look into it but that he had heard nothing further. The claim, made in March 1992, that he had told nobody about what had happened, would thus be replaced in 1994 by the assertion that he had told six people. Whereas in 1992 he had explained his reluctance to give police the first name of 'Jenkins' by saying that he did not want his friend to know about the sexual assault, in 1994 he told the court that Jenkins already knew but that he had died of an overdose three months before the police's visit. Whether 'Jenkins' ever existed appears never to have been established.

Although the story Surtees told police in 1992 was highly implausible, the more serious inconsistencies would not emerge for two more years. In view of the attitude of credulity they had been encouraged to cultivate, it was perhaps not surprising that the police appear to have taken Surtees at his word, and to have treated the statement about Howarth as though it were a serious and credible complaint. By this time they had managed to collect allegations of sexual assault against Howarth from seven different complainants, with the prospect of an eighth if the allegation made by Birley to Nelson was ever converted into an official complaint. They were also now in possession of a complaint about the man who had appointed both Stephen Norris and Peter Howarth to their posts – Matt Arnold. When these allegations were seen alongside the bizarre sexual allegations which had been made about Paul Wilson by Andrew Singer, and the claims made about Connie Bew by the art teacher Justin Soper, the picture which emerged was a serious one indeed. Alongside such evidence, even the suspicion that Bryn Estyn might lie at the centre of an organised paedophile ring might well have seemed moderate and reasonable.

These, however, were not the only sexual allegations which had emerged. At the outset the police had received an allegation against yet another former member of staff. For Andrew Singer, as well as accusing Peter Howarth and Paul Wilson of sexually abusing him, had also claimed that he had had a sexual relationship with David Birch. He told the police that, about six months after he had arrived at Bryn Estyn, Birch had asked him if he wanted to earn extra pocket money by cleaning his flat in the grounds. He said that he had done this and claimed that he had found homosexual magazines and posters in the flat. After about three weeks, he alleged that Birch had come into the flat and said something like 'Who needs a woman when you're here?' He had then supposedly accepted Birch's sexual advances and had oral and anal sex with him. This was allegedly repeated on three or four occasions and Singer said that he enjoyed what had happened and that he had had sex with Birch 'by choice'.[314]

Of all the complaints collected during the Bryn Estyn investigation, this allegation against an immensely popular member of staff whose heterosexual orientation was well known, was one of the most implausible of all. So unlikely was it that even Dennis Parry, who happened to know David Birch's family, has said that he did not believe Singer was telling the truth. When Birch's case eventually came to trial in 1995, the jury would take the same view. After hearing the evidence they deliberated only briefly before unanimously acquitting him.

In March 1992, however, the North Wales Police appear to have been in no doubt that the case against Birch should be pursued. Whether they believed that he too was part of the evil conspiracy which allegedly linked children's home to children's home across the length and breadth of North Wales has not been recorded.

What can be recorded is that, as dawn broke on Sunday 15 March 1992, a small army of police officers, numbering around forty, was making ready to carry out the largest police raid which had ever been executed in relation to allegations of sexual abuse in care homes. At 7.30, in an exercise code-named 'Operation Antelope', they swooped simultaneously on the homes of seventeen people, sixteen of whom were former Bryn Estyn staff, and five of whom were still working for Clwyd Social Services. Having arrested them all, they searched their homes and seized videos and photographs. In a curious development which has never been explained, one of the men arrested and subsequently released was reportedly an electrician from Norwich, who apparently had no connection with Bryn Estyn

Among those arrested were Peter Howarth, Paul Wilson, David Birch, Connie Bew, Matt Arnold and Stephen Norris. Ten other former members of staff, who had worked as teachers, as care officers or as nightwatchmen, also found themselves in custody that day, facing, in most cases, allegations of physical abuse.

Why the North Wales Police chose to make their arrests in this dramatic manner has never been made clear. The only plausible explanation, however, is that they still entertained a real suspicion that Bryn Estyn was at the centre of an organised paedophile ring, and it was this that made the simultaneous arrests necessary.

After staging such a dramatic dawn raid, and arresting so many suspects, there could be no turning back for the police. In order that they might vindicate such a strategy and justify the huge amounts of money which had already been spent on the investigation, it was now absolutely necessary to secure convictions. Although they did not know it at the time, one conviction would be obtained relatively easily. On 11 November 1993, Stephen Norris, who had been re-arrested in a bail hostel before fully serving his earlier sentence, would plead guilty to three offences of buggery, one of attempted buggery and three indecent assaults involving six Bryn Estyn boys. For Norris's Bryn Estyn colleagues this was a disturbing development which they regarded as a shocking aberration and as a matter for shame. Yet for the police a single conviction would not begin to justify the dawn raid they had just engaged in. For that to happen they would have to demonstrate that Norris's conduct, far from being an aberration, was something much closer to the norm. It was for this reason that, rather than signalling the end of the investigation, the arrests which were made on 15 March made it virtually imperative that the inquiry should now be continued and intensified.

37 Jackanory stuff

AS THE TASK OF INTERVIEWING the sixteen Bryn Estyn suspects neared completion that Sunday evening, one problem for the police was that, although the homes of all the suspects had been searched, no child pornography had been found. And there was no evidence for the existence of any paedophile ring. By the end of the day the police had no alternative but to release twelve of the sixteen without bringing any charges. Of the four who remained – Stephen Norris, Peter Howarth, Paul Wilson and David Birch, only Norris made any admissions.

In his long interview with the police that afternoon, Howarth repeatedly protested his innocence. At an early stage he was asked by one of the two officers interviewing him about his reactions:

> POLICE OFFICER: … there has been a number of complaints, detailed complaints, about that you had sexual relationships with boys at Bryn Estyn. How do you feel about those allegations? You must have a thousand thoughts going through your mind now.
> HOWARTH: I have. There is one main thought, I must be honest.
> OFFICER: And what's your main thought?
> HOWARTH: That someone's cooked this up.

Howarth went on to say that he felt one of the people who had 'got it in for' him was Ryan Tanner. He said that Tanner had phoned him up on two occasions and had taunted him about the Bryn Estyn investigation. Tanner had asked whether he was worried and had then laughed down the phone at him.

Again and again he dismissed the allegations put to him as fabrications. As he said of one statement, 'Make-believe, Jackanory stuff that is'. Later in the interview, one of the police officers made it clear that he thought Howarth was a homosexual:

> OFFICER: I'm saying to you that the, my perception of your time in Bryn Estyn, which is what I've just explained, yeh, I believe that you are homosexual.
> HOWARTH: Yeh, well I'm not.

OFFICER: I'm not making a judgment on that but I believe that you are homosexual and I believe that lads who were willing to partake in sexual activity with you that you would encourage and that you would have sexual relationships with those boys.

HOWARTH: That's not true.

Faced with repeated suggestions by the same officer that he was guilty, Howarth said this:

Well, I know you've made your mind up and you don't want to bother about the facts as far as I'm concerned. You have made your mind up, there is no doubt in my mind about that. Those statements that you've read out so far from those boys are totally untrue in every sense of the word, I haven't done any of those things, I completely deny them in every way, and you can look at me with your funny eyes as much as you like, it won't make any difference. They're not true.[315]

Howarth's protestations of innocence, however, seemingly did nothing to shake the belief of the interviewing officers, or of their superiors, that he was guilty of all or most of the sexual acts alleged against him. What his denials did make abundantly clear, though, was that the task of the police, if they wanted to be sure of securing a conviction, was far from over.

It did not take long for the next allegation to be secured. Three days after Howarth and fifteen of his former colleagues had been arrested, Simon Birley made a statement to the police in which he made officially the allegation which had already been reported in Dean Nelson's article (while omitting any mention of the chronologically impossible sexual contact with Wynne he had previously included).

Six days later, on 24 March 1992, the police were unsuccessful when they visited a former resident of Bryn Estyn, Daniel Mead. Mead made a statement in which he said quite explicitly that he had not been either physically or sexually abused during his time at Bryn Estyn. A mere three days later, however, Mead changed his mind and now claimed that he had been indecently assaulted by Howarth and physically assaulted by Wilson. Mead, who initiated a claim for compensation before Howarth's case came to trial, would find that his allegation would be rejected outright by the jury. However, from the point of view of the police, the circumstances in which the allegation emerged, and the fact that he had made two mutually contradictory statements within three days, could easily be explained by invoking the content of their January briefing session.

A week or so after Daniel Mead had made his second statement, the police visited yet another former resident of Bryn Estyn, Gary Waite, who lived in South Wales. Waite told them that he had been sent to Bryn Estyn at the age of eleven and that, about a year after arriving there, Howarth had persuaded him to stay on after one of his flat list sessions, and had then indecently assaulted him. This had supposedly happened repeatedly: 'I would then have to go and sit on his lap, he would then start to talk to me and pat my head.'

These words, conjuring up the picture of a small child being comforted by an adult, do not seem out of place in Waite's statement, according to which he was put into care when he was about eleven and spent four years in Bryn Estyn. In fact, however, Waite was fourteen when he was sent to Bryn Estyn and spent only two years there; he would have been fifteen at the time he describes. He was certainly not a small vulnerable child; he was a large and powerful adolescent. As Howarth recalled, he was 'hard as nails, a well built, solid lad'. Gwen Hurst, a teacher at the school, remembers him as 'a big-framed, stocky lad, like a rugby player'. A photograph of Waite taken at the time confirms this. It shows a powerfully built adolescent about five foot eight inches tall. It is improbable, to say the least, that any member of staff would have invited a boy of Waite's size to sit on their lap.

The implausibility of Waite's claims about Howarth were matched by a claim he made about a teacher who had supposedly slapped him around the head and face: 'He then picked me up off the ground and threw me several times about the room.' Once again, it was highly unlikely that any adult would have had the strength to pick the 15-year-old Waite off the ground and 'throw' him around the room. His statement then continued:

> The teacher who had hit me took me to see 'Strepsil' the matron, I think her name was Mrs Williams. I was then put in sick-bay. I believe that I may have been there for about five days. When I was there I wasn't allowed to see any of the other lads and I never saw anyone only Mrs Williams. When I left the sick-bay I believe that the bruising to my eyes had almost gone though I was still sore around my ribs.

The obvious objection to Waite's allegation is that any assault which resulted in two black eyes would have immediately come to the attention of senior staff. It would have been logged and an inquiry instigated. Yet no record of any such incident has been located. The part of Waite's story quoted here is an all-but transparent attempt to explain this circumstance away. Its clear implication is that Isabel Williams conspired with the teacher to hide Waite away until the evidence of the assault had faded. This is simply not credible. As we have already seen, Isabel Williams was not just the matron of Bryn Estyn, she was also highly regarded in the community, and in 1977 was made a magistrate. She remained a local magistrate for 16 years. As a matron she was both caring and conscientious and the suggestion that she would have engaged in the cover-up implicitly alleged by Waite defies belief. In fact the situation Waite describes, in which he spent up to five days in the sick-bay without seeing anyone other than Mrs Williams, lies quite outside the realm of the possible. As she herself has pointed out 'I would not have been on duty twenty-four hours a day for five days. There would have been other house mothers on duty when I was at home or doing other tasks, and any boy in the sick-bay would be monitored by myself and other members of staff.'[316]

Moira Jones, a house mother at Bryn Estyn from 1975 until shortly before the school closed in 1984, has also said that the situation described by Waite would have been impossible: 'Mrs Williams would not be there for five days without a break in any event. Anybody in the sick room was monitored by all of the house mothers on duty who would take meals and that sort of thing.'[317]

Isabel Williams also points out that no boy would have been kept in the sick-bay simply because he had black eyes but that this would certainly have been the occasion of an inquiry: 'I can say categorically that any boy with black eyes would have been reported to me and the matter would have been investigated. If the boy merely had black eyes he would not have been put in the sick-bay as he claims, and if his injuries were more than black eyes he would either have been referred to hospital or to Dr Wilkinson.'[318]

If the claim Waite made about Howarth was implausible, the claim he had made about the teacher and the matron was, or should have been recognised as, a transparent fabrication. In view of this it is interesting that, even before he made his allegations to the North Wales Police in April 1992, Waite was in touch with a solicitor. His claim for compensation was one of several which would be instigated before Howarth's trial began.

Once again, however, the police appear to have been persuaded by his story and Waite would soon find himself enlisted as a key witness in the prosecution case against Howarth.

Throughout their investigation the police continued to discover witnesses who had no complaints at all about their time at Bryn Estyn. Some three weeks after they had interviewed Waite, however, they were successful in uncovering another allegation against Howarth. On this occasion they had visited a 30-year-old former resident of Bryn Estyn, Nick Purnell, who claimed that Howarth had begun to assault him sexually while a number of other boys (whose names he could not remember) had been with him in Howarth's flat watching television. He said that after the boys had left, Howarth had performed fellatio on him and had asked him to reciprocate. Purnell said that he had declined to do so. He then said that the same thing had happened on a number of other occasions.

The idea that Howarth had started to make sexual overtures to Purnell while other boys were present in the flat seemed open to question. After some months, however, Purnell contacted the police again and gave a new account of the incident. He now said that the other boys had left the flat before any sexual approach had been made to him. He also said that his previous claim that he had not performed fellatio on Howarth had been incorrect and that he had in fact done so on a number of occasions.

At the Tribunal it would emerge that, in a successful claim for compensation, Purnell had made two much more serious allegations, saying both that Howarth had inserted objects into his anus and that he had buggered him.[319] Even though these claims had been made formally before Howarth's trial took place, Purnell had made no reference to them in the evidence he gave to the court.

The omissions and inconsistencies in Purnell's story came to light only at a much later date – in this case long after Howarth's trial. And once again the police evidently saw no reason not to place reliance on Purnell's evidence. He too was duly called as a witness for the prosecution.

With the additional evidence of Purnell, the criminal case which would be presented against Howarth at Chester Crown Court was virtually complete. However, this is not the full story. For there were other allegations against Howarth, some of which appeared in the first version of his trial indictment but which had been dropped by the time the case came to trial in 1994. The witnesses who did *not* appear at Howarth's trial were just as significant as those who did.

Purnell had made his second statement to the police at the end of October 1992. Just over a month later, on 4 December 1992, two police officers travelled to Cardiff Prison to interview yet another former res-

ident of Bryn Estyn. By a bizarre coincidence, which would play a significant role in helping to determine Howarth's fate, this witness had
exactly the same name as the boy who had been cited as a possible victim in the statement Ryan Tanner had given at the outset of the
inquiry. Both were called John Richard Evans.

To those who knew them at Bryn Estyn, there could be no confus-
ing the two boys. The John Evans who had featured in Tanner's statement (and in the 'minibus allegation' made by Alison Taylor) was white,
was born in 1966, and had no criminal record. The John Evans the
police visited in Cardiff Prison was black, was born in 1963, and had
been convicted of more than a hundred offences. Whereas the 'white
John Evans' has consistently said that he had never been sexually abused
by Howarth, the 'black John Evans', on being interviewed by the
police, made allegations of indecent assault and buggery. These allegations, made after a whole year of intensive publicity about the case,
were so general that they could not have been disproved from the few
details he gave. Evans, however, did make one very specific claim. He
said that he had been at Bryn Estyn with James Innes and that, on two
occasions, he had told Innes what Howarth had done to him. According to James Innes this was not true. If Innes was, as he appeared to be,
a truthful witness, Evans's claims were false. In the event, however,
Evans disappeared during Howarth's trial and his evidence was never
heard.

Another witness who did not give evidence at Howarth's trial, 29-
year-old Lee Steward, would soon become, along with Alison Taylor
and Ryan Tanner, one of the most important figures in the North Wales
story.

Lee Steward's entry into the story gave no indication of the central
role he would ultimately play. It took place on 30 March 1992, a mere
three days after Daniel Mead had made his second statement to the
police. In view of the fact that Mead and Steward had been at Bryn
Estyn at the same time, and that Mead played a small part in one of
Steward's allegations, this may well not have been a coincidence.

One of the most interesting features of the account Steward gave to
the police in the first of many statements was the identity of the first
care worker against whom he complained – Nefyn Dodd:

> I remember that the first member of staff I met at Bryn Estyn was a
> huge man called Nefyn Dodd, he must have been all of 25 stone and
> the first thing he said to me was, I'll never forget what he said: 'You

play ball with me and I'll play ball with you, or else.' And then he held up his clenched fist. He was only there for a short while, until he moved to a home in Bangor. Whilst he was there he hit me a couple of times and each time it was probably because I was misbehaving. He hit me with his clenched fists [on] the top of my head and I remember it gave me a headache. I think each incident took place in the dining room.[320]

Steward went on to give an account of Howarth's flat list and claimed that on a number of occasions Howarth had approached him while he was making the drinks in the kitchen and 'from behind he fondled my private parts ... .This happened a few times and I got the impression that if you turned him down he wouldn't pursue it. He never said anything at the time and never mentioned anything afterwards, and I tended to make sure that I was never in a room alone with him.'

This was the first allegation Steward had made against Peter Howarth, but it would be by no means the last. However, it was the allegation against Dodd which was the more revealing of the two. For although Dodd was indeed a big man, and would eventually, after contracting diabetes in 1980, put on weight rapidly until he was 18 or 19 stone, he was nothing like this weight in 1977 when Steward had first gone to Bryn Estyn. At the time Dodd was probably less than 15 stone. Steward's description has all the marks of one based on some recently acquired knowledge of Dodd rather than on his own recollection.

In directing his first two allegations against Dodd and Howarth, Steward had chosen the same targets which had been indicated by Ryan Tanner in the phone call he had made to Paul Wilson the previous autumn. It might well be that this was no more than a coincidence. Alternatively Steward's statement could well have been influenced not by Tanner himself but by the article in the *Independent on Sunday*. It was undoubtedly the case, though, that Tanner had not disappeared from the story. He was still playing an extremely significant role and by this stage had spoken to a number of former residents about the Bryn Estyn investigation. In most cases the content of these conversations has not been documented. But in one case it has.

This case has very serious implications. For it concerns the role played by Ryan Tanner in encouraging a former resident of Bryn Estyn to make an allegation not only against Peter Howarth but also against a mysterious, unidentified man who had some connection with Bryn Estyn. The second part of the story of North Wales was about to begin its slow unfolding.

38 The grey-haired man

THE PERSON WHO MADE one of the most revealing allegations in the entire North Wales investigation was a 25-year-old Wrexham man named Brendan Randles. In December 1982, when he was fifteen, Randles, a likable and happy-go-lucky youth, had appeared before Wrexham magistrates on a charge of burglary. He had been remanded into custody at Bryn Estyn where he spent a total of four nights.

In the years that followed, Randles made no complaints about his brief spell at the home. However, around Christmas 1988, he found himself living in the same part of Wrexham as Ryan Tanner and for a brief period he drank with him and his friends. Later, in the autumn of 1991, Tanner had given Randles's name to the North Wales Police as somebody who had once been at Bryn Estyn. Tanner recalls that he had bumped into Brendan in Wrexham soon afterwards. 'I remember Brendan saying to me "What the fuck are you doing talking to the police about me at Bryn Estyn?" I said, "Well, you were there, weren't you?"'[321]

Tanner gives no details of what else he may have said to Randles on this occasion. In January 1992, however, the police took a statement from Randles, in which he claims that when he arrived at Bryn Estyn he was introduced to a stockily built, grey-haired man who appeared to be in charge, but whose name he could not remember.

He then claims that, while he was having a shower, Tanner came in and accused him of going out with his girlfriend. He says that, with two other lads ('whom I can't remember'), Tanner had beaten him up. The grey-haired man is said to have watched this without attempting to intervene. The next day the man took him to the secure unit, placed his hand on Randles's penis and testicles, and tried to kiss him. Randles says he pushed him away and ran out the door. 'As I drew near to the door I saw Ryan Tanner walking towards the building. I didn't stop to talk to him.'

He says that he ran into the pool room but that the grey-haired man followed him and said, in a whisper, 'I'm going to fuck you tonight.' Later that evening the grey-haired man supposedly repeated these words to him several times when Randles had seen him through the door of his first-floor flat. Randles, however, says he returned to his dormitory where he spent the night without further incident. He goes on to say that in the morning he was taken to court where he told his mother what had happened to him. He was then bailed and says that the next day he told his girlfriend 'exactly what had happened'. He ends his statement with the following words: 'I couldn't sleep after what the man had said to me because I honestly believed that he was going to do to me what he said.' From Randles's first statement it is therefore clear that the threat which the grey-haired man had supposedly made was *not* carried out. The complaint was one of indecent assault only.

The police took this statement from Randles on Friday 22 January. The following Wednesday they interviewed Tanner. His version of events corresponded in some respects to that given by Randles, but some details were different. Nowhere in his statement did Tanner mention that he had been in contact with Randles since they had left Bryn Estyn. Randles, similarly, gave no indication in his statement that he knew Tanner.

In that Randles had been unable to identify the grey-haired man by name, it was highly improbable that his allegation of indecent assault could have formed part of any prosecution. However, within the next few weeks, Randles met Tanner and they spent the evening talking about Bryn Estyn. About two months after this, Randles made another statement to the police in which he revised the account he had given three months earlier.

Without offering any explanation of how he has identified him, he now refers to the grey-haired man as 'Mr Howarth'. Whereas previously he described encountering him in three locations – the secure unit, the pool room and the first-floor flat – the second and third of these alleged meetings now disappear. Randles claims that in the secure unit, 'Mr Howarth' actually carried out his whispered threat. He supposedly did so by stripping Randles, punching him in the stomach, and then, as he bent over in pain, anally raping him.

At this point a strikingly new element is introduced into the allegation. Randles says that, as he was being buggered, another man came into the room: 'I then heard the door open and then shut and I heard Mr Howarth speak to another man and say words to the effect "It's your turn."' Randles then claims that, without any preliminaries, the second man raped him anally while Howarth raped him orally. At this point it became evident 'that somebody was coming down to the secure room, I think it was Ryan Tanner although I'm not sure.'

The identity of the second man is left veiled in mystery. 'To this day,' says Randles enigmatically, 'I do not know who the man was, however I think he must have had something to do with Bryn Estyn although I didn't see this person whilst I was there.'[322]

This second statement was taken from Randles at the beginning of May. Three days later the police visited Tanner once again. On this occasion they apparently asked him specifically whether he had been in contact with Randles. The history of the contact between Randles and Tanner (or part of it) now emerged. About three weeks after he had made his first statement, Randles, who had been drinking, came round to Tanner's flat with a bottle of sherry. They talked about Bryn Estyn and Tanner says he asked Randles to tell him what had happened there: 'I tried to convince Brendan that whatever his problem was he was not the only one and others had made complaints. Brendan told me the police had asked him questions and Brendan said "What do you want me to say, that he's fucked my arse?" I then asked gentler questions about what happened.'

It would appear that Tanner had actually discussed with Randles complaints which had been made by others, and that he felt he was being put under pressure to go further than his original complaint and make an allegation of buggery. The reason why Randles's highly significant words had been preserved was that Tanner had actually taped part of the conversation: 'Brendan also knew that I was taping the conversation. I did this because I wanted to play it back to Brendan at a later date. If he should deny anything happened and also to assist the police in their investigation.'

The grey-haired man had not at this stage been identified. However Tanner evidently met up with Randles again and on this occasion he had shown Randles a photograph of Howarth: 'At a later stage I showed Brendan a copy of the *Independent* newspaper which had a photograph of Peter Howarth on the front page. Brendan told me that it was Howarth who had sexually assaulted him in the secure unit at Bryn Estyn.'

In the light of Tanner's police statement of 8 May, and of his subsequent evidence to the Tribunal, it would appear that he not only encouraged Randles to make a more serious allegation against 'the grey-haired man' at a time when he was drunk, but that he was himself responsible for bringing about the belated identification of this man as Howarth.[323] There is no clear evidence that Tanner, however reckless and ill-advised his conduct, had deliberately set out to manufacture a false allegation. On this occasion, as on others, it seems plausible to suggest that he was motivated by a kind of misguided idealism and that he may genuinely have believed that he was helping Randles to retrieve memories which had become buried, and that by doing so he was helping the police.

On any view, though, Randles's allegations were remarkable. His eventual claim that, before he had even spent 24 hours at Bryn Estyn, he had been viciously raped by two men, that he had remained silent about the assaults for nine years, and that he had been able to retrieve the memories only after drinking from a bottle of sherry at Ryan Tanner's flat, was one of the most far-fetched in the entire Bryn Estyn investigation.

One question, however, remains. This concerns the identity of the second man – the shadowy figure who was supposed suddenly to have appeared in the secure unit and, as if by some prior arrangement, to have joined in the alleged sexual assault on Randles. Who was this man, and why had he been belatedly introduced into a complaint in which he had originally played no role at all?

39 The second man

IT MIGHT WELL BE ASSUMED that, by the time Brendan Randles entered the story of Bryn Estyn, one of that story's authors, the journalist Dean Nelson, had returned to London, and that, for the time being at least, he would play no further part in the unfolding of the narrative.

Nelson had indeed left the Wrexham area in November 1991, after he had completed his research. There is no record of his having returned to Wrexham between then and 22 January 1992, when Randles made his initial statement, nor any reason to believe that he had done so. However, by coincidence, it was soon after the police had interviewed Randles that Nelson embarked on the second phase of his investigation

This phase had effectively begun when Ian Jack, the editor of the *Independent on Sunday*, had received a letter from Gordon Anglesea's solicitor threatening legal action. Anglesea was at this point being represented by the Wrexham solicitor, John Hughes, who had often visited Bryn Estyn during the course of his work and had a good knowledge of the home. When the initial letter to the paper brought no response, Anglesea had, at the suggestion of Hughes, sought advice from the barrister Andrew Caldecott. As a result of this advice a libel writ was issued towards the beginning of 1992. It was at this point that Jack had taken the decision to send Dean Nelson back to North Wales to see if he could find evidence that would justify the libel (see above, chapter 3).[324]

Nelson's task now was to scour the Wrexham area for any witness who might lend weight to his story by making an allegation of sexual abuse against Anglesea. Any witnesses he found now would, if the libel action continued, play a vital role in the newspaper's defence. If the case ever came to trial, they would almost certainly be asked to appear as witnesses for the paper.

Nelson's quest would lead him to contact a number of new witnesses. Understandably enough, however, Nelson began the second phase of his inquiry not by seeking out new witnesses but by making contact again with old ones. According to his own recollection, he set out for Wrexham again either at the end of January or in early February 1992. One of the first people he met up with was Peter Wynne. Nelson now interviewed Wynne again, this time focusing on Gordon Anglesea, on Anglesea's visits to Bryn Estyn, and any contact he had had with Peter Howarth.

Nelson immediately transcribed this interview. From the text of what was said it would appear that, once again, a conversation had taken place between Nelson and Wynne before the tape-recorder had been switched on. Nelson's opening question was: 'Do you remember a policeman ever visiting Bryn Estyn?' Because Bryn Estyn was the kind of institution it was, policemen of many different ranks visited it frequently. Wynne, however, replies without hesitation: 'Anglesea.'

Later in the interview Nelson asks him whether Anglesea was well known to the boys. Wynne says 'Oh aye, yeah.' Asked why this was, he says: 'I can't remember much, but I can remember some staff saying "If you're bad we'll get fucking Anglesea out." I can remember something about it but not much.' Here Wynne makes a claim which has not been made by any other Bryn Estyn witness, but which echoes Alison Taylor's claim about Anglesea being invoked as a bogey-man by Nefyn Dodd. In response to a question about whether he remembers Anglesea ever visiting Howarth socially, Wynne attempts to 'undo' the leading question by claiming spontaneity: 'I was going to say before you mentioned it. I know he was a good mate of Peter Howarth's. ... I'm sure they used to play golf together ...' This suggestion has frequently been made but never substantiated. There is no record of Anglesea, who did not play golf at this time, ever playing golf with Howarth. The claim that he did, however, does appear in Alison Taylor's dossier, where she writes that he was 'reputed' to have regularly visited the golf club with Howarth.[325]

What is clear is that Nelson was single-mindedly seeking any information which might link Anglesea to Howarth, particularly in circumstances which were compromising. Even though his interview with Wynne brought meagre returns in this respect, Nelson immediately faxed a transcript to the newspaper. A copy of this fax has been preserved. It was sent from the Posthouse Hotel in Chester on 5 February 1992.

The date is significant. It means that Nelson conducted his interview with Wynne a mere two weeks after Randles had made his first statement, and before his complaint assumed its final form. If Tanner's recollection of the timing of his sherry-drinking session with Randles is correct, this had taken place just a week or two after Nelson's interview with Wynne. There can be little doubt that Tanner, who was still in touch with Wynne, knew of Nelson's visit, and of its purpose.

The question which arises is whether Randles's revision of his statement was in some way related to the quest on which Nelson had so recently embarked. The scenario Randles described, in which Howarth was joined in an act of sexual abuse by another man, might appear to be bizarre and highly unusual. But similar scenarios would shortly figure again in the Bryn Estyn story. For just such allegations would be collected by Nelson in the course of his attempts to substantiate the libel against Anglesea.

When it comes to determining the intended identity of Howarth's companion, Randles's own words may be significant: 'I think he must have had something to do with Bryn Estyn,' he says in his second statement, 'although I didn't see this person whilst I was there.' This would suggest that the second man was not a member of staff but that he had some other connection with Bryn Estyn.

A further clue is provided by Randles's claim that at one point, when he screamed, Howarth said to him: 'Keep you mouth shut or you'll never get bail again. You'll get remanded.' Randles immediately goes on to offer a description of Howarth's unidentified companion. The alleged threat seems to imply that either the unidentified man or Howarth (or both), was in a position to influence the outcome of the bail hearing which was shortly due to take place. A police inspector might well be thought, whether rightly or wrongly, to be in just such a position.

Neither the coincidences of chronology nor these details are conclusive in themselves. However, they become a great deal more significant when considered in the light of a statement made by Alison Taylor. Writing to the editor of the *New Statesman* in November 2000, in a letter which claimed that an article I had written misrepresented Tanner's role in the Randles affair, Taylor said '[Randles], who alleged sexual abuse by an unknown "grey haired man", was shown a picture of Gordon Anglesea, not Howarth, but denied that Anglesea was the abuser.'[326]

Taylor's clear assertion that Randles was shown a picture of Anglesea strongly suggests that some attempt was made to elicit from Randles just the kind of allegation which Nelson was seeking. This attempt, if it took place, was evidently unsuccessful. Indeed, when Randles gave a description of the second man, in the statement he gave in May, it bore no resemblance to the recently retired police officer. Gordon Anglesea was clean-shaven and had a prominent red birthmark, the size of a man's hand, on the lower left-hand side of his face and upper neck. He would have been in his mid 40s at the time in question. Randles, however, described a slimly built man, aged between 30 and 35, who was six foot tall and had a 'full grey and black beard'. Given that this description bore no resemblance to anyone who might have been identified as a suspect, it is not surprising that the police appear not to have pursued this part of his complaint.[327]

The other part of Randles's complaint did form part of the first indictment against Howarth. Randles himself, however, did not live to take part in the trial. On 1 April 1994, two months before the trial, Randles was found at his home in Wrexham slumped over his sofa. By his side was a bucket, half-full of vomited blood. An inquest in June 1994 found that he had died from gross abuse of alcohol.[328]

The fact that Randles played no part in Howarth's trial did not weaken the case against him. In many respects, by removing one of the most implausible of all the allegations, and by effectively obscuring the manner in which it had been obtained, it strengthened it.[329]

As has already been noted, Randles was not the only man who made allegations of sexual abuse against Howarth which were destined to play no part in his trial. Lee Steward was another such witness and his story would become much more closely involved with the second phase of Nelson's investigation than that of Randles ever did. Before we examine the manner in which Steward's allegations developed, however, it is necessary to introduce a witness whose role in this part of the story would be even more important – Mark Humphreys.

40 The photograph

MARK HUMPHREYS HAD A NUMBER OF THINGS in common with Peter Wynne and Simon Birley. He too had initially told the police, when they questioned him in late 1991, that he had no complaints about his time at Bryn Estyn. Like Wynne and Birley, he was interviewed by Dean Nelson. Soon afterwards, like them, he changed his story and made a serious sexual allegation. These, however, were not the only things Humphreys had in common with Wynne and Birley. For, by the end of 1995, all three would be dead.

On 6 January 1994, Peter Wynne was found hanging from a door at his home. At the inquest, in April 1994, the verdict was suicide. Simon Birley died on 21 May 1995. He was found hanging from a tree. The inquest verdict was that he took his own life. Mark Humphreys died on 2 February 1995. He was found hanging from a banister at the bedsit in Wrexham where he was living. An open verdict was returned at an inquest in June of that year.[330]

The deaths of these young men, together with the deaths of Brendan Randles and a number of other former residents of North Wales care homes, have repeatedly been cited as evidence of the consequences of the sexual abuse they had suffered. Indeed this claim would play a key role in the press campaign which led to the setting-up of the North Wales Tribunal. The truth about what happened, however, is in some respects even more terrible than the claims repeatedly made in the press.

Mark Humphreys was born on 30 September 1964 and was 27 years old when the North Wales Police visited him at his home in December 1991. Remembered by his teacher at Bryn Estyn as a 'lovable rogue', he came from a large, close family. One of six brothers, all of whom were, confusingly, known as 'Sammy', he was also close to his two sisters, and for most of his life, to his mother Peggy, who was widowed when he was in his teens.

While he was still at school Mark sometimes worked as a newspaper vendor and it was at this point in his life that he was befriended by Gary Cooke, a former wrestler and male nurse, who has been convicted on a number of occasions of sexually abusing young boys in and around Wrexham. In August 1979, when Humphreys was 14 and Cooke was 27, a cache of indecent photographs belonging to Cooke was brought to the attention of the police. Cooke was subsequently convicted on various counts, including taking an indecent photograph of Mark Humphreys.[331]

On 13 May 1980, after being arrested for an offence of theft, Humphreys, who was then fifteen, was sent on remand to Bryn Estyn. On 3 June he was found guilty by Wrexham juvenile court. He was placed under a care order and returned to Bryn Estyn. He remained there until the end of August 1981 when he was a month short of his seventeenth birthday.

Since that time he had worked mostly as a market trader, travelling from town to town in North Wales while remaining based at Wrexham. He had three children of his own from two different relationships and was still close to the mother of his third child when he was first interviewed by the police in the early stages of the Bryn Estyn inquiry. Soon after this, however, he had moved in with another woman, Wendy, who had five children of her own, and whom Mark would marry in 1993.

When the police first visited him he made no allegations to them. Later, when it became clear that Gordon Anglesea's libel action could not be settled out of court, Humphreys made a statement for the libel trial in which he recalled the police visit: 'Towards the end of 1991 two officers came to see me and explained they were making enquiries about Bryn Estyn. I told them I could not help and that I had no complaints to make about my time in care.'[332]

It was around this time that the council house in which Mark and Wendy were living became dangerous after Mark knocked down a number of internal walls. They were forced to move and the council demanded money for the damage caused. On another occasion Mark, who sometimes drank heavily, smashed all the furniture in the house and was sent to a bail hostel in Bangor. These incidents were expensive and Mark, who frequently had money problems, became even more hard-pressed financially.

He was well known in the Queen's Park Estate in Wrexham, and some people would have been aware of the incident involving Gary Cooke which had taken place thirteen years before. According to Malcolm King, Mark's name was brought up at one point during a discussion at The Venture (the adventure playground/youth club where King worked), about abuse at Bryn Estyn. Somebody who knew Mark suggested that he might have been abused there because he was 'kind of odd'. As a result of this piece of speculation King has said that his deputy at The Venture, Colin Powell, attempted to talk to Humphreys:

> So Colin started on a series of visits to try and get hold of him, and he was always out … I can't think whether he did make contact with him, or whether he spoke to Wendy. Then young Gail Foley at that time made various forays – she's a BBC reporter, a radio reporter who I'd met a couple of times … she did a few reports. … She started asking around and I told her about Mark, I think she went to see him.[333]

It would appear that it was information gathered at The Venture which led Nelson to Mark Humphreys. Indeed during the Tribunal, Nelson said that he thought that King might have mentioned the name of 'Sammy Humphreys' to him as 'somebody who had been very much abused'. He said that he had called at a house which turned out to be Mark's brother's and that he had directed him to the house Mark had moved to: 'I went straight there and spoke to Mark and Wendy together.'[334]

Humphreys later recalled that this first visit took place in the evening of 18 June 1992. Nelson has said that he had not previously spoken to Humphreys, and that he had made no appointment to see him. From the comments of King, however, it would appear that, by this stage, either Wendy or Mark might well have been contacted by Colin Powell and that Mark had already spoken to the reporter Gail Foley. Indeed, Mark Humphreys subsequently said that 'someone from the BBC' had spoken to Wendy outside the school, and that the next evening Gail Foley and a male reporter had visited their home.[335]

It was Dean Nelson, however, who would succeed in eliciting an allegation from Humphreys. Although Nelson has always claimed that his first conversation with Humphreys, on 18 June 1992, was the subject neither of a note nor a tape, he did give an account of what had happened in a statement he made in October 1992:

> When I arrived Mark was in the house together with his common-law wife Wendy and their children. The children left the room and I sat down and spoke to Mark and Wendy. I explained what I was doing in terms of the story and asked if he had any experience of being abused I would like to interview him. I gained the impression that Mark had a disclosure to make, and that his wife was aware. Wendy made a remark to the effect 'Are you going to tell him?' whilst look-

ing at Mark. Mark replied to the effect 'I've got to tell someone.'

For the next hour and a half I spoke to Mark and explained that making a disclosure would be difficult and mentioned some of the experiences I had come across during my work on the story.[336]

From Nelson's own account it would appear that, only a matter of minutes after having been invited into the house, the journalist began explaining to Mark and Wendy that he was seeking an allegation of abuse. He then invited Humphreys to make such an allegation.

According to Nelson's police statement, no specific incidents were discussed at this point but Humphreys 'indicated in general terms that he had been abused'. Nelson immediately asked him if he would agree to a formal taped interview. They arranged for the interview to take place the next morning at Nelson's hotel – the Llwyn Onn Hall Hotel on the outskirts of Wrexham.[337]

The next day Nelson recorded an interview with Humphreys as had been agreed. The transcript of this interview shows that Humphreys's first difficulty is in recalling how long he was at Bryn Estyn:

> NELSON: Can you tell me what your name is and when you were at Bryn Estyn?
> HUMPHREYS: Mark Humphreys.
> NELSON: And when were you at Bryn Estyn?
> HUMPHREYS: Er – 1976.
> NELSON: Until?
> HUMPHREYS: 1981 or 2.
> NELSON: How old were you when you first went in there?
> HUMPHREYS: I don't know … 12, I think.
> NELSON: 12?
> HUMPHREYS: 11 or 12.
> NELSON: What was your first impression when you first went in there?
> HUMPHREYS: I thought it was OK when I first went in there.[338]

Humphreys goes on to say that after six months his impression of Bryn Estyn changed. One night he was allowed out and had come back late at about 10.30pm. Howarth met him downstairs and supposedly asked him to come up to his flat to move some furniture. Howarth gave him a glass of lager and then came up to him as he was sitting on the settee 'and tried to get my dick out of my trousers'.

Humphreys says that he responded by telling Howarth to 'fuck off'. He then 'leapt out of the room' and a few months later, in order to get away from Howarth, he absconded and was 'on the run for three months'. Humphreys goes on to talk about something a policeman had done to him while he was at the home. At the time, however, he says he did not know the man was a policeman and thought that he was the night watchman. Although no mention has yet been made of any name, Nelson asks: 'You thought he was the night watchman? Is it Gordon Anglesea?'

The fact that Humphreys evidently does not know this name and that it has to be supplied by Nelson might seem to undermine the entire allegation. However, he immediately goes on to give what appears to be persuasive evidence that he has identified Anglesea correctly, by giving a description of his distinctive birthmark: 'Yeah, well I didn't know his name, but all I know he was fucking scarneck, because he always used to have a scar on his neck, his birthmark wasn't it?' Asked where the 'scar' was, he says 'on the side of his face'; asked what kind of scar it was, he describes it as 'just like a red birthmark'.

He says that he realised the man was a policeman 'when I seen him one day with his stripes on his shirt'. He then says that one Christmas (he would later say that it was his second Christmas at Bryn Estyn), when most of the other boys had gone home, he was one of a group of ten who spent the Christmas period in the junior wing of the home, Clwyd House. One evening 'this fucking, well I'd say night security feller that's what I thought he was' came into his bedroom, 'tried to get my jamas down', then turned him over 'gripped hold of my dick like' and said 'oh that will do for now'.

Two days later, according to Humphreys, the same man, who seemed actually to work at Clwyd House, came back and tried to get into bed with him. 'I just said "get off" and that was it, he just got off me so then I went back over to the main school.'

Humphreys describes an occasion when, after being circumcised in the local hospital, he was returned to the sick-bay at Bryn Estyn. He claims that, while he was recovering from the operation, Howarth came into the room and started touching him in the area of the genitals. Once again he says his response was to run away.

Although the interview contains much else, including references to Humphreys's heavy drinking, these complaints are the only sexual allegations which are made. The allegations, even if they had been true, were so unclear that in some cases they barely amounted to a complaint of indecent assault. What Nelson did not know when he completed the interview, however, was that the version of events Humphreys had given could not possibly be true.

In fact Humphreys had been sent to Bryn Estyn not in 1976 at the age of eleven or twelve but in May 1980 when he was fifteen and a half. He left in August 1981, having spent not five years, but fourteen months there. Although the chronology given in his interview meant that he could not have been abused by Anglesea until his second Christmas, his time at Bryn Estyn included only one Christmas. He could not, however, have been abused at Bryn Estyn then, as he was on home leave from 18 December 1980 to 4 January 1981. On 20 December he was actually arrested by a police officer for shoplifting in the Wrexham branch of Asda.[339]

Humphreys's further claim that he had been on the run from Bryn Estyn for three months was difficult to credit. No record of any such absence appears in the Bryn Estyn log book, or in any other records. Had such a great escape ever taken place it would have been recalled by members of staff and boys alike, and it would also have resulted in considerable police activity. No record of any such activity has ever been discovered.

Practically the only feature of Humphreys's testimony which seemed plausible or compelling was his description of Anglesea's birthmark and his apparently vivid recollection of the man. There are repeated references to Anglesea's appearance throughout the interview. It is a point to which Nelson returns towards the end of his interview:

NELSON: If I brought you a picture of the copper, would you recognise him?
HUMPHREYS: Yeah I'd know him, yeah [inaudible], I can see his face now.
NELSON: Do you believe it was Gordon Anglesea?
HUMPHREYS: Definitely, definitely.

From this exchange it would seem that Nelson did not have a photograph with him and that he was referring to some future occasion. At the end of the interview this becomes quite explicit:

NELSON: If I come back and bring a picture back of Anglesea, will that be all right?
HUMPHREYS: Oh I know him, Not that I could draw but I know, you know what I mean, I'll never forget that fellow's face [inaudible] ever. ...
NELSON: OK. I will get a picture of him and come back to you and show you just to be sure.

The conversation on the tape gives the impression that Nelson intends to conduct another interview with Humphreys in which he will show him a photograph of Anglesea and will then tape-record his reaction to it. This indeed was precisely what he did when he held his second formal interview with Humphreys ten days later.

However, after Humphreys had been interviewed by the police, it became clear that Nelson had shown him a photograph of Anglesea beforehand. Subsequently, Nelson himself admitted to the police that the interview he conducted on 19 June at his hotel had a significant prelude of which no mention had been made:

> I had in fact picked Mark up at his home in my car to drive him to the hotel. Mark got into the car and before I drove off I gave him a photograph of Gordon Anglesea. The photograph was about half A4 size and was black and white. ... I did not speak to Mark but just handed the photograph to him. Mark said 'That's the bastard', and he became upset. ...[340]

It would be difficult to overstate the seriousness of this admission. It was not simply that it was now clear that both Anglesea's name *and* his description had been fed into the first interview by Nelson. This was grave enough. Nelson's most serious offence, however, was that he had engaged in a series of exchanges about showing Humphreys a photograph at some future point. In the light of his admission, it was now clear that these exchanges were charades. Their evident purpose was to disguise the fact that Nelson had *already* shown Humphreys a photograph, and to make it appear that he had a vivid memory of a man he barely knew, and whose name he could not remember.

Nelson said that the reason he had shown Mark the photograph was that he had mentioned having been abused by a policeman during the initial interview: 'I suspected Anglesea was the policeman he had mentioned the previous night and I was specifically investigating Anglesea in connection with a libel action against the *Independent*.' Whether it was in fact Humphreys who had first mentioned a policeman or whether, as seems more likely, it was Nelson, will probably never be known. What we do know is that the account Nelson gave to the police of what happened before the interview was significantly different from the account Humphreys himself would eventually give in the libel trial. Whereas Nelson went out of his way to say he did not speak as he handed Humphreys the photograph, Humphreys said that the journalist had said something like 'This is the bloke I'm after.'[341]

No less extraordinary than the attempt to conceal the showing of the photograph is the fact that, after the exchange already quoted, in which Nelson talks about the next interview, the journalist invites Humphreys to 'do that again' as if he is a film director asking for another take:

NELSON: If I brought you a picture of the copper, would you recognise him?
HUMPHREYS: Yeah I'd know him, yeah [inaudible], I can see his face now.
NELSON: Do you believe it was Gordon Anglesea?
HUMPHREYS: Definitely, definitely.
NELSON: *Just do that again.* If I showed you a picture of him you'd recognise him?
HUMPHREYS: I know him, yeah. I'll tell you now.
NELSON: Who do you believe it is?
HUMPHREYS: Him (sound of tapping).
NELSON: Gordon Anglesea, why do you believe it's him?
HUMPHREYS: I know it's him.

Here it would appear that, at the end of the first 'take', Nelson has noticed that he has asked a leading question (not for the first time), and that, by doing so, he has supplied Anglesea's name himself. The purpose of the second 'take' is apparently to eliminate the leading question so that Humphreys will actually be heard on the tape speaking Anglesea's name. However, even though Nelson successfully avoids the leading question, Humphreys, who apparently has great difficulty remembering a name which is unfamiliar to him, is unable to give a satisfactory answer. It is Nelson who ends up having to supply the name once again.

There would appear to be only two possible explanations for Nelson's conduct here. The first is that he is attempting to create a convincing exchange which can be selected from the tape and will pursuade those to whom it is played (including, perhaps, Nelson's editor). The second is that he is deliberately rehearsing Humphreys for the next interview at which he plans to show him the photograph as if for the first time and record his reaction. Either way the exchange is of a piece with the entire interview. There seems to be no other conclusion than that this interview and its invisible prelude was a deliberate exercise in journalistic sleight-of-hand. Its purpose was to create the impression that Humphreys's 'evidence' was dramatically better than it in fact was. If Humphreys had not told the police about the photograph, the exercise might well have succeeded.

Nelson, as has been noted, had used the technique of the invisible or unrecorded prelude to a recorded interview before. This time, however, he was much more circumspect than on earlier occasions, such as the 'glue-sniffing' interview with Peter Wynne. For there was no reference in the interview itself to any such prelude; from the tape alone nobody would have suspected its existence.

Nelson's exercise in witness management, however, was not yet complete. On 29 June, ten days after the meeting in the hotel, he interviewed Humphreys in Wrexham again. On this occasion he was evidently anxious both to obtain more serious allegations and to record Humphreys actually speaking Anglesea's name. In the latter quest Nelson was unsuccessful since Humphreys still could not recall Anglesea's name even when he was prompted to do so: 'His name doesn't stick in my mind, you know, his face does but his name doesn't.'[342]

However, the allegation which Humphreys made in his second interview against the man he remembered as 'the security guard' was dramatically different from what it had been ten days earlier. The crucial change related to the second incident, which was meant to have taken place at Clwyd House over Christmas. Whereas previously Humphreys had accused the man merely of trying to get into bed with him, he now said the man had 'pounced' on him and that 'he slided on top of me, spat on my bum ... and stuck his dick in, in it.' That this was supposed to be an accusation of buggery was made clear later when Humphreys referred to the time that he 'stuck his dick up my arse'.

A relatively minor allegation had now suddenly been transformed into one of buggery. The allegations against Howarth also became more serious and Humphreys subsequently signed an affidavit in which he made allegations of rape against both Howarth and Anglesea. Howarth, he now said, had actually raped him in the sick-bay while was recovering from the circumcision operation.[343]

On 18 August 1992, six weeks after he had sworn his affidavit, Humphreys was interviewed by the North Wales Police. This interview had apparently been requested by Humphreys, but had been arranged by Dean Nelson. Very unusually it took place not in North Wales, but in London at the offices of Oswald Hicks, the *Independent*'s solicitors. It would appear that Humphreys travelled to London with his family, with expenses being paid by the *Independent*.

The reasons for this unusual arrangement have never been explained. It was, however, quite clearly in the interests of Nelson that Anglesea should be prosecuted, and that there should be a criminal trial based on Humphreys's allegations. Were Anglesea to be convicted there would be no need for a libel trial. Given the difficulties Humphreys had in even remembering Anglesea's name, and given his tendency to drink excessively, it may well be that Nelson had come to the conclusion that his witness needed to be chaperoned (or coached) so that he could be presented to the police in the best possible light. What we do know is that Humphreys spent much of the morning before his statement was taken in the company of Nelson, who has said that he 'again talked to him about his allegations'. We also know, because Humphreys says as much in his statement, that, as on previous occasions when he was about to give evidence, Nelson had shown Humphreys the photograph of Anglesea.[344]

The statement which was taken by the police on 18 August seemed detailed and coherent. However, while the complaints against Anglesea remained similar to those in the second interview (and the affidavit), the complaints against Howarth had been transformed yet again. This time there was no allegation of rape in the sick-bay. But there was an entirely new allegation concerning a rape which had supposedly taken place after Humphreys had recovered from his operation. This had been the prelude to a series of sexual assaults: 'Over the next three years Howarth continued to bugger me when he had the opportunity. ... It is very hard to say how many times this happened but I would say about twenty times.'[345]

From his initial tentative claims about two or three minor indecent assaults, Mark Humphreys was now, a mere two months later, claiming to be the victim of a horrific series of serious sexual assaults extending over three years. It seems quite clear that one key factor in the development of his allegations was Nelson himself and the various meetings and interviews he had with him. But there appears also to have been another factor. Ever since the publication of Nelson's *Independent on Sunday* article on 1 December 1991, the police had been cooperating with the NSPCC helpline, which was under the direction of Viv Hector (see above, p. 209). Nelson also worked closely with this counselling service. During the Tribunal he said 'I was in contact with Viv Hector throughout my investigation, I took his advice on the handling of witnesses.' He also said that 'all' of his witnesses had been referred to Viv Hector at the helpline. In correspondence between the *Observer* and the Press Complaints Commission, Hector would himself be cited as one of the people who believed Humphreys's allegations. It would be reasonable to infer that these developed in the way that they did partly because of the counselling he received.[346]

One of the problems for Nelson was that neither he nor the NSPCC appear to have made even the most elementary attempt to check the allegations against the record of Humphreys's time in care. Had they done so they would have discovered that the allegations could not possibly be true. Since Humphreys's circumcision operation had taken place on 27 January 1981, and since he had left Bryn Estyn in August of that year, it is clear that he was not even at Bryn Estyn for most of the three years he claimed he was being sexually assaulted there by Howarth.

It was only when Mark Humphreys was interviewed by the police again, on 28 November, and informed of the actual dates of his stay at Bryn Estyn, that the impossibility of the events he alleged became – or should have become – clear. By this time, however, so many people (including, it would seem, some police officers) had invested belief in Humphreys's claims that the incidents he described had taken on a kind of reality. So much so, indeed, that it seems likely that Humphreys, with the help of the counselling he had received, had come to believe, or half-believe, in them himself.

Dean Nelson appears to have been drawn into this delusory world. An inexperienced journalist who had been sent unprepared on an extremely difficult assignment, he had already been lured into a series of catastrophic misjudgments. As a result he had created a story which had become so powerful, and so potentially destructive of his own reputation, that he seems to have been unable to assess it objectively. He had not only lost the ability to judge between what was true and what was false; he had also, it would seem, been driven to a kind of ethical collapse, where he found it difficult or impossible to judge what was journalistically permissible and what was not.

On a pragmatic level one thing was clear. In view of the many problems associated with the evidence of Mark Humphreys, problems of which Nelson must, at some level, have been aware, it would have been both foolish and dangerous for him to rely on his testimony alone. If the *Independent* was to have any chance of successfully defending a libel action (or if the North Wales Police were to have a realistic chance of prosecuting Anglesea) more evidence was needed. Both professionally and personally Dean Nelson had no option but to pursue more witnesses, and to do so with persistence and determination.

41 Pestered by the press

ONE OF THE INTERESTING FEATURES of Nelson's encounter with Mark Humphreys was that, although previously many of his key witnesses had been discovered through Alison Taylor, she appears to have played no role in his dealings with Humphreys. This does not mean, though, that she remained unaware of what was happening. In June 1992, shortly after his first interview with Humphreys, Nelson wrote to Taylor seeking any information she might have about a number of former residents of Bryn Estyn whom he named. The copy of the letter which Taylor submitted to the Tribunal was annotated in her hand with the following comment: 'Dean stated the *Independent* is in possession of a statement from a boy formerly in care relating to sexual assault by Anglesea and attempts are being made to secure one other such statement before publishing the story.'[347]

Although Alison Taylor would not be involved directly in this attempt to obtain a second statement, her working relationship with Dean Nelson was by no means over. Indeed, before long she would play a central role in one of the most extraordinary episodes in the entire Anglesea story. For the time being, however, it would appear that Nelson continued to investigate on his own. The direction in which his quest for more allegations against Anglesea now led him was indicated in another annotation on the letter he had sent to Taylor. She had written down not only the name Mark Humphreys, but also a second name – Lee Steward.

When Lee Steward made his first statement to the police, alleging that he had been hit by Nefyn Dodd and indecently assaulted by Peter Howarth, he was 29 years old. He had been born on Christmas day 1962. During a troubled and insecure childhood as one of eight children, he frequently had problems with his father who was an alcoholic and who, he told the Tribunal, used to beat him up regularly. On two occasions the NSPCC became involved with the family. In 1975 he was made the subject of a supervision order by the courts and had to report regularly to the probation service. In July 1977, at the age of 14½, he was placed under a care order. After spending the first two months at an assessment centre, Bersham Hall, he was sent to Bryn Estyn where he spent twenty months, from 27 September 1977 until 22 May 1979. When he left Bryn Estyn at the age of 16½ he remained subject to a care order, living at first in approved lodgings. In August he was sent back to a home – Chevet Hey – from where in October he was sent to a Detention Centre for two months. After this he was in various lodgings, spent time at Risley remand centre, and Neath Farm School until his care order finally expired on his eighteenth birthday in 1980.

Intelligent, imaginative and articulate, Lee Steward, through no fault of his own, lived through a troubled adolescence in which crime and punishment were recurrent themes. Evidently his estrangement from his own family had a powerful effect on him. Perhaps more emotionally insecure than many others who were in care with him, he became, as an adolescent, a highly skilled confabulator, who would make up stories both to try to get out of trouble and to excite and sustain the attention of adults. After he had left Bryn Estyn he spent ten days living in the flat of Gary Cooke while Cooke was away. It was Steward who, after being accused of theft by a man who had also stayed there, led the police to the cache of indecent photographs already referred to, one of which showed Mark Humphreys.

After his troubled adolescence Steward appears gradually to have become more confident. In his early twenties he started going out with a nurse, 'Jane', who had looked after him while he had been in hospital. He subsequently obtained a number of good jobs, working as the manager of a fast food restaurant and as a hotel manager. He and Jane married in 1988, and after three years of marriage she gave birth to their first child. Soon after this, however, she became depressed. On 1 April 1992, two days after Steward had given his first statement to the North Wales Police, she committed suicide, leaving her husband to care for their baby daughter.

It was during this particularly difficult period in his life, when he was looking after his three-month-old daughter and had no immediate prospect of employment, that Lee Steward was approached by Dean Nelson.

One of the reasons that Nelson later gave for trying to contact Steward was that he had heard a rumour that he, like Mark Humphreys, had been abused by Gary Cooke. This apparent link between the two former residents of Bryn Estyn seems to have predisposed Nelson to believe that Steward might be able to help him in the same way that Humphreys had.

On Sunday 16 August 1992, two months after he had first made contact with Mark Humphreys, and just two days before Humphreys was due to make his police statement in London, Nelson knocked on the door of Steward's home near Wolverhampton. He got no answer so he put a note through the letter box asking Steward to contact him. With this was a copy of his original *Independent on Sunday* article. The next day Nelson visited his house again. Once again he was unable to get any answer and once again he left a note.

According to Steward, these visits were followed by others during which Nelson had spoken to neighbours and children in an attempt to find out what kind of car Steward drove. On Thursday 20 August Steward phoned the North Wales Police to complain that he was being harassed by Dean Nelson. In a telephone conversation later that day he told Detective Inspector Rowlands that Nelson was trying to get him to say things about Gordon Anglesea, that he wanted him to go on an all expenses paid weekend to London and was offering the protection of a solicitor. On the following Monday Steward made a statement to the police in which he repeated his complaint:

> Since making previous statements to the police regarding the times I spent in care, I have been continually pestered by the press, mainly a man called Dean Nelson who is a reporter working I believe for the Independent Newspaper. Dean Nelson has visited my home on at least six occasions when I have been there myself. He has also called at this house on other occasions and spoken to friends of mine. I would just like to say that on the occasions that he had called at my house I never spoke to him personally. He did push notes through my door. I still have two of them. He has also phoned on numerous occasions to the extent that I have had to change my telephone number. The last time I had contact with him was by telephone, it was on Wednesday the 19th August 1992. During this conversation he said that he would like me to give him more information about Gordon Anglesea [and two other named police officers]. ... He offered me the services of a solicitor and a trip to London, all expenses paid, he then explained to me that police officers and a lad from one of the homes under investigation had been to London the day before and that the lad had made a statement about Gordon Anglesea but he felt he needed a little bit more and asked me if I would do the same.
>
> He explained to me that Gordon Anglesea had something to do with the homes, in particular Bryn Estyn at Wrexham and that he had information that Gordon Anglesea had sexually abused boys at the home, he then asked me if he had sexually abused me. I refused to dis-

cuss this matter with Dean Nelson over the telephone but I would like
to say that at no time did Gordon Anglesea ever sexually abuse me.
Dean Nelson wanted me to go to London today to speak to him
regarding this matter. He did say that I would have the same protection as the other lad, whatever that meant. Dean Nelson has also been
pestering my neighbours in an attempt to verify the fact that I live at
this address, he has also asked neighbours about which vehicle I own.

I have no intention of speaking to him regarding the homes but I
did tell him that if I did make a statement regarding the homes it
would be the truth and not something that he wanted me to say. In
my opinion I felt he wanted me to say things which were not the
truth.[348]

Steward's complaint to the police was a telling one. Although he was
clearly a gifted confabulator, quite capable of making false allegations
against innocent people, his phone call to the police, five months after
his wife's suicide, when he must still have been emotionally vulnerable,
could be construed as a cry for help. It was, perhaps, an attempt to resist
the temptation to make yet more false allegations.

Nelson, however, persisted in his efforts to make contact, and some
days later he persuaded Lee Steward to travel to London to meet him
at his home. As in the case of his initial discussion with Humphreys,
Nelson described this meeting as an 'interview about an interview'.
Once again no record of the meeting has ever been produced.

After arranging another meeting in London for which Steward failed
to appear, Nelson drove to Steward's home on 3 September. As before,
Steward would not come to the door. Instead, he telephoned the police
and spoke to a sergeant who recorded the following message: 'The reason why I've rung is because I am being hassled by Dean Nelson from
the *Independent* newspaper. He is actually parked up outside the house
in his car.'[349]

By the following day, for reasons that have never been explained,
Steward's attitude towards Nelson changed. At this point in his investigation Nelson was still spending time in Wrexham, where he was staying, as he had done before, at the Llwyn Onn Hall Hotel. On 4
September Steward telephoned the journalist at the hotel and they
arranged to meet in a pub in Wrexham. Nelson then returned to the
hotel with him and conducted a two-hour-long interview, the transcript of which occupies more than eighty pages.[350]

By the time he encountered Nelson, Steward had, of course, already
been interviewed by the North Wales Police during their Bryn Estyn

investigation (see above pp. 244–5). After making his first statement to the police in March 1992, he had made a second statement in April. In the first statement he claimed he had been physically abused by three different people, indecently assaulted by two male care workers (Peter Howarth and Stephen Norris), 'seriously abused' by Gary Cooke and said that two women care workers – one of whom had been called Claire – had had sex with him. In his second statement he made more allegations, of a more serious kind. He alleged a new series of indecent assaults by Howarth which had supposedly taken place in the sick-bay, and claimed that Norris had attempted to bugger him. He also claimed that he had been indecently assaulted by a senior care worker at Bersham Hall, and by his social worker during the journey there by car. In short, in his second police statement, he claimed that he had been sexually abused by seven people rather than five.

By the end of his interview with Nelson the number of people against whom Steward alleges sexual assault has risen to nine, while the number against whom he alleges physical assaults has risen from three to eight. At the same time, however, in the four months which have passed since he made his second police statement, it seems clear that the details of some of his allegations have slipped his mind. Interestingly, even though he mentions his social worker by name during the interview with Nelson, he makes no allegation of sexual abuse against him. More significantly still he appears to have forgotten about the allegation he had made against Stephen Norris and makes no complaint about him. Instead, he transposes the allegation he had made against Norris onto Howarth: 'On one occasion he tried to bugger me but, after a struggle, he didn't have much success.' When Nelson asks him for more details, he obliges, saying that it happened in the kitchen and that 'he undone my trousers, pulled my pants down and he tried to bugger me'. Although Steward has already indicated that the attempt failed, Nelson is clearly anxious to obtain a graver allegation than has yet been supplied. He asks: 'How close did he get?' When Steward replies 'Very close', Nelson asks a leading question:

NELSON: Did he get inside you?
STEWARD: Yeah, I would also like to point out at this time that I told the police that he only tried and he never succeeded.
NELSON: You told the police at the time?
STEWARD: No
NELSON: Recently?
STEWARD: Recently.

NELSON: You told them that he didn't succeed?
STEWARD: Yeah.
NELSON: Why?
STEWARD: Because they were such an insensitive lot of sods and my wife was ill at the time.

What appears to have happened in this exchange is that Steward, in response to Nelson's evident quest for a more serious complaint, actually makes use of his leading question to change his allegation in midstream. As he does so he recognises that he is contradicting what he had said to the police before (without apparently remembering that this was about Norris rather than Howarth). In an attempt to explain away the inconsistency, he now makes a complaint about police insensitivity which he has not made before, but which Nelson himself has frequently invoked in similar circumstances, and which he may well have discussed with Steward in the unrecorded 'interview about an interview'. Steward goes on to confirm implicitly that he is now in fact making a complaint of buggery by saying that he had told the police he had been abused but that 'I didn't say I was buggered'.[351]

At a later stage of the interview, in an evident reference to one of their previous unrecorded conversations, Nelson asks 'What about other outsiders, you mentioned a policeman?' This is clearly a cue to introduce the subject of Anglesea and, on this occasion, it is Steward rather than Nelson who is the first to speak his name. Nelson asks what he looked like. After eliciting only a general reply, in which Steward claims incorrectly that Anglesea had 'greyish' hair at the time, Nelson asks specifically 'Did he have any distinguishing features?' Steward then replies, 'Yes I know what you are going to ask me *and I have got to remember where* [italics added]. He certainly had a scar.' After this clear indication of some prior discussion of the point, Nelson attempts to obtain a description of Anglesea's birthmark:

NELSON: Where?
STEWARD: I can't remember you know, not off my head …
NELSON: Was his scar visible?
STEWARD: Hmm.
NELSON: Was it on his arms or part of his body or where?
STEWARD: Can't remember.
NELSON: Above the neck?
STEWARD: Can't remember, up here.

In this exchange, having carefully avoided leading questions and failed to elicit the whereabouts of the 'scar' (which Steward never refers to as a birthmark), Nelson eventually asks a leading question 'Above the neck?' It is at this point that Steward, as he would later confirm to the Tribunal, points to his neck and says 'up here'. The clear implication of the exchange is that Steward has no memory of Anglesea, and that Nelson's attempt to coach his witness into 'remembering' where his prominent birthmark was had failed.[352]

At this point Nelson shows Steward the photograph of Anglesea he had shown to Humphreys and which he may well already have shown to Steward:

STEWARD: That's the shit.
NELSON: Do you know who that is?
STEWARD: He hasn't fucking changed much. Where did you get that from?
NELSON: A newspaper.

The reason Steward is able to exclaim 'He hasn't fucking changed much', is that his description of a man with 'greyish' hair seems to have been based on Anglesea's appearance at the time of his retirement (when the photograph was taken), and not on how he looked thirteen years earlier at the time of his alleged encounter with Steward.

Asked about this encounter, Steward says it took place in an outbuilding in the grounds of Bryn Estyn which used to be the cadet hut. He says that Anglesea 'tried it on with me', by 'touching me up' but that when he had told him to 'fuck off', Anglesea had given him 50p and told him to keep quiet. In response to Nelson's questioning, Steward goes on to describe a second incident. He says that he was walking back to Bryn Estyn one evening when Anglesea pulled up in a car – 'Don't ask me what car because I couldn't fucking tell you' – and offered him a lift. He claims that Anglesea then drove off in the wrong direction and stopped in a lane. He then alleges that Anglesea masturbated him and made him engage in oral sex. When Nelson asks what happened next, he says 'It didn't go much further than that, it just carried on, sort of oral sex.' He claims that this time Anglesea gave him a pound and told him again not to say anything, or he would regret it. Asked when this happened, he says '1977-8', adding that it was at a time of year when the nights were dark.

Five days later, on 9 September 1992, Steward gave another statement to the police, saying that he wanted to tell them the full truth. He then gave yet another version of the incidents with Howarth, claiming that he was buggered twice. This had happened, he said, both on the occasion in the kitchen, and during the earlier encounter in the sick-bay. When he describes the two incidents involving Anglesea, there are significant changes to his story. In the first place the sequence of the incidents is reversed. More strikingly still, no mention is made of being picked up by Anglesea in his car. Instead the entire incident supposedly takes place in one of the sheds 'where they kept all the gardening equipment'. Whereas previously Steward specifically said that there was an act of oral sex which did not go any further, he now claims that he was buggered by Anglesea.

Having altered his second allegation and relocated it in place and time, Steward gives a revised version of the first allegation. This has the same location – the old cadet hut – but instead of describing an unsuccessful advance, he now claims that he was once again subjected to oral sex and buggery, and that he was again given money.

Two days after Steward had made this statement, Nelson conducted another interview with him. Mysteriously, although a transcript (or partial transcript) of this exists, the original tape recording has never been produced. At the libel trial no explanation was offered for the fact that this tape was missing. On the same day the interview was conducted, Steward made an affidavit in which the incident in Anglesea's car *was* described.

The gross inconsistencies between Steward's interview with Nelson and the statement he gave to the police on 9 September were never apparent at the time, for the simple reason that Steward refused to allow the police access to the affidavit he had given to the newspaper. On 17 November 1992 the police would conduct a long interview with Steward which was recorded on audio tape. During this interview he was asked whether he had made an affidavit to the *Independent* about Anglesea. He replied: 'To the *Independent,* no. I made an affidavit, I made a couple of affidavits which the *Independent* has seen, HTV has seen. I have got them and I do not intend, no matter what, any court order will not get me to hand them over.'[353]

During the Tribunal Andrew Caldecott QC, counsel to Anglesea, put it to Steward that he had kept the affidavit and the transcript of his newspaper interview from the police in order to hide the various inconsistencies these would have shown up. A striking feature of Steward's various statements and interviews is that he appears to have an almost photographic memory for car models and colours, and accurately described the cars which had belonged to a number of people fifteen years previously. Yet when he gave an account to Nelson of the incident which had supposedly taken place in Anglesea's car, he was unable to give any description of it and was also apparently acutely conscious of this omission – 'Don't ask me what car because I couldn't fucking tell you.' Caldecott suggested that it may have been for this reason that he did not repeat the allegation to the police. Had the interview and the affidavit been available to the police, he pointed out, they would have been made aware both of the allegation about the car and of the fact that Steward had been unable to 'recognise [Anglesea's birthmark] or remember it … until Dean Nelson told you where it was'.[354]

When Steward's refusal to release the newspaper documents is viewed in relation to the manifold inconsistencies these would have revealed, the case for doubting his claims seems almost complete. It is made almost unassailable when seen alongside his own declaration to the police on 24 August, that 'at no time did Gordon Anglesea ever sexually abuse me', and his suggestion that Dean Nelson 'wanted me to say things which were not the truth'.

However, there was another important feature of the evidence which concerned the question of dates. Lee Steward had been at Bryn Estyn from 27 September 1977 until 22 May 1979. In his interview with Nelson he specifically said that Anglesea had abused him in '1977-78'; he told the police that the first incident had taken place in 'late 1977' and that the second incident was 'a few months later'.

Yet the first connection Gordon Anglesea had with Bryn Estyn was when he was asked to set up the Home Office-run Wrexham attendance centre in September 1979. This was a centre to which delinquent young boys were sent for two hours at a time, for a maximum of 24 hours. Some of these boys were from Bryn Estyn. It was not until mid-November 1979 that Anglesea had first gone to Bryn Estyn itself, and it was not until September 1980 that Bryn Estyn became part of his 'section' within his duties as the operational inspector at Wrexham. In short Anglesea did not have any connection with Bryn Estyn until four months after Steward had left, and did not visit it until some two years after the date Steward gave for the first alleged incident.[355]

As in the case of Mark Humphreys, the allegations which Lee Steward made against Gordon Anglesea could not possibly be true. What all the evidence suggests is that they had been fabricated in response to pressure from Dean Nelson.

Some of the inconsistencies in Steward's evidence were, or should have been, plainly visible to Nelson himself. Others could have been uncovered by patient research. However, it would appear that no such research was undertaken. Nelson's willingness to accept Steward's testimony without making any attempt to seek out the facts which might have disproved it, was perhaps merely another sign of the journalist's increasing desperation.

If his treatment of Humphreys and Steward showed a lack of judgment, however, the nature of the approach he would make to his next witness was even more remarkable.

42 A memory prompt

WHEN NELSON CONTACTED ALISON TAYLOR in June 1992, he said to her that he was seeking just one more allegation against Anglesea before publishing a story. Although he had now reached this goal he appears to have felt misgivings about proceeding purely on the basis of what Humphreys and Steward had told him. Or he may simply have been unable to resist the prospect of recruiting another witness.

One day in September, probably soon after he had interviewed Lee Steward at the Llwyn Onn Hall Hotel where he was staying, Nelson made a telephone call to Alison Taylor in Bangor. He explained that he needed her help because he wanted to interview a Bryn Estyn resident they had both spoken to on an earlier occasion – Simon Birley.[356]

Nelson wanted to track down Birley and interview him for exactly the same reason he had recently been talking to Humphreys and Steward. Indeed, during the Tribunal, Taylor herself confirmed that the journalist's main aim that day had been to find evidence to substantiate the libel against Gordon Anglesea.[357]

Taylor, as might have been expected, responded positively to Nelson's request for help. On the agreed day she left her small terraced house in Bangor and made her way to the railway station. From there she travelled along the coastal line that leads through Gwynedd, past the headquarters of the North Wales Police at Colwyn Bay, to Chester. There she was met by Dean Nelson and together they drove to Wrexham. He explained to her that the *Independent* was being sued by Gordon Anglesea and she recalls that he was 'very edgy'.[358]

The attempt to locate Birley proved difficult and in the end they failed to find him. Given that Birley was highly suggestible, and had already responded to the joint influence of Nelson and Taylor, it is difficult not to reflect on what might have happened if they had succeeded in tracing him. He could very well have become the third former resident of Bryn Estyn to make grave sexual allegations against Gordon Anglesea.

Nelson and Taylor, however, did not abandon their quest for another witness. After their fruitless search for Birley, they decided to try another possibility. Having threaded their way through the Queen's Park Estate to an area known as The Dunks, they drew up outside a small council house. Leaving Alison Taylor in the car, Nelson went inside and began a discussion with another young man he had already interviewed – Peter Wynne.[359]

The visit might never have become known to anyone but for the fact that, months later, in January 1993, the police went to see Wynne to ask him about another aspect of the Bryn Estyn investigation. The story of Nelson's visit had then come out and was recorded in a statement. According to the account Wynne gave to the police, Nelson had begun his visit by explaining that Alison Taylor was in the car outside. He asked Wynne whether he would mind if she came in. Wynne said that he had no objection. Once Taylor had joined them, Nelson told Wynne that he had already found two or three people who said Inspector Anglesea had sexually abused them. He did not give their names, but said they had each signed affidavits and that he only needed one more person to be able to make a case against Anglesea. In Wynne's view it was obvious that Nelson wanted him to be the third person. He said the journalist told him that somebody had given him information that Anglesea had sexually abused him [Wynne] while he had been at Bryn Estyn. Nelson would not say, however, who his informant was. At this point, according to Wynne, Alison Taylor joined in the conversation and said that, while she had been working at Bryn Estyn, he – Peter – had been glue-sniffing down by the bank and that he had told her that he had been buggered by Peter Howarth and that Inspector Anglesea had also been involved.

When Wynne related the story of Nelson's visit to the police, he told them clearly that Taylor's suggestion was not true. Although he continued to maintain that he had been indecently assaulted by Howarth, he said he had not been buggered by him. So far as Anglesea was concerned, he knew who he was since he used to visit Bryn Estyn on occasions, but he had never spoken to him, and never had anything to do with him.[360]

If Wynne's account was accurate, it had very serious implications. The full gravity of what Wynne was saying only became clear when it was placed alongside what Taylor had said to the police on earlier occasions. In December 1991 she had given them a statement which referred specifically to Peter Wynne, in which she described a glue-sniffing incident and had claimed that he had told her that 'Peter Howarth fucks our arses'.[361] Neither in this statement nor in her dossier, however, was there any suggestion that Wynne had made an allegation against Anglesea. On the same day she had made the statement about Wynne, Taylor also made another statement about various police officers. In this statement she had specifically said that she had no complaint to make about Anglesea. It appeared to follow that, if she had indeed suggested to Wynne that he had made a complaint about Anglesea to her that day on the bank, then her suggestion was false.

That the North Wales Police thought this might be the case became clear on 11 February 1993, when, a month after Wynne had given his account of the visit, they interviewed Alison Taylor under caution on suspicion of attempting to pervert the course of justice. Asked whether she had visited Peter Wynne, she replied, having been given advice by her solicitor: 'No, you can't ask me if I have visited Peter Wynne, you can't ask me who I visit.' When asked again whether she had spoken to Wynne with Dean Nelson, she replied: 'Was that an offence?' She implicitly admitted that she had visited Wynne with Nelson, but denied that she had said anything about Anglesea. She went on to deny that Dean Nelson had said anything about Anglesea either. Asked what the purpose of the visit was, if Anglesea was not discussed, she said this was not relevant. Pressed again to describe the purpose of the visit, she said she was not prepared to answer this question. The interview, which Taylor had attended on a voluntary basis, and during which her solicitor intervened repeatedly and robustly on her behalf, then ended.[362]

Dean Nelson was not interviewed about this meeting until June 1993. He initially said that he was unable to recall for certain if or when he met Wynne with Taylor, but later added that he had 'a vague recollection of meeting Wynne at his home with Taylor'. But, far from denying that he had spoken to Wynne about Anglesea, Nelson implicitly confirmed that any interview with Wynne would have been about this topic: 'During my investigation I gained the impression Peter Wynne may have been abused to a greater extent than he told me. ... At this stage my enquiry was directed towards Gordon Anglesea, and the Howarth aspect was complete and an article published.' He said that he was unable to remember details of any meeting which may have taken place, but conceded that Taylor may have raised the subject of an allegation against Anglesea. He did so in terms which clearly implied that the meeting *had* taken place: 'I am not now able to recall any conversation and do not have any notes of what was said. I do however recall that he did not say anything new. I do not recall Taylor indicating to

Wynne that he had claimed to have been abused by Anglesea to her *but that does not mean that it was not said*' [italics added].[363]

One significant feature of Nelson's statement is that, having written it out initially, he had second thoughts and, after consulting a lawyer, deleted the following passage: 'The purpose in Taylor being present was that she felt that Wynne may reveal some further abuse if she acted as a memory prompt.' Asked during the Tribunal to explain this sentence, Nelson replied: 'Yes, I think that it would probably be fair that she thought that.' After reflecting on his own answer he then said: 'she thought simply by being there [she] might bring back some memories, and we were talking about something that happened a very long time ago. We are also talking about a subject matter that people often try to suppress.'[364]

The term 'memory prompt', however, implied that Taylor had come to the interview not as a silent presence, but in order that she might actively prompt Wynne to recall abuse he had supposedly forgotten. It was presumably because of the incriminating nature of these words that Nelson struck them out.

The further implication of Nelson's statement was that when Taylor, during her interview with the police, had denied that Anglesea had been mentioned during the visit, she was not telling the truth. In support of this view it is possible to invoke not only the testimony of Peter Wynne but that of Taylor herself. For when Taylor gave evidence to the Tribunal, four years after her police interview, she gave a quite different account of what had happened. Cross-examined by Benjamin Hinchliff, counsel for Anglesea, she accepted that Nelson had been concentrating on obtaining information about Anglesea, with a view to defending the libel action. She then specifically said that when she had joined Nelson in Peter Wynne's home after waiting in the car outside, Nelson was asking Wynne questions about Anglesea.[365] She went on to give a more detailed account of the conversation she said was taking place:

> He was asking him about, well, about Bryn Estyn, about Peter Howarth and Gordon Anglesea and he asked him if he had ever seen Gordon Anglesea at Bryn Estyn and Peter said, 'Yes.' He had seen him sort of several times, including at Christmas, I'm not sure whether it was Christmas lunches or pre-Christmas parties and Peter also said he was fairly sure there were photographs of the parties where Gordon Anglesea was seated between Peter Howarth and, I think, Len Stritch, I think he said.[366]

In the Tribunal, Taylor was reminded that, when she had been interviewed by the police, she had said specifically that the subject of Gordon Anglesea was not raised. Hinchliff now asked Taylor a simple question: 'Were you lying to the police or are you lying to this Tribunal?'[367]

Taylor replied that she wasn't lying on either occasion and attempted to divert further cross-examination on the point by suggesting that the transcript of the police interview was inaccurate. The most intriguing question, however, is why she had contradicted her own evidence so flagrantly and in a manner which left her exposed to fierce cross-examination of this kind. The answer may perhaps be found in another change of testimony, that of Dean Nelson. For when, in January 1998, Nelson submitted a statement to the Tribunal shortly before he was due to give evidence, the account he gave of the interview with Wynne was quite different from what he had told the police five years earlier. Whereas in his 1993 statement he had clearly said that he had no recollection of the conversation which took place, and that no note had been taken of it, he now said this: 'my recollection, *confirmed by a transcript of a tape recording of that interview*, annexed at Appendix 3, is that neither Alison Taylor nor myself put it to Peter Wynne that Gordon Anglesea was involved in sexual abuse' [italics added].

This testimony is significant, not least because the transcript which Nelson now produced was not in fact a transcript of the September interview at all. It was the faxed transcript of the earlier interview with Wynne in February (see above, p. 251). For reasons which perhaps only Nelson himself could explain, he was presenting to the Tribunal as a faithful record of the September 1992 interview a transcript of his February 1992 interview with Wynne, in which Taylor had not been involved.

During his Tribunal evidence Dean Nelson, while being examined by his own counsel, was placed in the position where he had no option but to confirm this:

ROBIN OPPENHEIM: The reason I am showing you this document is that you see on 4th February 1992, you saw Mr Wynne again?
NELSON: Yes.
OPPENHEIM: Having seen him previously and you will see in the two columns as a 'yes' and a 'yes and that refers to notes and tapes. Now, what I am going to suggest to you is that the transcript of the interview that we have at page 32 to 33 of the main bundle [presented as a transcript of the September 1992 meeting], relates to that [February]

meeting? ... Would that be probably right? ...
NELSON: Yes.[368]

The implications of this exchange appear not to have been noticed by any of the other barristers present.

It may or may not be a coincidence that, when Alison Taylor was asked at the Tribunal to say what Nelson had been discussing with Wynne when she had joined them, the answer she gave (see above) reflected some of the contents of this same transcript. For it was in the February interview that Nelson had established that Peter Wynne knew Anglesea as a visitor to Bryn Estyn and that he sometimes came there for the annual Christmas dinner. Since Taylor appeared at the Tribunal some months *before* Nelson did, it would seem either that some of the same ground was covered in the second interview as in the first, or that Taylor had foreknowledge of what Nelson was going to say and changed her own evidence accordingly. The evidence given to the Tribunal by both Nelson and Taylor was clearly misleading. Exactly how they came to mislead the Tribunal in this manner cannot now be determined.

What can be said is that, since there is no reason to believe the account Taylor gave in her police interview of what Nelson had said to Wynne, there is also no reason to believe her parallel claim that she did not herself discuss Anglesea. Indeed, it seems likely that the account which Peter Wynne gave to the police was substantially correct. If so, Alison Taylor had deliberately attempted to prompt him into making a grave allegation against Anglesea, by falsely claiming to recall a conversation which had never taken place.

The attempt, if it was made, did not succeed. Since Nelson and Taylor could see no real prospect of finding Simon Birley, who had been the original object of their quest that day, Nelson was left with the two witnesses he had already managed to track down – Mark Humphreys and Lee Steward.

Even with only two witnesses to support it, however, the case against Anglesea which Nelson had now put together was far more than a defence to a libel action. It was, potentially at least, a sensational story in its own right. His task now was to find a newspaper willing to publish it.

43 Lies and libels

WHEN DEAN NELSON AGREED to go back to North Wales in 1992, he did so, according to his own account, on the understanding that if he found evidence against Anglesea, the *Independent on Sunday* would print the story. Nelson himself would tell the Tribunal: 'I agreed to investigate further on the condition that we would publish any further information we obtained.' When, on Friday 11 September, he accompanied Lee Steward to Steward's solicitor so that he could swear the affidavit which had been prepared for him, a copy had already been sent to the news editor at the *Independent*. It was Nelson's fervent hope that when the new affidavit was placed alongside the evidence already provided by Mark Humphreys, the case for publishing the story would prove irresistible: 'With two affidavits on Anglesea we had enough evidence for the *Independent on Sunday* to defend the libel action, but according to my deal ... we also had enough to publish the story and expose him in the newspaper.'[369]

It was with this prospect in mind that Nelson set off to drive back along the M6 from Steward's solicitor's office in Telford, Shropshire, to the offices of the *Independent* in London. While he was driving his mobile phone rang. It was a message from the newspaper to say that the editor, Ian Jack, having considered the material Nelson had submitted, had decided not to run the story on the grounds that it might compound the libel against Gordon Anglesea.

It was Friday afternoon. With the *Independent on Sunday* running close to its Saturday deadline, it might have seemed that there was no hope of placing the story in another newspaper that weekend. Yet, perhaps because he was high on the adrenalin of a sensational story, Nelson appears to have been determined to attempt the seemingly impossible – to sell the story to the *Independent on Sunday*'s main rival – the *Observer*.

To persuade another newspaper to accept a story with such grave implications on the very eve of its publication deadline would have been virtually impossible but for one crucial factor. The *Observer* had already, only two weeks earlier, begun to publish stories about the

North Wales scandal. On 30 August it had printed a story under the headline '"200 VICTIMS" IN HUGE CHILD ABUSE INQUIRY', which related how Alison Taylor had been sacked in 1987 after trying to draw allegations to the attention of her superiors. The story, which noted that Taylor had 'now revealed details of her allegations', had been brought to the *Observer* by freelance journalist Brian Johnson-Thomas and rewritten by the *Observer* home affairs editor, David Rose.

The following week, on 6 September, a front-page story which approached even more closely the subject-matter of Nelson's most recent investigations appeared under the headline 'POLICE NAMED AS SUSPECTS IN SCANDAL OF CHILD ABUSE'. The story, whose substance had once again been supplied by Johnson-Thomas, dealt not with Anglesea but with serving officers: 'The officers, of junior rank, serve at different stations, including Wrexham and Holyhead. Det Supt Peter Ackerley, leading the inquiry, last night disclosed that a file on one officer had been sent to the Crown Prosecution Service.'[370]

The officer whose file had been referred to the CPS apparently served in Gwynedd and had become a suspect partly because of allegations of physical abuse made during the HTV programme of 26 September 1991 – the programme which featured Alison Taylor. In due course it emerged that the complaint against this officer was without substance. At least one of the other officers referred to had become a 'suspect' as a result of complaints made by Lee Steward.

The rest of the article was largely based on material from Taylor's 'Gwynedd County Council Analysis' or on sources she had cultivated. It claimed that 'one of the most shocking aspects of the emerging scandal is the fact that equally serious allegations were made years ago, and ignored by police and local authorities'. It then cited, without naming him, Peter Harbour's 1986 complaint, quoting verbatim from the aide-memoire Taylor had prepared for him at the time (see pp. 51–2).[371]

Whether it was purely coincidental that Alison Taylor, at a time when she was continuing to co-operate with Dean Nelson, had allowed crucial information to come into the hands of another freelance journalist, remains unclear. It was undoubtedly the case, however, that the two stories which had already appeared in the *Observer* had created the ideal journalistic context for Nelson, having been rejected by his own editor, to take his story to the *Independent on Sunday*'s rival.

Nelson's intermediary was David Connett, the staff journalist on the *Independent* who had brought him the story in the first place almost a year earlier. Connett knew David Rose of the *Observer* and, on the evening of Friday 11 September, he phoned him to offer him, at the very last minute, a sensational lead story for Sunday's newspaper.

Rose could immediately see that the story was a dangerous one in that, if the testimony of Mark Humphreys and Lee Steward turned out to be unreliable, it would be libellous. In journalistic terms, however, it was attractive. Above all, the approach from Connett offered the *Observer* an opportunity to take over from the *Independent on Sunday* what appeared to be an extremely important story.

Rose set out to check the story by making a series of calls to North Wales. He contacted not only Dennis Parry and Malcolm King but also John Marek, Labour MP for Wrexham, and Martyn Jones, the MP for the neighbouring constituency, Clwyd South West. Marek said he thought the allegations should be investigated by an outside police force. Inclining, like many local politicians, to the paedophile ring theory, he told Rose that 'the facts which are now emerging look every day more like a major conspiracy in Gwynedd and Clwyd'. Martyn Jones said that the alleged involvement of senior police officers would not help victims to speak out: 'If they've been abused by a policeman, they won't come forward to the same police force.'

Rose also spoke to a number of police officers, including John Tecwyn Owen, the deputy chief constable of North Wales. Owen confirmed that there had been allegations against both former and serving colleagues and that these had led him to seek advice from the Police Complaints Authority.

The soundings which Rose took from local councillors, members of parliament and the North Wales Police themselves, all seemed to strengthen the case for publishing. What Rose could not have known at the time was that, by talking to these sources, he was effectively seeking confirmation from an echo-chamber which Taylor and Nelson had themselves created.

Although Rose played a key role, the ultimate decision to run the story was taken by the editorial team in consultation with lawyers. Looking back on what happened that weekend, Rose now deeply regrets his own actions because of the damage the story did. 'The whole thing,' he says, 'was done in a dangerous rush. I think we all at the *Observer* got carried away with the idea of getting one over the *Independent on Sunday*, which at that stage was breathing down the *Observer*'s neck in terms of circulation. A story like that should have been given much more time. The fatal thing is that we didn't speak to anyone from the other side.'[372]

Although the decision to go ahead had been taken in principle, the story had still not been written. Saturday morning saw two journalists from a rival newspaper, Dean Nelson and David Connett, sitting beside the home affairs editor of the *Observer* as all three worked together to produce a publishable piece. Although the original intention had been to name Anglesea, the story which was printed refrained from doing so. Since Nelson and Connett could not be credited, the story was attributed to Brian Johnson-Thomas and David Rose. It appeared under the six-column front-page headline 'ABUSE VICTIMS ACCUSE POLICE':

> A former police chief has been named as a prime suspect in the North Wales child sexual abuse scandal, police sources in the region confirmed last night.
>
> Inquiries by the *Observer* suggest that the scandal – which detectives now believe involves half a dozen serving and retired police officers and more than 300 child victims – dwarfs in horror all previous cases of this kind. Local MPs are calling for an outside force to take over the investigation.
>
> The ex-police chief is due to be questioned this week as evidence emerges that staff in some children's homes in North Wales 'lent' children to convicted paedophiles for weekends.[373]

Even though he was not named, Gordon Anglesea would be immediately identifiable by anyone in North Wales who had followed the story from the beginning. The article went on to relate Steward's claim that he had arrived at Bryn Estyn only to be threatened and abused by members of staff, and that he had subsequently been buggered and forced to submit to oral sex by the police chief. It also included his claim that he had been taken to a flat by Gary Cooke and another man and that while they sexually abused him, they had shown him photographs of other adolescents being buggered. Steward was quoted as saying that later he had broken into Cooke's flat, stolen the photographs and taken them to the police: 'I was arrested for breaking and entering and held in a cell for several hours.'

Every detail in this latter claim was untrue. What had in fact happened, as has already been noted, was that, in the summer of 1979, Steward had stayed in Cooke's flat while Cooke had been away on holiday. One night Thomas Kenyon, the 'drop out' son of Lord Kenyon, had also stayed in the flat and had subsequently reported to the police that his watch, a pair of jeans and a five-pound note had been stolen. Steward was questioned by the police and admitted some of the thefts.

It was in an apparent attempt to mitigate these offences that he took the police to the flat and showed them the cache of photographs. His claim that he had broken into the flat and had subsequently been arrested for doing so was a fabrication. Although Kenyon initially said that he had sexual relations with Steward, who was then sixteen, Steward had denied this and Kenyon subsequently withdrew the claim, saying that he must have imagined it. Because Steward had made no complaint, no charges were brought against Kenyon.

In the article Steward's claims about Gary Cooke and the 'police chief' were placed alongside claims by Mark Humphreys, who was referred to as Glyn – 'a children's home inmate who asked not to have his true identity revealed'. Glyn was also said to have been raped by the police chief. The article was illustrated by photographs of Steward, of Bryn Estyn itself, and of Ryan Tanner, even though the latter played no part in the published story.

The article, printed across the front page under a quote from Malcolm King, 'We are looking at the biggest failure to protect children in British history', was finally approved for publication on Saturday evening. Once again a story which would have devastating implications for Gordon Anglesea, and for the newspaper which published it, was transmitted electronically to a number of different print sites and once again the presses started, irrevocably, to roll.

By the time copies of the *Observer* appeared in newsagents on Sunday morning, however, preparations for an even more direct and explicit television programme about the same allegations were already well advanced. David Williams, the reporter who had worked with Alison Taylor on the HTV programme about Tŷ'r Felin the previous year, now played a role in putting together a programme about Gordon Anglesea. In the programme both Lee Steward and Mark Humphreys would make their allegations in person.

If there were any residual doubts about the wisdom of broadcasting such a programme then it would seem that these were dispelled by the appearance of the *Observer's* story on 13 September. The following Thursday, HTV broadcast to a large part of Wales, including the area in which Gordon Anglesea lived, one of the most sensational programmes it had ever shown. Perhaps because the *Observer* had already referred to the police chief in terms which made him readily identifiable, the HTV journalists decided to go one stage further and name him. The presenter began by linking the new allegations to the ones which had already been broadcast by HTV:

In tonight's programme we examine shocking allegations that a senior
police officer in North Wales sexually abused children in care. We'll be
hearing from the two people who say they were assaulted by him and
we confront the man himself, Gordon Anglesea, who retired from the
force last year with the rank of superintendent.

The allegations made against him are contained in sworn statements
now in the possession of the police and they add to the growing and
frightening list of incidents of physical and sexual assaults on children
placed in care in homes throughout North Wales. Allegations are now
coming to light almost daily, but the roots of what is now a national
scandal go back to the late 1970s.

Twelve months ago, 'Wales This Week' broadcast an investigation
into the allegations of serious physical abuse in a number of homes in
North Wales. As a result of that programme, Gwynedd Social Services
called in the police who launched an investigation which has now
become part of the biggest enquiry into child abuse in Britain. In the
last week it has emerged that former police officers have been named
by victims. Several former child care officers in Clwyd have already
been convicted of sexual offences against children in care and others
are awaiting trial on similar charges.

The two people making allegations against Gordon Anglesea have
taken what is to them the unprecedented step of talking publicly about
what happened. One, because he feels so ashamed, prefers to remain
anonymous, the other has decided to reveal his identity. Both have
vivid recollections of the former police officer who sexually abused
them.[374]

The camera now cut to the silhouette of Mark Humphreys who had
been filmed in shadow. Although it is reasonably clear that Humphreys
had no memory of Anglesea when Dean Nelson first showed him the
photograph, he now seemed utterly sincere when he said: 'It's never
gonna come out of my mind. It is always gonna be there. I can see his
face and I can see him.'

The clip of Humphreys was immediately followed by film of Steward, who was fully lit and identified by his real name: 'He would use his
authority, you know, he would say once he had finished with you sort
of thing, he would sort of say, um, just remember who I am. You know,
so that you got the message that you couldn't go to anybody. To us he
was the police.'

After the presenter had repeated that the man accused of sexual
abuse was retired police superintendent Gordon Anglesea, the film cut
to a shot of Anglesea standing in the garden of his home. Asked to

respond to the allegations, he said that for legal reasons he could not do so but that he would refer all enquiries to his solicitor, John Hughes: 'He will make any statement deemed necessary, which will include, I am quite certain, an absolute and categorical denial of any such allegations.'

The thirty-minute programme went on to show Humphreys and Steward making their allegations of buggery and forced oral sex to the camera, sometimes in graphic detail. After a brief interview with Wrexham MP John Marek, who repeated his call for an outside force to take over the investigation, and after further shots of Gordon Anglesea, the programme ended, as it had begun, by showing the silhouetted form of Mark Humphreys: 'They ruined my fucking life to be honest with you, you know. I would just like to look him in the face and say "Why? Why? Why?"'

Gordon Anglesea and his wife Sandra watched the programme together in the sitting room of their seaside home in North Wales. Earlier that week they had already had to face the explicit allegations in the *Observer* in the knowledge that, although he had not been named, Gordon Anglesea would have been readily identifiable to neighbours and friends. The effect which the programme had on him is something he would describe in the evidence he gave in the libel trial which would ensue (see below, Chapter 56). Giving evidence then, Sandra Anglesea would describe how her husband looked the next morning: 'He had physically aged by about ten years, grey and gaunt. I have never seen a change in a person overnight to that extent.'

The HTV programme, however, did not mark the end of Gordon Anglesea's trial at the hands of the media. In the next two weeks the *Observer* would follow its sensational scoop with two further stories. On the following Sunday it ran another story about Steward and Bryn Estyn, revealing that he had now made a second affidavit in which he claimed 'he was raped at the home by another man who was the son of a prominent Welsh freemason who had formal connections with the police authority'. This was a reference to the incident involving Thomas Kenyon which had taken place, of course, not at Bryn Estyn but in Cooke's flat, and in relation to which no allegation of rape had previously been made. Kenyon's father, Lord Kenyon, had at one time been a magistrate and a member of the police authority. He was also a Provincial Grand Master of the Masons and in that capacity had argued against a North Wales Police order suggesting that any officers who were masons should consider withdrawing from the society. Although this disagreement had nothing to do with any case of alleged child abuse, it was now construed in a sinister light. The veiled implication of the *Observer's* story, which repeated the allegation against the 'police chief', was that Gordon Anglesea (who was also a mason) was linked to Kenyon and that both were part of a shadowy masonic conspiracy which, through its influence over the North Wales Police, had contrived to cover up grave acts of sexual abuse.

On the same day that this *Observer* report appeared, Alison Taylor wrote a letter to John Marek MP in which she developed this idea. 'I have been informed,' she wrote, 'that Superintendent Anglesea was not only supervising the 1986 investigation, but that he was also close to officers currently investigating allegations of abuse.' Since she knew full well that the 1986 investigation had been conducted by DCS Gwynne Owen, Taylor was now making the remarkable claim, which she must have known or suspected to be false, that the head of the North Wales CID had at the time been supervised by a uniformed officer who was junior to him.[375]

In the following Sunday's *Observer* the extent of the supposed conspiracy was enlarged still further. Having claimed on 6 September that four policemen were suspected of child abuse in North Wales, and on 13 September that six were, the paper now, on 27 September, ran a brief story (again by Brian Johnson-Thomas) under the heading 'PAE-DOPHILE RING "INCLUDES 12 POLICE"'. In the story which followed, the claim about the 'police chief' was repeated.

The HTV programme and the three stories in the *Observer*, however, were not the only libels occasioned by the interviews which Nelson had conducted with Humphreys and Steward. Another publication was about to join the pursuit of Anglesea. Partly because it was supposed to be an anti-establishment magazine, fearless in the pursuit of truth, its decision to take up the story would prove to be, in the long term, highly significant.

44 *Private Eye* and the Kincora legacy

ONE ASPECT OF THE NORTH WALES STORY which had a particular appeal to some journalists was the idea that a masonic conspiracy was helping to protect a paedophile ring. In this ring, care workers supposedly supplied children to paedophiles, who included policemen, local politicians and celebrities. This idea was a fantasy. Practically every element of it, however, had been present in an earlier scandal about a children's home – the Kincora working boys' hostel in East Belfast.

When the Kincora scandal had erupted in 1980, it was as the result of an article in a Dublin newspaper which claimed that there had been 'an official cover-up over the recruiting of boys at a Belfast children's home for homosexual prostitution'.[376] This led almost immediately to what was, perhaps, the first police trawling operation ever mounted in the British Isles. More than a hundred current or former residents of Kincora were interviewed by the Royal Ulster Constabulary, and some thirty of these made allegations of sexual abuse against one or other of the three members of staff at the home. Two of these men almost immediately admitted guilt in respect of some of the allegations.

In media coverage of the scandal it was repeatedly claimed that Kincora had been the centre of a paedophile ring in which boys had been supplied to other men outside the home, who included police officers, members of the security service, civil servants and Loyalist politicians. It was further claimed that this scandal had been covered up by the English establishment because one of the three men accused, William McGrath, had been an agent of MI5. The security services were supposedly intent on using Kincora to 'destroy' Ian Paisley.[376a]

Kincora and its implications continued to reverberate through the halls of British and Irish power for more than a decade. The facts of what happened may never be determined, though it does seem clear that some of the allegations were well-founded, and that there had been a refusal to investigate on the part of officialdom. McGrath, who protested his innocence almost to the end, had indeed been an intelligence agent. It is clear, however, that there was never any reliable evidence to support claims that boys had been 'lent' to people outside the home.

The journalist who has written the most substantial book about Kincora, former BBC reporter Chris Moore, has confirmed this. Although Moore is credulous in a number of respects, accepting at face-value almost all the allegations of sexual abuse which were made, he firmly repudiates the most sensational elements of the Kincora story at the very outset of his book:

> Since 1980 the name Kincora has been associated in the public mind with homosexual abuse of young men in care, but because of the nature of the media coverage of the story and some wild speculation about the events at Kincora there have been many misconceptions. For example, the word 'prostitution' has been used in relation to the abuses at the hostel in East Belfast but it is quite clear from the evidence of former residents that this allegation is without foundation. In statements to the authorities, those abused made allegations only against the three members of staff at Kincora who were subsequently convicted in court. Some made allegations against individuals at other state-run institutions which also resulted in convictions. No one alleged that he was taken to other men for sexual activity or that men came to Kincora to engage in sexual congress with the young men in care there.[377]

By 1992, however, the idea that Kincora had lain at the centre of an extensive paedophile ring had achieved considerable currency. Kincora had been given particular prominence in the pages of *Private Eye* where, under the new editorial regime of Ian Hislop, who took over the editorship in 1986, the investigative journalist, Paul Foot, returned after a long exile.

Foot had a particular interest in the Kincora story, which features in his 1986 book about the former British intelligence officer in Northern Ireland, *Who Framed Colin Wallace?* During the years following the publication of this book he was one of a small number of journalists who constantly raised the Kincora scandal. He was helped to do so by three left-wing Labour MPs, Ken Livingstone, Tam Dalyell and Dale Campbell-Savours who, with the occasional help of Michael Foot, repeatedly raised the matter in parliament.

Behind Paul Foot's interest in Kincora was his socialism and his famously generous disposition towards those who appeared to be victims of the establishment, or who belonged to the class of the disadvantaged or the oppressed. If the working class boys of Kincora had indeed been abused, and their abuse covered up by the intelligence services or the government, they were just the kind of victims who would attract Foot's heartfelt sympathy. But there was also another factor. As Foot's friend and fellow journalist, Nick Cohen, has written:

> Like Orwell and so many other rebellious sons of the establishment, Foot's hatred of the powerful was beaten into him. Even by the standards of England's public schools, Anthony Chenevix-Trench, his housemaster at Shrewsbury, was a flagellomaniac. Foot recalled: 'He would offer his culprit an alternative: four strokes with the cane, which hurt; or six with the strap, with trousers down, which didn't. Sensible boys always chose the strap, despite the humiliation, and Trench, quite unable to control his glee, led the way to an upstairs room, which he locked, before hauling down the miscreant's trousers, lying him face down on a couch and lashing out with a belt.'
>
> Naturally, Chenevix-Trench was promoted and became a headmaster, first of Eton and then of Fettes. Exposing him in *Private Eye* was one of Foot's happiest days in journalism. He received hundreds of congratulatory letters from the child abuser's old pupils, many of whom were now prominent in British life.[378]

Foot's own experience of being physically abused as a public schoolboy appears to have coloured his judgment of every similar allegation. In particular he seems not to have understood that the regimes of the public schools attended by the privileged were sometimes both meaner and emotionally crueller than the community homes attended by working class boys who had been placed in care.

Given Foot's own beliefs and background, and given that the North Wales story appeared to bear many of the hallmarks of Kincora, it was not surprising that *Private Eye* were interested in the claims about Bryn Estyn. What was rather more surprising was that the magazine should have taken a series of extreme claims almost entirely on trust.

Such intuitive journalism had certainly been the hallmark of Richard Ingrams, who had run the magazine, as Adam Raphael has written, 'on hunch, smell and prejudice'. Raphael quotes the view of Jane Ellison, a journalist who once worked for the *Eye*: 'Ingrams has always believed that he has an instinct for the truth of a story however defamatory and however insubstantial in terms of the facts. If it sounds right he will print it ... after a few moments of concentration accompanied by a paroxysm of facial contortion, he would utter the famous reply: "Put it in!"'[379]

On many occasions the Ingrams hunch was right and *Private Eye* enjoyed many notable successes with stories about John Poulson, Jeremy Thorpe and Reginald Maudling. But, as Raphael notes, 'balanced against this were many ill-judged vendettas and exposures of private lives which did nothing to advance the public interest.' Raphael suggests that with the retirement of Ingrams in 1986 the old era passed: 'The new editor, Ian Hislop, is a very different and more cautious character, who reportedly believes in checking his facts rather than trusting his sense of smell.'[380]

These words, however, were written three years before the magazine was approached, in January 1993, by Brian Johnson-Thomas with an updated version of the story about Anglesea. Perhaps because of the influence of Foot, or because similar allegations had already been printed in the *Observer* and broadcast on HTV, Hislop showed remarkably little caution. He seems indeed to have followed the example of his mentor Ingrams and published on the basis of intuition.

The story which *Private Eye* now printed focused on the idea that Anglesea's masonic connections might allow him to escape prosecution, and was printed under the headline 'THE OFF SCOT-FREEMASON?':

> North Wales detectives investigating the alleged involvement of no fewer than 12 serving and former colleagues in the country's biggest ever child sex abuse scandal are running into an unforeseen problem.
>
> The crown prosecution service (CPS) seems reluctant to prosecute anyone for well-documented cases of rape, buggery and indecent assault involving young boys who were in care over a twenty year period.
>
> The reluctance has nothing to do with the involvement of a number of the local great and good, as members of a paedophile ring, which regularly used homes, like the now-closed Bryn Estyn near Wrexham, to supply boys for sex to local celebrities.
>
> In late 1970s, Superintendent Gordon Anglesea of the North Wales Police was appointed to investigate an allegation of buggery made by [Lee Steward] against the son of a then member of the North Wales police authority. The Supt. found there was no case to answer. Coincidentally the police authority member and Supt Anglesea were prominent masons.
>
> Although senior police officers knew five years ago that Anglesea was alleged to have buggered boys in care at Bryn Estyn and that he had also forced them to have oral sex with him on several occasions, he has been enjoying a well-earned retirement.
>
> Even after being named in an *Independent* story over a year ago, featuring on the front page of the *Observer* last September, and being

named in an HTV broadcast, also in September, no action was taken until he 'voluntarily' agreed to an interview last month.

Since no fewer than six of his former colleagues have already been told that the CPS has returned their files marked 'no action', Anglesea is confident that no charges will be forthcoming.[381]

Practically every claim in this story was untrue. Although the North Wales Police were indeed investigating Anglesea, and although unsubstantiated allegations of sexual abuse had been made against three other police officers, the idea that twelve officers were being investigated in relation to sexual abuse was a fantasy.[382]

The claim that the CPS was reluctant to prosecute anyone for 'well documented cases of rape, buggery and indecent assault involving young boys' was also untrue. The only respect in which the claims were 'well documented' was that Humphreys and Steward had, at the behest of Nelson, signed affidavits containing their allegations. All the other documentary evidence, including the Bryn Estyn register, social service records, Steward's early police statements, *and* the transcripts of Nelson's interviews, would have suggested, had they been examined, that the claims made by Humphreys and Steward were false.

Private Eye's next suggestion, that 'a number of the local great and good' were members of a paedophile ring centred on Bryn Estyn was without any foundation. So too was the specific claim that Anglesea had been appointed to investigate a complaint of buggery by Steward. The incident referred to here was the one which had involved Thomas Kenyon. While it is true that Kenyon's complaint of theft against Steward had been investigated by the police in August 1979 and that this in turn led to the discovery of the indecent photographs, Gordon Anglesea had not been involved in any way. Interviewed in October 1992, the detective sergeant who had dealt with the incident at the time said this: 'As regards to ex-Superintendent Anglesea, he was an Inspector at Wrexham at the time of this investigation. He had no connection with this inquiry and took no part in any decision-making in respect of the prosecution of offenders or offences. He was a uniformed officer and would not have even seen the prosecution files which would have been viewed by a Detective Chief Inspector.'[383]

Even more important was that Lee Steward had never made a complaint of buggery. He had told the police that Kenyon had touched him upon the knee, that he had reacted by slapping him on the mouth and that they had slept separately without any sexual contact. Steward's claim that he had made a complaint of buggery at the time was a retrospective invention. The investigation which Anglesea had supposedly led, and whose outcome he had allegedly influenced, had not in fact taken place at all.[384]

It was not true either, as *Private Eye* claimed, that senior officers had known five years previously that there were sexual allegations against Anglesea. No such allegations had been made until Dean Nelson embarked on the second phase of his investigation early in 1992. Nor was it true that the police had taken no action until December 1992. Anglesea had first been interviewed in January 1992, a month after the original *Independent on Sunday* story had appeared.

It would be difficult to imagine any brief piece of journalism in which so many fabrications or fantasies had been presented as facts. Even if the inaccuracies had been restricted to those noted here, the article would have been virtually impossible to defend in any libel action. However, there was another factor which made the predicament of *Private Eye* even more serious. For the piece had another paragraph:

> Meanwhile Lee Steward, one of the few victims prepared to stand up and be counted, was recently beaten up by unknown assailants while visiting the Wrexham home of one Gary Cooke, aka Mark Jones, who was convicted of paedophile offences in 1980 while working in a children's home, convicted of buggery after being re-employed in another children's home after his release in 1986 and who is now working in an old people's home in Llay, near Wrexham.

This paragraph, like the others, contained serious errors. Although Gary Cooke was at one point employed by Bryn Alyn, a privately owned children's home in Wrexham, he was not working there at the time of his conviction in 1980; he was unemployed. Nor, it would appear, did he subsequently work at any other children's home.[385]

However it was not these inaccuracies which caused the greatest difficulty for *Private Eye*. The problem was contained in the claim that Lee Steward had been beaten up 'while visiting the Wrexham home of … Gary Cooke'. From these words it might be inferred that Steward had had a voluntary association with a convicted paedophile. It was because of this single sentence that *Private Eye* would find itself facing not one libel claim but two.

The first claim was from Anglesea. When it became apparent that the case was growing in size and complexity, Anglesea's local solicitor, John Hughes, had advised him to seek out a specialist libel lawyer. He had consulted the Police Federation who agreed to fund his action and gave the case to the libel solicitor Barton Taylor, of the London-based firm Russell, Jones and Walker. Writs were duly issued against the *Observer*, HTV and *Private Eye*.

The second claim for libel came from the very witness on whom *Private Eye* would necessarily have to depend if it was to defend itself successfully against Anglesea's action – Lee Steward.

The amount of money Steward demanded to settle his claim, and the manner in which his request was dealt with, would play a significant role in the libel trial to which *Private Eye*, along with the *Independent on Sunday*, HTV and the *Observer*, would eventually become a party.

45 More coals to Cardiff

THE ALLEGATIONS AGAINST ANGLESEA which Nelson had elicited from Mark Humphreys and Lee Steward would be the main evidence for the defence in the libel trial. But by the time this case came to court there would be another allegation.

Among the people who watched the HTV programme featuring Steward and Humphreys was Carl Holden, who, after Andrew Singer, had been the second man to make an allegation against Howarth, in September 1991.

A few weeks after the broadcast, Holden was visited by a BBC journalist, Debbie Stacey. According to the account he later gave to the police, she specifically asked him about Anglesea but he had not made any allegation against him. However, Holden said she had visited him again 'a couple' of times. In the libel trial, referring by name to another journalist, and not to Stacey, Holden would agree with Anglesea's counsel, Lord Williams,* that he felt the BBC was 'hounding' him in an attempt to get him to say more about Bryn Estyn.

In the end he relented and recorded an interview for television in which he made an allegation against Gordon Anglesea. Early in the new year, on 16 January 1993, he made a statement to the police. He claimed that he had caddied for Howarth at Wrexham golf course several times. On one occasion, when Howarth had been playing golf on his own, a man walked across the course and started talking to him. He said that Howarth had introduced this man as 'Inspector Anglesea', and that he abandoned the game of golf and walked back to the car park. He then drove Holden back to Bryn Estyn and Anglesea followed in his own car. Holden claimed that Howarth had told him to take his golf clubs up to his flat. He said that in the flat Howarth had taken down his (Holden's) jeans and that Anglesea had then started rubbing his penis while Howarth played with his buttocks. Holden said that he had pulled up his trousers and run back to his dormitory. He went on to claim that Anglesea had approached him on two further occasions but

---

* Gareth Williams QC was created a life peer in 1992

that he had told him to 'Fuck off' and he had gone away.

A significant feature of Holden's statement was the manner in which it brought his own role in the Anglesea case into very close correspondence with that of Steward. Having initially made a statement about Bryn Estyn in which he made complaints about Howarth which appeared to be false, he had subsequently talked on a number of occasions to a journalist who was specifically seeking information about Anglesea. In response he had given an entirely new version of events which included allegations against Anglesea.

Also significant was the fact that the incident which Holden described as the context for Anglesea's alleged indecent assault was apparently the same as one which had featured in his original statement about Howarth. For the third and final indecent assault which Holden had alleged against Howarth had also involved a visit to the golf course: 'For a few months [after the second alleged indecent assault by Howarth] Mr Howarth kept away from me until one day he asked me if I would caddy for him. I said I would because I knew I would get money and some perks. We went to the golf club and on our return I took his clubs to his flat. On this occasion Mr Howarth made another advance at me and grabbed my private parts with his hand. I pushed him away and ran out of his flat.'

It was on this occasion that Holden had supposedly made his dramatic escape from Bryn Estyn by jumping off a bridge onto a passing train. Although in both versions of the 'golf-club incident' Holden claimed that he had responded to a sexual advance by running out of Howarth's flat, in his statement about Anglesea he had escaped not to Cardiff but to his dormitory. The entire implausible story about the coal train had simply disappeared.

The only reasonable inference to be drawn from Holden's second statement and the circumstances which led to its being made is that, primed by the HTV programme featuring Humphreys and Steward, Holden had, like them, invented a false allegation and then attempted to weave it into the narrative he had already created about his time at Bryn Estyn. This view is reinforced if it is considered alongside the description of Anglesea which Holden gave in his police statement, in which he described Anglesea's hair as 'whitish'. This was not an accurate description of Anglesea's appearance twelve years previously, when the assault allegedly took place. However, it was an accurate description of the man who had appeared in the HTV programme in September 1992. Holden, in other words, had made almost the same mistake as

Steward, who had apparently based his description of Anglesea not on any recollection of the man himself, but on the photograph which Dean Nelson had shown him.

Holden's allegation against Anglesea was so evidently the product of contamination that it might be thought that it would not even be proffered as evidence in the libel trial. However, mindful perhaps that the evidence of Humphreys and Steward was itself visibly contaminated, lawyers acting for the defence recruited Carl Holden as an additional witness for the trial.

The cast of witnesses was now complete. Before this drama could be played out in the high court, however, the fate of a number of care workers, from Bryn Estyn and other homes in North Wales, who found themselves facing allegations trawled by the police, had first to be decided. In particular the trial of Peter Howarth would take place in Chester before the Anglesea libel trial began in London.

IV

THE TRIALS
(1994)

46 Waiting

SOME OF THE FORMER MEMBERS of Bryn Estyn staff who were arrested on Sunday 15 March 1992 were still employed by Clwyd Social Services as child care officers. Following standard procedures which effectively reverse the presumption of innocence, the director immediately suspended them. Liz Evans, who had gone to the police station voluntarily to answer questions, was also suspended even though she was never arrested.

The resulting sense of shock was felt far beyond the sixteen former care workers and teachers who had actually been arrested. Many of those involved had wives and children at home when the police had come to arrest them, and they too felt hurt and humiliated. They all had colleagues who, even though the police had in most cases not collected a single allegation against them, began to feel a stigma attaching to them. Simply because they had once worked at Bryn Estyn, they now became guilty by association with those who were, in fact, yet to be found guilty.

One of the most damaging views of Bryn Estyn, which now began to be widely held, would be expressed by Viv Hector, the director of the NSPCC helpline. According to the deputy editor of the *Observer,* he said he believed 'that the general view is that physical and sexual abuse were so high that it would be impossible to be there and not know.'[386] To anyone who held this view, any care workers or teachers who had worked at Bryn Estyn were not simply guilty by association; they were to be regarded as having been complicit in the horrific and systematic abuse which had supposedly taken place there. For ten years at least, this extreme but orthodox view of Bryn Estyn would place enormous stress on practically everyone who had any connection with the home.

One person who did her utmost to support her colleagues in the wake of the arrests was former teacher, Gwen Hurst. As a woman who had devoted her life to the care of others and who had worked tirelessly at Bryn Estyn to educate some of its most difficult residents, she was respected by her colleagues and by the wider community. She was also, as became evident during the Tribunal hearings, remembered with fondness, respect and appreciation by many of Bryn Estyn's former residents.

Having trained at Cardiff College of Education, Gwen Hurst had worked in a number of local secondary schools. She had also worked as a youth leader for Denbighshire County Council, and had come to know well the opportunities for young people in the Wrexham area. When, in 1975, she took up a post at Bryn Estyn, she brought this knowledge with her. In addition to her job as a teacher, she worked hard to link up Bryn Estyn residents with the larger community in Wrexham. On two evenings a week she would take a group of Bryn Estyn boys to a local youth club and, using her contacts, she was able to find opportunities for some of them to pursue their sporting interests in local clubs. Her aim was to give them a way of joining in with the local community in the same way they would have if they were living at home with their families.

Always going beyond the call of duty, Hurst was widely appreciated wherever she worked. After Bryn Estyn closed in 1984, she even enjoyed a brief moment of national fame for her role in organising child-care and nursery provision in the aftermath of the Welsh floods of 1990. Her contribution made such a deep impression on her colleagues and on those she helped that she was nominated for one of the Golden Heart awards given by Esther Rantzen of BBC television. The award was presented to her by Rantzen in December 1990.

From the moment the Bryn Estyn investigation was launched in August 1991 Gwen Hurst found the course of her life was changed. As union steward she was closely involved in seeking advice for those of her former colleagues who were now under suspicion. Having worked at Bryn Estyn for eight years, and knowing the care home intimately, she watched with mounting disbelief as local and national newspapers began to construct an image of the school which she knew to be untrue. Early in the development of the North Wales story she resolved that she would not rest until the true story of Bryn Estyn was made known.

Partly because she did not have any allegations made against her during the 1991–2 police investigation, and partly because she was a woman, Hurst was ideally placed to support colleagues who were facing false allegations. When John Jevons, as director of social services, held a meeting for former Bryn Estyn staff five days after the arrests, to encourage them to support one another, she was present. She became the mainstay of the Bryn Estyn Support Group, which soon became a self-help group, independent of social services. The group met monthly throughout the next year and it has continued to meet irregularly ever since. Gwen Hurst now looks back on what she and her colleagues had to endure almost with disbelief:

> I didn't realise it then, but I realise it now, that the vast majority of staff were in a state of shock. ... Some of us had to go to work, and it wasn't easy – well it was easy in one sense to face colleagues, certainly I wasn't feeling guilty about anything I'd done in Bryn Estyn, but it could create an uncomfortable atmosphere. ... It was very tough. It was all the publicity. The publicity was horrendous, in the papers and on television, I've never known anything like it. It hasn't been like that since. But we were hammered, absolutely hammered.[387]

On the Sunday that the police raid had taken place, Hurst had been contacted by the wives and families of many of those who had been arrested. Among those who got in touch was Claire Birch, the young wife of the man who had once been the best-loved member of staff at Bryn Estyn, but who now found himself in a police cell facing allegations of physical and sexual abuse. Claire, who was herself a care worker and the mother of three young children, the youngest of whom, Ginny, was 10 months old, was distraught. She could not understand on what possible grounds her husband had been arrested. She knew only that sexual allegations were involved, since the police had searched their house, even looking in the baby's cot in a vain attempt to find pornography.

When David Birch, after being forced to surrender his passport, was released from Wrexham police station that evening, he was at last able to tell Claire about the allegations which had led to him being arrested. She reacted with disbelief. Her greatest anxiety now was to protect her young children from the consequences of these false allegations. She was concerned above all that her baby daughter would not suffer as a result.

Such was the climate of intimidation which had been established that, to avoid any suggestion that they might be offering support to anybody who was actually guilty, the Bryn Estyn Support Group did not invite any of those who had been charged to attend its meetings. As a result David Birch and his family had to endure the two-and-a-half years before his case came to trial without any formal support from his former colleagues. Their life became an almost constant nightmare in which Birch says he felt he was being put under pressure by the police to say that he was guilty. It was his understanding that if he did so the charges of buggery against him would be dropped and replaced by charges of indecent assault. For David and Claire Birch the struggle to protect their children from the consequences of what had happened became paramount, and they tried hard to keep from them the realisation that their father's peace of mind and general confidence to face the world had been destroyed at a stroke.

Then, in April 1993, at a time when they seemed to have no emotional resources left to cope with any further setback, the Birch family was struck by tragedy. On Grand National day Claire's 19-year-old sister Gemma, who was looking after Claire's daughter, Ginny, now just thirteen months old, decided to drive in the car to the local bookmakers to put some money on a horse. As she drove down the main road she lost control of the car and hit a wall. Both she and the baby were killed.

Some months later, while David and Claire Birch were still trying to recover from this tragedy, they received, on a Friday, a telephone call from the police telling them that allegations had been made against Claire, relating to the time she had worked at Chevet Hey. She was told that if she did not report voluntarily to the police station for questioning she would be arrested. Then, when she rang the police, she was told that they could not see her until the following Wednesday. Unable to face spending the weekend without knowing what allegations Claire was facing, the Birchs rang their solicitor. He arranged for a police interview to take place that same day.

At the police station it became clear that a young man who had at one time been in care at Bryn Estyn, and who had been transferred to Chevet Hey, had alleged that a woman care worker, whom he was able to identify only as 'Claire' had had sex with him. It then transpired that the man who had made the complaint was actually two years older than Claire Birch who, far from working at Chevet Hey at the time, had still been at school studying for her O levels. What Claire Birch was not told was that the man who had made the allegation against the female care worker who shared her Christian name was Lee Steward. He had made this allegation in the very first statement he gave to the police more than a year earlier – on 30 March 1992.[388] David Birch remains convinced to this day that the decision to call his wife in for questioning was not simply the result of a careless mistake, but was part of a deliberate attempt to place yet more pressure on him.

As the Birchs waited impatiently for the trial, which they were confident would result in acquittal, Peter Howarth was preparing for his trial. A fundamentally lonely man even before he found himself facing allegations of sexual abuse, Howarth appeared to have become even more isolated in the months that had followed his arrest in 1992.

Gwen Hurst knew that she could not include Howarth in her support group. But, as the year wore on, she grew increasingly concerned about his well-being. Although she had never worked closely with him, and did not count herself among his friends, she decided to visit him in his Wrexham flat. She went with a woman colleague who had also once worked at Bryn Estyn. As it was nearly Christmas they took with them some mince pies she had baked. Howarth, who was clearly not in good health, was pleased to see them. The case itself was not discussed in any detail but Hurst recalls that Howarth said to them simply and emphatically 'I didn't do those things.'

One thing that did become clear was that very few witnesses had been contacted in relation to the forthcoming trial. Howarth, like many care workers who would find themselves facing trawled retrospective allegations, had no solicitor of his own at the time of his arrest. He was therefore being represented by the duty solicitor who had sat in on his police interview. While there can be no doubt that this solicitor prepared Howarth's case conscientiously, cases of this kind are extremely difficult to defend properly. They may demand scrutiny of 20,000 pages or more of social services documentation alone. At the same time, examining the course of the police investigation, and producing a coherent analysis of the allegations and the manner in which they came to be made, is itself a task of extraordinary complexity. Most solicitors are simply not equipped to deal with such cases. Indeed it is the very fact that such cases are virtually impossible to defend that has made police trawling such a threat to justice.

Hurst was concerned that, because of the magnitude of the task facing Howarth's solicitor, many key witnesses had not been contacted. She and her colleagues now tried to pass on to the solicitor details relating to former members of staff and residents who might be prepared to testify on Howarth's behalf. At least one former resident had not waited to be contacted. Keith Martell, a young man who had known Howarth well, and whose 1997 letter to Chris Saltrese has already been quoted, had been shocked to see a television news report showing Howarth on his way to court for the remand hearing. Martell immediately wrote to him, offering to come forward as a witness on his behalf:

Dear Peter,

Sorry to hear your bad news I was flabbergasted when I seen you getting into a taxi from the court on the television All the good work you
done for the boys in Bryn Estyn turned sour on you I don't believe
you did any of the things they say you done

    Peter if you want me to come to court on your behalf and say what
a good person you was you was allways good to me and I am sure most
of the other boys would come on your behalf See doing good for
people tends to backfire on you

    I hope you are well and if you want me to give evidence on your
behalf, I will come up and say how you help me with my problems
and how kind and pleasant you was to me and how you help me
through a bad spell Look forward to your reply

Yours faithfully

K Martell

Although his bail conditions did not allow Howarth to reply to this letter, his solicitor replied on his behalf and Martell was one of a substantial number of former residents who attended the trial in the
expectation of testifying on Howarth's behalf.

    As Howarth's solicitor attempted to prepare his client's case for trial,
another potential witness, who lived at the other end of North Wales,
was growing anxious about whether she would be called as a witness
for the prosecution. Although Alison Taylor would claim, many years
later, that she had had 'no involvement' with 'the allegations against
Howarth', at the time she was evidently anxious to play as large a role
as possible. On 18 February 1993 she even wrote to the chief crown
prosecutor dealing with the case. She sought an urgent reply to two
inquiries, one concerning the prosecution of Howarth and the other
concerning her willingness to give evidence about Gordon Anglesea,
should he become subject to a criminal trial. On the Howarth case she
wrote as follows: 'I understand that the above named has now been
committed for trial following upon investigations into alleged abuse of
children in care in North Wales. I have given a number of statements
to North Wales Police in respect of Peter Howarth, but have as yet
received no notification that I shall be required as a witness for the
prosecution at trial.'

    The CPS lawyer involved in these cases replied to Taylor's letter on 2
March. He listed thirteen statements which had been made by Taylor
to the North Wales Police between March 1986 and July 1992 and

added that he had also had sight of her dossier: 'Having reviewed those statements and the material contained in them, a decision was made not to use them as part of the prosecution case in relation to any of the existing defendants. The existence of the statements, therefore, has been disclosed to the defence as unused material.'

This decision may have been taken on the grounds that Taylor's evidence was mostly hearsay. But it is also possible that the CPS recognised that Taylor was an unreliable witness. This was certainly the view of the North Wales Police and it would be urged on their behalf years later at the Tribunal (see below, p. 442).

So far as Taylor's query about Gordon Anglesea was concerned, the CPS lawyer she was writing to, who was based in Colwyn Bay, was unable to help. In his reply of 2 March, however, he did make clear that a criminal prosecution of Anglesea had not been ruled out. 'That matter,' he wrote, 'is being dealt with by a member of the Crown Prosecution Service in the Police Complaints Division in London.'

It would only become clear years later, during the Tribunal, why the prosecution of Gordon Anglesea was under active consideration in March 1993. This was because, the previous month, the North Wales Police had themselves recommended that Anglesea should be prosecuted on the basis of the allegations made by Humphreys, Steward and Holden. Whether they had made this recommendation because they believed the evidence against Anglesea, or whether it was a strategic move designed to insure against future criticism, may never be revealed.

What is known is that their recommendation was rejected by the CPS. Having scrutinised the evidence, the senior lawyer concerned apparently came to the conclusion that the testimony of these three men should not be relied on in any criminal proceedings. Since Lee Steward and Carl Holden still featured at this point in the prosecution of Peter Howarth, the indictment which had already been drawn up now had to be re-drafted in order to exclude them from the case.

Steward and Holden were not the only potential witnesses against Howarth who did not, in the event, give evidence. As we have seen, in April 1994, not long before the trial started, Brendan Randles had already been found dead at his home. Even before then, towards the end of 1993, Peter Wynne's six-year-long, troubled relationship with his common law wife, and the mother of his children, had foundered. Having frequently been subjected to physical abuse by Peter, she had begun a relationship with another man. Wynne was evidently distraught at the idea that the woman whom he had at times treated so badly, but on whom he was emotionally dependent, might leave him. He sent a 13-year-old boy as an intermediary to her house, presumably with a message. But it would appear that on his return, on 6 January 1994, the boy found Peter Wynne hanging from a door at his home.

The idea that Wynne committed suicide because of the sexual abuse he had suffered is without foundation. Not only is there no credible evidence that Wynne ever was sexually abused at Bryn Estyn, but there is also clear evidence that he was emotionally distressed at the critical time for completely different reasons. Indeed one of the tragic aspects of Wynne's suicide was that, chief among the people to whom he might have turned during this period of emotional distress, were those who had once cared for him at Bryn Estyn, especially Liz Evans and David Birch, who might almost have been considered as surrogate parents. Yet, by making a horrific allegation against Birch (who was a friend of Evans), Wynne had effectively broken his ties with them. In short, it is at least possible that his false allegations were themselves one of the factors which led to his death.

The deaths of Randles and Wynne, and the decision not to call Alison Taylor as a witness for the prosecution, made it even less likely that the full facts about Howarth's case would ever emerge. For in the event the jury would learn virtually nothing about the role that had been played either by them, or by Ryan Tanner and Dean Nelson.

As the day neared when Peter Howarth would see for the first time the jury of twelve men and women who would decide his fate, a series of events had already conspired to tip the scales of justice decisively against him.

47 The trial

PETER HOWARTH HAD BEEN ARRESTED and charged on 15 March 1992. It was not until 14 June 1994 that his case came to trial. The trial took place in Chester Crown Court, in the courtroom where the Moors murderers, Myra Hindley and Ian Brady, had stood trial 18 years previously, after they had pleaded not guilty to a series of horrific crimes against children.

When Howarth was led into the dock he was accompanied by Paul Wilson. This was because the prosecution had used the allegation made by Andrew Singer – that Howarth and Wilson had handcuffed him and inserted a spiked object into his anus – to link the two defendants together in a single trial. Although the legal team representing David Birch had successfully resisted a proposal that he should be included in the same trial, the fact that Howarth and Wilson were arraigned together gave the prosecution an advantage. They had the opportunity – one which they did not fail to exploit – to suggest that this was not a trial of a corrupt individual, but of a corrupt institution – Bryn Estyn. At some points in the proceedings, indeed, it seemed almost as though the question before the jury was not whether Howarth and Wilson were guilty but whether Bryn Estyn had been a well-run care home.

The two defendants faced an indictment made up of 14 counts relating to allegations of indecent assault and buggery made by eight different complainants: Andrew Singer, Simon Birley, Martin West, John Duke, Gary Waite, Nick Purnell, Ian Surtees and Daniel Mead.

Wilson and Howarth were jointly charged with one count of indecent assault (the spiked dildo allegation). Wilson was charged with one other count of indecent assault relating to Singer (the crowbar allegation) and a further count of indecent assault relating to Daniel Mead. Howarth faced eight counts of indecent assault, each relating to a different complainant, and three counts of buggery (Singer, West and Duke). Although Wilson also faced a number of allegations of physical abuse, these were being dealt with separately.

As in any criminal trial, it fell to counsel for the prosecution to open the case against the defendants by putting forward a narrative in which

the guilt of the accused was assumed. It was perhaps a mark of the influence which had been exercised over the police investigation by journalists – and above all by Dean Nelson – that a central role was played
in this opening by the flat list. This was in spite of the fact that neither
Tanner's initial statement to the police in August 1991, nor the first allegations collected by the police, nor the two allegations which Nelson
himself had collected from Simon Birley and Peter Wynne, had made
any reference to the flat list. As has already been noted, this factor began
to figure in allegations against Howarth only after the publication of
Nelson's December 1991 article in the *Independent on Sunday*. In the
prosecution opening, however, it took pride of place:

> The list was used about four or more times each week and the proce-
> dure followed was for the selected boys to go to [Howarth's] flat after
> supper wearing pyjamas. Howarth, who wore pyjamas and a short
> dressing gown, insisted that no boy wore underpants, and would
> require any boy who was wearing underpants to remove them before
> he entered the flat. Howarth's explanation to staff who heard of this,
> was that it was unhygienic for boys to wear underpants, but the real
> reason was a sinister one: the prosecution say that he wanted the
> opportunity to see the boy's genitalia.

Although the prosecution have an obligation to advance statements
only when reliable evidence can be offered to support them, their
implicit claim that the 'no-underpants rule' was of Howarth's own
devising was false. By omitting any reference to the fact that Bryn Estyn
pyjamas had their flies sewn up half-way for reasons of modesty, the
prosecution were also able to make the highly prejudicial claim that
Howarth enforced this rule in order to gain the opportunity to see the
boys' genitals. In fact it was a general rule, enforced by all staff. The
claim made in the prosecution opening was never fully rebutted by the
defence who apparently remained unaware of the manner in which
Bryn Estyn pyjamas were modified.

The opportunity for the prosecuting counsel to create prejudice in
the minds of the jury is, in practice, a common feature of any criminal
trial conducted under the adversarial system. What renders such prejudice particularly dangerous in cases involving retrospective allegations
against care workers is the emotional power which can be derived from
combining sexual allegations made by different defendants. The effect
of a single allegation being presented in terms which confront the jury
with obscene or disgusting details of a sexual offence is in itself con-

siderable. But when, as happens in most police trawling operations, there has been a deliberate attempt to collect and bring to trial as many allegations as possible, the prejudicial power of such evidence becomes immense.

Although different alleged offences are normally tried separately in order to protect innocent defendants against the presumption of guilt, there are exceptions to this rule. The law has long held that in certain circumstances, if crimes are sufficiently similar, they can be tried together under the rules governing 'similar fact' evidence. Testimony about one alleged crime can then be offered as corroboration of another.

This approach to prosecution has always been fraught with dangers. These dangers were significantly increased by a change in the law which came about in 1991. Before 1991 it was necessary to show that there were 'striking similarities' between alleged crimes before one could be invoked as corroboration of another. In 1991, however, the House of Lords decided, in a case known as *DPP v P*, to dispense with the need for 'striking similarities'. Instead, it allowed allegations to be linked together merely through similar circumstances. This ruling actually made it much easier to secure convictions purely by advancing a sufficiently large number of uncorroborated allegations, and it was largely in response to it that police forces began to adopt trawling as their favoured technique for investigating care homes.

In practice, as Peter Howarth and his defence lawyers now found, this meant that it was possible for a criminal trial to be opened by a seemingly unending recital of repulsive sexual detail. In view of the manner in which child sexual abuse is now construed not simply as a crime, but as an unspeakable evil, any defendant exposed to such an ordeal is liable to find that by the end of the prosecution opening he or she has been effectively demonised in the minds of the jury. And although a potent mythology maintains that judges themselves are immune to the effects of such prejudice, there is no evidence that this is in fact the case. The reality in all too many cases is that, by the time the prosecution opening has been completed, both the jury and the judge may have been caught up in a current of prejudice so powerful that they are swept together towards a guilty verdict without being able properly to assess the evidence which is presented to them.

In the case of Peter Howarth the evidence which emerged during the trial, had it been dispassionately considered, could only have given rise to significant doubts. An interesting example was provided by the

testimony of Gary Waite. When he appeared in the witness box, there
were a number of striking differences between what he told the jury
and the statement he had given to the police two years earlier.

Whereas, according to his original statement, he had been twelve at
the time of the first incident he alleged, he now accepted that he would
have been fifteen. From the witness box he went on to describe what
he said was the first occasion on which Howarth had indecently
assaulted him. He claimed that this had taken place in the kitchen of
his flat, that he had started crying and that he had been taken back to
his dormitory by the night watchman. He then said that, about a month
later, something similar had happened. Asked by the prosecuting counsel, John Griffith-Williams QC, where he had been at the time, he said
'in the living room':

WILLIAMS: Whereabouts in the living room?
WAITE: On the settee.
WILLIAMS: Where was he?
WAITE: On the settee.
WILLIAMS: Where were you, in relation to him, on the settee?
WAITE: Sat next to him.

The significance of these questions can only be understood by reference to Waite's police statement, in which he had clearly claimed that
he had been indecently assaulted while sitting on Howarth's knee. The
prosecuting counsel was apparently trying to elicit this detail while
scrupulously avoiding any leading question. Since making this statement, however, Waite had discovered that he had been three years older
at the time than he had thought. He was the boy who had been
described by Gwen Hurst as having been 'a big-framed, stocky lad, like
a rugby player' at the time of the incident he alleged. It was perhaps for
this reason that he now gave a different account, which made no reference to sitting on Howarth's lap.

Cross-examined by counsel for Peter Howarth, Waite was asked
whether the incident in the kitchen had been his first sexual experience. He said that it had been, and claimed that it had been etched on
his memory ever since. He was then asked whether he had made any
reference to it in his original police statement. After being shown a
copy, he agreed that he had not. Nor had he mentioned the night
watchman, or bursting into tears. When reminded that he had said
Howarth had indecently assaulted him while he was sitting on his lap,
he revised the account he had given only moments previously and

claimed that sitting beside Howarth had been but a prelude to the alleged assault which had actually taken place when he was sitting on Howarth's knee.

During his evidence Waite was not called upon to relate the most implausible part of his allegations, which referred not to Howarth but to the unnamed teacher who had supposedly picked Waite up off the ground and thrown him several times around the room. But he *was* asked about the matron, Isabel Williams. In his statement she had played a disreputable role, having apparently concealed Waite's alleged black eyes and bruises by keeping him in solitary confinement for five days (a period of time which became 'close on two weeks' when he gave evidence to the Tribunal).[389] At Howarth's trial, however, Waite appeared to have forgotten that he had ever made this transparently false claim. Instead, the following exchange took place between the witness and Howarth's counsel, John Rogers QC:

ROGERS: And who was your house mother at Bryn Estyn, Mr Waite?
WAITE: Mrs Williams.
ROGERS: Was she also the matron, or is that another lady?
WAITE: That was the matron, yes.
....
ROGERS: And did you see her on a daily basis?
WAITE: Yes.
ROGERS: Did she treat you properly?
WAITE: Yes.
ROGERS: Did you trust her?
WAITE: Yes, yes.

What was not clear at this stage was the manner in which Waite had come to make his allegations in the first place. Towards the end of his cross-examination, Mr Rogers established that, by the time he made his statement, Waite, who lived in South Wales, was already aware that there had been an inquiry into Tŷ Mawr. The following exchange then took place:

ROGERS: And you knew there was already an investigation into Bryn Estyn, didn't you?
WAITE: Yes.
ROGERS: It was public knowledge – well, let me put it again: you knew that because of television programmes and because of newspaper reports, didn't you?
WAITE: No.

ROGERS: How did you know of it then?
WAITE: It was talk.

As can be seen from his answers here, Waite at first implies that he had not been influenced by any television coverage. However, when it was suggested that there was hardly likely to have been 'talk' about Bryn Estyn in South Wales, he admitted that it had been 'all over the telly', adding, in an apparent attempt to make his answer fit with what he had said previously, 'I was glad that I didn't watch it.' Re-examined by counsel for the prosecution, he clarified this claim, saying that his wife had heard about the Bryn Estyn investigation on the news. 'In fact, my auntie had seen it as well, and it came out that that's what was wrong with Gary.' At the trial no explanation was given of these words or of his further statement that he knew that the police were going to come two months in advance of their actual visit.

It was only when Waite gave evidence to the Tribunal in February 1997 that more light was shed on these comments. Contradicting what he had said during the trial, he told the Tribunal that he *had* seen television coverage of Bryn Estyn:

> I seen it on the news that there was things going on. I was taken aback, I was shocked with it. My wife noticed that there was something wrong and she said to me, she said, 'This is what has been the matter with you all these years Gary isn't it, something gone on in that school?' I didn't say nothing to my wife, she got in touch with a solicitor to get in touch with the police.[390]

If this account is true, it would appear that it was not Waite who first raised the idea that he was a victim of abuse, but his wife who, on seeing the television news, had jumped to the conclusion that her husband's problems could be explained by assuming that he had been abused at Bryn Estyn. He had then assented to her suggestion. This did not mean, however, that the police had played no role in eliciting the details recorded in his statement. At the Tribunal, Waite said that the police had 'pressed' him to make his allegations, even though he had begun by saying that nothing had happened:

> MERFYN HUGHES QC: ... but it was only when you went to the police that you were able to make the full disclosures that you did in your statement?
> WAITE: Only when they came to me, yes.

HUGHES: Sorry, I keep saying that – when they came to you?
WAITE: Yes, they pressed me for it. I still was denying that anything happened in Bryn Estyn, nothing happened. Then they done their police work and I broke down.
HUGHES: You broke down and you told them what had happened?
WAITE: Yes, sir.[391]

It also emerged in the Tribunal (though not in the trial) that Waite had at this stage been introduced by the police to a counsellor, and that he had discussed with her his allegations and his anxieties about appearing in court. Police officers had made several further visits to him and, when it came to the time of the trial, arrangements had been made for him to be accommodated in a hotel. On the night before he was due to give evidence the police had taken him to the court in a car and, together with his counsellor, 'supported' him throughout the trial.[392]

Even without the details which emerged at the Tribunal, there were so many implausibilities in the evidence Waite gave during Howarth's trial that no dispassionate jury could have been satisfied that his allegations had been proved beyond all reasonable doubt.

However, in this case, as in practically every retrospective care home trial, the operation of the law itself ensured that Waite's testimony could only be assessed within the prejudicial climate created by a series of similar allegations. Nor was the jury provided with any information which might help them to understand how the Bryn Estyn investigation had come about. Indeed, at the beginning of his summing-up His Honour Judge Gareth Edwards, having described John Jevons's decision to launch a police inquiry into Bryn Estyn as a 'drastic step', told the jury: 'We do not know, and we must not speculate, about what exactly triggered that action on Mr Jevons's part.'[393] Neither the role played by Alison Taylor, nor that of Ryan Tanner, in initially pointing the police towards Howarth as a suspect, was mentioned at any point during the proceedings.

It was in this historical and contextual vacuum that all the allegations against Howarth were presented. When Simon Birley gave evidence, the vacuum was maintained. Although Birley did say that he had made his allegation only after being interviewed by Dean Nelson, who had arrived with Ryan Tanner, no reference was made to the role of Taylor. Nor was there any mention of the crucial evidence linking Birley's allegation to that of Peter Wynne, which showed that the allegations the two men had originally made could not possibly be true.

One of the curious features of Birley's evidence was the language in

which he related his story. As he relentlessly laid detail upon sequential
detail, he linked them at almost every point with 'upons' and 'where-
upons':

> We went to Wrexham golf club whereupon we met a friend of his
> [Howarth's] ... after completing one round of golf, and that, we retired
> to the clubhouse for a lunch break and that, whereupon Howarth pur-
> chased two pints of lager for myself. ... Upon completion, he sort of
> said goodbye, and that, to his friend. Upon returning to Bryn Estyn ...
> he asked us if we'd like to go to his residence ... to watch telly, and
> that, for a while, like, whereupon both of us agreed that we would like
> to go there.[394]

After drawing attention to the manner in which Birley had 'gone
through everything as though you could not stop telling us precisely
what happened', and implying that his account was an untruthful one
which he had learned by rote, John Rogers QC, counsel for Peter
Howarth, asked him if he could remember making any contribution to
Howarth's retirement, which took place towards the end of his stay at
Bryn Estyn. Birley replied, somewhat curiously, 'I don't remember his
retiring, and even if I did I didn't make any contribution':

> ROGERS: You do not remember it at all? Certainly you would not have
> wanted to wish him well, would you.
> BIRLEY: I'd have had no pleasant feelings towards him, no.
> ROGERS: Well, he had sexually abused you, is that right?
> BIRLEY: Yes ...
> ROGERS: ... and you cannot remember anything about his retirement?
> BIRLEY: No.[395]

At this point Birley was handed a retirement card which Howarth had
been given when he left Bryn Estyn. It was apparently a card which had
been bought spontaneously. It contained the message 'With best wishes
on your retirement − and always', and was signed by just nine Bryn
Estyn boys, one of whom was Simon Birley. While admitting that the
signature on the card was his, Birley claimed that he could not recall
signing it. Rather more importantly, he was unable to provide any
explanation of why, along with a small group of boys, he had sent his
good wishes to a man who, if his allegations were true, he had come to
hate.

Later on in the trial Howarth would be asked about Birley. He said that he remembered him clearly. He knew that the boy was a glue-sniffer but this hadn't affected his attitude towards him. 'I just tried to bring him to his senses.' Birley had caddied for him, he said, at Wrexham golf club. He then recalled that, as well as signing the retirement card, Birley and the other eight boys whose names were on the card had clubbed together to buy him a tankard. It was inscribed 'To Mr Howarth. Best wishes for the future, from the lads at Bryn Estyn, 1984.' As Peter Howarth stood in the dock he was overcome by emotion. He broke down and wept. It was some minutes before the trial could continue.

Perhaps the most important of all the complainants was the man who had made the very first allegation against Howarth – Andrew Singer. Singer, a slightly built 26-year-old, was, in his manner, if not in the content of what he said, an impressive and plausible witness. However, there were a number of small but significant differences between the evidence which he now gave and what he had said in his police statement. His statement had clearly implied that all the acts of sexual abuse allegedly committed by Howarth on his own had taken place in the middle of the night, on occasions when he had left his dormitory, gone to Howarth's flat, and then returned to the dormitory he shared with Holden. When he gave evidence, however, although he began by describing these after-midnight visits, he referred also to going to Howarth's flat 'one evening'. Whereas in his statement he said that, after having been buggered by Howarth, he had bled for three or four days, in his evidence he said that he bled only for a couple of hours. In fact he transposed his evidence here to the incident involving Paul Wilson and the crowbar, telling the court that it was in relation to that incident that he had bled for three or four days.

In making the allegation about the crowbar, he said that Wilson had 'put the hooked, nail-extractor part up my back passage. A considerable way up. I felt pressure on my stomach. It was excruciatingly painful. I yelled out.'[396] He was shown a crowbar by Wilson's counsel and agreed that he was referring to an implement of just this kind. Even though evidence was produced which showed that extensive police searches had been unable to discover any venue on the canal near Llangollen which corresponded to Singer's description, and that they had not been able to find any former resident who had witnessed the alleged assault, Singer insisted that the incident he described was not an invention: 'It took place under the bridge.' He said that Wilson had told him to 'suck him off' but that he could not remember him making any other suggestion. He was then shown his statement in which he said Wilson had told him to suck off the other two boys as well, and he said: 'Well, now that you remind me, that is, in fact, the truth.'[397]

When Singer came to give his account of the incident in which he had allegedly been jointly assaulted by Wilson and Howarth in the latter's flat, he described, as he had in his statement, one of them coming into the room with a small box. But whereas he had originally said that the box had contained three pairs of handcuffs, which they applied to his ankles and his wrists, he now made no mention of handcuffs. He then reversed the roles he had ascribed to the two men in his statement, claiming that it was Wilson who had driven the spiked object into his anus with a dildo while Howarth held him. Asked why he had not tried to escape, he said that Wilson and Howarth had stopped him 'just by being there'. He was reminded that he had spoken in his statement of the three pairs of handcuffs and of being handcuffed with his ankles and his wrists behind his back. When it was suggested to him that he could not possibly have forgotten that, he replied 'I haven't forgotten, I'm just confused.' He then added 'I hadn't forgotten it. I just can't remember.'[398]

A particularly telling aspect of his evidence concerned a bizarre claim he had made in his initial police statement: 'After I left Bryn Estyn, I received a letter from Howarth saying he knew where I was and that if ever I told anyone about what had taken place at Bryn Estyn, he would find me and sort me out. I believed him. I destroyed the letter. I was living in Cardiff at the time.' In his evidence at the trial he claimed that this letter had been sent to him soon after he left Bryn Estyn while he had been at another children's home. He was then asked whether Howarth would ever be likely to take the risk of sending a letter like that to a children's home. He said:

> None of my letters has ever been intercepted. He did write such a letter – blow my legs off, things like that – and I just got rid of the letter. The letter was not on Bryn Estyn notepaper, nor was it signed by Mr Howarth. It's not signed at all as far as I can remember. It came from Wrexham.[399]

It was then pointed out to him that he had never previously said that the letter had been unsigned. Mr Rogers suggested that it was because the improbability of Howarth signing a letter like this and sending it to a children's home had been pointed out to him that he was now shifting his ground.

The cross-examination of Singer then moved to his return to Wrexham. In his statement he had said that, after he returned to Wrexham to live at the age of eighteen, about four years after leaving the home, Howarth had found him and visited his flat: 'He made threats to me and said I had to go to his flat. I went to his flat three times, twice with a friend and once alone.' His statement went on to say that, on the third occasion, when he had been alone, Howarth had got him drunk by giving him beer and that he 'believed' that he then had anal and oral sex with him.

When Singer gave evidence, however, he did not claim either that Howarth had visited him in his flat or that he had threatened him. He merely said that he had been in Wrexham for a couple of months and that 'either somebody told me his address or I met him'. He said that he had visited Howarth's flat on three occasions. On the first two occasions he had gone with the 15-year-old son of his landlady. The third time he had gone on his own. Asked by Mr Griffith-Williams why he had gone to Howarth's flat, he replied 'I don't know'. Asked by the judge to think again about this, he said that he went 'because I was still scared of him. I just went.' He said that, on the third occasion, 'He got me drunk. I ended up in the bedroom. We got undressed. We had sex. I was consenting to it and I've not seen him since.'

In cross-examining Singer, Howarth's counsel elicited from him that Howarth had a blue Datsun at that time. He then suggested to Singer that he had in fact met Howarth when he and his landlady's son had spotted Howarth driving by and had flagged him down. Singer said that he could not remember this but did not deny it. When asked whether Howarth had ever visited his flat, he now said that he had, but that he could not remember in what circumstances. When it was put to him that he had said in his statement that Howarth came to his flat in order to threaten him, and that he would presumably remember that if it had happened, he said, 'No, I wouldn't remember that.' When he was reminded again of what he had said in his statement, he said 'The statement is the truth.'[400]

When Howarth was called to give evidence he said that, in about 1987, Singer had waved him down while he was driving back from the golf club. He had then asked if he and the young boy who was with him could come and see Howarth in his flat. On the second occasion that they had come, the subject of Christmas arose and it transpired that Singer had not been included in his landlady's family celebrations. So that Singer would not spend Christmas on his own, Howarth said that he had invited him to come and have Christmas lunch with him. He said that they were just finishing their meal when the boy who had come with Singer on the earlier occasions arrived to collect him and they went off together.[401]

During cross–examination Singer was asked about his conviction for attempting to pervert the course of justice. Although he tried to equivocate, it could be inferred from his answers that he had indeed physically assaulted his own children, and then forced his common–law wife to sign a false confession which he had written for her. From his evidence in general it was quite clear that he was a habitual fabricator and fantasist. Many of his allegations were transparent inventions and there appeared to be no reason to believe any of the others, all of which were strained, far–fetched and implausible. Indeed, it might well be thought that no jury would ever rely upon his uncorroborated testimony to convict any defendant.

Any well–informed observer who had first–hand knowledge of Bryn Estyn and the young men who had given evidence against Howarth, would have found it very difficult to convict him on the evidence given to the court. A particularly significant observer in this regard was Howarth's co-defendant, Paul ('Paddy') Wilson.

Wilson had played an important role in the Bryn Estyn story. He had been contacted at an early stage by Ryan Tanner and asked to help 'get Howarth and Doddy', and he had been interviewed by Dean Nelson. He had told Nelson a series of calculated lies whose evident purpose was to help incriminate Howarth and Dodd – and by so doing to advance his own case against allegations of physical assault, some of which were well-founded. In his police interview he had repeated at least some of these lies and had portrayed Bryn Estyn as an ill–run institution in which discipline had broken down completely, and a blind eye had been turned to the possibility of sexual abuse. Many of his remarks reflected badly on Howarth and appeared to substantiate the case which the police had built up against him.

During the trial Wilson moderated the negative image of Bryn Estyn he had painted in his interview. But – for obvious reasons – at no stage did he admit, or come close to admitting, that he had painted this picture in order to save his own skin. Some of the comments he had made during his police interview were actually cited as evidence against Howarth. 'Be honest with me Paul,' one of the police officers had said to him, 'did you think at that time or in later stages that Mr Howarth was doing something to these kids?' Wilson had replied: 'I had suspicions but I couldn't prove anything. I didn't do anything about it.' Asked why not, he said that he had in fact contacted a local newspaper 'a long time ago'. This claim, which appears to have been another of Wilson's inventions, was repeated during the trial, though he now attempted to give the impression that he contacted a newspaper simply because he was 'concerned' about what was happening at Bryn Estyn.[402]

It was not surprising that, when Paul Wilson described to the court the phone call he had received from Ryan Tanner, he gave a significantly different account from that which he would give to the Tribunal. Instead of reporting Tanner as saying 'We're out to get Howarth and Doddy', he told the court: 'I asked what he wanted and he said he was trying to get Doddy *and others* – that is Nefyn Dodd – who worked at Bryn Estyn' [italics added]. At the same time, far from admitting that he had actually given an interview to Nelson, Wilson untruthfully told the jury that he had given 'no details' to the journalists who had contacted him.[403]

It seems possible that one of the reasons Paul Wilson had been willing to help Tanner and Dean Nelson build a case against Howarth was that he had begun to convince himself that Howarth might indeed have been guilty of sexually abusing boys. Had evidence emerged during the trial which seemed to confirm this view there can be little doubt that Wilson, who had played a small but significant part in putting Howarth in the dock beside him, would have been relieved.

However, as Wilson watched the case unfold against his former colleague, he appears to have become increasingly disturbed by the weakness of the evidence against him. His perspective on the evidence was clearly a privileged one, not least because he knew the truth about his own role and that of Nelson and Tanner. He also knew a great deal about the background of the witnesses who had given evidence against Howarth, and understood from his own fate that some of them were entirely capable of making false allegations of sexual abuse. Wilson had also been uniquely placed throughout the trial to observe Howarth's demeanour and his reactions to the evidence. Unlike the jury, he would have been privy to Howarth's utterances as they waited together to be brought into the court, or as they were led out from the dock. There was probably no person in the court better placed to judge whether Howarth was guilty or not guilty.

In due course Wilson reached a conclusion which he felt impelled to share. Late one night, when the trial was well advanced, he telephoned Gwen Hurst from his home. Hurst had given evidence on

Howarth's behalf. After her appearance in the witness box she had attended part of the trial with John Rayfield, a Bryn Estyn colleague and Methodist lay preacher, who had become a key figure in the Bryn Estyn Support Group. She recalls that when Wilson contacted her that night, he was in a state of extreme agitation. He told her that he believed that Howarth was innocent. She recalls clearly that, as he said this, the man who had been the toughest member of staff at Bryn Estyn, was weeping. By this stage, it would seem, Wilson, who was not fundamentally an immoral man, had been finally overcome by his conscience and by remorse at what he had done.

For the jury the task of assessing the evidence before them was more difficult. And there were certain pieces of evidence which, because they had not been effectively countered by the defence, inevitably had the effect of skewing the case against Howarth.

One key witness for the prosecution was Nigel Curtis. Curtis, it will be recalled, was the man who claimed that, as a boy at Bryn Estyn, he had walked into Howarth's flat through an open door to bring him lunch and had seen John Evans with his head between Howarth's legs. Howarth said that this was totally untrue. Asked about the claim that Curtis had left his meal on the floor, he said that 'If a meal had been left on the floor, the dog would have had it.' Howarth's denial, however, was clearly insufficient as a rebuttal of Curtis's evidence. If this evidence was untrue the jury might have expected John Evans himself to be called. Since Evans has said unequivocally that there was never any sexual relationship between him and Howarth, and that Curtis's evidence was a fabrication, it might well seem that the defence team would have summoned him as a witness.

However, they had made no plans to do so. The reason for this was simple – it arose from the fact that there had been two boys of the same name at Bryn Estyn. Noting from Curtis's statement that he claimed to have seen Howarth in a sexually compromising position with John Evans, the defence team had made the assumption that this was 'the black John Evans' who had alleged sexual abuse and who, at the outset of the trial at least, was due to be called for the prosecution (see above, p. 244). Only when Curtis actually gave evidence, and was asked specifically which John Evans he was referring to, did it become clear that it was the white John Evans.

Hurried attempts were now made to contact Evans, but he was on holiday in Spain. Howarth's solicitor did speak to him on his return, but although Evans said that Howarth had not sexually abused him, and that Curtis's evidence was untrue, he declined to come and give evidence to this effect. Contacted by telephone, in the middle of a trial, by a solicitor he had never met, and asked to give evidence at short notice, his response was perhaps only to be expected. It undoubtedly had a very significant effect on the trial, however. For it meant that the extremely damaging evidence given by Tanner's friend Curtis remained unchallenged.

Another crucial witness who was missing from the trial was David Birch. In ordinary circumstances he would have been a vital witness since he could have rebutted one of the most unlikely claims made by the complainants. This was the suggestion, made by John Duke, that after Howarth had allegedly buggered him, he had told Birch, who had responded by beating him up and pushing him into a pond. Since what was at stake was the truth or falsehood of an allegation which carried a life sentence, Birch was potentially one of the most important witnesses in the trial. Yet Howarth's counsel, perhaps understandably, took the view that Birch could not reasonably be summoned into the witness box since it would have emerged during cross-examination that he too was facing an allegation of buggery.

Yet another witness who did not appear was the man who had seen Howarth on television and had taken the trouble to write to him, offering to appear in court on his behalf – Keith Martell. Martell, not least because of the evident sincerity of the letter he had written, would have been an ideal character witness for Howarth. However, during his conversations with the defence team, he casually mentioned that, when he had been hitch-hiking through Wrexham, he had called on Peter Howarth late in the evening and had accepted Howarth's invitation to sleep on the sofa. In a trial where prurience and salaciousness had become vital instruments for the prosecution, the defence team decided at the last moment that they could not take the risk of allowing it to emerge in cross-examination that Martell had once spent the night in Howarth's flat. Since Martell was not called as a witness, the jury never had the opportunity of seeing the letter he had written (see above, pp. 305–6).

One piece of evidence which may have had an effect on the outcome of the trial was actually supplied by Howarth himself. Howarth said that on some occasions he would go swimming with the boys in the Bryn Estyn pool and that he would shower with them afterwards. 'Really?' exclaimed counsel. 'Are steps not taken to ensure that you are never found in any sexually compromising position?' 'Yes,' said

Howarth. 'Then why shower naked with the boys?' Howarth replied
that he would not have mentioned this if he thought there was anything wrong with it. 'It was a slip,' said counsel. 'No it wasn't,' said
Howarth.[404]

A number of care workers and teachers with experience of working
in community homes during the 1970s and early 1980s have since said
that they do not find this practice shocking, and that, while not common, showering with boys was something which did take place. However in the charged atmosphere of the trial, in which the slightest hint
of impropriety was being hungrily sought, and its significance magni-
fied by the prosecution, it would appear that Howarth's frank admission
had a damning effect. When I interviewed him in the summer of 1996,
Paul Wilson told me that, in his view, it transformed the entire atmosphere of the trial, turning it against Howarth.[405]

Another piece of evidence which was introduced into the trial was
given by a teacher who had worked at Bryn Estyn between 1977 and
1979. She said that on one occasion she had walked into the dining
room during the day and found Howarth and a boy whose name she
did not remember. She said that the boy was stripped to the waist, as
was common during the summer at Bryn Estyn, and that 'I witnessed
Mr Howarth in playful contact with [him].' She went on to say that 'his
mouth was in contact with the boy's back. He was gnawing it in— I
can perhaps best describe it, it is perhaps the way that I would do with
one of my children —in a sort of, I interpret it as, a playful intimacy.'

Howarth, when cross-examined about this incident said that he did
not remember it, but that it could have happened. 'I have chinned boys
on occasion, just for a bit of fun, just a bit of horseplay. ... I had chinned
boys before going to Bryn Estyn. I can't say when or where. It's just a
bit of horseplay. ... I wasn't gnawing the boy's back.' When it was put
to him that he wasn't a child's parent, he replied 'No I wasn't a parent
but I was *in loco parentis.* He went on to describe 'chinning' a boy as an
act of affection.[406]

Howarth's conduct may have been inappropriate and unwise, but
there was nothing in the action itself which suggested that it had been
a source of sexual arousal. There was certainly no way in which it could
be used to demonstrate that Howarth was guilty of the overtly sexual
and quite different acts with which he had been charged. Indeed what
was most surprising about the evidence was the fact that it was admitted at all. In that its prejudicial power seemed to be much greater than
its 'probative force' (its capacity to prove that a criminal act had been

committed), it was precisely the kind of evidence which would once have been rigorously excluded from a criminal trial on grounds of its irrelevance, and its potential to distract the jury from the issues which were actually before them.

Whether this particular evidence, or Howarth's own admission about showering, did indeed affect the outcome of the trial will never be known. What can be said with a reasonable degree of confidence is that a crucial role was almost certain to be played by the part of the trial which still remained – the judge's summing-up.

After a long and complex trial – two weeks in this instance – the summing-up can have the effect not simply of reminding the jury of the evidence but of focusing their attention on the case in a particular way. In the trial of Peter Howarth and Paul Wilson, what the judge did say to the jury – and, perhaps even more importantly, what he did not say – would, arguably, have enormous and lasting significance.

48 Judge and jury

THE ROLE OF THE JUDGE in his summing-up is to direct the jury on the application of the law and then to summarise the evidence in an impartial way so that they may reach their own conclusion on the facts. However, the summing-up given in the trial of Howarth and Wilson by Judge Gareth Edwards began by effectively pronouncing a verdict on Bryn Estyn itself.

One aspect of the regime at Bryn Estyn which clearly perturbed the judge was the fact that boys were allowed to smoke there. This policy, which was common in community homes throughout the country, was a pragmatic one. During the 1970s and 1980s, cigarettes, whose health dangers were by no means as widely recognised then as they are now, were a part of the culture of the kind of adolescents, many of them juvenile offenders, who were sent to Bryn Estyn. No total ban on smoking could conceivably have been enforced in an institution of this kind. To attempt such enforcement would only lead to a daily 'criminalisation' of the majority of the boys and to a massive expenditure of staff time and energy. It would also greatly increase the dangers of fire. Bryn Estyn, like many similar institutions, dealt with the problem of smoking by permitting it at certain times. This almost inevitably meant that cigarettes were used as a currency, and that sometimes members of staff would unofficially use cigarettes as rewards for good behaviour or co-operation.

This was one of the aspects of Bryn Estyn which Judge Edwards, who appeared to have little understanding of the day-to-day realities of life in community homes, singled out for criticism. He also seemed to have no awareness of the difficulties of recruiting staff to a sector of public service which was ill-rewarded both financially and in terms of status. He thus began his summing-up by levelling against Bryn Estyn criticisms which might well have been made of almost any institution of its kind:

Some of the witnesses from whom we have heard, who were employed at Bryn Estyn during these years, could see nothing wrong with the way the place was being run. I hardly imagine, members of the jury, that you will be able to take quite the same rosy-spectacled view. It is by no means clear that some of the senior care staff, or, indeed, with respect to her, the Matron, held qualifications appropriate to their responsibilities. Smoking by the boys, except perhaps the very youngest, was not only permitted but it would seem that by Mr Howarth, in any event, it was positively encouraged because he supplied boys with cigarettes.[407]

The judge went on to criticise the very existence of the flat list. In pointing out that this inevitably exposed Howarth to the possibility of false allegations, he was in one respect only repeating what some former members of staff had said in their evidence, and what others had said at the time. The matron, Isabel Williams, for example, recalls that, when she had said to Matt Arnold that Howarth was an unmarried man and that the flat list was therefore dangerous 'because of what people might say', Arnold had taken a different view. He said that it was precisely because Howarth was unmarried that he was able to give the boys a small taste of the home life of which they were all deprived: 'For what wife would ever put up with groups of teenage boys lounging around on her sitting-room floor watching television until late. Should we really put a stop to a practice which causes no harm and which confers considerable benefit on the boys, simply because of what some evil-minded persons might say? No, we should not.'[408]

Although Williams had appeared as a witness for Howarth, this particular piece of evidence did not emerge in the trial and the judge, in spite of a good deal of other positive evidence which had been placed before him, was unable to find any merits in the operation of the flat list. He immediately went on to point to evidence which in his view was clearly compromising: 'One boy, James Innes, and according to the witness Curtis, another boy, John Evans, spent a lot of time in Mr Howarth's flat, and not just at flat list times. Innes, undoubtedly, and Evans, according to Curtis, took baths in the flat, and eventually, as we know, James Innes actually moved in to live for a time in the flat, the only other occupant being Mr Howarth.'

In making these remarks the judge omitted to remind the jury that Innes had stayed in Howarth's flat briefly only after he had left Bryn Estyn; Howarth's flat had been used as a half-way house to help him get used to a more independent way of living, and Innes himself had given evidence in which he had made it clear that his relationship with Howarth had been one of friendship, with no sexual dimension.

Having referred pointedly to Howarth's admission that he had sometimes showered with the boys, the judge very properly pointed out that
residential care staff are 'particularly vulnerable to accusations made by
children of sexual interference'. But he then added: 'It may seem to
you, none the less, though it is entirely a matter for you, that if anyone
went out of his way to lay himself open to such allegations, Mr
Howarth did.'

The significance of these words only became apparent in the remarks
which the judge went on to make about Paul Wilson:

> It is, you may think, entirely otherwise with the other defendant, Mr
> Wilson; an outdoor pursuits man, happily married, very possibly, on
> the evidence you have heard, though it is a matter for you, arrogant,
> very probably, you may think, on the evidence you have heard, though
> again it is a matter for you, something of a bully. But there is no evi-
> dence of concern over favourite boys or about what was going on in
> the flat in his case. Whatever his faults may have been, there is you may
> think, no background pointer to the kind of conduct alleged against
> him on this indictment.

The clear implication of the judge's words was that Howarth's careless-
ness in laying himself open to allegations of sexual abuse and the fact
that he was a bachelor who had favourites, might in themselves be construed as 'background pointers' to his having committed acts of indecent assault and buggery. At this point Howarth's imprudence, which
was scarcely a matter of dispute, and his status as a single man, were
actually being used to incriminate him.

A remarkable feature of the first part of the judge's summing-up
concerned what he said about Singer. He was a crucial witness in the
trial for three reasons. In the first place he had made the first allegation.
Secondly, he alone had made allegations of a combined assault by
Howarth and Wilson, thus enabling the highly prejudicial joint trial to
take place. Thirdly, he was the least credible of all the witnesses, and the
only one who had a conviction for attempting to pervert the course of
justice. If Singer's evidence were presented in such a way that the jury
might be led to convict on the basis of it, then by any rational principle, convictions would follow in relation to almost every other complainant as well.

In the remarks with which he opened his summing-up, Judge
Edwards had already been careful to separate Singer's initial allegations
from those he made in his second statement:

You will recall that in his case, after he made a first statement containing allegations not dissimilar from those made by other complainants, he then made a second statement describing two utterly bizarre incidents, about the truth of which, though it is a matter for you − facts are for you − I suspect you may be entertaining strong doubts. The Crown themselves concede that the 'canal incident' and the 'dildo incident' may have been much exaggerated. I rather wonder whether you will be able to be sure that there is any truth in those allegations at all, but it is a matter for you.

Although the initial 'pre-crowbar' allegations were possessed of their own form of implausibility, the prosecution drew attention to two items of evidence which, in their submission, lent support to them. In the first place they pointed out that, during his police interview, Howarth repeatedly said that he could not recall Singer. Although he subsequently did say he remembered the boy, the prosecution argued that his initial failure of recall was not credible. Howarth, they said, had lied to the police for no other reason than that he had a guilty conscience about Singer.

Arguments like this, advanced by the prosecution on the basis of lies told, or allegedly told, by a defendant during a police interview are a common feature of criminal trials. As it is relatively frequent for defendants to say things which are not true for reasons which are quite innocent − or which have no bearing on the offences with which they are charged − a special judicial procedure has evolved for dealing with such prosecution claims. When such claims emerge during a trial, judges are generally required to point out to the jury during their summing-up that they must be approached with care.

The standard direction which judges are required to give to juries in appropriate instances has its origins in the case of *R v Lucas* and is known as the 'Lucas direction'. The basic direction, which should be 'tailored to the circumstances of the case', is as follows:

> It is alleged [admitted] that the defendant lied to the police [or X] in saying [that …], and you are entitled to consider whether this supports the case against him. In this regard you should consider two questions:
> You must decide whether the defendant did in fact tell [these] lies. If you are not sure he did, ignore this matter. If you are sure, consider:
> Why did the defendant lie? The mere fact that a defendant tells a lie is not in itself evidence of guilt. A defendant may lie for many reasons, and they may possibly be 'innocent' ones in the sense that they do not denote guilt, for example, lies to bolster a true defence, to protect

somebody else, to conceal some disgraceful conduct [other than] [short of] the commission of the offence, or out of panic or confusion. In this case the explanation for his lies is [... details of particular explanation given by the Defence].

   If you think that there is, or may be, an innocent explanation for his lies then you should take no notice of them. It is only if you are sure that he did not lie for an innocent reason ... that his lies can be regarded by you as evidence [going to prove guilt] [supporting the prosecution case].[409]

In the case of Howarth it could reasonably have been argued that, if he had indeed lied to the police, he may well have done so in an attempt to conceal circumstances which, while actually innocent, might be considered compromising by others. For it was a fact that Singer, who had been regarded as an effeminate boy, had been thought of as one of Howarth's favourites. Not only this but he had contacted Howarth again four years after he had left Bryn Estyn. They had met on three occasions, on one of which Singer had been alone with Howarth in his flat. In other words, while it is possible that Howarth had forgotten the boy's name, it is also possible that he may have been attempting to avoid discussing the renewal of a relationship with Singer, in circumstances which may have *seemed* incriminating even though they were actually innocent.

   In Howarth's trial, however, there was a simple but grave omission: the judge did not give the Lucas direction. Instead he told the jury: 'If, but only if you are sure that those answers by Mr Howarth were lies, and were designed to avoid answering questions about Singer because of a guilty conscience about what he had done to Singer years before, then the answers are capable of corroborating Singer's account on counts 6 and 7 [ie the counts of indecent assault and buggery]'. By failing to point out to the jury that it was relatively common for innocent defendants to tell lies to the police, the judge was misdirecting the jury in a manner which could have very serious consequences.

   This was not the only anomaly in the comments made by the judge. During his police interview Howarth had said that he would not generally be alone with a boy in his flat. In the trial itself, he said that Singer did sometimes call on him at his flat when he was on his own but that 'it's doubtful that I would invite him into the flat'. He said that this was because of 'an intuitive feeling', and added 'Singer was not often in the flat with me alone.'[410]

   The prosecution, however, were able to produce a log book entry, which showed that Singer had been reported to the police as missing one evening but that he had reappeared shortly before midnight saying that he had been in Howarth's flat. The log book entry recorded that Singer 'had been in PNH's flat all evening'. Confronted by this entry, Howarth said that he had no recollection of the incident and did not believe he had ever seen the log book entry. Given the prominence accorded to this piece of evidence both in the trial itself, and in the judge's summing-up, the full story behind the incident, which never emerged in the trial, needs to be given.

The first important consideration, which evidently escaped the notice of Howarth's legal team, was that, at the time the log book entry was made, Howarth was convalescing after an operation. The log book entry was dated Thursday 7 January 1982. A month previously, on 4 December 1981, Howarth had an operation to drain an abscess on his left heel. On Monday 4 January, he was examined by his doctor who noted that his leg was 'comfortable but is still non-weight-bearing'. At this point Howarth was not working. The doctor noted 'He is keen to get back to work and I do not see any reason why he could not. He ought to take things easy and rest his heel as much of the time as possible.' The exact time that Howarth went back to work is not recorded but, in the trial, he himself noted that his writing did not appear in the log book during this period; it would seem likely that he was still on sick-leave three days later, when Singer is said to have spent the evening with him.[411]

The background to Singer's disappearance on the evening in question is explained in another log book entry, written three hours after he had gone missing. Singer had recently been placed under a stricter regime than he had been used to. Earlier that evening there had been a row about this and it was then that Singer had vanished:

> Andrew was upset on the restrictions we had placed on him for this week. [We] explained in great detail this was a new term and whilst we accept Andrew has been left to his own devices, for the next few days he was to be restricted along with all the other boys. This Andrew neither liked nor accepted. I gave Andrew the benefit of being missing for two hours and then felt he had been given enough time to cool down. [We] then book[ed] Andrew out with police.[412]

Since Howarth's legal team had omitted to consult Howarth's medical records in relation to this incident, and since no reference was made to the other entries in the log book, the judge remained unaware of the full circumstances. In commenting on it, he began by misreporting what Howarth had said at the trial. Whereas he had clearly said that Singer 'was not often in the flat with me alone', the judge reported him as saying 'that he would not allow that boy alone in his flat'. He then went on to give the jury directions about the possible significance of this evidence:

> The evidence of the log book entry is capable of corroborating Singer's evidence on counts 6 and 7 but bear in mind that Mr Howarth says that the entry is all wrong and that nothing like that happened. If, however, you think that Mr Howarth must have seen that entry in the book, and took no steps to challenge it, then you would be entitled to regard it as stating the truth of the matter, and it would then appear to contradict something that Mr Howarth said to the police about not having Singer alone in his flat and something that he said in evidence to the same effect. Whether, in fact, it does corroborate Singer's account on either counts 6 or 7, of course, is entirely for you to decide, but that is a piece of evidence capable of corroborating Singer.[413]

In view of the fact that the relevant evidence had not been offered, the judge could not be blamed for failing to draw the jury's attention to one entirely innocent explanation of the log book entry – that Singer, who was clearly burning with resentment at the restrictions placed on him, had pretended to run away and taken advantage of Howarth's convalescence to 'hide' in his flat and watch television with him.

However, the fact that the defence had failed to bring forward the relevant evidence did not in itself explain the judge's words. For even without this evidence it should have been quite clear that there could be an innocent explanation of the log book entry. It was the judge's plain duty to allow for this. What was inexplicable was his direction to the jury that 'the log book entry is capable of corroborating Singer's evidence on counts 6 and 7'. The suggestion that evidence showing that A visited B's flat on a particular evening might in itself constitute *corroborative* evidence for the claim that A was sexually assaulted by B is nothing less than extraordinary. The judge's expressed view that the log book entry was capable of supporting a count of indecent assault and a count of buggery was not simply wrong from a common sense point of view; it was wrong in law. For evidence cannot constitute corroboration unless it offers confirmation of an essential feature of the act alleged. In this particular case the supposedly corroborative evidence did not correspond to Singer's original complaint even in its external detail, since, in his original statement, all the sexual abuse he had alleged had supposedly taken place after midnight. This account had only been modified at the trial itself, presumably after Singer had been made aware of the log book entry.[414]

The judge's misdirection of the jury was particularly significant in view of the fact that corroboration was an even more important issue then than it is now. Until it was abrogated by the Criminal Justice and Public Order Act of 1994, there was a requirement for judges to direct juries that it is dangerous to convict on the uncorroborated evidence of a complainant in any case involving sexual allegations. In Howarth's trial the judge had already discharged this duty:

> Now, members of the jury, a word of warning, as I said I would give you, about the evidence of the complainants, that is the young men who were boys at Bryn Estyn at various times between 1974 and 1984, and whose names appear on the indictment.
>
> I must warn you that it is dangerous to convict on the evidence of a complainant in a case of a sexual nature, and this is such a case, unless the evidence is corroborated. Corroboration means other evidence entirely independent of the complainant's evidence which confirms a relevant part of the complainant's account and tends to show that the offence alleged did happen and that the defendant committed it.
>
> You may, if you are sure that a complainant's evidence is true, convict on that complainant's evidence uncorroborated, so long as you bear in mind the warning I have given you, but you should first consider whether there is other independent evidence which corroborates his account. It is for me to tell you what evidence is capable of amounting to corroboration of a complainant's evidence, but it is for you to decide whether that evidence actually corroborates that complainant's evidence. ... [415]

Given this warning, given the implausibility of much of Singer's evidence and the medical impossibility of some of it, and given the fact that he had already been convicted for attempting to pervert the course of justice, it is difficult to believe that any jury, properly directed, would have convicted Howarth in relation to Singer's allegations, had these been considered purely on their own merits.

However, the fact that the judge wrongly told the jury that one particular aspect of Singer's evidence *could* be corroborated by the evidence available, effectively dissolved the warning about the dangers of convicting on uncorroborated evidence so far as Singer was concerned. It made it difficult for them *not* to convict.

Nevertheless, it would be unrealistic to suggest that proper directions to the jury would necessarily have led to Howarth being acquitted in respect of the other complainants, or even in respect of Singer himself. The crucial factor in the trial was the informal operation of what one senior police officer has called 'corroboration by volume' – or what might be called the 'no-smoke-without-fire principle'.[416]

In his summing-up, the judge reviewed the 14 counts brought against Howarth and Wilson in relation to the eight complainants. (Of these 14 counts, it will be recalled, 11 referred solely to Howarth, two solely to Wilson and one to Wilson and Howarth jointly.) He explained to the jury that, under the law governing 'similar fact' evidence, they were entitled, in considering whether any particular allegation was proved, 'to take into account the fact that other former residents at the school ... are making similar complaints of abuse against Mr Howarth.'[417]

The evidence of other complainants could be treated as corroborative so long as it was clear that it had been given independently:

> If you are satisfied that when considering one complainant's evidence there is evidence of a similar kind about Mr Howarth coming from other complainants, which is wholly independent of the evidence you are examining, not the result of collusion between complainants, and not the result of press or media contamination of the evidence, then you are entitled to ask yourselves whether Mr Howarth can really be so unfortunate as to be the victim of false allegations of so similar a nature coming from a number of witnesses giving their evidence independently.
>
> If the suggestion of such a coincidence strikes you as an affront to common sense, you are entitled to draw the conclusion that this can be no coincidence and that the allegation you are examining must be true. You are not bound to draw such a conclusion. It is entirely a matter for you to decide whether to draw that conclusion or not. Common sense may be your best guide here. But, if the evidence of these various complainants is independent, it may have occurred to you that it becomes then extremely difficult to explain it all away.[418]

While being cross-examined Howarth had succinctly expressed his own predicament: 'I think I am the victim of a terrible conspiracy. There must be collusion between the children. The media are also to blame.' These two sentences, the judge told the jury, 'come to the core of what you have to consider.' In the first place, he told them, they should consider the question of collusion.

The first suggestion of collusion was advanced by the defence in relation to the 'dog-walking' allegations of West and Duke. This possibility
was effectively dismissed by the judge who told the jury, 'West and
Duke did meet in Swansea Prison, probably in 1987, and certainly long
before any inquiry. They did not discuss Bryn Estyn'.[419]

The second question about collusion concerned Ryan Tanner, who
had in fact been present in the public gallery during the trial. Although
the defence team had at one point noted that he had been habitually
leaving the court whenever prosecution witnesses withdrew and raised
the possibility that he had been attempting to influence them, this suggestion had been withdrawn when it was declared by court officials
that no witness had ever left the court unaccompanied.

However, as the judge now reminded the jury, Tanner had featured
in some of the evidence given during the trial:

> Birley was spoken to by Ryan Tanner after Birley had initially been
> seen by the police and had made no allegation of sexual abuse. Ryan
> Tanner had apparently been in touch with the *Independent* newspaper.
> There is no suggestion that Tanner told Birley what to say, but it was
> after that visit by Tanner that Birley did make a statement of complaint
> to the police. There is no suggestion here, or certainly no evidence, that
> Tanner was acting as a go-between in relation to the complainants and
> no evidence that he has contacted any complainant other than Birley.
> It does seem likely, though we have no clear evidence about it, that he,
> that is Tanner, has been supplying background information about his
> years at Bryn Estyn to at least one newspaper. ... And Tanner has cer-
> tainly been taking a close interest in this trial, as you yourselves have
> seen.[420]

Because of the deaths of Brendan Randles and Peter Wynne, the fact
that Tanner had been in close contact with these two other complainants at least, and that he had actively prompted Randles to make
an allegation of buggery against Howarth, did not come before the
court. Although he was stepping beyond his role in doing so, the judge
now indicated to the jury the conclusion he thought they should reach.
This he did at various points during his summing-up, almost always
prefacing his remarks with the phrase 'It is a matter for you but ...':

> It is a matter for you but you may think that none of this really raises
> any evidence of collusion between the complainants or even the
> opportunity of collusion. All had gone their separate ways since leav-
> ing Bryn Estyn and although some did have overlapping periods of

residence, others were never there together and never knew each other.[421]

The judge's words notwithstanding, it remained a fact that West and Duke had known each other at Bryn Estyn and had not gone entirely separate ways since leaving; they had, on the evidence given by Duke, met on at least one occasion at Swansea Prison. The manner in which this evidence emerged was itself potentially significant. For Duke admitted that he had met West only after initially denying it, and after being placed under some pressure during cross-examination:

ROGERS: Have you been in contact with Martin West since you left Bryn Estyn?
DUKE: No.
ROGERS: Pardon?
DUKE: Not that I can remember, no.
ROGERS: Not that you can remember. I think you are now living in North Wales, in Dolgellau, but you were in Swansea certainly up to 1988, were you not?
DUKE: Yes.
ROGERS: And between 1986 and 1988 you served periods of youth custody, did you not? ... I am only asking you that because I want to know, did you during that time meet any former residents of Bryn Estyn?
DUKE: Oh, I don't know.
ROGERS: Pardon.
DUKE: I don't know.
ROGERS: You do not know.
DUKE: No. Could well have, but I might not.
ROGERS: You could well have. Just try and think and help us if you can remember who you met. [Pause] Cannot remember?
DUKE: West.
ROGERS: Pardon?
DUKE: West.
ROGERS: West. Martin West? Was that while you were doing youth custody together?
DUKE: While I was waiting for sentence, yes.[422]

While being re-examined Duke said: 'I was on remand a lot of times for which I didn't get convicted for, I got released. It might have been one of those times.' Asked whether he had met West before or after 1987, he said 'it may have been after'. Significantly, perhaps, he did not deny talking about Bryn Estyn, but instead said that he could not remember doing so.[423]

In offering his version of Duke's evidence during his summing-up, however, the judge gave the following account: 'I met Martin West,' he said, whilst serving a sentence at Swansea Prison and the record shows that my last prison sentence, or my last period in prison, was in 1987. I can't say if it was that year I saw West. I didn't talk to him in prison about Bryn Estyn.'[424]

One feature of this account is that it does not reflect Duke's reluctance to admit that he had met West at all, or his initial denial that he had done so. It also wrongly records Duke as saying he met West while serving a sentence, thus tying the meeting to 1987. Yet Duke had said that he had met West while he was *waiting* for sentence and had admitted that this might have been *after* 1987 when he had been on remand on several occasions without ever being convicted. Nothing in what he said ruled out the possibility that they might have met in prison in late 1991, when West was serving a sentence, shortly before the allegations were made.

The judge's version of the evidence was seriously misleading. At this crucial stage of his summing-up, he even omitted to remind the jury that West had claimed he could not remember Duke and had said he had not seen him since leaving Bryn Estyn. The latter point, indeed, was not made at any stage during the summing-up. Had the judge summarised the evidence accurately, this would almost certainly have made a difference. Had he directed the jury, as he ought to have done, that they should accord weight to the evidence of Duke and West only if they were sure they had not put their heads together to make false allegations, Howarth could well have been acquitted in respect of all four counts relating to them, including two counts of buggery.[425]

Having effectively dismissed the problem of collusion, the judge went on to discuss the question of media contamination. Although clear evidence had emerged during the trial that at least three witnesses – Duke, West and Waite – had seen or been aware of television coverage of the Bryn Estyn investigation before making their allegations, this evidence (whose potential significance had not been driven home by the defence) was again dismissed by the judge. Going once again beyond his role as an authority on the application of the law, he made another suggestion to the jury about how they should assess the evidence: 'Whether in the event there is any possibility of collusion between complainants, or contamination of their evidence by media coverage of the investigation, only you can decide. There is certainly you may think, though it is a matter for you, little, if any, evidence of it, and it may seem to you that the defence case fell short of actually suggesting it.'[426]

Having given a brief account of the evidence of Howarth and the evidence of Wilson, Judge Gareth Edwards concluded his summing-up: 'And now members of the jury, perhaps you would retire and consider your verdicts.'

What the judge did not deal with, because the evidence had not been presented by the defence, was the massive combined effect which Dean Nelson's article and the police investigation (as shaped by Tanner) had had on the emergence of the allegations against Howarth. Although the jury were invited to treat these allegations as having been made independently, not a single complainant had come forward of their own accord. All the allegations had been made in response to questioning by police officers, or a journalist, who were actively seeking complaints, and who had been influenced in varying degrees by Taylor's activities, by Tanner's statement, and by his self-proclaimed campaign to 'get' Howarth.

The principal reason why such grossly contaminated evidence had been allowed to become the basis of a criminal trial can only be found in the development of the law itself. It is to be found above all in the way in which the rules surrounding similar fact evidence have evolved, and been applied by judges up and down the land.

As the jury deliberated, they remained innocently unaware that the task which had now been entrusted to them would never have been given to any jury fifty years, or even five years earlier. And even the lawyers involved in the case almost certainly did not know the extraordinary history which lay behind the changes in the law that had made Howarth's trial possible.

49 Majority verdicts

IT WAS THE MIDDLE OF THE MORNING when the judge sent the jury out. The trial had begun on Tuesday 14 June. It was now Thursday 7 July. The previous evening Peter Howarth had packed his suitcase. As he had placed it in John Rayfield's car that morning, before being driven to the court at Chester, he hoped that he would be returning to his Wrexham flat that evening. There was still time for the jury to return a verdict that day. Peter Howarth, accompanied by John Rayfield who had never been a friend of Howarth's, but who had felt obliged to support his former colleague, settled down to endure the long and at times intolerable wait for the verdict.

After some hours, the parties involved in the case were summoned by tannoy to return to the courtroom. Peter Howarth took his place in the dock, and the twelve members of the jury filed in. A hush descended on the courtroom and the judge asked the foreman of the jury whether there were any verdicts on which they all agreed. They had, in fact, reached unanimous verdicts on six of the fourteen counts. They found Paul Wilson not guilty of indecently assaulting Daniel Mead – a young man who had been a particularly unconvincing witness at the trial. They also found him not guilty of sexually assaulting Andrew Singer with a crowbar and they found Wilson and Howarth not guilty of the joint assault involving handcuffs and a spiked dildo. In view of the judge's remarks during his summing-up, these verdicts were scarcely surprising.

So far as the other counts relating to Peter Howarth were concerned, the jury had been able to agree on only three. In all three cases they returned not guilty verdicts. One of the counts referred to an allegation of indecent assault by Daniel Mead, another to the allegation of buggery made by Andrew Singer – according to which he had been assaulted by Howarth on innumerable occasions in the middle of the night. The third count on which they returned a unanimous verdict of not guilty was the allegation of buggery made by Martin West. This part of the dog-walking scenario, at least, was not accepted.

The jury then retired to try to reach a decision on the remaining eight counts. When they returned it was to tell the judge that they had been unable to reach a unanimous verdict on any of these counts. It was soon clear that the trial would not be concluded that day. On the previous day Judge Edwards had advised the jury that, as a precaution, they should bring with them an overnight bag and any medication they were taking 'not that I am suggesting that your retirement should be very long, but I am aware that this is a 14 count indictment, of considerable significance and importance … .' The members of the jury were now sent to a hotel.

That evening, as he was driven home to his flat by John Rayfield, Peter Howarth was still in a position where, after an ordeal which had lasted two-and-a-half years, he could look forward to the possibility of being acquitted on all charges.

On Friday 8 July, Rayfield drove Howarth for the last time to Chester Crown Court. After an hour or so had passed, the jury, who had by this time been instructed that they could reach a majority 11–1 verdict, returned to the courtroom. By a majority of 11–1 they found Howarth guilty of having indecently assaulted six of the complainants – Simon Birley (who had been visited by Dean Nelson and Alison Taylor before making his allegation), Nick Purnell (who had changed his story between his first and second statements), Ian Surtees (who claimed that after he had been assaulted he had made the 14 mile journey to Deeside wearing his pyjamas), Gary Waite (who said he had sat on Howarth's knee), Martin West and John Duke (who had met in prison before they had made their dog-walking allegations).

The jury were still unable to decide on the two remaining counts – the specimen count of indecent assault relating to Andrew Singer and the allegation of buggery made by John Duke, which included Duke's claim that he had been pushed into the pond by David Birch. Eventually, almost certainly influenced by the judge's misdirection on corroboration, and his failure to give the proper Lucas direction in relation to Singer, they returned 10–2 majority verdicts in respect of both counts. Not only did they find Howarth guilty of indecently assaulting Singer, they also, crucially, found him guilty of the count of buggery in relation to Duke – a conviction which can still be punished by a life sentence.

Judge Gareth Edwards, before passing sentence on Howarth, described the crimes of which he had been convicted as 'utterly appalling'. He also expressed his view that the men who had complained would have been better off if they had never been sent to Bryn

Estyn but had been kept at home. He said that Howarth was entitled to no credit for being frank with the court since he 'had tried to get away with it despite the fact that men had to go through the ordeal of giving evidence, recalling dreadful and disgusting acts they would have preferred never to have to speak of again'. He sentenced Peter Howarth to ten years imprisonment on the charge of buggery and eight years on the seven charges of indecent assault, the sentences to run concurrently.

As soon as he had been sentenced, Howarth stood up in the dock and asked if the judge would permit him to make a statement. He wanted to tell the court – and the jury – that he was innocent of all charges. The judge refused him permission.

As Peter Howarth was led from the dock to begin his long prison sentence, Paul Wilson, of whose crisis of conscience in the middle of the trial the jury remained unaware, left the same dock and returned home to his wife and children.

50 Brides in the bath

IT MIGHT SEEM THAT the question immediately posed by the outcome of Peter Howarth's trial was whether there had been a miscarriage of justice. To put the question in these terms, however, is to make the assumption which we ordinarily and understandably do: that our system of justice is essentially fair and that, properly administered, and properly supplied with the relevant evidence, it will necessarily return a verdict which is itself just.

But, in the case of the trial of Peter Howarth, it would be wrong to see matters in this way. For the underlying issue is not to be found in any shortcomings, however serious, in the judge's summing-up, or in his conduct of the trial. Nor is it to be found in the manner in which Howarth's defence had been prepared. There were, it is true, a number of omissions or shortcomings in the defence case. But much of the evidence which has been presented in this book was simply not available to Howarth's barristers and would not have been discovered, however diligent their researches. The real problem with cases which are based on sexual allegations trawled from multiple complainants is, as many lawyers can testify, that it is impossible for defendants to receive a fair trial. However carefully the solicitors and barristers have done their work, however well the case is presented, there is always a grave danger that innocent defendants will be convicted.

It follows that the real question arising out of Howarth's trial concerns the fairness of the law itself. Even for those who have not been convinced by the evidence presented here that Howarth was an innocent man, his trial should serve to throw into relief a state of affairs which is, or ought to be, extremely disturbing. For at the very least it clearly illustrates that it is *possible*, according to our current laws, for a completely innocent person to be forced to stand trial on the basis of evidence which is grossly contaminated, and to face an almost unlimited number of horrific sexual allegations, all of which may be false. It illustrates, in short, how easy it is for an innocent person to be convicted on the basis of prejudice rather than proof.

What is perhaps most disturbing about this state of affairs is that it is against precisely this kind of danger that generations of learned judges and law lords have warned. Vigilant against injustice, these scrupulous lawyers gradually developed, over more than a century, a series of safeguards whose purpose was to prevent just the kind of injustice which is illustrated by Howarth's trial. The problem is that, in the last fifty years, these safeguards have been progressively removed until few or none remain.

The extraordinary history of these changes in the law has never been presented before. But this story is one which, like the story of North Wales itself, needs to be told. For it is an essential element in any explanation of how the witch-hunt that is the subject of this book came into being.

One of the most important stages in the development of the North Wales witch-hunt has yet to be related. For, a matter of months after the trial of Peter Howarth, there would be another trial in which a man would be faced in a courtroom by a series of horrific sexual allegations made by different complainants. Here, too, the jury would have to decide the question of a man's guilt or innocence on the basis of evidence which had been grossly contaminated. The fact that Peter Howarth had already been convicted would itself play a crucial role in the Anglesea libel trial. Perhaps most importantly of all, Howarth's conviction would lend credibility to the stories told by Mark Humphreys, Lee Steward and Carl Holden, in that all three had made sexual allegations against him as well as accusing Anglesea.

Howarth would himself, in the days immediately following his conviction, fleetingly re-enter the Anglesea story. For although the Crown Prosecution Service had, by this stage, turned down the proposal to bring a criminal prosecution against the retired police officer, it would appear that the North Wales Police were still hoping for developments which might cause the CPS to change its mind. Not long after he had arrived in the sex offenders' wing of Wakefield Prison, Peter Howarth would receive a visit from two police officers who were seeking evidence against Anglesea.

Before relating Howarth's response to his unexpected prison visitors, however, it is first necessary to explain how it was that he came to be in prison at all. This was not, ultimately, because of the efforts of Alison Taylor, Ryan Tanner and Dean Nelson, hugely significant though their role had been. It was because of a succession of judgments made by distinguished law lords, and because of one judgment in particular, composed by a judge who would eventually become one of the best-known law lords of all.

In seeking to answer the question of how Peter Howarth came to be convicted, we should recall that the reason different alleged offences are not generally tried together is to protect defendants against the prejudice this might give rise to. As two leading academic lawyers, Professor Sean Doran and Professor John Jackson, have written:

> It is fair to suggest that the impact on the jury of evidence that the accused has behaved in a similar way on occasions other than that of the alleged offence, or evidence that the accused has a general propensity towards this particular kind of wrongdoing, will in most cases be enormously damaging to the defence case.[427]

The effect of excluding such prejudicial evidence is to safeguard the presumption of innocence which forms – or should form – the point of departure for all juries when they come to consider their verdict.

The reason why dispensing with the presumption of innocence is rarely, if ever, contemplated is that there has long been a recognition that justice, whose purpose is to protect against social ills and to promote moral good, can, if not prudently administered, inflict harm on innocent citizens of a kind which is incalculably more damaging than the mere failure to punish a particular crime. By convicting innocent people of offences they have not committed, justice can itself become a form of inadvertent crime, more terrible for the fact that it is committed, or abetted, by servants of the state – by judges themselves.

By the end of the nineteenth century it was widely accepted that any attempt by the courts to admit evidence of a defendant's general disposition towards criminal conduct as evidence that they had committed a particular crime should be resisted. Similar facts, or counts relating to crimes similar to those with which the accused was charged, were therefore generally excluded from trials on the grounds that such evidence, while certainly relevant, does not in fact *prove* anything: the fact that a man has committed five burglaries in the past does not mean that he broke into a particular house last month. Because it is 'more prejudicial than probative', such evidence would actually undermine the presumption of innocence and make it more likely that innocent defendants would be convicted. To argue that because a man had a propensity to criminal conduct meant that he had committed a particular crime became known as 'forbidden reasoning'. Because of its prejudicial power, both 'propensity evidence' and evidence of prior (or subsequent) criminal acts was assiduously kept away from juries. How-

ever, during the twentieth century, and particularly in the years immediately preceding Peter Howarth's trial, the law on similar fact evidence
was subjected to a series of changes.

The modern similar fact principle assumed the form it did largely
because of the case of *Makin v Attorney General for New South Wales*,
which was heard in 1894. In this case Lord Herschell, the Lord Chancellor, reaffirmed the presumption that similar fact evidence would not
normally be admitted. He went on to outline the exceptional circumstances in which this exclusionary principle could be overridden. Evidence of similar facts could not be admitted merely because it seemed
relevant to the count on the indictment, but only if it was both relevant *and* made a significant contribution to proving that the particular
crime on the indictment had been committed.[428]

It is essential to note that the similar fact principle is not designed to
admit evidence because it is similar. It is designed to exclude evidence
even though it is similar. Only in exceptional circumstances, it was traditionally held, would it be just to override this exclusionary principle.
The case which Lord Herschell was considering was an example of
such an exception. In this case an Australian couple, Mr and Mrs
Makin, had been charged with killing a child whose body was found
buried in their garden. The Makins had taken in the child, in exchange
for money from the parents, to care for him. They denied killing the
child and claimed that he had died from natural causes. However, the
police made inquiries and found that the Makins had fostered a number of children in similar circumstances. They dug up the gardens of
several prior homes of the Makins, and found the bodies of twelve
more infants. In the trial the evidence of the twelve bodies was admitted in order to rebut the couple's defence. On being found guilty they
appealed against their conviction on the grounds that this evidence
should have been excluded. Lord Herschell ruled that it had been right
to admit the evidence on the grounds of its relevancy and its probative
value.

In practice the admissibility of the similar fact evidence in this case
turned on the improbability of there being any innocent explanation
for the presence of the bodies of the twelve other children in the gardens of the defendants' former homes. As a later judgment would put
it, the evidence had been admitted 'because a series of acts with the self-
same characteristics is unlikely to be produced by accident or inadver-
tence'.[429]

The case which, after *Makin*, was most significant in the development of the similar fact principle, was the celebrated case of *R v Smith*, which has come to be known as 'the brides in the bath'. This came about after a member of the public noticed a striking similarity between the ways in which two women had met their deaths.

On 2 January 1915, Joseph Crossley, the owner of a guest-house in Blackpool, read the newspaper report of an inquest which had taken place the previous day in London. It related how a man named John Lloyd had told the owner of the house where he was lodging that he was going out to buy some tomatoes for his wife's supper while she took a bath. When he returned he called out to his wife and, getting no answer, entered the bathroom and found her dead in the bath. A verdict of accidental death was recorded. The tragedy was all the greater because the couple had only recently married.

Crossley was struck by the similarity between the fate of Margaret Lloyd and a sudden death which had taken place in his guest-house about a year previously. On this occasion Alice Smith, who had recently married one George Joseph Smith, and had come on holiday with him to Blackpool, went from their room to take a bath and never returned. She was subsequently found dead in the bath and an inquest concluded that she had drowned accidentally after suffering heart failure. Believing that the striking similarities between these two cases might be more than a coincidence, Crossley wrote to the Metropolitan Police to point them out.

It transpired that the two husbands were one and the same, George Joseph Smith having adopted the alias of 'John Lloyd'. It was then established that a few years earlier, in July 1912, another recent bride, Bessie Munday, was found dead in her bath at a house in Herne Bay. Five days beforehand she had made a will in favour of her husband, Henry Williams (alias George Joseph Smith), by which he inherited £2,500. The police then discovered that both Margaret Lloyd and Alice Smith had taken out life insurance polices shortly before their deaths and that George Joseph Smith had been the beneficiary.

Smith was charged with Bessie Munday's murder, and evidence of the manner in which his two later brides met their deaths was deemed admissible. There seemed to be no other explanation of the similarities between the drownings than that all three women had been murdered by Smith. Smith was found guilty of the murder of Bessie Munday and was hanged at Maidstone Prison on 13 August 1915.

Although the similar fact principle originally had no connection to the field of sexual offences, the fact that corroboration of such offences is not normally available led some prosecution lawyers to invoke it. They attempted to use it to justify the admission not simply of similar acts or similar crimes but of similar *allegations*. Largely because they threatened some of the most fundamental principles of justice, these attempts were not initially successful. One occasion on which the attempt was made, however, is directly relevant to more recent judicial developments.

Peter Howarth's trial may have been unusual, but, in some respects at least, it was not unprecedented. Seventy years earlier, in a different part of Wales, another man who had spent much of his life catering for the needs of boys in a school about the size of Bryn Estyn, had found himself in a similar situation.

51 At the Monmouth Assizes

THE CASE OF R *v* BAILEY was heard at the Monmouth assizes in 1924, a few years after the introduction of new rules had permitted a number of different offences to be included on the same indictment. In order to safeguard the traditional similar fact principle, lawyers were permitted to object to such multiple counts if they believed it would prejudice the trial of their client. In this case, however, no such objections had been made. As a result Mr Bailey, a headmaster, found himself facing an indictment containing no fewer than 16 counts of indecent assault in respect of complaints made by 16 of his former pupils.

It was said in his defence that he was unpopular with the boys and their parents and that there had been a conspiracy amongst the boys to make the allegations. The judge noted that 'there is a great deal of want of cohesion about the evidence in respect of persons present on these occasions many of the boys say that so-and-so was present, and when the other boys come it does not appear that they say they were there.' In asking the jury to reach a verdict, however, he implied that they should reach their judgment by considering the case as a whole. They duly returned a general verdict of guilty on all counts, even though two of the complainants had declined to give evidence.

When the case came to appeal Lord Hewart, the Lord Chief Justice, indicated that in his view the hearing of so many counts together was gravely prejudicial:

> The general rule where there are many charges against a person is adequately and accurately stated in *Archbold's Criminal Pleading, Evidence and Practice*, 26 ed., p. 59: 'Though not illegal, it is hardly fair to put a man upon his trial on an indictment containing forty counts, involving several distinct charges of false pretences; for it would be almost impossible that he should not be grievously prejudiced as regards each one of the charges by the evidence which is being given upon the others'.[430]

In a passage of his judgment which would resound through twentieth-century legal history, and which is still quoted by some authorities today,[431] Lord Hewart carefully analysed the dangers of any trial involving multiple counts relating to serious criminal offences:

> The risk, the danger, the logical fallacy is indeed quite manifest to those who are in the habit of thinking about such matters. It is so easy to derive from a series of unsatisfactory accusations, if there are enough of them, an accusation which at least appears satisfactory. It is so easy to collect from a mass of ingredients, not one of which is sufficient, a totality which will appear to contain what is missing. That of course is only another way of saying that when a person is dealing with a considerable mass of facts, in particular if those facts are of such a nature as to invite reprobation, nothing is easier than confusion of mind; and, therefore, if such charges are to be brought in a mass, it becomes essential that the method upon which guilt is to be ascertained should be stated with punctilious exactness.[432]

He said that if the Crown had argued that the evidence on some of the counts was so compelling that a verdict of guilt would have been reached in any circumstances, such an argument would have given rise to serious consideration. However, they had made no such submission and it seemed clear that the jury's verdict had been directly influenced by the judge's directions. In his summing-up, said Lord Hewart, the judge had suggested 'that no distinction is to be drawn between one count and another, and that it is right and proper that in weighing the merits, or it may be the demerits, of the evidence, with reference to any particular charge, the jury should bring into the scale by way, if need be, of makeweight, whatever was to be collected from the evidence upon any other charge'.

This approach, said Lord Hewart, could not be justified. Ideally the counts should have been severed and tried separately. He clearly implied that an application for severance should have been granted. In its absence, clear directions to the jury were essential. Not only should the jury have been warned that they should act on evidence of this kind with extreme caution, but they should have been directed 'to weigh with great care the evidence with reference to each particular charge, being careful not to fall into the error of supplementing the evidence on any one charge by what might be improperly conceived to be helpful evidence on some other charge'. Because this had not been done, and because the jury had been wrongly directed to return a general verdict on all the counts, Mr Bailey's conviction was overturned.

The prescription that a jury in a criminal case must always reach separate verdicts on each individual count on an indictment remains to this day a fundamental principle of English law. However, there is one respect in which the law which applies now to cases of multiple allegations is fundamentally different from that which was in force at the time of Bailey's appeal.

During the appeal court hearing, counsel for the Crown argued that the convictions (which he himself referred to in the singular), ought to stand. He then cited the case of *Makin* as creating authority for the view that 'if the trial had proceeded on each count separately, the prosecution would have been entitled to call the other fifteen boys in order to give evidence of prior and subsequent acts by the appellant'.[433]

This argument, which had apparently been put in more detail in written submissions, was roundly dismissed by the Lord Chief Justice:

> It is said, on the part of the Crown that, after all, this was evidence proceeding from boys at the same school, and that the unity of the school provided a nexus which made the evidence upon any count available on any other count. It is a little difficult to follow that reasoning. One would have thought, on the contrary, that the very fact that this evidence did come from boys at the same school, especially if the master of that school was unpopular alike with boys and parents, might have provided ground for additional caution and a stronger warning.[434]

Lord Hewart was saying that the circumstances indicated that there was a real possibility of collusion between the witnesses or contamination of their evidence, and that it would be particularly dangerous to admit the evidence on the similar fact principle. The possibility that mere allegations should be admitted on a similar fact basis would clearly represent a significant and potentially dangerous departure from the law as it had been established in *Makin* and *Smith*. In the decades which followed the judgment in *Bailey*, it was, however, just this development which would increasingly be urged upon the courts, and to which not only the Court of Appeal, but the House of Lords itself, would ultimately succumb.

The pressure which was now placed upon the courts to lower the threshold for the admission of similar fact evidence, and to admit similar allegations as well, came from one source in particular. This was the anxiety of the courts, and to some extent of the public, that the relatively new crime of indecent assault, and the subsequent criminalisation of all homosexual behaviour, were not leading to as many convictions as they wanted.[435] One example of this judicial anxiety was provided in the original criminal trial of *R v Bailey*. In the course of his summing-up, the judge said this to the jury:

> You cannot as a rule convict people on charges of indecency with young people – male or female – as a rule you cannot convict them safely without some sort of corroboration, because otherwise a person cannot defend himself. A girl or a boy comes and says that 'A man did that to me.' And the man says 'I did not'. He cannot defend himself as a rule, and therefore unless there is something to turn the balance against him by way of corroboration, in practice a man in those circumstances gets off.[436]

The prevalence of this anxiety, and its tendency to push the courts towards some relaxation of the rules of evidence, is well illustrated by some remarks made by Lord Aitchison in a case heard by the Scottish courts in 1937. Here the legal background to the case was the requirement of Scottish law that convictions could not be made unless there were two witnesses to the crime in question:

> Now it is a well-established rule in our criminal law that you do not prove one crime by proving another or by leading evidence tending to show that another crime has been committed. That is a good general rule. But then when you are dealing with this class of crime, there is some relaxation of the rule, otherwise you might never be able to bring the crime home at all. Let me give you an illustration that is not at all unfamiliar – there are many cases of it, especially in our large cities – you get a degraded man who finds some little girl in the street, and he gives her a penny, and gets her to go up a close, and there he does something immoral with her, and then he sends her away. Nobody sees what he has done; there is only the evidence of the child. And then the same thing happens with another child, and again nobody sees that; and then there is a third child and the same thing happens again. Well, of course, if you had to have two witnesses to every one of these acts – they are all separate crimes – you would never prove anything at all.[437]

As a way out of what might seem to be an evidential impasse, Lord Aitchison went on to invoke the 'Moorov doctrine' which had been established in a similar case brought to the appeal court in 1930:

> But that is not the law. The law is this, that, when you find a man doing the same kind of criminal thing in the same kind of way towards two

or more people, you may be entitled to say that the man is pursuing a
course of criminal conduct, and you may take the evidence on one
charge as evidence on another. That is a very sound rule, because a
great many scoundrels would get off altogether if we had not some
such rule in our law. ...This is in substance what was laid down in the
High court in the case of *Moorov v HM Advocate*, 1930.[438]

Just as the Scottish courts specifically relaxed the rules of evidence in
an attempt to ensure that the 'scoundrels' accused in sexual cases would
not 'get off altogether', so there was strong pressure on English courts
to do the same. This pressure was intensified by a particular form of
prejudice. In the past twenty years our progressive emancipation – or
seeming emancipation – from certain forms of prejudice has taken
place so rapidly that we sometimes fail to recall the depth of prejudice
there once was towards homosexuality. We may forget that the death
sentence for buggery was abolished only in 1861. The attitude which
prevailed in England towards homosexuality during the early modern
period was more severe than it was anywhere else in Europe. Legal attitudes towards the 'sin against nature' were perhaps best summed up by
the jurist, Sir William Blackstone, who felt that the very mention of
buggery was 'a disgrace to human nature'.[439]

Those who have upheld the traditional safeguards of British justice
would point out that it is in just such circumstances that the presumption of innocence plays its most important role. For the greater the
public repugnance against a particular crime, the more necessary it is to
protect innocent people who are wrongly accused of that crime. Some
prejudices, however, can be so powerful that even judges and lawyers
may succumb to them. Because of the immense power of the prejudice
against homosexuality in the first half of the twentieth century, and
because of the repugnance towards the crime of child sexual abuse,
there was a grave danger that some of the most vital safeguards of
British justice would progressively come under threat. In particular the
similar fact principle, which has long been one of the cornerstones of
the presumption of innocence, might be permanently fractured.

Once this had happened there would be nothing to stop one innocent defendant finding himself faced in the courtroom by ten or even
twenty complainants, all of whom were making allegations against him
which were false, yet all of whose evidence could be invoked in support of any other charge.

It might well be thought that this possibility would not emerge until
the latter part of the twentieth century. Yet what happened at the Mon-

mouth Assizes in 1924 clearly illustrated that there were already cultural pressures in this direction. All that was needed now was for a judge of great energy and enterprise, who had little regard for the weight of judicial tradition, to take up the torch of prejudice which others had lit and the similar fact principle could be effectively destroyed.

It would not be long before just such a judge emerged.

52 'A particular perverted lust'

THE CASE WHICH BROUGHT ABOUT one of the most significant shifts in English law in modern history was an appeal brought in 1946 on behalf of one George Sims. Peter Howarth's trial, though seemingly far removed from the Sims case in time, could never have taken place in the way that it did without the precedent which this case created.

The newly appointed high court judge who, in drafting the historic 1946 judgment, would stamp his own prejudices on English criminal law, would eventually be elevated to the House of Lords and become one of the best known members of the modern judiciary. His name was Alfred 'Tom' Denning.

A man of great ability and industry, Denning had read mathematics at Magdalen College, Oxford, had served in the Royal Engineers during the first world war, and became a schoolmaster at Winchester. He then gained a first-class degree in law and rapidly rose through the ranks of the profession, often inspiring, by his own confident mastery of his briefs, deference in those who were senior to him. Denning was regarded by some as a radical figure. However, his attitudes were deeply traditional. He always maintained that retribution had an essential place in the penal system, saying that the ultimate justification of any punishment 'is not that it is a deterrent, but that it is the emphatic denunciation by the community of a crime'.[440] He had particularly strong views on homosexuality and maintained these fiercely throughout his life. In the House of Lords debate on the Wolfenden report in 1957, for example, he argued that, while natural sin was deplorable, unnatural vice was worse. Regretting that 'Hell fire and damnation hold no terrors nowadays', Lord Denning, as he had become, held that the law should continue to punish homosexual conduct, though 'discreetly'.[441]

The appeal which Denning found himself dealing with in 1946, two years after he had been made a high court judge, concerned this same 'unnatural vice'. It related to a trial in which the defendant had faced seven counts of sodomy or gross indecency relating to four different men. He was found guilty of offences of buggery in relation to three men but was acquitted on the other four counts. He appealed against

conviction on the grounds that, by introducing these different allegations in the same trial, the court had allowed the jury to convict him
on grounds of propensity rather than on the evidence which was actually given. It was argued that 'The effect of trying all the cases together
was to make the jury say: "This is a dirty old man, because four different persons have given similar evidence about him."'[442] It was submitted on behalf of the defendant that the allegations should not have been
tried together, and that in order to avoid the jury being improperly
prejudiced, there should have been separate trials.

This appeal was dismissed by the Lord Chief Justice, Lord Goddard,
who said that the case was such an important one that the court would
give its reasons at a later date. Although it was Lord Goddard himself
who read out the court's judgment, and is therefore usually credited
with having composed it, this was not the case.

It was in fact Denning who, perhaps because of the very strength of
his abhorrence for the crime, had put himself forward to take the main
responsibility for drafting what was clearly intended as a historic judgment. Lord Goddard, who once pleaded for the return of flogging, and
who would be criticised as one of the most illiberal and unfair judges
ever to hold the office of Lord Chief Justice, duly introduced the judgment as one which 'had been largely prepared by Denning J'.[443]

The judgment began by recognising what had clearly been set forward on behalf of Sims, namely that the entire appeal turned on the
question of whether the original judge ought to have ordered separate
trials. It was immediately contended that the inclusion of all the counts
in one indictment was perfectly proper under the Indictments Act of
1915, in that this permitted joining together 'a series of offences of the
same or similar character'. It was conceded that an exception should be
made to this if it were considered that the defendant would be prejudiced or embarrassed by having to face multiple charges. Interestingly
and significantly, Denning himself acknowledged that, in a case involving such grave and scandalous charges as had been brought against
Sims, it would not be reasonable to argue that such prejudice could be
cured by the judge's direction to the jury: 'In such a case as the present
… it is asking too much to expect any jury when considering one
charge to disregard the evidence on the others … [for] the prejudice
created by it would be improper and would be too great for any direction to overcome.'[444]

Since this crucial point was conceded, the only way that the conviction could be upheld was to argue that the evidence given on any one

count would in fact be admissible on any other on a similar fact basis.
This, of course, was the very point which had been argued by the prosecution in *Bailey* and which had been ruled out by Lord Hewart. In the
case of *Sims*, however, Denning cited the precedent established in
Makin in order to argue that where there was evidence of 'specific acts
or circumstances connecting the accused with specific features of the
crime', that evidence should be admissible. In this case he suggested
that just such a state of affairs existed: 'The evidence of each man was
that the accused invited him into the house and there committed the
acts charged. The acts they describe bear a striking similarity. This is a
special feature sufficient in itself to justify the admissibility of the evidence.'[445]

Although it gave general currency to 'striking similarity' as one of
the criteria for the admission of similar fact evidence, the judgment
itself gave no hint of what the alleged striking similarities might be in
the case under consideration. The observation made by J. R. S. Forbes
in his book *Similar Facts* that 'the similarities which so impressed the
court in *Sims* do not clearly appear in the report' is an understatement.
In fact they do not appear at all.[446]

What is clear is that the rationale according to which 'striking similarity' is put forward as a warrant for admissibility has been derived
from cases such as *Makin* and *Smith*. In these cases, each of the criminal acts introduced in evidence was, as it were, cut from the same similarly patterned cloth as the crime on the indictment, thus making it
logically improbable that they were not part of a single course of criminal conduct. However, in the absence of any details of what the acts
alleged against Sims actually were, it is quite impossible to assess
whether the 'striking similarities' asserted in the judgment were real or
imaginary. This in itself calls the soundness of the judgment into question.

What is perhaps even more dubious is the claim made in the judg-
ment that 'striking similarity' is a 'special feature *sufficient in itself* to justify the admissibility of the evidence'. For logically it cannot be right
to judge the admissibility of similar fact evidence solely by considering
the similarity between a series of alleged incidents which may not in
fact have happened at all.

The dangers of construing similarities as in themselves possessing
probative force are well illustrated by Howarth's own case. For of the
eight complainants ranged against him, only two made allegations
which were strikingly similar to one another. These were the 'dog-

walking' allegations made by Duke and West. Yet it was these complainants who turned out to have met in Swansea Prison, even though
West denied this and Duke at first attempted to. If anything, the striking similarity between their highly improbable complaints pointed to
the falsity of the allegations and not to their probative force.

It is not striking similarity in itself, then, which secures, or should
secure, admissibility. It is – or ought logically to be – the unlikelihood
that the allegations can have any other source than the criminal conduct of the defendant. For these allegations to be shown to have the
same degree of probative value as the facts in *Smith* or *Makin*, it would
be necessary to establish what Denning merely implies: that the four
men who accused Sims had never had any previous contact with one
another, that they had been unaware of the others' allegations, and that
they had independently and spontaneously made their complaints in
different towns or at different times. If it could first be shown that they
had acted quite independently, then the similarity in the facts of their
making such allegations would be compelling. Indeed, if it were beyond
doubt that all these conditions had been met, it might plausibly be
argued that, in this case, as in the case of *R v Smith*, the probative value
of the evidence of the four men was so great as to render irrelevant the
prejudicial effect of introducing their evidence collectively into a single trial.

What is striking about Denning's judgment though, is that he inverts
the process of reasoning which both logic and the legal precedents
demand. First he pronounces that the evidence is admissible on the
grounds of the alleged striking similarities alone, and only then does he
go on to consider the question of whether the allegations have been
made independently.

Before he even gets this far, however, he introduces another argument. In one of the most unusual pronouncements in British legal history, he suggests that 'sodomy is a crime in a special category', and that
therefore any allegation of sodomy made against a defendant who has
already been indicted on such a charge would be admissible as similar
fact evidence. In order to support this view he cites the words of Lord
Sumner which had been spoken in the course of an appeal heard in
1916:

> Sodomy is a crime in a special category, because, as Lord Sumner said:
> 'Persons who commit the offences now under consideration, seek the
> habitual gratification of a particular perverted lust, which not only

takes them out of the class of ordinary men gone wrong but stamps them with the hallmark of a special and extraordinary class, as much as if they carried on their bodies some physical peculiarity.' On this account, in regard to this crime, we think that the repetition of the acts is itself a specific feature connecting the accused with the crime and that evidence of this kind is admissible to show the nature of the act done by the accused. The probative force of all the acts together is much greater than one alone; for whereas the jury might think one man might be telling an untruth, three or four are hardly likely to tell the same untruth unless they were conspiring together. If there is nothing to suggest a conspiracy, their evidence would seem to be over-whelming.[447]

The most striking feature of this argument is the supreme confidence with which allegations of buggery are treated as a special category in respect of which the normal protection of the law can be removed from the person who is accused. Multiple allegations of sodomy are deemed *automatically* admissible on a similar fact basis.

Another remarkable feature is that, although Denning concedes the possibility that multiple allegations can be the result of a conspiracy, he suggests, contrary to all legal precedent, that such dangerous evidence should be put to the jury. Beyond this, perhaps the most telling feature of Denning's phrasing in the *Sims* judgment is his apparent assumption that an *allegation* of buggery is itself tantamount to evidence that an act of buggery has taken place. He thus refers to 'the probative force of all the acts together', when what he means is 'the probative force of all the allegations together'.

The overall effect of the judgment in *R v Sims* was, as J. R. S. Forbes has put it 'to place sodomy cases in a special, less demanding category for the purposes of similar fact evidence.'[448] The judgment also sought to give authority to an entirely new view of admissibility. For whereas previously similar fact evidence had been deemed admissible only to rebut a specific defence, such as mistaken identity or, as in the brides in the bath case, accident, it was now argued that it should be deemed admissible on account of its general probative value.

Although this new view might seem to have logical force, the fact that the judgment made no reference at all to the need to weigh pro-bative power against prejudicial effect inevitably lowered the threshold of admissibility. It is difficult to avoid the conclusion that a law which was designed to guard against prejudice had been radically weakened by a judge who was apparently intent on preserving and propagating prejudice of a particularly virulent kind. Innocent men wrongly accused of buggery were now to be treated with something of the same harshness Denning fully approved of in relation to those who were indeed guilty of such crimes. The judge who ruled on *Sims*, in other words, was recognisably the same judge who argued against the acceptance of the Wolfenden Report in 1957 and who believed that all homosexual conduct should continue to be regarded as both sinful and criminal.

That the judgment in *Sims* almost immediately gave rise to some judicial disquiet is suggested by the Australian case of *R v Jefferies* in 1947 in which Jordon CJ strongly dissented from the court's decision to admit evidence of homosexual behaviour with persons other than the complainant.[449] But it is perhaps a mark of the cultural power of the kind of prejudice expressed by Denning in 1946 that his attempt to place the crime of homosexual buggery in a special category, and effectively to undermine the presumption of innocence in cases involving allegations of buggery, was not properly challenged for almost twenty years. Even then the House of Lords panel which finally rejected it, still accepted some elements of the controversial and dangerous judgment of which it had formed a part.

As Peter Howarth tried to accustom himself to his new surroundings in Wakefield Prison, he remained unaware that his own case – and indeed the entire North Wales investigation – would almost certainly never have come to court in the manner that it did but for Denning's historic appeal court judgment, and the failure of subsequent appeal court judges to recognise just how dangerous that judgment was.

53 Striking similarities

BY THE 1970s IT HAD BECOME CLEAR to many members of the judiciary that the specialised application of the similar fact principle which had been devised by Denning and applied to cases involving homosexuality, needed to be reviewed.

The opportunity to reformulate the law as it applied to such allegations arose in 1975 when the case of *Boardman v DPP* came before the House of Lords. The case involved allegations of buggery and attempted buggery, made against a school teacher by three of his pupils. The appeal was heard by a particularly distinguished panel consisting of Lord Morris, Lord Wilberforce, Lord Hailsham, Lord Cross and Lord Salmon. The point of law which they had been asked to consider was this: 'Where, on a charge involving an allegation of homosexual conduct, there is evidence that the accused person is a man whose homosexual proclivities take a particular form, whether that evidence is thereby admissible although it tends to show that the accused has been guilty of criminal acts other than those charged.'[450]

The single question on which their Lordships unhesitatingly agreed was that the judgment in *Sims* was mistaken in one respect: there could be no question of homosexual offences forming a special class of crime for evidential purposes. Lord Cross noted that this view had already been expressed in passing by several of their Lordships in *DPP v Kilbourne* (1973) and said that he had no hesitation in agreeing with them: 'The attitude of the ordinary man towards homosexuality has changed very much even since *Sims* was decided, and what was said on that subject in 1917 by Viscount Sumner in *Thompson* – from which the view that homosexual offences form a class apart appears to stem – sounds nowadays like a voice from another world.'[451]

In other respects, however, the House of Lords now lent its authority to the judgment in *Sims* – in particular its willingness to admit as evidence not simply similar facts but similar allegations. At the same time it drew attention to the grave dangers which might follow from the change in the law. Lord Cross pointed out that there was a marked difference between cases which involved allegations and cases (such as

Makin and *Smith*) which involved counts of murder and undisputed evidence of previous deaths. In the original cases there was, he said, 'no question of any witness for the prosecution telling lies'.

Lord Cross went on to note that the crucial consideration in cases like *Sims* and the case currently before their Lordships, was that the similar fact evidence was disputed and that a series of allegations were all denied by the accused: 'In such circumstances the first question which arises is obviously whether his accusers may not have put their heads together to concoct false evidence and if there is any real chance of this having occurred the similar fact evidence must be excluded'.[452]

Lord Wilberforce underlined this view and warned against the danger that innocent defendants might find themselves facing a series of grave allegations, all of which were false. He clearly states his own view that the courts should be on their guard against the possibility that a series of false allegations might arise either from collusion or from a process of contamination. If there was any real possibility of this having occurred there should be no question of the similar fact evidence being admitted. Instead the judge should order separate trials.

The general test prescribed by *Boardman* was a cautious one. In deciding the question of admissibility, the judge should weigh the probative value of the evidence against its prejudicial effect. If the similar fact evidence was so weak, so unreliable or so contaminated that its capacity to prejudice a jury outweighed its probative value, then it should be excluded.

Their Lordships reinforced the caution embodied in this test by placing particular stress on the need (already acknowledged in *Sims*) for there to be 'striking similarities' between allegations before the possibility of their being admissible could even be considered. They thus accepted the highly dangerous precedent created by Denning, but did so only after insisting on two vital safeguards against the injustices it might lead to.

Where there were no striking similarities between the allegations, or where the allegations seemed not to have been made independently and therefore lacked probative power, the evidence was to be excluded. Lord Cross specifically advised judges against succumbing to the temptation to admit prejudicial evidence and then attempting to limit its power by directing the jury to put certain allegations out of their mind while judging the truth of others:

> [I]t is asking too much of any jury to tell them to perform mental gymnastics of this sort. If the charges are tried together it is inevitable

that the jurors will be influenced, consciously or unconsciously, by the fact that the accused is being charged not with a single offence against one person but with three separate offences against three persons. It is said, I know, that to order separate trials in all these cases would be highly inconvenient. If and so far as this is true it is a reason for doubting the wisdom of the general rule excluding similar fact evidence. But so long as there is that general rule the courts ought to strive to give effect to it loyally and not, while paying lip service to it, in effect let in the inadmissible evidence by trying all the charges together.

Boardman sought not simply to maintain the attitude towards the admission of similar fact evidence which had long been seen as crucial to the proper administration of justice, but actually to make it more stringent. It did so by stressing that probative power should always be weighed against prejudicial effect and that evidence which was more prejudicial than probative should be excluded. Whereas Denning's judgment in the case of *Sims* was redolent of prejudice and highly dangerous, the opinions of their Lordships in *Boardman* introduced vital safeguards which appeared to re-establish the possibility of justice and fairness even in cases involving allegations of homosexual behaviour.

Lord Morris recalled the words of Lord Sankey, who in 1934 had described the presumption that prejudicial evidence should be excluded as 'one of the most deeply rooted and jealously guarded principles of our criminal law'. Lord Morris went on to express optimism that it would be upheld. 'Judges,' he said, 'can be trusted not to allow so fundamental a principle to be eroded.'

However, although their Lordships had done their best to moderate the highly dangerous precedent created by Denning, by insisting on two vital safeguards against the injustices it might lead to, they had failed to recognise the extent to which the judgment in *Sims* radically threatened the very principles of justice itself. It would be the spirit of that judgment which would prevail. As a result, one of the safeguards put in place by *Boardman* would actually be removed by no other tribunal than the House of Lords itself.

This extraordinarily dangerous development in the law would take place in April 1991, a matter of months before the trial of Frank Beck, the launching of the Bryn Estyn investigation and the naming of Peter Howarth as a suspect. It would transform the law relating to sexual offences, and in doing so lay the foundations on which the practice of police trawling would be built.

54 Incest and injustice

ONE OF THE DOUBTS which must be raised about *Boardman* is why the possibility of collusion between complainants, or – more importantly – of other forms of contamination, received so little attention. Although this possibility was referred to in cautious terms both by Lord Wilberforce and Lord Cross, there was no real attempt to discuss how judges should deal with it. When the language and logic of all five law lords is scrutinised, it is difficult to avoid the impression that they failed to face up to this problem because to have done so would have meant confronting judicial history itself. They would have had to confront the fact that, in a number of decisions already taken by the higher courts, which had involved treating similar *allegation* evidence as though it were similar fact evidence, the safeguards which had been built up over centuries had been drastically compromised. The consensus, which Lords Wilberforce and Cross opposed in theory but not in practice, appears to have been that if there was no obvious indication of a conspiracy, then multiple allegations should go to the jury for them to determine their truth or falsehood, just as had happened in the case under consideration.

This principle, indeed, had already been endorsed by Lord Hailsham who had taken part in an appeal, *Kilbourne,* two years earlier. On that occasion he had said: 'When a small boy relates a sexual incident implicating a given man he may be indulging in fantasy. If another small boy relates such an incident it may be a coincidence if the detail is insufficient. If a large number of small boys relate similar incidents in enough detail about the same person, if it is not conspiracy it may well be that the stories are true. Once there is a sufficient nexus it must be for the jury to say what weight is given to the combined testimony of a number of witnesses.'[453]

It was this view which was endorsed, with qualifications, by their Lordships in 1975. We are thus confronted by the disturbing fact that, even in *Boardman*, which has sometimes been taken as the high water mark of caution in the matter of admissibility, the House of Lords assented to the logical possibility that an innocent defendant might find himself facing a series of allegations of sexual assault all of which were false. In order to be acquitted he would then find himself having to climb a mountain of prejudice so steep that he would almost certainly fail in the ascent.

In allowing such a state of affairs to come about it may well be that the five noble lords found themselves effectively in thrall to the opinions of those who had preceded them – especially the opinions expressed in *Sims* – and to a habit of mind developed in relation to factual cases such as *Makin* and *Smith*. They may also have judged that the likelihood of a conspiracy to make false allegations against an innocent defendant, or of any other form of contamination on the same scale, was so remote as to pose no real threat to justice.

But they may also have been influenced by another factor: that sexual offences, particularly homosexual offences against young people, are widely considered to be so abhorrent that most people, including members of the intelligentsia (and even of the Bar itself), are far less likely to demand fairness and justice for defendants than they are in cases of theft or burglary or even murder. There are therefore powerful pressures, to which even law lords may not be immune, to allow defendants who may be innocent to run the risk of prejudice in order to increase the chances of convicting those who are guilty.

Whether or not it is accepted that the House of Lords was unwittingly influenced by such factors in *Boardman*, as Denning and his colleagues undoubtedly had been before them, it would generally be conceded that the pressure to gain convictions in sexual cases increased as the twentieth century neared its end. Given the amount of attention during the 1980s to the crime of child sexual abuse, it is perhaps not surprising that the next crucial development in similar fact law took place in 1991 when the House of Lords considered a case involving allegations of incest. The case is known as *DPP v P*. Its outcome would be crucial not only for the father whose appeal was rejected, but for Peter Howarth and the hundreds of care workers who would soon find themselves following in his footsteps.

In the original criminal trial of *R v P*, which was heard in Stafford Crown Court in January 1988, the defendant, 'P', faced a number of counts of rape and incest as a result of allegations made by his two daughters. Given the fact that, on the one hand, the crime of multiple incest is a real one, and on the other hand that cases have been recorded where false allegations against a father have been made by two different daughters, the correct application of the similar fact principle was clearly a matter of great importance in this case.

The father applied to have the indictment severed so that he might be tried on counts relating to one daughter at a time. The judge, however, ruled that there were striking similarities between the allegations and, having apparently decided that collusion was unlikely, admitted the evidence of both daughters on a similar fact basis. P was convicted of one rape and a number of counts of incest in respect of each daughter. However, his appeal was allowed on the grounds that the striking similarities claimed at the trial did not exist. Crucially however, the Lord Chief Justice, Lord Lane, in delivering the appeal judgment, gave a powerful indication that he was unhappy with the outcome.

During the appeal hearing Michael Mansfield QC, representing the appellant, complained that it was almost a lottery whether separate trials would be ordered by the courts. These words were now turned back against him. Having suggested that the prosecution might wish to appeal to the House of Lords against the outcome of the appeal, the Lord Chief Justice made the views of the Court of Appeal clear:

> We have said enough to indicate that [this branch of the law] is an area which is difficult to understand and even more difficult to apply in practice. ... It seems to us absurd that counsel and judge should be spending time searching through committal papers, which may in the upshot not represent the evidence actually given, searching for 'striking similarities' such as to justify allowing the jury to hear evidence of that which they would naturally and rightly consider themselves entitled to know, namely that the defendant is charged with abusing not merely one but two or more of his daughters.[454]

Lord Lane, however, went even further than this:

> We see force in the suggestion adumbrated in argument before us that where the father has allegedly shown himself to be someone prepared to abuse sexually girls who are no more than children, in this case under the age of 13, girls who are moreover his own children, and to use his position of power over them in their own home to achieve those ends, this might provide a sufficient hallmark to render the evidence of one girl admissible in the case of the other where the danger of collusion can be discounted. In the current state of decided cases we are, we think, inhibited from so deciding.[455]

These words of the Lord Chief Justice might be said to mark as distinctive a turning-point in the history of the similar fact principle as the judgment in *Sims* in 1946. For what they clearly indicated was that the 'hallmark-of-vice' approach to similar fact evidence, which had originally been proposed by Denning in relation to alleged homosexuals, was now being proposed by the Court of Appeal in relation to those who were accused of being child abusers.

Once again an influential and very senior judge had suggested that the normal restrictions on similar fact evidence should be relaxed to make it easier to prosecute a particular class of sexual offence which was especially repugnant. Denning's suggestion that alleged homosexuals should be treated in this manner had eventually been rejected by the House of Lords, who had – after a delay of nineteen years – reaffirmed the need for striking similarities before any multiple allegations could be admitted. The outcome of Lord Lane's intervention, however, was different. The Director of Public Prosecutions almost immediately responded to his hint – one might better say instruction – and applied for leave to appeal to the House of Lords so that the conviction might be restored. the Court of Appeal granted this application and certified two questions as being of general public importance:

> (1) where a father or stepfather is charged with sexually abusing a young daughter of the family, is evidence that he similarly abused other young children of the family admissible (assuming there to be no collusion) in support of such charge in the absence of any other 'striking similarities'; and (2) where a defendant is charged with sexual offences against more than one child or young person, is it necessary, in the absence of 'striking similarities' for the charges to be tried separately?[456]

The appeal was heard in April 1991 before a panel of five: the Lord Chancellor (Lord Mackay of Clashfern), Lord Keith of Kinkel, Lord Emslie, Lord Templeman and Lord Ackner.*

The judgment given by Lord Mackay was unusual in that it consisted almost entirely of quotations from previous cases, mostly from *Boardman*. Having cited various pronouncements at length, Lord Mackay went on to offer his own view that whereas 'striking similarities' might be necessary in cases where the identity of the offender was at issue,

---

* Professor Colin Tapper has noted that, of the panel of five law lords, there were three 'whose only experience before their elevation was in Scottish law and one whose experience was exclusively in Chancery. Only Lord Ackner had had any substantial experience of English criminal law at trial or intermediate appellate level. ('The erosion of *Boardman v DPP*', *New Law Journal*, August 11 1995, p. 1224, note 15).

they were not necessary in other cases. Similar fact evidence was admissible in his view, if 'its probative force in support of the allegation that an accused person committed a crime is sufficiently great to make it just to admit the evidence, notwithstanding that it is prejudicial to the accused in tending to show that he was guilty of another crime'. Exactly how, in the absence of striking similarities, the claim that a person had committed one crime could be used to prove that he had committed another crime, was not a question which Lord Mackay addressed.

Even more remarkable than this omission was Lord Mackay's apparent belief that the need for 'striking similarity' proclaimed in *Boardman* only applied in cases which raised the question of identity. Since identity was not at issue in *Boardman*, this was clearly not so. Indeed, as Professor Colin Tapper has pointed out, 'Lord Wilberforce confined his speech in that case to "the present set of facts and cases of a similar character" and explicitly excluded from it "a case involving proof of identity".'[457] What makes Lord Mackay's pronouncement especially difficult to understand is that the demand for striking similarity as a criterion for the admission of similar fact evidence plainly did not have its origins in *Boardman* or even in *Sims*. It came in the first place from such cases as *Makin* and *Smith*, in neither of which had the issue of identity played any part at all.

The original point of the demand for such similarities was not to link a particular crime to a particular criminal, but to link one crime to another. For only if crimes could be shown to have strikingly similar features could the details of one reasonably be invoked as evidence for the other. If it could be shown that two different crimes shared the same unusual template, then the evidence relating to one might have probative value in relation to the other, as was clearly so in the brides in the bath case. Otherwise they were simply different crimes which, though committed by the same person, or alleged to have been, were logically and evidentially independent of one another.

Lord Mackay's insistence on confining striking similarity to the issue of identity entirely disregards this point. As Professor Tapper has noted 'it flies in the face of the ordinary operation of the doctrine of precedent'.[458] However there is another point it neglects, whose consequences are ultimately far more serious. If we are to understand the extent to which the judgment in *P* transformed the entire similar fact principle, it is essential to recognise that the concept of 'striking similarity' has a more complex function in 'similar allegation evidence' than

in 'similar fact evidence'. In cases which involve multiple sexual complaints, the striking similarities which *Boardman,* following *Sims,*
demanded of allegations, should not be seen as in themselves establishing an underlying unity between the various offences. For this once
again would be to assume that the allegations are true. In reality the
similarities merely establish the *possibility* that there is an underlying
unity between a number of alleged offences whose reality is not yet
established.

   It is because a similar allegation, unlike a similar fact, may be false,
that the judgment in *Boardman* lays stress on the need for striking similarities. It does so on the grounds that, while a group of vaguely similar allegations might come about as a result of accident or an ordinary
process of contamination, strikingly similar allegations are likely either
to be true, or the result of an organised conspiracy against the defendant. Allegations which indicated some relatively ordinary form of
indecent assault, with no striking similarities, might conceivably have
been made up independently and the defendant the victim of coincidence or misfortune – or a form of contamination which stopped short
of collusion.

   This much is recognised in *Boardman* itself. The point is so important
because the absence of striking similarities from a set of multiple allegations would greatly increase the chance that some other form of contamination had been at work. If we consider media contamination, for
instance, the mere mention in newspaper and television coverage that
a particular named man is being investigated on suspicion of sexually
abusing boys has limited potential to contaminate evidence. For it
could not plausibly be claimed as the 'common cause' of a subsequent
series of allegations whose unusual details exactly matched. However,
were 'striking similarity' to be dispensed with as a criterion of possible
admissibility, the opportunities for fabricating allegations against a suspect who had been publicly named would be massively increased.
Almost any allegation of indecency, however general or ordinary, would
now be admissible.

   Even though this point was never specifically made in *Boardman,* the
general consideration which lies behind it was clearly felt to be
extremely important, particularly by Lord Wilberforce and Lord Cross.
What Lord Mackay apparently did not recognise when giving judgment in DPP *v* P was that, by rejecting the traditional centrality of striking similarity, and creating a lower threshold for the admission of similar
fact evidence, he was removing a vital safeguard which had previously

kept potentially admissible evidence safe from certain forms of contamination.

In case the point should remain obscure, DPP *v* P itself provides an
excellent illustration of what is at stake. Much was made of the evidence which suggested that 'there was no real danger' that the two
daughters had colluded in making false allegations against their father.
It was pointed out that, although the dates of the offences alleged by
the two sisters overlapped, the elder sister had left home without knowing that her younger sister was allegedly being abused; thereafter she
had little contact with the rest of the family.[459] What neither the Court
of Appeal nor the House of Lords appears to have recognised was that,
in the absence of striking similarities between the sisters' allegations, the
spectre of collusion was not the most important factor. If, as was always
contended on behalf of the father, the allegations had been fabricated,
all that was necessary for vaguely similar 'copy cat' allegations to emerge
was for one sister to acquire some knowledge, possibly at second hand,
that the other was making an allegation. An active conspiracy to concoct allegations jointly was entirely unnecessary.

It was partly to guard against this kind of indirect seepage of false
allegations from one complainant to another that their Lordships in
Boardman had continued to insist on the criterion of striking similarity.
By abandoning it the Lord Chancellor, in giving judgment in the case
of DPP *v* P, inadvertently marginalised the significance of collusion
while simultaneously opening the evidential floodgates to every lesser
form of contamination which had previously been shut out from the
courts. The similar fact principle, once zealously guarded by the defence
as an essential means of keeping prejudicial evidence out, has, as a result,
become the favoured device of the prosecution, valued as an almost
ever-open conduit for letting prejudicial evidence in.

Had there been any real recognition of the need to protect innocent
defendants against the possibility of facing multiple false allegations,
the only course for the House of Lords to take would have been to
insist on rigorously assessing the credibility and reliability of multiple
allegations before admitting them in a single trial. In particular it
would have been necessary to adopt a much more sensitive approach
to any form of contamination, and to exclude evidence which might
have been contaminated in any way – including by the investigative
process itself. Yet it is quite clear from the judgment in DPP *v* P that no
such course was envisaged. Indeed, since the judgment gives no indication of where the allegations now declared admissible had acquired

their probative force, it is difficult to escape a disturbing conclusion. It would seem that the hidden assumption behind the judgment is that, for the purpose of assessing their admissibility, the allegations should be treated by the judge as though they were true. This reading of the judgment in *DPP v P* would eventually be confirmed by the Lord Chancellor himself when he gave judgment four years later in the case of *R v H*. The damage, however, had already been done.

As the jury in Chester Crown Court had deliberated over the allegations against Peter Howarth, they were not aware that the kind of police operation used to collect these allegations had come into existence only as an indirect result of the decision to dispense with the criterion of striking similarity taken in the House of Lords three years earlier. Until that crucial judgment, the kind of disparate allegations almost inevitably produced by police trawling would not generally have found their way into a single trial.

This very point, indeed, would eventually be implicitly acknowledged by the counsel to the North Wales Tribunal. In his opening address, Gerard Elias QC said this: 'In relation to allegations of sexual abuse ... questions of corroboration clouded the issue for much of the period, but at least since the House of Lords decision in *DPP v P* (1991), the prosecution of those against whom more than one similar offence (or type of offence) is alleged has been made procedurally and evidentially easier'.[460]

The prosecution of Peter Howarth was, for all these reasons, of a different kind from any that took place before 1991. Given the state of the evidence, and given the fact that no single count could conceivably have afforded proof beyond reasonable doubt that Howarth had committed the offence in question, it is reasonably clear that his conviction was founded on prejudice rather than proof.

If one examines the practical effects of the reforms which have been made to facilitate the prosecution of alleged sexual abusers, and to increase the chances of conviction, one is led almost inevitably to recall an earlier phase of legal history. For in the sixteenth and seventeenth centuries, one particular crime was defined by the authorities as *crimen exceptum* – an exceptional crime. In 1580 the great French legal scholar, Jean Bodin, wrote this of the crime of witchcraft:

> Therefore it is that somebody accused of being a witch ought never to be fully acquitted and set free unless the calumny of the accuser is clearer than the sun, inasmuch as the proof of such crimes is so obscure

and so difficult that not one witch in a million would be accused or punished if the procedure were governed by the ordinary rules.[461]

Bodin's view that the ordinary rules of justice should not be permitted to prevent the execution of those who were accused of witchcraft was a crucial factor in the development of the great European witch-hunt. What needs now urgently to be recognised is that, by gradually over-turning well-established judicial principles governing the admissibility of similar fact evidence, successive appeal court judgments have, since 1946, effectively established child sexual abuse as a new *crimen exceptum*. The case of *R v Peter Norman Howarth* was one of the first criminal trials to be conducted under the new rules.

The deliberate loosening of the rules of evidence meant that the very kind of injustice which the similar fact principle had originally been designed to prevent was now increasingly treated as a normal part of the court process. Since the courts themselves were now prepared in practice to convict people on the basis of contaminated evidence, made up of multiple uncorroborated allegations all of which might be false, it was only to be expected that the form of investigation which was best suited to collecting such dangerous evidence – police trawling – would undergo spectacular growth. In the years which followed the conviction of Peter Howarth, this is exactly what happened.

55 Paying a witness

ONE DIMENSION OF BRITISH SOCIETY which is not always understood by those who observe the workings of our judicial system is the intensity and depth of the faith which most ordinary people have in British justice. Most of those who are falsely accused do not lose this faith when they are charged. On the contrary they tend to repose even more faith in the fairness of the courts and their belief that they will not be convicted of crimes they have not committed. Peter Howarth was no exception. After the judge had sentenced him, he was taken down to a cell in the depths of Chester Crown Court. John Rayfield and Howarth's counsel, John Rogers QC, went down to see him. Rayfield recalls that Howarth was unable to speak. 'He was absolutely dumbstruck. He simply stared at us. I think he was in such shock that he just couldn't find any words at all. He couldn't believe what had happened. We spoke to him. I can't remember what we said. I think we said goodbye.'[462]

That night Howarth was held in Walton Prison in Liverpool. However, the prison authorities, fearing that he might become the victim of violence triggered by the massive local publicity given to the case, decided to transfer him. He was moved to a high security prison which houses a large number of sex offenders – HMP Wakefield.

Howarth's first action was to ask his solicitor to prepare an appeal. His dismay at the trial verdict was soon compounded by the response to this request. Having relatively little knowledge of the complex circumstances which had led to the Bryn Estyn investigation, unaware of the role which had been played by Alison Taylor and Dean Nelson, and without the benefit of the mass of evidence which would eventually emerge at the North Wales Tribunal, Howarth's counsel advised that there were no grounds for appeal. Although Howarth had the support of Gwen Hurst and John Rayfield, who both believed that he was the victim of a miscarriage of justice, he was now effectively without any legal representation.

However, the fact that Howarth had been convicted meant that he was an even more important figure in the North Wales story than he had ever been before. He had barely been in Wakefield a week when he was told by a prison officer that two visitors had come to see him. The men had made no prior arrangement. They had simply arrived out of the blue and requested an interview. When Howarth agreed to speak to them he discovered that his visitors were from the North Wales Police. Detective Superintendent Peter Ackerley, accompanied by another officer, had come to seek his help in relation to the allegations made against Gordon Anglesea. They were apparently looking for any evidence which might be used in a criminal prosecution of Anglesea. In a memo written on 22 July 1994, after visiting his client in Wakefield Prison, Howarth's solicitor wrote the following:

> You said that you had received a special visit from [the North Wales Police]. You were caught unawares. They asked you again about Anglesey [sic] and ... [whether] he had committed offences ... In terms you told them to get lost. You made it quite clear to them that Anglesey had not committed any offences. You got a prison officer to witness the fact that you were telling them this. At the end of the conversation they asked your permission to tell HTV where you were. You refused.[463]

Whilst Howarth declined to help the police for the simple reason that he had no evidence to give, another care officer, who had briefly worked at Bryn Estyn, was anxious to help in any way that she could. Alison Taylor's February 1993 offer to assist the CPS in relation to a possible criminal case against Anglesea had met with a negative response (see above pp. 306–7), but this did not rule out the possibility of her giving evidence in the civil case which was in preparation. She might yet, in short, appear as a witness in the libel trial.

Indeed, on 26 May 1994, even before Peter Howarth's trial had begun, Taylor had signed a proof of evidence for use by the *Independent on Sunday* in the Anglesea case. The first original feature of this statement was the account she gave of the regime at Bryn Estyn, as she had supposedly observed it during her three-month placement in 1982. This severely critical account included the following passage: 'Facilities at the home were poor with inadequate standards of comfort and privacy. A number of boys were particularly dirty and unwashed and some were infested with lice.'

According to the testimony of numerous former members of staff and former residents, this description was untrue. It was also wholly inconsistent with what Alison Taylor had herself said. In her many statements she had made no mention of the unhygienic, lice-infested conditions she now described. Nor, of course, did her description of the home correspond to what she had said in the Bryn Estyn log book in 1982, where she had nothing but praise for the home.

The next part of her statement was no less remarkable. Having pointedly referred to Howarth's 'flat list' (something she had not mentioned in her initial police statement), and to the fact that Howarth was about to stand trial on charges of child sexual abuse, she turned immediately to the subject of Gordon Anglesea:

> During my placement of [sic] Bryn Estyn, on one particularly fine day, whilst I was in the library at the front of the Home, I saw a car arrive. The driver, whom I did not recognise, entered the building and a short while later emerged with [the white] John Evans, one of the boys in residence. I asked one of the boys with me in the library whether he knew the driver. He told me it was Inspector Anglesea. I can recall instantly making a connection with the person mentioned on many occasions by Nefyn Dodd. I was curious to know what Inspector Anglesea was doing at the Home and I continued to observe him from the library. Then Peter Howarth emerged from the main building and all three (Anglesea, Howarth and Evans) drove away.
>
> I am sure the person I saw on that day was Gordon Anglesea because I saw him identify himself in the HTV programme 'Wales This Week' which was broadcast in 1992. There is no doubt in my mind that the man identified on the programme as Gordon Anglesea was the same man I saw at Bryn Estyn.[464]

Although Taylor has since attempted to explain away this statement by claiming that she was merely giving an account of an innocent event, this was clearly not how she construed matters in 1994. She very specifically linked Anglesea to Howarth in a context where, as she herself pointed out, the latter was facing criminal charges of child abuse. Since, according to her own story about the minibus (see above, chapter 27), she had supposedly learned soon after the encounter she now described that John Evans had himself been sexually abused by Howarth, the meeting, had it taken place, would have been highly significant and suspicious. It would, as she clearly intended it to, have raised as a possibility the notion that Anglesea had come to Bryn Estyn to collect Evans and Howarth, specifically to engage in an act of child sexual abuse.

Perhaps the most telling feature of Taylor's statement was that she had not mentioned the alleged sighting of Anglesea on any previous occasion. She had in fact had numerous opportunities to record it in the fifteen or so statements she made to the police about alleged abuse at Bryn Estyn between 1991 and 1994. In some of these statements she made detailed claims about each of the three individuals concerned. In the statement she made on 9 December 1991, for example, she claimed to remember a time when Howarth went out to play golf and took John Evans with him. This claim was itself implausible in view of the fact that, according to Taylor's own account in the same statement, 'Howarth had been confined to his flat either with a broken ankle or leg'. Her claim that 'when Mr Howarth was recovering from his break-age he would go out in the afternoons to play golf', seems inherently unlikely.

Yet, in spite of having made a statement which specifically described an occasion when Howarth had supposedly driven off with Evans, Tay-lor had made no mention, here or anywhere else, of any occasion when she saw Anglesea either with Howarth or with Evans or, indeed, on his own. On the contrary, all the information she had previously conveyed about Anglesea had been of a hearsay nature, and at no point had she ever hinted that she had met him or seen him.

Given the circumstances and the pervasive evidence of distortion and dishonesty (or delusion) in Taylor's allegations about related matters, the most plausible explanation of the claim she now made was that it was another opportunistic invention. Or, as Anglesea's counsel Ben Hinch-liff would suggest to Mrs Taylor at the Tribunal: 'that this supposed inci-dent at Bryn Estyn where you saw Mr Anglesea, so you say, Mr Howarth and John Evans is nothing more than a fabrication, that you never mentioned it in your police statements or your interview with Dean Nelson because it didn't happen, and that the first time that you mentioned it was in your witness statement prepared for the benefit of the libel action on 26 May 1994, which was 12 years later.'[465]

It is interesting that, in the event, Alison Taylor was not called to give evidence at the libel trial. In view of the fact that the newspapers defending the action did call at least one witness to give evidence of an even less substantial kind, it would seem entirely possible that Taylor was not called precisely because the lawyers recognised that she was not a credible witness, and that she might very well be destroyed in cross-examination. However there was one witness that the defence could not dispense with; this was Lee Steward.

Steward, however, had expressed reservations about giving evidence. The reasons he gave for his reluctance were set out in a letter written in May 1993 – more than a year before the libel action came to trial in

November 1994. The letter was sent by Steward's solicitors to the solicitors acting for *Private Eye*. Although it was not sent until four months
after *Private Eye* had published its article about Anglesea, its main purpose was to take issue with a particular paragraph in that article – the
paragraph which claimed that Steward had on one occasion visited the
flat of convicted paedophile Gary Cooke. Steward now said that this
paragraph libelled him. In conveying their client's complaint, Steward's
solicitors said he was alleging that he had been beaten up as a direct
result of the publication of this article:

> We write with reference to our telephone conversation this morning,
> [and] confirm we have now been able to take our client's further
> instructions. We also thank you for a copy of the article which you
> kindly faxed to us this morning. Our instructions are that prior to your
> clients printing this article our client was somewhat of a local hero,
> insofar as many of the other boys who had been at Bryn Estyn and the
> other various homes and were victim[s] of the paedophile ring, looked
> up to him as he had the courage to stand up against his abusers and file
> charges.
>
> Within a few days of the article being published in *Private Eye* our
> client was ostracised by many of his friends and acquaintances and
> became the target of both physical attacks upon himself and his prop-
> erty and, as you are aware, within approximately three to four days of
> the article being published our client was approached by four inmates
> of Bryn Estyn who accused him of selling his story to the press and
> then proceeded to violently assault him, told him if he said anything
> further he would be subjected to further violence. Nobody trusted
> him any longer, as they felt he was colluding with Gary Cooke, also
> known as Mark Jones.[466]

It would appear that no evidence has ever been produced to substantiate the story which Steward now told and that he has never identified
the former residents of Bryn Estyn who were supposed to have
assaulted him. In the circumstances, of course, *Private Eye* and its editor,
Ian Hislop, were scarcely in a position to question Steward's story, since
to do so would impugn the credibility of one of the very witnesses they
were relying on to prove their case against Gordon Anglesea.

The letter ended by offering *Private Eye* a way out of the libel action
which Steward was threatening: 'In the circumstances we feel if you
want to settle this matter out of court we would be looking for damages in the region of £55,000 to £60,000 plus reasonable costs.'

Not long after this letter was written, in June or early July of 1993,

Steward had a meeting with Ian Hislop in the presence of one of *Private Eye*'s solicitors. On 13 July 1993 Steward's solicitors wrote again to the solicitors representing *Private Eye*:

> We recently had a meeting with our client. He advised us that at the meeting that took place between himself and Ian Hislop and Mr Bays of your office, he was advised by Ian Hislop that whatever happened *Private Eye* would cover the cost of a new car, which we understand was pitched at £10,000. ... Our client would be prepared to accept £10,000 by way of settlement in addition to our costs.

Although Hislop subsequently disputed Steward's account of the meeting, it would appear that this letter was not replied to. On 18 November 1993, Lee Steward himself wrote to Hislop:

> My solicitor has written to your solicitors a number of times, your solicitors do not reply. You said you would like to get this matter sorted out. All we had to agree on was a figure. You wanted the matter sorted out as soon as possible, it's about time this matter was settled. It is not long now before we have to face Gordon Anglesea in court. I hope you are still prepared to fight this case. I'm sure we can win it. Remember if you need to contact me ... I am only too willing to help you in any way.
>
> Yours faithfully,
>
> Lee Steward

At this point, however, deadlock seems to have been reached. Almost a year passed without any settlement. In October 1994 *Private Eye,* who by this time were clearly anxious that a vital witness might not appear at the trial, suggested that the matter should be taken to arbitration. On 24 October Steward refused.

By now the date for the libel trial had been set; it was to begin in the high court in London before Mr Justice Drake on 14 November. There were only three weeks left before it was due to start. On 31 October *Private Eye*'s solicitors received a phone call from Steward's solicitors in North Wales. A note was made that the latter 'had letter from Lee saying "won't give evidence unless the *Eye* claim is resolved".' Steward's bargaining rested almost entirely on his claim, which *Private Eye* appears to have made no attempt to verify, that he had been beaten up by former Bryn Estyn residents as a result of the publication of the article. *Private Eye* was put in a position in which it either had to enter into a bargain whose dishonesty it must at least have suspected, or risk losing a vital witness. Steward was evidently aware of the strength of his own position. As he would eventually tell the Tribunal. 'My solicitor said to me that you carried the ace card, they need you, we shouldn't have a problem winning.'[467]

Private Eye finally capitulated; Steward's solicitors received a note indicating their 'preparedness to pay to your client the sum of £4,500 in full and final settlement of all his claims, plus costs.' The agreement was finalised on 7 November 1994. Exactly a week later, on Monday 14 November, one of the most important libel trials in recent history began in the high court.

56 Court 13: the libel trial

WHEN IT BECAME CLEAR that Gordon Anglesea's libel actions against *Independent Newspapers,* the *Observer, Private Eye* and HTV were going to be heard at one trial, the first three defendants (who were all London-based) decided to share barristers; their leading counsel would be George Carman QC. Respected and feared in equal measure for his ability to handle complex briefs, his shrewd way with a jury and his relentless cross-examinations, Carman was widely regarded as 'King of the Court'. The man who would eventually cross-examine and defeat the former cabinet minister Jonathan Aitken, in Aitken's notorious action against the *Guardian,* was the barrister who could be most relied on to find and ruthlessly exploit any weaknesses in the case of his opponents. He was celebrated above all for what has been called 'his wonderful capacity to destroy witnesses'. It is recorded that, during a gruelling session in the witness box, one plaintiff in another case, the South African journalist Jani Allen, said to him: 'Whatever award is given for libel, being cross-examined by you would not make it enough money.'

With the appointment of Carman (whose junior on this occasion was Heather Rogers) one thing seemed clear: Gordon Anglesea would find himself facing the most rigorous inquisition he could ever be submitted to.

It was to George Carman's London chambers that, in the weeks leading up to the trial, Ian Hislop of *Private Eye,* Ian Jack of the *Independent on Sunday* and a senior journalist from the *Observer* made their way. Of these journalists it was Jack alone who was familiar with the way in which the story had begun. And it was, of course, Jack who had made the fateful decisions to include the offending paragraph about Anglesea in the original story in December 1991 and, subsequently, to send Dean Nelson back to North Wales to search for more evidence.

Given his role in the story it is significant that, as the three journalists planned their defence with Carman, it was Jack who began to have doubts about the wisdom of continuing: 'I began to worry about the quality of our evidence,' he would write years later in the *Guardian,* 'but

repressed my thoughts because everyone else seemed so gung-ho (Is Ian
Hislop ever not?). To withdraw now would seem cowardly.'[468]

At one conference Jack did raise the possibility of settling out of
court. Carman responded by calling this a 'commercial question'. It
was, he said, quite possible to consider what settling out of court might
cost in financial terms as opposed to what losing the case might cost.
But beyond that there was the 'moral question'. It was Carman's view
that, if they were to settle at that point, the newspapers would give their
three witness the impression that they did not believe them. This could
be traumatic. Carman then mentioned something that had happened in
a previous case. If the three editors did decide to settle at this point, he
suggested, they would have to face the 'real possibility' that one of the
witnesses might kill himself.

It seems that the possibility that Mark Humphreys, Lee Steward and
Carl Holden might not be telling the truth was not seriously entertained by Carman any more than it was by Ian Hislop. Confronted with
the scenario that he might drive one of the three young men to suicide, Jack silenced his doubts. 'I never raised the question again. Who
wants death on their conscience?'[469]

As Jack and his colleagues consulted with Carman, Gordon Anglesea
was consulting with Barton Taylor, his solicitor. On several occasions,
sometimes accompanied by his wife Sandra, he visited the chambers of
the barrister selected to fight his case – Gareth Williams QC. Described
by one of his fellow barristers as 'having all the natural egalitarianism of
Welshness' and as a 'sparkling speaker' who is 'careful in debate, witty in
entertainment, always effortlessly eloquent', Williams was educated at
Rhyl Grammar School not many miles from Bryn Estyn. In 1992, not
long after the completion of his report into Tŷ Mawr (see above, chapter 2), he had been ennobled by John Major and was now Lord
Williams of Mostyn. He would later become leader of the House of
Lords, a position he held until his death in September 2003. In the trial
his junior would be Andrew Caldecott, the barrister consulted by
Anglesea about the original *Independent on Sunday* article.[470]

After carefully studying the evidence and after interviewing Anglesea and his wife at length, Lord Williams became deeply committed to
the case. Having already encountered the methods of Dean Nelson
during his Tŷ Mawr inquiry, he may have looked forward to the opportunity of cross-examining the journalist who might appear as the newspapers' leading witness.

But, as he probed into the relationship between Gordon and Sandra

Anglesea, and studied the reams of documents which had been disclosed in advance of the trial, there was one piece of evidence which, for the time being at least, remained invisible to him. Not until the trial was already in progress would Williams see for the first time a set of documents which were destined to play a vital role in the case.

Carman, who had made a speciality of confounding his opponents by suddenly producing new evidence, had managed to secure the disclosure of a cache of secret love letters written by Gordon Anglesea to Sandra – the woman who would become his second wife – at a time when she was still married. Carman had apparently come to the conclusion that by using this evidence of an adulterous affair he would be able to turn the jury against Anglesea. Yet, in reality, these letters provided striking evidence that, not long before he was supposed to have subjected three adolescent boys to a series of perverted sexual assaults, Anglesea had been conducting a passionate love affair with a woman. As he embarked on his legal duel, Williams could never have imagined that his opponent would soon place in his hand the very weapon he needed to help defeat him.

It was shortly before 10.30 am on Monday 14 November 1994, at the Royal Courts of Justice in The Strand, that the legal teams representing the four defendants and the plaintiff took their places at the front of Court 13 and waited for the judge, Mr Justice Drake, to make his entrance. Here, in the Victorian Gothic courtroom, with its stone walls, oak ceiling and high, leaded windows, a drama unlike any other in British legal history was about to unfold.

As the key witnesses in the case took their places behind the lawyers – on the left-hand side Mark Humphreys, Lee Steward and Carl Holden, and on the right-hand side Gordon and Sandra Anglesea, the limited number of places available to the press and the public rapidly filled up. Among those who would attend the trial over the next few weeks were Ian Hislop, and the proprietor of *Private Eye*, the comedian Peter Cook. Although the magazine had been the object of many libel actions in its brief history, this was clearly regarded as one of the most significant of them all.

Court 13, the most famous libel court in England, had in its time been the scene of more celebrated acts of perjury than practically any other courtroom in the land. To cite the best known instance, it had been the courtroom where Jeffrey Archer had repeatedly lied to the jury during his 1987 libel battle. Given the nature of the case about to be heard it was quite clear that more acts of perjury were about to be committed there. What most of those in attendance did not know was which side was most likely to commit them.

After the opening addresses by Lord Williams and George Carman it was Gordon Anglesea who was ushered into the witness box first. As he was examined by his own counsel, the bare outlines of his life were drawn in for the benefit of the jury. Anglesea was 57 at the time of the trial. He was born in North Wales and, after attending the local primary school at Buckley, near Chester, won a scholarship to Mold Alun Grammar School, ten miles away from Wrexham. Having decided that he wanted to be a policeman, he was accepted as a police cadet at the age of sixteen and completed his two-year training period before being called up for National Service in the Royal Air Force. In 1957 he went back to the police and gradually rose through the ranks, becoming a sergeant in 1969 and a uniformed police inspector in 1972. It was as an inspector that he occasionally had cause to visit Bryn Estyn during the course of his duties. He said that, to the best of his recollection, he never went there before 1980 and that in the next three years he believed he had been there about eleven times. Nothing of any great note had happened on these occasions.[471]

On the personal front he had married his first wife in 1959 and had two children with her, a girl and a boy. By 1975 the marriage was in difficulties and had all but broken down. It was at a New Year's Eve party at the end of 1975 that he first met Sandra. They fell in love almost at once. Sandra was married with three children. After a passionate romance they both eventually divorced and married each other on 26 March 1977.

After about two years, Gordon Anglesea's children from his first marriage, who were then in their late teens, came to live with him and Sandra. Their first child together, Elizabeth, was born with a serious medical problem; she died tragically in May 1983 at the age of four-and-a-half. It was during the time when he was anxiously pre-occupied by her health, that her father was supposed to have sexually assaulted the three adolescent boys who were now, fifteen years later, due to take the stand against him. Anglesea and his wife subsequently had another child, a boy, who was born in October 1985.

It was in that same year that Gordon Anglesea had become a chief inspector. He was subsequently promoted to superintendent, a rank which he held until his retirement in March 1991. He and Sandra had then settled down to enjoy his retirement in the peaceful seaside town of Rhos-on-Sea, where Anglesea was a pillar of the community. He was a member of the Methodist Church and the Rotary club, and a governor of two local schools. This happy retirement came to an abrupt end at the beginning of December. On Sunday 1 December 1991, Anglesea told the court, he attended church as usual and then called in at his local newsagents to buy the Sunday paper. He was going to buy the *Sunday Telegraph* as he normally did, but, as he bent down to pick up a copy of the paper, his eye was caught by the headline on the *Independent on Sunday*, 'NEW CHILD ABUSE SCANDAL'. Anglesea noticed that the story was about Bryn Estyn. As he quickly read through it he stopped at the paragraph which mentioned his name, the very paragraph which had caused Ian Jack, only eighteen hours earlier, to query the evidence on which it was based. Asked in court what effect it had on him, he replied: 'I was absolutely gob-smacked, horrified, because I couldn't understand why that should be printed and what connection I had with that particular scandal.'[472]

He took the newspaper home and showed it to his wife. She broke down in tears, left the house and went round to her mother's. Anglesea said that he was so incensed and so horrified that, even though it was Sunday morning, he immediately contacted the Wrexham solicitor, John Hughes, and asked if he would act for him.

Anglesea went on to relate how, in September 1992, he had read the full allegations published in the *Observer* where, without naming him, but clearly identifying him to those familiar with the story by describing him as 'a retired police chief', the paper had accused him of anally raping Lee Steward. Asked by his counsel how he felt, he said: 'I felt like a leper. I didn't want to go anywhere. I wanted to stay in the house. I felt people were looking at me and muttering behind their hands. It's a terrible experience, and not only [was] it a terrible experience for me, it was a dreadful experience for my wife and family, and in particular for my mother who is 81 years of age.'

A few days later HTV had broadcast their even more explicit programme, in which they had named Anglesea and confronted him in his garden before featuring the detailed and horrific allegations made by Mark Humphreys and Lee Steward. As he continued his evidence, Anglesea described how he had watched the programme at home with his wife. Asked once again how he had felt, he replied: 'Absolutely shocked, numbed, total and utter disbelief that a programme of such lies and falsehoods could be shown. I was totally distraught for Sandra, who was virtually inconsolable.'

Finally the article in *Private Eye* had been brought to his attention

and he said that this had had a similar effect on him. He told the jury
how he had felt compelled to go and speak to the various organisations
of which he was a member: the Rotary, the church and the schools
where he was a governor, describing the 'utter and total humiliation
and embarrassment he had felt' as he attempted to explain what had
happened to him. He went on to describe how Sandra had become difficult to live with and how the full and happy sex life they had once
had faded completely away. 'I feel unable to make love to her,' he said,
'because I feel dirty.' At one point Sandra left him. The next day his son
phoned him and told him she was in Birmingham. He spoke to her and
persuaded her to come home.

When Sandra Anglesea herself gave evidence she confirmed her husband's account. Having explained how neither of them had slept the
night after the HTV broadcast and how she had never seen anybody age
so quickly, she went on to describe the cumulative effect on her husband of the programme and the articles in the press: 'It's absolutely
destroyed his confidence. It's altered his personality. From a patient, loving husband he has become short-tempered, embarrassed to be with his
son in case anybody says anything about it; embarrassed to take him to
the swimming pool or go into the changing room because he thinks
people will talk.' Their sexual relationship which had been so splendid,
she said, had become virtually non-existent.[473]

Tall, lithe, attractive and utterly persuasive as a witness, Sandra Anglesea had evidently made a good impression on the jury. So much so that
when George Carman was offered the opportunity to cross-examine
her, he declined to ask her any questions at all.

Anglesea told the court that he had had very little connection with
Bryn Estyn and that his only visits there had been in an official capacity. As well as occasionally going there to caution boys, he had also
attended, in a purely formal capacity, two successive Christmas lunches.
He said that he had no contact at all with the three young boys, who,
as adults, had suddenly made allegations against him. He said that he
had always dealt with Matt Arnold the head, and that, far from having
a friendly relationship with Peter Howarth, he did not deal with him
at all. Indeed, he said that he did not even remember him.[474]

The last part of this evidence seemed unlikely. When I interviewed
Howarth in prison, he recalled Anglesea clearly and gave the impression
that he had dealt with him on a number of occasions. It would be quite
wrong, however, to conclude from this aspect of Anglesea's testimony
that he was attempting to conceal some guilty secret. It would be

entirely natural for anyone in his position, in danger of being damned by association with a man who had been convicted as a paedophile, to seek to minimise his contact with such a figure. The crucial question in the trial was not whether Anglesea's account of his contact with Howarth was irreproachably accurate, but whether there was any credible evidence that he had sexually assaulted any one of the three witnesses who now gave evidence against him.

In attempting to persuade the jury that there was such evidence, the defendants had necessarily to rely on the direct testimony of Mark Humphreys, Lee Steward and Carl Holden. The problem here was that these young men had no option, given the interviews, statements and affidavits they had already made, but to give evidence which was self-contradictory, inconsistent and, in some cases, wholly implausible.

Mark Humphreys was first in the witness box. Smartly dressed, he created a positive impression, seeming both sympathetic and vulnerable.[475] The difficulty he had when giving evidence, however, was principally as a result of the extraordinary manner in which Dean Nelson had interviewed him, and the blatant prompting in which he had engaged. Humphreys had no choice but to confirm that the journalist had repeatedly shown him a photograph of the man against whom he was seeking an allegation. And the tape of Nelson's interview, played to the jury, clearly demonstrated that it was Nelson who had supplied Anglesea's name to Humphreys and not the other way round.

One witness who had been called by Williams on behalf of Anglesea had already undermined much of Humphreys's testimony in advance. This was Gladys Green, the secretary who had had responsibility for maintaining the Bryn Estyn records, including the attendance registers. Seventy-five years old when she appeared in the witness box, she was, as Williams would later say in his closing address, 'sharp, astute' and 'as bright as a button'. Convincingly, she explained why her records, which meshed with, and could be checked against, records maintained centrally by the county, could be relied on for their accuracy. The problem for Humphreys was that the records clearly showed that his testimony was untrue.

He had not been a resident at Bryn Estyn for four years as he had originally claimed, and he could not have been abused during his second Christmas because his time at Bryn Estyn had spanned only one Christmas. Nor, according to the records, was it the case, as he now claimed, that having gone on home leave for that Christmas, he had been returned to the home by the police after having been arrested for shop-lifting. Mrs Green's meticulous records clearly showed that he had been at home and not at Bryn Estyn at the time he claimed he was abused by Anglesea. Nor was it the case that Humphreys had run away from the home and been missing for as much as three months. If Mrs Green's records were right the only conclusion open to the jury was that Humphreys's claims were not true.[476]*

Given the clear conflict between his testimony and the documentary evidence, it was not surprising that Humphreys frequently appeared confused. Although he remained both sympathetic and engaging, he seemed almost to be in a trance – as though he had mesmerised himself with his own evidence. At one crucial juncture he pointed to himself and said 'It must be true because it's in my head.'[477]

During cross-examination Mark Humphreys was asked why, if he had indeed been buggered, he had not made this allegation during his first interview with Dean Nelson. Humphreys said that Nelson had wept while recording this interview and he had not told Nelson originally of the buggery because he did not want to upset him further. 'Dean was a friend,' he said. Mr Justice Drake himself then asked why, since it was clear that Nelson was anxious to find out all that had happened, he had failed to mention the buggery. He again said it was to spare Nelson's feelings and also that he was ashamed. Williams suggested that the reason Humphreys had changed his evidence was that Dean Nelson had put pressure on him to do so. 'When Mr Nelson gives evidence, if he does, I shall ask him exactly what was going on.'

Dean Nelson, however, was never put into the witness box by the defendants. One possible explanation for his non-appearance was that they recognised that any cross-examination of the journalist was likely to result in their case being fatally undermined. Nelson's failure to appear in the witness box though, would ultimately prove almost as damaging.

The next witness to give evidence was Lee Steward. Like Humphreys, he was dapper and well dressed. He was intelligent and

---

* Because of the way in which defence lawyers and Mark Humphreys himself cast doubt on the accuracy of the Bryn Estyn records during the trial, Mark's mother would eventually check these against the records of the school he had attended before being sent to Bryn Estyn – St Christopher's. These records show that Mark was taken off the school register on 13 June 1980, when he was fifteen. There is a discrepancy of exactly a month between this record and the Bryn Estyn register which shows that Mark Humphreys was admitted to Bryn Estyn on 13 May. It seems possible that this discrepancy was due to the fact that Mark was initially sent to Bryn Estyn on remand; the school may have begun by treating his absence as temporary (Letter from St Christopher's to Margaret Humphreys, April 26 1996).

articulate but he sometimes gave his evidence in a bravado manner, which seemed unlikely to impress a jury. Significantly, permission was sought from the judge for Steward to take tranquillisers on account of the stress he was said to be suffering. Permission was granted on condition that the jury were informed. Then, after a break in which Steward took more tranquillisers, George Carman rose to ask for an adjournment on the grounds that the carer accompanying Steward reported that she had seen him overdosing, and she was afraid he would collapse and might need his stomach pumping out.

Mr Justice Drake declined the adjournment on the grounds that Steward was not alone in suffering stress and other witnesses had been subjected to comparable ordeals. After being seen to take another tranquilliser in the witness box Steward faltered, sat down and then fell to the ground apparently unconscious. Paramedics were summoned and the case was adjourned for the afternoon.

It was at this stage that George Carman turned to Ian Jack in the court urinals, and inquired 'What the fuck do we do now?'[478]

When Steward returned to the witness box the next day he seemed to be grey and less animated. According to one observer, the evidence he gave about the sexual assaults he alleged simply did not seem credible. However, asked by George Carman why he had come and given evidence against Gordon Anglesea, he said 'Because it's the truth.' Cross-examined by Lord Williams about his insistence on being paid by *Private Eye* before he entered the witness box and his threat not to give evidence at all, he replied: 'But I was only doing what you lawyers all do and making a threat to get my money, and I got it. I wouldn't in fact have carried it out. It's no good you attacking me on that, it's what all you lawyers do. Perfectly good tactics.'[479]

Steward was now confronted with a series of inconsistencies in his evidence. It became clear that his allegations had followed an inflationary spiral in which his declaration that he had *not* been abused by Anglesea, made when he complained to the police that he was being harassed by Dean Nelson, was replaced by allegations of indecent assault, which were in turn replaced by yet more serious allegations. Williams concentrated his questioning on Steward's original denial that he had been abused:

WILLIAMS: I'm taking you through that statement to the police. Listen to the following words: 'I would like to say that at no time did Gordon Anglesea ever sexually abuse me.' Is that true?

STEWARD: No, sir.

WILLIAMS: Well, a moment or two ago you said to me if it's in the statement it's true. 'I would like to say that at no time did Gordon Anglesea ever sexually abuse me.' That is true isn't it.

STEWARD: No, it's not ...

WILLIAMS: And that's what you were putting in this statement on the 24th August before Mr Nelson attended you, isn't it?

STEWARD: It's not true.

WILLIAMS: Do you think the truth is something that you play with according to the occasion?

STEWARD: Not at all.

WILLIAMS: Why did you say it, if it wasn't true, in a solemn sworn statement?

STEWARD: Very simply, North Wales Police have not carried out a full investigation. That proves that North Wales Police are corrupt, and that the force themselves, especially a lot of ones on the investigation, are really impossible to deal with.[480]

Challenged repeatedly about the multiple inconsistencies in his statements and affidavits, and about inconsistencies in the evidence he had given in the witness box, Steward replied: 'Would you like to tell me what I have got to gain out of this? ... I've got nothing to gain. I've certainly got a hell of a lot to lose. I've got no reason to lie whatsoever, and I'm telling you now, and I'll say it again, that man in the front abused me several times ... six at least.'

Williams, perhaps unused to being cross-examined by the witness, did not point out that Steward had already received £4,500 for giving evidence and had asked for £60,000. If the jury found in favour of the defendants Steward would have little difficulty in pursuing claims for criminal injuries. He would also be able to pursue a civil action against the North Wales Police (or against Clwyd County Council) – which could result in substantial damages – perhaps well in excess of £50,000.

Had he appeared as the sole witness in the case there can be little doubt that Steward, who clearly irritated Carman himself by his self-dramatising conduct and his tendency to walk noisily in and out of court, would have had his evidence dismissed out of hand by the jury. Something very similar might be said of Carl Holden – who was undoubtedly handicapped by having to give evidence after Steward's drug-induced collapse and his unimpressive performance in the witness box.

Holden's appearance was relatively brief. In cross-examination,

Williams elicited from him that he frequently drank fifteen pints of extra-strong lager a day and sometimes more. He suffered from black-outs and the shakes and also took amphetamines, sometimes dissolving these and self-injecting the liquid into his veins. Holden said that he was under the care of the community drugs team. He had last been an in-patient in the psychiatric hospital the previous year in order to 'dry out', but when asked whether this was in spring, summer, autumn or winter, he could not remember. Asked by the judge how he was able to afford fifteen pints of lager a day, he replied: 'It would be a bunch of us, a bunch of boys, and you would have that total on different days, and we – yes, we'd share it, and like, I'm no angel, I've been in trouble with the police, you know. I've broken into stuff to get money.' He went on to say that he never broke into houses or shops but that he did reg-ularly break into cars.

None of this bore directly on the credibility of his allegations against Anglesea. In this respect the difficulty faced by Lord Williams was that, although there is now clear evidence that Holden had fabricated his original allegations against Howarth, some of this was unavailable at the time. Besides, Howarth's conviction would have made it hazardous to pursue this line. Instead Williams focused on the fact that Holden had failed to make his allegation against Anglesea at the outset, and had made it to a BBC reporter only after he had seen Steward and Humphreys on television. Asked whether he felt the BBC had been 'hounding' him, Holden replied: 'A bit, yeah.' He then agreed with Williams that they had been 'hounding you, wanting you to tell some things about Bryn Estyn'. Although the cross-examination of Holden was constrained by the outcome of the Howarth trial, he was not an impressive witness.

Once the case for the defendants had been put, even Carman found it difficult to make, out of the evidence which had been given, a com-pelling argument against Anglesea. In a speech whose length seemed inversely proportionate to its substance, he had of necessity to urge the jury to disregard the details of the evidence and concentrate on the broader picture. He did, however, attack Anglesea on three points. The first of these concerned the manner in which he had left the police force. During his evidence, Anglesea had given no explanation of his reasons for resigning other than to say that it was nothing to do with Bryn Estyn. When he was being cross-examined by Carman, he was asked whether, on 13 March 1991, he had been interviewed by the chief constable. His answer was 'No, sir.' Asked whether he had been to the chief constable's office on that day, he again replied 'No, sir.' 'Well,' said Carman, I am suggesting to you that on the 13th March you were interviewed by the chief constable about your travelling expenses.' Once again Anglesea said 'No, sir.' It was at this point that Carman said 'And not by anyone else either?' To which Anglesea replied, 'Well, yes, by the assistant chief constable.' In his closing speech Carman said to the jury: 'Well that took a long time to come out, didn't it? That's hiding it, trying to avoid it, that shows that he's not quite the frank man he would have you believe.' Anglesea had simply said at the time: 'I was asked questions and I answered them accurately.' Once he had admitted to being interviewed, the story came out of how he had been called to the office over what was said to be a discrepancy of a few pounds in his expenses claims. As noted already, Anglesea has said that there was no irregularity and that he resigned in order to avoid being suspended in a manner he felt was unjust (see above, p. 142).

The problem for the defendants in the libel action was that, although Carman now attempted to persuade the jury that Anglesea had been 'economical with the truth', the truth when it did emerge actually provided an explanation of the entire Anglesea saga. It made it clear that the statement made originally in the *Independent on Sunday* that Anglesea had 'retired suddenly without explanation' had been true. The implication that he had retired because of events at Bryn Estyn, however, was now shown to be false. He had in fact resigned for reasons which, in terms of the libel case, were entirely innocent.

The second point on which Carman attempted to attack Anglesea was in relation to Howarth. Here the suggestion was that his claim not to have dealt with Howarth at Bryn Estyn was untrue. Once again, however, as already noted, there was an entirely understandable explanation for any attempt on Anglesea's part to understate his contact with a man who, so far as the jury was concerned, was nothing other than a convicted paedophile.

The third point concerned the manner in which Anglesea's account of the number of times he had visited Bryn Estyn had changed over time. Even before the *Independent on Sunday* article had appeared, Anglesea had been asked about this by Dean Nelson during a brief telephone call. At that point he had said he had only visited the home twice. Later, in the solicitor's letter which was sent to the newspaper, this figure rose to three. After retrieving his notebooks, however, Anglesea eventually said in his evidence that he had visited the home about eleven times. Although Carman now attempted to persuade the jury that Anglesea had tried to hide the true facts, it was by no means clear that his inaccuracies were caused by anything other than his difficulty in recalling events which had taken place ten years earlier. The further problem for Carman and the defendants was that, when the dates of Anglesea's visits were established, they merely confirmed what had already been urged in his defence – that he had not even been visiting Bryn Estyn during the period when Steward claimed he had been abused. Given this simple fact, and the fact that Humphreys's claims were also chronologically impossible, it was little wonder that Carman felt it necessary to place so much stress in his closing speech on the need for the jury to disregard the details and attend only to the broader picture.

It was in the first week of December that the climax of the trial came. It came not with the address of George Carman – the 'silver fox' – to the jury, but with the closing speech by Lord Williams. The question which the jury had to answer, he began by suggesting, was not *whether* the three men they had heard were 'basically telling the truth', as Mr Mathew (counsel to HTV) had put it. It was '*When?*':

> When Lee Steward swore in a police station in solemn form that Mr Anglesea had never abused him? When that was read out Mrs Anglesea cried did she not? Or when was Mark Humphreys telling the truth? When [on being questioned initially by the police in 1991] he said he had no complaints? And when was Mr Holden telling the truth? When he made a very detailed statement about Mr Howarth assaulting him, running away from Bryn Estyn, getting on the coal train, going down to Cardiff? These are questions that will not go away. I will come back to them in time.[481]

Before returning to examine these crucial inconsistencies, however, Williams invited the jury to accompany him on a short journey:

> I would ask you that we go together to the key to this case. It is a key to this case that is so devastating that Mr Carman, in a speech of many hours, did not refer to it, and this morning Mr Mathew, in his shorter speech, got nowhere near it. But you, of course, will not have missed it. The key is one document and one date. The one document, of course, is in your green bundle. It is the *Independent on Sunday* article. The date was 1 December 1991. So we are exactly three years now that these two poor people have borne this. 'NEW CHILD ABUSE SCANDAL', 1 December 1991. ... What is the other part of the key? The other part

of the key is in your red bundle. ... It is item number 4. ... Let us just look at those words. 'Transcript of first part of interview of Mark Humphreys by Dean Nelson,' wait for the date ... 'on 19 June 1992. What, therefore does that mean? As sure as the world is round, it means this. When the *Independent on Sunday* published that filth about Gordon Anglesea they had not got any evidence at all. They do not pretend they did ... they had no evidence from Lee Steward, they had no evidence from Mark Humphreys, they had no evidence from Carl Holden.[482]

This was the reason, Lord Williams suggested, that Dean Nelson's subsequent investigation had been left veiled in secrecy. This was the reason, he implied, that Nelson himself had been anxiously kept out of the witness box by the defendants: 'A decent newspaper, you might think, would investigate first and then publish. What you now know happened here, they published and then they went scraping for evidence. ... Now we see that they [did not] have ... a single piece of evidence, not even a couple of bits of notes on the back of a cigarette packet.'

The defendants, Williams pointed out, had chosen to hide their own actions behind the testimony of three young men who were, in effect, victims not of sexual assaults but of the newspaper's belated attempts to investigate the story it had already published. These three men, he suggested, were not simply 'deeply wounded by life' but were 'deeply fragile because of their lives ... and above all ... deeply, deeply suggestible':

> It is a terrible thing, you know, that has happened in this case: a newspaper – and it is not the *Daily Sport*, remember, or the *Sunday Sport* 'Elvis found alive on the moon' or 'Artichokes ate my grandchild'. It is not that sort of paper, is it? I hope it is a joke when I make it, but it is not fair, is it?
>
> What sort of country do we want to live in. Do we want to live in Russia or Poland where accusation is enough? What are we coming to? Just because newspapers are powerful, you know, and they have got money and the television is there with its cameras and hidden silhouettes; just because *Private Eye* is there publishing lies; it does not entitle them to do what they have done to this man.[483]

In Williams's view the whole manner in which Gordon Anglesea had been libelled by the press resembled an assault by a gang. After the initial attack on him by the *Independent on Sunday* other papers had 'just joined the mob': 'The *Observer* printed articles and joined the mob. HTV and *Private Eye* all joined in because they thought the man was wounded; they thought the dogs could be let on him. And it is a scandal.' What had happened, said Lord Williams, was a disgrace to journalism, not least because none of the editors or journalists concerned had been prepared to face cross-examination themselves:

> … it is an affront to decency, it is a wicked wrong to this man and his family, and in the end to this court, because not one of them has had the nerve to get up there, not one. It is a contempt of you. … They are willing enough to hide behind lawyers. … They are willing enough to put the three young men in the witness box. They are willing enough to have day-in, day-out cross-examination of Gordon Anglesea. They will not even get up there to answer a few questions that you might reasonably have wanted to know.[484]

Having accused the journalists of cowardice and contempt, Lord Williams concentrated his attack on Dean Nelson and on the way he had begun his interview with Mark Humphreys by showing him a photograph of Anglesea, and saying, before the tape started running: 'This is the man I'm after'. After citing various points on the tape where Dean Nelson talks about bringing a photograph to show Humphreys on some later occasion, even though he had in fact already shown him the photograph, Williams said this to the jury:

> Just assume you had this tape and listened to it and didn't know that that business with the photograph had gone on. You'd be completely misled, wouldn't you … There's something very odd going on here, I'm sorry to say, but not only is it odd, it's not straight …

He went on to direct the jury's attention to the passage in Dean Nelson's notes where he records Humphreys's attempt to draw a picture of Anglesea, saying, as he draws, 'This is how I see him, as I see him'. Any ordinary person who didn't know that Nelson had just shown Humphreys a photograph of Anglesea would, Williams suggested, be deeply impressed by the vividness of his recall:

> If you didn't know about the photograph you'd think 'Goodness gracious me, this is a young man remembering ten years earlier and he's drawing this fantastic diagram because it's never left his memory.' It's all a con. The only person who could tell you why that con was being practised is Dean Nelson. It's not Mark Humphreys's fault. I think it was Mr Carman who said that Mark Humphreys had been used and abused when he was a child. He's being used here, isn't he?

Williams went on to point out that ten days later, during the second
interview, which took place on 29 June 1992, Nelson was still maintaining the pretence about Humphreys having a vivid memory of
Anglesea:

> 'Do you recognise this picture?' [Nelson asks Humphreys] 'Yeah.' 'Why
> do you recognise this picture?' 'His face.'
>
>   So … more than a week after that first interview, he's still playing
> this game. What the devil's going on? I'm sorry to say this, and if Mr
> Nelson had been here I would have put it to him: there is wrong-
> doing here about the photograph and it's come out because Mark
> Humphreys actually said that the photo was shown to him and he was
> asked 'Is this the man?' … It's not right, is it? It's not fair and it's not
> straight.[485]

At one point Williams went beyond criticising Nelson for practising a
'con' and suggested that what the journalist had done was even more
serious:

> Then, after that, he plays games on the tapes: 'If I brought you a pho-
> tograph of the man, would you recognise him?' But he has just shown
> him the photograph. 'Will you draw him in my book?' 'Yes,' says Mr
> Humphreys. 'I'm not much of a drawer,' and he draws that diagram in
> the book. What is the point of that? He has shown him the photo-
> graph. The point of it is gross deceit. …
>
>   I want to say this as carefully as I can. Not in anger. If a policeman
> investigating a crime had done that, the case would be thrown out, the
> police officer would be thrown out of the police force and probably
> find himself in prison. … That is crookery. I'm sorry to say, members
> of the jury. It is crookery.[486]

Williams went on to deal with the testimony of Lee Steward, and the
manner in which Dean Nelson had managed to persuade him to
change completely his evidence about Anglesea. He focused, as any barrister would have done, on the statement which Steward had made to
the police on 24 August 1992. On at least two occasions he quoted
Steward's crucial words back to the jury: 'I refused to discuss this matter with Dean Nelson over the telephone but I would like to say that
at no time did Gordon Anglesea ever sexually abuse me. … In my
opinion I felt [Nelson] wanted me to say things which were not the
truth.'

The evidence of this statement was, suggested Williams, quite crucial:

This 24 August really is a killer, is it not? It blows Mr Steward straight out of the water. The 24 August statement is only a matter of days – three weeks – before HTV put their programme out. Mr Steward uses quite salty language on that tape [of his conversation with the police], so I must not use it myself but I can quote: 'Dean Nelson,' said Mr Steward, 'is a friggin' arsehole and he deserves to be shot.' I would not use those words, but I would alter them slightly: Dean Nelson has been deceitful and he deserves not to be shot, but he deserves to be cross-examined, does he not.'[487]

Williams then pointed to another gap in the evidence of the defendants. Although they agreed that on 11 September 1992 Nelson had conducted a further interview with Steward, the tape of this interview had never been produced: 'You have no explanation from Mr Nelson about what happened to that tape. Mr Nelson could have told us. He could have told us that he'd lost it, that he'd used it for something else, that he'd taped pop music over it, but you haven't had a word.'

Having dealt very briefly with the evidence of Carl Holden, he then turned to one of the most striking and moving aspects of the case. This concerned the cache of Gordon Anglesea's love letters which had not been disclosed until after the trial had started.

After the New Year's Eve party at the end of 1975, where Gordon Anglesea had met and fallen in love with Sandra, he had written her a series of passionate and heartfelt love letters. These letters had later been found by Sandra's husband who had made a formal complaint to the North Wales Police about the conduct of one of their officers, forwarding the letters as evidence. As a result Anglesea had been interviewed by the chief constable about his most intimate personal life.

For seventeen years the letters had been kept in the files of the North Wales Police. When the libel trial was already in progress, they were disclosed, along with some of the other contents of Anglesea's personal file. They had then been produced unexpectedly by Mr Carman, apparently in an attempt to portray Anglesea as a man who, because he had been unfaithful to his first wife, could not be trusted. Once the letters had been admitted, it was open to Williams to use them for a quite different purpose. He used them to demonstrate to the jury that the man who had given evidence before them was not a pervert but a full-blooded, heterosexual man who, only a short time before he had supposedly been abusing adolescent boys at Bryn Estyn, had been conducting a passionate affair with a woman. 'These are the letters,' said Williams to the jury. 'I won't read them all. I would prefer to ask you to read them yourselves. I know no one really likes to look at other people's love letters because they are so intensely personal and private, but he's been driven to this, hasn't he?' He went on to read extracts from the letters: '"My words are totally inadequate when endeavouring to express my feelings for you. It is sufficient just to look at you without speaking to know what is in my heart." I'm not reading every word,' said Williams, 'The next letter':

'Dearest, I find it difficult to express my feelings for you whenever I see you in company. The telephone enables me to say what I really feel for you, and I know as I write this letter I can never express adequately (inaudible due to coughing) … particularly when I hold you in my arms and we let ourselves touch each other by using our lips and eyes.

'Darling, to me you are everything that one could hope for. The ultimate in life is finding a partner, not just a partner but someone whom you can love deeply, someone who returns that love, someone you can respect. I know in my heart I have found what I have searched and longed for all my life. Yes, you, but sadly in the same way as I am tied so are you. This will not prevent me from taking you for my own. I know it is selfish and criminal to take someone else's wife, but I believe we are for each other.'

Williams looked up from the letter and addressed the jury:

I am just going to stop there. He doesn't pretend that he's a saint on a pedestal. He knew he was in the wrong. He said he was selfish and criminal to take someone else's wife, but the love they had for each other was what was the mainspring of their life. 'Oh no', say the newspapers, 'actually he's not the man that those letters show at all, he's a pervert'. Well, I'm sorry, whatever lawyers' words you have heard in this case, they don't match the eloquence of that, do they? They are not perfect grammar and I dare say he's got his punctuation wrong, but they are more eloquent than anything that could be said.

He goes on on the next page: 'Dearest darling Sandra, So many people are working for us. I cannot really believe that they all want us to be together in love having joys', and then it was illegible. Mr Anglesea actually, you will remember, said it was 'joys and sorrows'. … 'they all want us to be together in love having joys and sorrows'.

Once again Lord Williams looked up:

Do you mind if I just underline, in my mind anyway, the next few words: 'joys and sorrows of bringing up children in the right atmosphere.' 'Oh no', they say, these papers and the TV and the magazine. They say, 'Oh no, he's a pervert.'

He did bring up the children in the right atmosphere. There were five of them. Not every one of us, you know, would have the generosity and heart to bring up five children, not everyone of us. I'm not calling him a plaster saint, I'm saying he was a decent man to those five children. And in the middle of a love letter he writes to his intended wife, '… the joys and sorrows of bringing up children in the right atmosphere'.

I'm going on: 'Sandra darling, yes, I do want you for my wife. Yes, I do want your children. No, I won't be jealous if you shower some of your love on any of our children, but not all mind, you leave some for me, my love, and can I say here, spare me a thought. Blow me a kiss. Above all love me dearly.'

'Oh no', say the defendants, 'he's a pervert'. I am going on again – there's a page 6: 'My dearest, darling Sandra, We must make that decision soon or else we will be confined to a life of loving without touching, loving without seeing, knowing in our hearts that we long so much to be together.'

Having finished reading extracts from the letters, Lord Williams addressed the jury again:

Well, there might be some justice somewhere, and it may be that some of the people who have refused to give evidence have actually been able to listen to those letters. That's by the way. What a strange working providence has. I'm talking about the letters. When they were found they were shown to his boss in the police force. They were obviously embarrassing to him. He'd be in trouble. Then he had his interview that Mr Carman asked him about, and they were locked away then in his secret confidential file, mouldering away there for seventeen years. Seventeen years. So those embarrassing documents [from] seventeen years ago were then released by the North Wales Police for this case and this case only.

How strange it all is, because the embarrassing, affectionate and loving letters get released seventeen years later at his moment of accusation. He says they were deeply, physically and emotionally in love. Can you doubt that? Do you want to be that cynical, that disbelieving? If you do, there you are. What did Mrs Anglesea say? And, incidentally, Mrs Anglesea is not to be brushed aside in this case. She did not just give evidence, you know, about the effect on Gordon Anglesea. She gave evidence about their life. Mr Carman and Mr Mathew asked her no questions. I mean, she shines, doesn't she, with decency? She said that he had a strong sexual urge, that it was physical and emotional

love, that when he came home for his lunch they used to make physical sexual love. I mean, how do you make that up? Of course it's true.
She didn't just stand there talking to you about it. That's the man with
that sort of drive which I hope we can all recognise, or at least say we
can all remember, at least some of us! But that's the sort of sexual drive
that life is about, isn't it? You go home for your lunch – let me rephrase
that, some people go home for lunch, and they are so mad keen on
their wife, on their girlfriend, or whatever they call it now, partner – I
don't mind – you are so keen on your sexual partner that you have sex
at lunchtime.[488]

The love letters which Williams read out to the jury in Court 13 were
not, of course, proof of Gordon Anglesea's innocence. But they were
proof that the man who stood accused of abusing adolescent boys had
sexual drives and powerful feelings of attraction towards an adult
woman which were similar to those of normal heterosexual men. Mr
Carman had told the jury that 'some paedophiles are married'. 'Well I
don't know,' said Lord Williams. 'But paedophiles are not married like
that, are they?'

In the end, however, the case did not hinge simply on a subjective judgment about whether Gordon Anglesea was a man with 'normal' sexual
drives. It hinged on the testimony of three men who had all told contradictory stories, who had all gone back on their own evidence, and two of
whom had claimed that they had been abused by Anglesea at times when
either he or they had not been at Bryn Estyn. 'Which bit,' asked Williams,
'are you supposed to believe? The answer of the defendants is this: "Get a
big brush and brush away all the detail and do not bother about it." And,
of course, they have got to say that because when you look at the detail
you could not believe a word of it. It may well be that they just do not
know what the truth is and when they are telling it.'[489]

The case hinged, above all, as Williams pointed out, on the fact that
none of the three witnesses had made any complaint at all against
Anglesea until allegations were being actively sought out by a young
freelance journalist. This journalist was seeking to support a grave insin-
uation he had caused to be published without there being any facts to
support it. He had evidently been so desperate to find such allegations
that he had supplied the name of his suspect to his first witness. He had
then repeatedly shown him a photograph of Anglesea while pretending
that he had not. After which he had harassed and pestered his second
witness to such an extent that Steward had actually contacted the police
to complain about him.

In any ordinary trial the evidence would have been so clear and so compelling that the jury might have been expected to return a unanimous verdict in favour of Anglesea almost immediately. However, as the trial of Peter Howarth had already illustrated, the cumulative effect of horrific sexual allegations made by different complainants against the same person is enormously powerful. In the circumstances it was not surprising that the jury deliberated for nine hours before returning, on 6 December 1994, to give their verdicts. Two members of the jury, perhaps following the common and entirely false principle that 'there is no smoke without fire', found for the defendants. The other ten members of the jury found for Anglesea. Damages of £375,000 were agreed between the parties. When the costs of both sides were added, the total bill faced by the defendants was in the region of £3 million.[490]

All of the editors involved in defending the action were shaken by its outcome. Perhaps none was so badly affected as Ian Hislop, who had evidently sincerely believed in Anglesea's guilt.

57 The death of a witness

THE VINDICATION OF GORDON ANGLESEA at the libel trial should by rights have destroyed the entire North Wales story. For, as we have seen, until the jury returned their verdict on 6 December 1994, the most sensational claim made by the adherents of this story was that there had been a massive failure to prosecute sexual abusers in North Wales. This failure supposedly stemmed directly from the involvement of the North Wales Police themselves in the very paedophile ring they were supposed to be investigating. Given both the verdict and the compelling nature of the evidence, this sensational claim ought to have disappeared entirely. It should now have become generally known that the allegations against Anglesea were false, that they had been provoked by credulous journalists and made by three suggestible and deeply damaged young men.

However, this did not happen. The reason for this is very simple. While the judge and jury in a libel trial possess the power to dismiss false claims as libels and to punish those who have made them, this power is, by its very nature, limited. A successful libel action can, and usually does, have the effect of preventing any further publication of the allegations which have been deemed libellous. But no judge or jury has the power to change the beliefs of those who originated a libel, or to stop them from privately persisting in (or even quietly disseminating) a belief that the libel was well-founded. In the case of Gordon Anglesea there is evidence which suggests that some of the defendants in the action, including some of those who worked for *Private Eye* and the *Observer,* continued to believe that at least some of the witnesses who had given evidence in the high court were telling the truth.

The fate of one of these witnesses, Mark Humphreys, and the manner it was interpreted by the press, would powerfully reinforce these beliefs. After the libel trial, by whose result Mark and his wife, Wendy, had evidently set great store, Mark returned to North Wales. His marriage, however, had been in difficulties even before the trial took place. In the view of his family – in particular his mother and his two sisters – the emergence of his allegations against Anglesea had gone hand in hand with a change in his behaviour. He had become more moody and secretive, and his long-standing problem with drink became more severe.

Shortly after the trial, around Christmas, he and Wendy split up. For several nights Mark slept in a car. He then went to live in a bedsit and it is clear that at times he was both depressed and lonely. According to a solicitor he contacted at the time, 'he was desperate and asked me to write to Wendy to try and encourage a reconciliation'.[491] Although he told the same solicitor that he had no time for his family, he had kept in contact with his brothers and sisters and frequently saw his sister, Mandy, who lived near his bedsit. On 1 February 1995 he plastered a wall for her and that day she saw him three times. She recalls that he seemed happy. 'He didn't mention the allegations. It was as if he was putting the last couple of years behind him.'[492] Later that evening, however, it would appear that his mood changed. He left his local pub after a drinking session in which he consumed about nine pints. That night he was found dead, hanged from the banisters outside his bedsit in Wrexham.

It was not the first time he had attempted to end his life. He had tried to hang himself on one occasion before the libel trial. At his inquest a psychiatric social worker, who had seen him three days before he died and arranged an appointment for him to see a psychologist in February, said that he had taken an overdose of tablets on 12 January. He had also apparently tried to slash his wrists. The pathologist said that there were scars on his wrists which were between a week and a month old.

The reasons why Mark killed himself will never be known. What can be said with reasonable confidence is that, by making false allegations against Anglesea, he had profoundly altered the course of his own life and his relationships with those who had once been close to him – his wife, his mother, his brothers and sisters, and the mother of his children. Had he not made these allegations it seems possible that his troubled life would have continued.

Mark Humphreys's death did not go unnoticed by the press. On hearing news of it, Dean Nelson set off once again to North Wales – this time to attend the funeral. A few days later, Nelson wrote another story for the *Observer*. The story, spread over five columns, and illustrated by a large grainy photograph of Mark, was headlined 'NOWHERE TO HIDE FROM THE PAST'. Carefully peeling apart those elements of Humphreys's story which referred to Peter Howarth from those which referred to Anglesea, Nelson related the former as though they stood alone and were proven facts. The article made no mention at all of the recent libel trial, of the severe criticisms to which he himself had been subjected during it, or of the fact that Humphreys's allegations of abuse against Anglesea had not been accepted by the jury. Instead the story of Humphreys's life became a simple and tragic tale of abuse leading to a cruel and tragic death:

> Two weeks ago, 30-year-old Mark Humphreys put a noose [around] his neck and hanged himself from the banister outside his dingy North Wales bedsit. Everyone who knew him was shocked but no one was surprised. The clock had started ticking in 1976 when he was raped by a senior social worker at a Wrexham children's home; after that it was a matter of time.
>
> He had been put into local authority care because he kept running away from school – but when he left Bryn Estyn home at 16 he was illiterate and had been raped on at least 50 occasions by the deputy head, Peter Howarth. Others had molested him too.
>
> There was nowhere for him to hide. If he stayed at the home, he was brutally assaulted by those responsible for his care. If he ran away he had to run the gauntlet of sex offenders who habitually lay in wait outside the home's gates. ... He was first singled out by Howarth at the age of 12, shortly after he arrived at the home ... The rapes continued until he left Bryn Estyn. ... 'I went to tell somebody about this, but I couldn't. There were all these staff but I couldn't talk to any of them.'
>
> His instinct was right. Four senior staff have since been jailed for sexual assaults on children at Bryn Estyn. Had he decided to confide, his words would have been reported up the line – either to Howarth or to Stephen Norris, another manager, who has since been convicted for abusing children at Bryn Estyn and another home.[493]

The decision taken by the *Observer* to publish this article was a serious editorial misjudgment. The original articles which had led to the libel action had at least been published in ignorance of their factual inaccuracy. This article, however, of which practically every detail was false, unsubstantiated or misleading, was published two months after evidence calling its claims into question had been heard in open court.

During the libel trial, as we have seen, evidence had been placed before the court which showed that Humphreys could not have been raped by Howarth at Bryn Estyn in 1976 when he was twelve for the simple reason that had not been sent there until three years later – when he was fifteen. Nor was it the case that 'four senior staff' had since been jailed for sexual assaults on children at Bryn Estyn. Only two members of senior staff had been so convicted and one of these, Peter Howarth, continued to protest his innocence from his prison cell. (Of the other two members of staff convicted prior to the 1991 investigation – Gillison and Rutter – neither had been accused of assaulting any child at Bryn Estyn, and one appears to have been wrongly convicted [see above, p. 104]).

There was no evidence to support the reference to 'sex offenders who habitually lay in wait outside the home's gates'. Although the article went on to say that it was while he was at Bryn Estyn that Humphreys 'came to the attention of Gary Cooke ... a paedophile social worker', this was not true either. Cooke had met Humphreys before he went into care at a time when Cooke was an amateur wrestler and Humphreys was running a newspaper stand after school. It was at this point that social services had approached Humphreys's family because Cooke had paid Mark to let him take indecent photographs of him. In 1980 Cooke was convicted and jailed for this and for sexual offences against other boys. He was released only after Mark had left Bryn Estyn.

Most seriously of all, the *Observer*, by failing even to mention the libel action that it had lost, was guilty of misleading its readers about the context in which Mark Humphreys's allegations had been made and the fact that equally serious allegations had not been believed by a jury.

It is an indication of the ineffectiveness with which the press's conduct is regulated that the *Observer* was able to publish this article with impunity. Since Anglesea was not mentioned he could not sue; since Howarth had already lost his reputation as a result of his conviction, he could not take any action either. When Gwen Hurst complained to the Press Complaints Commission her complaint was dismissed after a barrage of sincere but misleading self-justification had been submitted to the Commission by the *Observer*'s deputy editor, John Price – formerly assistant editor at the *Independent*.

In the course of one of his letters, written on 30 March 1995, Price himself strongly implied that the *Observer* still believed that Mark Humphreys was a truthful witness:

The article published on March [sic] 12 was a personal piece of writing. Mr Nelson had interviewed Mark Humphreys on numerous occasions, gained his trust, and most of all believed his story. He was not alone in this: Viv Hector believed him, as did George Carman QC, Ian Jack, editor of the *Independent on Sunday*, Ian Hislop, editor of *Private Eye*, David Williams of HTV, and the solicitors and insurers representing all the newspapers and the television companies involved. He was a powerful witness who suffered greatly in recounting his story. It was certainly true that we had lost a libel action in which he had been a witness, *but it was testimony to his credibility as a witness that we defended the action all the way to the high court* [italics added].

The Press Complaints Commission appeared to accept this argument: 'Though the newspaper had lost a libel action in which the man was a witness,' they wrote to Gwen Hurst, 'this did not necessarily mean that the evidence given by him was untrue or to be disbelieved.' Remarkably, no criticism was made of the *Observer* for its failure to make any reference to the failed libel action. By publishing Nelson's misleading article it had engaged in precisely the kind of questionable journalism which, in other circumstances, might have been exposed by *Private Eye*. On this occasion, not surprisingly, no such exposé was published.

Months after Mark's death, on the day of his inquest in June 1995, his mother told local journalists that she did not believe Mark had ever been abused at Bryn Estyn. She said she believed he had made up his allegations in an attempt to gain compensation.[494] Mrs Humphreys, who believed her son had wronged an innocent man, repeated this view in a statement to the Tribunal and added that, three months after Mark's death, she had been visited by a young man who had been a friend of Mark's at Bryn Estyn. He too had made an allegation of sexual abuse during the police investigation. According to Mrs Humphreys he had said: 'Don't worry Peggy, nothing ever happened to Mark at Bryn Estyn and nothing happened to me either.'[495]

By the time Mark Humphreys committed suicide, Peter Wynne had already been dead for a year, having apparently been driven to hang himself by the belief that his long-suffering partner was about to abandon him. On 21 May 1995, Simon Birley, who had sunk deeper and deeper into drug addiction and glue-sniffing, was found hanging from a tree. As with Wynne and Humphreys, the exact reasons which had driven him to kill himself will never be known. Both he and Wynne had led lives so troubled that they might have been driven to suicide even if the North Wales investigation had never taken place. It is almost certainly the case, however, that in making false allegations against people who had once cared for them and who had genuinely tried, however inadequately, to help them, all three of these men had driven themselves – or been driven by those who encouraged them to make their allegations – even deeper into the misery which eventually over-whelmed them.

Their deaths, however, did nothing to halt the willingness of others to believe in the allegations they had made. Indeed, in the years to come, their suicides would feature as an essential part of the North Wales story. A powerful mythology would develop which portrayed sexual abuse in North Wales children's homes as so widespread that it had led not only these three men, but many more young people to kill themselves.

58 From Jillings to Waterhouse

THE CONVICTION OF PETER HOWARTH in July 1994 and the conclusion of the Anglesea libel trial in December 1994 both attracted national publicity. But, at the beginning of 1995, even with the death of Mark Humphreys, it would still not be accurate to describe the North Wales story as a national scandal. It was merely another child-abuse scandal which, while it had received a great deal of space in the national press, had never commanded public attention in the way that the Cleveland crisis had.

During the spring and summer of 1996, all this was to change. Of the factors which lay behind the change, the bald statistics of the investigation were in themselves significant. For one of the most striking features of the police inquiry was the huge disparity between the number of allegations made and the number of prosecutions which had resulted. Although the police investigation which had been launched in August 1991 had originally been focused on Bryn Estyn, it had soon developed into a much larger inquiry. This was partly because of the HTV documentary broadcast in September 1991, in which Alison Taylor, Ryan Tanner and others had made their allegations about Nefyn Dodd and Tŷ'r Felin. This had opened up a new branch of the investigation in Gwynedd. But the scale of the inquiry increased principally because police trawling operations are, almost by their very nature, self-reproducing. Simply because large numbers of former residents of care homes have attended two, three or even more different institutions, a trawling operation which initially targets one home will almost inevitably elicit allegations relating to other homes. Because of this domino effect, the North Wales Police found that, before long, they were investigating practically every care home in the two counties, including the privately-run Wrexham-based home, Bryn Alyn. Because of the sensational publicity given to the investigation by the *Independent on Sunday* and because of the level of abuse the police *appeared* to be uncovering, more resources were devoted to the investigation than had ever been envisaged at the outset

By September 1993, after two years of continuous investigation, when the main part of the inquiry had been formally completed, the North Wales Police had already taken some 3,500 statements from about 2,500 witnesses. According to their own figures, at least five hundred of these witnesses claimed they had been subjected to physical or sexual abuse while in care. Allegations were made against no fewer than 365 different people. Yet, by the end of 1995, only five North Wales care workers had been prosecuted as a result of these allegations and only four were convicted. Of these four, one – Stephen Norris – had already been convicted on charges of sexual abuse in 1990, while another – Paul Wilson – was convicted on charges of physical assault which did not even result in a custodial sentence. The largest investigation into child abuse ever mounted in Britain had resulted in only two new convictions for sexual abuse: those of Peter Howarth and (in 1995) of John Allen, the principal of the privately-run Bryn Alyn home. That somebody somewhere was seeking to prevent the full horror of what had happened in North Wales from becoming known seemed to many people an almost inescapable conclusion.

It was partly for this reason that there had been frequent suggestions, especially at the height of the 1991–3 investigation, that there should be a public inquiry. On a number of occasions the parliamentary under-secretary to the Welsh Office, Gwilym Jones, stated that the nature and remit of any inquiry would only be decided when all the trials had been completed. The clear implication was that some form of inquiry would take place.

It was with this in mind that Clwyd County Council decided to appoint an independent panel to conduct its own preliminary inquiry. One of its functions would be to undertake the preparatory work for any public inquiry and help to formulate the council's submission to that inquiry. Another function would be to advise the social services department of any urgent reforms which needed to be instituted immediately.

The independent panel was appointed by the social services committee following discussions between Councillors Dennis Parry and Malcolm King and the director of social services, John Jevons. The crucial decision about the choice of chairman was taken principally by Jevons. Anxious that the person appointed should have a detailed understanding of social services, Jevons accepted the suggestion of a colleague that the job should be given to John Jillings, who had recently retired as the director of social services for Derbyshire. Jillings was to be joined by two other experts in child-care – Professor Jane

Tunstill of Keele University and Gerrilyn Smith, a clinical psychologist, formerly of the Hospital for Sick Children, Great Ormond Street, who had been suggested by Malcolm King. At this stage Jevons envisaged an internal inquiry whose report would not be published.[496]

Although it was originally intended that the inquiry would report after about six months, its course in practice was very different. Soon after their appointment, the members of the panel decided they would advertise for former residents of Clwyd care homes to come forward to give evidence to them – a course of action which clearly had its dangers but to which the council reluctantly acquiesced. Very soon the Jillings inquiry began, as Jevons puts it, 'to take on a life of its own'. Jevons recalls that he became concerned about this and wanted to restrain the panel. Malcolm King, however, 'was delighted and wanted to encourage it'. King, according to Jevons, had accepted the conspiracy theory of what had happened in North Wales 'and was hoping that the Jillings team would … be instrumental in bringing the assumed wider horrors of abuse out into the open'. In Jevons's view the panel willingly accepted this change of direction and began to see themselves as accountable to Malcolm King and Dennis Parry, rather than to him and Andrew Loveridge as originally agreed. 'In fact from that point onwards the panel came to regard Andrew and me as hostile and obstructive to their new brief.' [497]

One complicating factor was the government's apparent retreat from the idea of holding a public inquiry. When the last criminal trial was completed in 1995, the Welsh Office announced that a barrister, Nicola Davies QC, would be commissioned to examine the relevant evidence and recommend whether there should be a public inquiry or not. When Davies reported in December 1995 she recommended an examination of child care procedures and practice. But she specifically concluded that there were no grounds for holding a public inquiry.[498]

The Jillings panel's view of its role now almost inevitably changed again and the question of their report being published became crucial. The main difficulty was that they were simply not equipped to conduct the kind of inquiry which might take the place of the public inquiry which now seemed to have been ruled out.

The huge number of allegations which had not led to convictions, and which were the main focus of the concerns expressed by local politicians, lay beyond the scope of the inquiry. When, in 1996, I asked John Jillings about the conclusions the panel had reached in relation to individual cases, he said that the panel had had no brief to investigate these. Asked specifically about the allegations made by Mark Humphreys, he replied 'I don't know about it. It's not my job to investigate individual cases. We hadn't got the authority to investigate that, we certainly hadn't got the resources to investigate it. It would have been quite improper for us to get involved in that.' He said that there would always be contentious cases but that 'it would be futile for us, because we hadn't got access to the material, to try and say whether this child or that child may or may not have been abused.'[499]

As Jillings intimates, much of the documentary evidence relating to the police investigation was simply not available to the panel. The North Wales Police had, quite properly, declined to give evidence to it on the grounds that this might prejudice the outcome of any subsequent trial or public inquiry. Moreover, the panel appears to have made little effort to take evidence from those who had been convicted of abuse or from care workers who had been accused but never charged. Nor was it empowered to grant legal representation to any of those against whom allegations had been made. It was not even obliged to allow such individuals the right to answer allegations at all. Those who made allegations to the panel could therefore not be cross-examined by barristers representing the accused, and no provision was made whereby those facing unfounded allegations could demonstrate their falsity.

According to John Jillings the various gaps and limitations in the inquiry he conducted were carefully set out in the report itself. One of the reasons that they have never been fully appreciated, perhaps, is that the report was never published. In the considered view of Jevons, who was still director of social services at the time the report was completed, the principal reason that the panel's findings were never published was the extremely low quality of the report they produced: 'In fact the work of that inquiry turned out to be, as far as I was concerned, a bit of a disaster – and I have no one but myself to blame for that. ... The choice of chair was wrong. The panel took a very, very long time. ... At the same time it appeared that the way they were investigating and drawing evidence was not something that would stand up to scrutiny ... because the interviews they were conducting, the way they were drawing conclusions was highly impressionistic. It didn't actually have the discipline attached to it that we had hoped it would.'[500]

One of the factors which undoubtedly sharpened Jevons's view of the finished report was that he was himself criticised in it in a manner which he considered grossly unfair. His view of the report, however, was shared by others. Andrew Loveridge, the county solicitor, is on record as saying that 'The initial reaction of the council was one of amazement [at] the number of inaccuracies contained therein and the style and content of the report'. Subsequently, during a debate in the Welsh Assembly, former parliamentary under secretary of state at the Welsh Office, Rod Richards, described the report as 'one of the worst I have ever read'.[501]

Clwyd County Council considered the report at the last meeting it held before its own dissolution. By this point it had received warnings from its insurance company that publication of the report might jeopardise its cover, and legal advice that it would risk libel writs from accused individuals who had been named. On 26 March 1996 it noted the contents of the report but referred the vexed question of its publication to the Welsh Office. In practice this meant that it would remain for ever under lock and key.

In view of the legal advice which had been received, the decision not to publish the report seemed an entirely reasonable one. Soon after this decision had been taken, however, a copy of the report was leaked to the newspaper which had originally broken the North Wales story – the *Independent*. By this time Dean Nelson had become a staff journalist on the *Observer*. In his absence a new freelance journalist, Roger Dobson, became enthralled by the revelations imparted to him by whichever councillor it was who leaked the report. According to the coverage given to the report, its authors, in spite of the fact that they had been unable to assess the veracity of the majority of the allegations before them, had apparently used the sheer volume of complaints as a basis for assessing the seriousness of the abuse that had actually taken place. The *Independent* quoted the report as saying that 'The history of allegations of serious abuse of children by staff was frankly appalling in its extent and persistence down the years.'

The coverage in the *Independent* indicated that the unpublished report had highlighted the claim that the deaths of twelve young men might be connected to abuse they had suffered while in care. It had apparently produced a list of these men, which included Brendan Randles, Peter Wynne, Mark Humphreys and Simon Birley. This was described as the 'most damning' evidence of all. The report was also said to have raised the issue of police involvement in the abuse, relaying the concerns felt in Clwyd itself, above all by Malcolm King, about the possibility that the abuse had been organised by a paedophile ring.

Although there were a number of good reasons for the non-publication of the report, the councillor who leaked it seems to have offered a different view. It was this view which was reflected throughout the coverage given to the story by Roger Dobson. The decision not to publish the report was thus represented as an act of censorship designed to prevent the truth from emerging. 'Paradoxically,' wrote Dobson in the *Independent on Sunday*, 'the latest attempt to suppress the truth may be what finally brings it the attention it deserves.'

The article in which these words appeared was published on 7 April 1996. Its publication marked the beginning of one of the most extraordinary campaigns ever run by a national newspaper in the recent history of British journalism. In a matter of days a special logo had been created showing a photograph of a distressed child alongside the heading 'Victims of the Abusers'. Over the next few weeks both the *Independent on Sunday* and the *Independent* used this device to flag story after story about allegations of child abuse in North Wales and elsewhere.

One of the reasons the newspaper chose to pursue this course was that, as it now revealed, the Jillings team had itself called for a judicial inquiry:

> It is the opinion of the panel that extensive and widespread abuse has occurred within Clwyd residential establishments for children and young people. An internal social service inquiry such as that of the independent panel cannot hope to address successfully the wider areas of concern which we identified during the course of our investigation, having neither the resources nor the authority to do so. This includes the suggestion that public figures may have been involved in the abuse of young people in Clwyd. … Our findings show that time and again, the response to indications that children may have been abused has been too little and too late. … Our criticisms in this regard apply not only to the county council, but also to the Welsh Office, North Wales Police and constituent agencies.

The *Independent* and the *Independent on Sunday* now made it their business to try and force such an inquiry on a reluctant government. Throughout the month of April their campaign seemed to gain momentum with every day. The power of accusation now appeared to be driving not simply a number of different complainants, but the entire newsroom of a respected national newspaper – together with its editorial policy.

In order to lend weight to its campaign for a public inquiry the *Independent* gave prominence to the other sensational claims that had been

made about North Wales. It implicitly endorsed the view that a paedophile ring had been operating in North Wales throughout the 1970s
and 1980s. More controversially, it also expressed the fear which had
been part of the story of North Wales from the very beginning – that
the membership of this paedophile ring might include some of the very
police officers who were supposed to be investigating it.

Although the judgment in the libel trial prevented the *Independent*
from naming Gordon Anglesea in this connection, there were perfectly
legal ways of circumventing this restriction. On 20 April, for example,
a front-page story in the *Independent* quoted leading barrister Allan
Levy QC as saying: 'What has come to light about the abuse in residential care homes, and what horrifies me is that there is no doubt that
there are groups of abusers working in these places, and the level of
involvement may go from workers right through to police officers.'

Although there has never been any reliable evidence to show that
any group of abusers has ever operated in English or Welsh care homes,
still less that police officers have been involved, the fact that this baseless idea had now been endorsed by a well-known barrister gave it
great authority. Three days later, in yet another front-page story, printed
under the headline 'POLICE QUIZZED OVER CHILD ASSAULTS', the *Independent* renewed its implied criticisms of the North Wales Police by
reminding its readers that, during the original North Wales inquiry of
1991–2, allegations of child abuse had been made against serving and
former police officers.

On Monday 22 April the newspaper intensified its campaign, printing no fewer than six articles about North Wales, including a front-page
story and a first leader entitled 'ROOTING OUT THE ABUSERS'. All these
pieces effectively appeared under the banner of the paper's front-page
headline which read 'PAEDOPHILES "CONTROL CHILDREN'S HOMES".'
On page 2 it published a large photograph of Bryn Estyn beneath the
headline 'THE BRYN ESTYN HOME WASN'T FIT FOR CHILDREN'. The main
article contained the following paragraphs, written again by freelance
journalist Roger Dobson:

> The children placed in residential homes in Clwyd, North Wales, in
> the 1970s and 1980s, were not, for the most part, delinquents, juvenile
> criminals, or uncontrollable. They were the innocent victims of
> domestic problems, sometimes four and five years old, who had been
> abused in their own families, or youngsters who had simply been aban-
> doned.
>
> What they needed was love and protection. But the world they went

into, as described in the report, was no safe haven. It was a brutal, abusive regime.

In reality there had been relatively few young children in residential care in Clwyd. At Bryn Estyn, to take the most important example, most of the boys were adolescents aged from thirteen to seventeen. Many were placed in care because they were considered uncontrollable, and a large proportion already had criminal convictions before they arrived. By painting a picture of innocent young children lost in a world of adult brutality, the *Independent* was obscuring the reality – that the vast majority of the serious allegations in North Wales had been made not by children but by adult men with records of criminal dishonesty. With few exceptions these allegations referred to a period in their lives when they would no longer have considered themselves 'children'. The picture created in the article was, in other words, false. It misrepresented the facts in a manner which could not but play on the reader's emotions. At the same time it obscured the real possibility that some of the allegations might have been fabricated.

The *Independent*'s campaign was also misleading in another way. The newspaper never pointed out that it was itself an interested party. After breaking the story of North Wales in December 1991, it had a continuing involvement which had led it to incur massive costs as a result of losing the libel case. As well as failing to disclose this crucial fact at any point during its campaign, the newspaper maintained a curiously inconsistent attitude towards the information it claimed was being suppressed. Although it had access to the Jillings report and could therefore have published details of the allegations made against named individuals, it did not do so. Presumably this was because its lawyers knew full well that any such action might result in another successful libel action against the paper. In other words the newspaper was suppressing information for some of the same reasons that Clwyd did not publish the report. The *Independent* was chastising Clwyd for not doing something the newspaper had the capacity, but not the courage, to do itself.

Such inconsistencies were not pointed out at the time and by the end of April 1996 the massive press campaign was beginning to have an impact. One of the bodies directly affected was the North Wales Police, who now suffered a renewal of the very kind of criticisms and unsubstantiated smears it had faced from 1986 onwards. As early as September 1992, the then Chief Constable, David Owen, had called for a public inquiry so that such unfounded criticisms (whose principal authors were Alison Taylor and Councillors King and Parry) might be laid to rest. On 20 May 1996, as the *Independent*'s campaign relentlessly continued, Owen's successor, Michael Argent, wrote to the Secretary of State for Wales, urging him to reconsider the decision not to hold an inquiry.[502]

Perhaps the most significant and decisive stage in the campaign, however, was still to come. On 9 June 1996, exactly two months after it had run its first full page story about 'the suppression' of the Jillings report, the *Independent on Sunday* published yet another front-page story. In a headline spread across seven columns it announced a disturbing sequel to the North Wales story: '300 VICTIMS IN SECRET CHILD SEX SCANDAL'. An exclusive investigation, it was claimed, had now uncovered a new scandal of abuse by care workers on a scale that was 'without parallel'. Inside the paper, under the headline 'OUR GULAG', the main story, spread over a full page, was introduced in large type: 'Victims of organised child abuse in Cheshire homes have at last told all. Their testimonies may unlock national paedophilia networks'. Beneath this in turn, Roger Dobson's article documented the new scandal. The opening paragraphs set out to explain the significance of its main headline. They did so by quoting the words of the man who had all but taken over the reins of the Jillings inquiry, and who had now persuaded a respected national newspaper to embrace his own conspiracy theories:

> It was just three months ago that Malcolm King, the chairman of social services in Clwyd, North Wales, declared: 'The evidence emerging is that children's homes were a gulag archipelago stretching across Britain – wonderful places for paedophiles, but, for the children who suffered, places of unending nightmares.'
>
> At the time it may have seemed a lurid and alarmist claim. There had been some isolated, if notorious cases, such as the Frank Beck affair in Leicestershire and the Pindown scandal in Staffordshire. The terrible saga of Clwyd – at least 100 children sexually abused over 20 years, of whom 12 subsequently died – was only just becoming known. It still seemed too much to suggest that this was a nationwide problem.
>
> But if anyone wanted to dismiss Clwyd as a freak, a one-off instance of systematic sexual mistreatment of children in care, they must now reckon with Cheshire. All the evidence now indicates that what has taken place there is actually worse than Clwyd, in the sense that it was on a larger scale.

Our gulag

After the Clwyd scandal, now we have Cheshire. Vulnerable children in homes have been sexually abused on an appalling scale. **Roger Dobson** reports

IT WAS just three months ago that Malcolm King, the chairman of social services in Clwyd, North Wales, declared: "The evidence emerging is that children's homes were a going archipelago stretching across Britain – wonderful places for paedophiles but, for the children who suffered, places of unending nightmares."

At the time it may have seemed a lurid and alarmist claim. There had been some isolated, if notorious cases, such as the Frank Beck affair in Leicestershire and the Pindown scandal in Staffordshire. The terrible saga of Clwyd – at least 100 children sexually abused over 20 years, of whom 12 subsequently died – was only just becoming known. It still seemed too much to suggest that this was a nationwide problem.

But if anyone wanted to dismiss Clwyd as a freak, a one-off instance of systematic sexual mistreatment of children in care, they must now reckon with Cheshire. All the evidence now indicates that what has taken place there is actually worse than Clwyd, in the sense that it was on a bigger scale.

The figures tell their own story. Six care workers have so far been jailed in separate court cases. Another nine trials are in the pipeline. Four residential establishments in the county are implicated. One hundred instances of abuse have come before the courts so far and the final figure for children abused may be 300 – nine in seven of those in care in those institutions. The squad of 24 detectives in Cheshire, conducting Britain's biggest investigation of its kind, is also studying links with Clwyd and Liverpool.

Who now could deny with any confidence the claim of a going archipelago stretching across Britain?

THE victims of these crimes were among the most vulnerable children in the county. Many came from broken homes, or homes where the parents could not cope. Some were rowdy children, officially declared beyond parental control, and some had already been abused by their parents. They were, all, in one sense or another, victims even before their came into public care.

Their allegations are mounting up today, rather than at the time in the 1970s and 1980s when residential children's homes – and the abuse – were at their height, for a clear, understandable reason. When a child is being abused he or she is often both threatened and made to feel guilty by the perpetrator. That guilt later turns into shame and a reluctance to discuss what happened. Many victims find that their failure to speak out at the time made them accomplices.

Most of today's complaints come from people in their thirties, a time when the lucky ones among them have settled down and found a stable lifestyle. They have begun to recognise the injustice of what happened to them. They see that they were not to blame, and in a climate of opinion where abuse is more openly discussed than before, they feel able to come forward.

The Cheshire inquiry has its origin in just such an instance. Four years ago, a young man walked into a police station and made a complaint about the abuse he had suffered. A second complaint followed some time later and the work got under way in earnest in February 1994, with a team of detectives based initially in Warrington.

A crucial decision was made at an early stage which was to determine the character and scale of the investigation: detectives decided to cast their nets wide. Instead of limiting inquiries to original complainants, they went looking for victims. One officer explained: "We decided that ... the last thing we wanted was somebody knocking on the door six months after we finished and saying, 'You never came to see me'."

So they set out to trace every single young person who had been in care in the area since the mid-1960s. The list came to 2,500 names. "The aim was to trace and speak to them all, to ask them about their experiences. We left nothing to chance. It has been a detailed, thorough inquiry," said the officer.

In each case, the police explained that they were investigating the specific homes and they asked: did they have any complaint to make about their time there? When evidence of abuse emerged, registered letters were sent which had to be signed for, showing they had been received. Those who received letters but made no contact were assumed to have no complaints. In all, just over 2,000 people were contacted and more than 300 made allegations that they had been sexually abused.

The investigation has resulted in the following convictions:

● Alan Langshaw, care worker, pleaded guilty at Warrington Crown Court to 30 counts of serious sexual assaults and indecent assaults against boys aged under 16 at homes in Cheshire and Liverpool. Jailed for 10 years.
● Colin Dick, care worker, guilty of nine counts of serious sexual offences and indecent assault against children at one home in Cheshire. Jailed for three-and-a-half years.
● Roy Shuttleworth, care worker, found guilty of 15 counts of serious sexual offences and indecent assaults on boys in a care home in Cheshire. Jailed for 10 years.
● In addition two men have been jailed

in Liverpool in prosecutions arising from the Cheshire inquiry. They are: Philip Savage, who was given 12 years, and Edward Stanton, now serving 15 years.

To take just one of those cases in more detail: Shuttleworth, who was jailed just a week ago, molested boys over an 11-year period starting in 1974 when he first got a job at the home. Now 63, he abused them both sexually and mentally. In court, he denied 11 charges of serious sexual offences and in-

CHESHIRE may be the biggest scandal so far, but there are grounds for believing that

victed abusers to talk. "In the ideal world, and on TV, one of these offenders would break down in court and tell us everything," said the officer. "But no one has said anything. There were guilty pleas, but no one has told the story. There have to be some links – everyone networks at some stage – but no one has ever said anything."

decent assault and claimed that the former residents were making up the allegations to get money from the Criminal Injuries Compensation Board.

One 33-year-old witness in the case told the court that he had been unable to tell his father about what Shuttleworth had done to him, it was only when his father had died and he was standing at the graveside that he poured out his feelings. Judge Robin David, passing sentence, told Shuttleworth that his behaviour had been beneath contempt.

Detectives have explored the idea that the perpetrators of these crimes belonged to organised paedophile networks, but they have been hampered by the refusal of all the con-

Independent on Sunday, 9 June 1996 'Our Gulag' (see pp. 414–15).

CHILD ABUSE SCANDAL

‘The Bryn Estyn home wasn’t fit for children. It has made my life since leaving a complete misery’

The unpublished Clwyd report reveals the full horror of life in residential care, **writes Roger Dobson**

The full horror of young lives blighted, terrorised, and in some cases destroyed by years of sexual and physical abuse in children's homes is revealed in the report into one of Britain's biggest child abuse scandals.

For many of the young children, their lives were a living nightmare, the report says. Even when in desperation they ran away to escape the abuse, their stories were not believed and they were almost always returned to their abusers.

The children placed in residential homes in Clwyd, North Wales, in the 1970s and 1980s, were not, for the most part, delinquents, juvenile criminals, or uncontrollable. They were the innocent victims of domestic problems, sometimes four and five years old, who had been abused in their own families, or youngsters who had simply been abandoned.

What they needed was love and protection. But the world they went into, as described in the report, was no safe haven. It was a brutal, abusive regime.

"The history of allegations of serious abuse of children by staff was frankly appalling in its extent and persistence down the years," says the report by three leading and independent child care specialists – which has so far not been published.

Most damning of all is the list of 12 young men who have died and whose deaths were linked to their lives in care.

Most of these deaths were not when the abuse was occurring, the report shows, but took place around the time of the investigation and trials of the men found guilty of abusing children in Clwyd.

The list reveals that nine of the 12 died after the police investigation and in some cases after men had been charged. Some of the young men who died had been involved in making statements or giving evidence.

The team says: "We are of the opinion that perhaps insufficient thought has been given to the psychological or psychiatric stress of appearing in court as a witness in high-profile cases."

The stark list of those who have died appears on one page of the 300-page report and the inquiry team says that even this list "is not comprehensive".

R1: Fell to his death from a railway bridge. Former resident of Bryn Alyn Home.

R2: May, 1978, committed suicide aged 16 by taking an overdose of pain killing tablets. Former resident of Bryn Alyn.

R3: March 1985, was found dead in a flat in which he was living in poverty, aged 21. Former resident of Little Acton Assessment centre.

R4: April 1992, died in a fire aged 32 in premises in which he lived in Sussex. The inquest verdict – unlawful killing. Former resident of Bryn Alyn.

R5: June 1992, found dead aged 18 in a bed-sitter. Cause of death, acute respiratory failure due to solvent abuse. Former resident of Bryn Alyn.

R6: January, 1994, committed suicide by hanging, aged 27.

R7: April, 1994, died aged 27 from alcohol abuse. Allegations that he had been the subject of a serious sexual offence. Former Bryn Estyn resident.

R8: July 1994, found dead in a car, aged 18. Former foster child in Clwyd where he allegedly suffered from maltreatment.

R9: November, 1994, committed suicide aged 16 by hanging.

R10: February, 1995, died from and apparent heroin overdose aged 37. Former resident of Bryn Alyn where it was alleged he had been sexually abused.

R11: February, 1995, hanged himself aged 31. Allegations of sexual abuse against care workers.

R12: May, 1995, found hanging aged 27. Allegations that he had been sexually abused by a senior care worker. Former resident of Bryn Estyn.

The inquiry team members said they had interviewed some former residents who said their experience in the homes was positive "but on the whole, those interviews which we undertook and the statements which we read, gave a clear indication that the residential care experience for a significant number of young people was little short of a living nightmare".

The inquiry team interviewed a number of young people as well as reading statements made earlier. One young man, now in his twenties, who spent some time at the Bryn Estyn home, told the team: "Bryn Estyn wasn't fit for children. It has made my life since leaving a complete misery. I spent some time in hospital because of suicide attempts. It has made me unable to form a loving relationship."

Another said: "It scares me now looking at kids of that age. I look at my kids and think, how could somebody do what they did. But I know it is true."

Commenting on visits from headquarters officials to homes, one young man said: "It was always suits, always men. We were told to smile. It would have been nice if it had been a woman."

Another said: "Bryn Estyn was the Colditz of residential care. If you ever rocked the boat you were left alone."

Yet another said: "Years later I was talking to a cousin who was at the same home as me. I didn't know he was my cousin then. He said, 'I remember you, you were the boy with no shoes'. They wouldn't let me have shoes because of running away."

Paedophiles were ‘free to perpetrate evil’

ROGER DOBSON

The widespread sexual abuse of hundreds of children in care by workers may remain hidden for decades, because the victims have been convinced by paedophiles that they will never be believed, according to a senior police officer leading the inquiry into child abuse in Cheshire.

Detective Inspector Terrence Oates described the insidious methods used by the paedophiles who found jobs in children's homes in the area. They made their victims feel completely isolated to ensure their credibility was undermined, so avoiding exposure.

"It is part and parcel of paedophile activity to convince the boy that he is the only one and that if he does tell anyone, they won't believe him, because look at who he is compared to who the perpetrator is," DI Oates said.

The allegations are only emerging now, according to DI Oates, because victims have finally found the confidence to come forward following a host of prominent scandals across the country, including Staffordshire, Leicestershire and London.

An unprecedented number of people have been interviewed in the Cheshire investigation, covering alleged abuse in the Seventies and Eighties. The police have traced 1,847 out of the 2,331 former residents at the homes and have taken 2,000 statements.

The children were already in care because of traumatic circumstances, and in a large number of cases they had been placed there because they had suffered sexual or physical abuse within their families.

But many of them were also difficult to handle because of their experiences, and their accusations were not believed.

DI Oates said: "There is no doubt that in that period when the abuse was at its height, a lot of the residential care workers were so poorly paid that it was an easy avenue for these paedophiles ... They had a captive audience and no one believed the kids. They were free to perpetrate their evil.

"These victims [went] away believing that they were the only ones, and never talked about it," he added, "that is often why these allegations are now being made several years later, after young people realised that what happened to them was wrong.

"There is evidence too that some [abusers] have risen fairly high up in social services and so when allegations started to come in they were in the ideal position to stop it in its tracks.

"Some of these lads were moved from one home to another where they were abused, and the perpetrators moved from home to home too. It is essential that we root out the paedophiles that still work in the childcare arena."

Allan Levy QC, a leading childcare barrister who chaired the "Pindown" inquiry in Staffordshire, says paedophiles are still operating in children's homes. He wants better policing of the homes but says that the Department of Health is cutting back on inspectors.

House of shame: The Bryn Estyn home, described in the Clwyd report as 'a living nightmare' Photograph: Tom Pilston

Indecision over bid for social services council

NICHOLAS TIMMINS
Public Policy Editor

Health ministers remain undecided on whether to introduce a general social services council to provide statutory registration for individuals working with children, the elderly and disabled which would allow those who abuse their clients to be struck off.

John Bowis, the junior health minister, has said he has "an open mind" on the issue. But a commentary the government plans to publish on the issue is likely only to canvass options, not provide outright backing for the idea.

Work on revising the central index which the Department of Health maintains of individuals who employers believe should be debarred from working with children is still not complete eight months after it was commissioned. Mr Bowis announced a review of it last August after the Islington child abuse cases demonstrated its ineffectiveness.

But a report on what should be done – and whether employers should have new rights of access to criminal records – has still not reached his desk.

On the broader issue of registration, ministers are understood still to be undecided whether to go for a statutory council rather than a voluntary registration scheme. Key questions about which groups of staff a statutory council should cover remain unanswered.

The department is currently considering two reports – one from the National Institute of Social Work and a study of the issues that need to be addressed before a council is set up that was commissioned from the management consultants Price Waterhouse. Ministers plan to publish them, together with their own commentary on the options.

Support for a formal registration system – in effect some form of general social services council modelled on the lines of the General Medical Council and its nurses' equivalent, is growing, with past opposition from local authority employers and the growing private sector reducing.

Sussex Health Care, a private nursing home group, said yesterday that it believed a registration system may now be needed after employing as a care assistant a former nurse who had been convicted of rape but did not disclose that on his application form.

Home sacks rapist, page 7

John Bowis: junior minister with 'open mind' on council

Redwood paper seeks tax cuts

COLIN BROWN
Chief Political Correspondent

A 20,000-word policy agenda, including a call for tax cuts, is to be issued by John Redwood, intensifying pressure on John Major to adopt a right-wing agenda for the general election.

Mr Redwood is determined to set out his policy priorities before the Conservative manifesto is finalised, in the hope of influencing the Cabinet over the direction of the Tory campaign.

It will highlight the battle for the soul of the Tory party. The One Nation group of Tory MPs is to publish its own agenda for the manifesto next month as a direct rebuttal of Tony Blair's claims that Labour is the party of the centre.

Mr Redwood is anxious to ensure that the Tories strengthen their appeal to the traditional Tory voters, who supported Margaret Thatcher through three elections, by highlighting the distinctive policies that set apart the Tories from Labour.

His radical right-wing agenda may be seen as a further plank in the campaign for the leadership. Mr Redwood is also preparing for talks with Sir James Goldsmith, the international financier, over his threat to field Referendum Party candidates against Conservatives.

Sir James yesterday repeated his threat to stand against David Mellor in his Putney constituency on the ITV *Jonathan Dimbleby* programme. Tory leaders have refused to agree to a referendum on Britain's withdrawal from the EU. Sir James said he will not "back off" for Mr Redwood.

The threat of Sir James to Tory chances in crucial marginals may be leading to a more Euro-sceptic tone from the Government. Downing Street yesterday dismissed as "ridiculous" a report that Mr Major had described Britain's EU partners as "a bunch of shits" over the ban of UK beef exports.

Sir James: Renewed threat to stand in David Mellor's seat

Mr Redwood believes that the Government has got to fulfil its pledges to cut taxes if it is to regain the trust of the voters. He has called for £5bn in tax cuts.

Michael Heseltine, the Deputy Prime Minister, yesterday dismissed Mr Redwood's argument that tax cuts could be financed by efficiency savings. He also tried to turn the attack on to Labour over taxation, after a poll showed many Labour MPs support Clare Short's view that those earning more than £40,000 should pay more tax.

He accused John Prescott, the deputy Labour leader, of supporting Ms Short by agreeing on the BBC *Breakfast with Frost* programme that a fair tax system was one in which some paid less tax, and others more.

Man dies as police try arrest

A 47-year-old man collapsed and died yesterday as police attempted to arrest him in a street in north London.

The incident happened at Whetstone after police were called to a report that a man was damaging a car.

The report was delivered at 1.08pm saying that a man had been throwing bottles at traffic and one had hit a car.

Two officers traced the man, later named as Ziya Mustafa Bitirim, from north London, and were reportedly attempting to arrest him when he collapsed.

After the officers and an ambulance crew failed to revive Mr Bitirim he was taken to Barnet General hospital where he was pronounced dead.

A spokesman for the Police Complaints Authority said last night that it had begun an investigation after having had the matter referred to it by the Metropolitan force.

A post-mortem examination last night at Finchley Memorial hospital into Mr Bitirim's death proved inconclusive and further tests are being carried out today.

Brigadier Anthony Vivian, of the PCA, said the inquiry would be headed by Superintendent Michael Partington of the Metropolitan Police Complaints Investigation Bureau.

He added: "A full investigation will be carried out and the detailed results prepared for the coroner's inquest."

A Scotland Yard spokeswoman said that Mr Bitirim was being arrested for breach of the peace and for his own safety when he collapsed.

IN BRIEF

Investigators probe death crash

Investigators were yesterday examining the wreckage of an autogyro light aircraft which fell from 1,000ft, killing its pilot. Retired company director Charles Kendall Park, 65, from Bakewell, Derbyshire, lost control when his rotor blades jammed during a rally at Long Marston airfield, Warwickshire, at the weekend. Investigators from the Air Accident Branch removed the aircraft for tests at their laboratory in Farnborough, Hampshire.

£20m plea to save historic waterway

British Waterways is to ask the Environment Department for £20m to save the Caledonian Canal, after surveys showed repairs are needed at many of the 29 locks on the 200-year-old waterway. The 60-mile canal runs through the Great Glen from Corpach, near Fort William in west Scotland, to Inverness in the east.

Blackmailer clue in bank bomb blast

Detectives were last night investigating whether a blast outside a Barclays branch was the work of the blackmailer known as Mardi Gra, who has been waging a letter-bomb campaign against the bank. Three people were slightly injured when the device exploded in a flowerbed without warning at the height of the Saturday afternoon shopping rush at Ealing Broadway, west London.

Hundreds pay tribute to Muslim leader

Muslims paid tribute to the controversial hardline leader Kalim Siddiqui, who died last week. Speakers described him as "the leading Muslim of his generation" at the service in Stoke Poges, Buckinghamshire. Siddiqui gained national prominence when he backed the fatwa on the author Salman Rushdie and demanded that Britain chop off the hands of thieves.

Man shot with antique rifle

A 51-year-old man was treated for a neck wound caused by an antique .22 rifle fired in his home in Holmbury St Mary, near Guildford, Surrey. Two other residents at the address, a 62-year-old man, who called the police, and a woman of 57, were being questioned. Police also found an old hand-grenade, which army experts detonated.

Oldest citizen dies aged 113

Britain's oldest person has died aged 113. Annie Scott, a widow since 1937, celebrated her birthday last month. She died at the Church of Scotland home in Reay, near Thurso, Caithness, where she had lived since 1972. She was born in Dungannon, Co Tyrone, married in 1915 and trained as a teacher but gave up when her daughter Nan, now 79, was born. In 1971 she moved from Ireland to join her son Tom, now 76, in Scotland.

Former student wins Oxford Union appeal

A former Oxford Union president barred from office for alleged electoral malpractice has won his appeal. Jonathan Wolf, 21, of Corpus Christi college, who was accused of preventing one electoral candidate from speaking while aiding another, said he felt "totally vindicated" by the appeal tribunal's decision and added that he would "definitely not" be going into politics or law.

Independent, 22 April 1996

The article went on to reveal that the Cheshire investigation had already secured six convictions with the promise of nine prosecutions still to come. The investigation had then spread to neighbouring Merseyside where 'Operation Care' had already obtained two convictions and where many trials were in the pipeline.

This story was accompanied by one of the most unusual illustrations which has ever appeared in a quality British newspaper. Printed as a sidebar down the length of the page was a cartoon silhouette of a leering, large-nosed man with his hands close to the throat of a tearful young boy. Only by reading the text alongside did it become clear that this was not an attempt to revive the ancient anti-semitic charge of ritual murder, but that the man was supposed to be one of the members of a new evil conspiracy – the national paedophilia network which was referred to in the story's headline. Although the article contained no evidence for the existence of this network and although no such evidence has been found since, the headline created an entirely different impression. In a strident editorial the paper renewed its call for an inquiry. 'The case for a full public inquiry into sexual abuse in children's homes,' it wrote, 'is now unanswerable.'

A mere three days later, on 12 June, the *Guardian*, which until now had remained silent, featured, on the front page of its second section, photographs of five men, including Frank Beck and Peter Howarth. Beneath the single word headline 'BETRAYAL' the following text appeared: 'These men sexually abused children in their care. Their secrets were hidden for up to 20 years. Today, one is dead and the rest safely behind bars, but how many more stories of broken trust remain untold?' Inside the paper, journalist Christopher Elliot, after reporting as a fact the allegations which Mark Humphreys had made against Peter Howarth, went on to record his tragic death, to repeat the claim that 12 men had died because of sexual abuse they suffered, and to endorse the call for a public inquiry.

On 13 June 1996 a presenter on the BBC radio programme *The World at One* suggested that we might have to face up to the possibility that abuse in children's homes was 'the norm' rather than the exception. By this time, however, the *Independent*'s campaign had already achieved its main objective. At a cabinet meeting that morning, as *The Times* would later report, the prime minister, John Major, had to 'read the riot act' to his ministers to force them to take action in relation to children's homes. On 17 June 1996 William Hague, secretary of state for Wales, announced that a full Tribunal of Inquiry would examine the question of the alleged abuse of children in care in North Wales. In July the Tribunal was formally appointed by parliament and it was announced that Sir Ronald Waterhouse, a retired high court judge, with local Welsh connections, had agreed to serve as its chairman. He was to be assisted by Morris le Fleming, a former chief executive of Hertfordshire, who had served on the Leicestershire Frank Beck inquiry, and by Margaret Clough, formerly of the Social Services Inspectorate.

By some criteria, what the *Independent* had achieved was a major triumph. To mount a campaign which brings into being a Tribunal of Inquiry is no everyday journalistic achievement. As befits an instrument of government that is used but rarely, a Tribunal of Inquiry has formidable powers. It has full powers to compel reluctant witnesses to give evidence, and to force public bodies and private individuals to produce documents they would prefer to keep hidden. In practice it also has at its disposal massive financial resources which it can deploy to staff its own secretariat and to fund the legal representation of those it calls to give evidence. There could be no doubt at all that, if power is the key to truth, then the Tribunal would end by unlocking the entire story of what had happened in North Wales. It would enable one of the darkest rooms of our recent history to be illuminated for the first time.

V

WATERHOUSE:
ERRORS OF JUDGMENT
(1996–2000)

59 Care goes on trial

IT IS 10.30AM ON TUESDAY 21 January, 1997. As more than thirty barristers and solicitors sit expectantly in the front rows of the Flintshire County Council chambers in Ewloe, North Wales, as members of the public and local officials settle down in the seats behind them, and as thirty or more journalists peer down from a packed press gallery onto the empty platform below, it is becoming clear that the largest, the longest and the most expensive Tribunal of Inquiry in the entire history of the United Kingdom is not going to start on time.[*]

Fifteen minutes pass. The words 'Rise please' are spoken by the usher and, amidst a rustle of papers and a general stirring, Sir Ronald Waterhouse, the retired high court judge who has been appointed by parliament to preside over the North Wales Tribunal, comes onto the platform. Having made his way to its centre, followed by the two other members of the Tribunal team, he inclines his head briefly towards those in front of him. As the rows of barristers and solicitors bow back, and as members of the public shuffle uncertainly behind them like unpractised worshippers at a funeral, Sir Ronald settles into his chairman's seat. 'I'm sorry about the slight delay,' he says, 'but I understand that there's a hitch with my computer.'

With these words, the North Wales Tribunal of Inquiry officially began. With the help, and occasionally, as now, the hindrance of modern technology, the Tribunal was due to probe into some of the most disturbing allegations ever brought before a public body of this kind. Previous tribunals had dealt, for the most part, with events which could be circumscribed in time and space – with Bloody Sunday in Northern Ireland for example, or with the Aberfan disaster. The North Wales Tribunal, however, was charged with the duty of establishing the truth about a long series of allegations concerning the sexual and physical abuse of children in care homes throughout North Wales. For by the end of 1996 an astonishing number of people – some 650 in all – had

---

[*] At this point, the second Bloody Sunday Tribunal (the Saville inquiry), which was to last far longer and cost much more, had not been announced.

complained as adults about abuse they said they suffered in North Wales during the 1970s and 80s. Of these complainants 180 were due to give evidence to the Tribunal. Although Bryn Estyn was still at the centre of the inquiry, the allegations by now involved thirty different homes and were directed against 365 people, of whom 80 care workers and teachers might be called by the Tribunal to give evidence. In the forthcoming months the Tribunal would have placed before it, in vivid and sometimes obscene detail, complaints of beatings, of sadistic cruelty, and of the heterosexual and homosexual seduction of children by adults. It would hear allegations of the systematic infiltration of children's homes by an organised network of paedophiles, as well as claims that this network included a number of serving police officers – Gordon Anglesea in particular. Anglesea himself would give evidence in public and so too would some of those who had stood trial – including David Birch, Paul Wilson and Peter Howarth. In theory at least many of the key complainants, including Ryan Tanner and Lee Steward, would appear. There would also be an opportunity for lawyers to cross-examine some of the people without whom the Tribunal would never have been convened – Alison Taylor, Dean Nelson, Malcolm King and Dennis Parry, to name but the four most important.

In the nature and complexity of the problem it was dealing with, in the number of witnesses it planned to call, in its estimated £10 million cost, and in the time it was expected to take – an entire year to hear all the evidence, followed by several months to compile the report – the North Wales Tribunal of Inquiry into Child Abuse was unique. In the seventy-five years since such tribunals had been introduced by parliament to investigate the most grave and intractable public scandals, no other tribunal had ever been conceived on such a scale.*

To most observers those chosen to conduct the inquiry were eminently well qualified to do so. As a recently retired high court judge, Sir Ronald Waterhouse would undoubtedly possess just the kind of judicial gravitas which would be required of the chairman of such a sensitive inquiry. Because he had presided in family and in criminal courts

---

* On the second Bloody Sunday Tribunal, see previous footnote. So far as cost is concerned, £10 million was the amount initially allocated by the Welsh Office to the North Wales Tribunal. The final cost was estimated as being £12.8 million. This figure, however, did not include the costs of many of the major parties such as the police, health agencies, successor authorities and insurers who were paying their own administrative and legal expenses, and doing so in most cases out of the public purse. The full cost of the Tribunal may therefore have approached £20 million.

his experience of the legal issues involved was considerable. He also had a record of social concern and had in the past stood as a parliamentary candidate for the Labour Party.

Sir Ronald's leading counsel on this occasion was to be Gerard Elias QC a distinguished prosecuting barrister with a long record of public service. A senior member of the England and Wales Cricket Board and chairman of their disciplinary board, Elias was capable of severity when it seemed necessary while also striving to maintain a sense of fairness. The Tribunal's legal team would also include Brian McHenry, from the Treasury Solicitor's Department.* A capable lawyer of great charm, who was also a member of the Church of England's General Synod, McHenry was appointed as solicitor to the Tribunal and was widely regarded as a model of fairness.

The experience possessed by the Tribunal team seemed essential, since a major problem was posed by the sheer number of allegations which had to be considered. The alleged criminal conduct which the two Bloody Sunday Tribunals have been required to investigate was on a minor scale compared to the allegations brought before the North Wales Tribunal. In the case of Bloody Sunday, all the alleged criminal acts had happened in the same place and on the same day. The relevant tribunals were expected to investigate just one complex crime or alleged crime, committed jointly by a number of people. Sir Ronald Waterhouse, in contrast, was dealing in effect with at least 365 defendants, only eighty of whom were actually going to give evidence. And, in principle at least, he was dealing with more than six hundred complainants who had made between them as many as two thousand different complaints relating to alleged criminal acts supposedly committed over a period of more than twenty years.

By any ordinary criteria the task which the Tribunal faced was exceptionally difficult. However, it appeared to be made easier by the widespread belief held by journalists, politicians and the public that abuse had taken place in North Wales children's homes on a horrific scale and that the principal problem lay in the failure of the authorities to make adequate acknowledgment of this fact.

* The Treasury Solicitor's Department is the main legal department of the government. It acts under the remit of the Attorney General and is staffed by lawyers who are civil servants and whose function is to provide legal services to the government. One of its roles is to organise, and provide staff for, tribunals of inquiry and to brief the barristers who are appointed to assist the tribunal chairman. The treasury solicitors and the barristers they brief are sometimes referred to as the treasury team.

This assumption appeared to have been reflected in the terms of reference which had been set for the Tribunal. These were:

> to inquire into the abuse of children in care in the former county council areas of Gwynedd and Clwyd since 1974;
>
> to examine whether the agencies and authorities responsible for such care, through the placement of the children or through the regulation or management of the facilities, could have prevented the abuse or detected its occurrence at an earlier stage;
>
> to examine the response of the relevant authorities and agencies to allegations and complaints of abuse made either by children in care, children formerly in care or any other persons, excluding scrutiny of decisions whether to prosecute named individuals;
>
> in the light of this examination, to consider whether the relevant caring and investigative agencies discharged their functions appropriately and, in the case of the caring agencies, whether they are doing so now; and to report its findings and make recommendations to [the secretary of state].

In that the Tribunal was instructed to inquire into 'the abuse of children' and not into 'alleged abuse', there seemed to be a presumption that abuse on a massive scale had taken place in North Wales. Given the wording of these terms of reference the Tribunal could be forgiven for concluding that its principal task was to confirm the reality of such abuse and not to investigate whether it had taken place.

This was not, however, how it defined its own role in its public pronouncements. During his opening statement to the first preliminary meeting of the Tribunal, on 10 September 1996, Sir Ronald Waterhouse, attempted to set out how the Tribunal would approach its task. He observed that one of the reasons why it had been set up was that speculation had continued 'that both sexual and non-sexual abuse has occurred on a much wider scale than was revealed in the criminal trials.' In view of this, he said: 'The Tribunal's first duty, therefore, in accordance with paragraph (i) of our terms of reference will be to try to assess the scale of that abuse over the period of existence of the two county councils.'[503]

This task, however, was clearly an enormously difficult one. The danger which now faced the Tribunal was a version of the danger which beset the trial of Mr Bailey in the Monmouth Assizes in 1926. That danger, as we have seen, was eloquently summarised by Lord Hewart when he observed that 'It is so easy to collect from a mass of ingredients, not one of which is sufficient, a totality which will appear to contain what is missing'. Lord Hewart went on to note that in that case the jury had effectively been invited to bolster up a series of weak allegations by taking them in bulk (see above, pp. 349–50).

The North Wales Tribunal was facing the same kind of judicial problem on a much larger scale – in which more than a thousand 'unsatisfactory' allegations were under consideration. There was clearly a grave danger that a totality might be derived from these ingredients which 'appeared to contain what was missing'. The only possible safeguard which might be adopted by the Tribunal was the one which had been prescribed by Lord Hewart. Ideally the members of the Tribunal should have taken great care to consider each allegation separately and to reach individual verdicts on all the allegations.

However, they did not do so. Their approach was exactly the contrary of this and was spelled out quite clearly in their report. Having pointed to the sheer volume of the allegations, and the long delay involved, Sir Ronald Waterhouse says this: 'We do not consider that it would be either practicable or appropriate for us to attempt to reach firm conclusions on each specific allegation that has been made to us.' He goes on to say 'it would have been impracticable and wastefully expensive to undertake a detailed examination of each specific incident'.[504]

In other words, what had long been considered a fundamental principle of justice was ignored. It was ignored not because the North Wales Tribunal was deferring to some higher principle. It was ignored because to comply with it would have been too difficult and too expensive.

The fact that the Tribunal undertook at the very outset a task which was extraordinarily difficult (and perhaps impossible), and that it proceeded to ignore the essential safeguard which might have rendered its procedures less dangerous, did not augur well for its outcome. But the Tribunal also laboured under another handicap which is part of the very nature of such inquiries. For what must be recognised is that a Tribunal of Inquiry has always been, and is likely to remain, primarily an instrument of government. In 1966 the Salmon Commission, which had been set up to review the tribunal system, declared that only a 'nation-wide crisis of confidence' should be investigated by a statutory Tribunal of Inquiry. The implications of this should be clear. Whenever a Tribunal of Inquiry is set up it has a particular purpose. That purpose is not to make a public crisis of confidence deeper. It is to restore confidence.

What must be pointed out, however, is that, whenever politicians borrow the robes of justice in order to conduct the business of government, they set out on a very dangerous path. And whenever judges allow their robes to be borrowed in this way they almost inevitably run the risk of undermining justice. The Waterhouse Tribunal may well have promised to restore confidence in the government by creating the illusion that a thorough inquiry into events in North Wales was at last about to be conducted. But in this particular instance there was clearly a very real risk that it might do so only by concealing the truth which it had been appointed to uncover.

The only parallel it seems reasonable to draw is with an earlier Tribunal of Inquiry – the first Bloody Sunday Tribunal. When that Tribunal was set up in January 1972 by the Conservative government, its purpose too was to use the judiciary in order to restore confidence in the government. To undertake this task it appointed no other person than the Lord Chief Justice, Lord Widgery. Among the scandalous revelations which would eventually destroy the credibility of that Tribunal was the discovery in 1996 – 24 years on – of documents showing that on the very eve of that inquiry, Lord Widgery had met with the prime minister, Edward Heath, and with Lord Hailsham, and that they had discussed how the Tribunal would be conducted. The clear purpose of that secret meeting had been to steer the inquiry in a direction favourable to the interests of the Army – and by doing this to restore confidence in a beleaguered government.[505]

Of course nobody would suggest that any secret meeting took place in 1996 or 1997 between Sir Ronald Waterhouse and John Major. What might reasonably be suggested, however, is that, in the climate of moral panic which prevailed, there was no need for such a meeting. It was abundantly clear what conclusions the Tribunal was expected to reach. There had already emerged a powerful consensus among apparently informed observers that abuse had taken place in North Wales on an unprecedented scale. There also seemed to be clear evidence that there had been a repeated failure to acknowledge this on the part of the authorities. The real crisis of confidence in the government had come about not because there had been abuse but because there had apparently been repeated attempts to cover it up. What was now needed above all was an official acknowledgment of what practically no senior politician, social worker or police officer seemed to doubt – that exten-

sive abuse had taken place in North Wales care homes and that countless innocent children had suffered as a result.

In the climate of prejudice which had been created against care
workers in general, and Bryn Estyn care workers in particular, there
were, in short, massive pressures on the Tribunal to reach a particular
conclusion. By doing so it would confirm the version of events which
had already been outlined powerfully by the national press – and in particular by the *Independent* – and by the 'suppressed' Jillings report.

In theory at least, one of the roles of any Tribunal should be to resist
such pressures. In this respect we should recognise that it is not only the
chairman of a Tribunal who has a duty to remain impartial but the
entire Tribunal team. The counsel to the Tribunal – in this case Gerard
Elias QC – had a quite different role from that of leading counsel in a
criminal trial. Under the adversarial system barristers are explicitly
appointed as advocates of a particular case. It is not their impartiality,
but their partiality which is sought. Gerard Elias, best known for his
abilities as a fierce and implacable prosecutor, was very familiar with
such a role. He was the barrister who had successfully obtained the
convictions of six men from Pembrokeshire who were among twelve
defendants facing allegations that they were part of an organised ring
dedicated to the satanic sexual abuse of children. (The six men who
were convicted continued to protest their innocence long after their
conviction, but in 1995 the appeal of all but one of them was turned
down by a panel of appeal court judges, one of whom was Sir Ronald
Waterhouse.) The case has since been described by Byron Rogers, as
'one of the greatest, and the most bizarre, miscarriages of justice in our
time'.[506]

However, Elias had now been cast in a quite different role. For a Tribunal of Inquiry is not, or should not be, an adversarial exercise. Its procedures should be *inquisitorial*. The counsel who are appointed to assist
the Tribunal are therefore expected to approach their role impartially.
Their duty is to *inquire* – to seek out the truth on whichever side it may
lie.

Those former members of Bryn Estyn staff, including Gwen Hurst
and John Rayfield, who sat in the public gallery on the opening day,
naturally hoped that the Tribunal would find itself able to fulfil this
function. They looked forward to the whole question of allegations
against care workers having a fair hearing in a forum whose investigative powers were massive and whose impartiality seemed beyond question. Although they did not all subscribe to the same view, some at least

still felt that the truth about North Wales could not now fail to emerge.

At 11.45 am on Tuesday 21 January 1997, as Gerard Elias QC rose to his feet, the members of the public and journalists who were present (as well as most of the barristers) remained unaware that the Tribunal lawyers had already taken a strategic decision which would profoundly affect the content and the fairness of the opening statement Elias was about to make.

60 No stone unturned

GERARD ELIAS'S OPENING STATEMENT was possibly the longest ever delivered to a Tribunal of Inquiry. Occupying 214 pages of typescript, it took two days to deliver. This delivery was made in measured tones to a packed press gallery and was prominently reported by national newspapers and television and radio news.

But, perhaps because most of the journalists present had little or no experience of Tribunals of Inquiry or were unfamiliar with legal convention, the most revealing feature of Gerard Elias's statement was never commented on in the reports which appeared. This was that, with the apparent approval of the chairman, he had effectively disregarded the convention that Tribunals should be non-adversarial. For it was the opinion of a number of lawyers who listened to Gerard Elias's statement that this was a speech for the prosecution. In some parts, it is true, considerable care was taken to disguise the prosecutorial zeal which seemed to underlie it. Mr Elias even used the extremely odd phrase 'preliminary conclusions' to stress that the examination of the evidence had not yet been completed. He also boldly promised that the Tribunal team would 'leave no stone unturned in its search for the truth'.[507]

As the opening statement unfolded, however, it became apparent that in some crucial cases 'preliminary conclusions' were being treated as established facts, and that allegations were being accepted as historical accounts even though the witnesses had yet to be cross-examined.

Although those responsible for the research on which the opening statement was based may have tried to remain independent of earlier reports, they do not appear to have succeeded. Like the Jillings report, the opening statement of counsel to the Tribunal suffered acutely from 'confirmatory bias', with its authors paying attention only to those kinds of evidence which appeared to confirm the intensely negative view of North Wales care homes which had already been widely disseminated. As a result the distinctive character of some of the care homes, including Bryn Estyn, was submerged beneath a black tide of rumour and uncorroborated allegations which were treated all too frequently as facts.

Particularly questionable was the manner in which allegations of sexual abuse which had been dropped by the prosecuting authorities, or had actually been dismissed by a jury, were adduced as if there was some direct relationship between the weight and volume of allegations and the amount of abuse actually being perpetrated. The assumption appeared to be that if allegations were piled up high enough they would somehow validate themselves and the problem of corroboration could be dissolved. This was the strategy which was employed first to blacken the character of institutions in Clwyd and Gwynedd, and then to besmirch the reputations of almost all who worked in them.

An excellent example of the way in which the opening statement oscillated between provisional and prosecutorial modes is provided by the following passage about Bryn Estyn:

> 138 complainants have alleged abuse whilst at Bryn Estyn. ...If those allegations are true or largely true, they reveal sexual and physical abuse on an almost unimaginable scale. The picture which emerges from dozens of witness statements, made both to the police and to the Inquiry team, is of an environment in which systematic violence was permitted to occur, and in which Norris and Howarth were permitted to practise their perversions apparently immune from discovery. It is small wonder that within such an environment, bullying and brutality between the boys flourished, sometimes in extreme forms, and that dozens of boys recall their time at the home as being deeply unhappy.[508]

Mr Elias begins here by obliquely acknowledging that we do not yet know whether or not the 138 Bryn Estyn complainants are telling the truth. But he almost immediately goes on to describe the picture which emerges from the allegations in terms which implicitly endorse their veracity. By the end of the passage allegations are being treated almost as though they are facts. Even though hundreds of former Bryn Estyn residents had made no complaint of abuse, and even though a significant number of these had recalled their time at Bryn Estyn with fondness and even gratitude, no mention is made of such contrary testimony.

In fact the sceptical point of view about the allegations in North Wales was neither expounded nor even outlined. The possibility that a very large number of the 650 allegations made in North Wales had been fabricated was apparently considered such a taboo subject that it could not be publicly addressed.

It might well be thought that the apparent one-sidedness of the Tribunal opening was accidental – or alternatively that it reflected the mature judgment of the lawyer who delivered it. It would seem, however, that the real explanation lay elsewhere: the one-sidedness was, in part at least, a deliberate contrivance which had been adopted by the Tribunal team for strategic reasons.

This at least is the conclusion reached in a book written by three social work academics. In their *Public Inquiries into Abuse of Children in Residential Care*, Brian Corby, Alan Doig and Vicki Roberts point out, quite rightly, that any public inquiry has a theatrical dimension: 'The terms "stage management", "audience", and "actors" are used [by us] intentionally to emphasise that one of the main functions of Tribunals of Inquiry (and the North Wales one is no exception) is to satisfy the public on issues of key concern. Justice, above all, has to be seen to be done. Tribunals in this sense are public performances which need to be presented before an audience.'[509]

What gives these comments a particular significance is that they were made on the basis of inside information. The authors had actually spoken to an unnamed barrister who was part of the North Wales Tribunal team:

> The notion of stage management was brought home to us following an interview with one of the Treasury counsel team, who made it clear that the main perceived initial difficulty was that of gaining sufficient trust with the complainants to encourage them to come forward to be witnesses. Put bluntly, without achieving this, the show could not go on. Without complainants there was no possibility that the Tribunal could carry out its remit, which was to satisfy the general public that everything possible had been done to ensure that all available knowledge and information was out in the open. The history of alleged cover-ups and the general climate of suspicion made this a sine qua non. This need, therefore, was a driving force behind much of the early pre-hearing work and was also much in evidence in the hearings themselves.[510]

To anyone who observed the early stages of the Tribunal closely, this account is likely to ring true. As soon as the Tribunal was announced a number of the key complainants recognised that they held a powerful position. This was strengthened further when they formed organisations such as OCEAN (Official Campaign for Ending Abuse Nationwide) and NORWAS (North Wales Abuse Survivors), which became, in

effect, complainants' unions. A key role was played in their emergence
by Ryan Tanner and Lee Steward, who were assisted by Malcolm King.
Steward in particular attempted to dictate to the Tribunal the terms on
which he would give evidence, and his non-appearance as a witness
remained a possibility throughout the opening days of the hearings. The
approach taken in Elias's opening statement had, it would seem, been
directly shaped by such threats. Corby, Doig and Roberts write that 'the
Tribunal made it clear at the outset that it accepted that children in care
in Clwyd and Gwynedd had been abused physically and/or sexually on
a major scale'. They go on to say that 'this acceptance of the scale of
abuse was initially *a device to encourage reluctant witnesses to come forward*
[italics added].'[511]

This approach was fraught with dangers, not least because it meant
the Tribunal began by deferring to the very witnesses whose evidence
it was supposed to be testing. One danger was that, by extending to
potential complainants an implicit promise that their evidence would
be accepted, the Tribunal was creating the ideal conditions for even
more false allegations to be made. A related danger was that, since the
tactical 'device' was itself a presumption of guilt, this presumption
would colour the Tribunal's entire view of the evidence. This appears in
practice to be exactly what happened.

A central section of the Tribunal opening concerned the character of
the head of Bryn Estyn, Matt Arnold. Having discussed the allegations
of abuse at Bryn Estyn, Gerard Elias posed what was clearly seen as one
of the key questions for the Tribunal to answer: 'If the majority of the
allegations are true, how was this situation allowed to develop?' Since it
was being assumed, in advance of any evidence being heard, that the
majority of the allegations *were* true, it followed that the question must
be answered. The first explanation offered was that Matt Arnold, the
headmaster, although he had arrived at Bryn Estyn with a high reputation, had failed to tackle the problems he found there. 'There is considerable evidence,' Elias claimed, 'that he turned a blind eye to the
problem of abuse at the home, suppressed evidence of abuse, and was
also prepared to act dishonestly to protect staff who may have been
involved in that abuse.'[512]

To justify this extremely serious allegation Elias went on to give a
highly tendentious and inaccurate account of two incidents which had
taken place in Bryn Estyn. He portrayed Matt Arnold as a man who did
not have the welfare of the boys at heart, and who appeared to be principally concerned with covering up any complaints and concealing

them from the authorities. Perhaps the most grotesque aspect of the Tribunal's attempt at character-assassination was the simple fact that Matt Arnold had died in 1994, and was not legally represented at the Tribunal. Counsel to the Tribunal was therefore in a position to deliver a seriously inaccurate and misleading account of the two incidents without there being any real danger that this account would be contested.[512a]

The attempt to destroy the reputation of Matt Arnold was not only grossly ill-informed but it seemed to go far beyond any merely strategic device. It was one of a number of indications that the extraordinarily powerful narrative that had been created during the preceding five years had already been accepted by some of the key figures in the Tribunal team.

Because large groups tend to multiply the power of the orthodoxies they inherit, there was clearly a danger that the entire Tribunal would find itself more and more in thrall to the received view of North Wales. The gravest danger of all was that this view might become effectively unchallengeable within the Tribunal. This would happen not because of the strength of the evidence in its favour but because those who attempted to challenge it – including solicitors and barristers who were ostensibly independent of the Tribunal team – would find themselves marginalised or subtly ostracised. In other words they would experience precisely the pressures towards conformity which have been described by sociologists as 'Groupthink'.*[513]

One lawyer who seemed likely to pose a threat to the consensus view was the barrister representing Peter Howarth. The Tribunal had originally envisaged that Howarth, as an 'abuser', would be obliged to share his representation with other convicted care workers – principally Stephen Norris. Howarth resisted this on the grounds that it would be inappropriate and prejudicial for a man who was still protesting his innocence to share legal representation with a man who had pleaded guilty. By this point Howarth's legal papers were in the hands of a leading criminal defence solicitor, Adrian Clarke, of Bindman and Partners. His initial brief was to study Howarth's case with a view to appealing

---

* These words were written several years before the term 'groupthink' was given a much wider currency (in June 2004) by the report of the US Senate Intelligence Committee on pre-war intelligence regarding Iraq's possession of weapons of mass destruction. For more discussion of the nature of groupthink, see endnote.

against his conviction. With the announcement of the Tribunal, Clarke's role suddenly changed. The priority now was to ensure that Howarth would receive proper legal representation throughout the Tribunal. At first it seemed that the Tribunal would refuse this on grounds of cost. They may also have been concerned that granting full representation to Howarth might undermine the strategy which had been adopted in Elias's opening and have the effect of deterring complainants from giving evidence. At the last moment, however, the barrister Courtenay Griffiths, a talented junior counsel, now a QC, volunteered to travel to North Wales at his own expense to put the case for separate representation to the Tribunal.

The case he put was a powerful one. It rested on the observation that Bryn Estyn was at the heart of the Tribunal and that Peter Howarth was at the heart of Bryn Estyn. Since Howarth was, in effect, the most important figure in the Tribunal and since he faced a large number of allegations in addition to those on which he had been convicted, it was essential, in Courtenay Griffiths' submission, that he be granted adequate representation.

Although a number of lawyers predicted that this application would be refused, Griffiths put his arguments with such force that it would have been extremely difficult for the Tribunal to decline his request. To have done so would have been to run the risk that a decision made by the Tribunal itself might be taken to judicial review. With considerable reluctance, Sir Ronald Waterhouse granted the application. Although Griffiths himself was forced to withdraw from the Tribunal due to a clash of engagements, Howarth was now represented by another extremely able barrister, Anthony Jennings, then a leading junior, now also a QC.

The issue which almost immediately arose was whether Howarth's counsel would be permitted to raise questions about his conviction. This point was central to the entire conduct and credibility of the Tribunal. As I myself had argued in an article about the dangers of police trawling in the *Guardian* on the eve of the Tribunal:

> One of the most urgent tasks which faces the Tribunal of Inquiry in North Wales is to examine the evidence which has led to the convictions already obtained, and to interrogate with the utmost scepticism the principle of what one senior police officer has called 'corroboration by volume'. Since the Tribunal is not a court of appeal and cannot overturn convictions, there can be no doubt that it will embark on this task only with extreme reluctance. This reluctance should be over-

come. For a Tribunal which meekly accepts its own powerlessness to assess some of the most important evidence in front of it, can scarcely be said to be conducting an inquiry at all.

For the sake of all seven of the care workers from the north west (including Cheshire and Merseyside) who continue to protest their innocence from their prison cells *and* for the sake of those who really have been abused while in care, the Tribunal should consider all the evidence which is before it, rather than a pre-selected extract from it. Only if it does this can it hope to put together the whole picture of what has happened in North Wales. After so many failed or incomplete inquiries nothing less will now suffice.[514]

However, it was soon made clear that Howarth's counsel would not be permitted to question his conviction in any way. One of the most telling episodes in the Tribunal came on Day 7, when Anthony Jennings was cross-examining one of the complainants from the Howarth trial, Gary Waite:

JENNINGS: The wearing of pyjamas in the evenings. It was a house rule, wasn't it?
WAITE: That's right.
JENNINGS: That in the evening you would remove underwear and get changed into your pyjamas?
WAITE: Yes, it was a house rule that you put on pyjamas.
JENNINGS: It was also a house rule that before you got dressed for bed, in other words before you put on your pyjamas, you would hand over your underwear?
WAITE: I don't recall handing over my underwear to anybody …
JENNINGS: I suggest that as a matter of course as a matter of daily routine, by the time any of you young men came to go to Mr Howarth's flat in the evening, you would not be wearing underwear?
WAITE: You can suggest what you like. I'm telling you.
MR TIMOTHY KING QC (Counsel to Waite, Tanner and others): Sir, I hesitate to interrupt but I have to ask on behalf of my client where this cross-examination is going in the light of the conviction which is recorded here. If the purpose of the exercise is to reopen the facts behind that conviction, then this is very much contrary to what the indication was by the Tribunal.
THE CHAIRMAN: What is the answer to that, Mr Jennings?
JENNINGS: The answer to this, first of all, sir, is that, as you have been told (may I say in ringing terms), no stone is to be left unturned to discover the truth in this inquiry. You have—
CHAIRMAN: That is not an answer to the question.

JENNINGS: It is an introduction to the answer to the question. You have
to—
CHAIRMAN: Are you challenging Howarth's conviction?
WAITE: Of course you are.
JENNINGS: I am challenging the facts as put forward by this witness.
CHAIRMAN: What aspect of the facts?
JENNINGS: The inconsistencies between what he has said on previous
occasions and what he has said today.
CHAIRMAN: What are the facts that you are prepared to accept?
JENNINGS: I am not prepared to accept any facts.
CHAIRMAN: Then I am not going to permit cross-examination on the
basis of inconsistency if the underlying purpose is to demonstrate that
the conviction was unsafe or unsatisfactory.
JENNINGS: Sir, with respect, the purpose is to establish the factual mate-
rial that is put before this Tribunal by this witness.
CHAIRMAN: What evidence has he given that you seek to challenge in
terms of a reflection upon your client?
JENNINGS: Sir, I seek to draw out a number of inconsistencies.
CHAIRMAN: Are you challenging that the behaviour that he describes
occurred?
JENNINGS: Yes.
CHAIRMAN: Despite the fact that he has been convicted of such behav-
iour?
JENNINGS: Yes, and no doubt, sir—
CHAIRMAN: *I am not going to permit it* [italics added].[515]

The import of the chairman's ruling was clear. It meant that, although
he was quite prepared to allow any witness to use the Tribunal to make
new allegations against care workers (or against Gordon Anglesea), even
if those who were so accused had already been vindicated in a court,
he was not prepared to allow counsel to elicit evidence that might call
into question Howarth's conviction. This ruling highlighted the question which was begged by the entire proceedings – whether it was in
fact possible to hold a thoroughgoing inquiry into the North Wales
allegations at all.[516]

The restriction on the questioning of convictions notwithstanding,
the fact that Peter Howarth had been granted separate representation
did at least suggest that some aspects of his central role would be properly illuminated. Throughout the month of April 1997, having been visited on a number of occasions in Wakefield Prison by his new lawyers,
Peter Howarth had maintained his determination to give evidence to
the Tribunal in person. Innocently unaware of the depth of the hostil-

ity he would encounter, he seemed to believe that justice, which had eluded him for so long, was now within his grasp. As the time for his appearance drew closer it seems likely that the stress was mounting. One morning he collapsed from a heart-attack in his prison cell. At about six o'clock in the evening of 24 April 1997, before any member of his family could visit him, he suffered another heart-attack and died.

Had such a death taken place during a criminal trial, Howarth's legal representation would, of course, immediately have ceased. But so too would the criminal proceedings against him. In the Tribunal the case against Peter Howarth continued. But his legal representation was withdrawn shortly after his death. Although his counsel was invited to make a closing submission on his behalf, a number of crucial phases of the Tribunal now took place in circumstances where the central figure in the story was effectively without legal representation. From the point of view of those who believed in Peter Howarth's innocence, no more disastrous development could be imagined; the withdrawal of his representation meant that the truth – or at least a very important part of it – was left without an advocate.[517]

When Anthony Jennings eventually came to make his closing submission, he prefaced it by saying 'I am not making submissions concerning those who gave evidence at the criminal trial resulting in a finding of guilt.'[518] Complying with the narrow conditions imposed by the Tribunal, he did not present any evidence that might be construed as an attempt to question Howarth's convictions. A challenge to the Tribunal's conclusions had been successfully headed off.

In the very early stages of the Tribunal, however, there was another potential threat to the received view. This came from the barrister representing one of the best-informed parties in the entire Tribunal – the North Wales Police.

61 A mason-free zone

WHEN, AT 12.20 ON THURSDAY 23 January 1997, Andrew Moran QC rose to make the opening statement on behalf of the North Wales Police, it was already clear to those who had looked through the advance press copies that he had one main target in his sights. For his statement addressed among other issues, the role of a key protagonist in the North Wales story who had been mentioned only once (and in passing) in the two-day opening statement of Mr Elias – Alison Taylor.

The North Wales Police were acutely conscious that one of the main reasons the Tribunal had been called into being was that allegations had been made against them. They had faced, ever since 1986, but particularly in the years following the 1991–2 investigation, repeated charges that they had failed to investigate allegations thoroughly and, indeed, that they had actually covered up abuse. Rumours had circulated that the force was riddled by freemasonry and that this, together with the participation of its own officers in an alleged paedophile ring, had been one of the principal motives for the alleged police cover-up.

Andrew Moran, who of all the barristers in the Tribunal had the most vigorous and powerful delivery, made it clear that his principal task, on which he intended to embark at once, was to ensure 'that fanciful, untruthful and unsupported allegations reflecting upon the integrity of the North Wales Police are publicly shown to be just that'.[519] A number of these allegations, Moran pointed out, had been made forcefully by Councillor Dennis Parry in the *Independent on Sunday* article of 1 December 1991. They had related to the manner in which the North Wales Police had allegedly failed to investigate thoroughly the Tŷ'r Felin allegations brought forward by Alison Taylor in 1986.

To show that these allegations against the police had been unfounded, Moran explained that their failure to secure convictions had been due not to any defects in the Tŷ'r Felin investigation, but to problems they had encountered with the evidence brought forward by Taylor. He then went over ground which will already be familiar (see above pp. 306–7):

To give a flavour of the difficulties, the first victim referred to by Mrs Taylor, Jennifer Dunlop, was said by Mrs Taylor to have been given a severe beating by Mr Dodd and was badly bruised on her back and trunk. Other members of staff who were there at the time are reported to be aware of this incident, as were the other children in residence at the time. Jennifer was seen by the police on 10th June 1986 by a woman police constable, not in the presence of Joseph [Nefyn] Dodd at Tŷ'r Felin, as has been suggested, but with her foster parent, guardian. … She, the foster parent, countersigned her statement. She said, 'It is fair to say that whilst I stayed at Tŷ'r Felin at no time was I treated in an unreasonable or unfair manner. Never was I smacked by any member of staff for any reason. I heard the boys got smacked when they were naughty but the girls were never smacked. On no occasion did Mr Dodd lift a finger towards me, or even threaten to do so.'

So, wherever the truth lies, what more can the police do? How should they react in those circumstances? Mrs Taylor referred to another victim in her statement, and I will confine myself to these two examples. The reference was in these terms: that she, Mrs Taylor, on 3rd February 1986 had, herself, received a first hand complaint from the boy, Michael Thomas, that Mrs Dodd had thumped him on the shoulder and knocked him into a chair. The incident was alleged to have occurred after Michael Thomas and other boys had run away from the home and had been in trouble. Mrs Dodd was seeking that they should apologise to the officer then in charge, a Miss Jandrell. The boy was seen by Detective Chief Superintendent Gwynne Owen and he demonstrated what had occurred: the putting of the flat of a hand on a shoulder and being pushed down into, what we know to have been a soft chair behind him, sitting into a sitting position. But there was also a witness seen, Mrs Gillian Roberts, and she made a statement. Of this thumping on the shoulder and knocking into a chair she said in her statement, 'Mrs Dodd asked them to apologise to Mrs [sic] Jandrell for the trouble caused. The three other boys apologised, Michael Thomas did not. He smiled defiantly and would not apologise. Mrs Dodd had Michael by the shoulder of his clothing and pushed him into a soft easy-chair and told him off for his cheek. That's all the so-called assault amounted to. It was nothing more than what I would apply to my own child. It was not an assault by any stretch of the imagination.'

Having given these two examples in detail, so there could be no question of the Tribunal not being aware of the problem, Moran drove home the predicament in which the police had been placed:

Again, we say, wherever the truth lies, and we – that is the North Wales Police – in the light of what they discovered in 1991, hold no brief for Mr Dodd, but the conduct of the North Wales Police and its response to information must be judged by what happened when it took steps in response to that information. There you see two illustrations. That is not to say that no evidence was forthcoming from any complainant or on any complaint. Some eight suspects were considered, including Dodd. It was not, as had often been represented, an investigation confined only to Mr Dodd. Evidence was carefully pursued but found then to be non-existent in some of the cases, or of doubtful quality.[520]

Having given a general description of the main 1991–93 police investigation, Moran went on to offer a forceful rebuttal of the claim that freemasonry within the North Wales Police had led to a systematic cover-up of the allegations in general, and the allegations against Gordon Anglesea in particular. He now revealed that the North Wales Police had recommended the prosecution of Anglesea. It was the CPS who had rejected this recommendation (see above, p. 307):

Despite the verdict in the libel trial – which no doubt the CPS would point to [to] vindicate their decision – in which the authors and publishers could not even discharge the burden of proving on a balance of probabilities that Mr Anglesea was guilty, the recommendation was justified at the time and nails the lie of masonic influence and favour. Sir, I am instructed to add, irrelevant though it should be, that none of the following is a Freemason: the current Chief Constable, Mr Michael Argent; the former Chief Constable, Mr David Owen; the current Deputy Chief Constable, Mr J T Owen; the former Deputy Chief Constable, Mr R E Evans; the Assistant Chief Constable, Mr T J W Cooke; the former Assistant Chief Constable, Mr R Heseltine; and from CID command, those charged at the head of the list, an important one of those charged with overseeing the investigation of criminal offences, Detective Chief Superintendent R G [Gwynne] Owen; Detective Chief Superintendent and Acting Assistant Chief Constable G R Williams, Detective Superintendent and Acting Detective Chief Superintendent G Jones, Detective Chief Superintendent Peter Ackerley, the man himself in charge of the investigation, and Detective Chief Superintendent Colin Edwards, crime operations. It should not be taken that any senior officer in the North Wales Police not mentioned is a freemason, but these are the senior officers of whom enquiry has been made in relevant positions during relevant periods in the control of the North Wales Police. Where then, please, we ask is the masonic influence? Freemason[s] at the top of the North Wales Police? There are none. ...Mason-free zone, we would say.

He went on to describe the role played by Dean Nelson and Alison Taylor in the quest for allegations against Anglesea:

> It was stated by one witness, now sadly deceased, Peter Wynne, who confirmed that he had never been abused by Anglesea, that this reporter Nelson had visited him in about August 1992 in company with Mrs Alison Taylor, and that Mrs Taylor had suggested to him, as if by way of reminder, that he, Wynne, had reported to her when she worked at Bryn Estyn in 1984 that Howarth had buggered him and that Anglesea had been involved. What on earth was Mrs Taylor up to, we ask the Tribunal to consider? More importantly, how does it help this Tribunal to make an appraisal of how witnesses came to make allegations against Mr Anglesea or other persons, for that matter? Mrs Taylor – and the chronology has to be carefully picked out of this – Mrs Taylor was the person who, on leaving Bryn Estyn (she had worked there) wrote in the log a lengthy entry of thanks to Mr Arnold and all of the staff for all of their help during her three-month stay in Bryn Estyn. She who made a comprehensive statement on child abuse to Detective Chief Superintendent Gwynne Owen in March 1986, who has compiled a dossier, and made numerous statements to the police before ever mentioning that she was the recipient in 1984 of a complaint by Wynne to her of Anglesea's involvement in him being buggered.
>
> It surely did not just slip her mind.[521]

In any ordinary circumstances these striking pronouncements about the role played by a social worker in bringing forward a series of false or unsubstantiated allegations of child abuse might have been expected to attract the attention of the national press. On this occasion, however, the national press remained silent. In some cases they had little alternative but to do so, for the *Independent* and the *Observer* in particular had relied on Alison Taylor as a source.

The only significant media comment on the opening statement of the North Wales Police was published in *Private Eye* in the 'Footnotes' column edited by Paul Foot. The article, printed under the headline 'WHAT A MORAN!' carried a photograph of Andrew Moran in his wig. It also bore a larger photograph of Alison Taylor being presented with an award earlier that year by the Campaign for Freedom of Information. The caption read as follows: 'NO GAGS ON ME: Alison Taylor, receiving a freedom of information award from Steven Norris MP on 12 February. The citation said she "was dismissed for trying to expose child abuse in North Wales, and refused to accept a financial settlement containing a gagging clause".'

As we have seen, *Private Eye*'s original story about Anglesea had been published under the headline 'THE OFF SCOT-FREEMASON' and had clearly implied the existence of a masonic conspiracy which had organised a wide-ranging cover-up of allegations of sexual abuse, particularly those directed against Anglesea. It might have been expected that *Private Eye* would at least now report the North Wales Police's explicit denial of this allegation. However, no mention was made of this, or of the claim that the upper ranks of the North Wales Police should be recognised as 'a mason-free zone'.

Instead, the piece was a concerted defence of Taylor. It noted that Moran 'had attacked her again and again by name', and that he had suggested 'that Mrs Taylor had stirred up muck where none existed'. This, said the *Eye,* was 'an unlikely proposition'. It then homed in on Moran's claim that when Mrs Taylor had made her original 1986 complaints, 'she was not herself a witness to any assault'. 'Wrong,' said *Private Eye*, 'She had provided eye-witness evidence to one assault …'. The reference here was presumably to the alleged assault on Lewis Harper. Since neither this allegation, nor any other relating to an assault she had supposedly witnessed, was included in the complaints Mrs Taylor made to the police in 1986, it was reasonably clear, from this claim alone, that the source of the *Private Eye* story was Alison Taylor herself. As it had done previously, *Private Eye* was evidently accepting on trust an account of what had happened in North Wales without checking the facts for itself.

Without producing any evidence to substantiate its claims, the magazine went on to contest a number of Moran's other points. Its most striking claim, however, was the one with which it ended: 'Moran alleged that Mrs Taylor had deliberately withheld an allegation made to her by a boy in care. Wrong. The boy never made that allegation.'

This could only be a reference to Peter Wynne. The account of what Moran had said, however, was a complete misrepresentation. He had said quite clearly that Peter Wynne had confirmed to the police that 'he had never been abused by Anglesea'. The clear implication of his remarks was not, as now reported, that Mrs Taylor had deliberately withheld an allegation which had been made. It was that, accompanied by the journalist Dean Nelson, she had deliberately 'reminded' Wynne of an allegation which had *never* been made. In short, as Andrew Moran would eventually put it in his closing submission, she had gone to see Wynne 'to try ... to suborn him into making a false complaint against Mr Anglesea'.[522]

Taylor herself knew very well that this was what the North Wales Police were alleging. She knew this because she had subsequently been interviewed under caution on suspicion of attempting to pervert the course of justice (see above, p. 193). The story in *Private Eye,* however, contained no reference to this fact. It would appear either that *Private Eye* knew about this interview and had failed to mention it, or that the informant on whom they were relying had omitted to draw this crucial information to their attention.

The article ended by claiming that Mrs Taylor 'has plenty of other evidence that she is being smeared by the powerful group of people in the area who pretend that all child carers in North Wales are innocent of any abuse.' Who this group might be was not revealed. Since Andrew Moran, acting on behalf of the North Wales Police, had robustly upheld the guilt of a number of accused care workers during his opening statement, it was not clear that there was any basis for this comment at all.

The appearance of the *Private Eye* article, and the simultaneous silence of the rest of the press, made quite clear that there was likely to be no support in the media for any criticism of Mrs Taylor. On the contrary, in *Private Eye* Mrs Taylor had a significant supporter whose power and influence should not be underestimated.

Private Eye's article can scarcely have escaped the attention of the Tribunal lawyers. It seems entirely possible, however, that a strategic decision had already been taken by the Tribunal team about how it should approach Taylor's testimony. It was certainly the case that, when Mrs Taylor eventually came to the Tribunal to give evidence herself, she was treated with considerable indulgence both by counsel to the Tribunal and by the chairman.

In his closing statement Mr Moran claimed, as was perhaps inevitable given the extent to which the North Wales Police had followed the path of investigation which Mrs Taylor had indicated, that she had played a significant and positive role in some respects: 'We can also acknowledge that, as outrageous and unsubstantiated as many of the allegations in her dossier and press comments were, and however many innocent people have been defamed by those statements, including officers of the North Wales Police, she has contributed to the exposure of abuse, the identification of abusers and a cleansing process in which this Tribunal is playing a major role.'

However, although the North Wales Police softened their stance in this respect, they by no means withdrew the serious allegations which had been made against her. 'In such circumstances,' Andrew Moran continued, 'it is vitally important for those who were the victims of false allegation and innuendo, including the North Wales Police, that false allegations be shown to be just that and that her true conduct and motives now be shown and reported on rather than some rose-tinted portrayal that she would have the world receive'.[523]

It is highly significant that at this point Mr Moran was brusquely interrupted by the chairman, who asked 'What is the meaning of that?' In an evident attempt to defend Mrs Taylor, the chairman suggested that 'One of her difficulties is that she does not approach life as a witness, she approaches it as a journalist'. Sir Ronald, who throughout the Tribunal was frequently forgetful, was apparently at this point under the impression that she *was* a journalist. When Mr Moran gently corrected him by suggesting 'or a novelist', the chairman persisted: 'I think it's fair to say "journalist", then she tends to embrace in her comment a lot of things that would come to her attention, but she is not writing a witness statement, so to speak, when she is making her submissions.'

By the end of the Tribunal, although the North Wales Police had softened their approach to Alison Taylor, Mr Moran's underlying attitude remained robust. The chairman, however, seemed reluctant to entertain even a hint of criticism of her.

62 Trial by ambush

ANTHONY JENNINGS AND ANDREW MORAN were not the only barristers who sought to resist the powerful pressures exerted over the course of the Tribunal by Sir Ronald Waterhouse and Gerard Elias. Among the barristers who tried with considerable diligence and spirit to submit Mrs Taylor and others to searching cross-examination were David Knifton (counsel to a number of former Bryn Estyn care workers), Barrie Searle and Alistair Webster QC. However, it would be wrong not to call attention to the role played in the Tribunal by one lawyer who, although not a barrister, made a significant attempt to influence its approach – the solicitor Chris Saltrese.

As the son of the head of a care home himself, Saltrese was acutely conscious throughout the Tribunal that the kind of regime which was being ascribed to Bryn Estyn bore no relationship to the regime in the midst of which he himself had been brought up at a community home in Merseyside.

Saltrese had been introduced to the nature of police trawling when a colleague and friend of his father, the former head of another Cheshire community home, had actually been convicted as the result of a police trawling operation. After his conviction Saltrese had volunteered to look at the trial papers to assess the prospects of an appeal.

He concluded that the reason some thirty different complainants had all made similar allegations against the same innocent man was that the process of evidence gathering had been unwittingly conducted by the police in the medium of suggestive or leading questions. An interview he conducted in prison with one of the witnesses had offered a disturbing confirmation of this hypothesis (see below, chapter 66).[524]

Because of his knowledge of what could happen during such police operations, Chris Saltrese was aware that the same dangers would have been present in the North Wales investigation. Yet it was clear, as he followed the course of the Tribunal, that such dangers were not being given any attention at all. So disturbed was he by this omission, and by some of the remarks made by Sir Ronald Waterhouse, that he felt he had no alternative but to write to Sir Ronald expressing his grave anxiety about the dangers of trawling operations. After relating his own experience of investigating one particular trawling case, Saltrese went on to outline his more general concern. He was not suggesting, he said, that police officers set out deliberately to create evidence. His concern was that, by asking leading questions, police officers might be inadvertently creating the very allegations they subsequently collected.

In support of this view he enclosed the letter he had received from Keith Martell, in which he had said he was 'dumbfounded' when the police told him he would get compensation if he had been abused (see above, p. 222). He also cited the Tribunal statement of another former Bryn Estyn resident, John Evans, who made it clear that, when he had been interviewed by the North Wales Police, *they* had told *him* that he had been abused by Peter Howarth. When Evans pointed out that this was not true, he too had been told that he might receive compensation if he did make an allegation of abuse (see above, p. 224).

Saltrese concluded by suggesting that police trawling methods could all too easily lead to miscarriages of justice and that this was directly relevant to North Wales because of the case of Peter Howarth: 'Having read the used and unused evidence in the Howarth case, and having listened to some of the complainants give their evidence to the Tribunal, it is my view that there is every possibility that Peter Howarth was an innocent man, wrongly convicted.'

The chairman's response to this letter was instructive. Two weeks after receiving it he asked that the Tribunal should sit in chambers. Saltrese was then reprimanded in front of his fellow lawyers. Any submission, the chairman suggested, should be based on evidence before the Tribunal that was subject to cross-examination. He made it clear that, although he had read the letter, he considered that it did not form part of any evidence before him and that it would have 'no impact' on his mind.

When this ruling was made, the Tribunal had already been hearing evidence for a hundred days. At no point had any question been raised about police trawling methods, even though these methods lay at the very heart of what had happened in North Wales. It was clear that Saltrese had written his letter out of frustration at the manner in which the Tribunal had continually avoided this most crucial of issues.

What amounted to the ritual 'punishment' of Saltrese, for daring to draw this subject to the attention of the Tribunal, effectively ensured that no other lawyer raised the subject of police trawling again. This does not mean, however, that Saltrese was the only lawyer who remained critical of its approach. Perhaps the most significant of all the criticisms made against the Tribunal was reserved for its closing moments. It was made by one of the few barristers whose experience was in family rather than criminal courts – Anna Pauffley QC.

Although, in the early stages of the Tribunal, Pauffley had shown no signs of dissidence at all, and had diligently complied with its procedures, she had apparently become increasingly disillusioned with the Tribunal's approach. In a closing address which was striking for its vehemence and its brave criticisms of the conduct of the inquiry, she launched a full-scale attack on the manner in which the Tribunal lawyers ('the Treasury team') had discharged their duties:

> Sir, then I come on to my fourth submission: has the approach of the Treasury team been impartial and balanced? We say that it should have been if it was genuine in its desire to conduct an inquisitorial, as against an adversarial process. It has been evident from the first day of the proceedings, we say, that the Treasury team had a case that they were to pursue. The opening made by Mr Elias set the scene. [In] the section of the opening entitled, 'Highlights and Summary', he said this: 'Without intending to pre-judge the evidence which is to be heard by the Tribunal, or to influence its view of it in any way, the content, volume and consistency of statements made by complainants appear cogent and very impressive. If as a whole, or in substantial part, they are accepted by the Tribunal then it may be that they', and then this next part appeared in bold type in [press copies of the opening statement] 'will compel the conclusion that children in care in Clwyd and Gwynedd, during the period under review were abused physically and/or sexually on a scale which borders on wholesale exploitation.'
>
> It was a memorable phrase, which unsurprisingly was widely reported not just locally but across England and Wales. It was surprising that such a sensational phrase was used in the light of what Lord Justice Salmon had had to say about counsel's openings in his report, and I then quote from paragraph 109 to 111. Paragraphs which we say contain sound advice: 'In its discretion the Tribunal will direct whether or not counsel instructed on its behalf should make an opening statement indicating the progress which had been made in the investigation before the evidence is heard. The statement should be an impartial summary of the investigation and avoid any comments which are likely to make sensational headlines. It should be emphasised that until the evidence is heard it would be wrong to draw any conclusions.'
>
> How much better it would have been, we say, if that advice had been followed. Instead, at the beginning of every significant phase, there has been an opening which would seem to have been drafted with sensa-

tional headline opportunities uppermost. *Accordingly, we submit that from the first day of the Tribunal's sitting the die has been cast, witnesses were taken through their evidence-in-chief and complaints were made about abuse they maintained they had suffered.* It mattered not that there may have been material that showed probable inconsistency, the complaint was sympathetically led. It mattered not if that witness also had good things to say about care staff, even if he or she was a Salmon letter recipient. That evidence was not led in-chief very largely. *There has been an almost morbid preoccupation with anything that might have been wrong with the system and criticisms of individuals. Seemingly the Treasury team was not interested in eliciting the positives, the good examples of child care, they were intent on finding out about the bad practice, the mistakes that were made. There has been no balance* [italics added].

In these words Anna Pauffley expressed forcefully many of the conclusions that had already been reached by some observers before the opening statement had even been completed. For it had seemed at the time almost inevitable that, where the Counsel to the Tribunal had led, the Tribunal itself would follow.

From Pauffley's impassioned closing address it seemed she felt that this was just what had happened:

> Sir, the person who is accused of criminal wrongdoing is entitled to a proper trial, usually a jury trial, with all of the safeguards that exist within the criminal justice system. He would not be tried alongside 150 or so other defendants, his trial would not take over 15 months to complete, evidence could not be adduced against him after he had himself given evidence, he would not have to share his counsel with the 105 other defendants, he would have advance disclosure of the relevant material and access to all unused material, evidence of complainants would not have been adduced in response to a series of pleadings …
>
> There has been little effort, as we said, to try to achieve fairness, perhaps fairness was never really attainable because of the enormity of the task facing the Treasury team.[525]

Not only did Anna Pauffley suggest that, for many of the care workers involved, the Tribunal had been 'the late twentieth-century equivalent of the medieval stocks', she also suggested that what seemed sometimes to have been in operation was 'trial by ambush'.

Sir Ronald Waterhouse took exception to these strictures, claiming that the suggestion that there had been little effort to achieve fairness was 'wholly unwarranted'. There can indeed be little doubt that the members of the Tribunal team genuinely believed they had been fair to all parties. The problem was that their attempts at fairness were premised on the assumption that there had indeed been widespread abuse. It was this assumption which was grossly unfair.

Anna Pauffley's words would continue to echo long after the Tribunal proceedings had been brought to an end. If her portrayal of these proceedings was in any significant respect accurate, then the very last thing that could be expected to emerge from the Tribunal report, when it was eventually published, was the truth.

63 Lost in care

THE NORTH WALES TRIBUNAL had begun taking evidence in January 1997. It had been envisaged that it would hear evidence for a year and that its report would be published around Easter 1998. In the event it did not complete its hearings until April 1998. The writing of the report then took much longer and the projected publication date was repeatedly put back.

The delay led to speculation that the Tribunal might be reconsidering its assessment of the evidence. Among those who were aware of the damage being done by police trawling operations, there were even moments of optimism. Generally, however, a more sceptical view was maintained and it was widely expected that when the report did appear it would do little more than translate into 'findings' the 'preliminary conclusions' which had been set out by Gerard Elias in his opening statement.

When the publication date of the report, *Lost in Care*, was fixed for February 15 2000, most national newspapers had already prepared extensive feature articles based on the assumption that the Tribunal would confirm the claims of widespread abuse. This is precisely what happened. At the heart of the report lay the conclusions the Tribunal had reached about Bryn Estyn. The testimony of the many former residents who had spoken positively about their time there was all but disregarded. Instead the Tribunal focused on the allegations of abuse.

Their method of assessing these allegations is never properly explained in the report. However, shortly before the Tribunal formally began its public hearings, in January 1997, Sir Ronald Waterhouse had been interviewed on BBC2's *Newsnight* by Rosie Waterhouse (no relation) – the journalist who had played such a significant role in discrediting allegations of satanic abuse (see above, p. 88). She had raised the possibility that a significant number of allegations in North Wales had been fabricated in an attempt to gain compensation. She then asked Sir Ronald how he would tell the difference between a true allegation of sexual abuse and a false one. He answered that he would seek to do so on the basis of his 'experience of life'. An experienced senior police officer privately expressed concern that Sir Ronald had made no reference to scrutinising the evidence and using this to judge between truth and falsehood.

This seeming lack of regard for traditional evidential standards is reflected in some of the report's comments about alleged victims. Above all it is clear that the members of the Tribunal treat allegations of sexual abuse as a special category which are not to be assessed in the same way as the evidence of other crimes. Their comments on 'witness B' – who is in fact Lee Steward – are particularly significant. Although a significant number of the allegations Steward makes against the hundred or more adults he now accuses of abusing him are demonstrably false, the members of the Tribunal say this in their report:

> We are satisfied that B has suffered a long history of sexual abuse before, during and after his period in care and, to a significant extent until he left care, of physical abuse. As a result he has been, and remains, severely damaged psychologically; he has been greatly affected also by the sudden death of his young wife in very sad circumstances on 1 April 1992, leaving B with a very young child to bring up. A major problem is that the damage is reflected in B's personality *in such a way that he presents himself as an unreliable witness by the standards that an ordinary member of a jury is likely to apply* [italics added].

What this seems to imply is that, whereas implausibilities in a witness's evidence would usually be grounds for disbelieving them, such doubtful testimony can actually result from sexual abuse, and can therefore be construed as evidence that a crime *has* taken place. Although most juries would not see things in this way, the members of the Tribunal imply that they can see beyond appearances to a reality that most jurors would miss. In making this suggestion it is reasonably clear that the Tribunal members are accepting uncritically articles of doctrine promulgated by 'experts' on sexual abuse.

They go on to enumerate various criticisms of the complainants which were made during the Tribunal on behalf of care workers, including the suggestion that they had been motivated by the hope of compensation and the idea that they may have conspired together to fabricate allegations. However, these criticisms are cited only to be dismissed out of hand:

> Despite these substantial criticisms and other allied attacks upon the credibility of individual witnesses, including the paucity of direct corroboration in relation to most specific incidents, we have been impressed

generally by the sincerity of the overwhelming majority of the complainants that we have heard and their own conviction that they are telling the truth about what occurred to them in care. Indeed, no one who has sat through the Tribunal's hearings and listened to their evidence impartially can have failed to have been impressed by what they have said and their stated motivation now in coming forward to give evidence.

In invoking the apparent sincerity of the complainants and the compelling nature of their allegations, the Tribunal members seemed unaware that these very features are frequently found in *false* allegations. One example of this was provided soon after the publication of the report. When, on 7 April 2000, Roy Burnett had his conviction for rape quashed by the Court of Appeal after serving fifteen years in prison, Lord Justice Judge said this: 'The crimes of which he was convicted almost certainly never happened at all. The complainant, *apparently persuasive and compelling*, convinced the jury that she was telling the truth when there was probably no rape or assault' [italics added].

Precisely because of the strength of the emotions associated with rape or abuse, and because of the psychological effect of obscene testimony, it is perhaps easier for witnesses to make false *sexual* allegations, than false complaints of a more mundane kind. In an appeal court judgment in 2003, overturning a conviction in a sexual abuse case, the Lord Chief Justice, Lord Woolf, acknowledged that sincerity on the part of a witness should not be taken as a guarantee of veracity:

> The reason the jury convicted [in the case before us] was almost inevitably because they felt the complainant was speaking the truth and the defendant was not. No doubt they took into account that generally people do not make allegations of this sort years after the event unless they believe them to be true. However, those who try cases know that sometimes – and this is in the experience of each member of this court – honest witnesses can convince themselves that something happened in their youth when it is subsequently shown that what they remember cannot be true.[526]

In attempting to use the apparent sincerity of witnesses as a means of judging their truthfulness, the members of the Tribunal were effectively ensuring that they would fail in their essential task of assessing the scale of abuse.

There was another respect in which an attempt by the Tribunal to establish the scale of abuse failed – and did so in a remarkable manner. During his opening statement, Gerard Elias QC gave a striking account of a form of investigation the Tribunal was undertaking which was, as he put it, 'entirely of our own making'. The Tribunal had, he said, identified a random sample of 600 adults who had been in care in the two counties of Clwyd and Gwynedd during the period under scrutiny. Investigators had already begun to trace and approach these individuals 'to enquire as to the way they were treated whilst in care'. It is quite clear that the assumption behind the setting-up of 'the random 600' inquiry was that if abuse had indeed taken place 'on a scale which borders on wholesale exploitation' this could now be confirmed by an objective sample. Indeed Elias specifically said that the inquiry into the random 600 was one of three parallel investigations which would enable the Treasury team 'to put statistical information before the Tribunal in the form of schedules to assist it in the task of identifying the nature of the abuse which existed in North Wales and its scale'.[527]

Mysteriously, however, the main body of the Tribunal report, when it appeared three years later, contained not a single reference to the random 600 inquiry. It was only in Appendix 4, on page 870 of the report, in a section headed 'Notes by the Chairman of the Tribunal on its procedures' that its existence was acknowledged at all. Yet Sir Ronald Waterhouse gave no indication of the outcome of the inquiry. It is only by combing through the Tribunal transcript that it is possible to discover what happened. On day 190 of the Tribunal proceedings, junior counsel to the Tribunal, Mr Treverton-Jones, belatedly admitted to the chairman that the attempt to trace and interview 600 randomly selected potential witnesses had been abandoned after only 111 people had been contacted. The reason for this was that very few had made allegations of abuse. Or, in the words of Mr Treverton-Jones: '… a clear pattern had emerged that really our inquiries were not significantly adding to that which the police had revealed during their major investigation.'[527a]

Of the 111 who were contacted, only five gave evidence to the Tribunal. Of these, four made allegations which were either lacking in any convincing detail, or which appeared, on the basis of other evidence that emerged during cross-examination, not to be true. The fifth gave a portrait of Bryn Estyn which corresponded closely to that which had been painted in the media. His own allegations, however, were relatively minor, and during cross-examination serious doubt was cast upon their veracity. The random 600 inquiry, in other words, led to a significant number of witnesses making statements that nothing had happened to them. But it produced not a single credible witness alleging serious physical or sexual abuse.[527b]

If the Tribunal had indeed been conducting an open-minded inquiry it seems clear that it would have persevered with the exercise. For the very fact that the initial findings suggested that there had been relatively little abuse meant that these findings were, potentially, a vitally important corrective to the received view. However, apparently because it was not providing the evidence of abuse that was being sought, the entire project was halted. Although counsel to the Tribunal had claimed that the purpose of the exercise was to help establish the scale of abuse, it is clear that its real purpose had been to confirm that the scale of abuse corresponded to the preconceptions of the Tribunal lawyers, as expressed in the opening statement. When it became apparent that the exercise was going to yield the 'wrong' answer, it was hastily abandoned. Not only was it abandoned, but its results, which suggested that the entire picture painted in Mr Elias's opening statement might be mistaken, were not given anywhere in the Tribunal's report.

Once again there were clear signs in the Tribunal's approach of 'confirmatory bias' and of reluctance to accord significance to any evidence which did not seem to accord with the view that 'wholesale abuse' had taken place. The consequences of the Tribunal applying this approach were predictable. Bryn Estyn was portrayed in the report in much the same way as it had been by countless journalists. It was presented as a bleak, forbidding and cruel institution – the ideal venue for sexual perversion on an almost unimaginable scale. 'The evidence before us,' the Tribunal members wrote, 'has disclosed that for many children who were consigned to Bryn Estyn, in the ten or so years of its existence as a community home, it was a form of purgatory or worse from which they emerged more damaged than when they had entered and for whom the future had become even more bleak'.[528]

At the heart of the report was the figure of Peter Howarth. The authors noted that, in spite of 'the weight of evidence which has now emerged against Howarth' and 'the transparent sincerity' of many of those who gave evidence against him, a small number of former members of Bryn Estyn staff 'still refuse to believe that Howarth was guilty of any sexual misconduct.' In order to discredit this point of view, the Tribunal quoted, as an example of fanciful speculation, the words of John Rayfield, who had suggested that those who made the allegations had been 'carefully trained' and that there had been a 'conspiracy'.[529]

The Tribunal omitted, however, to cite Rayfield's rather more substantial suggestion that a significant role in propagating false allegations had been played by Alison Taylor, Lee Steward and others, and that 'the North Wales Police were given false information about abuse at Bryn Estyn, and took unusual steps to investigate it'. On the strength of their selective reading of the evidence, the Tribunal bracketed John Rayfield and Gwen Hurst together in their report and wrote that 'we are unable to sympathise with the persistent ostrich-like response of these two witnesses (and some others) to the very substantial body of evidence placed before the Tribunal'.[530]

While firmly dismissing the views of these two former members of staff, the Tribunal made no mention of the fact that a significant number of former residents of Bryn Estyn had shared the view that Peter Howarth had been an innocent man. Nor did they record the fact that none of these witnesses, a number of whom had been prepared to give evidence on Howarth's behalf at his trial, had been invited to give evidence to the Tribunal. Perhaps more importantly still, they made no mention of the fact that, in their own proceedings, Howarth's counsel had in effect been forbidden to question his conviction at all.[531]

Instead they went on to present, as though it were a finding made on the basis of the evidence given to the Tribunal, the conclusion which had been reached six years earlier at the criminal trial: namely that Howarth was guilty. It was the Tribunal's view, widely quoted in the press coverage which followed, that the consequences of Howarth's abuse were 'immeasurable':

> The lives of these already disturbed children were grossly poisoned by a leading authority figure in whom they should have been able to place their trust. They felt soiled, guilty and embarrassed and some of them were led to question their own sexual orientation. Most of them have experienced difficulties in their sexual relationships and their relationships with children ever since and many have continued to rebel against authority. Even more seriously, their self-respect and ability to look forward to the future have been shattered.[532]

Of the grossly contaminated state of the evidence against Howarth, and of the part played by Ryan Tanner, Alison Taylor and Dean Nelson in furthering the case against him, the Tribunal report spoke not a word.

In one or two respects, the report did succeed in setting the record straight. It roundly dismissed the suggestions that there had been a masonic conspiracy to cover up allegations of sexual abuse. At the same time it rightly exonerated the North Wales Police from the persistent charges of 'cover up' which had been levelled against them in respect of the 1991–2 investigation.

On the question of Gordon Anglesea, the Tribunal was less perceptive and much less robust. As was expected, it endorsed the findings of the original libel trial. However, it did so in terms so weak that some came to the conclusion that the Tribunal's findings on Anglesea had been carefully drafted in order that the original allegations would *not* be laid to rest.[533] 'Having considered all [the] evidence with very great care,' Sir Ronald Waterhouse wrote, 'we are unable to find that the allegations of sexual abuse made against Gordon Anglesea have been proved to our satisfaction ...' Given that the evidence indicated that a well-intentioned but overzealous journalist had pressurised damaged former residents into fabricating allegations against an innocent man, the Tribunal's findings fell far short of the complete vindication which Anglesea might reasonably have expected. Indeed, one of the most extraordinary features of the Tribunal's chapter on the Anglesea case is that Nelson's part in it is dealt with and dismissed in a single paragraph. No real description of his role is offered, and no criticism whatsoever is made of his conduct.[534]

So far as the role of Alison Taylor was concerned, we have seen that, in the closing statement made on behalf of the North Wales Police, the Tribunal was specifically asked 'that false allegations be shown to be just that'. In the report however, the Tribunal restricted its criticisms of Mrs Taylor to noting, in passing, that some of her allegations had been 'exaggerated'. Their specific conclusion with regard to the Tŷ'r Felin allegations was favourable to Mrs Taylor: 'Alison Taylor's complaints about Nefyn Dodd and John Roberts, although at times exaggerated, have been substantially vindicated by our own findings. In the event Dodd's position as her line manager placed her in great difficulty and she would have failed in her duty to the residents in care if she had remained silent.'[535]

In which particular ways the Tribunal considered Mrs Taylor's complaints to be 'exaggerated' is not specified. What is interesting, though, and perhaps significant, is that the Tribunal, while adopting a generally credulous approach to allegations, did exercise considerable scepticism about the complaints made by one of the most important of the witnesses – Ryan Tanner.

So far as Tanner's complaints about John Roberts, the teacher, were concerned, the evidence, as we have seen, was quite clear: Tanner had accused Roberts of physically abusing him repeatedly at Tŷ'r Felin during a period when Roberts was not in fact employed at Tŷ'r Felin. In the light of this evidence even the Tribunal, who referred to Tanner as 'D', felt obliged to cast doubt on the allegations:

> The difficulty about the allegations of D against John Roberts is that the documentary evidence before the Tribunal suggests that D was only at Tŷ'r Felin for eight days during Roberts' period there. As we have said earlier, D's major stay at Tŷ'r Felin was for about eight weeks at the beginning of 1978, over 18 months before Roberts was posted there.* D's only other admission to Tŷ'r Felin was for about eight days at the beginning of June 1981, said to have been at his mother's request; and it seems clear that D's allegations relate essentially to the earlier and longer period in 1978. D remained adamant in cross-examination that John Roberts assaulted him as described and he complained of being slapped by Roberts in the first of his statements to the police before us, made as long ago as 8 August 1991. … In these circumstances there must be considerable doubt about the veracity of his allegations against Roberts.[536]

What is troubling about this very reasonable scepticism is that there is no evidence that the Tribunal considered with any care its real implications. Given that Tanner had played such a significant role in the entire North Wales story, and had been closely associated with Taylor throughout, the fact that a crucial part of his testimony appeared not to be true was, potentially, enormously significant. The Tribunal report makes no attempt to pursue the point.

What is perhaps even more disturbing is that, although the report suggested that Alison Taylor's role with regard to Gwynedd had been 'substantially vindicated', Taylor's role in relation to the Bryn Estyn investigation was scarcely examined at all. The fact that she made a number of claims in relation to Bryn Estyn which appeared to be not simply exaggerated, but entirely false, was passed over without comment.

One of the most troubling features of Taylor's role, namely her involvement in the false allegations made by Peter Wynne and Simon Birley, was not even put before the Tribunal in evidence. One reason

---

* In suggesting that Tanner's major stay at Bryn Estyn lasted 'for about eight weeks' it would appear that Sir Ronald is privileging the evidence of Tanner's memory over the documentary records. These indicated that Tanner had been remanded to Tŷ'r Felin not in December 1977, but on 1 February 1978 (NWTT, p. 3704).

for this may well have been that, by the time Taylor herself gave evidence to the Tribunal, Peter Howarth was dead. Because his legal representation had been withdrawn, the barrister who might have noticed this aspect of the evidence, and drawn out its extremely important implications, was simply not present; the truth, on this occasion as on others, had been left without an advocate.[537]

But other troubling evidence *had* been put before the Tribunal. The various claims which Taylor had made about John Evans, Andrew Singer and the minibus were explored in detail and the members of the Tribunal were fully aware that Evans had explicitly rejected both Taylor's account and the idea that he had been abused by Howarth. The Tribunal were also aware of the clear evidence that Taylor had visited Wynne in the company of Dean Nelson and of Wynne's claim that she had attempted to place in his mouth a false allegation against Anglesea. They knew that Taylor had been interviewed under caution by the North Wales Police on suspicion of attempting to pervert the course of justice. As we have seen, Andrew Moran, on behalf of the North Wales Police, had specifically underlined this fact in his closing address.

Yet, while other allegations against a variety of care workers were discussed in detail in the report, even where there was no substantiation of them, the very serious allegations levelled against Alison Taylor throughout the Tribunal proceedings were passed over in almost complete silence.

In view of these omissions it was scarcely surprising that the report's claim that Mrs Taylor had been 'substantially vindicated' in relation to the allegations against Dodd and Roberts was taken by most national newspapers as signifying an endorsement of her entire role in the North Wales investigation.

On the morning of 16 February 2000, the day after the report's publication, the North Wales scandal received massive publicity in every national newspaper. Sensational front-page headlines abounded. According to the *Daily Mail,* the report had laid bare 'Britain's worst-ever paedophile scandal'. The newspaper added that '40 of the monsters are still at large'. The *Mirror's* single-word headline was 'DAMNED', printed over a recent three-quarter-page photograph of Ryan Tanner, who, it was reported, had suffered 'six years of hell' in North Wales care homes.[538] The *Express,* meanwhile, carried a picture of the 10-year-old Tanner. 'This little boy,' it wrote, 'and hundreds like him were cruelly abused in children's homes over nearly two decades.' Several newspapers, translating the number of those who had made allegations into the number of victims, reported that 650 children had been physically or sexually abused in North Wales.

Almost all newspapers featured the role of the whistleblower without whom, it was widely reported, the Tribunal would never have come about. The scandal was only exposed, wrote the *Guardian*, 'after Alison Taylor, a children's home head in Gwynedd, pressed her concerns at the highest levels. The inquiry report finds that her complaints have been "substantially vindicated". But for her, there would have been no inquiry into Gwynedd and possibly not into Clwyd either.'

'I NAILED CHILD SEX PERVERTS' was the *Sun* headline printed in bold across its front page beside a colour picture of Taylor, the 'brave mum' who had blown the whistle on the 'evil abusers' who had 'lurked in the shadows for years'. The *Daily Telegraph* carried a picture of Taylor under the headline 'I HAD THE PROOF BUT THEY WOULDN'T LISTEN.' The picture and headline were accompanied by a half-page profile which gave a markedly incomplete account of her role, omitting almost all the allegations on which she had been cross-examined most sceptically during the Tribunal.

Meanwhile, in the *Daily Mail,* Bryn Estyn was presented by journalist Rebecca Fowler as 'the Colditz of care':

> As the iron gates clanked shut behind them and they looked up at the forbidding mansion for the first time, the boys who were sent to Bryn Estyn children's home in North Wales were all gripped by the same thought. This was the end of the world.
>
> And it was. For more than a decade it was at the centre of Britain's biggest child abuse scandal where the corruption cast a shadow so evil it shattered the lives of a generation of children.

Having recounted a catalogue of physical and sexual abuse alleged by one witness, the story ended with these words: 'Imagine his story multiplied perhaps 200 times and you get an idea of the hideous scale of the scandal.'

What the story did not reveal was that none of this particular witness's allegations had ever been substantiated or even brought before a court. For the witness in question was Lee Steward. Since it had endorsed (with reservations) Steward's overall credibility, the Tribunal itself bore at least some responsibility for the attention given to the claims he had subsequently made to the press.

The general manner in which the Tribunal report was received was perhaps best encapsulated in the newspaper where the entire story had

begun, just over eight years previously – the *Independent*. Page three of
the newspaper was illustrated by a large photograph of Alison Taylor
stroking her cat in a sunlit sitting-room. In the bottom left-hand corner was a smaller photograph of Tanner. An article about Tanner gave
his account of how brutal abuse in a series of homes had turned him
into an 'animal'. The main article, written by Roger Dobson, related the
story of how Alison Taylor had first triggered the 1986 investigation in
Gwynedd and then helped to bring about the major 1991–2 investigation in Clwyd amidst widespread speculation that a paedophile ring
was operating. It went on to report, as a factual account of life in North
Wales care homes, the claim made by Gerard Elias: 'The child entered
the system bewildered, and left it … brutalised … sexually damaged,
abandoned.' Nowhere in its coverage that day did it record the fact that
the Tribunal had found that there was no paedophile ring centred on
care homes, or the equally significant fact that it had upheld the findings of the libel trial in respect of Gordon Anglesea.

The Tribunal, set up to establish the truth about what happened in
North Wales, had in practice given its own imprimatur to the very kind
of inaccurate, ill-informed journalism which had helped to create the
scandal in the first place. Its report did not discuss the problem of false
allegations in any depth and barely acknowledged that these posed a
problem at all. It failed utterly to examine the dangers of police trawling and at no point did it even acknowledge the possibility that trawling operations might lead directly to miscarriages of justice.

Of course there could be no doubt at all that in North Wales, as in
every other part of the country, some children had been abused while
they were in care. There was some sexual abuse and some physical
abuse. It is right that this should be seen as a matter for shame, and that
all possible steps should be taken to improve safeguards. But instead of
facing up squarely and unflinchingly to the mixed reality of what life
in North Wales homes had, in fact, been like, the Tribunal had come
close to endorsing the fantasy which Alison Taylor, Dennis Parry, Malcolm King and others, with the help of a number of damaged and suggestible young men, had created.

Whereas the members of the Tribunal had accused Gwynedd
County Council in particular, and the authorities in general, of constructing 'a wall of disbelief' around the allegations made by Mrs Taylor, they had themselves succeeded in constructing a wall of disbelief
around the evidence of widespread fabrication and fantasy which had
been presented to them almost daily during the two hundred days of

the Tribunal.

Taylor herself was one of the few beneficiaries of the report. Even before the Tribunal had started hearing evidence, she had received an award from the BBC journalist and child abuse campaigner, Esther Rantzen. In 1996 she had been chosen for the first *Community Care* Readers' Award. A year later she was given one of the annual awards made by the Campaign for Freedom of Information. Now, with the publication of the report, she received almost universal acclaim. The view of her role which emerged was perhaps best summed up by the organisation Caring for Children in the comments they made at the time:

> The only person to come out of the whole saga with a really positive image is Alison Taylor, who blew the whistle, not only once but time and again. She went to the top to make her points. She gathered information systematically. She sacrificed her career when the authorities disliked what she was saying.
>
> Understandably, her story has been seized upon in one newspaper after another, each with lengthy interviews or quotations. This is a subject which has the type of scandal on which tabloid journalism can thrive, but in all the papers which quote her, Alison offered balanced, insightful remarks, making telling points in a straightforward way and providing factual information.
>
> She deserves every credit.[539]

Two months after the publication of the Tribunal report, Taylor was one of a number of people who, in front of a star-studded audience at the London Hilton, which included guest-of-honour Tony Blair, were presented with a *Daily Mirror* 'Pride of Britain' award by ITN newscaster Trevor McDonald. In their citation the judges wrote: 'For her determination to see justice done, Alison has been called "the whistleblower". We have another name – "heroine".'[540]

Ironically, the very Tribunal which had been convened in order to investigate whether a massive cover-up had taken place in North Wales, had itself ended by covering up the truth.

VI

FRAGMENTS
OF A WITCH-HUNT
(1994–2004)

64 The photograph album

THERE IS ONE SENSE IN WHICH the publication of the Tribunal report in February 2000 brought to an end the story of North Wales. It might therefore seem that 'the story of the story', which I have set out to tell in this book, is itself now complete. It would, however, be misleading to give this impression. For to recount the story of North Wales without conveying some idea of its influence and consequences would be to misrepresent history itself. The investigation launched by the North Wales Police in August 1991 may well have been, at the time, the largest inquiry into child abuse which had ever been conducted. But, before many years had passed, it would be overtaken by other trawling operations which arrested many more people and gained many more convictions.

In attempting to convey some of the historical background to the North Wales investigation, I tried in an earlier chapter to show its complex historical roots. These go back to the emergence of the modern child protection movement in the 1960s, in response to the work of Henry Kempe and his 'battered child syndrome', and to the subsequent development of what I have called the 'Californian model' of child sexual abuse. An even longer historical perspective would trace this modern child protection movement back to Victorian London, and to its essentially religious and revivalist roots in the work of the father of modern investigative journalism, W. T. Stead, and his close friend and admirer, Reverend Benjamin Waugh, the founder of the NSPCC.[541]

Because of the immense significance of historical factors like these, it would be wrong to suggest that the rapid spread of the technique of trawling throughout Britain was 'caused' by what happened in North Wales. For it is impossible to distinguish clearly between those historical events which flowed directly from North Wales and those which simply developed out of the same broad historical and cultural influences. What is beyond question, however, is that the North Wales story and the centrality and authority accorded to it from 1991 onwards, exercised a powerful influence over the development of police trawling as a technique of investigation. With the publication of the Waterhouse report in 2000 it would scarcely be an exaggeration to say that the story became one of the canonical 'scriptures' of the contemporary child protection movement, influencing both social workers and senior police officers in almost equal measure.

The influence of North Wales, however, made itself felt long before Sir Ronald Waterhouse's report appeared. The very fact that Wrexham, the main geographical focus of the 1991-3 investigation, is situated in the extreme north-east corner of Wales meant that the North Wales Police were investigating only a few miles away from the areas covered by two English police forces – Cheshire and Merseyside. Inevitably there were links between the three forces and between the relevant social services departments. It was also the case that the local newspapers and television stations often ran the same stories, with developments in the Wrexham investigation being covered extensively in Cheshire and on Merseyside. There were also other links, one of the most significant being the fact that it had been a consultant from Cheshire social services, John Banham, who had mooted the possibility of a paedophile ring based on Bryn Estyn at the same time that Alison Taylor was making similar suggestions to Councillor Dennis Parry. While it was undoubtedly the case that theories of 'organised abuse' were widely held at this period by child protection workers throughout the country, Cheshire Social Services Department appears to have been particularly susceptible to such ideas. In 1987 it had been Cheshire social workers who had launched the first satanic abuse investigation in Britain.[542]

One other crucial link with North Wales was through Greystone Heath, a former community home and approved school in Warrington, Cheshire, which had closed some years before. It had already become part of the North Wales story, as it was here that Stephen Norris had been working when he applied for a job at Bryn Estyn, a post which he took up in 1974. For those given to constructing evil conspiracies this fact alone was enough to point the finger of suspicion at Greystone Heath. What made the argument more compelling was that one former member of staff at Greystone Heath had already fallen under suspicion.

In 1986 a senior care worker, Alan Langshaw, was accused by two boys in his care of indecently assaulting them. Langshaw, who was employed by the Liverpool-based organisation, the Nugent Care Society (formerly Catholic Social Services), and who at this time was head of St Vincent's in Formby, vehemently protested his innocence. A number of his colleagues, including some senior employees of Nugent Care, went out of their way to support him. They represented him as a man who had been wrongly accused and even as the victim of a witch-hunt. The police eventually decided that there was insufficient evidence to prosecute, and Langshaw, who had been suspended, was re-instated. One clinical psychologist in Liverpool, David Glasgow, however, had provided therapy to the two boys and was convinced they were telling the truth. He was so disturbed by the failure to prosecute or even suspend Langshaw that he caused questions to be asked in the House of Commons. Even so Langshaw continued to work with children.

Eight years later, early in 1994, a persistent offender, Tim Keeley, who had once been in care at Greystone Heath, found himself in the custody of the Cheshire Police. At this point the North Wales investigation was still in progress and the trial of Peter Howarth and Paul Wilson was pending. There is no record of whether the subject of sexual abuse was introduced by the police or by Keeley, but, whether prompted or not, Keeley told the police that nine months earlier he had been driving his car in Widnes when he had seen Langshaw leaving the magistrates' court with a boy. This, he said, had brought back the horror of the sexual abuse Langshaw had inflicted on him at Greystone Heath during the 1970s. Over the next few days he accused no fewer than seventeen other care workers of abusing him.

By the time Keeley made his allegations the Cheshire Police had already begun investigating abuse in children's homes. Given the charges of cover-up which had been levelled against the North Wales Police, and given the seriousness of the allegations being made, it was not surprising that they now launched a major investigation. In a sideways reference to the name of the institution on which it was focused (Greystone), they called it Operation Granite.

Before long Langshaw found himself facing more than thirty allegations of sexual abuse. As is almost inevitable in any police trawling operation, a significant proportion of these allegations appear to have been false. However, by Langshaw's own account, at least half of them were true. In November 1994, therefore, on the advice of his barrister, he pleaded guilty to all 33 counts of sexual assault which included a number of counts of buggery.[543]

The two boys, it now seemed, had been telling the truth all along. Langshaw's Roman Catholic employers, however, had been unable to bring themselves to believe that a man of such seeming probity could have performed the acts alleged or that he could have lied to them so brazenly. They chose to believe his denials and to disbelieve the teenagers who had been courageous enough to complain.

As the journalist Christian Wolmar has noted, Langshaw expressed remorse and regret for his actions and acknowledged that he had to attempt to reform his sexuality completely.[544] The ultimate result of the investigation into Langshaw, however, was disturbing. There was, once again, no paedophile ring. But Langshaw had not been the only member of staff who was guilty of abuse. An older care worker, Dennis Grain, who had worked at Greystone Heath for nine years until May 1980, had also been guilty of serious sexual abuse. Grain eventually pleaded guilty to seventeen offences of indecent assault and buggery and was sentenced to seven years in prison.

Grain's admissions and Langshaw's decision to plead guilty to all the allegations made against him, gave the Cheshire investigation a solid core of reality. Just as the conviction of Stephen Norris in 1990 helped to launch the North Wales investigation, so the convictions of Langshaw and Grain in Cheshire led eventually to an even larger investigation in which the Cheshire Police entered into co-operation with a neighbouring force, the Merseyside Police.

If ever proof were needed of the reality of 'denial' in sexual abuse cases and of its consequences for vulnerable young people, it may be found in the case of Alan Langshaw. Within the Nugent Care Society, the effect of its initial misjudgment during the Langshaw affair was traumatic. The outcome was the discrediting of those who might have counselled moderation in the crusade against sexual abuse which now developed in the north west.

In a BBC *Panorama* documentary, broadcast in March 1997, the presenter, Alan Urry, attempted to explain the 'success' of the approach adopted by the police – an approach which was still seen as startlingly new:

> Past child abuse investigations had usually relied on victims contacting police. In the north west inquiry, once a member of staff had been identified as a suspect, police set out to find former residents who were at the home at the same time …That proactive method started producing dramatic results. Soon those traced by police were naming as abusers other child care staff at other homes. By March 1995 two neighbouring police forces, Cheshire and Merseyside, were working together.[545]

The programme then cut to a shot of Detective Superintendent Albert Kirby, the officer who, in 1993, had investigated the murder of James

Bulger by two 10-year-old boys, and who subsequently led the first phase of the Merseyside inquiry:

> We never ever realised what we were going to uncover. We thought it was going to be an inquiry that was, you know, relatively short in the length of time it would take, but once we actually started and we realised the magnitude of it ... we decided very early on that we would interview wherever possible every single boy that an individual was likely to have abused whilst he was in the employment of the particular home.[546]

At an early stage, senior police officers sought to learn from the experience of others. Detective Inspector Terry Oates, who led the Cheshire investigation, has described three particular investigations, into Frank Beck, Castle Hill and North Wales care homes, as having provided 'the backbone to our inquiry'. The most important was clearly the latter: 'North Wales Police were finalising their inquiry as we began ours, so liaison at senior management level was made and best practice sought.'[547]

However there were some extremely important differences between the new investigation and its prototype in North Wales. One of these was that, whereas in North Wales the investigation had been conducted entirely by the police, the inquiry in Cheshire and Merseyside was conceived as a 'joint investigation', in which, although the police remained in control, they would seek the full co-operation of social workers at every stage. The *Panorama* programme explained that the records of thirty years of the care system were gathered 'at a secret and secure location'. Social workers from Liverpool and Cheshire 'were then brought in to investigate members of their own profession'. Among them was the deputy director of Cheshire Social Services, David Whitehead, who had in the past taken a keen interest in theories of 'organised abuse'. Whitehead now appeared on camera:

> We feel very strongly that we have got to make sure that everything that can possibly be done to set right the things that went wrong in the past has to be done, whatever the cost of that and however embarrassing that might be, we have got to make sure that we've finally once and for all dealt with the skeletons in these cupboards.[548]

Perhaps at the suggestion of social workers, Cheshire police held two training seminars. The first of these, in October 1995, was addressed by two speakers who had taken part in the Castle Hill inquiry in Shropshire. The second was held for an invited audience of police officers, social workers and CPS lawyers, and featured a presentation by the well-known sexual abuse consultant, Ray Wyre, on questions relating to the use of expert evidence by the prosecution.[549]

One very significant dimension of the Cheshire investigation was the policy adopted towards the large number of former residents who were in prison. Potentially such prisoners were a prolific source of allegations. Terry Oates, however, has reported that police officers found that some prisoners were reluctant to make any complaints: 'In the early stages of the inquiry difficulties were encountered in obtaining disclosures from inmates of prisons. This was due to the lack of privacy between the prisoner and the interviewing officer.'[550] Another explanation for the difficulty in obtaining disclosures, of course, might be that the prisoners in question had not been abused and therefore had no allegations to make. This explanation, however, is not considered at all in Oates's written account. Instead, it is assumed that the reason the prisoners are not 'disclosing' is that they are inhibited by their prison surroundings. Oates and his team of police officers and social workers were not prepared to accept what they perceived, quite sincerely, as an obstacle in their path. They therefore set out to remove it:

> After consultation with the Home Office Prison Liaison Section, it was accepted that where it was necessary to interview an individual who was either *likely to disclose or believed to have been a victim*, the arrangements were made for that person to be taken to a designated police station, the prisoner being given a 'cover story' prior to their return to prison. Victim support in these circumstances proved extremely difficult. However a network of prison/police liaison officers was contacted and, together with prison doctors and prison psychiatrists, these problems were overcome [italics added].[551]

The implications of this bold departure from normal police practice need to be considered carefully. Perhaps the most important point is that, for the majority of prisoners, 'imprisonment' means just that. The liberty to leave the prison and have a taste of what the outside world has to offer is precisely what is most rigorously denied to them. For this reason few would be likely to decline a trip to a police station were it to be offered.

A prisoner's experience of such visits might well be very positive. Police stations can, in certain circumstances, be relatively attractive places. For a prisoner to find that they have almost free access to unlimited cigarettes, chocolate and cups of tea and coffee in a place outside the prison walls may be gratifying to a surprising degree. It may also be a relief to be able to talk to a sympathetic woman rather than a man. Oates himself implicitly acknowledges this when, in an understated comment, he writes that: 'A male victim is just as likely to disclose to a female officer as to her male colleague and there have been some instances where victims have made their preferences known. As a consequence it is felt that any inquiry team should be composed of mixed gender staff.'[552] If, as is possible, the police station interview takes place in a rape counselling suite, there may be easy chairs or soft furnishing for the prisoner to relax in. There can be little doubt that, in most cases, the police succeeded in doing exactly what they had set out to. Through their prison 'exeat' scheme, they had created an ideal version of what Peter Ackerley called 'the climate to facilitate people to tell us what went on.' As Terry Oates himself suggests, if a prisoner who had been abused was too embarrassed to talk about it in a prison visiting room, then he was much more likely to speak out in the relative comfort and privacy of a police station.

What Oates and his colleagues do not appear to have considered, however, was the problem which has already been encountered in relation to the North Wales investigation. There was, in short, a real danger that, in creating the right climate for 'disclosure', the police were, quite inadvertently, creating the ideal conditions in which false allegations might be made. In these circumstances, where police officers were sincerely, and even eagerly, anticipating that a genuine allegation would be made, and asking questions with this in mind, then almost any prisoner who was in the least degree suggestible would be liable to make a false allegation, if only to oblige his 'hosts'. Once again the knowledge that this might ultimately bring financial gain could only increase the temptation to create a story of past abuse.[553]

Another respect in which the Cheshire Police went out of their way in order to create the climate for 'disclosure' was in their use of social workers. As in the North Wales investigation, all former residents who were seen during the course of the inquiry were given a card with the details of an NSPCC helpline. In Cheshire, however, there was much greater input from social workers at all stages of the inquiry. At some points, social workers were deliberately used in an attempt to obtain allegations from former residents of care homes who appeared to be reluctant to make such allegations. We know this because it is actually stated by DI Oates that this was part of the police's policy: 'While the investigation is the primary role of the police,' he writes, 'the skills of the social worker should be utilised to their best advantage, particularly when dealing with *potential victims who may be reluctant to disclose*' [italics added]. As a matter of routine, 'social services liaison officers' were supposed to 'be available to advise and assist inquiry police officers and potential witnesses/complainants in successfully and sensitively achieving disclosure of material statements.'[554]

One of the almost inevitable consequences of deploying social workers in this manner was that the police would be unaware of the extent to which the evidence they subsequently collected had been contaminated through prior questioning by another agency. It was largely because this policy of joint investigation had, for the very best of motives, been adopted in Cheshire and on Merseyside, that this new trawling operation was even more dangerous, and even more likely to generate false allegations than the North Wales investigation had ever been.

It was also dangerous for another reason. This was because of the sheer scale on which it was conceived. When they had launched their investigation in August 1991, the North Wales police can have had little idea of what was to come. In Cheshire and Merseyside, as the views of Detective Superintendent Albert Kirby would suggest, there may initially have been a similar failure to foresee what could happen. It would seem, however, that in Cheshire at least, the police rapidly became aware that they were embarking on a huge operation. More importantly still they appear to have accepted this, and to have done so almost in a spirit of emulation. In other words, the North Wales inquiry became a template not only in terms of its techniques but also in terms of its size. In his article about the Cheshire investigation which appeared in the *Independent* in June 1996, under the headline 'OUR GULAG' (see above, pp. 414–15), the freelance journalist Roger Dobson described the approach which Oates and his colleagues adopted:

> A crucial decision was made at an early stage which was to determine the character and scale of the investigation: detectives decided to cast their nets wide. Instead of limiting inquiries to original complainants, they went looking for victims. One officer explained. 'We decided that … the last thing we wanted was somebody knocking on the door six months after we finished and saying, "You never came to see me."'
>
> So they set out to trace every single young person who had been in care in the area since the mid-1960s. The list came to 2,500 names.

'The aim was to trace and speak to them all, to ask them about their experiences. We left nothing to chance. It has been a detailed, thorough inquiry,' said the officer. In each case, the police explained that they were investigating the specific homes and they asked: did they have any complaint to make about their time there? When personal calls failed, registered letters were sent which had to be signed for, showing they had been received. Those who received letters but made no contact were assumed to have no complaints. In all, just over 2,000 people were contacted and more than 300 made allegations that they had been sexually abused.

Once again, as in North Wales, the assumption that a paedophile ring might be at work appears to have been central to the entire investigation. But, as Dobson's article made clear, there was not, in fact, any evidence of such a ring:

Detectives have explored the idea that the perpetrators of these crimes belonged to organised paedophile networks, but they have been hampered by the refusal of all the convicted abusers to talk. 'In the ideal world, and on TV, one of these offenders would break down in court and tell us everything,' said the officer. 'But no one has said anything. There were guilty pleas, but no one has told the story. There have to be some links – everyone networks at some stage – but no one has ever said anything.'[555]

In view of the manner in which Bryn Estyn had already been demonised as an institution at the centre of a paedophile ring, in which sexual abuse was supposedly rife, it was perhaps only to be expected that the Cheshire Police would form a similar fantasy-image of the home where Langshaw and Grain had both worked – Greystone Heath. This they clearly did. When one of the innocent suspects they were interviewing said that he had never seen any sexual abuse of the boys, the police officers expressed astonishment. One of them reportedly said of the staff: 'They were all at it.' One observer of the investigation, a local clergyman, drew attention to this response at the time of the criminal trials: 'This reveals a great deal of the minds of the investigating officers. From the very first day they are already convinced to their own satisfaction that every member of staff is guilty. When allegations are made it is the duty of a police officer to try to ascertain the truth. These policemen apparently see their job as trying to nail down every single person against whom allegations are made. Justice is not served by a one-sided search for evidence to convict.'[556]

The same improbable scenario of 'total abuse' was at least half-accepted by the social workers who, in the aftermath of Langshaw's admissions, had rapidly gained power and influence within Nugent Care. Having mistakenly sided with a care worker who was actually perpetrating sexual abuse, the Nugent Care Society now entered into equally ill-judged co-operation with the Cheshire Police in an investigation which, as in North Wales, would eventually reach far beyond the home on which it was initially focused.

So far as Greystone Heath itself was concerned, the Cheshire Police succeeded, according to the journalist Christian Wolmar, in collecting allegations against no fewer than 33 former members of staff.[557] Some of these allegations were demonstrably false. In November 1994 police officers visited a 27-year-old former resident of Greystone Heath, James White. Having discovered that potential complainants often found it difficult to recall the names and faces of those who looked after them, the police had come with a photograph album from which White picked out a photo of Dennis Grain. He went on to make an allegation of indecent assault against Grain, saying that this 'big man' (Grain was about 15 stone) had pinned him to the wall one day and started to play with his penis. This had happened, he said, on two further occasions.

A week later White made another statement to the police. He said that he had been thinking about what had happened and wished to say that there were some details he had left out because they were embarrassing. He went on to make an allegation of attempted buggery and also alleged that Grain had attempted to force him to suck his penis.

A month later the Cheshire Police visited White again. By this time they had established that Dennis Grain had left Greystone Heath in May 1980, almost two years before White had arrived there in February 1982. White now made a third statement, saying that he had been upset and confused when he had made his first statement. He later went on to make a fourth statement in which he maintained that the abuse he had described had indeed happened, even though he had been mistaken about Grain. The person he had described in his first statement as 'a big man', whose 'heavy body' he had referred to in his second statement and who was 'well built' according to his third statement, was described, in his fourth and final statement, as having been of 'medium to slim build'.[558]

Given that Grain was in fact guilty, James White's false allegation made little difference. The problem with the method of investigation, however, was that it was just as likely to encourage the making of false allegations against members of staff who were completely innocent.

One such care worker was Roy Shuttleworth. A former miner and champion swimmer, Shuttleworth had worked as a long-distance lorry driver until his wife Irene persuaded him to take a job alongside her as a house parent at Greystone Heath. From that point on the couple did everything together. They were enjoying their retirement when, during 1994, the Cheshire Police, armed with their photograph album and an entirely false allegation made by Tim Keeley, began to collect a series of allegations against Shuttleworth.

One former resident made a detailed and compelling statement, describing how Shuttleworth had forced him to masturbate him in the shower. Only later did the police realise that this man had actually left Greystone Heath seven years before Shuttleworth began to work there in 1974. He had made the statement because the police had arrived 'out of the blue' and shown him photographs of Shuttleworth, saying that they were investigating claims that he was a paedophile.

Another of the men who complained, Jim Ryan, said that Shuttleworth had bent him over his bed and started to bugger him. He had screamed and bitten Shuttleworth's finger so hard, he fell to the floor in agony. He claimed that another care worker, Phil Fiddler, came running in to see what was happening and that Shuttleworth had escaped suspicion by telling Fiddler that Ryan had attacked him.

When Ryan told this story at Shuttleworth's trial in 1996, the jury believed him. Some two years later he gave evidence at the trial of Phil Fiddler. This time he claimed that Fiddler bent him over his bed and started to bugger him. He said he had screamed and bitten Fiddler's finger so hard that he fell to the floor in agony. Another member of staff had then rushed in and Fiddler had escaped suspicion by telling him that Ryan had attacked him.

What Ryan did not know as he told his story in court for the second time, changing only the name of his alleged abuser, was that Fiddler's solicitor, David Woods, had attended the earlier trial of Shuttleworth and had obtained a transcript of Ryan's evidence. Since his carbon-copy evidence clearly showed that he was lying, the jury acquitted Fiddler of all charges. Another former resident later said that he had met Ryan in prison, where he boasted that he was making false allegations for money, adding: 'You should try it yourself.'

By this time, however, Roy Shuttleworth had been convicted on eleven counts of sexual assault and buggery and was serving a ten year sentence for crimes he had not committed. When, in October 2000, he

was visited in prison by the *Observer's* David Rose, he showed the journalist a collection of the letters he had received from his wife Irene. 'My
darling, innocent Roy,' one began, 'I am as much in love with you as
the day we met nearly 40 years ago. My only wish is to spend what life
we have left together. I only hope nothing happens to either one of us,
because I know the other will die of a broken heart.'

In fact Irene, who had been endlessly anxious and active in seeking
her husband's liberty, had died of a heart-attack the previous year. Shuttleworth had been allowed to attend her funeral handcuffed to a prison
officer. 'My life is in fragments,' he told David Rose, 'I am in darkness.
What those men's lies have taken away can never be put back.'[559]

Apart from Langshaw and Grain, two of Shuttleworth's former colleagues, Brian Percival, who worked as a store keeper, and Keith Laverack, a senior residential social worker, were also convicted. Percival was
supported at the time by his vicar, who carefully documented the case
and, on Percival's conviction in 1996, wrote a passionate letter to the
Home Secretary which contained one of the first critiques of police
trawling ever written. On legal advice the letter was held back until the
outcome of Brian Percival's appeal. In the event it was never sent, since
Percival's conviction was overturned by the Court of Appeal in 1998
and he was able to return home to his wife. Keith Laverack has meanwhile protested his innocence from his prison cell. Partly because of the
sheer number of allegations collected against him, Laverack was sentenced to 17 years. Wherever the truth about his case may lie, there can
be little doubt that many or most of the allegations trawled against him
were completely false.

In one other case, which involved a former care worker who is now
confined to a wheelchair, a series of allegations which had apparently
been fabricated was abandoned after lawyers representing him successfully argued that his trial would be an abuse of process.* In some twenty

---

* An abuse of process can be defined as an attempt to prosecute somebody which is
so unfair and wrong that it violates the very principles of justice. In the context of
trawling cases, abuse of process hearings normally consider pre-trial submissions from
the defendant's lawyers that the prosecution should be abandoned because allegations
have been made after such a long time that it is impossible for a care worker to
defend himself. This is usually because key documents have been destroyed and crucial defence witnesses have died or cannot be traced. However, because of the abhorrence for child sexual abuse, most judges are very reluctant to accept such arguments.
In that they give licence to unfair trials based on dangerous evidence, most abuse of
process hearings in trawling cases themselves constitute an abuse of process.

other Greystone Heath cases, allegations have not led to criminal charges, presumably because they are either demonstrably false or so unconvincing that they would be unlikely to lead to a conviction. However, many of those who were accused and not charged have had their lives permanently blighted. Some, like Phil Fiddler, who was charged and acquitted on two separate occasions, will never work in their chosen profession again.

It would be wrong, however, to give the impression that the effects of Operation Granite were limited to Greystone Heath. Partly because Dennis Grain had once worked at Danesford, a community home in Congleton run by the National Children's Home (NCH), a new Cheshire inquiry was set up. This time its name would be determined by the fact that two of the care workers who were now considered suspects were Methodists and helped to run the local Boys' Brigade.

65 Operation Bugle

THE INVESTIGATION WHICH WAS MOUNTED into Danesford, a highly-regarded community home run by the Methodist children's charity, NCH, had much in common with the original North Wales investigation and with Operation Granite. Once again the spectre of a paedophile ring was raised, and once again police began interviewing former residents in search of a malign conspiracy.

On this occasion one of those arrested was a woman, Jenny Hall*. She was in her bedroom, about to get up, when the knock at the door came. 'I looked out of the window and saw two police officers. I went to the door and they asked for a word about the home I used to work in. I said "Yes, but do you mind if I get dressed?" The police refused. I was standing there in my nightie.'

In a matter of minutes Jenny Hall was taken in a police car to Warrington police station. Three officers remained at her home and searched the house in front of her husband and her two bewildered children, aged two and four. Hall was held by the police for eight hours, during much of which time she was confined to a cell. 'The attitude of the police,' she later told a journalist, 'was appalling. They refused to make me drinks. They didn't even answer the bell. They wouldn't even let me have pictures from my purse of my little ones. They said there was no telling what the likes of me would do with such things.'[560]

While at Danesford, Hall had worked closely with a colleague she trusted and respected, who was openly gay. Now they were jointly charged with having attacked a boy with a screwdriver so that his nose was ripped and bled profusely. Her colleague, Adrian Coates*, was also charged with a number of indecent assaults which she was convinced he had not committed. Although she was asked repeatedly to do so, she declined to give evidence against him on the grounds that she had never seen or suspected any wrong-doing and she believed him to be completely innocent.

Jenny Hall was eventually acquitted by a jury. It was only after her

---

* This name has been changed.

trial that the police returned to her a collection of photographs they had seized. One of these timed and dated photographs was of the boy she and Coates had supposedly assaulted earlier that day with a screwdriver. It clearly showed that his face was unmarked, conclusively proving that the most serious count against her was false. There was no reason why the police, who were evidently looking for photographs which might indicate paedophile activity, would have registered the significance of this photograph, but they had inadvertently deprived her of a vital piece of evidence.

Adrian Coates, meanwhile, was tried on a number of counts of indecent assault. One local court reporter, who has covered some 20,000 cases of all kinds, told me that this was the only case in which he had ever become emotionally involved. When the guilty verdict was given, Coates broke down in the dock and his family wept. Having heard all the evidence, the reporter said he felt that it should not have been possible for any jury to find Coates guilty beyond all reasonable doubt, and that he was almost certainly innocent. According to his account, even the judge, who said during the trial how impressed he had been by letters from those formerly in Coates's care, spoke of how these letters suggested 'love in the true sense of the word'. Coates continued to protest his innocence from his prison cell but found himself facing further trawled allegations. This was at a time when his mother was ill with cancer and, after taking advice, he told his friends and supporters that he had decided to plead guilty to the new charges in order to avoid a second trial and a lengthened sentence.[561]

The real focus of Operation Bugle, however, was the local Boys' Brigade, in which two Danesford care workers, Brian Hudson and Danny Smith, were officers.

Brian Hudson was the group leader who was effectively in charge of the Woodlands unit in Danesford – a unit for young, disturbed children from the age of ten upwards. Hudson had begun his association with Woodlands as a caseworker to some of the boys. This brought him to the unit on frequent visits and his involvement gradually increased. When he took over the position of group leader he had already formed good relationships with most of the members of staff in the unit. He rapidly established himself as a strong and effective leader who, though often forthright, was sensitive and perceptive about the boys in his care and fair both with them and with his staff. Because he combined considerable strength of character with great warmth, many of the more difficult boys responded extremely well to him and would frequently seek him out as a source of comfort and encouragement.

Partly because of Hudson's leadership, staff in Woodlands remained highly motivated and confident in the face of problems which would have defeated many less resolute teams. As a result they managed to deal very effectively with a group of boys whose potential for disruption was huge. While many of the boys' problems remained intractable there can be no doubt that the Woodlands unit was, by any standards, a success.

The main source of the stream of allegations which would eventually engulf Danesford and lead to the large-scale police investigation of 1994-5 can be identified quite clearly. In fact the crucial events originally had no association with Hudson's Woodlands unit. They concerned his colleague Danny Smith. In June 1989, two Danesford boys made complaints of indecent assault against Smith. When these allegations were taken to court they did not result in a conviction. But the allegations were serious and, because of the way they were handled, they had a lasting and ultimately tragic effect.

When the allegations were made, Smith was immediately suspended. This in itself was understandable. However, he was also evicted from the house he occupied in the grounds of Danesford and installed in a hostel in a town thirty miles away from Congleton, where he knew nobody. Smith's colleagues were then warned by their employers that they should have no contact with him.

Hudson was in no position to know whether the allegations against his colleague were true or false. But, because he regarded the way his colleague had been treated as a betrayal of natural justice, he made arrangements for him to stay in bed-and-breakfast accommodation in Congleton. Then, disregarding warnings he received from NCH management, he collected Danny Smith from his 'exile' and brought him back with him to Congleton. It would seem that the help which Hudson extended to Smith was resented by NCH managers and seen by at least some of them in a sinister light. From this point onwards Hudson was apparently viewed with suspicion.

In late 1989, several months after the allegations had been made, a fateful development took place in the Woodlands unit. Ever alert to any behaviour which the boys in the unit tried to conceal, Woodlands staff became aware that sexual activity was taking place between some of the boys on the unit. This was reported by Hudson to senior managers within NCH who decided to institute an inquiry. These managers now decided that, in view of the allegations which had been made against

Smith, they should call in an outside agency to conduct the inquiry and specifically inquire into any possible adult involvement in the sexual abuse which Hudson had reported. Since Smith himself had very little direct contact with the boys, it would appear that the adult on whom suspicions were now focused was Hudson himself.

The investigation which followed was led by the principal officer for children's services for the area. The investigation established that two of the boys, Mark Cowie, aged 15, and Jonathan Hatton, aged 13, had engaged in buggery and three other younger boys had had sexual approaches made to them.

After all the boys had been interviewed it was found that there was no adult involvement in this sexual abuse, and the social workers who conducted the inquiry said that they had no anxieties about the staff at Danesford. However, this conclusion was reached only after both Cowie and Hatton had been explicitly asked whether they had been sexually abused by Brian Hudson. The lesson which they could not but learn from such questions was that Hudson was not trusted by these social workers, and that they might be receptive to sexual allegations which were made against him.

Three years later, in 1992, at the time of widespread publicity about North Wales, Mark Cowie told his social worker that he wanted to tell the newspapers about Danesford in order to make money. He then made a series of highly implausible allegations. He claimed that he had been taken on a summer camp by Hudson (to a part of Wales which Hudson had never visited), that he had been padlocked in a tent, and that Hudson had a double bed in his own tent where sexual improprieties took place. Shortly before Cowie made his allegations, a psychiatrically disturbed former resident of Danesford had complained about five members of staff there (including Hudson), claiming that they had taken part in an orgy with him.

In a meeting which took place on an unknown date between NCH, Cheshire Social Services, and Cheshire Police, it was decided to investigate Hudson and 'Operation Bugle' was born. At an early stage of this investigation Mark Cowie was interviewed extensively by the police. Although in 1989 he had stated quite explicitly that there had been no sexual impropriety with Hudson, he now made several entirely new allegations which were quite different from those he had made to social workers in 1992. Later on in the investigation Jonathan Hatton was also visited by police officers and he subsequently made an allegation against Hudson. A number of former residents of Danesford also made allegations in response to police questioning.

In July 1995 Brian Hudson and Danny Smith were both arrested on the morning of the day they were due to take a Boys' Brigade group on their summer camp. They found themselves facing a series of allegations of sexual abuse including some counts of buggery. Smith also faced counts of physical abuse. Three months later there was an unusual twist to the story when, in September 1995, the police held a meeting with parents who had sons in the Boys' Brigade. They evidently felt confident they would gather new allegations from this source. At this meeting, which was also attended by social workers, they spoke of the threat posed by paedophiles, referred to Hudson and Smith by name, and even handed out copies of a pink leaflet called 'Coping With Sexual Abuse'. The leaflet was published by Cheshire County Council and many parents were shocked to find it contained a section on how to claim from the Criminal Injuries Compensation Board. It specifically explained that 'You are still able to get compensation *even if the person who assaulted you is found not guilty*' [italics added].

The main effect of the meeting, which had clearly not been the police's intention, was to unite the parents in support of Hudson and Smith. After the meeting, although many parents did question their sons, not a single new allegation was made against either of them.

Notwithstanding this dramatic failure to gain further allegations, police now proceeded with their case. After learning that Hudson was on remand in Walton Prison, one of the complainants against him, Shane Morris, evidently realising the serious consequences of the false allegation he had made, bravely rang Hudson's home. He spoke to a close friend of Hudson and told her that his allegation was not true and that he wished to withdraw it. She recorded this phone conversation and suggested to him that he went to a solicitor and made a statement to this effect. He did telephone a solicitor to inquire about this. At this point, however, he was visited once again by the police. After this visit he changed his mind again, and said that he wanted to go ahead with his allegation. In order to explain why he had phoned Hudson's home he now claimed that Hudson had offered him £100 to withdraw his allegation. Hudson, however, had actually been in prison on remand at the time he was supposed to have made this offer.

Hudson's case was finally heard in Chester Crown Court in July 1996, almost exactly two years after Peter Howarth had stood trial in the same court. Although he was found not guilty on most of the nine counts, which included two counts of buggery, he was found guilty on a number of charges of indecent assault (including those made by Cowie and Hatton) and was sentenced to three and a half years.

Smith also stood trial later in 1996. After the jury was unable to reach a verdict, he was retried the following year. He was found guilty on a number of counts of physical and sexual abuse and sentenced to ten years. Because of the manner in which the evidence emerged, it is impossible to say whether Smith was guilty of any of the counts or whether he too, like Hudson, was an innocent victim of police trawling.

Seven years after Brian Hudson was convicted I posted on my website an article about the Danesford investigation which had originally been published in the *Guardian Weekend* magazine in May 1998. A few days later I received an email from one of the former residents of Danesford who had been interviewed by the police during their investigation:

Hi Richard, just been on your website reading about Brian Hudson. I'll only refer to him, as I only knew him. In 1976 I arrived in Danesford after being in care in North Wales. I stayed there for three years. I was in Westholme the house Brian was a house parent in, so I think I came to know him pretty good. Also I was in the Boys' Brigade so I can speak with authority, although while I was in the BB I spent most of my time stealing the tea money so I could buy fags, a habit I have since given up, stealing that is.

The point of this email is to give you an incite into how the police behaved whilst interviewing me. I lived in Wrexham when they came. My life was good. I owned my own house, car, had a job. Basically doing good considering the background I had. Also my daughter was newborn at the time. I arrived home from work one day to find a card pushed through the letter box saying DC so-and-so wished to speak to me and he was from Operation Bugle. I contacted him and arranged to make an appointment.

He arrived and introduced himself. I can't remember his name but that ain't important, he basically said he was investigating child abuse allegations at Danesford especially Brian Hudson and did I have anything to tell him? Well I told him Brian was the only member of staff I had any time for, I was a bit of a tearaway whilst there, stealing cars, running away, even to Ostend on one occasion. But Brian was the only one to not preach. He would be firm and not let me get away with anything. Even now I can't think of a bad thing. He did tell me off, maybe be angry when I let him down, but abuse me? No.

The policeman told me some allegations had been made by people about abuse Brian had done. I asked him who. He wouldn't say except to say these people had given my name to him and said I was one of his favourites!!! So I asked him if he thought that made me a victim of abuse.

I gave him a rundown of all the times I could remember being with Brian on my own – places away from the home on my own, even to foster parents in Brian's home town of Oldham. Nothing untoward happened. He wouldn't believe that nothing had happened and kept repeating that there was something I wasn't telling him. I asked the policeman if Brian was a child abuser why didn't he do anything to me when I was alone with him. He said maybe you wasn't his type!!!!! Made me feel sick.

I made a statement to the affect nothing had happened. The policeman ... repeated he thought I had something to tell him. That was the last I heard. I was in care in Bryn Estyn, Box Lane, Chevet Hey, amongst other places some good, some bad. The worst I saw was the odd belt round the head, the odd threat – no abuse. No one I know complained, except X who was in Bryn Estyn and I worked with him in Y and he well told lies as any one who worked there will tell you. He has had his compo [compensation] and somebody suffered to make that possible. Now I'm not stupid but young people were abused by whom I don't know. But Brian as far as I'm concerned was alright. If you are in contact with him tell him I was thinking of him at the time this was going on and pass my e mail address on. I would love to hear from him so I can tell him one of his tearaways made good.

Although it might seem that this man would have been an ideal witness for the defence, the police visited him only after Hudson had been convicted. This was at a time when, perhaps disappointed by the relatively short sentence of 3½ years, they were apparently attempting to gain more allegations for a second trial. Even though they may have been disappointed by his sentence, the Cheshire Police were undoubtedly pleased to secure this conviction, and evidently believed that Hudson was guilty. Hudson, however, was a relatively junior care worker. By the time he was convicted, the Cheshire trawling operation had netted a much bigger catch.

66 Unused evidence

THE MOMENT IN HIS CAREER which Terry Hoskin looked back to with the greatest pride was when, in 1979, accompanied by his wife Brenda, he attended a garden party at Buckingham Palace. He had spent a large part of his working life caring for troubled children and adolescents. Largely as a result of his work as the head of St Aidan's in Widnes during the 1970s, this Roman Catholic community home established a reputation for combining firmness with a deeply caring approach to its residents – who included some of the most difficult young offenders in the north west. During his headship Hoskin was highly regarded by Nugent Care, his employers. He had been invited to the palace at a time when he was serving as national president of the Association of Community Homes. This position reflected his standing in a profession where close co-operation with police officers was a matter of routine.[562]

What the man who visited Buckingham Palace as a leader of his profession never suspected was that he would eventually spend several years as the guest of Her Majesty in a very different establishment, put there by the same police force he once worked hand in hand with.

One of the most disturbing aspects of Terry Hoskin's conviction was that, of the many men who made allegations against him, only one, a 31-year-old former resident of St Aidan's, approached the police himself. The fact that a man had actually gone to the police to make an allegation, rather than waiting for them to come to him, was unusual. But so too were the circumstances out of which the allegation – the first to be made against Hoskin – had emerged. The former resident who made the complaint was a troubled young man who had, not long before, slashed his wrists with a kitchen knife after his wife had asked him to leave, attempted to hang himself in a police cell, spent three weeks in psychiatric hospital and three months in prison. During this period he had gradually pieced together, with the help of his probation officer, a 'memory' of having been abused by Terry Hoskin. He had then given a statement to the police. It was this statement, containing a number of demonstrable untruths, which led the police, in March 1994, to ask Hoskin to come to a police station to be interviewed.[563]

The conversation which took place focused on the use of the cane at St Aidan's. Like Bryn Estyn, St Aidan's had once been an approved school where corporal punishment was routine. When approved schools became community homes in 1974, responsibility for them passed from the Home Office to local social services departments. At this point many community homes, including Bryn Estyn, gave up corporal punishment. But some social services departments continued to authorise the use of the cane and this was the case at St Aidan's. The regulations stipulated that boys should always be caned over their clothes, that no more than six strokes should be given, and that another member of staff should always be present. As head, it was Hoskin who caned the boys.

The police officers put to him a number of allegations made by the 31-year-old former resident, who claimed that, fifteen years previously, Hoskin had repeatedly caned him on the bare buttocks. He said that this happened late at night, when no one else was present. He claimed that these canings culminated in a series of indecent assaults and an act of buggery. The man making the allegations, the police said, was Roy Phillips. They asked, 'What's your recollection of Phillips?' After a moment's thought Hoskin replied, 'He was, I seem to recollect, a nice-looking lad who lived fairly locally ... He was a nice enough kid, I mean I'm amazed.'

Hoskin found the whole interview bizarre and distressing, but he remained confident that once the police had made all the necessary inquiries, they would realise that something was wrong. He therefore submitted with resignation to the procedure which was so familiar to many of his former charges; he was fingerprinted; he had his picture taken. A photograph of a distinguished grey-haired man wearing a dark blazer became part of police records.

Had Phillips's allegation been made a few years previously it is likely that it would have been investigated as an individual complaint and recognised as a false allegation. By March 1994, however, the example set by the neighbouring North Wales Police was all but impossible to ignore. The result was that Phillips's allegation triggered an extraordinary trawling exercise and Terry Hoskin's visit to the police station proved to be the first of many. On each occasion he would be bailed to report back and each time he returned he was confronted with new allegations.

Hoskin soon felt overwhelmed by events beyond his control. For, with the appearance of that first accusation, it seemed as though a dam had been breached and an endless black river of allegations had begun to flow against him. As the months passed the allegations mounted until he found that he had been accused by more than forty former residents. Nineteen of these were included on Hoskin's indictment and nine more were due to give 'similar fact' evidence. In the event four of these witnesses failed to appear for the trial so the figure of 28 complainants was reduced to 24. Most of these were prisoners or ex-prisoners and none had ever attempted to complain until the police, or social workers, approached them.

In the end the inconsistencies and implausibilities in the complaints were overpowered by the sheer number of witnesses called by the prosecution. Terry Hoskin was convicted on all twenty-one counts of physical and sexual abuse. His wife Brenda, his son Simon, and his daughter Niki were in court to hear the verdict. 'When Dad was sentenced to eight years,' recalls Niki, now a solicitor, 'I just screamed.'

One man who was also in court was a senior social worker from Nugent Care who had co-operated closely with the Cheshire police and helped to make possible their entire trawling operation. He was stricken with doubt about the case of Terry Hoskin, and when I spoke to him in the headquarters of the Nugent Care Society in Liverpool in 1996 he pointed to Hoskin's case as a possible miscarriage of justice. So serious were his misgivings about the fact he may have helped put an innocent man in prison, that he had found it necessary to seek spiritual advice. This senior Roman Catholic social worker chose not to express his doubts in public. Evidently terrified of what the consequences might be, he has since preserved a complete silence.

By the time this guilt-stricken social worker spoke to me, however, Hoskin's case had aroused the scepticism of a friend of the family, the solicitor Chris Saltrese. Saltrese knew very well that sexual abuse did sometimes take place in care homes. His own father worked for Nugent Care and had direct knowledge of the Langshaw case. But neither Saltrese nor his father found the case against Hoskin at all persuasive. When he was convicted Saltrese offered to examine the papers. Finding that the statements relied on by the prosecution were full of inconsistencies, untruths and impossibilities he became sceptical about the way the police had investigated Hoskin. 'The more I studied the evidence,' he says, 'the more disturbed I became.' He then started to read with meticulous attention the evidence which had *not* formed part of the prosecution case at the trial.

Careful study of the 'unused evidence' made it quite clear that the case presented in the trial had been arrived at only by a process of careful editing. For obvious reasons the prosecution had discarded the more blatant fabrications. Some were so far-fetched that nobody was likely to take them seriously. One man claimed that he had been taken to St Aidan's on a stretcher and wheeled into a small room on a trolley: 'I spent a total of nine days at St Aidan's. I was drugged and strapped down all the time. … I was buggered regularly by men who I presumed worked at St Aidan's … One occasion seemed like eight or nine men. As one man rolled off me, another would roll on.'

Many of the allegations which were used for the trial, however, did seem to support one another. Saltrese's task was to understand how so many apparently interlocking allegations had been made against a man who appeared to be innocent. Was there a conspiracy? He spent hours on the telephone to Walton Prison in Liverpool. He was eventually able to establish that, out of about 30 complainants he investigated, seventeen had spent time in Walton in the previous three years and might therefore have had an opportunity to collude. However, he was not satisfied this was the answer. Even if all 40 complainants had passed through Walton, that would not prove a conspiracy. He thought there probably had been a degree of co-operation between small groups of complainants, but there was no evidence of a full-scale conspiracy.

It was only when he placed all the statements from the unused evidence in which *no* complaints had been made, alongside those in which complaints had been made that he began to see a pattern.

A statement taken by a police officer is a special kind of construction. Although it is presented as a straightforward record of what one person has said, it is, in just about every case, the record of a conversation; it is a report of a dialogue which has been edited into a monologue. As Saltrese now recognised, the art of reading police statements forensically depends on reconstructing the part of the conversation not recorded – the words spoken by the police but attributed to the witness. Negative statements tend to 'stain' police questions, so that what is normally invisible becomes visible. In other words if a witness's statement reads, 'I was never caned by Mr Hoskin', this is almost certainly because the witness answered 'No' to the question: 'Were you ever caned by Mr Hoskin?' There were many such examples in the unused evidence and the more closely Saltrese studied this, the more convinced he became that it could unlock the entire investigation. 'It was quite clear from the statements,' he says, 'that police officers were specifically asking potential witnesses whether they had been abused by named individuals. They were not only introducing names, but also ideas.'

This might explain certain features of the statements that would otherwise be difficult to account for. In the trial it was notable that only two of the fifteen complainants had described Hoskin's clothes. Both said he usually wore blazers. But this was not the case. 'During his time at St Aidan's, Dad always wore suits,' said Niki. 'Usually they were light-coloured suits. He only started wearing a blazer after we moved to Hesley.' Similarly, of the fifteen complainants, only half gave a description of Hoskin, and, of these, five said that his hair was grey. During his time at St Aidan's his hair was brown. It was grey, however, in the photograph the police had taken of him at the outset of the investigation. The grey-haired man wearing a blazer was not someone any of the complainants had encountered while at St Aidan's. It was, however, the person the police encountered in March 1994.

One of the statements which puzzled Saltrese was made in prison by Paul Edwards, then 31, a former St Aidan's pupil. His statement contained the allegation that he was caned 'on the bare buttocks' by Mr Hoskin, but surprisingly continued: 'I cannot remember Mr Hoskin touching me in an indecent manner or suggesting anything indecent to me while I was at St Aidan's. Again, I have no complaints to make against Mr Hoskin.'

Saltrese was able to trace Paul Edwards without difficulty; he was in prison. Saltrese gave Edwards a copy of the statement he had made and Edwards immediately said that it did not match his own memories of St Aidan's. He then wrote out a fresh statement: 'After such a long time, I would not be able to remember the name of the headmaster without police prompting,' he wrote. 'Nor do I recall ever being caned on the bare backside.'

Edwards explained that prisoners do not like being seen talking to policemen, and he would have signed the statement simply in order to get rid of them. But he did clearly recall one detail of the interview: 'I remember the police asking if, when caned by Mr Hoskin, did he ever touch me with the cane in an indecent manner? i.e. did he put the cane between my buttocks or touch my genitals? I replied no to this, jokingly asking the police would I get compensation if I said yes. They replied along the lines of "I suppose so".'

Saltrese's visit to Edwards seemed to confirm his hypothesis that, by asking leading questions (perhaps without even recognising that they were doing so), the police had actually suggested to witnesses the kind of indecent assault which Hoskin had been accused of in the first place.

If Edwards – either to ingratiate himself with the police, or to gain compensation – had accepted their suggestion, then he too might have been standing in the witness box as one of Terry Hoskin's accusers. Nobody would then have suspected that a highly specific detail of the case against Hoskin had inadvertently been supplied by the very police officers who were supposed to be investigating it.

Having analysed all the allegations in the case in minute detail, Saltrese was convinced that they were products of the investigation itself. They were, in his view, the all-but inevitable precipitate of police methods which were saturated with leading questions and inadvertent cueing. Saltrese then went on record as saying that he was '100% confident that Terry is a completely innocent man', a view he has continued to hold ever since.

When I interviewed him in prison, Hoskin was not always able to conceal his anger about what had happened to him and his family. 'I seriously thought that I'd come out at the end of the trial a free man', he said, 'I knew I'd done nothing, and I thought the statements would be knocked down one by one.'

At the time he was first interviewed, Hoskin was already aware of the police investigations into care homes:

> I thought, I'm sorry, you've picked the wrong one this time – someone who's probably one of the best residential care workers they've come across. But, by God, they won in the end, didn't they?
>
> After 32 years of serving this country, of looking after its most difficult kids, here I am doing eight years. Can you imagine how I feel? I've lost all respect for the police. And the judge congratulated them at the end! While I was banged up in Walton that night, those men would have been out celebrating. It's appalling.
>
> I have refused to join a therapy programme for sex offenders because I am not a sex offender. I could be eligible for parole after four years, but to do that I have to show remorse and I can't show remorse for something I've not done. They may send me off to Siberia because of that, thinking I'm being awkward. But I'm not being awkward, I'm just being honest.
>
> I survive because of my belief in myself, and in Chris, who is working for the truth to come out, and obviously my family, who are super. I still believe that goodness will shine through in the end.

Hoskin's confidence remains unshaken by the fact that the Court of Appeal rejected his first appeal. The case, like so many others, is destined for the Criminal Cases Review Commission.

If we examine the conduct of the Nugent Care Society, first in the Langshaw case, and then in relation to Operation Granite and the various Cheshire investigations which grew from it, including the case of Terry Hoskin, it is tempting to conclude that it has been guilty of folly and misjudgment on an exceptional scale.

That conclusion, I believe, is one which we should resist. For while Nugent Care should be criticised, it is important to place such criticism in perspective. The folly and misjudgment which is indeed reflected in the policies of Nugent Care is nothing other than our own. For the story of Nugent Care is, in one respect, the story of our own confusion. As a society, we too have swung from an attitude of almost systematic disbelief in the reality of sexual abuse towards an equally dangerous position where, at the most extreme, we react to allegations of sexual abuse with a kind of systematic credulity.

To say this is not to suggest that Operation Granite (or any similar investigation) is not an effective way of convicting those who are genuinely guilty of sexual abuse. Langshaw and Grain were not the only genuine abusers sent to prison as a result of the Cheshire investigation. A significant proportion of those charged pleaded guilty for no other reason than that they were guilty. The problem with the kind of investigation that was pursued was that it provided absolutely no reliable way of distinguishing between those who were guilty and those who were not. It relied on the courts to do that. Paradoxically, however, the very investigative methods used by the police, and the fact that none of the interviews they conducted were tape-recorded, meant that the courts had no proper way of determining where the truth lay. A police investigation which was intended to safeguard the lives of innocent children had become a powerful instrument for destroying the lives of innocent adults.

If the Nugent Care Society is to be criticised for acquiescing to methods of police investigation which are misguided, then this criticism can only reasonably be made if we are prepared to accept that we have ourselves acquiesced to a process of demonising paedophiles which is profoundly dangerous. For whenever supposed criminals are hunted down primarily because of the demonic image we have projected onto them, the pursuit of justice all too easily becomes a witch-hunt in which the innocent suffer alongside the guilty.

The great tragedy was that the massive trawling operation set up by the Cheshire Police in imitation of their colleagues in North Wales, was not the end of the story. It was merely the beginning.

67 Policing in reverse

LIKE THE NORTH WALES INVESTIGATION, the Cheshire trawling operation grew exponentially until it traced more than two thousand former residents, almost all of whom were treated by the police as potential victims. From its beginnings, however, as we have seen, it was closely linked to the parallel investigation being conducted by the Merseyside Police.

The Merseyside force had, under the direction of DS Albert Kirby, conducted some of the inquiries relating to St Vincent's, where Alan Langshaw had worked. As these inquiries started to snowball and affect other institutions, the Merseyside Police concluded that there was a need to follow the example of North Wales and Cheshire and set up a major investigation of their own.

In 1996 the chief constable of Merseyside took the decision to set up Operation Care, which would become the largest and best known trawling operation in the country, and would be held up to the media and to police forces nationally as 'a model of best practice in its field'.[564] Detective Superintendent John Robbins, who had been the deputy head of Merseyside CID, was appointed to take charge of this operation. As in the case of North Wales and Cheshire, there were two main reasons for the spectacular growth of the Merseyside operation, which would eventually trawl allegations against more than 500 care workers and collect allegations from more than 700 complainants. The first reason was that sexual abuse in children's homes was a real problem to which police resources had never previously been devoted on any significant scale.

Although trawling operations were hugely inefficient in their deployment of scarce police resources, they were undeniably effective in identifying and securing the conviction of some genuine abusers. Because the huge injustices perpetrated by the system remained invisible to the officers concerned, Operation Care was almost immediately perceived as a success. In defending it, senior Merseyside police officers have frequently – and quite correctly – pointed out that a significant number of care workers who were accused as a result of Operation

Care, actually pleaded guilty to some or all of the counts with which they were charged. Thus, of the five hundred care workers who were accused, at least twenty pleaded guilty – and almost certainly were guilty of the majority of the counts to which they pleaded.

The second reason for the 'success' of the operation, however, was quite different. The key factor was the attitude of Detective Superintendent John Robbins to the verification of allegations. It might be thought that, in view of the gravity of the complaints being collected, a concerted effort would be made to identify any inconsistencies or impossibilities contained in the allegations. Such statement-checking may on occasions have been carried out. But frequently it was not. It was certainly not seen as the principal means of verification.

When I interviewed Robbins in 1996, some months after Operation Care had begun, and asked how allegations were verified, he replied that 'Corroboration is generally done by volume'. The clear presumption was that it was not the task of the police to seek to *disprove* any particular allegation, or to look for evidence which might call it into question; the principal task was to try to discover more allegations against the same person. If these were forthcoming then they would be treated as offering substantiation of the original allegation. The possibility that the gathering of such allegations might simply illustrate how easy it was to generate false allegations was apparently never seriously considered by Robbins and his team.

Robbins himself told me that the manner in which he was conducting the investigation was 'the reverse of normal police methods'. Usually, he explained, police officers start with a crime and are unsure who committed it. In trawling investigations, however, this process is reversed. What he clearly meant by this was that you start with a suspect or an allegation and end up by discovering a number of crimes which had not previously been reported.

What Robbins told me in 1996 is now deeply embarrassing to senior police officers as his characterisation of trawling was entirely accurate. It remains accurate now. Of course it is quite true that, in the course of investigating serious crimes such as murder, the police may go to great lengths to discover fresh witnesses who have not come forward of their own accord. But, in this case, the police are seeking evidence about a crime whose reality is not in doubt. In trawling operations they are seeking crimes which have not been reported – and which may not have taken place at all. There is a difference between conducting a search for witnesses and conducting a search for complainants. As Robbins himself clearly recognised in 1996, the latter approach turns traditional police methods on their head.

A fascinating perspective on this is provided by the journalist Christian Wolmar in his book *Fogotten Children: The Secret Abuse Scandal in Children's Homes* (2000). Robbins, he says, recalled how, as a young officer, he would take absconders back to children's homes: 'Maybe these kids were being abused. If they had said that, I don't think a lot would have been believed. I would have looked at what they were in for, and if they were there for being dishonest, I would have thought that they were trying to justify their running away.'

What is most revealing is how the head of Operation Care, interviewed by this journalist four years after he had spoken to me, describes his approach. Wolmar quotes the following words: 'I'm used to a whodunit situation – there has been a crime, but we don't know who has done it. This is different. We know who has committed a crime, but how much has he done.?'[565] In these extraordinary words Robbins is not saying that trawling means starting with a *suspect* and then trying to find the crime. He actually says that it means starting from a position where you *know* someone is guilty.

What Robbins's own characterisation of trawling suggests is what any dispassionate examination of it will reveal. All too often the officers involved in such inquiries embark on their quest for evidence in exactly the frame of mind conveyed by Robbins's words: they feel that they *know* that certain care workers are guilty and the only question which remains to be answered is *how* guilty. Investigations thus sometimes start out not simply with a presumption of guilt but with a *conviction* that certain care workers are guilty and must, at almost any cost, be shown to be so.

In 1999 a booklet about trawling techniques entitled *You told me you loved me* was published jointly by the Merseyside Police, the Cheshire Constabulary, the City of Liverpool Social Services Directorate and Cheshire Social Services. It is described as 'An account and analysis of the Joint Investigations into Institutional Child Abuse carried out in the north west of England from 1993 to 1999'. It contains the following oblique acknowledgment of the truth of what Robbins told me in 1996 about trawling being the 'reverse' of normal police methods: 'Critics have pointed out that these operational methods represent a departure from normal police practice. This may be true but the methods have been scrutinised by the judiciary in trials without criticism to date.'

It is significant that the authors of the booklet (which features a photograph of Robbins, who may well have contributed to its drafting) have attempted to limit the self-inflicted damage done by Robbins's accurate analysis. They have done so by misattributing it to 'critics' of trawling who have, in fact, merely been quoting it.

In practice trawling is not a form of investigation; it is a technique for ensuring that prosecutions can be brought in relation to long-delayed allegations, and for maximising their chances of success. This much is implicitly acknowledged in *You told me you loved me*. It is pointed out that, once a police force has adopted trawling as a technique, a single complaint of abuse will, almost automatically, trigger a full investigation: 'It is arguable that in times past, a single uncorroborated allegation may not have produced such a response. Indeed it was probably the case that the fact that the allegation was uncorroborated often resulted in the matter being given a much lower priority for action. Experience has shown that in many (but not all) cases, *proactive inquiry can uncover further allegations*' [italics added].[566]

Although it has since been denied, it is quite clear from these words that the 'uncovering' of further allegations was originally seen as the central task of trawling operations. Again and again the former residents who are contacted in this way are referred to in the booklet as 'potential victims'. At no point is the problem of false allegations even discussed.

Whereas care is taken with most ordinary police investigations to focus on a limited set of objectives and to prevent inquiries getting out of control, it was accepted from the outset that trawling, or 'dip sampling' as Robbins preferred to call it, was self-reproducing. In a paragraph headed 'Mushrooming technique', *You told me you loved me* explains how each witness should be treated as a means of propagating the names and addresses of more witnesses. The starting point, we are told, is with the known victim(s): 'From their information the tracing of other ex-residents becomes possible. This technique is used to build up a database in the absence of comprehensive records for an establishment. This is a conscious act to improve the records but it is not to be confused with the mushrooming "effect" where an enquiry may be made in respect of a particular establishment and result in allegations about a different suspect or even establishment, thereby instigating a whole new enquiry.'[567]

Once the 'mushrooming technique' was adopted, it was possible, as the case of Terry Hoskin illustrated, to collect an almost limitless number of allegations against a suspect. The 'mushrooming effect', however, meant that new suspects were always being identified, and sometimes even a small number of allegations sufficed to convict them. Des Traynor, a residential social worker at Dyson House, a secure unit on Merseyside, found himself arrested as a result of complaints of buggery trawled from only two former residents, both of whom had long records of criminal dishonesty, both of whom had worked as male prostitutes and both of whom, during the period that their allegations were made, lived in the same city – Manchester.

In the circumstances there was absolutely no way that a conspiracy between the two complainants could be ruled out. The possibility of 'indirect collusion', whereby police officers had inadvertently transferred an allegation from one complainant to the other, could also not be ruled out. Bewildered by his arrest and never thinking that such allegations might actually lead to a conviction, Traynor accepted the advice of his union that he should use their solicitors. He found himself represented by a solicitor who had virtually no experience of criminal cases, no understanding of the nature of police trawling, and little concept of how to mount a defence. He advised him to say nothing at all to the police – not even to deny that he had committed the offences. The solicitor, indeed, may well have been influenced by the view which was likely to be taken by the jury – that there was no smoke without fire.

Traynor's trial lasted little more than a day. On the slenderest imaginable evidence, this devoted father of two young daughters found himself sentenced to eight years in prison. As he was led from the court he cried out that he was innocent. While he was in prison he was able to assemble evidence which demonstrated that his first accuser had lied on oath at another criminal trial. Largely because legal aid becomes available for delayed appeals only once leave for appeal has been granted, however, Traynor has yet to submit his appeal formally.

Traynor was convicted on 3 July 1996. It so happened that the edition of the *London Review of Books* which appeared the next day carried a review of Chris Moore's *The Kincora Scandal*. The reviewer was Paul Foot, who wrote that, in Cheshire and in Liverpool, stories of abuse in children's homes 'have emerged piecemeal from a series of carefully separated trials in which the accused – all of them staff at the homes – have pleaded guilty to a series of charges of buggery, rape and indecent assault on the children in their care'. Even though there had already been five cases (excluding Traynor's) in which the defendants had pleaded not guilty, this fact was simply not reported. Instead, Foot went on to write that one Cheshire solicitor 'represents a hundred young people who say they have been abused in county council homes – *and no one denies their claims*' [italics added]. The clear implication was that the huge number of allegations made in Cheshire and Liverpool had not been contested in any way. No indication was given that the vast majority of these claims had not been made spontaneously at all, but had been collected as a result of police trawling operations.[568]

When a respected campaigner against miscarriages of justice wrongly reports not-guilty pleas as admissions of guilt, and represents evidence which has been grossly contaminated by the investigative process as having 'emerged piecemeal from a series of carefully separated trials', the signs of acute moral panic are already visible.

Foot's reference to the Cheshire solicitor (which did not make clear that he was seeking compensation for his hundred clients) was one indication that the police and social services were not the only professionals involved in sustaining this moral panic and driving it forwards. Some lawyers were also deeply involved. Unusually, though, the police also took a close interest in the question of compensation and went out of their way to ensure that obstacles standing in the way of claims were, if possible, removed. Police officers even held a series of meetings with the very solicitor to which Paul Foot's article referred – Peter Garsden of the firm Abney Garsden McDonald. In addition to dealing with civil claims made by his own clients, Garsden was also co-ordinating claims made by other solicitors' firms throughout the north west.

'It very quickly became apparent that it was important for us and the police to have a symbiotic relationship,' Garsden told David Rose. 'For example, the police would want us to refer any new complaints of abuse that they didn't know about to them, because it would help them in their process. We depended on them, because we wanted as much information about the pending criminal trials as possible.'[569] Rose reported that Garsden had appointed a 'press relations officer', one of whose tasks was to get articles placed in the local media. Such articles sometimes made it clear that victims might be able to claim thousands of pounds in damages. In the course of his researches Rose even discovered that one former Greystone resident had lodged a claim with Garsden's firm as a direct result of seeing this publicity. Only after he had made his statement for the lawyers did he agree to talk to the police.

In some cases, the relationship between lawyers and police was even closer. 'The police have been very helpful,' Rose was told by solicitor Keith Robinson, who was handling over 100 abuse claims. 'I have had several clients who have been referred to me by officers. They will often supply important documents, such as unused material from a trial and supporting evidence.'

By 2000 Peter Garsden's firm was already co-ordinating 700 civil claims, about half of which were clients of his own firm. In part the motivation for dealing with these claims was a financial one. The interim funding for work on the claims is provided by legal aid. In any case which is successfully settled, however, the money advanced by legal aid is returned and the work is re-invoiced by the solicitor to the local authority (or insurance company) which is held to be liable. The work is then charged at a much higher rate to allow for its supposed difficulty and stressfulness. As Garsden's firm's website announced at one point: 'There is undoubtedly investment in the future in that when these actions are successful and costs are settled, the mark-ups we will be requesting are considerable.'[570] This work would ultimately involve legal fees running into millions of pounds. It would be wrong to suggest, however, that money is Garsden's sole motivation. He is clearly driven by an idealistic desire to help 'victims', and this appears to blind him to the possibility that many of those who allege abuse may not in fact be victims at all. He has suggested that all the allegations he is dealing with must be true because nobody would be prepared to submit themselves to the ordeal of giving evidence in court unless they were telling the truth. When giving evidence to the Home Affairs Select Committee, he told MPs: 'I do not believe there is one person who is sitting there in prison who is blameless, and has not committed any act of abuse; no I do not.'[571]

Perhaps more interestingly still, given the reluctance there is to acknowledge the continuities between ancient and modern witch-hunts, Garsden, like the zealots of an earlier age, appears to believe that he is, quite literally, fighting the forces of Satan: 'I believe that we're messing with the Devil, because you know, child abuse is evil, and the people that get involved in it are powerful, manipulative people. And they will do their level best to stop us succeeding and stop us getting justice for the victims.'[572]

Such was the burning zeal by which Peter Garsden was consumed in his fight against this imagined conspiracy that, in 1997, he became one of the leading members of the Association of Child Abuse Lawyers (ACAL), an organisation for lawyers who specialise in supporting allegations of sexual abuse – particularly in relation to civil claims for compensation. As is acknowledged on its website, the founder of ACAL, barrister Lee Moore, believes that she is a victim of ritual abuse herself and that she 'experienced Satanic ritual abuse throughout childhood'. An article about Moore in the *Times Educational Supplement* implied that she initially had no memories of the twelve years, from the age of three to fifteen, when she had been brought up inside what she later identified as a satanic cult; her experiences during this period had been so traumatic that she had 'dissociated' herself from them. It was only after she had a nervous breakdown forty years later that she had, 'with the help of her psychiatrist, pieced together her life of fear growing up in an organised abuse ring', where she had been 'abused by carers, friends and acquaintances both male and female'.[573]

Anyone who believes that they spent twelve years of their childhood being abused inside a satanic cult, that they repressed the memory of this abuse and only recovered it forty years later with the help of a psychiatrist, deserves the utmost sympathy and understanding. What is truly disturbing, however, is that a delusion of this kind has helped to give rise to a professional organisation of lawyers which is now acting as a pressure group for others who make allegations of abuse.

Far from being perceived as a fringe or fanatical organisation, ACAL has managed to establish a considerable measure of respectability. In 1998 it secured St John's College, Cambridge as the venue for its inaugural conference. It then approached a number of distinguished speakers, asking if they would be prepared to donate their time without receiving any fee. Among the speakers who accepted this invitation were the social worker Barbara Kahan, who had co-authored the original Staffordshire Pindown report, and Gerard Elias QC. Elias was joined on the platform by Ernest Ryder QC who had been his assistant at the Tribunal.

Although Elias and Ryder subsequently told me that they were unhappy about the conference's extremely one-sided approach to the question of child sexual abuse, and would decline any further invitation from ACAL, their presence was in itself sufficient to confer respectability on the proceedings. The conference took place in March 1999 and was chaired by the journalist Christian Wolmar.[574]

The list of conference delegates included not only lawyers but senior police officers (among them Peter Ackerley of the North Wales Police). At the very centre of the programme was a presentation by John Robbins, who was introduced as a pioneer investigator whose methods had already exerted an influence on police forces throughout the country. Robbins gave no intimation that he had any doubts about the reliability and integrity of the trawling methods he was describing. His seeming confidence may have had a particular origin. For at this point he must already have known that Operation Care was about to make the most important of all its arrests.

68 Going to jail with a clear conscience

WHEN OPERATION CARE was launched in 1996 it initially focused on a small number of children's homes. However, simply because most people who have been in care passed through more than one institution, and because of what John Robbins called 'the mushrooming effect', it was almost inevitable that any investigation targeted on one home would spread to others.

By January 1999 the number of children's homes under investigation by Operation Care had reached the extraordinary figure of 76. Throughout the relentless expansion of the investigation, however, its centre seemed to remain constant; the homes run by the Catholic organisation Nugent Care were those against which trawling techniques were directed most assiduously.

In September 1997, the following letter was sent to some 500 former residents of St George's, a former community home (reclassified as a special school during the 1990s) situated in the prosperous Merseyside town of Formby:

Dear ———,

OPERATION CARE

I am the senior investigating officer of the above operation which is currently investigating allegations of child abuse reported to have taken place within a number of residential establishments in the Merseyside area.

I am aware from records provided to me that in times past you have been a resident at St Georges/Clarence House School in Formby, whilst in the care of a local authority. I am concerned that there is a possibility that such abuse may have taken place whilst you were in residence there.

If you have any information or if we can help with any complaint you may have, please respond by completing and returning the attached slip using the enclosed pre-paid envelope or by contacting a member of my staff using the above telephone number.

MAY I TAKE THIS OPPORTUNITY OF ASSURING YOU THAT

ANY INFORMATION GIVEN OR COMPLAINT MADE WILL
BE TREATED IN THE STRICTEST CONFIDENCE.

If you do not wish to communicate with the Police or Social Services
at this time, but feel you would like to discuss any events which have
taken place, you may wish to use the independent and confidential
counselling service offered by BARNARDOS COUNSELLING 0151-707-
1327. If they cannot assist I am sure they can put you in touch with a
counselling service which can.

Please reply by [25ᵗʰ September 97]

Thank you for your assistance in this matter.

Yours faithfully,

J.H. Robbins, Detective Superintendent

The consequences of this mail-drop, in which a police force was applying tried and tested marketing techniques to the gathering of evidence
for a criminal prosecution, would be huge. St George's was destined to
become the Bryn Estyn of Operation Care. It would be turned, in the
imagination of the Merseyside Police at least, into a 'house of horrors'.
Eventually no fewer than 91 former members of staff would have allegations made against them.

The reasons why St George's came to be demonised in this way are
far from clear. One factor was that it had always been one of the largest
community homes in the country, accommodating as many as 120 boys
in the 1960s. Another possible reason was that, very unusually, one of
the ex-members of staff was a national celebrity; David Jones, the former Wolverhampton Wanderers football manager and Everton player,
had worked at St George's in the 1980s.

However, there was another factor which might have influenced the
police even though it was never explicitly acknowledged by them. This
was the fact that the solicitor who had emerged as the most effective
and articulate opponent of police trawling, who had spoken against it
on BBC Radio 4's *Law in Action* and on *Newsnight*, himself had an association with St George's. Chris Saltrese, who was based on Merseyside,
had been brought up in St George's, where his father, Nick Saltrese, had
been the head, and his mother had worked as a house mother. It can
hardly fail to have occurred to the Merseyside Police that if the home
over which Saltrese's father had presided could be exposed as a haven
for paedophiles, then one of their most persistent opponents would be

effectively discredited. Clearly this was not the prime factor in the decision to investigate St George's; this followed almost ineluctably from the setting-up of Operation Care itself. But, once St George's did enter the frame of investigation, it is entirely possible that Robbins and his team may, perhaps quite unwittingly, have been influenced by the Saltrese connection.

One of the first allegations the Merseyside Police collected in relation to St George's came, unusually, from a former resident who had returned as a member of staff. Two years after Steven Bryanton had taken up his appointment in 1994, two female members of staff complained of persistent sexually offensive remarks made to them by him. Bryanton was formally told of these complaints by a senior colleague, Mike Lawson. Rather then returning to work, where he would possibly have faced an inquiry, he responded by taking sick leave. He then resigned.

Soon after this Bryanton was visited by police officers who were following up responses to their trawling letter. The officers were evidently applying the 'mushrooming technique' and had obtained Bryanton's name from a former resident who had received one of the letters. In response to their questions he now made an allegation, claiming that Lawson had sexually abused him while he was a resident at the home in the early 1980s.

Mike Lawson, who had previously been a sergeant in the Liverpool City Police, and had been a member of staff at St George's for twenty-two years, now became a prime suspect. At 6.30 am on 2 June 1997, five officers from the Merseyside Police arrested him. As his wife and youngest daughter, Becky, who was then ten, looked on bewildered, Lawson was driven away in a police car.

Given the circumstances in which the complaint had been made, and the fact that Bryanton had returned to St George's of his own free will to work under the very man he subsequently accused, the allegation clearly invited a degree of scepticism. Had it been properly investigated, documents would have shown that, contrary to what he was now claiming, Bryanton had not in fact been in Lawson's unit at the time he claimed he had been abused. Other discrepancies would also have shown that the allegations could not be true. However, having committed themselves to a methodology in which one allegation, however unreliable, would trigger a hunt for more, the Merseyside Police now began to trawl in earnest. As a result, seven former residents also made allegations against Lawson.

As soon as the first allegations were made, Lawson and his solicitor, knowing what had happened elsewhere, began to prepare rebuttals. They alerted local politicians and the local member of parliament to what had happened. Mike Lawson, whose hobby is organising re-enactments of Civil War battles, and who has a national reputation for the brilliance of his historical reconstructions, now embarked on a battle of his own. His aim was to clear his name and to call attention to what was happening throughout the north west and in many other parts of Britain.

As Lawson's case developed, however, the Merseyside Police's relentless trawling was already resulting in allegations against others. On 23 December 1997, when the Christmas presents were already under the tree, Basil Williams–Rigby, another former member of staff, was visited by three police officers. They said they were investigating allegations of sexual abuse and seemed particularly concerned about the safety of his six-year-old son – the youngest of his four children.

Williams–Rigby's father had been a member of the central management committee for the Catholic Children's Society. His son remembers him as an exceptionally generous man who every year sent a large tin of Quality Street chocolates to each of the homes the society ran. One year in the early 1970s, Basil volunteered to deliver the presents. As a direct result of the gratitude expressed to him as he did this, he decided to stop working for his father's construction company and take a job in a home. Eventually he became a houseparent at St George's – a social worker who lived on the premises with his family.

Interviewed by the journalist Bob Woffinden in March 2003, Baz Rigby, as he was known by the boys, recalled his time at the home almost with nostalgia:

> It has been painted recently as a bad school – but it wasn't. When there was a potato shortage, in the 70s, we went out to local farmers, to buy potatoes so that we could give the boys chips. Then I went and bought the frame of a go-kart, with my own money, assembled it and we used to spend hours going round the field at the back. They would stand in an orderly queue, to take a turn, it was a tremendous activity for them.
>
> I was concerned that these children were looked after. They were from rough-and-tumble backgrounds, streetwise children, but likeable rogues, let's say. You couldn't think aloud sometimes. I remember saying I had two bald tyres on my Mini. The kids said, 'Don't worry, Mr Rigby, you're good to us, we'll sort it out'. I instantly knew that somewhere in Liverpool that weekend there'd be a Mini jacked up with its

tyres gone. To prevent that happening, and even though I was sorely pressed financially at the time, I had to go straight out to get new ones.[575]

Because he had gone out of his way to help the boys in his care, Williams-Rigby had made himself vulnerable to the kind of allegations he now faced. He found it almost impossible to take these seriously:

> When my solicitor sent me the statements of complainants, I couldn't read them. It upset me to think that I could be accused of something like that. I just went like a lamb to the slaughter, thinking that these people wouldn't continue with these idiotic lies. That wasn't the case, was it?
>
> There was one witness I was staggered by. He used to be a very frightened kid, I boosted his confidence. He'd done reasonably well for himself – I thought at the time, that's something that I gave him. He'd actually kept in touch. The police approached him on more than one occasion. He said nothing like that had ever happened. I'd phoned and asked him to be a character witness – he agreed straightaway: 'What a stupid set of allegations. I'll help you anytime, Baz, you've helped me enough in the past'.
>
> Then, he succumbed to temptation. I think it was just the money. He got three thousand pounds – or three thousand pieces of silver, as I think of it.

As Basil Williams-Rigby waited in disbelief for his trial, the Merseyside Police continued to collect allegations against others. One person who would inevitably find himself in the line of fire was the former head of the home, Nick Saltrese.

When I first spoke to Chris Saltrese, in May 1996, I asked him why he had worked for so long and with such dedication on the case of Terry Hoskin. 'It's really very simple,' he said. 'There, but for the grace of God, goes my father.' Three years later, on 13 May 1999, Saltrese's worst fears were realised when his father was arrested. Although the allegations against him were without substance, Nick Saltrese knew better than anyone that they should be treated with the utmost seriousness. He arranged to be represented by Bindman's, one of the leading firms of defence solicitors in the country.

In a decision which may well have been designed to avoid embarrassing the Merseyside Police, the allegations, which were false, would eventually be dropped. For two years, however, as the home he had once presided over was progressively demonised, Nick Saltrese lived with the knowledge that he might have to stand trial and face the possibility of being wrongly convicted.

Saltrese's arrest did not mark the end of the St George's investigation. On 17 June 1999 newspapers throughout Britain reported the most sensational news in the history of police trawling: the arrest of David Jones, then the manager of Southampton FC For the first time, a nationally known figure had been arrested for allegedly abusing boys in a children's home.

The news was broken to Jones and his wife Ann shortly before the arrest and only days after Ann's brother-in-law had been killed in a tragic accident at work: 'We were half way up the M6 on our way to my brother-in-law's funeral,' Ann Jones recalls, 'when Dave's secretary called on the mobile phone. She said Merseyside Police wanted to speak to him. That was the first we knew that his name had come up as part of a child abuse investigation. My heart just sank and I felt physically sick.'[576]

By October her husband was facing nine charges of physical and sexual abuse. The offences had supposedly taken place fifteen years earlier when Jones, after an injury had put a stop to his career as professional footballer, had worked briefly at St George's. Over the succeeding months, as the investigation intensified, the tally of counts gradually rose so that David Jones found himself facing 22 charges arising out of allegations made by six complainants. Three of these charges related to physical abuse and nineteen to sexual abuse. 'It was the worst thing somebody could possibly accuse you of,' his wife told a newspaper. 'He said he'd rather be up for murder than something like this because he's so anti-abuse.'

As the police attempted to strengthen their case against David Jones by collecting more allegations against him, Williams-Rigby's case, which followed a much more rapid trajectory than Mike Lawson's, came to trial in August 1999.

Williams-Rigby was supported throughout the trial by his wife Diane, and his three eldest daughters, who were then aged 27, 21, and 14. Two years after the trial, the eldest daughter, Rebecca, would recall the moment when she realised her father was going to prison. 'He said "how can I prove my innocence?" and I just hugged him and said "you can't, Dad". Then I knew for certain that he wasn't coming home.'

When the jury returned their verdicts on the 47 counts her father faced, Rebecca's intimation proved correct. Although acquitted on 25 counts, he was found guilty on 22. He was sentenced to twelve years in prison.

In some respects the conviction of Williams-Rigby, coming as it did so close to the arrest of David Jones, was to prove a turning point in the history of police trawling. A number of former St George's members of staff were dismayed by what to them was quite clearly a miscarriage of justice, and concerned at the manner in which a witch-hunt appeared to be developing. At a gathering around her kitchen table that included friends and relatives of Williams-Rigby, one of these former members of staff, Liz Mills, suggested that they should form an organisation to fight against what was happening on Merseyside. The organisation was FACT (False Allegations against Carers and Teachers). It began to hold weekly meetings and sought to bring the realities of police trawling to the attention of the local member of parliament, Claire Curtis-Thomas, the Labour MP for Crosby.

Claire Curtis-Thomas's constituency, formerly that of Shirley Williams, includes the site of St George's in Formby, a commuter town a few miles up the coast from where the Mersey runs into the sea. If you look south from the sand-dunes on Formby beach you can see the North Wales coast stretching out from Rhyl towards Bangor. With binoculars it might even be possible to make out the tall radio mast which towers above the headquarters of the North Wales Police at Colwyn Bay.

It was there, in August 1991, eight years before the conviction of Basil Williams-Rigby, that the Bryn Estyn investigation had been launched. With the conviction of Williams-Rigby, however, those who lived in Formby no longer needed to look to North Wales to appreciate the huge power which is gained by those who make allegations of sexual abuse. As a result of the trawling methods adopted by the Merseyside Police, they found themselves living in the midst of their own witch-hunt. In an article about Operation Care and its effect on the town, the *Formby Times* quoted one local resident as saying 'Anyone who has worked in care is waiting for that knock on the door and living in fear.'

One of FACT's earliest public meetings was held in a school hall at St Helens in March 2000. The meeting was chaired by Harry Fearns, the brother-in-law of Basil Williams-Rigby. At one point Mike Lawson spoke movingly about the allegations he faced. 'I can sleep easily in my bed at night,' he said, 'because I know I'm innocent.'

Two months later, on 2 May, Lawson's sixtieth birthday, his trial began at Liverpool Crown Court. In an attempt to counter the prejudicial force of the allegations made by the eight complainants, Lawson's legal team pointed out that thousands of boys had passed through the home while he worked there, yet the police had only found eight who had made allegations against him. They also called 46 witnesses to give evidence (mainly character evidence) on his behalf. The judge remarked that he had never known a case in which so many defence witnesses had been called.

However, this impressive evidence was undermined by the fact that the judge permitted the jury to be told of the conviction of Basil Williams-Rigby, and that 91 former members of staff had been accused. The jury was even given the names of about twenty people who had been arrested or were facing charges. One of the names was that of Nick Saltrese, whose wife had worked as a house mother and had given evidence (as Mrs Saltrese) on behalf of Lawson. Since she would almost inevitably have been identified by the jury as the wife of a suspected paedophile, this disclosure called her evidence into question. The same was true of two other defence witnesses whose husbands had been arrested and whose names were also included in the list. Far more importantly, since the jury were never told that, with the exception of Williams-Rigby, not one of the 91 accused people had actually been found guilty of anything, they were left to conclude that the home in question was riddled with abuse.

At his trial Lawson faced an indictment of 29 counts relating to the eight complainants. When the jury returned their verdicts, they found Lawson guilty on 17 counts of indecent assault relating to seven complainants. The only complainant whose allegations were dismissed out of hand was Steven Bryanton, without whose complaint the case against Lawson would never have been constructed at all. Mike Lawson was sentenced to a total of seven years imprisonment. 'I go to jail with a clear conscience', he told the judge.

The conviction of Mike Lawson added urgency to FACT's campaign. It decided to hold its next meeting at the very heart of the new witch-hunt – in Formby itself.

At the local church hall, on a Sunday in July 2001, there was half-an-hour before the meeting was due to start. Liz Mills and her helpers had been working all morning preparing sandwiches and laying out the hall; they were clearly optimistic about the number of people who might come. Each of the 250 seats bore a FACT leaflet. With only a sprinkling of cars in the car-park such optimism seemed unwarranted.

Half an hour later every seat was taken. People were standing in the aisles and crowding every doorway. Claire Curtis-Thomas MP took a

seat in the front row. Among the speakers were Chris Saltrese and barrister Mark Barlow. Barlow was clearly disturbed. A few days earlier his
client, Barry Strettle, had been convicted. Barlow described to the audience, which included Barry's wife, Doreen, his feelings as he met his
client after the jury had given their verdict. He had evidently been
deeply moved. 'Good hard-working people find themselves accused of
foul crimes which they cannot defend properly,' he said. He was in no
doubt whatsoever that Strettle was an innocent man, wrongly convicted.

Because Mike Lawson, who had addressed the previous FACT meeting at St Helens so eloquently, was unable to attend, his place was taken
on the platform by his wife, Geraldine. She explained that three weeks
ago her husband had been sent to prison for seven years. Passionately,
angrily, she called for police trawling operations to stop. 'I know I was
emotional,' she said afterwards, 'but at least that might bring home to
people that it is a family which is involved, not just a name and a number, which is all Mike is to them now.'

FACT members went on to call for a government inquiry into police
trawling. One name which was not mentioned during the meeting was
that of Southampton football manager, David Jones. But the case was
very much on everyone's mind. Some of the people at the meeting
knew Jones during the time he was a residential social worker. Nobody
knew any details of the 22 allegations of child abuse he was facing, but
everybody at the meeting presumed he was innocent.

This may well be because the members of FACT had prejudged his
case. But they also knew that the presumption of innocence was the
most fundamental principle of British law, and that, for most people
facing allegations of child sexual abuse, this principle had already been
destroyed.

69 The football manager

AS THE DAVID JONES TRIAL approached, the subject of trawling began to receive serious interest from the media. The *Daily Mail* published a sympathetic two-page feature on the David Jones case which included an interview with Jones's wife, Ann, and a large colour photograph of the couple with their four daughters.

What was perhaps most significant about this article was not its publication but the response it provoked. The *Daily Mail* received so many letters, most of them complaining about police trawling operations, and many of them from Merseyside, that it sent its chief reporter, Michael Seamark, to investigate the larger story which lay behind the David Jones case. Seamark spent several days in Liverpool and was deeply disturbed by what he discovered. Much of the material he gathered was stored up to be used at the end of the David Jones trial.

Seamark was not the only journalist now working on the story. The investigative journalist Bob Woffinden, who specialises in miscarriages of justice, and with whom I had written an article for the *Guardian* magazine in 1998 to mark the publication of my brief book *The Great Children's Home Panic*, had now looked into a number of trawling cases which he wrote about in the *Guardian* and elsewhere. Another investigative journalist, David Rose, whose role in the Anglesea case has been noted here, read the book soon after it was published. Rose, who had long been interested in miscarriages of justice, was working for BBC's *Panorama*. He had been alerted to the practice of police trawling by a barrister friend who was representing Andy Shalders, a former care worker from Yorkshire, who was facing a large number of counts of sexual abuse made some thirty years after the complainants had been in care.*

Rose decided he would try to persuade the BBC to make a

---

* Andy Shalders, who in the view of his solicitor Chris Saltrese, was undoubtedly innocent, was eventually found guilty on 22 (out of 36) counts of sexual abuse and sentenced to 15 years' imprisonment. He had served just over a year of his sentence when, on 11 October 2002, he died of a heart attack in HM Prison Albany. He was 55.

programme about allegations in care homes from the kind of critical perspective which no television programme had ever adopted. Against very considerable odds he was successful in persuading the *Panorama* editor to commission such a programme.

The programme, which focused on the case of Roy Shuttleworth, put before the British public graphic and compelling evidence that an innocent man had been convicted as a result of a police trawling operation. As well as raising disturbing questions about police methods, it drew attention to the worrying links between police forces in the north west and Peter Garsden and other local solicitors.

The documentary, presented by Rose and produced by Gary Horne, represented such a significant intervention into the debate and threatened to raise such troubling issues that the Merseyside Police made a last-minute attempt to prevent it being broadcast. The *Panorama* investigation was scheduled for Sunday 26 November 2000. It had been timed to fit in with the trial of David Jones, due to begin in Liverpool Crown Court at the end of that week. A few days before the broadcast, the BBC was approached by the Merseyside Police who requested a preview. This was refused but pressure on the BBC continued to build with approaches from the Liverpool Crown Prosecution Service and from the office of the Attorney General – a position at that point held by the counsel to Gordon Anglesea, Lord Williams of Mostyn. The BBC, however, held firm to its decision to transmit the programme. It made it clear that since it did not touch on any of the specific facts of the David Jones case, it would not be likely to constitute contempt of court.

The programme undoubtedly contributed to the change in attitudes towards police trawling which had been taking place since the announcement of Jones's arrest. When Jones's trial began later that week, the atmosphere in and around the court was quite different from that which had prevailed in earlier trawling trials.

In many trials, including Peter Howarth's, former residents had entered the witness box to make a series of false allegations in the knowledge that there was little or no public awareness of the extent to which such complaints were being fabricated. There was certainly no media interest in the possibility of this being so. In the case of the David Jones trial, the massively prejudicial publicity about 'wholesale abuse' in children's homes was now counterbalanced by a new awareness of the dangers of trawling. David Jones himself was an extremely sympathetic figure, widely perceived as an ordinary and decent family man. In this respect he was like many who had already stood trial. He, however, was famous and was believed by a number of journalists to be completely innocent. Those who were due to make allegations against Jones were placed under immense pressure.

Apparently in response to this pressure, the first witness, a man with more than fifty criminal convictions, thought better of his allegations and failed to appear. The police were given twenty-four hours to trace the second defendant – who had also failed to appear – but were unable to do so. One former resident of St George's who did make it into the witness box was a troubled young man with an earlier conviction for arson. He had spent seven years working as a homosexual prostitute in order to fund a £150-a-day cocaine habit. Appearing in the trial as a woman, he was half way through a series of sex-change operations which were being carried out while he was serving a seven-year sentence for armed robbery. According to a fellow former resident of St George's, he had actually said that he was making false allegations against Jones in order to pay for these operations.[577]

The next witness who was due to appear was the first to have made allegations against Jones. When he announced that he no longer intended to give evidence, the prosecution recognised that their case had collapsed. They actually acknowledged, in the words of David Aubrey QC, that 'It was only after publicity given to Mr Jones arising [out of the first allegation] that others came forward.'

Mr Justice Clarke, the Recorder of Liverpool, addressed the man standing in the dock. 'David Jones,' he said, 'not guilty verdicts have been entered in respect of all charges against you. I would just like to say this means you leave this court as you entered it – an innocent man.' In the public gallery, Jones's supporters broke into spontaneous applause. He looked towards his wife who had stood by him throughout the long ordeal leading up to the trial. A few moments later, the couple shared a single kiss at the back of the courtroom and left by a rear door.

That evening radio and television news broadcasts featured the acquittal of David Jones as their lead item, and almost all included reports about police trawling and the dangers it posed to innocent care workers. The next day a number of national newspapers addressed this subject. The *Daily Mail* in particular gave unprecedented space to the story, locating it firmly in the context of other trawling cases. Under the banner headline 'END OF THE NIGHTMARE' and beside a picture of David Jones and his wife outside the court, the *Mail*'s front-page story began as follows:

Major questions hung over the way child abuse cases are investigated last night after the trial of soccer boss David Jones dramatically collapsed. Crucial witnesses failed to turn up to face defence claims that they had invented their stories in the hope of winning pay-offs ...

Lawyers involved in a series of similar cases on Merseyside say that [Jones] is not the first innocent victim of the system of 'trawling', where police investigating allegations about a children's home contact other former residents to ask if they have complaints.

The paper went on to quote a number of Merseyside lawyers on the dangers posed by these cases, ending with the words of Chris Saltrese:

The English legal system assumes a man is innocent until proven guilty. But, in this case, that burden has effectively been reversed. A defendant facing allegations from five, ten or fifteen complainants has a mountain of prejudice to climb.

Unfortunately most defendants in these cases are not successful in doing so. I think the conviction rate in these type of cases is 90 per cent which is disturbingly high. Sheer volume will prevail. Jurors are loathe to acquit where they think there is a scintilla of evidence that the offence has been committed.

There may be 100 innocent people in jail. I know up to 20 people who I think are innocent who have been convicted. The national position doesn't bear thinking about.

Any dispassionate observer of the BBC *Panorama* programme, of the trial at Liverpool Crown Court and of the media coverage of its collapse, might have concluded that the witch-hunt that had begun in North Wales nine years previously was over. For at last, it would seem, the tide of opinion had turned.

But any observers who did reach such a conclusion would soon be proved wrong.

70 The net widens

ON THE WEEKEND FOLLOWING the acquittal of David Jones, the Sunday newspapers carried extensive coverage of the case. Exclusive interviews with Jones and his wife were negotiated with the *Mail on Sunday* and the *News of the World*. The latter's interview appeared under the headline 'CHILD SEX COPS KILLED MY FATHER'. In it David Jones related how the details of his arrest had been released to the press before he had a chance to break the news to his family. His father had first learned what had happened while watching a TV news bulletin in Portugal where he was holidaying with his wife. Days later he was taken ill with a stress-induced stomach ulcer. He went into hospital two days after returning from Portugal and never recovered. 'I will always stand by this,' said David Jones, 'My father died because of this case. And yes, I do blame these people, the people who made these allegations, the people who decided to release the information. … This case was the last thing Dad and I talked about. Then he slipped into unconsciousness and never recovered.'

On the opposite page of the *News of the World*, Ann Jones related how the allegations had led to demands from social workers to question their four daughters to find out whether he had abused them. 'This was the worst possible thing they could have accused Dave of because it was so personal,' she said. 'To suspect a father of committing such a crime on his own children was almost too much to bear. He was devastated – we both were.' She went on to describe how her husband had reacted to the allegations:

When Dave was first questioned about it in Liverpool he returned home and immediately had a shower. He said he imagined it was like when a woman gets raped – he felt dirty and he wanted to wash it off.

When he was finally charged he came home and looked absolutely dreadful, bedraggled and somehow older. He just kept shaking his head.

My reaction was complete shock, then tears, then anger. That anger hasn't left me since. I know they were only out to get Dave because he was a big fish.

There'd be times when I'd break down crying if a certain song came

Merseyside Police

Operation Care
Upton Police Station
Arrowe Park Road
UPTON, Wirral, L49 0UE

Tel: 0151 777 2456
Fax: 0151 777 2466

4ᵗʰ September, 1997

Dear M/S ▬▬▬▬▬

OPERATION CARE

I am the senior investigating officer of the above operation which is currently investigating allegations of child abuse reported to have taken place within a number of residential establishments in the Merseyside area.

I am aware from records provided to me that in times past you have been a resident at St.Georges/Clarence House School situated in the Formby area of Merseyside, whilst in the care of a local authority. I am concerned that there is a possibility that such abuse may have taken place whilst you were in residence there.

If you have any information or if we can help you with any complaint you may have, please respond by completing and returning the attached slip using the enclosed pre-paid envelope or by contacting a member of my staff using the above telephone number.

MAY I TAKE THIS OPPORTUNITY OF ASSURING YOU THAT ANY INFORMATION GIVEN OR COMPLAINT MADE WILL BE TREATED IN THE STRICTEST CONFIDENCE.

If you do not wish to communicate with the Police or Social Services at this time, but feel you would like to discuss any events which have taken place, you may wish to use the independent and confidential counselling service offered by BARNARDOS COUNSELLING 0151-707-1327. If they cannot assist I am sure they can put you in touch with a counselling service which can.

Please reply by *25ᵗʰ SEPTEMBER 97*

Thank you for your assistance in this matter.

Yours faithfully,

J.H. ROBBINS
Detective Superintendent

Merseyside Police: Operation Care trawling letter which led to the arrest of David Jones, Mike Lawson, Basil Williams-Rigby and to the collection of allegations against 88 other former members of staff at St. George's, Formby (see pp. 499-500).

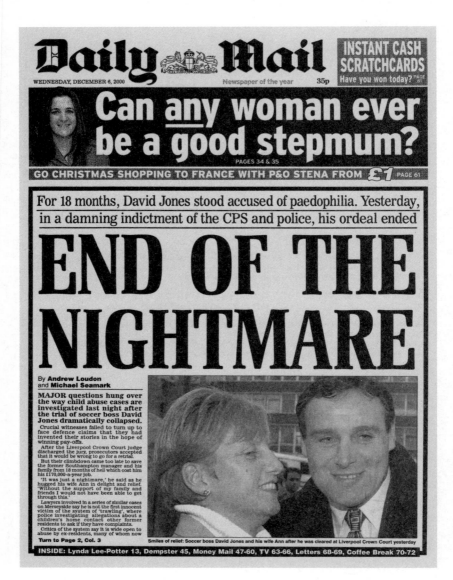

Daily Mail, 6 December, 2000: the trial of David Jones collapses (see pp. 509–10).

on the radio – like Hey Jude, a favourite of ours from school. It was like a snake growing inside of me, taking me over and I could do nothing about it.[578]

The *News of the World* interview with David and Ann Jones powerfully conveyed the larger tragedy suffered by entire families when one innocent person is falsely accused of sexual abuse. Yet neither such personal coverage nor the unprecedented publicity given to the nature and dangers of police trawling operations was sufficient to halt the police investigations which had, by this time, covered the entire country in a trawling net.

Even the St George's investigation itself continued. One reason it could not be stopped in its tracks was that the Crown had obtained a court order preventing St George's from being identified in the press. It was therefore never possible to report which home had attracted allegations against 91 members of staff, or to document the gradual process whereby almost every one of these allegations was dropped by the police or Crown Prosecution Service. Because journalists do not like stories which are shorn of such details, the police investigation into St George's was never exposed as the witch-hunt it undoubtedly was. The police themselves appear to have remained blind to the true nature of their operation.*

But the careful suppression of publicity by the prosecuting authorities was not the only reason that care home investigations continued virtually unaffected by the collapse of the David Jones trial. By the beginning of 2001, trawling had long left behind its original geographical limitations and had become a massive network of related investigations, stretching across the entire country and possessed of the kind of

---

* Of the 91 people against whom allegations were made, one former care worker (in addition to Basil Williams-Rigby and Mike Lawson) would eventually serve a prison sentence in relation to such allegations. He decided in his police interview to confess to having had a consensual gay sexual relationship with a former resident after he had left care. The police subsequently trawled for more allegations and were successful in eliciting from the same former resident an allegation that he had been sexually abused by the care worker at the age of 12. The man said that this was completely untrue and pleaded not guilty to all the allegations formally made against him. He was found guilty. One other former member of staff was convicted of one count of indecent assault and one count of wilfully assaulting a young person under sixteen. He was sentenced to twelve months' imprisonment suspended for two years. It thus seems possible that 95% or more of the allegations collected in relation to St George's were entirely false.

momentum which made them impossible to stop. The 'mushrooming effect' explicitly acknowledged by Robbins was, in short, now happening nationally

The North Wales investigation itself provides one of the best examples of the manner in which trawling operations almost always 'propagate' or 'breed' allegations. As has been seen, this investigation was launched without a single allegation having been made to the police at the time against fifteen of the sixteen Bryn Estyn care workers who were subsequently arrested. The exception was Stephen Norris who had already been convicted in relation to another home. The allegations against the other fifteen members of staff were in effect 'bred' by the investigation itself and in particular by the fantasy out of which the investigation grew – namely that a paedophile ring was operating in children's homes in North Wales. Indeed, all 365 allegations which emerged were bred in the same way.

This pattern, in which trawling operations lead to the progressive multiplication of suspects, is characteristic. In many instances a single completely unreliable allegation, which is subsequently discredited, shown to be impossible, or rejected by the prosecution themselves, is allowed to trigger massive police investigations whose main effect is to encourage the proliferation of further unreliable allegations – and eventually to trigger entirely new police operations either in neighbouring forces, or in completely different parts of the country.

Once the North Wales investigation was underway it was all but inevitable that it would spread not only north and east to Merseyside, Cheshire, Lancashire, Yorkshire and Northumberland, but also south to South Wales, Somerset, Devon and Cornwall. The former staff of one home in Wales had every reason to believe they had been 'inoculated' against the trawling operations which were spreading through the principality. Tŷ Mawr in Gwent had, after all, been investigated by Lord Williams and effectively cleared of any charges of serious abuse.

This finding, however, appears to have made no impression on the Gwent Police. In 1998 they launched Operation Flight, perhaps the most intensive of all trawling inquiries. By the year 2000 this trawl, in which 30 police officers were involved full-time, had produced allegations against more than 100 former members of staff. According to Detective Chief Inspector Terry Hapgood, who then headed the operation, inquiries were continuing: 'The investigation, although we've been going 2½ years now, is still very much in its infancy and there's still a long way to go... In round figures we're looking at approximately

7,000 people that actually went through Tŷ Mawr and the remit we've been given is to interview as many of those as we can trace. We're not a third of the way through yet.' At that point some 5,000 people remained to be contacted.

Meanwhile the neighbouring South Wales Police force had sixty officers dedicated to Operation Goldfinch. This grew out of an inquiry set up in 1996 to investigate allegations of abuse at a single care home. As almost always happens, this inquiry generated allegations against other homes and in April 1997 Operation Goldfinch was launched to investigate further. By 2000 it covered a total of 81 homes. Detectives said at that point that they had identified 581 suspects. Ten had already been convicted and had received a total of 85 years imprisonment. The scale of the inquiry was such that it eventually required an establishment of 46 police officers and support staff.

Many of these inquiries were vitalised and sustained by the massive publicity which surrounded the setting up of the North Wales Tribunal in 1996 and its opening hearings in 1997. When the Tribunal finally published its report in February 2000, the renewed publicity served in effect as an advertising campaign directed towards potential complainants, and many more came forward to make civil claims. Sometimes these new allegations became the basis of new criminal investigations and yet more trawling operations were launched.

A Tribunal set up to investigate a national scandal – the 'cover-up' which had allegedly taken place in North Wales – had, in practice, served to revive, intensify and enlarge the moral panic which had led to its creation in the first place.

So many different police trawling operations have now been launched, and so difficult are they to keep track of, that Gwent Police set up 'the Historic Abuse Database', a national archive under the direction of Chief Superintendent Ian Johnston. In 2001 Johnston confirmed that, out of 43 police forces in England and Wales at least 32 had 'major abuse inquiries' running. Trawling operations which are completed or still in progress include Operation Flight in Gwent itself, Operation Care on Merseyside, Operation Goldfinch in South Wales, Operation Cleopatra in Greater Manchester, Operation Lentisk in Devon, Operation React in Bristol and Avon, Operations Courier, Clyde and Pudsey in North Yorkshire, Operation Camassia in West Midlands, Operation Orchid in West Mercia, Operation Harpoon in Nottinghamshire, Operation Screen in West Yorkshire, Operation Rose in Northumberland, Operations Lapwing, Aldgate, Kite and Juno in

Humberside, Operation Diamond in Lincolnshire, Operation Panorama in Avon and Somerset, and Operation Nevada in Lancashire. Some forces have had more than one inquiry. The Metropolitan Police, for example, were at one point conducting at least 6 different trawling operations simultaneously. These included Operation Middleton which started in Lambeth, but rapidly became a nationwide inquiry seeking to trace an alleged paedophile ring which, according to a newspaper headline, had supposedly claimed thousands of victims.[579]

All these investigations had a genealogy which linked them, at least indirectly, to North Wales. In the case of the investigation by the South Wales Police there was an additional link. John Jevons, who had been director of social services for Clwyd when Alison Taylor approached Dennis Parry in 1991, had subsequently become director of social services for Cardiff. In 1996 he was approached by another 'whistleblower', who once again raised the possibility that a paedophile ring was operating in the children's homes for which he was responsible.

Jevons, a devout Methodist who had originally trained as a mathematician, was a capable and efficient manager. Used to dealing with a multi-million pound budget and managing a staff of several thousand, he was, perhaps of necessity, remarkably trusting of officialdom. He saw it as his role to pass on not only allegations to the police but also alarmist and unfounded claims about paedophile rings. He appears not to have recognised the extent to which, in doing so, he was lending his own authority to such claims. Having played a key role in helping to trigger a moral panic in North Wales, this conscientious public servant now once again helped to mobilise a Welsh police force amidst press reports that the new investigation was seeking to apprehend the members of a paedophile ring.[580]

Some of the complaints collected in South Wales were, of course, true. They thus helped convict social workers who had indeed betrayed the trust placed in them. But it is quite clear that many complaints were fabricated. Those who find it difficult to believe that anyone would deliberately invent an allegation of sexual abuse should ponder the case of Richard Scott. Scott was once a social worker in South Wales; he was arrested during the course of Operation Goldfinch, and his trial took place in April 2000.

Many of those who were close to Scott, or had worked with him, believed unreservedly that he was an innocent man. This view was shared by his legal team. At the last moment they managed to track down Michael Selby, a former resident of the home where Scott had worked. Selby spoke highly of Scott and praised the standards of care at the home. He was clearly going to be a key witness for the defence and he gave a strong statement over the phone. He then inquired why people would make allegations if they were not true. It was suggested that one possible motive was compensation. Selby asked what amounts were involved and the inexperienced solicitor conducting the interview suggested the relatively low sum of £10,000. Later that same day this key defence witness walked into his local police station and made an allegation of indecent assault against Richard Scott. He immediately became a prosecution witness. Although Selby's evidence was discredited in court, Scott was convicted on the testimony of others and sentenced to 4½ years.

The story of the witness who changed sides starkly illustrates the dangers of police trawling operations. The temptations for potential witnesses are heightened by the manner in which police officers make their approach. In an aide-memoire compiled for the South Wales inquiry, officers are instructed to disguise the fact that they are policemen during their approach to a potential witness:

> Officers should be as casual as possible both in their dress and approach to a possible victim …
>
> It may be necessary when visiting a victim's home only to give your first name, in which case, one officer should attend and ask the victim to meet you in an area which is not crowded by members of the public.
>
> Never ask a uniformed officer or a local CID officer to attend on your behalf to seek out a possible victim.

The most revealing feature of the South Wales Police protocol is that potential witnesses are repeatedly referred to as 'victims'. The implicit assumption is that *all* former residents of care homes are likely to be victims; the main task of police officers is to coax them into 'disclosing' abuse. Officers are told that they should not necessarily take 'no' for an answer:

> You may have a 'gut feeling' that a *victim* will not disclose after an initial meeting. Be prepared to leave your name and a telephone number where either you or someone connected with the enquiry can be contacted. Explain that you are giving the *victim* time to think and that you will call back or telephone if the *victim* allows it [italics added].

One former resident of Headlands in South Wales has described his own experience of Operation Goldfinch:

> I saw nothing of any abuse happening at Headlands. It was just not like that. ... The police are trying to make something sinister out of the simplest things.
>
> ... When I spoke to the police I told them that if I wanted a few grand I could jump on the bandwagon too and get some compensation. These people don't seem to realise the consequences of saying what they are just for the sake of getting some money if the people are going to go to prison for 15 years. ...
>
> The staff were like parents really ... I did not have a bad time at all. They did not ill-treat you. They taught you right from wrong ... .
>
> I think this investigation is getting out of hand. The CID visited me for three days on the trot. I told them I had nothing bad to say about any of the staff, so I don't know why they kept coming back, it was crazy.
>
> They were throwing names at me. They were trying to see if I would say anything different. They kept on encouraging me, saying 'is there anything you have not told us' and things like that.
>
> I was not going to make anything up for them.[581]

Although the intention behind the repeated visits is to give those who were abused the opportunity to tell the truth, it is clear that this witness felt that he was being put under pressure to say that things that were *not* true.

In the Headlands investigation itself, the original complainant made a series of wholly implausible allegations, including the claim that he had been sexually abused by a train driver, Brian Green, in the cab of his train while he was driving it. It was eventually established by the police that Brian Green did not exist. By this time, however, a massive investigation had taken place. Its purpose was to gather as many allegations as possible against the members of a paedophile ring which had no more reality than the spectral train driver. As a result of this investigation, seven men found themselves facing a total of some three hundred allegations. These included a claim that one residential social worker had sexually assaulted a boy with a cucumber, and that the same social worker had witnessed a murder, and protected the murderer by his subsequent silence. So little faith did the police have in the veracity of their own complainants that they did not even dig up the patch of ground where the alleged murder victim was supposed to be buried.

In spite of the evidently false claims made by some of the complainants, the police pressed on with the prosecution. Six of the seven men were charged, four of them jointly. In a process which lasted more than three years, the cases were brought to trial at Cardiff Crown Court where they collapsed spectacularly in February 2001. A set of allegations made by a complainant who was shown conclusively to be a fantasist and a compulsive fabricator, had been allowed to trigger a massive trawling operation which had led to the collection of around 300 false allegations, and which had cost the taxpayer several million pounds.

The human cost of this case, as of every similar case, was far greater than the financial cost. One of the defendants, Arthur Rowett, an 80-year-old man, died before his name could be cleared. Another, 50-year-old Simon Smith, died after hitting his head against a radiator when he stumbled and fell while he was being interviewed in a police station. The careers of the four other men have been destroyed, and their lives blighted. In two cases, social workers threatened to separate fathers from their own children, and indeed from their wives, by removing them from the family home.

In one of the most disturbing episodes in the entire saga, the judge who directed that the three remaining defendants should be acquitted, made no comment on the horrific ordeal suffered by all seven men, and offered no endorsement of their innocence. Whereas the judge in the David Jones trial told the football manager that he would leave the court without a stain on his character, the judge who presided over the spectacular collapse of the Cardiff trial gave no such reassurance.

Most disturbingly of all, one of the men who walked free from Cardiff Crown Court in February 2001, Tony Burke, found himself facing trial again later in the year. The South Wales Police had managed to trawl another set of allegations from four men in their forties, two of whom were brothers. These complaints related to events which had supposedly happened at a care home where Tony Burke had taught thirty years earlier. Even though almost all documentary evidence had disappeared, and key witnesses had died, an application to have the trial stayed as an abuse of process was rejected by the judge.

Partly because significant evidence casting doubt on the reliability of the allegations was not presented at his trial, Tony Burke was convicted in December 2001 and sentenced to 8½ years in prison. His wife Claire, a social worker, and his three young children, have now joined the many thousands of innocent family members and friends who are the indirect victims of trawling operations, and whose punishment can never be undone by any appeal court.

71 Artists in dishonesty

AS THIS BOOK WENT TO PRESS in January 2005, Tony Burke, who corrected an earlier version of the typescript in his prison cell, received the news that his appeal, which had been heard in November 2004, had been turned down. He thus found himself in the same position as the man who is unquestionably the most prominent victim of Operation Goldfinch – Derek Brushett. A former Welsh Office inspector, Brushett has already entered the story of North Wales briefly as the trusted mentor of Carl Holden (see above, p. 119).

What Derek Brushett could never have imagined when he was being interviewed by the North Wales Police in relation to Carl Holden's allegations, was that the same police force would soon trawl a complaint against him. This complaint would lie uninvestigated in the files of the North Wales Police until it was unearthed by lawyers preparing papers for the Tribunal.

Once it was passed to the South Wales Police, however, a massive trawling operation was launched and before long Brushett, a conscientious and highly respected social services inspector, was bemused to find himself facing 44 separate allegations made by 26 complainants, none of whom had come forward of their own accord. Represented by solicitors who clearly did not understand the nature of the case, and who had prepared no effective defence, Brushett was convicted in November 1999 and sentenced to fourteen years in prison.

The reaction from Derek Brushett's community was immediate and dramatic. In the village of Dinas Powys on the outskirts of Cardiff, more than 300 people, including teachers, lecturers, businessmen, a hospital consultant and all four local GPs, banded together to oppose trawling operations and to fight for justice.

Friends of Derek Brushett (FoDB) is led by former French teacher Gail Saunders, who explains that one of the group's aims is to raise public awareness: 'We've been horrified at how ignorant the public is about how these men are being convicted,' she says. Early in 2000 the group held a silent demonstration during which they walked fourteen times around the village green, once for every year of Derek Brushett's sentence. The group has successfully lobbied MPs and local politicians, and intends to continue its campaign until Brushett's conviction is overturned.

Such wrongful convictions are tragic in themselves. What compounded the tragedy and made such injustices seem permanent is that, at the time Derek Brushett was sentenced, only one conviction obtained by trawling had been overturned on appeal.* One of the main reasons for this is that the entire judicial system continues to operate on the assumption that trials involving multiple allegations are the product of traditional methods of investigation. Allegations which are in fact the product of trawling are treated as though they have been made spontaneously by unrelated individuals. Yet in the cases of Derek Brushett, Roy Shuttleworth and Terry Hoskin, and in countless other cases, the vast majority of the complainants are linked by one crucial fact: they have all been visited by police officers before making any complaint. Brushett, Shuttleworth and Hoskin were all granted leave to appeal but all three (along with many others) had their appeals rejected. As late as December 2002, more than a decade after the appearance of the *Independent on Sunday*'s story about Bryn Estyn, the possibility that a police investigation might be responsible for contaminating evidence on a quite massive scale had still not been recognised by any British court of law.

There had, however, been some signs that trawling operations were causing judicial unease. In York Crown Court in June 1999, Judge Jonathan Crabtree dismissed a care home case altogether. 'The courts must draw a line somewhere,' he said. 'Is every teacher in England to lie awake at night wondering which child they have offended twenty years ago might suddenly decide to go to the police and complain? Anyone who is in charge of children is vulnerable to allegations of assault from some dissatisfied or angry child, and if no complaint is made for months or years how can any teacher, social worker, nurse defend themselves? How is he or she going to be able to ... prove his or her innocence after so much time has passed?'

However, Judge Crabtree's remarks demonstrate the clear persistence of the habit of mind which inhibits or even prevents understanding of the real dangers of police trawling. For even in this relatively enlightened pronouncement the assumption is made that it is the 'children'

---

* This was the case of Brian Percival, the store keeper at Greystone Heath, who had won his appeal in 1998, (see above, p. 474).

who, after many years, 'suddenly decide to go to the police and complain'. What Judge Crabtree does not recognise here is that in care home investigations the complainants, who are actually adults, scarcely ever go to the police. The police come to them.

Given this strong residue of traditional attitudes it is interesting that, some two months later, in another legal pronouncement on the same issue, Judge Crabtree (although he still talks about 'children') does recognise one of the points missed in his initial remarks. On 10 August 1999 he opened the trial of Roy Fawcett, a former residential social worker in North Yorkshire, by cautioning the jury. Police forces which had 'fished' for allegations of sexual abuse in children's homes, he said, were in danger of garnering 'false accusations, childhood fantasies and dreams'. He told the jury that: 'Over the past three years or more police forces around the country have been investigating possible child abuse at many children's homes going back 20 or 30 years. They are not waiting for complaints. Instead they have asked children who used to live there if they have any complaints to make regarding abuse, both physical and sexual.' The Judge said that it was not surprising that many of those asked had said 'yes'. He said that some of the widespread accusations were true, but others were false. He asked the jury to keep this in mind and put out of their minds everything they had previously heard about abuse in care homes.

By warning the jury in this way Judge Crabtree was attempting to restore balance and fairness to a trial of the kind where most defendants are left to cope, unprotected, with the massive prejudice against care workers which has been generated by the media in recent years. Roy Fawcett was acquitted on all the counts he faced. He is perhaps the only care worker in recent years who, as the result of this prudent warning to the jury, had any real chance of receiving a fair trial.

Other cases where the evidence, viewed dispassionately, suggests that the defendants are completely innocent, have had very different outcomes. To investigate such trials is to enter a grotesque Alice-in-Wonderland world in which known criminals, sometimes with long records of deception, swear solemn oaths on the Bible and give testimony which sends decent men to prison. It is a world in which lies told to gain love and attention are ratified by the court, and where honest service to other people is penalised with prison sentences of up to eighteen years. It is a world where the cash motive and the compensation culture have triumphed over justice.

One of the complainants in the case against Roy Shuttleworth (see above, pp. 473–4) actually had a previous conviction for conspiring to gain money by deception from the Criminal Injuries Compensation Board. This man had deliberately slashed an accomplice's back with a Stanley knife. Partly because he had got drunk first in order to overcome his inhibitions, the wound he inflicted was so severe that it required 102 stitches. The plot to gain compensation came to light in the casualty department of the local hospital when the 'victim' began to talk to the nurse about how much he hoped to receive for each stitch.

In spite of the doubts that might reasonably have been raised about the credibility of the assailant, Shuttleworth was convicted on the basis of his unsupported testimony and, as we have seen, was sentenced to 10 years in prison. Almost all the other complainants in his case either were or had been heroin addicts.

In another case, former care worker Brian Johnson found himself facing a number of allegations of physical and sexual abuse trawled by the South Wales Police. It became clear that the prosecution themselves did not believe the highly implausible allegations of sexual abuse which had been made against Johnson. He was therefore offered a deal according to which, if he pleaded guilty to some counts of physical abuse, all the sexual counts would be dropped. Johnson declined to plead guilty to physical assaults he said he had not committed. His case then went to trial; he was found guilty on a number of counts of sexual abuse, was sentenced to 15 years, and was led from the court shouting out that he was innocent.

One allegation against Johnson and his co-defendant Geoffrey Morris (who pleaded guilty to a number of counts) involved a claim of satanic abuse: a black cloak, an altar and the drinking of blood were supposedly used as ritual preludes to sexual assault. Although the jury rejected this allegation, they accepted another from the same man that actually ran counter to the evidence before them. The man claimed that Morris had driven him in a minibus to a venue where he was sexually abused by both Morris and Johnson. Even though Morris could not drive, and even though this was accepted by the Crown, the jury convicted Johnson on this count.

Another witness was a woman who claimed that Johnson had indecently assaulted her. Her psychiatric records suggested that she was unable to distinguish between truth and fantasy and that she had made numerous allegations which were not true. Ten years previously, after making an allegation of rape which had resulted in a police investigation, she eventually admitted that she had made up the entire incident. At Johnson's trial, however, she claimed that the rape had taken place after all. In spite of a great deal of other evidence, including the testimony of her former foster mother, which completely undermined the credibility of this witness, Johnson was found guilty of indecently assaulting her.

It was only after his first appeal had been turned down that Johnson's lawyers discovered details about the criminal past of his principal accuser which had never been disclosed at the time of the trial. On one occasion this man, who was well-known to the police as a burglar, had been still inside the house he was burgling when two police officers arrived. Instead of giving himself up or attempting to escape, the man climbed into one of the beds in the house and, when asked by the police what he was doing there, calmly told them that he lived there. Only when he was asked to get out of bed did it become apparent that he was fully clothed and still wearing his shoes. It was on the basis of the word of this witness, who was clearly an artist in dishonesty, that the jury had convicted Johnson of horrific sexual crimes he had not committed. At the time of writing, Johnson is still in prison waiting for the CCRC to refer his case back to the court.

Such cases are in many respects typical. The majority of convicted care workers who continue to protest their innocence were found guilty on the basis of uncorroborated evidence given by men with convictions for crimes involving dishonesty – or even, in some cases, murder or armed robbery. In a survey of such cases, the All Party Parliamentary Group for Abuse Investigations obtained the following information from solicitors: in the 32 prosecutions in question there were 282 complainants. 92 per cent of these people were known to the police, 84 per cent had convictions, and at least 34 per cent were interviewed while they were actually in prison.[582]

Of course it is not the case that a complainant's criminal background necessarily indicates that his or her complaint is untrue. The most balanced appraisal of the dilemma posed by such allegations is perhaps that of the Canadian judge, the Honourable Fred Kaufman. In his 2002 report on the compensation-driven abuse allegations made in relation to care homes in Nova Scotia, Kaufman says this:

> Sexual abuse claimants should not be regarded as immune from the temptations and incentives – particularly monetary – that move human beings generally, just because they allege sexual abuse. The fact

that young offenders may be targeted for abuse because of their vulnerability, and because they are less likely to be believed, does not mean that their institutional history for deceit or criminality should be discarded in evaluating their credibility. The fact that abused young offenders may be reticent to report their victimisation while in an institutional setting should be considered in assessing the importance, or lack thereof, of an untimely [ie long-delayed] complaint, as should the fact that their complaints may only have been forthcoming after the Government created expectations of compensation for abuse.[583]

In Britain perhaps the most disturbing of all the cases involving complainants with a history of dishonesty is that of Paul Hadfield. Hadfield, 49, was a quiet unassuming man. Dedicated to his work, he held the kind of liberal or left-leaning views which led him to sympathise deeply with the damaged young men he looked after. Until 1997, he was officer-in-charge of Hillrise Children's Centre in Hereford and Worcester and a number of his colleagues regarded him as the best residential social worker they had ever known. In 1997 however, a young man he had worked with as an adolescent made allegations of sexual abuse against him.

Paul's sister Jenny Varley, the deputy head of an infants' school, recalled the moment when he first told her what had happened. 'I went over to see Paul one day. We always used to go and walk the dog. He'd said to me previously "There's something I want to talk to you about but I don't want to discuss it over the phone". So we went out and he said "Somebody's made these dreadful allegations".' When he explained the kind of allegations they were, and who had made them, Jenny immediately felt confident. 'My reaction was just disbelief. This can't come to court. How can anyone believe someone who has a history of lying? I didn't believe that it would go any further.'

The man who had made the allegations, Mark Walmer, had been convicted of fraud. In 1996 he had obtained a wheelchair and persuaded a friend to pose as his full-time carer and to push him into the local Elim Pentecostal Church. Here, over several months, Walmer convincingly passed himself off as a brain-damaged invalid with a mental age of six months.

There can perhaps be no clearer instance of a deception which appears to have been undertaken principally to gain attention and affection – of 'lying for love'. However, in this case, as in some others, there was also a financial element. After some months Walmer and his accomplice made up a story that they had been burgled and that money they had saved towards a new wheelchair had been stolen. A special wheelchair fund was set up for him and hundreds of pounds were raised.

By the time he had received this money Walmer was beginning to feel trapped in his role. One day, when the pastor was away on holiday, he arranged for his friend to push his wheelchair down to the front of the church. As the congregation prayed for him he suddenly stood up. He then started to walk and to talk, claiming he had been miraculously cured. There was amazement and great rejoicing among the congregation, and thanks were offered to God.

The deception was only exposed when Pastor Barry Killick, having returned from holiday and suspecting that, on this occasion, no miracle of healing had been wrought, insisted on taking Walmer to a GP – who concluded that his 'symptoms' were part of an elaborate charade. Walmer and his friend were later found guilty of fraud. The judge described Walmer as a 'scoundrel' and sentenced him to eighteen months. The story was widely reported under such headlines as 'Long Stretch for Lazarus' and 'Con the Baptist'.

One feature of the story, however, had not been reported. No sooner had Walmer been forced by the pastor to confess than, in an attempt to excuse his conduct, he began to make allegations of sexual abuse against the members of the church who had cared for him. These allegations were entirely false. When he subsequently made allegations against Paul Hadfield, however, the police launched a trawling operation. They obtained other allegations and the case came to trial in January 1999. The jury were unable to reach a verdict but the Crown Prosecution Service insisted on a second trial.

This meant that all the complainants had, in effect, a dress-rehearsal. Mark Walmer benefited from this most. Many who watched him give evidence found that his performance in the second trial was powerful and disturbing. When it was put to him that he had reacted to the exposure of his wheelchair scam by making allegations of sexual abuse, he lied on oath, saying that this had not happened. When he was asked whether he was seeking compensation, he lied again. Only when the defence barrister revealed the details of a civil claim he had already submitted did Walmer admit that he was seeking money.

Another witness, Ian Jonson, also claimed that he had been sexually abused by Hadfield, but the abuse he alleged in the first trial could not have taken place. In the second trial Jonson changed his evidence to make his allegation more plausible. But he went on to admit that Paul

Hadfield's name had been given to him by the police officer who questioned him.

By the end of the first week it was clear that the prosecution did not believe their own witnesses. As in the case of Brian Johnson, they offered Hadfield a deal. If he would plead guilty to some of the cruelty charges, they would drop all the sexual charges. Hadfield refused. 'I am not going to plead guilty to something I didn't do,' he told his sister, Jenny.

In the event the jury could not reach a decision in relation to Walmer. But they found Hadfield guilty of sexually abusing Jonson. Hadfield was devastated. He subsequently wrote a note in which he suggested that he would never have been found guilty had it not been for Walmer's 'carefully choreographed' performance and the effect it had on the jury. What should also be underlined is that Jonson's allegation would never have been made at all had the police not responded to Walmer's original complaint by trawling.

In September 1999 Hadfield was due to return to the court for sentencing. A friend, Tony Kokke, had arranged to pick him up from his house but found him slumped in his armchair. Using his botanical knowledge, Paul Hadfield had killed himself with a lethal mixture of plant toxins. 'He went to his death protesting his innocence and I want that to be a matter of public record,' said Kokke at the inquest. 'I found a letter waiting for me at home which stated that he felt his life had been destroyed by the justice system and that he could no longer go on.'

In a letter to his eldest sister Jean, Paul Hadfield wrote:

The past two and a half years have been disastrous for me and I am left without a career, without a job, and branded as a pervert and a criminal. ... The only things that have kept me sane are the knowledge that I am innocent, the support of my family, and the support of friends, colleagues and ex-colleagues who in high numbers have made it clear that they do not believe the allegations, and insist that the specific allegations of which I was convicted could not have happened. Sadly, although I am truly blessed by having known these good and caring people, as soon as the allegations were given any real credence my life was over.

I have worked hard and committed myself to caring for children. Some of these kids were great despite their difficulties, the majority were OK, but a very small percentage are the dregs of our society. The police appeared to select that small percentage.

I now feel that, despite meeting and working with some of the finest people who exist, my life has been a total waste and I regret ever going into child care.

He went on to express the hope that his friends would contact the press:

I would like maximum publicity to be given in order to help others and to help the general public understand just what type of child we are likely to be dealing with and how vulnerable we are. I would like questions asked about how the police question potential complainees and how the system is open to abuse... There is so much wrong with the way retrospective allegations of sexual abuse are investigated and the public perception of sexual abuse in the 70s and 80s and something must be done about this.

72 The long march to freedom

PAUL HADFIELD IS BUT ONE of many residential social workers who have been convicted by the courts *in spite* of evidence which suggested that they were innocent. It would seem that in almost every case judges and juries have treated trawled complaints, which would never have been made at all but for the action of the police, as though they were spontaneous allegations.

By the year 2001 the demonisation of residential social workers, which effectively began in North Wales in 1991, had been carried by social workers, by zealous police officers, by crusading journalists and by the Waterhouse report itself, into every corner of the country. Thousands of completely innocent care workers found themselves facing allegations of physical or sexual abuse and as many as a hundred of these (perhaps more) had been wrongly convicted as a result.

Such was the image of evil which had been projected onto care homes and those who once worked in them that it was possible for a single determined individual to mobilise an entire police force.

Alison Taylor provides but one example of such an individual. Even as the North Wales Tribunal report was published, the investigation which she had played such a major role in triggering was continuing and at least three more former care workers in North Wales were facing trial. In August 1999, Roger Griffiths, formerly principal and proprietor of Gatewen Hall School, New Broughton, Wrexham, was sentenced to eight years imprisonment. His former wife, Anthea Roberts was also sentenced to two years. Both continue to protest their innocence, as does Richard Groome. In a bitter irony the latter was sentenced to eight years in July 2000 after he had himself voluntarily come forward as a witness to the North Wales Tribunal because he believed child care practices were in need of improvement.

As the North Wales investigation continued to claim innocent victims, another inquiry, in some respects even more bizarre, was unfolding in Devon. This too had come into being largely as the result of the efforts of a single individual.

In the mid 1990s, Gerry Houlden, a former resident of Forde Park

School at Newton Abbot in Devon, had attempted to sue Devon County Council for the treatment he said he suffered there, and for the school's alleged failure to provide him with a proper education. However he has said that at the time the council 'told me to go away'. He was not deterred, however. As he later told David Rose, 'The only way forward, as I saw it, was I had to speak to other people.'[584]

Houlden now used local radio and newspapers to 'advertise' for other alleged victims. By early 1997 he says that 65 former residents of Forde Park had contacted him and he wrote to all of them urging them to start civil actions against the council. He also lobbied the police but at first they said that they were not prepared to launch any inquiry because of the time which had passed – thirty years in some cases – since the offences which were now being alleged.

Concerned that it was not being taken seriously, the 'Forde Park Survivors Group', as Houlden's organisation was called, went back to the press. A number of lurid newspaper features now appeared, some of them making outlandish allegations that pupils had been forced to endure brain operations as part of a sinister regime of experimentation carried out behind closed doors on defenceless residents. After the group had also organised lobbies of parliament, Devon and Cornwall Police finally launched an investigation which they named Operation Lentisk.

It was at this point that there was another significant development in the Devon investigation. The group which Houlden had founded, many of whose members were now making allegations of sexual abuse, managed to secure the services of a local solicitor, Penny Ayles. As David Rose has reported in the *Observer*: 'Between December 1999 and April 2001, Ayles organised three mass "case conferences" for the survivors at an Exeter hotel. There, she and the barristers in the case told the claimants how their case was going and explained the damages they could expect – up to £50,000 for buggery, but only "single figures" for mere physical assaults.'

Soon after these meetings had been held, a series of trials took place and four men, Patrick Fitzgerald, John Maybery, Derek Hooper and Brian Ely faced allegations made by former residents of Forde Parke, some of whom were members of Houlden's organisation. Although Fitzgerald, ably defended by barrister Linda Strudwick, was acquitted, Maybery, Hooper and Ely were sentenced to a total of thirty-three years imprisonment. All three men have continued to protest their innocence and the conviction of John Maybery has already been overturned by the Court of Appeal. At the time of writing, however, Derek Hooper and Brian Ely are still in prison serving 15-year sentences, and yet another human tragedy brought about by police trawling continues.

For more than ten years, police trawling operations, the most bizarre and dangerous development there has ever been in modern policing methods, were allowed to go from strength to strength, virtually unchallenged by journalists, social workers, police officers, politicians or judges.

By launching trawling operations, and piling up huge numbers of allegations against individual care workers, police forces had found a way of effectively destroying the presumption of innocence.

There were, of course, some cases where justice was done even in the midst of prejudice. The case of Robin Reeves in Oxford, who was acquitted in 2000 after facing 34 counts of sexual abuse, was one of them (see Introduction, p. 5). And, in Newcastle during the same period, solicitor Gill Rutherford and her team of six barristers successfully defended some twenty cases. In one of these cases four care workers appearing in a joint trial were found not guilty. They were later to be seen on Newcastle Quayside drinking with the members of the jury who acquitted them, who were clearly disturbed that the case had ever been brought.

It was undoubtedly significant, however, that all the counts involved in this Newcastle trial, as in most of the Operation Rose cases, were of physical abuse. One of the jurors actually told a care worker whom she had helped to acquit that if the allegations had been of sexual abuse, she would almost certainly have found him guilty.

In the preponderance of allegations of physical abuse it collected Operation Rose was exceptional. Most trawling inquiries collect large numbers of sexual allegations. Their horrific nature and their tendency to induce prejudice meant that, for almost ten years, from the conviction of Frank Beck in 1991 onwards, acquittals in care home cases remained relatively rare.

For all this period it was practically impossible to persuade the mainstream media to take criticism of police trawling operations seriously.[585] However, with the collapse of the David Jones trial in December 2000 and the relentless spread of such operations from police force to police force, those who voiced concern about police methods found, almost for the first time, that their concerns were given serious attention and

that at least some politicians were prepared to express their own concerns in public.

Some of the most significant support for these concerns came from
Claire Curtis-Thomas MP. Although her political advisers warned her
that to take up this cause would be to commit political suicide, she has
drawn tributes from MPs on all sides of the house for her work. She was,
however, by no means the only politician to become involved. By January 2005, twenty had joined the All Party Group on Abuse Investigations that she chaired, including Austin Mitchell, Tim Boswell, Edward
Garnier QC, the former shadow Attorney General, and the shadow
health spokesman Earl Howe, who has developed a deep understanding of the problem of false allegations.

One of the most helpful political developments came with the publication of the report of the Home Affairs Select Committee. On 31
October 2002, a long campaign, fought by hundreds of former care
workers and championed by Curtis-Thomas, seemed finally to have
been vindicated by a House of Commons report. The gravest series of
miscarriages of justice in British legal history was at last given some
measure of official recognition.

Bob Woffinden, David Rose and I gave evidence to the first main
session of this inquiry. After three months, during which it took oral
and written evidence from many individuals and organisations including senior police officers, the Home Affairs Committee concluded that
what it called 'a new genre of miscarriages of justice' has arisen from
'the over-enthusiastic pursuit' of allegations of abuse relating to children's homes. 'I am in no doubt,' said the chairman, Chris Mullin MP,
'that a number of innocent people have been convicted and that many
other innocent people, who have not been convicted, have had their
lives ruined.' During the inquiry it was suggested by witnesses that as
many as a hundred former care workers had been wrongly convicted
as a direct result of police trawling operations, and the weaknesses in
the laws of evidence which these exploited.

The Committee's strong report, which robustly questioned many
received views, recommended a series of safeguards to protect people
who are investigated during the course of trawling operations. It called
for the compulsory audio or video recording of police interviews with
alleged victims, anonymity for the accused and wider powers for the
Criminal Cases Review Commission to enable alleged miscarriages of
justice to be reviewed.

In a vital section of its report, which seemed to have far-reaching implications, the Home Affairs Committee accepted the view that the law on similar fact evidence should be reformed. It recommended to the Home Office that multiple allegations made by different complainants should not be admitted into a trial before a jury unless there are 'striking similarities' which justify their being heard together. This would restore the relatively cautious approach adopted by the House of Lords in 1975 in the case of *Boardman*, and undo the dangerous relaxation of the evidence rules which was introduced in 1991. What made the Home Affairs Committee's recommendation even more important was that it simultaneously urged that the presumption favouring severance in sexual abuse cases should be restored. In other words, where there are no striking similarities between allegations, the counts should be 'severed' and heard in separate trials in order to avoid prejudicing juries.

That the Home Affairs Committee should have reached such conclusions was a major triumph for all those who had campaigned against police trawling. That the government's response to these recommendations should have been one of complete rejection came as no surprise.

A witch-hunt of the power and intensity of that which has raged in Britain for so long does not disappear overnight. It would be naive to suppose that those who have staked their political reputations on policies which have inadvertently furthered that witch-hunt, would be likely to renounce their views simply in response to a report by a select committee.

What has been much more encouraging than the view of the government has been the response of the judiciary. In a passage of its report which was addressed directly to the judiciary, the Committee acknowledged that 'many of these recommendations are simply closing the door after the horse has bolted.' It was, said the Committee, 'all the more important, therefore, that the Criminal Cases Review Commission and the appeal court take a robust approach to the review of suspected wrongful convictions.'

It was perhaps no coincidence that the first two trawling appeals to be heard after the publication of the Home Affairs Committee report appear to have been approached with unusual attention by the three appeal court judges involved.

One of these cases involved two different appeals which were heard together by the same court. The men who were appealing were none other than Basil Williams-Rigby and Mike Lawson. After a long and complex hearing in which new evidence was brought forward, and in which the court expressed grave concern at the prejudicial manner in which unsubstantiated allegations against a massive number of St George's workers had been introduced into the trial, the court quashed both of the convictions.

Lawson and Williams-Rigby were free to return to their families and their friends who had so faithfully supported them. On the same evening they were interviewed on the BBC *PM* programme. To an audience still largely unaware of the true nature, or even the existence of police trawling, Mike Lawson said this:

> If you're accused of an imaginary crime, allegedly committed on an unspecified date years ago, then of course it's virtually impossible to defend yourself other than truthfully saying it didn't happen. When I was a detective, if a murder had been committed, you'd set out to find who'd done it. But in these cases the police are actively soliciting complaints by sending letters to people in prison. Sadly some of these chaps are succumbing to the temptation... I don't feel bitter but feel sorry for those who have told lies; they have been tempted by the system.

Basil Williams-Rigby told reporters:

> My feeling is one of exhilaration. It has been three years and seven months. I have counted the days. Our long march for freedom has finished. But we will be starting another long march to stop others being caught up by similar trawling operations. There are hundreds of innocent people in prison because of it. This method can never be justified.

Just a few days earlier, the Court of Appeal had quashed another trawling conviction. This time the man who walked free was John Maybery. In this case the appeal court made an explicit reference to trawling and its dangers:

> The evidence that was put before the jury in this case was the result of investigations over a significant period of time and was produced in large part from the results of questionnaires which had been sent to former children at the school.
>
> The case therefore presented what is now unhappily a common problem for the courts, namely, a case of sexual abuse which of itself is always a potentially difficult offence for a jury to consider because of the usually private nature of the events surrounding the allegations, which is made the more difficult because of the very substantial delay which has occurred, in this case some thirty years. There is no doubt

that much concern has been expressed about the ability of the courts to deal fairly with allegations which are of such antiquity. The Home Affairs Committee has produced a report in which it identifies a number of features which cause concern and those are features which have caused concern to the courts over the years and have been the subject matter of directions to the jury to seek to obviate the particular difficulties which old offences such as these create. The particular problems that were identified by the Home Affairs Committee, quite apart from the problems created by delay itself, relate to *the fact that in many cases the evidence is produced by trawling for witnesses which carries with it the risk of instilling into those who are providing the information, in effect, the indication that certain answers may be expected by those who are making the inquiries.* The fact is that it is not easy to be able to make a proper inquiry into the way in which the evidence has ultimately emerged in a way which enables a court to evaluate the quality of the evidence satisfactorily. There are also problems that arise as a result of the fact that in many such cases a number of allegations are tried together with the inevitable consequence that there is the prejudice to a defendant of what may appear to be the coincidence of similar allegations.[586]

In the Maybery judgment, for the first time in British judicial history, both the existence of police trawling and its dangers were explicitly recognised. The long march to freedom had finally begun.

73 Fragments of a witch-hunt

One of the obstacles which has for so long blocked the route of 'the long march to freedom' of which Basil Williams-Rigby speaks has been the received version of the story of North Wales. Until now this obstacle has been rendered all but immovable by the ratification of that received version by Sir Ronald Waterhouse's Tribunal of Inquiry.

The fact that an official inquiry should have functioned to conceal the truth about North Wales rather than reveal it, should not ultimately be surprising. What the Tribunal hearings and the report help to illustrate is something of which historians have long been aware. Witch-hunts do not generally happen *in spite* of the contributions made by judges and official inquiries. They often happen because of these contributions. It was in 1742 that Montesquieu, wrote, 'There is no crueller tyranny than that which is perpetrated under the shield of law and in the name of justice.'[587]

From the day that the *Independent on Sunday* published its sensational story about North Wales, what had come into being was a narrative of immense power. Given the fact that this story was rapidly accepted by politicians, senior police officers and social workers, it was all but inevitable, in view of its ingredients, that a witch-hunt would result.

To refer in the twenty-first century to the creation of a 'witch-hunt' may seem to some people intemperate or historically inaccurate or both. In a debate about police trawling in the House of Commons in October 2002, John Denham MP, the Minister for Policing, Crime Reduction and Community Safety, took exception to the terms used by several members of parliament in the debate to which he was responding: 'I must say ... that the widespread use of expressions such as "witch-hunt" does this complex and important issue no justice. I would not like to give credence to the idea that it is being dealt with in the atmosphere of a witch-hunt.'[588] Other commentators have also taken exception to the idea. It is often said that it is easy to overdo the comparison between the zeal to hunt paedophiles and the witch-trials that took place at Salem in 1692: 'After all,' as one journalist has written, 'witches do not exist, but paedophiles most disturbingly do.'[589]

To say this, however, is to misunderstand the nature of witch-hunts. Historically, witches *did* exist. There was never any doubt about the reality of those who, throughout the early Middle Ages, practised ritual magic or attempted to work supernatural harm. What turned mild anxieties about practitioners of magic into the great European witch-hunt was the gradual emergence of a demonological fantasy. Under the influence of this fantasy, ecclesiastical zealots saw witches not as the real and relatively harmless human beings they were, but as members of an imaginary world-wide conspiracy – an evil and highly organised cult, whose supremely powerful members flew through the air to gatherings where they worshipped their master, Satan. Even in Britain, where the vision of an orgiastic Sabbat was never developed as it was on the continent, the belief grew up that witches were in league with Satan, and that they were part of a devilish conspiracy given to preying on innocent children and undermining Christendom. Once this powerful idea began to grip the minds of learned men, the empirical reality on which it was based became all but irrelevant. So too did the requirement for reliable evidence or proof. Because of the sheer evilness of the crime in question, the balance of justice was systematically and deliberately tipped in favour of the supposed victims of those who were said to be witches. Once this had happened, completely innocent men and women could find themselves arraigned and burnt as witches even though they had never attempted to cast a spell or practise ritual magic at all. Those who *had* practised magic or experimented with the occult (and to that extent were 'guilty') were almost as much victims of a witch-hunting mentality as the wholly innocent people who were accused with them. For it was the demonological fantasy of what they had done, as opposed to the reality, that had become the principal reason both for hunting them down and punishing them with such exceptional rigour.

During the last 30 years, because of the depths of our enduring anxieties, we have managed to demonise those who sexually abuse children in almost exactly the same way. What makes the fantasy so powerful is precisely the fact that paedophiles exist. There can, or at least there should, be no doubt that child sexual abuse is one of the most serious social problems of our age, and that it is more widespread than many people are prepared to accept. But onto this palpable and disturbing reality we too have projected a fantasy. According to this fantasy those who sexually abuse children are seen not simply as human beings who have committed criminal acts, but as the ultimate incarnations of darkness, evil and cruelty. So powerful has this fantasy become and so urgent is our need to rid the world of anyone who might conceivably be a paedophile, that the requirement for evidence has all but disappeared. It is for this reason that the innocent are almost as likely to be arraigned as the guilty.

When, in the late 1970s and 1980s, social workers in California – and later in Britain – allowed themselves to be gripped by the belief that young children were falling victim to systematic sexual abuse by organised satanic cults, they unwittingly revived the demonological fantasy which lay at the heart of the great European witch-hunt. It was this fantasy that many highly intelligent people embraced as a reality.

When this fantasy was discredited during the early 1990s, the belief system it belonged to did not disappear. Instead it was 'desatanised'. In 1993, two young nursery nurses, Dawn Reed and Christopher Lillie, who worked together in the Shieldfield nursery in Newcastle, found themselves the victims of a version of the same fantasy. Wrongly accused of perpetrating vile forms of sexual crime on the young children they cared for, they were portrayed as part of a sinister ring whose members abused children behind black doors. It was this secularised version of an ancient demonological fantasy which drove the persecution of Reed and Lillie onwards for nine long years, sometimes placing their lives in danger. Although they were acquitted in a criminal trial in July 1994, Newcastle City Council refused to accept the verdict and appointed a review team of psychologists and social workers who found them guilty over the heads of the court. It was only in August 2002, after a six-month libel trial in which they successfully sued the four authors of the city council's report, that their reputations were finally restored.[590]

Shieldfield, however, was not the only context in which a 'desatanised' version of an ancient demonological fantasy claimed innocent victims. For there had already emerged, elsewhere in Britain, some two or three years before Reed and Lillie were first accused, an even more dangerous variation on the same theme. This was the belief that children's homes had been taken over by paedophile rings.

As has already been noted, this belief did not originate in North Wales; its first coherent expression had been in 1980 in relation to the Kincora working boys' hostel in East Belfast. It had been in this connection that rumours first began to circulate about the existence of a paedophile ring whose members were so distinguished that they had effectively been guaranteed immunity from investigation and prosecution.

The notion that the great and the good had been co-opted by an evil conspiracy was not in itself a modern one. A very similar notion had been part of the great European witch-hunt. In his commentary on the *Malleus Maleficarum,* the fifteenth-century witch-finders' manual written by two Dominican monks, the modern scholar Sydney Anglo draws attention to this aspect of the fantasy. Not only, he notes, were witches supposed to satisfy their own 'filthy lusts'; they also pandered to the carnal desires of great men:

> And it was through such men, whom the witches protect from other harm, that 'there arises the great danger of the time, namely, the extermination of the Faith'. ... Here we see the whole conspiracy laid bare. Men of the noblest birth, governors, the rich and the powerful, are all in thrall to their demonically dedicated lovers. Thus witches are themselves protected. Thus they increase in power.[591]

The potency of this kind of conspiracy-thinking resided in the fact that it placed enormous psychological pressure on those who were rich and powerful – and on magistrates themselves – to visibly redouble their efforts to arraign witches wherever and whenever they could. Any citizens who did not support this crusade might attract the suspicion that they were wedded to evil themselves.

When the *Independent on Sunday* published its story in 1991, suggesting that an evil paedophile ring based at Bryn Estyn was being covered up by the very police force which was supposed to be investigating it, and when it clearly implied that one senior police officer was a part of this ring, it was giving currency to the same ancient fantasy. When, as happened eventually, rumours of the involvement of senior conservative politicians began to circulate, the fantasy became even more potent.[592]

It was just such a fantasy which *Private Eye* endorsed a year later when it joined in the attempt to name and shame Gordon Anglesea, and alleged the involvement 'of a number of the local great and good, as members of a paedophile ring' which supposedly preyed on boys at Bryn Estyn (see above, pp. 292–4).

For conspiracy-thinking of this kind to be translated into a witch-hunt, it was not necessary that every detail of the fantasy should be believed unreservedly by all who were exposed to it. As in the great European witch-hunt itself, it sufficed that it should be driven forward by a small number of zealous believers who would persuade the civil authorities to adapt their procedures in order to accommodate their zeal.

By the time Alison Taylor had persuaded Councillors Malcolm King and Dennis Parry to wed themselves to her cause, the power of the new witch-hunting fantasy was already considerable. When the director of social services, John Jevons, suspended disbelief in the idea of a paedophile ring based at Bryn Estyn, the power of the fantasy was greatly increased. When the North Wales Police were mobilised to investigate the alleged ring, its momentum was already vast.

In that beliefs about paedophile rings and 'organised' sexual abuse had already been widely disseminated among social workers and the newly formed child-protection divisions of police forces, it was always likely that the North Wales story would have an effect far beyond the region itself. When large-scale police trawling operations spread first to Cheshire and Merseyside, and then from police force to police force until practically the entire country was affected, the making of a modern witch-hunt was all but complete.

If it is the case, as I have suggested, that the route of 'the long march to freedom' has been blocked by the received version of the story of North Wales, then it is this same obstacle which has sometimes prevented us from recognising that what has happened is indeed the creation of a witch-hunt.

In writing this book I have set out to remove that obstacle. Inevitably, because of the facts of the story, I have given a great deal of attention to the role played by Alison Taylor. But it would be wrong to conclude from this that it is my intention to pin the blame for what happened in North Wales on one person. The most disturbing feature of the North Wales story is not to be found in the conduct of Mrs Taylor herself. It is to be found in the massive and repeated failure of the authorities, of the police, of journalists, of politicians and, most critically, of a £15 million Tribunal of Inquiry, to expose her conduct or to recognise the extraordinary dangers it posed to innocent people. Far from being opposed, indeed, Alison Taylor was presented to the public as a heroine whose respect for the truth was so great that she had wrecked her own career in order to bring her complaints to public attention.

It may be the case that the North Wales story would never have taken the form that it did without the intervention of Alison Taylor. But to hold her responsible for the entire complex tragedy which has subsequently unfolded would be unjust. We certainly cannot blame Mrs Taylor for the fact that journalists, newspaper editors and judges have chosen to repose trust in her and to treat her distortions, innuendoes and fabrications as though they were reliable facts.

Ultimately the responsibility for the witch-hunt that resulted does not rest with a single residential social worker nor even the single journalist who did so much to advance it in its early stages. Nor should it rest with the local councillors and social workers or the police officers who took part in it directly. The responsibility must rest with all those of us who, in varying degrees, failed to oppose it with sufficient vigour or with sufficient timeliness and who, by our own credulity, tardiness or relative inaction, inadvertently colluded with the production of a narrative which was both false and dangerous.

What renders the story of North Wales even more disturbing is that, although it does indeed illuminate the making of a modern witch-hunt, the witch-hunt in question is but one among many. To place our own historical predicament in perspective we should perhaps recall the experience of our ancestors who lived in towns and cities in sixteenth- and seventeenth-century Europe. Those who found themselves in the midst of a witch-hunt then must almost invariably have believed that they had been caught up in some local aberration. It was only when historians had the chance to gather up the fragments of these local witch-hunts and piece them together into a single narrative that the idea of the great European witch-hunt came into being.

Today we live in the midst of a similar fragmented witch-hunt which is taking place throughout the Western world. Its extent and intensity are not generally recognised for the simple reason that the whole story has never been told in one place.

However, as we have seen, police trawling operations did not come into being in Britain without significant precursors. They were preceded by satanic abuse investigations which, both in Britain and in North America, claimed a massive number of innocent victims, some of whom are still serving prison sentences for crimes they did not commit. These satanic witch-hunts were themselves closely allied to other similar movements, especially the recovered memory movement. As this developed, from about 1980 onwards, therapists throughout the English-speaking world and beyond inadvertently encouraged hundreds of thousands of young adults to make false retrospective allegations of rape and sexual abuse against parents and other family members. Yet more false allegations (and we are talking of very large numbers) have been made in the course of marriage break-ups and custody disputes. All too often these too have been ratified by the courts.[593]

Nor do the kinds of sexual abuse crusades enumerated here exhaust the taxonomy of modern witch-hunting. One campaign which has gathered momentum rapidly over the past decade is the one now being conducted against the Roman Catholic Church. Once again it must immediately be acknowledged that some of the allegations which have been made against Roman Catholic priests – possibly the majority of the early ones – are genuine. Others, including a number based on bizarre recovered memories, are quite evidently false.

The church has greatly exacerbated its own predicament by adopting policies of concealment and denial towards cases where priests have sexually exploited the young people in their spiritual care. On too many occasions the Church has sought to suppress the facts. Out of naivety or moral dishonesty or both, it has created situations in some dioceses where known sexual offenders were given new opportunities to re-offend rather than being stopped.

The folly of the policies adopted by the Church in the past, however, should not be allowed to disguise the fact that the Catholic Church has now been demonised. The process of demonisation has inevitably made it into a target for a growing number of allegations.

Naive onlookers may assume that all these claims are being made spontaneously. However, a significant proportion are being generated by lawyers who have discovered that sexual allegations have given them access to the deep pockets of the Catholic Church, and who are actively encouraging potential clients to make new complaints. According to Patrick Schiltz, associate dean of the law school at the University of St. Thomas in Minneapolis, the current frenzy of allegations – which is particularly intense in the United States – stems from a decade-long campaign by plaintiff lawyers. 'It's like warfare,' he says. 'Phase One was for plaintiff lawyers to maximise bad publicity and destroy the credibility of the Church. Phase Two is to use that publicity to push for legislative changes. Phase Three will be to collect.'[594] An analogous process also appears to be taking place, particularly in North America, in relation to other churches, especially the Mormon Church and the Jehovah's Witnesses.[595]

The pattern which has resulted, in which a core of genuine complaints has come to be surrounded by a large and growing number of false allegations, is one which has significant parallels with the pattern of care home allegations in Britain. In Canada, as noted in the introduction, a massive number of compensation-driven false allegations have been made in relation to care homes. And in Australia the first trawling investigations have already been launched.

Another country which has developed a particularly intense and dangerous crusade against child abuse is the Republic of Ireland. Here, as in almost every modern instance, the collective fantasy which has been progressively developed has a core of reality. The beginnings of the story go back to 1994 when the authorities in Northern Ireland sought the extradition from the Republic of Father Brendan Smyth, a Catholic priest who was facing a number of counts of child sexual abuse to which he would eventually plead guilty. It would appear that he had previously been protected against allegations by his own Norbertine order, which had moved him from parish to parish as complaints arose, and failed to alert the police. Perhaps because of the age of the allegations, which went back twenty years, there was a delay of several months during which the Irish Attorney General took no action in relation to the extradition request. Unfounded reports began to circulate in Dublin that the process was being deliberately delayed in response to a request made at the highest level by the Catholic Church. An Irish opposition deputy, Pat Rabbitte, then referred in parliament to the possible existence of a document that would 'rock the foundations of this society to its very roots'. He apparently had in mind the rumoured existence of a letter written by the Primate of All Ireland, Cardinal Cathal Daly, to the Attorney General in Dublin. In this letter the Cardinal had supposedly interceded on behalf of Father Brendan Smyth and requested the delay in his extradition which had in fact taken place. No evidence has been produced that any such letter ever existed. Yet, as a direct result of the rumours which now swept the country, the Attorney General and his successor were forced to resign and the Fianna Fail government of Albert Reynolds fell, amidst talk of a dark conspiracy involving politicians, members of Opus Dei, the Knights of Columbus and others. This conspiracy was allegedly seeking to cover up the activities of paedophile priests.

It should not be necessary to labour the similarities between the imaginary conspiracy which led to the fall of an Irish government, and the imaginary conspiracies which were invoked in the early stages of the story of North Wales. The Irish story then developed in a manner which paralleled the development of the North Wales story. In 1996 the producer and director, Louis Lentin, made a television documentary about abuse in children's homes which was shown by RTE, the main public service broadcasting station in Ireland. It focused on the brutal regime which was said to have been operating during the 1950s at St Vincent's Industrial School, Goldenbridge, one of a network of children's homes or detention centres which were funded by the state

and run by the Catholic Church. The documentary featured allegations made against Sister Xavieria, one of the nuns belonging to the
Sisters of Mercy order which ran the home. The woman 'survivor' at
the centre of the film claimed that, on one occasion, she had been
caned by Sister Xavieria so severely that the entire side of her leg was
split open from her hip to her knee. She says she was treated in the
casualty department of the local hospital and believes that she received
80 to 120 stitches. No medical evidence has ever been produced to
substantiate this claim. The surgeon who ran the casualty department
at the hospital in question has given evidence which renders it highly
unlikely that such an incident ever took place. Apart from anything
else, he points out that caning would not have caused a wound of this
kind, which would have required surgical treatment under a general
anaesthetic and not stitches in a casualty department. Yet although the
evidence suggests that the woman's memory was a delusion, her testimony was widely believed at the time. In the wake of the broadcast,
atrocity stories about Goldenbridge and other industrial schools began
to proliferate.[596]

In April and May of 1999 RTE broadcast a much more extensive
account of the industrial schools in the form of a three-part documentary series, *States of Fear*, which was written, produced and directed by
the journalist Mary Raftery. The programmes contained much historical material which appeared to be soundly based. They portrayed the
industrial schools as part of a grossly underfunded and chaotic child-
care system, in which Dickensian conditions had prevailed for decades
longer than most people would have assumed possible. Most of the
schools had clearly been inadequate both pastorally and educationally.
Corporal punishment was frequently used and it seems beyond doubt
that some regimes were both repressive and brutal. The programmes
also featured a series of claims by former residents of the schools that
they had been physically or sexually abused by members of orders such
as the Christian Brothers, the Sisters of Mercy and the Sisters of Charity. References were also made to a number of unexplained deaths
which allegedly took place in these schools. Raftery herself has explicitly rejected the 'bad apple' theory which seeks to explain the acts of
abuse which were alleged as aberrations from a system which was
essentially benign:

> Were this true, it would be a valid point. However, the scale of the
> abuse of children within the industrial schools system was so vast as to

pose the most fundamental questions about the nature of religious orders in this country ... [C]hildren were savagely beaten and treated with extraordinary levels of cruelty by their religious carers in almost every single one of the fifty-two industrial and reformatory schools which existed in Ireland for most of the twentieth century. Very large numbers of the boys in particular were sexually abused and raped by male members of religious orders into whose care they were entrusted.

It is undoubtedly the case that by no means all nuns or Brothers within institutions were cruel to the child detainees. However, it is equally clear that those who did not either beat or abuse children *did not stand in the way of the often sadistic excesses of their fellow religious** [italics added].[597]

The series provoked a huge public response. As Raftery puts it, 'Outrage at the crimes committed against these children was expressed continuously for the three weeks of the series, across acres of newsprint and hours of radio broadcasts all over the country.'[598]

The reaction of the government was swift. On 11 May 1999, the date that the final programme in the series was due to be broadcast, the Irish prime minister, Bertie Ahern, made the following statement: 'On behalf of the State and of all citizens of the State, the Government wishes to make a sincere and long overdue apology to the victims of childhood abuse for our collective failure to intervene, to detect their pain, to come to their rescue.' Little more than a week later the minister for education, Michael Martin, announced the establishment of a Commission to Enquire into Childhood Abuse, chaired by a high court judge, Miss Justice Mary Laffoy. The Commission's proceedings, however, became bogged down in legal argument and delays over documents. In September 2003, after the government had proposed that the Commission would investigate only sample allegations of abuse instead of the 1,700 complaints which were before it, Mary Laffoy resigned.

In 2002 the government set up the Residential Institutions Redress Board of Ireland, whose purpose was 'to make fair and reasonable awards to people who, as children, were abused while resident in various institutions in Ireland'. The maximum payment to any individual was set at the very high level of €300,000 (or £200,000). By November 2004 it was reported that the Redress Board had already received

---

*The word 'religious' is used here as a (plural) noun in the Catholic sense of 'someone who is bound by religious vows' – usually a monk or a nun..

4,633 applications 'and continues to receive applications at a steady rate'. As was noted in the introduction to this book, an Irish government report compiled in 2004 estimated that the potential final number of claimants could be around 8,900, at a cost of €828 million in compensation payments. In view of the fact that, as this report was being compiled, the Cheshire-based solicitor Peter Garsden was advertising for British-based Irish complainants on his website, and teams of lawyers were already preparing to scour Australia, New Zealand (and, presumably, North America) in search of more allegations from expatriate Irish citizens, it is entirely possible that this estimate will be exceeded.[599]

In this case it seems beyond doubt that many children and young people did suffer abuse in the Irish industrial schools, not least because of the draconian extent to which corporal punishment was sometimes permitted and used. At the same time, however, there is clear evidence that large numbers of incidents have been fabricated, imagined or retrieved as 'memories' as a result of counselling or other forms of suggestion. It would indeed be remarkable if the creation of the Redress Board, which has extended extraordinarily generous terms both to complainants and to their lawyers, did not lead to an unusually high level of false allegations.

What has certainly happened already in Ireland is that journalists and politicians have inadvertently created a witch-hunt of their own – one in which the members of religious orders have effectively been demonised and in which false allegations have already played an extremely significant role. Just as in Britain, the narrative which was created about North Wales was wholeheartedly accepted by a number of distinguished and excellent journalists, including Paul Foot and Nick Davies, so in Ireland a narrative in which a great deal of history is mixed with a great deal of fantasy or fabrication, appears to have been adopted, with few reservations, by some of the country's leading journalists.[600]

Meanwhile, although it might be thought that 'the great children's home panic' is purely a phenomenon of the English-speaking world, similar allegations have also surfaced in continental Europe, above all in Portugal.

Whereas in Britain well-known politicians were sometimes named as being involved in the North Wales scandal but not proceeded against, in Portugal the situation is very different. There the scandal has affected both the leader of the Portuguese socialist party, Eduardo Ferro

Rodrigues, and his political protégé, 38-year-old former social security minister Paulo Pedroso.

Pedroso was a highly regarded politician who had often been spoken of as the natural heir to the leadership of the party and a future prime minister. In May 2003, however, he was arrested and spent several months in prison on remand, facing 15 allegations of sexually abusing adolescent boys formerly resident in the state-run Casa Pia network of children's homes. Although all charges against Pedroso were dropped in May 2004, it seems entirely possible that Pedroso's political career has been destroyed.

One Portuguese newspaper actually implicated Ferro Rodrigues himself in the scandal, by claiming – on the basis of no reliable evidence whatsoever – that the leader was present on an occasion when boys were being abused, and witnessed this abuse without participating in it.

The scandal is not a new one. For months, after the arrest in November 2002 of a former Casa Pia employee, Carlos Silvino, who allegedly raped young boys, Portugal was racked by rumours that the Casa Pia homes had been infiltrated by a paedophile ring. This ring supposedly supplied young boys to be sexually abused by well known politicians and celebrities. Carlos Cruz, one of the country's most famous television presenters, was arrested, as was Jorge Ritto, the former ambassador to South Africa. Also imprisoned on remand were a lawyer, a doctor, and the former director of the homes, Manuel Abrantes. All were accused of abusing children in a paedophile ring whose existence had been covered up by the authorities. Lisbon lawyer Francisco O'Neill Marques has said: 'Rich and powerful people have been detained. It makes me proud to be a lawyer.'[601]

As in Kincora and North Wales it would appear that there may be a small core of reality to the accusations of abuse made in relation to Casa Pia. But, as in North Wales, it is already quite clear that Portugal has been swept by a wave of false allegations, many of them trawled by well-intentioned police officers. And, as in North Wales, it is not the rich and powerful people initially named who have suffered most. Early in 2003 a 92-year-old man, Francisco Pedro, a simple peasant farmer from the interior of the Algarve, found himself caught up in the moral panic which spread out in ripples from the Casa Pia accusations.

Late in the summer of 2002, after Pedro, who was almost blind, had reprimanded some children for throwing stones into the village pond, the mother of one of the children burst angrily into his home and struck him. When his family complained to the local police that the woman had assaulted a defenceless old man, she responded by accusing Pedro of sexually abusing her 2½-year-old daughter. This, she now said, was the reason she had hit him.

Given the background to the accusation and the fact that the scene of the alleged crime was in full view of the village café, it seems unlikely that this accusation would, in normal circumstances, have been taken seriously. However, shortly afterwards, the Casa Pia scandal erupted and, almost exactly twelve years after the North Wales scandal was first publicised in the *Independent on Sunday*, Portugal began to experience its own children's home panic.

In February 2003, even though the scene of the alleged crime had never been investigated, the police arrested Pedro. He was charged with having sexually abused the daughter of the woman who had struck him. He spent the entire day in court, where two television crews filmed him and where he was asked by journalists when he had last had sexual intercourse with his wife.

Shamed and humiliated by the publicity, and anxious about his looming trial, he retreated into himself. A few weeks after he had been arrested, Pedro committed suicide by strangling himself with his own shoelaces. Weeks later his son contacted some of the journalists who had been at the court and suggested that they should report this outcome of their earlier coverage. The journalists declined to do so. As a matter of policy, they said, they did not give publicity to suicides lest, by putting the idea into people's heads, it might encourage others along the same path.

Instead of reporting on the suicide of 92-year-old Francisco Pedro, they continued to write, sometimes in graphic detail, stories about child sexual abuse.[602]

In Portugal the 'great children's home panic' is a relatively new phenomenon. In Britain it is already some fifteen years old. Perhaps the greatest danger we now face is that we might underestimate the damage we have already inflicted on our system of justice in our attempts to secure convictions in relation to the crimes we most abhor.

What is at stake ultimately is the presumption of innocence itself. One of the most succinct statements of the rationale behind this principle, which has been cited on a number of occasions in the House of Lords, was made by Mr Justice Sachs, sitting in the South African constitutional court in the *State v Coetzee* in 1997:

There is a paradox at the heart of all criminal procedure, in that the more serious the crime and the greater the public interest in securing convictions of the guilty, the more important the constitutional protections of the accused become. The starting point of any balancing inquiry where constitutional rights are concerned must be that the public interest in ensuring that innocent people are not convicted and subjected to ignominy and heavy sentences massively outweighs the public interest in ensuring that a particular criminal is brought to book. … Hence the presumption of innocence, which serves not only to protect a particular individual on trial, but to maintain public confidence in the enduring integrity and security of the legal system.[603]

Many observers in Britain believe that the real danger we now face is that the New Labour government, in its concern to re-balance the scales of justice in favour of 'the victim', is committed to a course which will lead to the overturning of this principle.

Unfortunately these observers are wrong. The truth of the matter is much more grave. For the truth is that, in respect of many sexual offences, this principle has already been abandoned

As we have seen already, in a series of judgments made between 1975 and 1995, their Lordships have themselves progressively removed a series of safeguards which once protected innocent defendants facing multiple allegations of sexual abuse. The effects have already been catastrophic. In practice, partly because of the state of public opinion and partly because of these legislative 'reforms', the presumption of innocence no longer applies to trials involving sexual offences; it has been replaced by a presumption of guilt.

An extraordinary endorsement of this state of affairs came during a televised discussion in the aftermath of the Waterhouse report. Sir William Utting, a former chief inspector at the Social Services Inspectorate and a past president of the National Institute for Social Work, said 'It may be that innocent people are convicted but we ought to be more worried about the guilty who might get away.'[604]

In Britain, generally speaking, trials involving sexual allegations made by multiple complainants reflect the illiberal views Utting expresses. Such trials are not examples of justice at work; they are cruel charades in which the outcome is determined by prejudice rather than by evidence. Among those many innocent defendants who have been convicted in this manner, and among their families and friends, confidence in what Mr Justice Sachs calls 'the enduring integrity and security of the legal system' has already, and rightly, been utterly destroyed.

If the damage which has been has inflicted on our system of justice is incalculable, so too are the costs in personal terms which the resulting witch-hunt has inflicted on its many victims, in Britain and the world over.

The sheer scale even of that fragment of the witch-hunt which is concerned with care homes and police trawling is difficult to grasp. According to figures produced by the Association of Chief Police Officers in response to parliamentary questions posed by Claire Curtis-Thomas, by May 2001 police forces in England and Wales had obtained allegations from approximately 5,750 former residents of care homes. Since these figures did not include investigations which had been completed before January 1998, it may safely be assumed that, by the end of 2004, complaints had been trawled from at least 10,000 former residents of care homes. The majority of these have made several allegations. If we extrapolate from this figure, we can estimate that between 7,000 and 9,000 care workers (and possibly more) have already had accusations made against them as a result of these investigations. Most of these care workers have not been charged with any offence, but many of these have still had their lives blighted by false allegations. And, in the last fifteen years, as many as a hundred may have been wrongly convicted.[605]

All the evidence suggests that the majority of the many thousands of allegations which have been collected by police trawling operations are false.

Police trawling is but one fragment of a larger witch-hunt. If we add the false allegations which have been made in all other contexts, including recovered memory cases, satanic abuse investigations, marital and custody disputes, and the huge and growing number of allegations made against teachers, then the figures start to grow dramatically.

There are, of course, no hard, global statistics for the total number of teachers and care workers, celebrities and doctors, fathers and grandfathers, stepfathers, brothers, uncles and mothers who have found themselves the victims of false allegations. But, in the English-speaking world alone, the number of false allegations of sexual abuse made in all contexts in the last thirty years must certainly be numbered in hundreds of thousands and has probably already reached millions.

Even if accurate figures were available, they would not express what has really been happening in the Western world during this time. In attempting to convey the reality of a tragedy of this kind, we might do worse than recall the words of the former Soviet official, Victor

Kravchenko. Having given statistics for the millions who were arrested, exiled or executed in the Soviet Union during Stalin's Great Purge, he wrote this:

> But even these colossal figures don't sum up the tragedy. They're big but they are cold. ... One must think of the victims not in such impersonal terms, but as individuals. One must recall that each of these multitudes had relatives, friends, dependents who shared his sufferings; that each of them had hopes, plans, actual achievements which were shattered. To the historian of tomorrow, to the sociologist of today, these are statistics. But to me, who lived through it, the digits have bodies and minds and souls, all of which were hurt, outraged, humiliated.[606]

The implied comparison here with what took place in Stalin's Russia may seem extreme. In some respects it is. In the Soviet Union in the first half of the twentieth century, millions of innocent victims were actually killed; in the current world-wide witch-hunt the number of those falsely accused who have been driven to suicide can probably be numbered in hundreds or in thousands. But, whatever the true figure may be, there can be little doubt that many, many more people have been driven to contemplate suicide as they have suffered the seemingly endless anguish and terror of being falsely accused. Ultimately, all that can be said is that the amount of sheer human misery which has been inflicted in this manner will remain incalculable.

One of the factors, however, which makes this modern witch-hunt uniquely terrible is that it has claimed, and continues to claim, two sets of victims. For it is not only those who are falsely accused who suffer anguish and misery. Among the other victims are all those who genuinely have been abused.

Because of the huge number of false allegations which have been made in the last thirty years, the veracity of almost all allegations of abuse may begin to be called into question. As a result many people who have made truthful complaints of having been abused in children's homes, of rape, or of incest, may find that they are disbelieved or may fear that they might be. They may feel, in consequence, that they have been robbed of their own integrity and their own history. That, too, is a tragedy and we should not underestimate the distress which such disbelief can cause.

One of the most disturbing features of the modern child protection movement is its seeming inability to recognise that it has itself created the conditions for such a new climate of disbelief. For once we take the view that anyone who makes an allegation of sexual abuse has a right to be believed, we inevitably invite false allegations. If we do not carefully investigate every complaint of abuse with an open mind, and if we permit trawling operations and other investigations which actually encourage the making false allegations, then the entire currency of complaints is debased and even those who make genuine allegations may find themselves disbelieved.

The remedy for such unwarranted disbelief is not to castigate those who point to the fact that false allegations have been made. It is to recognise that the responsibility for creating the inflationary spiral of disbelief which is described here lies principally with those who make false allegations and with those who create the conditions that encourage them.

For one of the greatest failings of the modern child protection movement is that, in its zeal to believe *all* allegations, it has betrayed the very children it seeks to protect and ushered in the return of the climate of disbelief it sought to banish for ever.

The tragedy which is now unfolding as a result of false allegations of sexual abuse, with their two sets of victims, is far from over. If we do not take action to reintroduce reason and restraint into our system of justice, and into our child protection procedures, then that tragedy will continue to grow inexorably. And, to the historian of tomorrow, the great European witch-hunt of the sixteenth and seventeenth centuries will be as nothing when compared with the world-wide witch-hunt that took place in the twentieth and twenty-first centuries.

VII

REFLECTIONS ON
CULTURAL HISTORY

74 'Attacking the devil'

IN OFFERING AN ACCOUNT of the manner in which one of the most important of our modern myths – the 'official' story of North Wales – was created, and in attempting to convey the character and proportions of the witch-hunt that grew out of it, I have completed one part of the undertaking on which I embarked at the beginning of this book.

There remains, however, a significant task which, though it cannot be discharged fully here, should at least be attempted. The nature of this task will be familiar to anyone who has ever consulted a detailed map of their destination in order to plan a journey. The problem with detailed maps (such as the one I have offered in this book of the North Wales story) is that, unless they are accurately located in a much broader context, they can actually end by providing the illusion of orientation rather than the reality. If we do not know the shape of the continent in which we are travelling, or have already mistaken our bearings, a detailed map may sometimes help us to get more lost than we ever were before.

There is a danger that the detailed history which is contained in this book, might, if no attempt is made to situate it in a larger context, have precisely this effect. The problem is an acute one because, for all our sophistication as members of a 'rational' and 'scientific' culture, we seem to lack any broad understanding of our own cultural history, or any real insight into our cultural psychology. Yet it is just this kind of understanding we need if we are to grasp the implications of the detailed historical map I have tried to provide in the main body of this book.

In an attempt to supply this larger context, we might begin by noting that the single most important idea which has appeared, however fleetingly, in almost all the most zealous modern campaigns against child abuse is not the simple belief that young and vulnerable children are being exploited. It is the conviction that this is being done in a clandestine manner by some group or organised conspiracy. Whether we look to the 'satanic panic' of the 1980s, the scandal which came to surround Kincora in Belfast, the non-existent paedophile ring centred on Bryn Estyn, the alleged infiltration of the Irish government by agents of Opus Dei, or the Casa Pia scandal in Portugal, we encounter, in only slightly different forms, the same underlying idea.

Although the proximate origins of this interest in organised abuse can be found in the child protection movement which emerged in the United States – above all in California – during the 1970s, the fascination of our culture with dark conspiracies goes back much deeper into our history. It actually goes back further than the demonological fantasies associated with the witch-hunts of the sixteenth and seventeenth centuries, or even than the devilish conspiracies envisaged in medieval Christian anti-semitism. For we will find just such a preoccupation at the heart of what was once considered the most sacred repository of all cultural orthodoxy in the West – the New Testament.

It is C. S. Lewis, perhaps the most prominent popular writer on Christianity in the second part of the twentieth century, who has provided one of the most interesting perspectives on this aspect of the Bible:

> One of the things that surprised me when I first read the New Testament seriously was that it talked so much about a Dark Power in the universe – a mighty evil spirit who was held to be the Power behind death and disease, and sin. The difference is that Christianity thinks this Dark Power was created by God, and went wrong. Christianity agrees with Dualism that the universe is at war. But it does not think this is a war between independent powers. It thinks it is a civil war, a rebellion, and that we are living in a part of the universe occupied by the rebel. Enemy-occupied territory – that is what this world is. Christianity is the story of how the rightful king has landed, you might say landed in disguise, and is calling us all to take part in a great campaign of sabotage. When you go to church you are really listening in to the secret wireless from our friends: that is why the enemy is so anxious to prevent us from going. He does it by playing to our conceit and laziness and intellectual snobbery. I know someone will ask me, 'do you really mean, at this time of day, to reintroduce our old friend the devil – hoofs and horns and all?' Well, what the time of day has to do with it, I do not know. And I am not particular about the hoofs and horns. But in other respects my answer is 'yes I do.' I do not claim to know anything about his personal appearance. If anybody really wants to know him better, I would say to that person 'don't worry. If you really want to, you will. Whether you'll like it when you do is another question.' ... Christians, then, believe that an evil power has made himself for the present the Prince of this World.[607]

These remarkable words serve to remind us of the absolute centrality of demonology – of belief in the devil and his powers – to the historical Christian faith. In short, if we try to trace the genealogy of the
deepest preoccupation of the modern child protection movement, we
find it leads back to the very heart of our traditional religious orthodoxy.

A preoccupation with the works of the devil and the manner in
which he has supposedly infiltrated the ordinary institutions of our
world is not simply present in the New Testament. It remained a staple
part of the orthodox Christian imagination for most of the last two
thousand years. In all its most significant manifestations up to the time
of the Reformation, the Christian church never ceased to imagine the
culmination of history as an apocalyptic battle in which Satan and the
powers of darkness were finally defeated and the pure reign of God was
established for all eternity.

Such apocalyptic fantasies were once the very essence of religious
orthodoxy, and it was in the white-hot religious zeal which was associated with them up to the sixteenth and seventeenth centuries that our
modern 'rational' consciousness was originally forged. Yet, as C. S. Lewis
implies, there came a point in the history of Christianity when the
devil and all his works began to disappear. In Britain and much of
Europe the decline of hell and the gradual disappearance of traditional
Christian demonology began in the seventeenth century but was most
marked during the nineteenth century.[608] By the end of the 1960s it
was almost complete. Indeed, by now, many practising Christians are
almost completely unaware of the centrality which fantasies about dark
powers and apocalyptic battles once enjoyed in the Christian church.
As the religious scholar S. G. F. Brandon has written: 'The secularisation
of Western society has coincided with a growing uncertainty among
Christians, of most denominations, about their traditional eschatology.
Although the ancient concepts of Judgment, Heaven and Hell are still
current in hymns and prayers, and are enunciated in the reading of the
Bible, the imagery in which they were originally presented is now
found embarrassing.'[609] In this respect our modern cultural predicament
has been most succinctly and poignantly expressed by the novelist John
Updike: 'Alas we have become, in our Protestantism, more virtuous
than the myths which taught us virtue; we judge them barbaric.'[610]

Today we tend to explain the 'disappearance' of the devil from our
contemporary world-view by invoking the triumph of rationalism. Yet
this represents a fundamental misunderstanding both of our cultural

history and of our cultural psychology. The principal objection to it is that it fails to take account of the fact that the Judaeo-Christian tradition is itself one of the principal sources of modern rationalism. The dream according to which human irrationality is finally defeated and replaced by the reign of reason has always been at the heart of Christian apocalyptic fantasies. It was Christianity which fostered the view that human irrationality and human viciousness, though part of our 'fallen' nature, were not part of our essential spiritual and rational identity. In the eternity of God's kingdom which was to be established at the end of history, they would be banished for ever. It is religion, in other words, which has encouraged us to believe in an unrealistic version of human nature according to which all human unreason (traditionally personified as 'the Beast', the 'Whore of Babylon', or 'Satan') can be bound for a thousand years (the 'millennium') or somehow permanently excised from human nature. 'Rationalism' is, in this sense, the greatest of all the irrational delusions which has been promoted by our religious tradition.

The alternative to the modern myth which explains the decline of demonology by reference to our increasingly rational outlook is to recognise that demonology has not in fact declined at all. It has simply been relocated in another part of our culture where it remains just as central to our modern consciousness as it ever was in the past.

This is what we might expect if we adopt the kind of perspective on our own history which might be taken by a cultural anthropologist. Any anthropologist who studied the extraordinary continuity of our culture's preoccupation with dark alien forces over the last two thousand years might very reasonably come to the conclusion that they were studying an aspect of human nature itself. This is not to say that such preoccupations are written into the DNA of the human species. But there is, at the very least, strong circumstantial evidence to suggest that a preoccupation with dark conspiracies is part of our cultural identity. If such a preoccupation is part of 'human nature', or of what might be termed, less traditionally, the 'cultural physiology' of the human brain, it would follow that we remain just as susceptible to demonological fantasies as our ancestors who lived in an age of faith.

It may well be that the Christian church has largely renounced its interest in doing battle with Satan, and in the traditional trappings of biblical demonology. But, in Britain at least, the organised Christian church now plays relatively little role in our national life. The modern child protection movement, by contrast, plays a significant role and, if

At the heart of all apocalyptic fantasies is the idea of a final and decisive battle between the forces of Christendom and the forces of evil – frequently symbolised by the many-headed 'Beast of the Apocalypse'. In this sixteenth-century Lutheran woodcut Christ is shown trampling triumphantly on a three-headed version of the apocalyptic beast. One of the heads is that of the pope, who spews out monks and demonic spirits. The second is that of the devil disguised as an angel. The third is that of a Muslim, specifically of the Turk, who was seen at the time as a sign of the last days, and as identical with Gog and Magog, the hosts of Satan who figure in Revelation 20:7.

Apocalyptic fantasies played a crucial role both in the English Civil War and in the Newtonian movement and remain part of the hidden inheritance of modern rationalism. In the seventeenth-century engraving reproduced above, which projects a massive fantasy of male domination, the place of Christ has been taken by Oliver Cromwell, who is shown standing in triumph on the dead body of the Whore of Babylon and the defeated reptilian form of the seven-headed beast – the Roman Catholic Church. In some seventeenth-century versions of this image – which is already a clear example of the 'pornography of righteousness' – the woman's breasts and nipples are exposed. As Dan Jacobson has written, in words which might well be applied to W. T. Stead and the modern child protection movement: 'A conviction that one is writing or speaking on the side of virtue can license an indulgence in fantasies that virtue itself would ordinarily compel one to forswear.'

we are to understand our cultural predicament it is essential that we should understand the extent to which this movement has in practice tended to take over very large parts of the role traditionally played in our society both by Christian doctrine and by Christian demonology.

If we trace the modern child protection movement back to its origins in Victorian London this conclusion might seem rather less surprising. One of the main founders of this movement has long been clearly identified. He was the Reverend Benjamin Waugh, a congregational minister in London's East End, who created the Society for the Prevention of Cruelty to Children (SPCC) in 1884. Five years later, in 1889, this became the NSPCC with Queen Victoria as its patron. Until this time cruelty to children which stopped short of causing death had not been an offence in Britain. 1889, however, saw the first British legislation against such cruelty, popularly known as the 'Children's Charter'. Subsequent legislation gave NSPCC inspectors, or 'cruelty men', the power to remove children from their homes providing that the consent of a JP was first obtained.[611]

Even before Waugh had turned his society into the NSPCC, he had become deeply involved in one of the most zealous child protection crusades ever fought. For he was a friend and supporter of the journalist W. T. Stead, whose campaign against child prostitution both enthralled and scandalised Victorian London. It was Stead's notorious series of *Pall Mall Gazette* articles on this subject, 'The Maiden Tribute of Modern Babylon', which would eventually lead to the passing of the Criminal Law Amendment Act of 1885. It was this act which, principally in order to outlaw child prostitution, increased the age of consent for girls from thirteen to sixteen, and in doing so laid some of the essential foundations of the modern child protection movement.[612]

The roots of Stead's mission were to be found in his own deep puritanism. He was not simply an avowed Christian from Puritan stock whose own father was a Congregational minister; he was devoted, with a passionate religious love, to Oliver Cromwell. 'The memory of Cromwell,' Stead wrote in 1899, 'has from my earliest boyhood been the inspiration of my life':

> To say that he ranked far and away before all the saints in the calendar, was to say nothing. My devotion to the Apostles and the Evangelists was but tepid compared with my veneration and affection for the uncrowned king of English Puritanism. Nay, I can to this day remember the serious searchings of heart I experienced when I woke up to a consciousness of the fact that I felt a far keener and more passionate

personal love for Oliver Cromwell, than I did even for the divine figure of Jesus of Nazareth.

Cromwell was so near, so human, so real. And above all, he was still the mark for hatred, scoffing and abuse. You never really love anyone to the uttermost until you feel that other people hate him and misjudge him …[613]

Like Cromwell, Stead came early in his life to believe that he had been vouchsafed a high and holy duty to battle against the armies of Satan – and in particular the rich, the powerful and the aristocratic who to him personified the forces of evil. When, in 1872 at the age of 22, he was made editor of the newly founded *Northern Echo* newspaper in Darlington, Stead reacted with a kind of religious exultation. 'What a glorious opportunity of attacking the devil,' he wrote to a friend. He later said that he 'felt the sacredness of the power placed in my hands, to be used on behalf of the poor, the outcast and the oppressed.'[614]

With the help of the new railway network, Stead rapidly turned the *Northern Echo* into Britain's first truly national newspaper, attracting the attention of leading politicians, including the former and future prime minister, Gladstone. Then, in 1885, after moving to London and becoming editor of the *Pall Mall Gazette*, an influential daily newspaper, Stead became involved in the campaign against child prostitution.

At this point a series of proposals designed to outlaw child prostitution by raising the age of consent from thirteen to sixteen had already been incorporated into a Criminal Law Amendment Bill which was introduced into the House of Lords under Gladstone in 1883. The bill, however, ran into serious opposition, was reintroduced in a watered-down form and then appeared, in 1885, to be facing defeat in the House of Commons.

It was at this juncture that the Salvation Army's Bramwell Booth (the son of the founder, General William Booth) intervened and decided to ask Stead to help. Having taken a deep interest in the question of prostitution, Booth introduced the journalist to a number of young girls who had been lured into prostitution and persuaded him of the rightness of the cause. Since Gladstone's government had already collapsed in June 1885 to be replaced by an interim Conservative administration, there were only weeks to go before parliament would be dissolved and the bill would have to be abandoned. Any press campaign now to force the bill through parliament would, of necessity, have to be of a sensational and unprecedented kind.

In a decision which effectively marked the beginning of modern investigative journalism, Stead chose to launch his own inquiry into the night streets and brothels of London. After a hastily conducted investigation, he compiled a lengthy report which he planned to publish in four successive daily instalments. Living in a Victorian age where the proprieties of the public press were decently observed by all god-fearing editors, Stead knew that he was about to attract notoriety by breaching them. He therefore shrewdly chose to advertise his infamy in advance. On Saturday 4 July 1885, just before the first instalment was due to appear, the *Pall Mall Gazette* carried a solemn editorial under the heading 'Notice to our Readers: A Frank Warning'. Having explained the perilous state of the Criminal Law Amendment Bill and the need to mobilise public opinion, Stead announced his intention to publish in the paper 'an infernal narrative' of modern sexual vice: 'Therefore we say quite frankly today that all those who are squeamish, and all those who are prudish, and all those who prefer to live in a fool's paradise of imaginary innocence and purity, selfishly oblivious to the horrible realities which torment those whose lives are passed in the London Inferno, will do well not to read the *Pall Mall Gazette* of Monday and the three following days.'[615]

This announcement that a Victorian daily newspaper was about to deal, in unprudish detail, with some of the gravest forms of what Stead called 'sexual criminality', created, as it was clearly intended to, an unprecedented frisson. By Monday, a good part of London, and indeed of the entire nation, waited expectantly for the journalistic sensation which had been promised. Stead began by introducing what he called the 'maze of London brotheldom' within which labyrinth there wandered 'like lost souls, the vast host of London prostitutes, whose numbers no man can compute, but who are probably not much below 50,000 strong.' He went on to talk of the existence of a 'white slave trade' in the streets of London: 'It is a veritable slave trade that is going on around us; but as it takes place in the heart of London, it is a scandal – an outrage on public morality – even to allude to it. We have kept silence far too long.'

After breaking this silence with a series of sensational descriptions of the vices of London, Stead ended his first instalment with what was to be the highlight of the entire series – an account of how he had, with the assistance of a reformed procuress and her brothel-keeper acquaintance, managed to buy a 13-year-old girl for £5. The brothel-keeper, said Stead, had in fact purchased the child for a sovereign from her mother, who was 'poor, dissolute, and indifferent to everything but

drink'. She had then sold the child to the procuress for an advance of
£3 with £2 payable when she had been certified as a virgin. Stead
described how the girl had been taken to a midwife to be examined
and, having been pronounced intact, had then been prepared, with the
help of chloroform to ease the pain, for her purchaser:

> From the midwife's the innocent girl was taken to a house of ill fame,
> No. ——, P——— street, Regent-street, where, notwithstanding her
> extreme youth, she was admitted without question. She was taken
> upstairs, undressed, and put to bed, the woman who bought her put-
> ting her to sleep. She was rather restless, but under the influence of
> chloroform she soon went over. Then the woman withdrew. All was
> quiet and still. A few moments later the door opened, and the purchaser
> entered the bedroom. He closed and locked the door. There was a brief
> silence. And then there rose a wild and piteous cry – not a loud shriek,
> but a helpless, startled scream like the bleat of a frightened lamb. And
> the child's voice was heard crying, in accents of terror, 'There's a man
> in the room! Take me home; oh, take me home!'
>
> And then all once more was still.[616]

The child, referred to in the article as 'Lily', was in no danger since the
purchaser was Stead himself. 'That was but one case among many,' he
wrote, 'and by no means the worst. It only differs from the rest because
I have been able to verify the facts. Many a similar cry will be raised
this very night in the brothels of London, unheeded by man, but not
unheard by the pitying ear of Heaven ...'

The long first instalment of 'The Maiden Tribute' was, without
doubt, the most sensational piece of journalism which had appeared in
living memory – or perhaps ever. Because Stead had carefully prepared
the ground on the preceding Saturday, the response was instant. Just as
a skilled evangelical preacher knows how to bring members of his congregation to the altar rail to confess their sins – or to take communion
– so Stead, preaching from his pulpit in Northumberland Street, just off
the Strand, knew how to bring communicants to *his* altar rail. Except
that those who pressed most keenly against the offices of the *Pall Mall
Gazette* on Monday had come not to repent of their sins but to replen-
ish their retail stock. Motivated by profit rather than piety, they were
newsboys who had already sold the first printing of the paper and
sought the second or the third or the fourth. Hundreds lay siege to the
Pall Mall Gazette offices and 'fought with fists and feet, with tooth and
nail ... for the sheets wet from the press'. This did not mean, however,

that the freshly printed papers supplied to them would serve merely secular ends. In the view of Reverend Benjamin Waugh a more sublime force was at work. Recounting how he had taken Stead to a refuge to meet some young victims of sexual crime, the founder of the NSPCC recalled the journalist's reaction:

> As we went out of the Shelter his eyes filled with tears: he lost strength, his knees failed him, and I felt him lean upon my arm as with the weariness of a broken-hearted, bowed-down old age. Then it was – in that moment of quiet woe – that I felt the homage for him which has deepened through all the strange weeks which have passed since.
>
> 'And the Papers will say nothing about these cases,' I added: 'the details are too revolting.'
>
> Then the woe changed, and the silence broke, and erecting himself with the thrill of an awful indignation, he burst out, 'Mr Waugh, I will turn my Paper into a tub; I will turn stump orator, I will. I will damn and damn. I'll cease to be a Christian; I'll be a prophet, and damn, and damn!'
>
> With all the impetuosity of a pure child there was blended the majesty of a rare man. It was extraordinary. I was awed.
>
> 'You must not cease to be a Christian to damn,' I responded out of genuine admiration; 'prophets did not damn; it was Jesus who first spoke that word. To damn nobly we must be His disciples, and be hot with the feel of His God in us.' And then I was almost sorry that I had spoken to so sublime a woe, and he said, 'I'll be a disciple of anybody who will teach me to damn this wickedness.'
>
> I seemed to feel a wind, as of a prophet sweeping by me in a chariot of fire, so utterly and sublimely in earnest was he, and so intense was his woe.[617]

For Waugh, as indeed for Stead himself, it is clear that 'attacking the devil' and 'damning wickedness' were one and the same, and that it was in doing both that they vitalised their religious faith. For Waugh, indeed, it was almost as if the copies of Stead's *Pall Mall Gazette* articles which poured off the presses for four days in July 1885 conveyed the body of Christ to the newspaper's readers yet more surely than did the communion wafer to those who celebrated mass in a more orthodox manner. Waugh himself later declared that he loved Stead 'with some of the love with which I love my Redeemer.'[618] This view, however, was not universally shared. On the morning after the first sensational part of Stead's 'Maiden Tribute' appeared, most newspapers were silent. But the *Manchester Guardian* judged it 'prurient', and W. H. Smith's, who enjoyed a virtual monopoly of railway news-stands, refused to sell the paper on the grounds of its obscenity.

In some respects their judgment was sound. The articles Stead produced contained virtually no explicit sexual detail. The sub-headlines he used, however, which included 'The Violation of Virgins', 'Confessions of a Brothel-keeper' and 'Strapping Girls Down' were sensational in themselves. And, in that the substance of his articles endlessly described prostitution, and the rape of young girls, what he wrote was, quite literally, pornographic. It was also, as the *Guardian* suggested, deeply prurient. Above all, the articles projected an image of the massive sexual power of men, while simultaneously portraying women as weak, passive and defenceless. Seeming almost to relish the rapacious sexuality he so vigorously condemned, it was Stead's genius to have created a new Victorian genre, the pornography of righteousness. The fact that W. H. Smith's banned it from their shelves and the city solicitor attempted to ban its sale in the city of London, only made its appeal more powerful. On this occasion the lurid pornography which the country's largest newsagent refused to sell was distributed enthusiastically by the Salvation Army.

As the *Northern Echo* journalist and historian Chris Lloyd has noted, Stead used sex to sell newspapers. He was, perhaps, the first British newspaper editor to do so; he was certainly the most influential and he may well have done so quite deliberately: 'Sex passion ... like steam,' he wrote in 1898, '... is the driving force if it is kept within bounds. In excess, it bursts the boiler.'[619] In 1885, at least, Stead's calculated use of sexual sensationalism for political ends proved successful. His articles produced uproar in London, and the government, perhaps sensing that inaction might lead to insurrection, almost immediately agreed to reopen debate on the Criminal Law Amendment Bill. MPs were urgently summoned back from the country and even before the *Gazette*'s presses had stopped rolling, the home secretary moved the resumption of the second reading. Within a month, on 7 August 1885, the bill to raise the age of consent received its third and final reading. A week later it passed into law.[620]

One of the reasons Stead remains so important in any attempt to understand our cultural history is that he stands at the crossroads that lead from a traditional Christian outlook, where the Church of England and the non-conformist churches still possessed institutional power, to a new secular age. It is Stead himself, with his constant and earnest comparisons of the editor's chair to the preacher's pulpit, who points to one of the most important developments. Historically, the demonology of Christianity had always played a crucial psychological role in maintaining the vitality of Christian belief. By projecting the image of an evil enemy, preachers were able to galvanise the beliefs of their followers and unite them in solidarity against satanic powers which were perceived as a dark external threat. Stead's role in the battle against child prostitution showed how the preacher's role in 'damning wickedness' had, as the twentieth century approached, been passed to the newspaper editor. In many respects the publication of his 'Maiden Tribute' articles in 1885 marked the birth of the modern child protection movement. They signalled that the age of mythological or Dante-esque journeys into a traditional Christian hell was over, and that the new secular demonology would be developed not by the church but by newspapers following in the footsteps of Stead – who himself referred to his articles as 'the story of an actual pilgrimage into a real hell'. Just as the Old Testament prophets had used the pornography of righteousness in the Bible, and had, in this sense, used sex to sell a moral message, so newspapers would increasingly do the same thing as the twentieth century developed.

But there was another respect in which Stead's new puritanism would set a pattern for the future. For one striking feature of his 'Maiden Tribute' articles was that the most sensational allegation they contained, namely that Stead had purchased a 13-year-old girl from her mother for the purposes of prostitution, was completely untrue. Stead had introduced the relevant section of the article with the following words: 'I can personally vouch for the absolute accuracy of every fact in the narrative.' He then closed his account of the incident with a similar assurance which has already been cited: 'That was but one case among many, and by no means the worst. It only differs from the rest because I have been able to verify the facts.' It transpired, however, that, far from being in a position to vouch personally for the story of how the girl was purchased, Stead had not in fact been present at any stage of the transaction, and had witnessed only its apparently successful outcome.[621]

Instead, the entire scheme had been carried out for him by a woman, Rebecca Jarrett, who had claimed to be a reformed prostitute and procuress. She had also played an essential role in his investigation and had been perhaps the most important of all his informants. Because, on this occasion, as in so many journalistic investigations, Stead had been working to a deadline, he seemed to have had no alternative but to place immense trust in what she told him. But when the mother of the 13-year-old came forward to claim that her daughter, Eliza Armstrong, had been abducted, the true story gradually emerged. Stead and Jarrett were charged with abducting the child and stood trial at the Old Bailey, where Jarrett was cross-examined by the Attorney General, Sir Richard Webster QC. Under cross-examination, it gradually became clear that Jarrett's story about being a reformed procuress was untrue. Asked where her brothels had been, she gave, with some reluctance, a number of addresses. Her claims were checked, and in all cases they turned out to be fabrications. More importantly still, her account of how she had obtained the services of the 13-year-old girl also appeared to be untrue in almost every particular. The girl's mother said that she had not been paid any money for her daughter and she had parted with her only because she had been led to believe that she was going into respectable service as a housemaid. All the evidence pointed to the conclusion that the most important of all Stead's collaborators had deceived him. And he, crucially, in his anxiety to find evidence for the evil of whose reality he was already convinced, had allowed himself to be deceived.[622]

Interestingly and significantly, the evidence of Stead's untruthfulness which emerged at the trial did not diminish the regard that Reverend Benjamin Waugh held for him. Indeed, the more Stead was publicly reviled, the more valiantly Waugh declared his support for him. Both, it would seem, belonged to the long Puritan tradition according to which truthfulness was to be judged by the conscience alone, and untruthfulness could be justified so long as the cause was sufficiently righteous.

75 Patriarchalism and the new puritanism

IT SHOULD NOT BE NECESSARY to labour the parallels between the child protection campaign launched by W. T. Stead in July 1885 and the campaign launched by a newspaper more than a century later in December 1991, in which Dean Nelson and Alison Taylor played such significant roles. The parallels are important, however, because it is only with their help that we may accurately locate the detailed map of the North Wales story which has been offered in these pages in a larger context.

One commentator who has made this task easier is a journalist who was himself writing for the *Independent* in 1996, during the period it was conducting its lurid campaign for a public inquiry into the North Wales allegations. Soon after this campaign had reached a successful conclusion, Bryan Appleyard, who had evidently remained sceptical of the newspaper's stance, wrote a thoughtful article about images of childhood under the title 'Return of the Angel'. In a passage which evidently referred to the very newspaper in which it appeared, Appleyard noted that 'children today are seen as being at unprecedented risk from a world-wide epidemic of paedophilia':

> Whole pages of broadsheet newspapers are routinely devoted to today's crop of paedophile horrors. Why have we fastened on to child abuse as the defining evil of our day? The answer is obvious. Just as a moral, intellectual and cultural vacuum obliges politicians to adopt the child as the only absolute good, so it obliges everybody else to adopt the abuse of the child as the only absolute evil. Look at how social workers became obsessed with satanic child abuse – dressing up this evil, borrowing the imagery of religion to make it as foul as possible. Child abuse was all they had. There was nothing else on which they could all agree to vent their sense of evil and which they knew would inflame ours. It worked. Perhaps we have dropped the horns and cloaks out of embarrassment. But the sheer intensity of our interest and concern makes the same point – this crime above all others fulfils our need for evil.[623]

Appleyard's sober reflections on the role played by the devil in secular child protection campaigns is highly significant. But it is the story of Stead and Waugh which explains how this situation has come about. For what this story should make clear is that the modern child protection movement was, in its origins in Victorian London, not simply a social purity campaign, but a revivalist religious movement possessed of quite extraordinary power and intensity. Those most closely associated with Stead and Waugh wholeheartedly shared their religious commitment. They included Bramwell Booth of the Salvation Army and Josephine Butler, a campaigner for women's rights, who was herself described by one of her followers as 'a woman Christ to save us from our despair'.[624] Without fully realising what they were doing, these zealous religious revivalists created, at the end of the nineteenth century, a form of Christianity which was ideally suited to a society which was undergoing rapid secularisation. Where the traditional iconology of the crucifixion had once been they placed the image of the abused child. And where the devil had once reigned they enthroned the child abuser. The immense practical advantage of this new form of Christianity was that, while retaining the imaginative potency of traditional religious faith, it rendered belief in supernatural entities such as God optional or unnecessary. It was, in short, a revivalist faith which could be professed without embarrassment even by those who had no faith.[625]

Within this new secularised form of Christianity, a particular form of late Romanticism, with its idealisation of the child and the child's supposed innocence, has gathered strength. In it all adults are seen as potential threats to children, with the greatest threat of all being posed by child sexual abuse. Onto a real crime, whose actual consequences have never properly been understood, the anxieties of an entire society have been projected. As a result the threat posed by a form of sexual behaviour which was once under-reported has been grossly exaggerated. At the same time our obsessive concentration on the possibility of sexual abuse has tended itself to eroticise children and disseminate the kinds of sexual fantasies about them we purport to oppose.

In our public obsession with child sexual abuse we have contrived actually to promote, and repeatedly force into everyday consciousness, the very form of sexual crime we claim to abhor. The long-term consequences of this oblique public assault on the very taboo we claim to value most are impossible to calculate. They may well, however, be far greater than we can begin to imagine.

Like any society which has developed fantastic notions of purity or innocence, we have increasingly nurtured fantastic notions of evil; it is within these dark collective fantasies that we have located the figure of the paedophile. So anxious have we become that we might fail to protect our children against the threats posed by real and imaginary paedophiles that we have developed an extraordinary and elaborate folklore. This claims to be able to detect the symptoms of abuse and unfailingly to identify the evil-doers in our midst.

What is most dangerous about this child-protection folklore is that its unverified and frequently false tenets are now widely accepted and disseminated in colleges and universities and have become adopted as unquestionable orthodoxies by countless therapists, psychologists and social workers. The enormous historical potency of this new revivalist movement has been due, in part, to the fact that it has been fed not only by the evangelical zeal of the British non-conformist tradition (as personified by Stead and Waugh), but, in more recent years, by a particular kind of New England puritanism which had already absorbed the influence of Freud and psychoanalysis.[626]

One significant event in the development of what must be called the 'demonology' of the modern child protection movement took place at a particular historical moment, 17 April 1971. It was on this day that the New York Radical Feminists, a group which had at most some 400 members, began a two-day conference about rape in New York. Susan Brownmiller, who would later write the classic feminist work on rape, *Against Our Will,* was one of many prominent feminists attending the conference and she later described in vivid terms the effect of a speech given by the social worker Florence Rush. 'I have been to many feminist meetings,' Brownmiller wrote, 'but never before, and not since, have I seen an entire audience rise to its feet in acclaim. We clapped. We cheered.'[627]

During the course of her speech Rush had outlined statistics which suggested that the sexual abuse of children in general, and father-daughter incest in particular, was much more widespread than generally acknowledged. But it was with her conclusion that she set her audience alight. In words which would perhaps prove even more important in the history of child protection than W. T. Stead's 'Maiden Tribute' articles, she put forward a view of child abuse which had never previously been expressed in public. She suggested that child sexual abuse was deliberately permitted by patriarchal societies, and clearly implied that it was the cornerstone of patriarchal authority:

> Sexual abuse of children is permitted because it is an unspoken but prominent factor in socializing and preparing the female to accept a subordinate role: to feel guilty, ashamed and to tolerate through fear, the power exercised over her by men ... The female's early sexual experiences prepare her to submit in later life to the adult forms of sexual abuse heaped on her by her boyfriend, her lover, her husband. In short the sexual abuse of female children is a process of education that prepares them to become the wives and mothers of America.[628]

These words, received so rapturously by Rush's New York audience, powerfully conveyed the outrage of many women at the *real* subordination they suffered at the hands of men. Partly because of this resonance, their distorted view of child sexual abuse as having been virtually institutionalised by patriarchy was often accepted uncritically by feminist thinkers in the 1970s.

Some radical feminist writers now put into circulation extraordinarily high prevalence figures for child sexual abuse. Catherine MacKinnon, the Harvard lawyer, maintained that 4.5% of all women are victims of incest by their father but suggested that this figure should be increased to 40% if other male relatives and friends were included. 'In fact,' she wrote, 'it is the woman who has not been sexually abused who deviates.' Harvard psychotherapist Judith Herman dedicated her 1981 book, *Father-Daughter Incest*, to the women 'estimated by us to be in the millions, who have personally experienced incestuous abuse.'[629]

Without realising the depth of her own underlying cultural orthodoxy Rush had in effect re-created a traditional form of evil. Even more than that of Stead and Waugh, her vision was ideally suited to a secular, post-Christian, post-Marxist and feminist age. As Rael Jean Isaac has written:

> Now [women who attended the conference] could show that feminists had uncovered the great American secret: behind the picket fences, hidden by those starched suburban curtains, fathers were raping daughters to prepare them for their proper role in society. Beyond racism, imperialism, and capitalism lay the true root of evil – patriarchy.[630]

Although it may be tempting for some to represent the new vision as an example of man-hatred which was feminist *by inspiration*, to do so would be entirely to miss its cultural resonance and potency. What made Rush's vision so powerful was the fact that, in some respects at least, it was *not* distinctive. Traditionally, patriarchal religious hierarchies have always sought to control human sexual behaviour by demonising men as sexual predators and then using such propaganda to disseminate the ideal of chastity among women. Stead himself had inclined to just such an approach. New England progressive thinkers now followed exactly the same patriarchal pattern – and did so in the name of feminism.*

Because the new puritanism of the child protection movement so closely resembled that of traditional revivalist movements, it had a strong appeal to religious conservatives – the very kind of campaigners whose beliefs resembled those of Waugh and Stead. But because it was combined with some of the doctrines of psychoanalysis, it rapidly attained an even greater intellectual plausibility.[631]

The vision which resulted implied that there was a massive and secret conspiracy, first to sexually abuse girls and young women, and then to conceal that abuse by denying that it had ever taken place, or by terrifying the victims into silence and repression. The version of evil conjured up in this way might well be compared to medieval Christian visions of the power of Satan, in which the devil was seen as the head of a clandestine and evil conspiracy whose secret followers were everywhere, working constantly for the enlargement of his kingdom.

According to this vision, the world was in thrall to the forces of evil. This evil was dark, dangerous and immensely powerful. But if the forces of good could unite against it, it might be banished and the world finally redeemed from evil.

This was the underlying message which emerged repeatedly from the child protection movement which gathered strength in both Britain and America throughout the 1970s and 1980s. The message was

---

*Katie Roiphe, an American feminist writer of a more robust and perceptive kind, has captured well the continuity between traditional purity campaigners and the new puritanism of campus feminists such as Catherine MacKinnon. She describes one of MacKinnnon's anti-pornography lectures in the following terms: 'As MacKinnon talks, the ideal of social purity burning in her inflamed rhetoric, you can hear the legacy of the nineteenth century in her voice. ... At the height of her emotional pitch, the room fills with palpable tension. The audience is intimidated, enraptured, captivated. Even the skeptics like me are silent and listening. As MacKinnon talks about her antipornography ordinance, her eyes burn, her face flushes, her hair begins to fall from her bun. She is fire and brimstone. She is a Puritan preacher with a strong jaw and her words carry all the positive and negative associations attached to the Puritans – discipline, dogma, sharp lines, New England autumns, and a furious gray path to grace. She surpasses the level of intensity beyond which there is no doubt God is on your side' (Katie Roiphe, *The Morning After: Sex, Fear and Feminism*, Hamish Hamilton, 1993, pp. 149–50).

not simply an implicit programme for social reform; it was an apocalyptic fantasy.[632]

Men and women in the grip of apocalyptic fantasies have throughout history tended to behave in ways which are profoundly irrational. On some occasions they have become murderous fanatics, at other times they have launched impossible crusades or fomented revolutions which have destroyed the very ideals of liberty they have invoked. But at almost all times they have been prepared to disregard visible evidence and rearrange reality until it conforms with the delusory world-view they have embraced.

When, on 10 June 1991, four men met in the office of Dennis Parry at Shire Hall in Mold in the county of Clwyd, they either embraced, or willingly suspended disbelief in, a secularised apocalyptic fantasy which was a version of those already current within the larger child-protection movement – namely that a particular children's home in North Wales had been infiltrated and taken over by a conspiracy of paedophiles. Precisely because this fantasy was sustained by a series of doctrines and orthodoxies which had grown up in Britain and America over a period of more than a century, its delusory nature was not at first apparent either to the police force which was asked to conduct an investigation, or to the journalist who was asked to write about it.

Indeed, to varying degrees, both police officers and journalists fell under the influence of this fantasy, at least to the extent that they began to 'create' the very evidence which was needed to sustain it. Because the fantasy was being elaborated in the midst of an avowedly sceptical and scientific society a great many doubts about some of its more extreme propositions were expressed at practically every stage. But it was almost as though each public profession of scepticism made room in the rational conscience for the private indulgence of credulity. And, for the most zealous believer, the chairman of social services, Malcolm King, it would seem that there was barely any room for scepticism at all.

As King drove the fantasy onwards and upwards, as Taylor supplied the evidence which the fantasy demanded, and as Nelson duly and credulously reported it, newspaper editors and politicians began to believe it. This appears to have happened to such an extent that at one point, during the spring and early summer of 1996, the entire newsroom of the *Independent* appears to have been gripped by a delusion, and after publishing article upon article which bore only the most tenuous relation to the truth, forced the government to hold a public inquiry.

By now the fantasy had become so powerful that reality itself seemed to disappear in order to make way for it. In spite of the fact that the Tribunal was presented with a substantial amount of evidence which indicated that large numbers of allegations were false, this evidence appears to have been completely invisible to those who scrutinised it. Because its members were themselves evidently in the grip of a delusion, the Tribunal eventually produced a report whose findings were an almost complete inversion of the truth.

This in turn created the conditions in which a witch-hunt that had already gathered significant momentum was given an even greater impetus, and police forces throughout Britain were responsible for encouraging and collecting thousands of false allegations against innocent care workers.

In seeking to bring our current witch-hunt under control we should above all resist the temptation to fall victim to one of the greatest fallacies of all − the idea that it is the destiny of all rational societies to leave behind them superstition and unreason and to pass into an era where witch-hunts and persecution have no place. This, as I suggested at the outset, is one of the great delusions of modern rationalism. The sobering truth is that the more confident we become in the rigour and restraint of our own rational disposition, the more likely we are to become blind to those irrational impulses which are part of the very essence of human nature and which are destined to endure as long as human nature itself endures. It is only if we recognise that the tendency to succumb to apocalyptic fantasies, or to engage in witch-hunts, is part not of our savage, but of our civilised nature, that we are likely to recognise them when they recur in the future − as they undoubtedly will. Vigilance in this respect is, and always will be, necessary.

The witch-hunts of the sixteenth and seventeenth centuries were conducted and encouraged by many learned men who numbered amongst them bishops, monks and magistrates. The witch-hunt which took place in North Wales in the last decade of the twentieth century was certainly not the creation of one person. It was driven forward by many highly educated people who occupied responsible positions. They included journalists, broadsheet newspaper editors, social workers, police officers, local councillors, members of parliament, solicitors, barristers and judges.

One of the lessons taught both by our more remote and by our recent past is that it is just those people who are most confident of their rightness and their rationality who are likely either inadvertently to foster some of the most dangerous of all our delusions, or to enter into complicity with them by their silence or neglect.

One of the other lessons taught by history is that it is precisely this lesson that we have been most reluctant to learn. The story of North Wales should be studied carefully because it illustrates the point more vividly and more powerfully than any other comparable episode.

But it should also be studied because it constitutes one of the most terrible instances of collective ingratitude which is to be found in our recent history. For decade after decade, we expected that one of the most poorly regarded and poorly paid groups of workers in our society would look after some of the most difficult and disruptive children with conscientiousness and care. To an astonishing extent this is what tens of thousands of dedicated care workers actually did. They worked in obscurity, often with immense patience and generosity, to give such children a second chance. They did so principally, one suspects, not because of the meagre salary they were paid, but because in many, if not most cases, they were motivated by idealism and a sense of the service they owed to society.

In the closing years of the twentieth century, however, rather than recognising retrospectively that we had grossly undervalued care workers, we compounded our historical ingratitude by demonising them. Many people appear to have come to the conclusion that, in the absence of significant financial rewards, one of the major factors motivating residential care workers to join an underpaid and low-status profession was the opportunity it might afford for sexual contact with young people. This notion, which in the overwhelming majority of cases is entirely false, has helped to shape the attitude of an entire society.

In all too many cases it has led us not belatedly to recognise the virtues of care workers but wrongly to attribute to them vices which they do not have. Again and again we have imprisoned care workers for imaginary crimes which neither they nor anyone else have committed.

Many of these innocent care workers, like many others wrongly accused of sexual abuse, are in prison still. Our long-term aspiration must indeed be to learn the historical lesson which will reduce the chances of other innocent people being forced to join them in the future. But our most urgent and immediate task is to bring about their release.

If, by telling the story of North Wales, this book helps in some small way to change the climate of moral panic which has led to so many innocent people being imprisoned, it will have succeeded, in part at least, in what it set out to do. But only if it conveys something of the complexity and the enormous scale of the larger historical tragedy of which the North Wales story is but a part, will some of its wider aims be achieved.

For the current witch-hunt is not the product of some shallow and temporary aberration which floats upon the surface of our culture. As I have tried to show, the modern child protection movement out of which it has grown is itself a revivalist movement, deeply rooted in some of our most ancient religious orthodoxies. It is, in effect, a modern secular church which is just as powerful as traditional churches have been in the past, and whose doctrines are almost as pervasive.

To say this is not to imply that we should now turn upon the most active members of this secular church and demonise them as the 'enemy within'. This would merely be to invert the current witch-hunt and to pursue it in a new guise. What it does mean is that we should face up to the fact that the revivalism of the modern child protection movement is something which goes deep into our own cultural history and our own psychology. It is only if we first understand the extraordinary depth and inclusiveness of this movement, and the extent to which we have all been influenced by it, that we are likely to be able to moderate its destructive power and deal effectively with the threat it poses both to innocent people and to justice itself.

Return to North Wales

BEFORE I COULD COMPLETE this book there was one final visit I needed to make. In the summer of 2000 I was given by Gwen Hurst a copy of a memorandum written by Liz Evans. It was her description of a chance meeting with a former Bryn Estyn resident exactly a week after the publication of the report of the North Wales Tribunal. This was at a time when publicity about Bryn Estyn had been at its height. Liz Evans still worked for social services, and she had written up her encounter partly for the benefit of her employers. Her account was so important, and seemed to sum up the entire story so well, that I felt it should be quoted verbatim as the Afterword to this book. Because I had not seen Liz Evans for about five years, I decided that, rather than telephone her, I should go and see her to ask her permission.

It was October 2004; I had lost count of the times I had visited North Wales in pursuit of a story which seemed never to have an ending. On this occasion, however, I had a feeling of finality as I travelled to Wrexham from Oxford by train.

Liz Evans had just returned from work when I arrived at her home and we began, inevitably, to discuss Bryn Estyn. I told her how, in July, I had been telephoned out of the blue by Ryan Tanner. Having completed a degree course in criminology at Bangor university, he had been reading an article about the North Wales Tribunal on my website and wanted to know more about a reference I had made to some documents which related to him. The phone-call led to our meeting up in a hotel bar in Gwynedd where we talked for about four hours. I found Ryan to be intelligent and immensely engaging. He was clearly a gifted story-teller and related a number of accounts of past incidents which were utterly compelling and which presented him in a relatively good light. It was only after our meeting, as I set these accounts alongside evidence from other sources, that it began to become clear that they did not necessarily correspond to the truth.

I imparted to Liz Evans something of what had taken place, together with my feeling that, in spite of everything, there was something likeable about Ryan. She agreed that he had great charm. She also said that they had frequently clashed at Bryn Estyn over his bullying of other boys. Interestingly, however, she recalled that this bullying often had a moral dimension and cited the occasion he had punished another boy for stealing eggs from a nesting bird. When I said that my meeting with Ryan had confirmed the impression I already had that, even though he appeared sometimes to make things up deliberately, he had come quite genuinely to believe in a number of events which had never taken place, she accepted that this was a possibility.

Like almost everyone who had worked there, Liz Evans had been deeply affected by the launch of the Bryn Estyn investigation in 1991 and the fourteen years of accusation and innuendo that ensued. But she did not seem to be bitter. So far as Ryan was concerned she knew his difficult side all too well. But it was clear that she had cared about him when he had been at Bryn Estyn, and that in some respects she still did. 'I have fond memories of him,' she said.

Our conversation eventually turned to the chance meeting she had had in February 2000, only a matter of days after the Tribunal report had been published. She said she was happy for me to use the account she had written at the time. We decided, however, that it would not be right to identify the person concerned, so his name and some of the details in the note which follows have been changed:

RECORDING OF A CONVERSATION WITH JOHN DAVIS ON 22 FEBRUARY 2000 AT 1.15 PM

Whilst I was in the queue at Somerfields supermarket in X, I recognised a person in the next queue but was not sure of his name. I noticed that he recognised me too and he came over to me whilst I was at the kiosk and said, 'Liz' and reminded me he was John (Davis, a resident of Bryn Estyn in the early 1980s when I worked there as a Residential Child Care Officer). He asked me how I was and he said he'd like to talk to me outside and would wait for me to finish in the queue. When I went out he was on his mobile phone and called me over and invited me to sit in his car as I was obviously cold. I got into a top of the range Land Cruiser.

John told me how he had 'jumped on the bandwagon' and said he had received £91,000 compensation and still had to go for a further medical before the last instalment would be released. He said he had alleged that he'd had 'the arse shagged off me' and 'as we didn't jump on the bandwagon until later it was easy because so many statements had been made and people convicted'. When I asked who he meant by 'we', he said Jack O'Neill, 'but that Jack O'Neill had actually been abused elsewhere'. He said that John Smith Solicitor had dealt with everything for him as he had all his life.

He wanted to know how I was and Rob Jones and Dave Birch in particular and said if there was anything he could do to help he would. I said it was obviously very difficult for Dave Birch as he was one of the 28 named in the press as a risk to children and he again asked me to let him know if he could do anything in support. He said he thought we had been really good to him at Bryn Estyn and Birch in particular … He said he hadn't believed what Dave Birch had been accused of in court and he thought Bryn Estyn had been a great place. He said it was 'doing his head in' reading about it in the papers and none of it appeared the same as his memories. He said I must be finding it difficult as some people think all who worked there were perverts and all the boys, had been 'shagged rotten'. He didn't want everyone thinking that about him. He said he thought 'they'll destroy you in work', and if there's anything he can do to help he will.

I asked him if he'd seen the *Lost in Care* report and said that if it would help he could come and see the office copy. He said he didn't want people seeing him come into our offices and I said if he phoned my direct line I could meet him and take him straightaway into one of the rooms which are also used by housing and the registrar. He wanted my home phone number but I told him how, obviously, I was very wary of people and their motives these days and would only give him my work number. I told him he could phone anytime as he said it helped to talk to someone who knew the truth.

He went on to ask if I thought all the abuse alleged against Peter Howarth had occurred. He said he didn't think so and how everyone used to fight to get on the flat list but he was never allowed. I said I thought that was because he was so naughty and he agreed …

He gave me his mobile phone number and asked me to give it to Dave Birch and tell him to phone him to see if he could help.

When I said I needed to go as I'd only popped out for two minutes to get my lunch he said, 'Yes you'd better go, you never know who's watching with a camera these days.'

John Davis was one of many ex-residents of Bryn Estyn who made sexual allegations against Peter Howarth. The total has risen since Howarth was convicted in 1994 and now stands at more than thirty.

In the light of Davis's words, which contain their own tribute to Liz Evans and her colleagues, the secret of Bryn Estyn – that it was an ordinary community home where the majority of the staff did their best to look after the difficult adolescents in their care – can perhaps, finally, be acknowledged.

Democracy, justice and legitimate violence

Some moderate proposals for reform

IN THE LAST QUARTER OF THE TWENTIETH CENTURY, in a number of appeals heard between 1975 and 1995, the House of Lords delivered a series of judgments which radically transformed the original similar fact principle. These judgments, as we have seen already, had the effect of removing a set of safeguards which once protected innocent defendants facing multiple allegations of sexual abuse. In 1994, in the Criminal Justice and Public Order Act, parliament introduced another change in the law. Until this time there had been a mandatory requirement on the courts that in all cases involving sexual allegations, the jury should be warned that it was dangerous to convict on the basis of uncorroborated testimony. This warning served to remind juries that people do make false allegations and to focus the attention of the prosecution on the quality of the evidence which had been collected.

The corroboration warning was still current at the time Peter Howarth stood trial (see above, p. 333) and his case itself demonstrates that such warnings may have relatively little effect in trials involving multiple allegations made by different complainants. But the abolition of the corroboration warning undoubtedly did have a significant effect on trials of 'domestic' cases in which a single complainant, often a daughter or stepdaughter, made uncorroborated allegations against a man. Many more convictions were obtained in such cases and there can be no question but that a significant number of those who were found guilty were entirely innocent.

Yet another development affected the attitude of the courts towards the question of 'delay'. One significant judicial ruling on the question of 'delayed' prosecutions of alleged child sexual abuse was made in 1990 by Mr Justice Judge (now Lord Justice Judge). The case, *R v LPB*, was an abuse of process hearing in relation to offences allegedly committed by a stepfather against a girl who complained only many years later when she was an adult. Mr Justice Judge gave a ruling which discriminated in favour of prosecutions based on late allegations of child sexual abuse, even where no corroborative evidence was available. He stated that delay in reporting child sexual abuse in the home was 'wholly understandable' because '[d]elay is directly connected with and may be a consequence of the offences ...'. He went on to say that he found it difficult to conceive of any circumstances in which a delay, however long, in the reporting of child sexual abuse, should ever lead to the proceedings being stayed in advance of the evidence being heard at trial. His further pronouncement that '[t]he delay here is the result of reticence by the alleged victim in reporting the allegation' is clearly based on a presumption of veracity. For, as Margaret Jervis has pointed out, in a memorandum to the Home Affairs Committee, a delay in reporting abuse has only occurred if the allegation is true; if it is a false allegation there has been no delay because there was never any offence in the first place.[633] Since a presumption of veracity about the complainant is a presumption of guilt in relation to the defendant, Mr Justice Judge was coming perilously close to turning one of the fundamental principles of British justice on its head in order to render it more likely that people could be successfully prosecuted on the basis of allegations of child sexual abuse.

Subsequent rulings in the higher courts overturned this judgment and confirmed that, in theory, stays should always be granted where the defendants could demonstrate, on the balance of probabilities, that they would not receive a fair trial because of the difficulties caused by 'delay' (which might include the disappearance of documents and the unavailability or death of witnesses).[634] In practice, however, it appears that the attitude adopted by Mr Justice Judge in 1990 continued to prevail in the courts. Throughout the next decade and beyond, the courts were extremely reluctant to exclude any allegation of sexual abuse on grounds of 'delay' alone, even when there has been a gap of thirty years between the alleged offence and the complaint. Again and again trials which are manifestly unjust because the accused has no hope of defending himself against a series of 'delayed' allegations were ordered to proceed by the judges concerned.

That there is at least some recognition of the dangers of the present state of affairs within the judiciary itself has been made clear on a number of occasions. Some of the most significant pronouncements on the question have been made by the Lord Chief Justice, Lord Woolf. On 23 November 2001, the *Independent* published an article by its legal affairs correspondent, Robert Verkaik, under the headline 'MANY CHILD ABUSE CONVICTIONS COULD BE UNSAFE, SAYS WOOLF':

> Dozens of men convicted of sexually assaulting children years after the alleged offences may be victims of miscarriages of justice, the country's most senior judge has warned.
> Lord Woolf, the Lord Chief Justice, said child abuse allegations 'were easy to make' and might be motivated by claims for compensation ...
> Lord Woolf said serious concerns had already been raised by the

Criminal Cases Review Commission over a number of paedophile convictions. In an interview with the *Independent*, Lord Woolf said the allegations involved 'very old offences' from former residents of children's homes. He said many of the recollections 'may not be accurate', especially when they were 'tempted' by awards from the Criminal Injuries Compensation Board and the police were asking 'Did anything happen to you?'

Plans to relax the rules of evidence so that juries could be made aware of previous convictions could add to the risk of miscarriages of justice in child abuse cases, he warned.

Lord Woolf urged judges to use their discretion to make sure juries did not hear overtly prejudicial evidence. 'With paedophiles it can be very difficult – the natural reaction is one that we have got to protect the children and juries will be affected by this. It may be that in some respects in relation to some sexual offences the balance has gone the wrong way already,' he added.[635]

Lord Woolf subsequently described the headline as misleading, but he accepted the substance of the story. He later returned to the same theme in a context where the authenticity of his pronouncements was beyond dispute. In February 2003 he presided over an appeal court hearing concerning the case of Mr B, who had been accused by his adult stepdaughter of abusing her when she was aged between 7 and 11. As the complaints were not made until at least thirty years after the alleged incidents, Mr B's lawyers applied to have his trial stayed as an abuse of process. This application was rejected by the judge and he was convicted.

The appeal court judges made no criticisms of the trial judge or of his decision to allow the trial to go ahead. However, they had clearly noted that the allegation of abuse had first been made to a psychiatrist and that there was at least a possibility that the woman had imagined the incidents. It was during his judgment in the case of *R v B* that Lord Woolf expressed the view which has already been quoted, to the effect that 'honest witnesses can convince themselves that something happened in their youth when it is subsequently shown that what they remember cannot be true' (see above p. 450). Because there were clearly doubts in the minds of the judges, they took the unusual course of quashing the conviction because of these doubts. In doing so, Lord Woolf delivered the following remarks which bear directly on the presumption of innocence and its importance:

> However, there remains in this court a residual discretion to set aside a conviction if we feel it is unsafe or unfair to allow it to stand. This is so even where the trial process itself cannot be faulted. It is a discretion which must be exercised in limited circumstances and with caution. When we exercise that discretion we must be conscious that we

are not only involved in deciding where justice lies for the appellant.
We must do justice to the prosecution, whose task it is to see that the
guilty are brought to justice. We must also do justice to the victim. In
this case we are particularly conscious of the position of the victim. If
she is right, she was treated in a most disgraceful way by someone
whom she should have been entitled to trust: her stepfather. For years,
for understandable reasons, as we have already indicated, she felt unable
to make public what had happened. She is entitled to justice as well.
But we also have to do justice to the appellant. At the heart of our
criminal justice system is the principle that while it is important that
justice is done to the prosecution and justice is done to the victim, in
the final analysis the fact remains that it is even more important that
an injustice is not done to a defendant. *It is central to the way we administer justice in this country that although it may mean that some guilty people
go unpunished, it is more important that the innocent are not wrongly convicted*
[italics added].[636]

The difficulty which Lord Woolf felt in expressing these views may be
judged by the care he takes to stress the importance of 'doing justice to
the victim'. Thus, at the very point when the presumption of innocence
is about to be restored to the appellant, Lord Woolf feels it necessary to
say that the stepdaughter may be right after all and that Mr B may have
treated her 'in a most disgraceful way'. He even refers to her as 'the victim' in spite of the fact that the judgment he is delivering is an acknowledgment of the fact that there is no compelling evidence that a crime has
been committed. In this he follows a trend which is now disturbingly
common among social workers, police officers, lawyers and the Crown
Prosecution Service. In all these professions there seems often to be an
inability to break a pattern of thought and speech which automatically
identifies any person making an allegation of sexual assault as a 'victim' –
even when there is no tangible evidence of a crime, or when the evidence
actually points the other way. It should be noted that this gravely prejudicial habit of thought and language itself implies – and enacts – a reversal
of the presumption of innocence.

All this having been said, the Lord Chief Justice's attempt to reaffirm
what had always been recognised as the fundamental principle of British
justice is extremely significant. The fact remains, however, that neither
Lord Woolf's words, nor the judgment of which they form part, begin to
measure up to the seriousness of the crisis whose existence they seem
obliquely to recognise.

During the nineteenth century and the early part of the twentieth,
judges tended to be acutely conscious of the principle enunciated by Lord
Woolf partly because they were more aware than are most judges today of

the true function of a judge in a democratic society. In earlier times, when the mystificatory notions which surround the idea of 'freedom' were not as much a part of people's consciousness as they have become today, most judges were aware that the administration of justice frequently entailed the legitimation of violence against those who had broken the law. Until the abolition of the death penalty in Britain in 1965, judges could not help but be aware that they were, potentially at least, agents of the most extreme form of violence. Its abolition did not mean, however, that judges ceased to be implicated in the lawful and necessary violence of the state.

The nature of such violence now tends to be obscured by the myths of modern liberalism and by the unthinking acceptance of such misleading notions as 'democratic freedom' and 'the free world'. What we in the West all too frequently forget is that the kind of 'freedom' which prevails in democracies is very far from being a form of untrammelled liberty. It is the historical product of one of the most disciplined and orderly of all religious movements. In Britain and America in particular our democratic institutions and traditions are deeply rooted in Puritanism, and in just the kind of God-fearing, law-regulated standards of behaviour that Puritanism sought to inculcate.

The failure to understand that the very freedom which those of us who live in Western democracies are expected to cherish depends on a kind of internalised violence, was well illustrated by some of the words of US defence secretary Donald Rumsfeld, at the height of the chaos which followed the invasion of Iraq in 2003. The turmoil and looting were, he suggested, merely signs of freedom. 'Stuff happens,' he said. '… It's untidy, and freedom's untidy. Free people are free to make mistakes and commit crimes and do bad things. They're also free to live their lives and do wonderful things.'[637] It would seem here that even an experienced politician has been so blinded by the rhetoric of modern liberalism that he has, momentarily at least, actually forgotten that in the United States people are not free to commit crimes, and that those who do break the law are violently restrained, imprisoned and sometimes killed by the all-powerful state which can alone ensure the harmony and stability of a 'free society'.

Violence, it should be noted, is inherent even in those judicially approved punishments which stop short of capital punishment. When judges impose the briefest prison sentence they are inevitably authorising the use of violence in certain circumstances. If any convicted person attempts to preserve their liberty, perhaps on the grounds that they are in fact innocent, they may be physically seized and even hit with truncheons until they comply with their sentence. Although the threat of violence may rarely be enacted, the threat is ever present. Merely to be arrested is to experience something of this violence and even those who have only been threatened with arrest may actually feel as though they have been beaten up, and may react with the kind of shock which the reality of such violence would occasion. In any democracy one of the principal roles of judges is to be the official and proper instigators of such state violence. The fact that it falls to others – police and prison officers – to enact the violence which is implicit in their sentences may help to obscure the violence of the judge's role, but it does not remove it. When the American campaigner against miscarriages of justice, Hans Sherrer, writes that 'The violence judges routinely engage in makes the carnage of serial killers insignificant in comparison', he is guilty of hyperbole. But this hyperbolic utterance comes closer to the real role of judges (especially in the United States where the death penalty is still in force) than many more orthodox and anodyne views.[638]

Contrary to what is implicit in the words of Donald Rumsfeld, the principal difference between democracies and dictatorships is not that the latter are based on repressive state violence while the former are not. It is that the forms of state violence sanctioned by democracies are, in theory, carefully regulated and delivered from arbitrariness and undue oppressiveness by an independent judiciary whose powers are ultimately defined by an elected state assembly.

As already noted, judges used once to be much more aware of their role as the lawful agents of the state's violence than they have been in recent years. It is partly for this reason that both British and American judges were traditionally so scrupulous in seeking to control and moderate their own powers. Above all, they upheld the presumption of innocence out of an oblique recognition that those who are wrongly convicted suffer not simply an injustice but inevitably become the actual or potential victims of state violence.

The great tragedy which began to overtake the administration of justice during the twentieth century appears to have been brought about by the confluence of two different kinds of pressure. On the one hand the increasing mystificatory power of liberal myth-making has helped to obscure the true nature of democratic states. To the extent that liberal myths have rendered almost invisible the role played by state violence in maintaining democratic 'freedom', it may be that judges have tended to become less scrupulous about their own role in legitimating such violence. At the same time, the demonisation of sexual offenders generally, and of paedophiles in particular, has placed an increased pressure on the judiciary to abandon traditional safeguards against miscarriages of justice.

The removal of the corroboration warning and the effective destruction of the similar fact principle have created a situation whose gravity would be difficult to overstate. In certain circumstances innocent people may now quite easily find themselves arrested, tried and imprisoned on the basis of false allegations made by convicted criminals who are either tacitly encouraged or suborned by agents of the state. As a result, the distinction between the kind of justice which is found in democracies and the kind found in dictatorships has been blurred. Indeed, in relation to some kinds of sexual allegations the distinction has been almost obliterated. As many imprisoned care workers know to their cost, we no longer have the kind of justice system which is appropriate to a democracy. In the sphere of child abuse allegations, we have a justice system which resembles, in its arbitrariness and oppressiveness, that of a dictatorship.

However, the dismantling by the judiciary of traditional safeguards against wrongful convictions in sexual cases appears to have come about because of error, ignorance and prejudice on the part of a small number of judges rather than because of any deliberate policy. Precisely because of this, there is at least a possibility that the judiciary may still find it within itself to restore those safeguards. The pronouncements of the Lord Chief Justice which have been cited suggest that it is not yet time to abandon hope in this respect.

The central reform which is now necessary, without which the current witch-hunt will continue, is the restoration of the similar fact principle. When, in 1975, the House of Lords delivered its judgment in *Boardman* (see above pp. 360-2), there were certain pronouncements which, had they been followed rigorously, would themselves have served to preserve the principle. Lord Wilberforce, for example, suggested that the criteria for the admission of similar allegation evidence would only begin to be met when 'the facts testified to by the several witnesses bear to each other such a striking similarity that they must, when judged by experience and common sense, either all be true, or have arisen from a cause common to the witnesses or from pure coincidence.'

The need to restore the demand for 'striking similarities' has been canvassed implicitly in the main body of this book (see pp. 368-9).[639] Just as important, however, is the stress Lord Wilberforce's words place on the importance of establishing whether the similarities in a series of allegations might stem not from their factual accuracy but from 'a cause common to the witnesses':

> I use the words 'a cause common to the witnesses' to include not only (as in Sims) the possibility that the witnesses may have invented a story in concert but also that a similar story may have arisen from a process of infection from media of publicity or simply from fashion. In the sexual field and in others this may be a real possibility: something much more than mere similarity and absence of proved conspiracy is needed if this evidence is to be allowed. This is well illustrated by the case of DPP *v Kilbourne*, where the judge excluded 'intra group' evi-

dence because of the possibility, *as it appeared to him*, of collaboration between boys who knew each other well. This is, in my respectful opinion, the right course, rather than to admit the evidence unless a case of collaboration or concoction is made out.[640]

These words both recognise the logic of the original similar fact principle and seek to preserve it. For unless it is clear that a series of allegations has been made quite independently, the fact that there are multiple allegations does not prove anything at all. Lord Wilberforce was not alone in making this point; Lord Cross expressed a similar view. In words which have already been cited, he noted that the crucial consideration in cases like *Sims* and *Boardman* itself was that the similar fact evidence was disputed and that a series of allegations were all denied by the accused: 'In such circumstances the first question which arises is obviously whether his accusers may not have put their heads together to concoct false evidence and if there is any real chance of this having occurred the similar fact evidence must be excluded.'[641]

The problem with *Boardman* is that these eminently sound pronouncements are effectively ignored in the judgment which is eventually given. The case was one which involved allegations of homosexual indecency made by three pupils against a teacher, where the possibility of conspiracy could not reasonably have been ruled out. Yet their seemingly ringing endorsements of the original similar fact principle did not lead either Lord Wilberforce or Lord Cross to dissent from the majority view which dismissed the appeal. Instead they both endorsed the view of their fellow law lords, while expressing the fear that the case may be setting the standard of striking similarity 'too low' (Lord Wilberforce), and that it was 'very much a borderline case' (Lord Cross).

The overriding impression is that the significant truth which Lords Wilberforce and Cross had spelled out so clearly was overwhelmed in practice by precisely the kind of prejudice against homosexuality which their Lordships had attempted to eschew and which had originally determined the reasoning of Lord Denning in *Sims*. In short one is led to suspect that the two noble lords failed to translate the clearly expressed principles into practice because of the fear or repugnance inspired by the offences which were alleged.

However, precisely because the views expressed by Lords Wilberforce and Cross reflect the original spirit of the similar fact principle, they have been endorsed by a number of more recent authorities. By far the most significant case in this respect is that of *Hoch v The Queen*. This Australian case, whose appeal was heard in 1988, involved allegations of indecent assault made against a care worker by three boys who had been in the same children's home. The judge had rejected an application to sever the indictment and hear the allegations separately. The trial had therefore gone ahead and the accused was convicted.

The appeal court held that the potential value of the similar fact evidence lay in the improbability of witnesses giving accounts containing marked similarities unless the alleged indecent assaults had occurred. However, in a ruling which was entirely consonant with the comments of Lords Cross and Wilberforce in *Boardman*, which it specifically cited, the court went on to hold that if the possibility of collusion could not be ruled out, this would deprive the evidence of its probative value and render it inadmissible. It so happened that the three complainants in the case had a close relationship (two were brothers and the third was a friend) and therefore would have had the opportunity to concoct their accounts. There was also evidence that one complainant had an antipathy towards the accused. In view of these circumstances the court held that the evidence of each of the three complainants lacked the probative force necessary to render it admissible as similar fact evidence in relation to the other offences charged:

> Similar fact evidence which does not raise a question of improbability lacks the requisite probative value that renders it admissible. ...
>
> [T]he evidence, being circumstantial evidence, has probative value only if it bears no reasonable explanation other than the happening of the events in issue. In cases where there is a possibility of joint concoction there is another rational view of the evidence. That rational view – viz. joint concoction – is inconsistent both with the guilt of the accused person and with the improbability of the complainants having [individually] concocted similar lies. It thus destroys the probative value of the evidence which is a condition precedent to its admissibility.

In an amplification of this ruling, which led to the quashing of the defendant's conviction, the presiding judges made quite clear the rationale which lay behind their view:

Admissibility of evidence of this kind depends not only on similarity between the acts which the prosecution seeks to prove but, more importantly, on the non-existence of 'a cause common to the witnesses'.

> If there is a real danger of the concoction of similar fact evidence it is consistent with the attitude which the law adopts towards evidence of that kind that it should exclude it upon the basis that its probative value is depreciated to an extent that a jury may be tempted to act upon prejudice rather than proof. That consideration is of special importance in cases where the fact to be proved is inferred not from

similar facts which have been clearly established but from the con-
catenation of the testimony of a number of witnesses who depose to
the occurrence of similar facts. The credibility of that testimony bears
directly on the probative force of the evidence. Several witnesses all
giving evidence to a similar effect are generally easier to believe than
one witness. But if the witnesses have put their heads together that is
not the case.[642]

The soundness of this ruling and its consonance with the original similar
fact principle is best appreciated by considering what appears to have happened in the trial itself. Here the defendant, whom we may, and indeed
should, presume to have been innocent, had found himself facing three
complainants all of whom were, according to his own evidence, making
false allegations of indecent assault. During the trial indications of possible collusion had emerged and the judge had found it necessary to warn
the jury explicitly 'of the danger of conspiracy between the boys'.[643]
However, because of the nature of sexual abuse cases it seems likely that
the huge prejudicial power of the evidence which had been presented had
overwhelmed the jury and prevented them from weighing properly the
evidence indicating that the allegations were, or might have been, fabricated. If the allegations had indeed been jointly concocted, an innocent
man had been convicted as a result of prejudice rather than proof. Ultimately the responsibility for this wrongful conviction, had it not been
overturned by the appeal court, would have rested not with the jury but
with the judge (or the judiciary as a whole) for failing to preserve the
logic of a legal principle expressly designed to avoid just such miscarriages
of justice. By maintaining that principle the ruling in *Hoch* was upholding
nothing other than justice itself.

Subsequent judgments in the Australian courts have clarified what
should be evident from the underlying principle – namely that 'concoction' should be construed broadly. As it was put in R v OGD (2000): 'Concoction is not limited to the circumstance where the witnesses might have
agreed, in what was referred to in *Hoch* as a conspiracy, to give false evidence; the term is wide enough to include concoction by a potential witness, in isolation, but after becoming aware of the allegations against the
accused person.' The same judgment also stressed that the decision in *Hoch*
ultimately turned not on the presence of a proven conspiracy, nor even on
the probability of such a conspiracy, but on the *possibility* of concoction:
'In the majority judgment, Mason CJ, Wilson and Gaudron JJ held that the
possibility (as distinct from the probability or real chance) of concoction
would have rendered the evidence inadmissible also.'[644]

The general conclusion reached in *Hoch*, which is squarely based on the
words of Lords Cross and Wilberforce in *Boardman*, is that wherever there

is a possibility that multiple allegations may be explained by joint or separate concoction, or indeed by any form of contamination, then the evidence in question is dangerous and should not be put before a jury in a single trial. It follows from this basic principle that different allegations obtained against a single defendant by a police trawling operation should automatically be deemed inadmissible in a single trial for the very simple reason that such allegations necessarily bear a rational explanation other than the guilt of the accused – namely that they may be the product of the investigation itself.[645]

To suggest such an approach is not to propose some new judicial formula. It is simply to reaffirm the original formula whose rationale was that it sought to avoid the possibility of innocent defendants being wrongly convicted.

If the original similar fact principle was restored, it would inevitably mean that police trawling investigations would cease to have any operational rationale. This in turn would mean that some care workers who were genuinely guilty of committing abuse fifteen or twenty years ago might escape conviction. That, however, has always been recognised as the price of justice. For, to cite the words of Lord Woolf again: 'It is central to the way we administer justice in this country that although it may mean that some guilty people go unpunished, it is more important that the innocent are not wrongly convicted.'

In practice, by refraining from trawling investigations, which use a huge amount of police and social services time, and whose overall cost (including the cost of trying and in some cases imprisoning, large numbers of innocent people) runs into hundreds of millions of pounds, police forces could make resources available for other forms of child protection work. Such work could then address the real problems of sexual and physical abuse which undoubtedly do exist and the investigation of which has for some years been starved of resources by reckless expenditure on 'historic' inquiries. Some chief constables, indeed, have already adopted just such a policy. Their wise example is unlikely to be universally followed however, so long as the doors of the courts continue to be held open to the kinds of dangerous evidence which trawling operations inevitably collect.

While the restoration of the original similar fact principle would have a significant effect on the practice of police trawling and on trials involving multiple complainants, it would have relatively little effect on trials involving uncorroborated allegations made by a single complainant. In relation to such trials it should be noted that the abolition of the corroboration warning in 1994 took place, in part at least, in response to understandable pressure brought by feminists. As Lord Woolf observed in the course of the judgment in R v B, 'Before the change in the law, judges often explained why corroboration was looked for: namely that allegations of sexual abuse are easily made but difficult to refute. However, this was, understandably, thought to be unnecessarily offensive to women who are normally the victims of such offences.' Since 1994, however one thing which has become abundantly clear is that men are also adept at making false allegations. Because of the large number of wrongful convictions which appear to have arisen in 'domestic' cases, there are now strong grounds for parliament to legislate to restore the corroboration warning – and indeed to introduce additional safeguards.[646]

One further reform which is an essential element of any attempt to restore justice to the prosecution of the offence of child sexual abuse concerns the question of compensation. Because our courts currently permit very large payments to be made to witnesses who make allegations of sexual abuse in criminal cases, and because there is no way of verifying these allegations, we have created a system which cannot but undermine justice. For there are now significant financial incentives to make false allegations of abuse. As a result, both the Criminal Injuries Compensation Authority and, more seriously, the civil courts can, and frequently do, reward criminal acts of perjury by conferring large financial benefits on those who commit them. The only way to deal with this situation in a manner which is consonant with ordinary principles of justice is to remove the very possibility of perjury ever being rewarded financially. Compensation, in short, should never be paid in circumstances where there is not unequivocal and indisputable proof that a crime has been committed and that an injury has been sustained.[647]

This is not an extreme suggestion. It is a moderate proposal, one of whose effects would be to make it more likely, by removing one of the main incentives to false allegations, that genuine victims of sexual abuse would be believed.

None of the proposals for reform which are outlined here is revolutionary. If they are adopted, the current witch-hunt will begin to falter and may eventually fade. If, however, judges, who are the gate-keepers of justice, continue to admit into their courts the kind of contaminated, prejudicial and dangerous evidence which has been accepted all too frequently in recent years, then the witch-hunt will continue.

If that happens, then a system of justice which, rightly, has been revered for centuries, will increasingly be held in contempt by all those innocent people, and their supporters, who continue to suffer under it.

Bryn Estyn: my *alma mater*

AS THIS BOOK WAS about to go to press I found in my files a typewritten document which had long been missing, presumed lost. It is an account of Bryn Estyn written in April 1992 by a former resident for the solicitor acting for one of the members of staff arrested on 15 March. It presents a warts-and-all portrait of the home which is both critical and affectionate, written by a 31-year-old man who is now a social worker (see quoted extract on pp.168–9). It later transpired that its author was 14 when he went to Bryn Estyn, not 12 or 13 as he had written, and that he was there for two years, not four. He arrived in February 1975, at a time when Arnold and Howarth were already in post. The text of his note (which is published here with his permission) has been edited for length but is otherwise reproduced as it was written:

BRYN ESTYN SCHOOL

Bryn Estyn was to all intent and purpose a classic example of a 'Total Institution'. It provided almost everything for the child in an environment that could give a child were he receptive and willing, an eclectic education in the broadest sense of the word. In some respects warmth love and care played a small part in this. There were in excess of 70 boys at the time I arrived there. In nearly all cases we were there as a result of a care order from a juvenile court, some for criminal offences, others because of serious family breakdowns and a whole lot of others in between. The idea that any boy there had come from a 'normal' home environment would be quite misleading to say the least. In many cases the boys were often a hundred miles or so from their families and therefore no continuity or real work could be done in trying to patch up a particular problem, or do any intervention work in order to secure an early return to the boys home. The average stay at Bryn Estyn was at least 18 months and in a lot of cases several years.

Indifference and lack of cohesive planning meant that in some cases where boys from other cultures / ethnicity and of different faiths were residents, no special care or attention was given and in some cases children lost their entire previous identities over a period of time. Like any institution, it had a heirachy amongst both the staff-group and of course amongst the boys as well. This usually meant that the younger more vulnerable boys were controlled quite informally. I must add by the older and harder boys. This of course was normally encouraged by the staff who I surpose thought it would lead to an easier life for them.

There was little if no self-advocacy amongst the boys and what little there was of course tended to be seen as 'devient' behaviour and a threat to the working order within the school. Individuality suffered greatly and this raised tensions at times – sometimes leading to anger, frustration and even violence. This violence was often misdirected. and unserious in nature, but often led to a feeling of being 'incarcerated', and of being forced to participate in activities they did not want to do.

In most cases, the staff group were both pleasent, amiable and funny. I have no doubt that the welfare and the care for the boys was the motivation behind working there, and of course human nature as it is, this led to a certain informal and of course formal (housemaster) relationship between boys and individual members of staff. In fact today we would see it as effective 'keyworking' by most, and perhaps in some cases as being a little 'inappropriate' at best or as in some cases putting oneself in a vulnerable position and at risk of accusations ... Very few members of staff as I recall were either qualified or very experienced in, dealing with at times quite disturbed adolescents, and in fact there was a very marked difference in both opinion and approach by different staff group teams. This of course led to both confusion and manipulation by the boys which again meant disturbances in the running order of the day.

What was the ethos behind the school? Certainly it did a good job of holding kids there, attempting to educate them and through example showing positive life images as opposed to the negative ones which they boys had been surrounded by. In my day we had a Fraudian psychiatrist who was kept quite busy and in some cases added to the confused state of the boys even more.

What then were its good points?

– A real sense of warmth security and care (for many the first time.)
– A place of never-ending stimulation.
– The opportunity to relax, take stock and think about the future
– The opportunity to experience new environments such as: education; pottery; woodwork; painting & decorating; outdoor pursuits; nature & the environment; sports; and a host of others.

There was an undeniable sense of being wanted. Of course one could argue that this was due to the statutary responsibilities on the staff, but their interest and in many cases compassion all led me to believe that they really did care. Again many boys were unable at the time to realise this, as I suppose in some ways I was at the time, and the frustration of being so far from home meant that little concern was shown by the boys for the efforts that the staff group tried to make their stay there more pleasent.

I can see the positive aspects of Bryn Estyn now because having spent approximately 4 years there and now at 31 having had the benefit of both working in personal social services, voluntary agencies and counselling organisations, I see a clear number of reasons why I believe the school was in its way a success. I am now working to start a BA course at University in the fall and certainly without much doubt I feel able to critizise perhaps analytically people who are currently not only casting quite often stereotypical images of CHE's (Community Home with Education on the premises) but are also because of current allegations of abuse at the school bismirching the good characters of many of the previous staff members and indeed the resident boys as well. I hope to show objectivity towards my 'Alma Mata' but give what I feel is factual reminiscence of my time there.

The post-mortem examination of Bryn Estyn School must show a vindication of the staff and the resident boys, once the legal system has finished with its investigations. This is not only crucial to credibility for former boys and staff, but in some ways has significant effects on how we as a society deal with children within the care system who do not fit into the foster-parent system or the intermediate treatment system, never mind the quite abhorrent system of Young Offender institutions that are wholly unsuitable for certain adolescents, and shows clearly the need for another form of intervention of which Bryn Estyn despite its obvious flaws, provided such an environment.

I feel able to comment briefly on the present interest in Bryn Estyn school in a little more detail. I was sent to Bryn Estyn because of a care order imposed on me because I was a 'rent-boy'. In fact I had not turned 13 when I arrived at Bryn Estyn school (Or had just turned 13) and of course these details were in my file for all staff to see. At the school I was 'actively seeking sex' from other boys, perhaps quite unaware of any concrete sexual identity at the time and certainly both consenting to what I suppose would be seen as heavy petting in this day and age. I suppose I am saying that I was an 'easy' target for any member of staff who had a taste for young boys and I can certainly state that at no time did a member of staff either make a pass at me or assault me in any way. Because I was close to several boys there, and rumours, inuendos and gossip being what it is, I am certain that had any member of staff been involved in such activity at the time I was at the school, I would have known about it and I believe the staff would have found out. I also think that being 'the devil you knew' would have meant that at some time I would have been approached even in a half-hearted way. ... It also seems to me that such activity just does not start like that, it seems from evidence elsewhere that the process is a long drawn out affair, which also has circumstantial evidence, inuendo and gossip there from the start. We are talking here of allegations made often more than 12 years ago which because of the highly motivated and principled staff group would certainly have meant an earlier detection and reporting of the abuse if it did occur.

As to the allegations of physical abuse, certainly one of the people charged [Paul Wilson] I believe was quite capable of such actions because I remember him to be a care officer who showed little concern to the boys, often did quite irresponsible things like climbing without appropriate clothing or equipment, and in my view not in the right job ... Generally I suppose at times some staff acted inappropriately in some situations, remember at that time there was no such concept as professional practice, indeed formal RSW [residential social worker] training was quite a new thing and therefore actions taken were often wholly wrong for the situation at hand.

So what is this all about? Who is telling the truth? Of course I cannot catagorically deny that this sort of thing never took place, I can only comment on my time there and how I feel that little truth should be placed on allegations that may or may not have happened in many cases 10 or 12 years ago, unless substantial evidence is available, especially testimony by an independent witness. Someone recalling for example that 'a number of boys frequently went to the Deputy Headmasters' private quarters to watch TV and have a little late supper' although of course is relevent, specific boys, specific nights, etc is just not available to the normal human memory, and some doubt must therefore be raised as to the credibility of using such recollections as the basis of actual abuse having occured. It has been put to me that the incentive at this time has been the possibility of compensation through a civil suit against, Clwyd Social Services, recent claims elsewhere seem to confirm this. The recent cases of abuse elsewhere fresh in mind with the incentive of a possible financial settlement plus an over-active and certainly confused reminiscence can of course lead to feelings that something must have occured, because 'I think it did occur.'

I certainly have no feelings of allegiance towards anyone of the charged individuals, though perhaps I do have sympathy. If I do have any allegiance at all, it is to the former staff and children who have had their respective characters bismirched by the allegations and the media interest in the school. Inuendos of 'colluding' with or 'ignoring' what was going on could be associated with either former staff or children and this must be seen for what it is. The professional integrity of the former staff must be upheld, and the characters of the former residents must be protected.

April 1992

Chronology of the North Wales story

1973	May	• Matt Arnold made head of Bryn Estyn
	October	• Bryn Estyn becomes Community Home
	November	• Peter Howarth appointed third-in-charge
1976	September	• Alison Taylor deputy officer-in-charge, Tŷ'r Felin
1977	January	• Haydn Jones, officer-in-charge, Tŷ'r Felin, leaves
		• Taylor made acting officer-in-charge, Tŷ'r Felin
	November	• Dodd (Bryn Estyn 1974-7) made o-i-c, Tŷ'r Felin
1978	February	• Ryan Tanner (10½) remanded to Tŷ'r Felin 21 days
1980	September	• Taylor leaves for CQSW course in Wrexham
1981	September	• Ryan Tanner (14) placed at Bryn Estyn
1982	March	• Taylor starts 10-week placement at Bryn Estyn
	June	• Taylor makes congratulatory entry in logbook
	August	• Taylor officer-in-charge at Tŷ Newydd, Bangor
1984	23 May	• Taylor called to formal disciplinary hearing
	29 May	• Taylor alleges boy assaulted by Tŷ'r Felin teacher
	August	• Bryn Estyn closes due to re-organisation
	September	• Taylor calls police in re bump and bruise
	October	• DI Gregson concludes the allegation is unjustified
1985	November	• Memo refers to Tŷ Newydd's 'imminent' closure
	20 November	• Graham Ennis (15) suddenly moved to Tŷ Mawr
1986	2 February	• Girl claims Ennis had sex with Jane Harkness
	4 February	• Dodd 'clears' Jane Harkness by telephone
	February	• Taylor takes new allegations to Cllr Marshall
	20 February	• DCS Owen visits Marshall and meets Taylor
	26 March	• Taylor details second-hand allegations in statement
	April-Sept	• Owen finds complaints false or unsubstantiated
	23 July	• Birley tells Owen he has not been sexually abused
	October	• Owen's report to the CPS criticises Taylor
	December	• Gwynedd CC informally suspends Taylor

1986	29 December	• Ex-resident makes more second-hand allegations; Owen fails to substantiate any of these
1987	13 January	• Taylor officially suspended
	17 January	• Taylor tells Mrs Thatcher she saw abuse herself
	June	• Height of Cleveland child sexual abuse crisis
	October	• DCS Owen submits second report to CPS: 'There is every likelihood … she will manipulate others in the future to make similar complaints'
	3 November	• Taylor dismissed by Gwynedd County Council
1988	29 February	• Taylor writes to health minister, Tony Newton; she describes, for the first time, a brutal assault she claims she witnessed in 1980
	May–June	• Nottingham satanic abuse allegations
	July	• Butler-Sloss Cleveland report published
1989	March	• Investigation into Frank Beck is launched
	June	• Yorkshire TV approach Taylor to make film
	12 September	• Taylor and Tanner filmed for Yorkshire TV
1990	February	• YTV abandon Gwynedd film for Castle Hill
	April	• Young woman makes allegation against Rutter
	15 June	• Male resident of Cartrefle accuses Stephen Norris
	5 October	• Norris pleads guilty to indecency against 3 boys
1991	7 May	• YTV screens Castle Hill film on care home abuse
	24 May	• Nelson reports Tŷ Mawr suicide in *Independent*
	30 May	• Publication of Staffordshire Pindown report
	31 May	• Headline: 'PINDOWN VICTIMS TO SEEK DAMAGES'
	May/June	• Taylor takes her allegations to councillor Parry
	10 June	• Parry and King hold crisis meeting with Jevons
	17 July	• 'Paedophile-ring letter' sent to chief constable
	30 July	• Fred Rutter convicted of rape and indecent assault
	2 August	• Police launch investigation into Clwyd homes
	4 August	• Tanner, alerted by Taylor, tries to make statement
	8 August	• Tells police Singer & Holden victims(?) of Howarth
	20 August	• Police trawl complaint against Howarth from Singer who also accuses David Birch
	September	• Parry contacts *Independent*, alleging police cover-up
	12 September	• Peter Wynne tells police he has encountered no sexual abuse: '…I enjoyed my time at Bryn Estyn'
	15 September	• Police trawl allegation against Howarth from Holden

1991

19 September	• Parry meets journalist Dean Nelson at London hotel
24 September	• Singer makes crowbar and spiked-dildo allegations
26 September	• HTV film: complaints re Dodd by Taylor & Tanner
October	• Birley tells police he has never been abused
12 October	• Nelson meets Taylor at her home in Bangor
7 November	• The *Independent* formally commissions Nelson
November	• Taylor tells Nelson Wynne was abused at Bryn Estyn
November	• Tanner phones Wilson: 'out to get Howarth & Doddy'
12 November	• Nelson interviews Paul Wilson about Bryn Estyn
14 November	• Police warn Taylor re contacting witnesses
15 November	• Wynne tells Nelson he was not sexually abused Nelson notes: 'I did not believe him'
16 November	• Birley, who has been in contact with Taylor, tells Nelson that Howarth abused him
	• Wynne, coaxed by Nelson, accuses Howarth
30 November	• Frank Beck receives five life sentences
1 December	• The *Independent on Sunday* publishes article
2 December	• Police merge Clwyd and Gwynedd inquiries
6 December	• Bryn Estyn helpline starts, staffed by NSPCC
December	• Tanner & Wynne launch compensation claim
10 December	• Police visit M West. 1st dog-walking allegation

1992

22 January	• Brendan Randles alleges abuse by unnamed man
23 January	• Police see John Duke. 2nd dog-walking allegation
February	• Nelson returns to seek evidence against Anglesea
5 February	• Nelson faxes new Wynne interview to *Independent*
Feb-March	• Tanner shows Randles photograph of Howarth
5 March	• Police see Surtees. 14-mile-run allegation against H
15 March	• 16 former Bryn Estyn staff arrested in dawn raid
24 March	• Daniel Mead tells police he was not abused
27 March	• Police return; Mead makes allegation against H
30 March	• Police visit Steward. He alleges indecent assault
6 April	• Police visit Waite who alleges indecent assault
23 April	• Steward makes sick-bay allegations re Howarth
30 April	• Police visit Purnell who alleges indecent assault
5 May	• Brendan Randles names assailant as Howarth; now alleges rape by him and unidentified man
8 May	• Tanner admits helping Randles make allegations
18 June	• Nelson elicits vague allegations from Humphreys

1992	19 June	• Nelson shows photo of Anglesea to Humphreys who alleges Anglesea and Howarth abused him
	29 June	• Nelson re-interviews Humphreys. He alleges rape
	18 August	• Humphreys seen by N Wales police in London
	20 August	• Steward tells police Nelson is harassing him. Says 'at no time did Anglesea ever sexually abuse me'
	24 August	• Steward goes to London. Meets Nelson at his flat
	3 September	• Steward complains he is being hassled by Nelson
	4 September	• Steward tells Nelson Anglesea abused him
	9 September	• Steward makes new, graver allegation to police
	11 September	• Steward swears affidavit prepared by Nelson
		• *Independent on Sunday* declines to publish story
	13 September	• Story is published by the *Observer* on front page
	September	• Nelson, seeking 3rd allegation against Anglesea, questions Wynne, with Taylor as 'memory prompt'
	17 September	• HTV: Humphreys & Steward accuse Anglesea
		• Holden watches Humphreys & Steward on TV
	Oct–November	• Carl Holden is visited by BBC journalists
	30 November	• BBC films Holden accusing Anglesea

1993	8 January	• Wynne tells police of visit by Nelson & Taylor
	27 January	• *Private Eye* names Anglesea and alleges cover-up
	11 February	• Police interview Alison Taylor re Wynne, on suspicion of attempting to pervert course of justice
	March	• CPS drop case against Anglesea, who is now suing HTV, *Independent*, *Observer* and *Private Eye*
	April	• Nefyn and June Dodd are arrested but not charged
	13 May	• Steward threatens to sue the *Eye*. Wants £60,000
	June/July	• Steward meets Ian Hislop and asks for new car
	22 September	• Norris pleads guilty to indecent assault or buggery of 6 Bryn Estyn boys

1994	6 January	• After his partner leaves, Wynne hangs himself
	12 January	• Clwyd CC sets up independent Jillings inquiry
	1 April	• Randles is found dead: 'gross abuse of alcohol'
	26 May	• Taylor makes statement for Anglesea libel trial
	13 June	• Trial of Howarth and Wilson on sexual charges
	8 July	• Howarth found guilty, 10 years. Wilson acquitted
	31 October	• Steward says he won't give evidence unless paid
	7 November	• *Private Eye* pays Steward £4,500 to settle claim
	14 November	• Anglesea libel trial begins in London

1994 28 November • Wilson pleads guilty to 3 physical assaults

6 December • Libel jury returns verdict in favour of Anglesea

1995 12 January • David Birch is acquitted on two sexual charges

2 February • Mark Humphreys commits suicide

9 February • John Allen, of Bryn Alyn, convicted of indecent assault against six former residents. Six years

21 May • Simon Birley commits suicide

1996 22 February • Clwyd receives Jillings report & seeks legal advice

26 March • The council accepts advice not to publish report

1 April • Clwyd County Council dissolved

7 April –June • Using a leaked copy of Jillings, the *Independent* runs campaign to press for public inquiry

13 June • BBC radio suggests abuse in children's homes 'may be the norm rather than the exception'

• PM 'reads riot act' to cabinet to force inquiry

17 June • William Hague announces Waterhouse Tribunal

1997 21 January • The Tribunal opens in Ewloe, Flintshire

24 April • Peter Howarth dies of a heart-attack in prison

1998 7 May • The Tribunal holds its last hearing

1999 30 September • Report handed to secretary of state for Wales

2000 15 February • Tribunal report published as 'Lost in Care'

16 February • Massive coverage in the national press, much of it featuring Tanner and Taylor. The latter's vindication by Waterhouse is widely reported

11 April • Alison Taylor is presented with a *Daily Mirror* Pride of Britain Award at ceremony held in the Hilton, attended by prime minister, Tony Blair

People and places

Brief reference notes are provided here for the main people and care homes in the North Wales story. An asterisk [*] indicates that a name has been changed.

CARE HOMES

Gwynedd

Tŷ'r Felin: A small, purpose-built community home in a large council estate in Maesgeirchen, on the northern outskirts of Bangor. Initially built in 1973/4 as an observation and assessment centre, it gradually became a dual-purpose institution, providing places for twelve or more children (boys and girls), half for assessment and half for longer term residence. Education was provided in one classroom by one teacher. After the retirement of Nefyn Dodd in May 1990, Tŷ'r Felin became almost entirely a residential home. It was closed in the autumn of 1995 and demolished in March 1997.

Tŷ Newydd: A stone, lodge-type building about a mile south-east of the Maesgeirchen estate where Tŷ'r Felin was situated. It was originally used as a hostel for young men but was re-opened as a community home in 1982 to provide accommodation for about ten boys and girls who attended local schools or Tŷ'r Felin for their education. The officer-in-charge from its reopening in 1982 until her suspension on 1 December 1986 was Alison Taylor. It would appear that she inherited a building which was in a run-down condition. The home was closed in January 1987.

Y Gwyngyll: A purpose-built community home in a small private housing estate at Llanfairpwll (Llanfair PG) in Anglesey, about three miles from the suspension bridge over the Menai Strait which links the island to the mainland. It opened in January 1979 and provided accommodation for sixteen boys and girls – and sometimes more.

Queen's Park: A small community home situated in a council estate near the centre of Holyhead, Anglesey, which provided accommodation for up to eight boys and girls in five quite spacious bedrooms. At the time that Graham Ennis was abruptly transferred to Tŷ Mawr in November 1985 there were about five children in residence.

Clwyd

Bryn Estyn: The building in which Bryn Estyn was housed is a large mansion on the outskirts of Wrexham. It was built in 1904, in the style of an Elizabethan manor house, by a successful Wrexham brewer. From 1942 onwards it was an approved school for boys from the Merseyside area. In October 1973 it became a local authority community home with education on the premises. In 1975, under its new principal, Matt Arnold, Bryn Estyn held 64 boys of whom 15 were accommodated in Cedar House, a unit for boys of working age, and the rest in the main building. There were 44 members of staff including 8 teachers and 18 houseparents. The home took boys from Clwyd itself, from South Wales, Mid Wales, Gwynedd and occasionally Cheshire and Merseyside. In 1977 the working boys unit was closed and Cedar House became a wing for the younger Bryn Estyn boys. A year later this 'junior' wing of Bryn Estyn was moved to Clwyd House, a new purpose-built unit in the grounds of the main building. Although numbers declined in subsequent years, sometimes to almost half this number, Bryn Estyn continued to take many of the same kind of boys who would have been sent to an approved school in an earlier era, and a large proportion were sent there on care orders after committing criminal offences. In the last eighteen months of its existence, with the shadow of closure hanging over them, and with the principal, Matt Arnold, ill, the Bryn Estyn staff appear to have become demoralised and standards declined. In the view of some who worked there, however, the home continued to function well until this point.

Gwent

Tŷ Mawr: Tŷ Mawr was situated on the edge of the small village of Gilwern not far from Abergavenny in Gwent. Like Bryn Estyn, it was originally an approved school run by the Home Office. In 1974 it became a community home under the control of Gwent County Council. Before 1983 there were about 100 boys in residence but over the next few years the numbers were reduced to almost half of this. In 1991, after articles by Dean Nelson had been published in the *Independent* suggesting that Tŷ Mawr was driving vulnerable young people to suicide, the Secretary of State for Wales announced an inquiry into the home which was to be conducted by Gareth Williams QC and John McCreadie. Although they recommended the closure of Tŷ Mawr on the grounds that it had outlived its usefulness, they found that there was no truth in the most serious charges which had been made against it. In describing the home, they also noted that 'There is no perimeter fencing of any sort.' This was important, they said, because 'a contrary impression has sometimes been given by press photographs'.

CARE HOME EX-RESIDENTS

Gwynedd

Birley, Simon, (d. May 1995): see below, under *Clwyd*

Dunlop, Jennifer*: One of the complaints Alison Taylor brought forward in March 1986 concerned this girl, who was a resident of Tŷ'r Felin. According to Taylor, Jennifer had been assaulted by Nefyn Dodd and, as a result, was badly bruised on her body; she had, Taylor said, been 'beaten black and blue'. However, when she was interviewed by DC Joanne Bott in the presence of her foster mother, she said that no such incident had happened: 'It is fair to say that whilst I stayed at Tŷ'r Felin at no time was I treated in an unfair or unreasonable manner … On no occasion did Mr Dodd lift a finger towards me, or even threaten to do so.'

Ennis, Graham*: In 1985, Ennis, who was 15 at the time, was a resident at Queen's Park, a small community home at Holyhead in Anglesey. In November, when the officer-in-charge was on extended sick leave, rumours began to circulate that he was having sex with a young female member of staff, Jane Harkness*. On 20 November Ennis was abruptly removed from Tŷ'r Felin and driven in a taxi to Tŷ Mawr in South Wales. He later claimed that he had been moved 'to keep my mouth shut about the fact I was sleeping with her'. When the officer-in-charge, Beryl Condra, returned to work in February she was told by another resident that, before his sudden transfer, Ennis had been having sex with Harkness. When Harkness was interviewed by Dodd and another officer she denied that there had been any sexual relationship. Dodd subsequently produced a memorandum in which he claimed that the head of Tŷ Mawr, Christopher Phelan, had, at his request, conducted an investigation into the matter and had found the allegations to be untrue. The details of Dodd's memo are highly questionable and he appears to have done everything he could to exonerate Harkness, one of whose relatives worked for the county council. Ennis, meanwhile, continued to maintain that his allegation was true.

Harbour, Peter*: Harbour spent a year at Tŷ'r Felin and was then moved to Y Gwyngyll in Anglesey. In March 1986, when he was 16, he made a false allegation against Gerry Norman, a care officer who had previously been in the marines. He claimed that Norman had hit him, causing an injury, but he had in fact inflicted the injury himself. He phoned the director of social services, Lucille Hughes, and, after she had arranged for a car to collect him, made his complaint to her in person. He then decided he did not wish the police to pursue the matter. This incident took place just a week before Alison Taylor made a statement to DCS Owen on 26 March 1986. The second-hand complaints she set out included one allegedly made by Harbour. According to Taylor he had complained that when he was at Tŷ'r Felin, Nefyn Dodd and the teacher, John Roberts, regularly punched, slapped and kicked him in order to entertain the other children. Harbour had made no mention of this in his recent meeting with the director and, when interviewed by the police, declined to make the complaint formally. However, he was subsequently moved to Tŷ Newydd, where Taylor was officer-in-charge. She prepared an aide-memoire for him in which he alleged assaults even more vicious than those previously described. Having done this, she called the police and DC Joanne Bott took a statement from the boy which closely followed the one Taylor had prepared for him. Given all the circumstances, it was reasonably clear that the complaints which Harbour made in this statement were entirely without foundation.

Harper, Lewis*: Harper was put into care at Tŷ'r Felin on 1 May 1980 when he was thirteen years old and remained there until December of the same year. While he was at the home he gained a reputation for making false allegations. On one occasion he made a hoax 999 call in which he reported that a man had jumped into the Menai Strait, a claim which led to the scrambling of an RAF helicopter. When he left Tŷ'r Felin he spent a year at Bryn Estyn, from January 1982 to January 1983, during all of which time Ryan Tanner was also there. In January 1988, in a letter to the health minister, Tony Newton, Taylor claimed that she had seen Nefyn Dodd viciously assault Harper using his fists and a cane. She had made no mention of any such allegation to DCS Owen in 1986 but it now underwent a series of transformations. When Taylor was cross-examined about her claim at the Tribunal a great deal of evidence emerged which suggested that it was untrue.

Mason, John*: Mason was in care at Tŷ Newydd at the time Alison Taylor was officer-in-charge. In May 1984 he returned from Tŷ'r Felin, where he was attending school with what was subsequently described as 'a bump and a bruise which later faded'. Taylor later obtained a statement in which he claimed he had been hit by the teacher, John Roberts. When the police investigated this complaint they could not substantiate it and were sceptical of Taylor's motives in bringing forward the allegation (see Gregson, DI, under police officers).

Tanner, Ryan*: Ryan Tanner was in care at Tŷ'r Felin, Bryn Estyn and at Y Gwyngyll. After his parents had split up when he was a young child, he became, by his own account, 'a tearaway' and began to steal money from electricity meters at the age of eight. On 1 February 1978, when he was 10½, he was placed on remand at Tŷ'r Felin for 21 days. He was then placed under a care order and transferred to another home in Gwynedd – Eryl Wen. In September 1981, at the age of fourteen, he was sent to Bryn Estyn where he met Alison Taylor during her three-month placement at the home. In June 1983 he was transferred to Y Gwyngyll in Anglesey where he spent 15 months before moving into approved lodgings. He was eventually discharged from care in May 1985, three months before his eighteenth birthday. After spending 10 months in prison for drug dealing he says that he came out 'a reprobate – drinking, fighting and taking drugs'. He and Alison Taylor played key roles in the 1991–93 police investigation and in the North Wales Tribunal. After the Tribunal was over he completed a degree course in criminology at the university of Bangor. Although Tanner has made allegations of brutality and physical violence against a large number of people, none of these has ever led to a successful prosecution and some of his claims are clearly untrue. Tanner has never alleged that he was sexually abused although he was once wrongly reported as having done so.

Thomas, Hannah*: Was in care at Tŷ'r Felin at the time Taylor was deputy to Nefyn Dodd. At the end of December 1986, not long after DCS Owen had completed his investigation into Taylor's complaints, Hannah Thomas contacted a police constable saying she knew of more complaints. She then made a statement setting out four new second-hand allegations, including a claim that Dodd had thrown a nine-and-a-half stone boy over the goalposts on the Tŷ'r Felin football pitch. When DCS Owen investigated these new claims he was unable to find any evidence on which a criminal prosecution might be based. During the 1991–93 investigation Hannah Thomas made a statement to the police saying that before she contacted the police in 1986 she had been approached by Taylor and encouraged to do so. Taylor has always denied this.

Thomas, Michael*: When Alison Taylor made her statement to DCS Owen in 1986 her most recent complaint concerned this Tŷ'r Felin resident. She said that, according to the boy, June Dodd had 'thumped him on the shoulder and knocked him into a chair' when he had refused to apologise for causing trouble in the home. When interviewed by Gethin Evans, the boy made no complaint of being hit. Gillian Roberts, a care officer who had witnessed the incident, said that Mrs Dodd had simply pushed the boy into a soft easy chair: 'That's all the so-called assault amounted to. It was nothing more than what I would apply to my own child. It was not an assault by any stretch of the imagination.'

Clwyd: Bryn Estyn

Birley, Simon, (d. May 1995): Placed in care at Bryn Estyn in October 1982 where he remained until the home closed in the summer of 1984. Subsequently in care at Tŷ Newydd near Bangor during the time Alison Taylor was officer-in-charge. After the two-cans-of-shandy innuendo (chapter 8), he told DCS Owen in 1986 that he had not been abused and repeated this to the North Wales Police in 1991. Subsequently, after contact with Taylor, he made an allegation against Peter Howarth to Nelson. He later appeared in Howarth's trial as a complainant.

Duke, John*: former resident of Bryn Estyn who made allegations of indecent assault and buggery against Peter Howarth in February 1992, six weeks after similar allegations had been made by Martin West. Both sets of allegations involved taking Howarth's dog for a walk. Duke and West knew each other at Bryn Estyn and met again while they were both in prison.

Evans, John Richard* ('the white John Evans'): Born in South Wales, Evans was in care at Bryn Estyn in 1981–82 and got to know Howarth well. Alison Taylor claimed that Evans had told her that he had been abused by Howarth throughout his time at Bryn Estyn. He was supposed to have made this allegation on his last day at Bryn Estyn, after being taken to the station in a minibus. Evans has since said that he did not know Alison Taylor, that Howarth never abused him and was 'a good bloke'.

Evans, John Richard* ('the black John Evans'): This ex-Bryn Estyn resident, who had more than 100 criminal convictions, made allegations against Howarth after being visited in prison by two police officers in December 1992. He disappeared during Howarth's trial and did not give evidence.

Harper, Lewis*: see above under *Gwynedd*

Holden, Carl*: Holden was at Bryn Estyn from the spring of 1981 to the autumn of 1982. His time there overlapped with that of Ryan Tanner, who pointed the police towards him as a possible victim of Howarth. The police interviewed him in September 1991 in a community drugs centre in Cardiff. He became the second person to make an allegation against Howarth, and in his statement he described jumping off a railway bridge in Wrexham into the truck of a coal train which took him to Cardiff. He subsequently made an allegation against Gordon Anglesea after having watched Mark Humphreys and Lee Steward accuse Anglesea on HTV.

Humphreys, Mark (d. February 1995): Mark Humphreys came to the attention of social services in 1979 when he was fourteen after a cache of indecent photographs, including one of him, was discovered in the home of the 27-year-old sex offender, Gary Cooke. On 3 June 1980, after being arrested for theft, Humphreys was placed in care at Bryn Estyn and remained there until the end of August 1981. When initially visited by the police in 1991 he said that he had no complaints about his time in care. He began to make allegations against Peter Howarth after being visited by Dean Nelson. He only made allegations against Anglesea after Nelson had shown him a photograph of the retired police officer and supplied his name. He appeared as a witness for the newspapers in the Anglesea libel trial in 1994. After the trial he and his wife Wendy split up. In February 1995 he committed suicide.

Mead, Daniel*: This former Bryn Estyn resident was visited by police officers in March 1992 and told them that he had no complaints about his time at Bryn Estyn. Three days later he changed his mind and made allegations against Peter Howarth and Paul Wilson. He then made a claim for compensation. His allegations were not believed by the jury in Howarth's trial.

Purnell, Nick*: Purnell was at Bryn Estyn from March to December 1976. In April 1992 he was visited by police officers and made an allegation of indecent assault against Howarth. He said that Howarth had started to make sexual overtures to him in the presence of other boys. He subsequently altered his evidence about this. He also took a civil action against Clwyd County Council in which he made an allegation of buggery against Howarth. Although this and other serious allegations were made before Howarth's trial, he made no reference to them in the evidence he gave to the court.

Randles, Brendan (d. April 1994): In December 1982, at the age of fifteen, Randles was remanded to Bryn Estyn after being charged with burglary and spent a total of four nights there. In the autumn of 1991 Ryan Tanner gave Randles's name to the police as a former resident of Bryn Estyn. Tanner subsequently encouraged Randles to make allegations of sexual assault against Peter Howarth. In 1994, before the trial of Howarth had taken place, Randles died of gross abuse of alcohol.

Singer, Andrew*: Singer was a resident of Bryn Estyn at the same time as Carl Holden and Ryan Tanner. He was sent there in March 1981 and left at the end of June 1982. As a young man he became involved in a child abuse case when his own children were found to have injuries. He pressurised his wife into making a statement to the police taking the blame but was found out and convicted of attempting to pervert the course of justice. When police officers visited him in 1991, after having been pointed in his direction by Tanner, he made serious allegations of sexual abuse against Howarth.

He subsequently alleged that he had been sexually assaulted with a crowbar by Paul Wilson and subjected to a joint sexual assault by Howarth and Wilson which involved handcuffs and a spiked dildo. Singer was a witness at Howarth's trial in 1994. In 1997, although he was scheduled to give evidence to the Tribunal on several occasions, he failed to appear.

Steward, Lee*: After a troubled and insecure childhood, Steward was placed under a care order at the age of fourteen. He spent twenty months at Bryn Estyn, from September 1977 to May 1979. After leaving Bryn Estyn he spent ten days living in the flat of Gary Cooke while Cooke was away. After being accused of theft by another occupant of the flat, Steward led the police to a cache of indecent photographs taken by Cooke. These included a photograph of Mark Humphreys. Steward was visited by police officers in March 1992 and made allegations against Howarth and Dodd. Shortly after this his wife committed suicide, leaving him to care for their young daughter. His allegations multiplied and became more serious especially after he was interviewed by Dean Nelson. After initially complaining that this journalist was 'pestering' him and attempting to get him to say things about Gordon Anglesea which were not true, his attitude changed and he made a series of allegations against the retired police officer. He was not called as a witness in Howarth's trial after being ruled out by the Crown Prosecution Service. But he did appear as a witness in the 1994 libel trial after first attempting to secure £60,000 in libel damages from one of the defendants, *Private Eye*.

Tanner, Ryan*: see above under *Gwynedd*

Waite, Gary*: Waite was placed in care at the age of fourteen and was at Bryn Estyn from October 1975 to July 1977. One documented version of his social services record shows his stay at Bryn Estyn, incorrectly, as running from 1 January 1973 to 31 December 1978. When police officers visited Waite in April 1992, he made an allegation which appears to have been based on this incorrect record, claiming that, when he was about twelve, he had been invited by Howarth to sit on his knee and that an indecent assault and an act of buggery followed. In fact Waite would have been fifteen at the time he describes and the teacher, Gwen Hurst, recalls him as 'a big- framed, stocky lad, like a rugby player'. It became apparent at the Tribunal that Waite had made his original complaint after he and his family had watched television coverage of the Bryn Estyn allegations, and only after receiving a visit from police officers.

West, Martin*: Former Bryn Estyn resident who made allegations against Howarth after being visited by the police in prison where he was serving a three-year sentence. The allegations were made on 10 December, nine days after Dean Nelson's article had been published in the *Independent on Sunday*; they involved the claim that West had regularly taken Peter Howarth's labrador dog for walks in the grounds of Bryn Estyn.

Wynne, Peter (d. January 1994): Peter Wynne's parents split up when he was a child in a manner which left him almost homeless. He was taken into care at the age of eight, was then fostered but could not settle and so returned to care. He was sent to Bryn Estyn at the age of twelve and, because of his small stature and fiery temper, was frequently bullied, especially by Tanner. After leaving care, falling out with Tanner and attacking him with a 12-inch bayonet, he served a short prison sentence. When Wynne was first visited by the police in September 1991, he told them that Bryn Estyn 'was the best home I was in' and said that, apart from two minor incidents, 'I enjoyed my time at Bryn Estyn'. He spoke highly of several members of staff, including Liz Evans. However, soon after this, he teamed up with Tanner and made an allegation about a broken 'chandelier', some of whose details were demonstrably untrue. At this point Tanner and Wynne were using the same solicitor and their claim for compensation was reported in the local press. When Wynne was first interviewed by Dean Nelson, in November 1991, he told him that he had not been sexually abused. Nelson, however, did not believed him and returned the next day in an attempt to obtain an allegation from him. Once again, some of the details in the allegation Wynne now made were demonstrably untrue. Wynne was due to appear as a prosecution witness in the trial of Peter Howarth. In January 1991, however, after his relationship with his partner (and the mother of his children) had broken down, he committed suicide.

CARE WORKERS, SOCIAL WORKERS AND TEACHERS

Gwynedd

Condra, Beryl: Condra was officer-in-charge of Queen's Park, Holyhead from 1985 until her retirement in June 1997. She was critical of Dodd's regime in general and also with particular reference to his conduct in the Graham Ennis affair (see above, Ennis, Graham).

Dodd, Nefyn (b. 1936, d. June 2000): Officer-in-charge, Tŷ'r Felin Assessment Centre, Bangor (November 1977–May 1990). Previously worked at Bryn Estyn (1974–77, with break for training). Like the teacher, John Roberts, he became the victim of a series of false allegations of physical assault, many of which were brought forward or made by Alison Taylor. Taylor also falsely accused him of possessing child pornography. During the 1991–3 investigation a number of false sexual allegations were made against him. Although Dodd was arrested during this investigation, he was never charged with any offence.

Dodd, June: Married Nefyn Dodd in 1961 when she was working as a seamstress at Bersham Hall near Wrexham. It was she who introduced her husband, who originally worked as an operating theatre technician, to residential care. After Nefyn was appointed to Tŷ'r Felin, she joined the staff as a residential care officer and subsequently gained a Certificate in Social Services (CSS) social work qualification. In the statement which she made to the police about Michael Thomas, her colleague, Gillian Roberts, said: 'I would like to point out that Mrs Dodd was very fair, but firm with all the boys.'

Jones, Haydn: Officer-in-charge, Tŷ'r Felin Assessment Centre, 1975–77; went on sick leave in January 1977, at which point Alison Taylor became acting officer-in-charge.

Compton, Edward*: Assistant house parent at Tŷ'r Felin from May 1976. Officer-in-charge at Y Gwyngyll from September 1981 until December 1985.

Evans, Gethin: Evans was head of children's services at Gwynedd County Council. In March 1986 he investigated the complaint Taylor had made concerning Michael Thomas and found that it could not be substantiated.

Hughes, Lucille: Director of Gwynedd Social Services from October 1983 until March 1996 when she took retirement.

King, Larry: King was a principal officer for Gwynedd Social Services. He knew both Dodd and Taylor socially and has expressed the view that Taylor's resentment of Dodd's policies at Tŷ'r Felin sprang principally from the fact that she was not herself in charge. Although Taylor has consistently said that she was a reluctant applicant for the post of officer-in-charge, King disagrees: 'She wasn't very reluctant … She would have taken charge immediately if Dodd has disappeared.'

Norman, Gerry: A former marine who became a care-officer at Y Gwyngyll in Anglesey. In March 1986 he was falsely accused by a 16-year-old boy, Peter Harbour, of physically assaulting him. A week later Alison Taylor made a statement to DCS Owen in which she brought forward a number of second-hand complaints.

Parry, D. A. (David Alan): Deputy director of Gwynedd Social Services, in charge of residential care and children's services, 1976–81; Alison Taylor's line manager while she was at Tŷ'r Felin.

Roberts, John: Roberts was employed as Tŷ'r Felin's only teacher from September 1979 until July 1985. Like Nefyn Dodd he became victim of a series of false allegations of physical abuse, some of which were second-hand complaints brought forward by Alison Taylor. Ryan Tanner has also made a series of allegations against him. Since Tanner left Tŷ'r Felin before Roberts was ever appointed (and denies ever having returned), it is clear that these allegations are false.

Taylor, Alison Gwyneth (b. 1944): Appointed deputy officer-in-charge, Tŷ'r Felin Assessment Centre, Bangor, in September 1976; became acting officer-in-charge in January 1977 after Haydn Jones had taken sick leave. Applied unsuccessfully for the position of officer-in-charge, summer 1977. Resumed duties as deputy in January 1978 when Dodd took up the post she had held temporarily. Left to do CQSW course in September 1980. Training placement at Bryn Estyn in Wrexham, March–June 1982. In August 1982 she became non-resident officer-in-charge at Tŷ Newydd, a small care home on the outskirts of Bangor. Made statements to the North Wales Police in 1984 and 1986. Dismissed from her post in 1987. Played a major role in the 1991–93 Bryn Estyn investigation in Clwyd and later in the Tribunal. In the years after her dismissal she became a crime novelist and a columnist for *Community Care*.

Clwyd

Arnold, Matt (d. 1994): Appointed headmaster of Bryn Estyn in May 1973 when it was still an approved school. Remained in this post until the home was closed in 1984. Arrested in Operation Antelope on 15 March 1992. Released later that day on bail and never charged.

Bew, Connie: Appointed residential social worker at Bryn Estyn in 1976 and left when the home closed in 1984. She was one of those arrested on 15 March 1992 after a former colleague had falsely claimed that she used to allow boys to fondle her. Like most of those arrested, she was released later that day and never charged.

Birch, David: After leaving school, Birch, who excelled as a sportsman, and once swam for Wales, completed a diploma in physical education. He also worked with deprived children in the Bronx and as a junior youth leader in Wales. In 1979, at the age of twenty-one, he started work at Bryn Estyn as a residential child care officer. He was an extremely popular member of staff and some boys, including Peter Wynne, looked on him as a father-figure. He worked at Bryn Estyn until it closed in 1984 and subsequently worked at Chevet Hay. During the course of the police investigation Andrew Singer made highly implausible allegations of sexual abuse against him. A number of other residents, including Peter Wynne, made false allegations of physical abuse. Birch was arrested on 15 March 1992 and, in spite of the tenuous nature of the case against him, the police pushed on with the prosecution. When his criminal trial took place in January 1995 he was rapidly acquitted by the jury in relation to the complaints of sexual abuse. The allegations of physical assault were never proceeded with. By the time his trial came, he and his family had spent almost three years living under the shadow of false allegations whose consequences were only extended and exacerbated by the Tribunal hearings.

Dodd, Nefyn: see above under *Gwynedd*

Evans, Liz: After doing a teacher-training course at Cartrefle College, and working for a time as a supply teacher, Liz Evans joined the Bryn Estyn staff as a residential child care officer in 1979 at the age of twenty-three. She told the Tribunal that she recalled the home as having a generally happy atmosphere and said that she believed that most of the boys enjoyed their time there. She formed good relationships with some of the more difficult boys, including Peter Wynne, and remained at Bryn Estyn until September 1984. In October she was transferred to Bersham Hall and, after completing a CQSW course, she became a social worker for Clwyd County Council, and then a senior social worker for Flintshire County Council. During the 1991–93 investigation various false allegations were made against her and, although she was not arrested, she went to the police station voluntarily to answer questions and was suspended from her employment. During the Tribunal hearings a number of former residents specifically praised her and the Tribunal report notes that 'most of the witnesses who referred to her described her as a kind, caring and sympathetic member of staff' (LOST IN CARE, p. 118).

Howarth, Peter (d. April 1997): Howarth was born in Doncaster in 1931. He worked at first as an accounts clerk and, while employed by the Cementation Company, began doing welfare work for them. After working at a school for maladjusted children in Surrey, he was appointed as housemaster to an approved school and subsequently took a one-year residential course in childcare at Ruskin College, Oxford. In 1966, soon after finishing at Ruskin, Howarth was invited by his part-time tutor, Matt Arnold, to apply for a job in Axwell Park, an approved school in the north east. Subsequently he followed Arnold from Axwell to Bryn Estyn. He joined the Bryn Estyn staff in November 1973 as third-in-charge and became deputy head three years later. Howarth eventually retired at the end of July 1984. Even though he was visited by the journalist, Dean Nelson, in November 1991, he was never interviewed either by journalists or police officers and appears to have had little or no knowledge of the Bryn Estyn investigation until he was arrested on 15 March 1992. On the allegations made against him, see the entries for Birley, Duke, Evans, Holden, Humphreys, Mead, Purnell, Randles, Singer, Steward, Waite, West and Wynne. His trial began in Chester Crown Court on 14 June 1994. He was found guilty on seven counts of indecent assault and one count of buggery and was sentenced to a total of ten years' imprisonment. He died of a heart attack in prison on 24 April 1997 while he was waiting to give evidence at the Tribunal.

Hurst, Gwen: Having completed her training as a teacher at Cardiff College of Education in 1964, Gwen Hurst worked in a number of secondary schools in the Wrexham area before leaving teaching to bring up a family. She also worked as a youth leader for Denbighshire County Council. When, in 1975, she returned to full-time work, she took up a post as a teacher at Bryn Estyn where she also became, in effect, Bryn Estyn's main youth worker. On two evenings a week she would take a group of Bryn Estyn boys to a Wrexham youth club. She also tried to link them back into the community by putting them in touch with local sports clubs. She worked at Bryn Estyn until it closed and then continued as a social worker, enjoying a brief moment of national fame (in the form of a 'Golden Heart' award from Esther Rantzen of BBC television) for her role in organising child-care and nursery provision in the aftermath of the Welsh floods of 1990. As a UNISON steward she became involved with many former members of staff who were arrested or found themselves facing allegations after 1991. She became the leading figure in the Bryn Estyn Support Group and, early in the development of the North Wales story, she resolved that she would not rest until the true story of Bryn Estyn was made known.

Jevons, John: Jevons was appointed director of social services for Clwyd County Council in April 1991. Three weeks after this he took part in the meeting in Dennis Parry's Shire Hall office out of which eventually emerged the decision to launch the Bryn Estyn investigation and to raise with the North Wales Police the possibility that a paedophile ring might be operating in Clwyd children's homes. On 30 September 1995 Jevons left Clwyd to become director of social services for Cardiff. In 1996 he was approached by a whistleblower and once again took concerns to the police which led to a major trawling operation – this time conducted by the South Wales Police.

Norris, Stephen: Norris, who had previously worked at Greystone Heath in Cheshire, was 38 when, in March 1974, he became a joint houseparent with his wife at Cedar House, a unit for boys of working age at Bryn Estyn. When the working boys unit was closed and Cedar House became a wing for the younger Bryn Estyn boys in 1977, Norris was appointed a senior houseparent there. A year later he was made head of Clwyd House, a new purpose-built unit to which the younger boys, previously resident in Cedar House, were transferred. When Bryn Estyn closed in 1984 Norris moved to Cartrefle, a small community home at Broughton, about ten miles north of Wrexham, where he became officer-in-charge. He was suspended in June 1990 after a boy complained to a member of staff that he had been sexually abused by Norris. When he appeared at Chester Crown Court on 5 October 1990, Norris pleaded guilty to five specimen charges of indecent assault committed against three boys in his care. He was sentenced to three and a half years' imprisonment. During the main 1991 investigation more allegations were made against him and he was one of those arrested (in his bail hostel) on 15 March 1992. On 11 November 1993, at Knutsford Crown Court, he pleaded guilty to three offences of buggery, one of attempted buggery and three indecent assaults involving six former Bryn Estyn boys. He pleaded not guilty to ten other counts and was sentenced to a total of seven years' imprisonment.

Rayfield, John: Rayfield became a Methodist 'local' [lay] preacher in 1958. Before going into residential work, he was employed as a sales representative for a timber importer. He began to do voluntary work at Bryn Estyn when it was still an approved school in the early 1970s. This had come about through contact with Isabel Williams, a member of his Methodist church who had recently been appointed as matron. In March 1974, at the age of 51, Rayfield changed career and he and his wife became full-time house parents at Cedar House, the Bryn Estyn unit for working boys. When this unit closed he continued to work as a care officer, and in 1978 completed a one-year part-time CETSW training course in residential care at Stockport College. He retired when Bryn Estyn closed in September 1984. After the arrests of 15 March 1992, Rayfield, against whom no allegations had been made, offered his support to those who had been falsely accused and became an active member of the Bryn Estyn Support Group.

Wilson, Paul (d. 2001): 'Paddy' Wilson was born in Ireland. He was 24 when he took up his post at Bryn Estyn in 1974. He proved to be extremely talented as an organiser of outdoor activities for the boys and had a good knowledge of camping, canoeing and hill-walking. He was also, however, regarded by many Bryn Estyn boys as a bully; a number of former residents who enjoyed their time at Bryn Estyn have singled him out as the one member of staff who should not have been working with young people. In November 1991 he was telephoned by Ryan Tanner who wanted his help 'to get Howarth and Doddy' and mentioned a journalist who had come up from London to do a story about Bryn Estyn. Wilson subsequently met Dean Nelson and gave him an interview in which he presented the journalist with a deliberately distorted and self-serving account of the home.

Dodd and Howarth were presented in a bad light and Bryn Estyn was portrayed as an institution where violence was the norm. During their 1991–92
investigation, the police collected many allegations of physical assault involving Wilson. They also trawled from Andrew Singer two bizarre complaints
which included the claim that Wilson had sexually assaulted Singer with a
crowbar. As a result Wilson found himself standing trial alongside Peter
Howarth at Chester Crown Court in June 1994. During the trial he came
to the conclusion that Howarth was an innocent man and had something
approaching a crisis of conscience. He was found not guilty on the sexual
charges against him. In November 1994 he pleaded guilty to a number of
counts of physical assault. He was sentenced to a total of fifteen months'
imprisonment but the judge suspended the sentence for a period of two
years. As the Tribunal report comments: 'In fairness to Wilson it should be
said finally, … that the judge made that decision not only because of Wilson's pleas of guilty … but also because of the good character that Wilson
had established in the intervening years. After referring to the positive
aspects of Wilson's work on outside activities at Bryn Estyn, he said "I also
take into account that since you have become a mature man you have done
much on a voluntary basis for youngsters in the Chirk area, giving up many
hours, indeed many days, of your time to work with them, with the result
that you have fully earned the warm testimonials which have been presented
to the Court by parents, and by persons in responsible positions in North
Wales, who know of the work you have done.'''

JOURNALISTS

Jack, Ian: Jack began his career as a journalist on a small weekly paper in
Scotland in the 1960s. Between 1970 and 1986 he worked for the *Sunday
Times* as a reporter, editor and foreign correspondent. He was a co-founder
of the *Independent on Sunday* in 1989 and edited the paper between 1991 and
1995. His press awards include Journalist, Reporter and Editor of the year.
In 1995 he became the editor of *Granta*, the magazine of new writing. He
has written interestingly of the atmosphere of 'quiet desperation' which
sometimes prevails in the offices of Sunday newspapers on a Saturday afternoon: 'Nothing much has happened anywhere in the world: it rarely does
on a Saturday … Oh for another poll tax riot (a Saturday), or an IRA bomb
in the City of London (a Saturday also), or that wonderful and rare thing, a
genuine, copper-bottomed, well-researched scoop!' The Sunday newspaper
editor's greatest anxiety, he suggests, is about how to fill 'the great hole – the
lead story hole – on the front page' ('"Sexing up" those slack Saturdays'
Guardian, 23 August 2003). Of all the journalists involved initially in the creation of the North Wales story, Jack is the only one who has publicly
expressed doubts about his role.

Nelson, Dean: Before he was commissioned by the *Independent on Sunday* to report on allegations of abuse in North Wales, Nelson had already written articles for the *Independent* as a freelance. In particular he had reported on Tŷ Mawr, a community home in Gwent. These articles, which appeared in the *Independent* in May 1991, suggested that a harsh and uncaring regime was driving young boys to self-harm and suicide. An inquiry later commissioned by Gwent County Council, and undertaken by Gareth Williams QC, came to the conclusion that this view of Tŷ Mawr was not justified. By the time the report was published, however, Nelson had already been sent to North Wales. Partly because he had no time to conduct a thorough inquiry himself, he made extensive use of Alison Taylor and Ryan Tanner as sources and placed great reliance on what they told him. When the reference to Gordon Anglesea in his article of December 1991 resulted in a libel writ, Nelson was sent back to North Wales to see if he could find evidence to substantiate the libel. He eventually found two highly suggestible and deeply damaged young men, Mark Humphreys and Lee Steward, to whom he showed photographs of Anglesea, and who made a series of increasingly grave allegations against him. When the libel trial took place in London in November and December of 1994, Humphreys and Steward appeared as witnesses for the defendants but Nelson never appeared himself to face cross-examination. He apparently continued to believe in the allegations made to him by Humphreys and Steward even after evidence of the untruthfulness of these allegations had emerged. When Mark Humphreys committed suicide in 1995, Nelson wrote an article in the *Observer* in which he repeated Humphreys's allegations against Howarth as though they were true, even though Humphreys had not even been at Bryn Estyn for most of the time he claimed Howarth was abusing him there. By this time Nelson had become a staff reporter on the *Observer* where he later became the paper's Scotland editor. After a spell editing the Scottish edition of the *Sunday Times*, he moved to London in 2003 to head the paper's Insight team.

LOCAL COUNCILLORS

King, Malcolm: King once worked for Clwyd County Council as a social worker specialising in Intermediate Treatment or 'IT' – an approach which aimed to keep juvenile offenders out of care or prison. After resigning from this post, he became the manager of a charitable organisation called 'The Venture' – a combined adventure playground and youth club based on the Queen's Park Estate in Wrexham; later he also became a Labour county councillor and chair of social services. A fervent believer in the paedophile ring theory of abuse in children's homes, King played an extremely significant role in the process of decision-making which led to the launching of the 1991–93 police investigation. After a copy of the unpublished Jillings report had been leaked to the *Independent* in the spring of 1996, he also featured frequently in the campaign run by that newspaper to force the government to hold a public inquiry into the North Wales allegations. In May 2000 King became chairman of the North Wales police authority.

Parry, Dennis: A retired steelworker who became a Labour councillor in 1981, Parry became a member of the North Wales police authority in 1990 and was soon well-known as a critic of the North Wales Police. He was brought up in a children's home himself and would eventually become an executive member of NSPCC Wales and a member of a charitable organisation called Abuse Watch. In the spring of 1991, soon after he had become the leader of Clwyd County Council, he was contacted by Alison Taylor who told him 'that she had some complaints and grievances against the North Wales Police and would I meet her on them'. At the meeting which then took place, Alison Taylor outlined to Parry her version of the 1996/7 investigations into allegations of abuse in Gwynedd care homes; according to Parry she also talked about connections with Bryn Estyn. It was this conversation between Taylor and Parry which led to the crucial meeting in Parry's office in Shire Hall in Mold out of which emerged the decision to write a letter to the North Wales Police which mentioned the possibility of a paedophile ring operating in Clwyd children's homes. After his conversation with Alison Taylor, Parry appears to have become convinced that the police in North Wales were covering up abuse and was quoted in Dean Nelson's article of 1 December to this effect: 'I'm disturbed about the way these young people are being interviewed. We are fighting a machine trying to cover things up.'

POLICE OFFICERS

Ackerley, Peter, Detective Superintendent: Officer in charge of major North Wales Police trawling investigation, 1991–93, and of subsequent related inquiries. He has now retired from the force. In 2001 he was awarded the Queen's Police Medal in recognition of his work during the 1991–93 investigation.

Anglesea, Gordon, Superintendent: Anglesea became a sergeant in the North Wales force in 1969 and a police inspector in 1972. His first connection with Bryn Estyn was in 1979 when he was asked to set up an attendance centre in Wrexham for delinquent boys. He first visited the home in late 1979 and made occasional visits after that. In March 1991 he retired from the force and in December of the same year the *Independent on Sunday* published Dean Nelson's libellous reference to him. At this point there were no allegations against him. Allegations only emerged after Nelson returned to

North Wales in 1992 in an attempt to find evidence to defend the libel action which was being taken against the *Independent*. The libel trial in which Anglesea was vindicated took place in the Royal Courts of Justice in London and ended in December 1994 (see also entries for Steward, Holden and Humphreys).

Bott, Joanne, Detective Constable: took part in 1986 and 1987 Tŷ'r Felin investigations with DCS Gwynne Owen.

Gregson, Roy, Detective Inspector: Investigated John Mason's 'bump and a bruise' allegation in 1984. He came to the conclusion that 'This incident has been blown up out of all proportions' and that Alison Taylor 'started the wheels in motion purely to 'get one back on her employers'.

Johnson, Lorraine, Detective Chief Inspector: Specialised in child protection and family work and helped to lead the training session held in January 1992 by the North Wales for the major 1991–93 investigation.

Owen, Gwynne, Detective Chief Superintendent: Owen was head of North Wales CID from 1980, when he was promoted to DCS, until his retirement from the force in July 1988. He led both the 1986 investigation into Gwynedd children's homes, triggered by Alison Taylor, and the re-investigation launched in 1987 in response to the complaints of Hannah Thomas. At the conclusion of this second inquiry, Owen wrote as follows in his report to the CPS: 'The officer's view regarding Taylor remains unchanged and there is every likelihood that she will manipulate others in the future to make similar complaints, in an effort to keep the matter in the public domain, and in the belief that if sufficient mud is thrown some will stick.'

Notes

TMCHI = Tŷ Mawr Community Home Inquiry, Report by Gareth Williams QC and John McCreadie M.Ed., 1992, Gwent County Council.

NWTT = North Wales Tribunal Transcript.

LiC = Lost in Care: Report of the Tribunal of Inquiry into the abuse of children in care in the former county council areas of Gwynedd and Clwyd since 1974 ('the Waterhouse report'), HMSO, 15 February 2000. (References are to paragraph numbers, followed by page numbers.)

GCCA = Gwynedd County Council Analysis, 1991 (Document prepared by Alison Taylor, unpublished, Tribunal document 10992)

BUTLER-SLOSS = Elizabeth Butler-Sloss, Report of the Inquiry into Child Abuse in Cleveland 1987, London, HMSO, 1988.

HLP = Howarth's Legal Papers. In 1996, while he was in prison, Peter Howarth signed over to me the legal papers relating to his criminal trial.

HTT = Howarth Trial Transcript, *R v Peter Norman Howarth*, Chester Crown Court, July 1994.

1   I am half-quoting here the words of one of the scholars who has contributed most to our understanding of the role played by collective fantasies in Judaeo-Christian culture – the French historian Léon Poliakov. Poliakov made it his life's work to study that phenomenon which contains so much of our cultural history, and which speaks so eloquently and so disturbingly about our cultural psychology – anti-semitism. Throughout all the centuries of Christian history, he writes, there has functioned 'that terrible mechanism of projection that consists in attributing to the loathed people of God one's own blasphemous desires and unconscious corruption' (Léon Poliakov, *The History of Anti-Semitism*, vol. 1, Routledge and Kegan Paul, 1974, p. 274).

Poliakov's most distinguished colleague in this country, the British historian Norman Cohn, has done more than any other scholar to illuminate the role played in history by collective fantasies and this book would almost certainly not have been written had my own interest in witch-hunts not been awakened by Cohn's work some thirty years ago. See Norman Cohn, *Europe's Inner Demons: An Enquiry Inspired by the Great Witch-Hunt*, Paladin, 1976; *The Pursuit of the Millennium: Revolutionary Millenarians and Mystical Anarchists of the Middle Ages*, Paladin, 1970; *Warrant for Genocide: the Myth of the Jewish World Conspiracy and the Protocols of the Elders of Zion*, Penguin, 1970. As I have noted in the preface, all three books seek to establish the role played in history by collective fantasies and all three are concerned with 'the urge to purify the world through the annihilation of some category of human beings imagined as agents of corruption and incarnations of evil' (*Europe's Inner Demons*, p xiv).

In the original editions of his works Cohn inclined towards psycho-analytic explanations, and sought to interpret collective fantasies in the light of the theories of Freud and Melanie Klein. This leads almost inevitably to a view that modern examples of the witch-hunting mentality arise out of a kind of collective regression, as a result of which archaic modes of thought which have long been buried in our cultural unconscious suddenly return to dominate our behaviour. His own rationale for accepting the 'collective regression hypothesis' is to be found in the conclusion to *Warrant for Genocide*, 'A Case-Study in Collective Psychopathology':

> There are in fact many people who never cease to be small children in their emotional lives. Such individuals need authority figures whom they can idealise and trust unreservedly, as they once did their idealised parents; but they also need 'bad' authority figures, scapegoats on whom they can blame all their misfortunes and whom they can hate and attack with a clear conscience. Moreover such individuals tend to identify with the idealised parent-authority and to see themselves, too, as altogether perfect.
>
> In the grip of such fantasies men can develop into murderous fanatics. But what dominates the minds of murderous fanatics is to some extent present in the minds of almost everybody. In medieval Europe normal religion was experienced largely in terms of 'good' and 'bad' parental figures. This is less true in the twentieth century; but even today, people who have attained a relatively high degree of maturity may, in situations of stress, find themselves again using these infantile emotional mechanisms. Worse still the process can occur on a mass scale. Where there is widespread suffering and, above all, a widespread sense of disorientation and impotence, a wholesale regression to infantile modes of thinking and feeling can occur quite easily. And when it does, nightmarish fantasies of 'bad' parents can still influence the attitude and behaviour of a modern society [italics added]' (pp.287–8).

This view is clearly consonant with the idea that witch-hunts belong essentially to pre-rational modes of thought and that civilised societies will tend to grow out of them. While I have immense admiration for the work of Norman Cohn and the extraordinary manner in which he combines a rich historical imagination with meticulous scholarly research, I disagree with him fundamentally on this point. I would only add that Cohn has now retreated from his more psychoanalytical hypotheses and, in his ninetieth year, takes the view that there is too great a gap between the psyche of the individual and the conduct of entire societies to warrant the application of psychoanalytic hypotheses to history. The most recent paperback edition of *Warrant for Genocide* does not contain the conclusion from which the words cited above are taken.

2   See Joshua Trachtenberg, *The Devil and the Jews: The medieval conception of the Jew and its relation to modern anti-semitism,* New Haven, 1944.

3   Even our contemporary preoccupation with the threat from paedophiles has deeper historical roots than is generally recognised. Writing in 1951, the American journalist Howard Whitman warned that 'Children in alarming numbers have been the victims of molesters, exhibitionists, perverts and pedophiles. The sex hoodlum, hanging around schools with comic books and bubble gum to lure his victim, has imbued parents with a stark new fear.' According to Whitman the nation faced 'the grotesque, baffling problem of pedophilia'. He warned that people in positions of trust in churches or schools sexually molested large numbers of their charges, raising the possibility that covert paedophiles had infiltrated institutions in order to gain access to children. As Philip Jenkins comments, in his book *Moral Panic: Changing Concepts of the Child Molester in Modern America,* (Yale, 1998), 'It all sounds strikingly familiar' (p. 53).

4   A study of the headlines which have accompanied news stories in Britain about sexual abuse and paedophiles indicates just how literal the process of demonisation has sometimes been. Headlines such as 'Demons of the dark', 'Paedophile ring organised abuse at "evil" home' and 'Dealing with the devil' are relatively common.

5   The figure of 'hundreds of millions of pounds' is an estimate which includes costs incurred by the police, by social services, by crown and civil courts, by the CPS, by the Court of Appeal, by the North Wales Tribunal, by the prison service, by the CCRC, by the probation service, by the legal aid board, by other agencies and by psychiatric and medical reports. So far as civil claims for compensation are concerned, one firm in Cheshire alone, Abney Garsden McDonald, was already co-ordinating 700 cases by the year 2000.

6   Richard Webster, *The Great Children's Home Panic,* The Orwell Press, 1998

7   On 16 November 2004, the *Irish Times* reported that the Residential Institutions Redress Board (the state compensation scheme for victims of institutional child abuse) had received 4,633 applications to date 'and continues to receive applications at a steady rate'. The government estimate referred to was made in the 2004 annual report of the Comptroller and Auditor General.

8   Almost every other Canadian church has also been hit hard financially by these claims. As in Britain, some lawyers in Canada have begun actively to seek out complainants. In December 2000, to cite but one significant example, the Saskatchewan Law Society found it necessary

to reprimand one of its members and fine him $15,000. This lawyer's firm is responsible for bringing forward more than half of the 7,000 lawsuits which have been filed against church organisations that ran Indian residential schools. His offence was that he had solicited complaints from former residential students with misleading letters likely to create 'an unjustified expectation' of the levels of compensation which might be achieved.

9   *Report of the Internal Investigations Unit (Police and Public Safety Division – Nova Scotia Department of Justice) regarding the investigation into alleged abuse of residents of Provincial youth facilities*, pp. 357–8. This report was submitted to the deputy minister of justice in December 1999. It has not been published but, in October 2000, after pressure from a solicitor representing accused care workers and from journalists, a severely edited version of the report was released under the provisions of the Freedom of Information Act.

10   The Internal Investigation team go so far as to suggest not only that those who have made the allegations should not be described as 'victims', but they should not even be referred to as 'complainants'. Since in most cases they have not made complaints to the police, but only claims for compensation to the government, they should be referred to as 'claimants'.

11   On the conclusions of the Tribunal, see below, chapter 63. It remains the case that, although allegations were made against 365 different people as a result of the 1991–2 police investigation in North Wales, the original allegations resulted in only one new conviction for sexual abuse – that of Peter Howarth. Later John Allen, the head of the private Bryn Alyn home was convicted and later still other care workers in North Wales were found guilty – though most continue to protest their innocence. It is partly because the original 1991–3 investigation resulted in so few criminal trials that the North Wales Tribunal was set up.

12   On the views of former members of staff at Bryn Estyn, see below, chapter 46

13   Ian Jack, letter to the author, 24 January 1997

14   Peter Wilby, telephone interview, June 1997

15   The stories appeared in the *Independent* on 27 and 31 May 1991. The 'Pindown' regime was devised by an individual care worker, Tony Latham, as a means of dealing with children who were absconding or whose attitudes were held to be particularly aggressive or challenging. It was operated in the home in Stoke-on-Trent where Latham himself worked between 1983 and 1989. It was also used for a matter of months at three other homes run by Staffordshire County Council. The disciplinary system in which Pindown consisted was supposed to be based on the idea that the most difficult children would be given intense individual attention. In practice, however, it tended to be a repressive

regime in which children were sometimes isolated in an area cordoned off as a 'pindown' unit, had to wear shorts or night-clothes and were deprived of many privileges. The Pindown inquiry, conducted by Allan Levy QC and Barbara Kahan, whose report was published in May 1991, concluded that the regime was 'intrinsically unethical, unprofessional and unacceptable'.

16 The Tŷ Mawr inquiry was held by Gwent County Council in response to a direction from the secretary of state on 27 June 1991

17 TMCHI, pp. 4, 33

18 TMCHI, p. 88

19 TMCHI, p. 33

20 TMCHI, pp. 37–38

21 TMCHI, pp. 39, 42

22 TMCHI, p. 41

23 TMCHI, p. 41

24 TMCHI, p. 51

25 TMCHI, p. 58

26 TMCHI, p. 24

27 Telephone interview with former member of staff, March 1997

28 As above

29 Interview with Ian Jack, January 1997

30 Alison Taylor, 'An eerie silence', *Community Care*, 5 August 2004

31 Alison Taylor told the Tribunal that she gave up her university course because of domestic circumstances (NWTT, p. 16247); she subsequently said that her daughter was adopted (p. 16286).

32 'My Shout' by Alison Taylor, *Daily Post*, Conwy, 10 June 2004, p. 8

33 Interview with D. A. Parry, Bangor, 11 November 1996; interview with Alison Taylor, Bangor, 11 November 1996

34 Interview with Parry, as above

35 Interview with Nefyn and June Dodd, Bangor, 11 November 1996

36 NWTT, p. 16694: 'It is the expectation of the Authority that in all establishments the Officer-in-Charge and Deputy are expected to be totally co-operative in their relationships so that the interests of both residents and staff are properly safeguarded and I am restating that customary expectation so that there is no doubt about it, or ambiguity.'

37 NWTT, p. 17174

38 NWTT, p. 17174

39 NWTT, p. 16458. These words are quoted from a copy of Alison Taylor's survey 'Perceptions of Care' which she gave to Bryn Estyn care worker John Rayfield on completing her placement. Confronted by this document at the Tribunal, she denied that she had given it to Rayfield (NWTT, pp. 16457–80).

40 NWTT, p. 16468

41 Police statement, 8 August 1991

42 LiC, p. 509 (note). For a discussion of the chronology of Ryan Tanner's period in the care of Gwynedd social services, see chapter 18.

43 NWTT, pp. 3610–1. From the contemporary documents which are available, it would appear that Tanner's behaviour did not become a serious problem until considerably later. In 1981, during the period he spent in Y Gwyngyll, a home in Anglesey, Dodd, acting in his role as area supervisor, wrote another report on Tanner which contained the following observations: 'There has been evidence of late of his inciting other, often younger children, into delinquent and anti-social activities. Whilst at the centre there have been reports from other children of bullying and intimidation.' It was shortly after this report was written that Tanner was transferred to Bryn Estyn (NWTT, p. 3615).

44 O. G. Evans, 23 May 1984, Tribunal document 9108/23/125

45 Police report, 10 October 1984

46 NWTT, pp. 16485–6. One aspect of the evidence given by Alison Taylor to the Tribunal about the 1984 incident was perhaps even more revealing. While being cross-examined by counsel to the Tribunal, she repeated the version of events she had already given on a number of occasions, making the striking claim that, when she had informed the director about the incident, and about the fact Mason wished to make a complaint, no action whatsoever had been taken: 'The only acknowledgement I received was this memorandum from Mr Robinson about the insurance claim.'

Taylor's claim in this respect is untrue. Her original note to the director had given no indication that an allegation of assault was being made and merely reported that the boy had sustained an injury. In the case of any accidental injury it was a matter of routine that an insurance claim form would be filled in. The director's administrative assistant, Henry Robinson, duly sent Taylor a blank form, and endorsed the memo with the words 'Accident form sent, 30.5.92'. The memorandum specifically noted that the form was being sent on 30 May in response to her original memo dated 26 May. The first intimation that the incident was anything other than an accident came in her subsequent letter which was not received by the director until 4 June.

The crucial document needed to demonstrate this was the letter itself, which referred to Mason's complaint for the first time and was clearly dated 29 May. However, the copy of the letter supplied to the Tribunal was so dark as to be almost entirely illegible. The date cannot be deciphered and the only words it is possible to make out are 'Dear Miss Hughes' and the heading of the letter, 'John Mason'. The fact that this document was effectively missing meant that the untruthfulness of Taylor's claim became invisible to the Tribunal. So too did the context of her actions. For, as another, legible copy of the letter makes clear, the final paragraph contained a reference to the troubled circumstances which surrounded Taylor's complaint as well as a frank acknowledgment of the delay which, at the Tribunal, she sought so resolutely to deny:

> I apologise for the delay in notifying you of this matter: however, in respect of the circumstances surrounding myself at present I felt it to be wise to take advice prior to bringing this matter to your attention.

The director of social services for Gwynedd, Lucille Hughes, would subsequently suggest that this paragraph, plainly a reference to the disciplinary action being taken against Taylor, contained the 'real reason' for her actions. The disappearance of this paragraph from the evidence placed before the Tribunal was therefore extremely significant. From the clear reproduction of a label affixed to the letter by a Tribunal clerk, it is evident that the document, which is apparently a photocopy of Taylor's own carbon copy, was actually supplied to the Tribunal in this illegible state. In the circumstances it was almost inevitable that the Tribunal lawyers would assume that the insurance form had been supplied in response to the (illegible) letter of complaint and not to the original memo which intimated no complaint. This is exactly what happened, as can be seen from the following exchange between Ernest Ryder, counsel to the Tribunal, and Taylor:

> RYDER: [To the witness] The report to Miss Hughes is sadly unreadable on the copy the Tribunal has. We know the letter is written to Miss Hughes, page 164 of the bundle, and her response [enclosing an insurance claim form] is the page later, page 165?
> TAYLOR: Which in fact came from a Mr Henry Robinson in the sort of admin department at social services. It has his initials in the reference at the top of the memo (p. 16342).

Here, although Taylor avoids answering Ryder's question in the affirmative, she effectively confirms the incorrect inference he has drawn. It should perhaps be observed that illegible photocopies of documents are occasionally supplied in criminal cases among unused evidence which the police have been forced to disclose to the defence. From time to time, as some experienced defence lawyers are in a position to confirm, documents are supplied in an unreadable form in an attempt to conceal significant evidence. Whether or not something similar was done here cannot be determined on the evidence currently available.

47 Letter from Mr Davies, county personnel officer to Taylor, 2 July 1985; Letter from Taylor to Davies, 23 May 1985 (Tribunal documents, 10593/46/181; 10593/44/176)
48 Memo from Lucille Hughes to Taylor, 26 November 1985

49 NWTT, p. 16323
50 NWTT, p. 25984
51 She also said that two documents – a memorandum to Gethin Evans concerning an alleged assault upon a girl, and a copy of a memorandum from her on the same subject – had been deliberately removed from her personal filing cabinet. She said she believed this had been done because the information contained in them might embarrass the social services department. No evidence was produced to support this claim (NWTT, pp. 25985–6)
52 NWTT, p. 25993
53 NWTT, pp. 25992–3
54 NWTT, p. 395
55 Extract from Alison Taylor's memo to the director of social services, 4 February 1986
56 NWTT, p. 396. The last sentence was omitted from the passage quoted in the Tribunal and has been added from the original text of Gillian Roberts' statement, made on 15 May 1986.
57 'I can categorically say that I was unaware of any allegation of mistreatment to [Michael Thomas] during his stay at Tŷ Newydd, and at no time has Mrs Taylor or any other member of staff discussed with me an allegation of assault on [Michael] by a member of staff at the Assessment Centre.' Report by PC Evans, schools liaison officer, 12 September 1986; see also NWTT, pp. 26004–5.
58 Police statement, 26 August 1986; see NWTT, p. 26018
59 As is normal when police officers interview children, and as is stipulated by the Police and Criminal Evidence Act of 1984 (PACE), the boy was interviewed in the presence of an appropriate adult, in this case the acting officer-in-charge of Y Gwyngyll.
60 'Donald Peter Harbour', Police statement, 10 June 1986
61 NWTT, pp. 26034–5
62 Pearl Worrall, police statement, 1986
63 As above
64 Police report, 19 March 1986
65 Norman himself, rightly or wrongly, believed that the story had not been made up by Peter alone:

> I believe Peter and X [another resident] thought up the assault story. X's reason was just to get rid of the authority [X] cannot handle. However, Peter, although going along with X's reason, also was seeking attention … The death of the other boy usurped his position in the home and he felt no-one cared or noticed him. However, his telephone call to the director solved his problem. As Peter sees it, the director sent her car for him, gave him an interview and bought him chocolate. He immediately shot to the top

of everyone's notice parade. Peter succeeded. He even withdrew his charges from the police. The question is, how will Peter cap this in the future as this dies in the past?

Norman expressed these views in 1991. He may not at this time have been aware that his rhetorical question had, in one respect at least, already been answered.

66   Tribunal document 10599/12/206

67   As correspondence with the personnel officer suggested, one particular difficulty staff at Tŷ'r Felin experienced concerned Taylor's frequent absences. According to Robert Sussams, Taylor suffered periodically from severe headaches. It would frequently happen, he said, that members of staff who were on duty, and who were expecting to be relieved by Taylor, would be telephoned by a member of her family, who would say that Mrs Taylor was not well, and would therefore not be able to come into work on time. A member of staff would then be expected to stay on at the home beyond the end of their shift until Taylor arrived in about two hours' time. As the appointed time drew near, Sussams said, it would sometimes happen that there would be another tele-phone-call to say that Mrs Taylor was still unwell and would not be able to come in until later in the day.

The frequency with which such absences occurred caused consider-able irritation and frustration to Taylor's colleagues. Eventually, after dis-cussing the matter with some of her fellow members of staff, the deputy officer-in-charge, Ann Ashton, decided to seek guidance from Nefyn Dodd. Robert Sussams went with Mrs Ashton to the meeting with Dodd. When Taylor discovered what had happened she was said to have been furious. According to Sussams she held him responsible for insti-gating the meeting with Dodd and told him that the matter should have been taken up through her rather than behind her back.

The meeting between Sussams, Ashton and Dodd apparently took place during the early part of 1985. It was in July 1985 that Sussams him-self was seen behaving towards a young girl in a manner which was clearly unacceptable. According to one of his colleagues, Gillian Roberts, there had been an occasion in the dining room when Sussams had reprimanded a twelve-year-old girl, Helen Jones, who had appar-ently answered back or muttered something under her breath. Roberts said that Sussams had responded by slapping Helen on the face with the back of his hand. According to Roberts tears had immediately welled-up in the girl's eyes, but she had apparently soon forgotten about the incident and carried on eating her meal.

Gillian Roberts had subsequently mentioned this incident to one of her colleagues, Susan Jones, who had in turn informed Taylor of what had happened. Taylor had reported the matter to Dodd, saying that

Helen had informed her of another occasion when Sussams 'had hit her around the head some time previously when she was upstairs with him'. In drawing this incident, as witnessed by Gillian Roberts, to the attention of Dodd, Taylor was evidently acting quite properly and responsibly. However, it was at the same time as she complained about this episode that she also made complaints about an occasion when Sussams had supposedly had an argument with Helen's brother, and about an even earlier incident. She said that, on 13 June, Simon Birley, a boy who had previously been in care at Bryn Estyn, and who was now almost seventeen, had consumed a number of cans of shandy while in the company of Sussams. See the continuation of the chapter. See also Tribunal document, 9108/71/163, cited below.

68   Report by Larry King, 6 August 1985

69   Simon Birley, statement, 23 July 1986; see NWTT, p. 26020

70   NWTT, p. 26102

71   In view of this it is significant that, on 2 December 1986, Alison Taylor wrote a letter to the deputy chief constable, copying the letter both to her union representative and to the councillor who had received the two statements. One of the 'complaints' she made in this letter was that a copy of Harbour's statement had been seen by members of the social services department. She implied that WDC Bott was responsible for putting the statement into circulation. Taylor later made this complaint explicitly (NWTT, p. 16619). The North Wales Police replied to Taylor, informing her that their copy of the statement had not been given or shown to any person outside the police force. If this information was accurate (and there is no reason to suggest otherwise), the only conclusion that may be drawn is that Taylor herself was responsible for putting Peter Harbour's statement into circulation, and that she had written her letter of complaint to the police in an attempt to disguise this fact.

72   *Bangor Mail,* 2 December 1986

73   'Child abuse allegations sent to Attorney General', *Community Care,* 28 November 1986

74   From a summary of the views of colleagues, Tribunal document, 9108/71/163. See note about Robert Sussams above.

75   Tribunal document 9108/61/152

76   'Council silent on suspension', *Bangor Mail,* 7 January 1987

77   'Hannah Thomas', statement, 29 January 1987

78   Another boy with the same surname had been at Tŷ'r Felin for two days, but when he was traced during the 1991–2 investigation he had no complaints about the regime there; see NWTT, pp. 26067–71.

79   NWTT, pp. 20672–3

80   During the Tribunal Owen was criticised for assuming that the goal-posts were of regulation height, even though he was unable to cite the evidence for this assumption. In this particular instance the criticism

seems to be a just one. On the other two allegations, see NWTT, p. 26077

81 'Hannah Thomas', statement, 17 December 1991

82 NWTT, p. 26103

83 Michael Walzer, *The Revolution of the Saints: a study in the origins of radical politics,* Weidenfeld and Nicolson, 1966, p.284

84 The psychology of false allegations appears to be little studied. One academic who has interviewed women who make false allegations is Professor Keith Soothill of Lancaster University. In an excellent *Guardian* article about Nadine Milroy-Sloan, the woman who made a false accusation of rape against Neil and Christine Hamilton, Dea Birkett quotes these words of Soothill: 'Women tend to make false allegations to get themselves out of trouble rather than to get men into trouble. They lie when they feel constrained, when they're in a tight spot. ... The whole thing gets out of hand and there just isn't the opportunity for the woman to bail out. The process begins to take over. ... A woman can get into a situation she doesn't understand and then try and make sense of it somehow by constructing a story. ... As people probe you, you fit in other features, make it tighter. You get more and more convinced. You begin to think it must have happened like that. Evidence to the contrary only bolsters your false belief ... The more the world is against you the more the paranoia sets in. She'll say, "Well, nobody ever believes me!" Then she produces the very situation where that is the case. So the paranoia continues and develops. That's the cycle she's in.' (Dea Birkett, 'An unshakeable delusion', *Guardian Weekend*, 7 February 2004).

85 LiC, 33.30, p. 498

86 LiC, 33.34, p. 499; NWTT, p. 18845

87 LiC, 33.39, p. 500; at the Tribunal Evans referred also to an 'atmosphere of fear' and compared the children to mice, 'scurrying here and there when we visited'. But these observations were not made in his original report. Under cross-examination he accepted that the phrase 'an atmosphere of fear' would be better replaced by 'regimentation' (see NWTT, p. 18844).

88 NWTT, p. 19178

89 NWTT, p. 19178; LiC, 33.43, pp. 501–2

90 LiC, 33.44, p. 502

91 NWTT, p. 19174

92 NWTT, p. 26115. In his evidence to the North Wales Tribunal, DCS Owen suggested that he had reached the conclusion in 1986 that Nefyn Dodd was not a fit person to be in charge of a children's home and that he had communicated this view to the director of social services Lucille Hughes. However, in his contemporary reports there is no trace of such a judgment, and in cross-examination Gwynne Owen accepted that he may not have said this to Miss Hughes at all (NWTT, p. 26123).

93 NWTT, p. 26108.

94   Given the nature of the campaign waged against Dodd, it is extremely
      difficult to assess the extent to which physical chastisement was used by
      him or if, indeed, it was used at all. One of the most striking aspects of
      the evidence relating to this issue is that, in spite of the large number of
      allegations against him, many of Dodd's former colleagues have testified
      in unequivocal terms that they never witnessed him inflict any form of
      physical violence on any of the young people in his care. What is par-
      ticularly impressive is that this view was endorsed during the Tribunal
      hearings by a number of former colleagues who were openly critical of
      his regime. This having been said, it is also the case that, particularly in
      the wake of the 1986–7 investigation, some care workers and social
      workers who were hostile to Dodd clearly came to believe that the
      view of him as a tyrant, who habitually engaged in physical abuse, was
      accurate. Some of the unsound allegations which were brought forward
      by Taylor had apparently begun to circulate among discontented and
      resentful members of staff with the result that fiction was frequently
      retailed as fact.
          Since 1986 a large number of people, mostly former residents, have
      made allegations of violence they say they had witnessed or suffered
      themselves. Some of these claims, including some made by former
      members of staff, are clearly untrue. In assessing the others we inevitably
      encounter the problem which arises whenever false allegations prolifer-
      ate. In these circumstances the entire currency of complaints is debased
      and even genuine allegations are liable to be disbelieved. The most cred-
      ible allegations against Dodd are among the least serious. One former
      member of staff, who was interviewed by Owen during the course of
      his second, 1987, investigation said that on two occasions during a two-
      year period she had witnessed Dodd slapping children across the head.
      It was perhaps partly because the evidence of this witness seemed per-
      suasive that Owen himself eventually wrote, in his 1987 report, that it
      was his 'opinion' that Dodd occasionally resorted to physical chastise-
      ment of children in order to maintain discipline. He went on to say that
      he did not believe that 'such incidents … amounted to gratuitous vio-
      lence directed at individual children' (NWTT, p. 26110). Wherever the
      truth may lie there is no compelling evidence that Dodd ever commit-
      ted any criminal offence or came near to doing so.
95   See NWTT, p. 12732
96   NWTT, pp. 12732–3
97   LiC, 36.30, p. 554
98   LiC, 36.30, p. 554
99   LiC, 36.17, p. 550
100   NWTT, p. 24093
101   NWTT, pp. 12647, 24094
102   NWTT, pp. 24060–3, 18559, 18498–9

103   LiC, 36.20, p. 551

104   NWTT, pp. 18496–18502. For Dodd's cross-examination in relation to this incident, see pp. 19252–19269

105   NWTT, pp. 12727–8

106   LiC, 36.23, p. 552. Interestingly a conclusion which is in some respects similar to that expressed here was reached by the Tribunal, which did not have access to the account Ennis had given in 1989. In their report the members of the Tribunal record that they 'are left in some doubt as to whether [Ennis] was interviewed at all at Tŷ Mawr about the matter'. However, without questioning Phelan's honesty as a witness, they conclude that 'the balance of probability is that he did speak to [Ennis] at Tŷ Mawr about his relationship with [Harkness] and that [Ennis] may have denied to him that he had sexual intercourse with her'. The report goes on to express 'grave reservations about the way Phelan is alleged to have reported his conversation according to the note prepared by Dodd' (LiC, 36.21, 36.26, pp. 551–3).

107   Notes of Mandy Wragg, Yorkshire TV researcher, see chapter 13.

108   In their report the members of the Tribunal do not accept Ennis's explanation of why he was moved. They write that Ennis:

> did not indicate how anyone with sufficient authority to arrange his transfer could have known of his alleged relationship with [Harkness] by 20 November 1985. Moreover, he advanced a rather different explanation later in his evidence to the effect that he had been present when [Harkness] was beating another boy resident's head against a bedroom wall. He continued: 'I threw her off, I threw her across the room and told her to lay off him because there was no need for it, and I didn't talk to her after that. Within a fortnight I had been moved down to South Wales' (LiC, 36.15, p. 550).

The Tribunal members seem not to have appreciated the significance of Ennis's claim that he had told Stephen Adderley, another boy at the home, about what had happened. According to Alison Taylor, a log book entry at this time said: 'Stephen Adderley spoken to by Jane [Harkness] about the lies he had been telling.' Taylor adds that 'there is no indication as to the nature of these lies' and claims that 'at this time … J Harkness was in daily contact with J N Dodd and June Dodd' (Alison Taylor, GCCA, p. 114).

Taylor is not generally a reliable source. However, if her claim about the log book entry is correct, then, on this occasion, her account rings true. What Taylor was evidently unaware of, and what the Tribunal report neglects to record, was that the name of the boy who was allegedly being chastised by Harkness was Stephen Adderley. It is difficult to avoid concluding that, after Ennis had stayed up with her until the early hours of the morning, Harkness had found herself engulfed by the kind of gossip which threatened to destroy her career. After she had battled unsuccessfully to silence its secondary source, Dodd was prevailed on to remove its primary source by abruptly transferring Ennis to Tŷ Mawr. (It should be noted that the members of the Tribunal say in their own report that it is impossible for them to reach any firm conclusion in relation to the allegations against Harkness.)

109 Tribunal document 10607/9/239C

110 Letter to Rt Hon Margaret Thatcher MP, 17 January 1987; Tribunal document 10601/1/217–8. Some words in the final paragraph of the first page of this photocopied document are illegible.

111 10 January 1988, Tribunal document 1608/1/228; after a long delay this letter was eventually answered on 28 March 1989 by the Colwyn Bay office of the Crown Prosecution Service.

112 Letter to Tony Newton MP, minister of health, 29 February 1988, Tribunal document 10601/9/229–233

113 During the North Wales Tribunal Tanner was asked directly how Yorkshire Television had got in touch with him. He replied that they had contacted him through his mother, who lived in Anglesey. But he did not initially offer any explanation of how they had located his mother. At a later stage in his evidence Tanner claimed that 'Alison Taylor had been to my mam's looking for me.' According to Wragg, however, Taylor had in fact located Tanner 'through an old contact' (see NWTT, p. 3623, pp. 3755–6). In her evidence, while being cross-examined by David Knifton, Taylor confirmed that she had been responsible for renewing contact with somebody she had first met seven years previously during her 1982 placement at Bryn Estyn:

> KNIFTON: When did you first meet Ryan Tanner?
> TAYLOR: Well, Ryan was in care at Tŷ'r Felin but I think that was the period you referred to when I was off sick so, actually, my first recollection of Ryan as an individual was at Bryn Estyn.
> KNIFTON: When did you meet him again, at a later stage, after he had left care?
> TAYLOR: I think probably about 1990, simply because other young people were saying: 'You have got to talk to Tanner.' And I didn't know where Tanner was.
> KNIFTON: You contacted him, I think, in connection with a 'First Tuesday' documentary, is that right?
> TAYLOR: Yes because Yorkshire Television had approached me through the Children's Legal Centre.
> KNIFTON: You found in him a kindred spirit, somebody who shared your goal?

TAYLOR: I found that Ryan had been through the mill, like a lot of the others and had a lot to say, yes (NWTT, p. 16412).

114 Telephone interview with James Cutler, February 2001; telephone interview with Mandy Wragg, February 2001; programme research notes supplied by Wragg.

115 Ian Hacking, *Rewriting the Soul: Multiple Personality and the Sciences of Memory*, Princeton University Press, 1995, p. 60; Lynley Hood, *A City Possessed: The Christchurch Civic Creche Case*, Longacre Press, Dunedin, 2001, pp. 44–5

116 Debbie Nathan and Michael Snedeker, *Satan's Silence, Ritual Abuse and the Making of a Modern American Witch Hunt,* Basic Books, 1995, p.14

117 Debbie Nathan and Michael Snedeker, as above. The first chapter of their study of the satanic scare in the United States, provides an excellent account of the emergence of what I have called 'the Californian model of child protection'. I have drawn freely on this account in the paragraphs which follow. I have also drawn on my own earlier account in *The Great Children's Home Panic,* The Orwell Press, 1998, pp. 35–42.

118 Roland Summit, 'The Child Abuse Accommodation Syndrome', *Child Abuse & Neglect* 7 (1983), p. 191. Summit's views are discussed by Nathan and Snedeker, as above, pp. 20–1, 26–7.

119 Stephen J. Ceci and Maggie Bruck, *Jeopardy in the Courtroom: A Scientific Analysis of Children's Testimony,* Washington DC, American Psychological Association, 1995

120 By far the best accounts of the development of satanic abuse allegations are those which deal with the American origins of the scare. See in particular Nathan and Snedeker, as above. See also Jeffrey S. Victor's excellent *Satanic Panic: The Creation of a Contemporary Legend*, Open Court, Chicago, 1993.

121 Richard Webster, 'A global-village rumour', *New Statesman,* 27 February 1998, pp. 45–6 (www.richardwebster.net/speakofthedevil.html); See also Nathan and Snedeker, as above

122 The words quoted are those of the journalist Rosie Waterhouse in an article published in the *Independent on Sunday*, 12 August 1990. Waterhouse was one of the first journalists to direct proper scepticism towards the claims made about satanic cults, and the *Independent on Sunday* was one of the few newspapers which did not succumb to a delusion which achieved considerable currency elsewhere in the press. It was this record of proper scepticism which gave the *Independent on Sunday's* later reports about paedophile rings in children's homes so much authority.

So far as the resilience of the belief in satanic abuse is concerned, it should be noted that one of the main refuges of this belief now is in psychotherapy. See Valerie Sinason ed., *Treating Survivors of Satanist Abuse*, Routledge, 1994. A number of journalists and academics also apparently retain their belief in satanic abuse. Perhaps the most intellectually sophisticated recent contribution towards what might be called the 'new theology' of satanic abuse can be found in the work of Sara Scott. See her *The Politics and Experience of Ritual Abuse: Beyond Disbelief,* Open University Press, 2001.

123   *Working Together Under the Children Act 1989,* DOH, 1991, was produced jointly by the Home Office, the Department of Health, the Department of Education & Science and the Welsh Office; J. S. La Fontaine, *Speak of the Devil: Tales of Satanic Abuse in Contemporary England,* Cambridge University Press, 1998, p. 11.

124   It is quite true that the Butler-Sloss inquiry concluded, from the evidence then available, that the anal dilatation sign was 'abnormal and suspicious'. Yet this was in 1988. In 1989 the publication in the United States of research by the paediatrician Dr John McCann showed that reflex anal dilatation was actually present in half of his control group of *non-abused* children. This finding was later confirmed by parallel studies conducted by British paediatricians which indicate that the anal dilatation reflex is actually part of a wide spectrum of *normal* signs. See Nathan and Snedeker, pp. 196–7.

125   The Joint Enquiry Team report ('Joint Enquiry Report to the Director of Social Services and the Chief Constable', Nottinghamshire County Council, June 1990, unpublished but see below) went on to suggest that parts of the social services department appeared to have developed an 'unshakable' belief in satanic ritual abuse through which they were unwittingly encouraging children to allege bizarre acts of abuse which had never taken place. 'This could lead eventually,' the report concluded, 'to grave injustice, and, if unchecked, it has the ingredients of a modern "witch-hunt".' In the view of the team, all the elements necessary to such a witch-hunt were already present. These included 'rigid, preconceived ideas, dubious investigative techniques, the unwillingness to check basic facts'. In a telling and prophetic passage, the 1990 report noted that 'Recently claims have been made in the social work press that sexual abuse is occurring in 75% or even 100% of the nation's children's homes and the same report considered ritual abuse in this context … If this country followed the precedent of the USA the next step would be extensive allegations of ritual/satanic and sexual abuse against residential and day care workers.' The JET report was never published. The report was, however, made available on the internet in 1997 at www.users.globalnet.co.uk/ ˜dlheb/Default.htm under the heading 'Broxtowe Files'.

126   Beatrix Campbell, *Unofficial Secrets: Child Sexual Abuse – the Cleveland Case,* Virago, 1988, p. 78

127   See 'Crusade or Witch-hunt', my review of Mark D'Arcy and Paul Gosling, *Abuse of Trust: Frank Beck and the Leicestershire Children's Homes*

Scandal, Bowerdean, London, 1998; *Times Literary Supplement,* 22 January 1999; www.richardwebster.net/crusadeorwitchhunt.html

127a On Pindown, see note 15

128 NWTT, p. 24865

129 Alison Taylor, GCCA, p. 78. Eventually, during her Tribunal evidence Taylor would accept that this document consisted largely of hearsay and speculation. According to Dennis Parry, however, when she handed over a copy of this document to him during their meeting, no such qualifications were made: '[S]he showed me the document, and as far as I was concerned, the document was a piece of evidence I needed to look at and to pass on to whoever' (NWTT, p. 24922).

130 NWTT, p. 24866

131 Interview with Malcolm King, Wrexham, 14 November 1996

132 Fred Rutter, who protested his innocence throughout his trial and claimed that he had been 'fitted up' by a number of young women who were motivated by the hope of gaining compensation, was found guilty on 30 July 1991 on four counts of rape and two of indecent assault and sentenced to twelve years imprisonment.

133 John Jevons says he believes that Banham did not initially use the phrase 'paedophile ring': 'By the time John Banham came to report his conclusions he was reporting them to me. I do not recall John ever saying that a paedophile ring was operating at Bryn Estyn. He was much more cautious in his approach, indicating that a number of concerns led back to Bryn Estyn and that there might have been abuse on a more systematic scale' (John Jevons, personal communication, December 2003). However, it was this term which rapidly gained currency and was used repeatedly by Malcolm King – and by Dean Nelson. It was also evidently endorsed by Jevons himself when, on 17 July 1991, the letter drafted by Loveridge was sent to the chief constable (see below, notes 134 and 141). It should perhaps be noted that the phrase 'systematic' itself, when applied to abuse, is a kind of social work code which is often used to dress up conspiracy theories in more moderate-sounding language.

134 John Jevons (personal communication, December 2003) has said of his own attitude and that of Loveridge and senior social services managers: 'We started (and I believe maintained) an agnostic view both about the general theme and specific allegations. The whole approach was not to believe the unbelievable, but to suspend disbelief – i.e. neither to automatically believe nor to dismiss allegations or suspicions out of hand, but to subject them to test.' He appears not to recognise that to adopt an attitude of open-minded agnosticism in the face of extremist conspiracy theories can be highly dangerous – especially when no reliable tests are available. It is also difficult to reconcile his words with the contents of the letter which was sent to the chief con-

stable in which the *possible* existence of a paedophile ring was explicitly canvassed. This would seem to be not so much agnosticism as flirt-
ing with belief. Before alarmist and moral-panic-inducing cries of
'paedophile ring' (even if qualified by 'perhaps') are uttered by senior
council officers, a certain evidential threshold should first be reached.
In the case of the Clwyd investigation, as in many comparable investigations, it never was.

135 Interview with Malcolm King, Wrexham, 14 November 1996
136 Interview with King, as above
137 NWTT, p. 24870
138 Jevons, personal communication, December 2003
139 As above
140 On this disagreement see, for example, the cross examination of Dennis Parry by Andrew Moran QC, NWTT, pp. 24923–36
141 This letter has sometimes been referred to as having been sent by the
chief executive. According to Jevons, however, it was written by
Loveridge.
142 LiC, 2.23, pp. 16–17; NWTT, pp. 188–9
143 According to Jevons, some part at least of Taylor's role was subsequently explained to Detective Superintendent Ackerley (personal
communication, December 2003). Jevons insists that Taylor was in any
case not the main source of his concern at this stage. He accepts, however, that the case was different for Malcolm King.
144 Fred Rutter's conviction for four offences of rape and two of indecent
assault was one of the earliest to be achieved by a police trawling operation. Having protested his innocence throughout the first part of his
sentence, Rutter was eventually advised by his solicitor that, in the
absence of new evidence, he would not be granted leave to appeal. He
was now faced with the dilemma which confronts all those who have
been wrongly convicted. If he continued to protest his innocence and
refused to accept therapy as a sexual offender, he would almost certainly be denied parole. His choice was therefore a stark one. Either he
could continue to protest his innocence and end up serving nine years
(after remission) of his twelve-year sentence. Or he could feign guilt
and accept therapy. In this case he would almost certainly be released
on parole after six years. Rutter, a happily married man with two
daughters, one of whom was about to get married, had always been a
pragmatist. He opted for the latter course, was released in 1997 and
attended his daughter's wedding as a free man.
145 It has since been overtaken in this regard by 'Operation Care', the retrospective investigation into care homes subsequently mounted on
Merseyside.
146 See above, chapter 9
147 NWTT, pp. 3622, 3757. As can be seen from the passage cited here, on 3

March 1997, Tanner clearly told the Tribunal that Taylor accompanied him when he went to the police station to make his first statement. The very next day, however, on 4 March, the point was taken up by Stephen Bevan, counsel for Peter Howarth:

> BEVAN: You have told us that Taylor accompanied you when you made that statement, is that correct?
> TANNER: You're wrong.
> BEVAN: I am wrong?
> TANNER: You're wrong.
> BEVAN: I'm wrong in what regard?
> TANNER: I never stated Alison Taylor came with me to make that statement, ever. I would have been lying if I said that.
> BEVAN: So she was not with you when you made that statement?
> TANNER: She was not with me. My ex-girlfriend was with me (NWTT, pp. 3756–57).

Here it would appear that Tanner had thought better of his evidence the previous day and was attempting to give the impression that he had never said what he did. The manner in which he does so is instructive. The sheer boldness with which he contradicts the barrister who is cross-examining him seems almost to undo the reality of what had been said the day before.

In fact, however, Tanner was telling the truth on both occasions since he was referring to two different occasions – one in Bangor on 4 August 1991 and the other in Mold on 8 August 1991. On the former occasion he had been accompanied by Taylor and his girl-friend, on the latter by his girl-friend only. As Taylor herself writes in her 'Gwynedd County Council Analysis', '[Tanner] attempted to make a complaint and statement at Bangor Police Station on 4 August 1991, and it was refused'. It was as a result of Taylor's approach to a member of the police authority, who then intervened with the deputy chief constable, that arrangements were made for Tanner's statement to be taken at Mold four days later (NWTT, p. 16670; GCCA, p. 96). It would have been very easy for Tanner to have explained this while giving his evidence to the Tribunal. By not doing so he used an entirely truthful account of his second attempt to make a statement to obscure some of the details he had already given of the first occasion.

148 NWTT, p. 3757
149 See NWTT, pp. 3709–10
150 Placing such a young boy on remand was an unusual course and was taken only when a child had an extensive record of criminal conduct, as was true of Tanner. His care order was imposed for burglary and theft from a meter, and 23 other offences were taken into considera-

tion (LiC, p. 509). In order to fit in with court timetables the normal period of remand was 21 days – precisely the period which, according to the records, Tanner spent at Tŷ'r Felin. Although Tanner continues to dispute the record of his stay at Tŷ'r Felin and has said that he does not believe it accords with the law, it actually follows exactly the pattern which one would expect.

It must be said that the Tribunal report merely confuses matters further. It says this: 'The records are not clear but it seems that [Tanner] went there [Tŷ'r Felin] for eight weeks assessment in or about December 1977. On 22 February 1978 he was made the subject of a care order and, on completion of the assessment, he was transferred to Eryl Wen community home' (LiC, 33.70, p. 509). The claim which is made here notwithstanding, there was no indication given in the Tribunal hearings that there was anything 'not clear' about the records. It was simply that Ryan disagreed with the dates which were recorded and which were clearly set out by counsel to the Tribunal, Gerard Elias (NWTT, pp. 3480–5). The Tribunal report is, it would appear, pleading a lack of clarity in the records simply in order to accommodate Tanner's own version of events. Remarkably, the report offers no explanation of how a ten-year-old boy came to spend ten weeks in an assessment centre prior to being made the subject of a care order when only one 21–day remand order is recorded. The Tribunal is presumably not alleging that Tanner was illegally abducted by Gwynedd Social Services for a period of seven weeks. There is an alternative explanation: the records are correct.

151 NWTT, pp. 3593–4, 3704–7
152 Even the Waterhouse report, having set out its version of the facts, notes 'In these circumstances there must be considerable doubt about the veracity of [Tanner's] allegations against Roberts' (LiC, 33.96, p. 516). On the progressive inflation of the complaints Tanner made against Roberts, see NWTT, pp. 3707–8. Both Tanner and Taylor have attempted to deal with the problem over chronology by suggesting that John Roberts had worked at Tŷ'r Felin as a supply teacher before taking up his permanent post. There is no evidence that this was the case.
153 NWTT, pp. 3610–1
154 Yorkshire Television research notes supplied by Mandy Wragg in March 2001
155 Telephone interview with Mandy Wragg, 8 February 2001
156 *Wales This Week*, HTV, 26 September 1991
157 NWTT, pp. 3709–10
158 NWTT, pp. 3620; 3569–70
159 See the extensive literature on the phenomenon of 'false memory'; in particular the recent work by Harvard psychologist Richard McNally, *Remembering Trauma,* Harvard University Press, 2003.

160 NWTT, pp. 3707–8
161 See, for example, Mark Pendergrast, *Victims of Memory: Incest Accusations and Shattered Lives*, HarperCollins, 1996, passim
162 Statement made to Howarth's solicitor, June 1994
163 As above
164 This counsellor gave a police statement on 1 October 1991
165 Telephone interview with Derek Brushett, July 2001
166 NWTT, p. 4002
167 Derek Brushett, police statement, 19 February 1993
168 Various documents relating to this incident are contained in the legal papers of Peter Howarth
169 Police statement, 8 February 1993
170 *Guardian*, 'Protesters target NYPD in Haitian torture case', August 18 1997
171 The last possibility, involving the putative recovery of repressed memories, seems sometimes to play a significant role in care home investigations. See 'Freud's False Memories: Psychoanalysis and the Recovered Memory Movement' which forms the Afterword to my *Why Freud Was Wrong: Sin Science and Psychoanalysis*, Fontana Press, 1996; www.richardwebster.net/freudsfalsememories.html
172 Michael Mansfield, Foreword to *Fitted In: The Cardiff 3 and the Lynette White Inquiry,* by Satish Sekar, The Fitted In Project, London, 1997, p. vii
173 NWTT, p. 1005
174 NWTT, p. 999
175 NWTT, pp. 1307–8
176 NWTT, pp. 1403–4
177 NWTT, p. 1367
178 NWTT, pp. 1409–10
179 NWTT, pp. 1463–4
180 Dennis Roy Parry, 'Response to North Wales Child Abuse Tribunal of Inquiry', not dated [1997]
181 Evidence of Dean Nelson, NWTT, p. 24521
182 NWTT, pp. 24527–8
183 NWTT, p. 24945
184 NWTT, p. 24942
185 NWTT, pp. 24220–1
186 NWTT, pp. 24943–4
187 NWTT, p. 24945
188 'The network, run by secret services of NATO members, was apparently set-up in the 1950s at US instigation to create a guerrilla resistance organisation in the event of a Soviet invasion or communist take-over in Nato countries.' John Palmer, *Guardian*, 10 November 1990. Gladio was the name given to the Italian branch of a network with the harm-

less official name, Allied Co-Ordination Committee, set up with British help in the 1950s, operated by the secret services and partly financed by the United States CIA.' Richard Norton-Taylor *Guardian*, 16 November 1990.

189   NWTT, p. 24949

190   NWTT, pp. 24930–2; see also the evidence of Detective Superintendent Peter Ackerley, pp. 25515–25530. This crucial evidence has disappeared from the North Wales Tribunal report, which gives a seriously misleading account of the episode. See LiC, 51.61, p. 766.

191   NWTT, p. 24586

192   NWTT, pp. 25416–7; LiC, 2.24, p. 17

193   NWTT, p. 24523

194   NWTT, p. 24588

195   NWTT, pp. 24589, 24566. Nelson's suggestion that he met Tanner 'endlessly' apparently refers not only to the research he undertook before the publication of his article but also on his return to North Wales in 1992.

196   Police statement, 7 January 1992

197   NWTT, p. 16433

198   NWTT, p. 16436

199   NWTT, p. 16432

200   NWTT, p. 16423

201   NWTT, p. 16434

202   NWTT, p. 19640

203   NWTT, p. 12591

204   Wragg also notes that 'Lewis remembers boot-licking incident that Peter Jones [see below] talks about, but can't recall why.'

205   See NWTT, p. 16565. One further mystery remains. If Alison Taylor's claim about having witnessed an assault on Lewis Harper was a fabrication, how was she able to claim, as she did to Dean Nelson in the autumn of 1991, and to the police in January 1992, that the same incident had been witnessed by another member of staff, Peter Jones?

Peter Jones worked as an untrained care worker at Tŷ'r Felin from August 1979 to September 1981. However, his career had been effectively blocked by Nefyn Dodd, who had a low opinion of his abilities as a child care officer. Because of Dodd's intervention during a job interview, Jones did not gain the promotion he sought and was transferred sideways to another post. Shortly after his transfer Jones was convicted of fraudulently using a credit card and of deception and, in April 1982, he resigned in disgrace. Five years later, on 8 March 1987, he was interviewed by the North Wales Police in connection with the 1986–7 investigation into Tŷ'r Felin. In his statement he made it clear that he had not witnessed any physical abuse: 'I never saw any physical manifestations of the ill treatment of children' (NWTT, pp. 15911–2, 15922).

However, at some point during 1989 it would appear that Jones was contacted by Taylor in relation to the Yorkshire Television programme. Taylor then arranged a meeting between Jones and Mandy Wragg, a meeting which, according to Wragg, was cloaked in secrecy and surrounded by elaborate precautions reminiscent of spy stories and thrillers. At this meeting Jones made a number of claims which contradicted his 1987 statement to the police. He claimed on the one hand that he had seen Dodd hitting out at one child (whose name he said he could not remember), 'and giving him a really vicious backhander'. He also said this:

> On another occasion I walked into the room and Lewis Harper was kneeling at Dodd's feet. Dodd had made him lick his shoes. John Roberts was standing next to Dodd, he'd witnessed the whole thing. Dodd always gave that kid a hard time. In fact I saw Lewis with blood in his mouth a few times (verbatim quotation from report written by Wragg in the summer of 1989).

It was after this meeting that Jones made his first appearance as one of the *dramatis personae* in Taylor's allegation. This was in spite of the fact that Jones has apparently never claimed that Taylor was also present. In March 1992, Jones was interviewed by the North Wales Police again. On this occasion, as in his 1989 interview with Mandy Wragg, he claimed to have some knowledge of an incident similar to the one which Alison Taylor had described. He did not claim, however, that he had been present in Dodd's office, or that he had witnessed the assault, or even, as he had told Wragg three years earlier, that he had actually walked into the room. His evidence amounted to the claim that he had heard a disturbance, that he had 'peeped' round the door of Dodd's office 'and there was the two gentlemen I have named [Nefyn Dodd and John Roberts] with Lewis Harper at their feet'. Jones further claimed that Harper had subsequently told him that he had been made to lick the boots of both Dodd and Roberts, and that this had happened on numerous previous occasions.

Since this evidence did not match that of any other witness, and since, at the time of the alleged incident, Lewis had only been at Tŷ'r Felin for a matter of days (and therefore could not have been subjected to such treatment on 'numerous occasions' before), Jones's evidence could not be used to corroborate Taylor's allegation. It is presumably for this reason that Taylor, who has on a number of occasions said that Jones was present during the alleged assault, has more recently changed her account yet again to say that Jones witnessed 'an almost identical assault' (letter to the editor of the *New Statesman,* unpublished, November 2000. By the time she made her Tribunal statement, Taylor had already weakened her claim by saying that 'Peter Jones *may* also have witnessed the incident').

Very significantly Jones made no mention in his Tribunal evidence of the fact that he had been contacted by Taylor in 1989. Nor did he claim, as he had done then, that he had seen Harper with blood in his mouth. For these reasons and others, it is clear that Jones's evidence to the Tribunal, which contradicts both his own police statement, and the claim made by Taylor during her interview with Dean Nelson, should not have been relied on. His story had quite clearly been developed at some time after 1987 and apparently only emerged after his contact with Taylor.

206 See, for example, NWTT, pp. 22618, 24940–1

207 NWTT, p. 24587; when I first interviewed Taylor in July 1996 she said that she had supplied a copy of the document to the *Independent on Sunday* at the time they were researching the initial story. See also Nelson's evidence at NWTT, p. 24752

208 GCCA, p. 25

209 Police statement, 18 November 1992

210 LiC, 34.18, p. 533

211 One example is provided by the case of Barry Doughty. Taylor had already brought forward one complaint relating to Doughty in 1986, citing the claim of a fellow resident who said he had been 'battered' by Nefyn Dodd. At the time Doughty had made it clear that the claim was untrue, describing the author of the claim as 'a liar who disliked Nefyn Dodd' [see above, p. 47]. In her dossier, however, Taylor renewed and enlarged the original claim. Doughty was now supposed to have been 'persistently and brutally beaten at Tŷ'r Felin'. A number of former residents had allegedly 'witnessed Barry's being thumped in the testicles by John Roberts'. Yet Barry Doughty, who had already made one statement to the police saying that nothing had happened, now made a second in which he specifically denied being assaulted by Roberts.

According to the dossier Peter Hart was another former resident of Tŷ'r Felin who was 'alleged by several children to have been brutally beaten by J. N. Dodd on many occasions. It has also been alleged that a care officer once, under the excuse of alleged restraint, ground a broken bottle into Peter's hand, causing very serious injury.' Yet, when Hart was interviewed by the police, he had no such complaint about his treatment at Tŷ'r Felin (NWTT, p. 16614).

212 NWTT, pp. 16614–5

213 Nelson-Taylor interview, pp. 19. This transcript was supplied to the Tribunal without a date. The interview was apparently conducted at some point during Nelson's November visit to North Wales.

214   Nelson–Taylor interview, p. 2

215   Interview with D. A. Parry, 11 November 1996; NWTT, p. 16710

216   GCCA, pp. 22–3; a more detailed version of the allegation will be found on pp. 106–7

217   NWTT, pp. 16746–51. The incident is summarised in the Tribunal report thus: 'As far as we are aware, there was only one allegation of abuse made by a resident of Tŷ'r Felin during the period when Taylor was acting officer-in-charge. The allegation was made in March 1977 by a highly disturbed girl, who had been transferred from Tŷ'r Felin to Silverbrook Treatment Centre at Pontypridd, Mid Glamorgan the previous month. She alleged that she had had sexual intercourse with [Compton] two or three times whilst she had been resident at Tŷ'r Felin and had become pregnant as a result. It appeared, however, that she had made similar allegations against a different person earlier. The matter was investigated by the deputy director of social services (David Alan Parry) and he was "completely satisfied that the relationship between [Compton] and (the girl) was completely innocent in all respects and that the allegations made were completely unfounded". Mid Glamorgan and Hughes were so informed and no further action was deemed to be necessary. We have seen the background documentation and do not criticise this decision' (LiC, 33.14, p. 494).

218   In reality there are no classic behavioural symptoms of sexual abuse which are recognised generally by all psychiatrists.

219   Nelson–Taylor interview, p. 5

220   NWTT, p. 16447; Silverbrook was not in Abergavenny, but in Pontypridd.

221   Whereas, in the version of events given to Nelson, Taylor says Dodd told her the incident had been investigated, she specifically told the Tribunal that she had not been told anything about an investigation:

> MR RYDER: Do you believe there was any investigation at all into this report?
> TAYLOR: No, I think [Tricia] was shifted to keep her quiet, as later happened with [Graham Ennis], and when she continued—
> CHAIRMAN: I am most anxious to know if you know whether there was any investigation such as Mr. Dodd seeing [Tricia Everett] and saying 'What is all this?'?
> TAYLOR: I wouldn't necessarily know, sir, because I wasn't around all the time. *I never heard anything* [italics added] (NWTT, pp. 16355–6).

222   See NWTT, pp. 16443–4, 16704–6; LiC, 33.14, p. 494

223   GCCA, p.22; the claim about a vice ring was usually reported by Taylor as an allegation and was attributed on one occasion to Paul Wilson.

224   GCCA, p. 20
225   NWTT, p. 16452
226   NWTT, pp. 16448–9
227   GCCA, p. 54
228   NWTT, p. 16455
229   GCCA, p. 52
230   Interview with Paul Wilson, August 1996; See also NWTT, pp. 8409–11
231   NWTT, pp. 3672–3
232   LiC, 10.06, p. 100
233   Statement supplied by a witness who eventually gave evidence to the Tribunal
234   NWTT, pp. 647–9
235   NWTT, pp. 649–50
236   NWTT, p. 650
237   NWTT, pp. 8413–4
238   Police statement, 30 April 1993; the rationale given here appears to have faded away but the practice to which it gave rise continued as an informal Bryn Estyn tradition.
239   Police statement, 24 April. 1992
240   The same explanation may also apply to the claims which Wilson would eventually make about Dodd during his police interview in 1992. He specifically claimed that Dodd used his belly to push boys along and that he treated boys who didn't speak Welsh less favourably than boys who did. These claims, though made by no other witness, were, of course, almost exactly the same as those made by Ryan Tanner in his first police statement. See NWTT, p. 8430.
241   That the Chairman of the Tribunal and counsel to the Tribunal apparently believed Wilson's testimony, and took it as indicating that the Bryn Estyn staff had some knowledge of the sexual abuse supposedly being perpetrated by Howarth, becomes apparent on day 58 of the Tribunal when the document containing the transcript of Nelson's interview with Wilson is discussed. See NWTT, pp. 8055–9
242   GCCA, p. 100
243   Nelson–Taylor interview, pp. 16–17
244   NWTT, p. 16466–7
245   NWTT, p. 16572–3
246   This decision appears to have been taken in mid June; an entry in the log book for 15 June reads 'MH to leave 25.06. Mother very pleased.' During her Tribunal evidence Taylor said that she thought she left Bryn Estyn on 6 June 1982 but she was not sure (NWTT, p. 16466). The dates of Alison Taylor's placement at Bryn Estyn were in fact 15 March 1982 to 4 June 1982. The farewell entry Taylor wrote in the Bryn Estyn Logbook (see Chapter 6) is undated but appears to have been written some days after her placement had formally ended. If this is the case it

suggests either that she returned to Bryn Estyn after her placement had ended or that she extended her stay by some four days, in which case John Evans would have returned to Bryn Estyn by the time she left. There is no doubt at all, however, that he did not leave Bryn Estyn again until the end of the month. What this means is that the incident described by Taylor cannot have taken place.

247   Nelson eventually interviewed Evans in the spring of 1992 when he was seeking information against Anglesea. He reported Harris as telling him what he has consistently said to others: that Howarth was 'a good bloke' and did not abuse him (NWTT, p. 24612).

248   NWTT, p. 24524

249   Nelson–Taylor interview, p. 17

250   NWTT, pp. 7540, 7626

251   NWTT, pp. 9060–1

252   GCCA, p. 101

253   NWTT, pp. 24590–1

254   Dean Nelson's transcript. This quote is used in Nelson's newspaper article. See *Independent on Sunday*, 1 December 1991, p. 3.

255   Dean Nelson, letter to the *New Statesman*, published March 20 2000. One section of Wynne's formal interview clearly suggests that this was not the only respect in which Nelson may have contaminated Wynne's testimony. After Wynne has described Howarth's alleged assault, Nelson puts the following question: 'Did he [Howarth] ever say anything about "you know what the other lads say about me"?' Nelson's leading question has clearly been derived from his interview the previous day with Simon Birley, who would eventually, in his police statement, quote Howarth as having made just such a remark. Wynne's answer to Nelson's question is revealing:

> NELSON: Did he ever say anything about 'you know what the other lads say about me'?
> WYNNE: You said something about it earlier about one of the other lads saying it. I can remember something about it. But I can't remember fully … But when you said about it, it was like I was there, it's hard to explain. I do remember something about it. But I can't fully remember.

From this exchange it is quite clear that Nelson has discussed with Wynne some of the things which have been said by 'other lads', one of whom is evidently Birley. It may be noted that the only other likely candidates for this description are Evans and Singer, since they are the only 'other lads' who are supposed to have made similar allegations.

Given the subsequent disappearance of crucial parts of Wynne's original story and the clear presence of some elements of contamination, the only inference which may reasonably be drawn is that Nelson himself imparted at least some elements of Birley's story to Wynne, that he may well have related to him both Taylor's account of the minibus 'allegations' and her version of the glue-sniffing incident, and that the complaints which Wynne went on to make were based on these suggestions.

256 HTT, 23 June 1994, p. 50

257 NWTT, pp. 9060–1. In his evidence at the trial of Peter Howarth, Birley says that when Nelson came he was accompanied by Ryan Tanner.

258 NWTT, p. 25528

259 NWTT, pp. 25528–9

260 NWTT, p. 25529

261 GCCA, p. 48

262 NWTT, pp. 16599–16600

263 Mark Hall, police statement 5 June 1992. See also NWTT, p. 16608

264 GCCA, p. 47; see NWTT, pp. 16596–7

265 GCCA, pp. 51–2

266 Nelson–Taylor interview, p. 3

267 NWTT, pp. 27285–6

268 NWTT, p. 16625

269 NWTT, pp. 25534–5

270 Jean La Fontaine, *Speak of the Devil: Tales of Satanic Abuse in Contemporary England*, Cambridge University Press, 1998, p. 103

271 NWTT, p. 25445

272 NWTT, p. 1144

273 Telephone interview, 21 November 2000

274 NWTT, p. 8035

275 Williams, cited at NWTT, p. 8501

276 NWTT, pp. 1161–1169

277 Ryan Tanner, police statement, 16 August 1992; interview, 10 August 2004

278 The Western Mail, 'Social work job applicant shocked over reference to Soham case' Rhodri Clark, 17 February 2004

279 NWTT pp. 3525–6

280 LiC, 10.45, p. 110

281 Police statement, 22 September 1992; the police had checked with Wynne on 16 August 1992, see NWTT, pp. 9042–3

282 Telephone interview, November 2000

283 NWTT, p. 2454

284 NWTT, pp. 8032–3

285 NWTT, p. 25457

286 NWTT, Statement of John Richard Evans, p. 5

287 This claim was made by Tanner during a meeting he had with the director of social services and others (including Malcolm King), on 27 June 1995. At one point Tanner said that the police had told him that

Paul Wilson would be charged with indecent assault on the basis of one of his allegations. He complained that nothing happened: 'I was told I would get loads of money for this by the police. They won't talk to me now – I'm like an abuser. I've had nothing but harassment from the police' (NWTT, p. 3648).

288 NWTT, pp. 758–9
289 NWTT, pp. 780–1
290 Transcript of Nelson-Wynne interview, 15 November 1992
291 NWTT, p. 25427
292 NWTT, pp. 26523–4
293 NWTT, p. 26482
294 In a telephone interview I conducted with Detective Superintendent Ackerley in May 1996
295 NWTT, p. 25443
296 see Phillip Jenkins, *Intimate Enemies: Moral Panic in Contemporary Great Britain*, Aldine de Gruyter, 1992, pp. 110–111)
297 Jeremy Laurence, 'Bentovim's Technique', *New Society*, 28 November 1986, cited in Lynley Hood, *A City Possessed: The Christchurch Civic Creche Case*, Longacre Press, Dunedin, 2001, p. 60
298 BUTLER-SLOSS, p. 40
299 BUTLER-SLOSS, p. 43
300 Jevons, personal communication, December 2003
301 NWTT, p. 26527
302 NWTT, p. 26535
303 NWTT, p. 25869
304 This study, which strongly suggests that the model of progressive disclosure is misleading, was made in 1995 by two American psychologists, April R. Bradley and James M. Wood. Their study was published under the title 'How do children tell? The disclosure process in child sexual abuse' (*Child Abuse and Neglect*, Vol. 20, No 9, pp. 881–891, 1996). The study was introduced by an editorial, written by the child psychiatrist David Jones, 'Gradual disclosure by sexual assault victims – A sacred cow?' (pp. 879–80). Jones notes that the study calls into question 'the commonly held view that most accounts of sexual abuse gradually unfold over a period of time'. Bradley and Wood had examined 234 cases where sexual abuse had been confirmed: 'The authors were looking for evidence that a developmental sequence of unfolding revelation of abuse was to be found, using a scoring system specifically designed to reveal this process, if it were to have been present. Despite this they did not find gradual disclosure (p. 879).' The majority of the 234 cases made full or partial disclosures during the initial investigative interview.
305 On the origins of Freud's theory of repression see my *Why Freud Was Wrong: Sin Science and Psychoanalysis*, Fontana Press, 1996. On ritual abuse see Debbie Nathan and Michael Snedeker, *Satan's Silence: Ritual*

Abuse and the Making of a Modern America Witch Hunt, Basic Books, New York, 1995, p.132 and passim. Jean La Fontaine, *The Extent and Nature of Organised and Ritual Abuse,* HMSO, 1994; *Speak of the Devil: Tales of Satanic Abuse in Contemporary England*, Cambridge University Press, 1998

306 Richard Webster, 'A global-village rumour', *New Statesman,* 27 February 1998, pp. 45–6; Nathan and Snedeker, as above, passim

307 BUTLER-SLOSS, pp. 39, 42

308 La Fontaine, p. 155. This remark is applied specifically to the making of allegations of satanic abuse but it is clearly also relevant to any false allegation.

309 La Fontaine, p. 154

310 See NWTT, p. 25456

311 Another development took place on 3 March when two plain clothes police officers paid a visit to Eamon Bowskill, a former resident of Bryn Estyn who had already made one statement to them just before Christmas in which he had complained that a man called Morris or Norris had indecently assaulted him one evening when he had been alone in bed. Bowskill now described more incidents, including another alleged sexual assault by another member of staff. In order to explain why he had not included these details in his first statement he explained that he had since spent some time in hospital and said that 'it was during these days in hospital and the following nights at home that these incidents have come back to me'.

He now claimed that he had spent one night in the secure unit at Bryn Estyn and that a member of staff had brought him his supper on a tray and had then indecently assaulted him. He said that he could not remember the name of this member of staff but that he was second in charge of the home, had a golden Labrador dog and played golf. Quite clearly this description was of Peter Howarth. Bowskill then went on to describe a second incident in which he claimed the same man had indecently assaulted him in the showers. He also claimed that, on the day after the police had taken their first statement from him – 23 December 1991 – he had gone to his local pub and seen the man called Morris or Norris having a drink there.

It would eventually transpire that the history of Bowskill's complaint was more complicated than the police record itself suggested. The first complaint he made had been on 9 December 1991 when he had arrived without an appointment to see an official at Shire Hall. It transpired that at this point, eight days after the publication of the *Independent on Sunday* article, and four days after the launch of the NSPCC helpline, Bowskill had seen an item on a television programme about the Bryn Estyn investigation. He had then contacted the helpline about an accident he had had while he was at Bryn Estyn and the

NSPCC had suggested he contact Shire Hall. During his interview at Shire Hall he had made no allegation against either Norris or Howarth. But he had claimed that he had been sexually assaulted by one of the night staff. It subsequently emerged not only that the Norris allegation he made to the police later the same month was a revised version of this earlier allegation, but that Stephen Norris was still in prison at the time and therefore could not have been in the local pub the following evening. When it also transpired that there was a police record of Bowskill having already made a false allegation against a close relative, his testimony was effectively discarded and would play no part in Howarth's trial (NWTT, pp. 1909–43). Emerging as it did, however, at a particularly significant time, it may initially have played an important part in seemingly reinforcing the case against Howarth in the eyes of the police.

312 Police statement, 5 March 1992
313 Police statement, 11 March 1992
314 Police statement, 20 August 1991
315 Police interview, 15 March 1992, p. 189
316 HLP, Legal papers of Peter Howarth, statement made to Howarth's solicitor
317 As above
318 As above
319 see NWTT, pp. 2857, 2864–82
320 Police statement, 30 March 1992
321 Ryan Tanner, statement, 8 May 1992
322 Randles goes on to revise his account of what happened when he attended court the next day. Whereas in the first statement he said that he told his mother what had happened, in this statement he does not. Whereas in the first statement he says that he had told his girl-friend 'exactly what had happened', in this statement, given thirteen weeks later, he says 'I didn't tell her what happened with Mr Howarth and the other man.'
323 In his evidence to the Tribunal, given five years later in March 1997, Tanner gave a slightly different account of the same events, one which, nevertheless, confirmed the broad picture he had given initially. While being cross-examined by David Knifton, Tanner said this:

> He [Randles] told me he had been sexually abused by Peter Howarth. After I showed him a picture he said 'Yes, that's Howarth', because I thought I would tape it in case he tried denying it because he liked a drink, Brendan did. So I thought if I got it on tape he could either deny it to the police, that would be to his downfall or—

At this point Tanner was interrupted by Knifton. Tanner then confirmed to him that the photograph of Howarth he showed to Randles was the one in the *Independent* (NWTT, p. 3625).

324   Interview with Ian Jack, January 1997
325   GCCA, pp. 51–2. During the interview Nelson conducts with Wynne the following exchange takes place:

> NELSON: Do your ever remember him going up to Howarth's flat at all?
> WYNNE: No. Someone told me, can't remember who, that the nightmen, someone asking me if I remember it happening, that was that X [one of the night staff] used to pick out lads from the dorms, I don't remember this, X going round picking out lads, and then them lads would be moved from that bedroom, and go missing for hours. And Anglesea was meant to be involved in that with Howarth.
> NELSON: Who said that?
> WYNNE: Honestly I can't remember.
> NELSON: How long ago did they say that?
> WYNNE: Over this investigation stuff.
> NELSON: Recently? last couple of weeks? Since you met me?
> WYNNE: Yeah, just after you went [ie in November 1991].

The source of this unfounded allegation is never established, and Wynne effectively retracts his own tentative suggestion that it may have been the police. But there would seem to be little doubt that the answers Wynne gives to Nelson have been influenced by the claims of Alison Taylor. Whether this influence was direct, whether it had been passed on by Tanner, or, indeed, by Nelson himself, remains uncertain.

326   The relevant part of Taylor's letter reads as follows: 'Webster claims that [Tanner] "himself recorded a conversation with one man, to whom he had shown the picture of Howarth from the *Independent on Sunday*". [Tanner] recorded a conversation with [Randles] and subsequently handed the recording to North Wales Police as evidence. [Randles], who alleged sexual abuse by an unknown 'grey haired man', was shown a picture of Gordon Anglesea, not Howarth, but denied that Anglesea was the abuser.' This attempt at rebuttal is interesting, not least because the claim that Randles was *not* shown a picture of Howarth would, in the light of Tanner's own evidence, appear to be untrue. Since the grey-haired man was clearly identified in Randles's first statement as a senior member of the care staff, the only purpose in showing him a photograph of Anglesea would have been in an attempt to identify the mysterious second man.

327   Brendan Randles, statement, 5 May 1992

328 NWTT, p. 28203

329 Without a witness who could give live testimony the CPS evidently concluded that there was no realistic prospect of a conviction in relation to this charge. Although in theory Howarth's lawyers could have introduced evidence relating to Randles and Tanner, in practice most defence lawyers will avoid exposing their client to an additional allegation they would not otherwise have to face.

330 NWTT, p. 28203

331 A key role was played in this affair by Lee Steward, who had been staying in Cooke's flat at the time. See below, chapter 43.

332 NWTT, p. 24605

333 Interview with Malcolm King, Wrexham, 14 November 1996

334 NWTT, p. 24606

335 Police statement, 7 November 1992

336 Dean Nelson, police statement, 12 October 1992; NWTT, p. 24628; in his evidence to the libel trial Humphreys would eventually say that he thought Nelson had been taking notes during their conversation. But when Nelson gave evidence to the Tribunal some three years later, he claimed that he had made no record of the conversation.

337 Police statement, 12 October 1992: 'We did not discuss specific incidents but ... during this interview we agreed that Mark would visit the the Llwyn Onn Hall Hotel the following day. I was staying at the hotel. Before I left Mark indicated in general terms that he had been abused and that [it] involved a policeman. He agreed that I could have a formal taped interview with him.' In view of Humphreys's subsequent confusion over the issue it is by no means clear that he did indicate that his supposed abuser was a policeman.

338 Nelson transcript, 19 June 1992. The transcript was disclosed for the libel trial and for the Tribunal.

339 NWTT, p. 9080

340 Nelson, police statement, 12 October 1992; Humphreys first mentioned Nelson's use of the photograph in the statement he gave to the police on 18 August 1992. He referred to the photograph again in his statement of 7 November 1992.

341 Mr Justice Drake, summing-up, Anglesea libel trial, p.65

342 The transcript of the relevant portion of the interview reads:

> NELSON: Who did the abuse? Who abused you?
> HUMPHREYS: Howarth.
> NELSON: Howarth?
> HUMPHREYS: Yeah.
> NELSON: The deputy head of the home?
> HUMPHREYS: That's it.
> NELSON: Were there any others?

HUMPHREYS: Eh, well what I thought he was a security guard at the time but now I believe he's a policeman.
NELSON: Do you know what his name is?
HUMPHREYS: His name doesn't stick in my mind, you know, his face does but his name doesn't.
NELSON: Do you know his name now?
HUMPHREYS: No.
NELSON: Do you recognise this picture?
HUMPHREYS: Yeah.
NELSON: Why do you recognise this picture?
HUMPHREYS: His face.
NELSON: How do you know his face.
HUMPHREYS: The one I seen in Bryn Estyn.

343   So far as the allegations against Howarth were concerned, the situation was confused. While the first allegation was unchanged, the complaint Humphreys made about what happened to him after he had been circumcised had become more obscure. Humphreys said that Howarth had come to see him in the sick bay:

> He said 'So let's have a look.' I said 'Look at what?' He said 'What you've had done.' I think I was embarrassed [inaudible]. It was hurting me, you know what I mean and he did it to me as well and I was in a lot of fucking pain.

What Humphreys was trying to say here is simply not clear. The very next day, however, on 30 June, Nelson took Humphreys to a solicitor's office in Barmouth in order to swear an affidavit. Before doing so he once again showed Humphreys the photograph. Not surprisingly, given what had been said in the interview the day before, the affidavit contained an allegation of buggery against Anglesea. Rather more surprisingly, Howarth was also now accused of rape: 'On one occasion he raped me (forced anal intercoursed me) while I was recovering in the Bryn Estyn hospital ward from a circumcision operation.'

No satisfactory reason has ever been given for the appearance of a serious allegation in an affidavit on Tuesday when no such allegation had apparently been made in the interview which had taken place on Monday. One possible explanation is that, since Nelson himself appears to have been largely responsible for compiling the text of the affidavit which Humphreys signed, the allegation of rape was one which he formulated on the basis of an interpretation of Humphreys's words. In short, Humphreys's statement that 'he [Howarth] did it to me as well' may have been construed as meaning that 'Howarth did to me the same thing that Anglesea had already done'. Whether he intended to or not, Humphreys now signed an affidavit which made an allegation of rape not only against Anglesea but also against Howarth.

Wherever the truth may lie in relation to this particular question, there can be no doubt that there are significant differences between the contemporaneous shorthand notes which Nelson made of the interviews he conducted, and the transcripts which were eventually made of the relevant tape-recordings.

During the Tribunal, Geoffrey Nice QC, appearing as counsel for Gordon Anglesea, drew attention to the following passage in Nelson's notes of his first interview, in which he records Humphreys as saying:

> I've got a bad memory but I can remember everything from back then. Gordon Anglesea was a policeman. He was well liked and he was over everyone. I thought he was a night watchman when he came, not a policeman. When I had been there 8 months I called him scarneck because of his birthmark. I thought he was the nightman at Clwyd House.

As Nice pointed out, there are significant differences between what is written here and the transcript of the relevant part of the interview, some of which has already been quoted:

> HUMPHREYS: I can remember everything (inaudible) it's always on my mind (inaudible). To be honest with you I've got a bloody bad memory … You know, coppers stick to their own, forget it at the end of the day you know, he was well fucking, when he was a police … I didn't know he was a … policeman he was well fucking right wasn't he. Like he was over everybody wasn't he. You see I never knew he was a policeman when he first come to Bryn Estyn, you know who I thought he was? A night watchman.
> NELSON: You thought he was the night watchman? Is it Gordon Anglesea?
> HUMPHREYS: Yeah, well I didn't know his name, but all I know he was fucking scarneck, because he always used to have a scar on his neck, his birthmark wasn't it?

What has happened in this transposition is that a version of events which is full of uncertainty, and in which Humphreys makes it clear that he did not know the name of the man he said had abused him, becomes a clear account in which Humphreys is effectively credited with saying precisely the words he was unable to speak: 'Gordon Anglesea was a policeman'. In the Tribunal, Nelson sought to minimise the significance of this change by saying that wherever there were differences, the transcript of the interview would always take precedence over his contemporaneous note and would be deferred to. The chairman of the Tribunal appears to have accepted this explanation.

What was not pointed out was that, according to the transcript itself, Nelson's notes of the interview had a specific and very important function. At one point in the first interview, Nelson actually says 'if later, when I type up the notes of this interview, would you be prepared to sign them as an affidavit, that it's true?' Humphreys replies 'I'll sign them.' What this exchange should alert us to is that the making of an affidavit, like the creation of a police statement, is not a straightforward process in which the witness's own words are faithfully recorded; it is a process of redaction in which the witness's words are edited, and to some extent refashioned, by the person who actually writes the text of the affidavit. From the comments which he makes in the interview, it would appear that it was Nelson who was ultimately responsible for the form of words which Humphreys signed and that, presumably for reasons of speed, much of the affidavit would be based on Nelson's notes, which were immediately available, rather than on a transcript, which had to be laboriously prepared.

344 Humphreys, police statement, 18 August 1992; NWTT, pp. 24639–40. Nelson, police statement, 22 December 1992. In this statement Nelson claims that they did not discuss the *details* of Humphreys's allegations and says that he cannot recall whether he again showed him the photograph of Anglesea on 18 August, the day of the police interview in London. According to Humphreys's statement of 18 August, he did: 'Today I have been shown a black and white photograph by Mr Dean Nelson. Mr Nelson has shown me this photograph several times before and I can say that it is a photograph of the man I knew as the security guard at Bryn Estyn. The man who attacked me in my room. In the photograph the man was wearing police uniform and it was just of his face and upper body.

345 Police statement, 18 August 1992

346 NWTT, pp. 24725, 24659. The reference to Hector will be found in the letter from John Price to the PCC which is quoted in chapter 46.

347 NWTT, p. 24635; the reference here is to the possibility of the *Independent* publishing a second story as a follow-up to the December 1991 article. In the event, as will become clear, the newspaper declined to do so.

348 Police statement, 24 August 1992

349 NWTT, p. 24656

350 NWTT, p. 24681

351 Steward also intensifies, in a similar manner, his allegations of physical abuse against Nefyn Dodd, and his complaints about Gary Cooke. Having originally claimed that Dodd had hit him on the head on two occasions, he now describes an incident in which Dodd supposedly

gave him 'one hell of a pasting', punching him and kicking him and leaving him with bruising and a black eye. He makes explicit allegations of buggery against Cooke and another man, and connects these with the time he was in care at Bryn Estyn. He claims, in effect, that information was passed to Cooke by members of staff about the times he would be allowed out of the home in order to be sexually abused by Cooke and his friend.

352 NWTT, p. 5875
353 NWTT, p. 5929
354 NWTT, pp. 5910, 5930. However, it should perhaps be noted that a reference to the allegation involving the car was made in the story about Steward which appeared in the *Observer* on 13 September 1992
355 LiC, 9.19–20, pp. 92–3
356 NWTT, p. 16645
357 NWTT, pp. 16643–4
358 As above
359 As above
360 The relevant portion of Peter Wynne's police statement of 8 January 1993 reads as follows:

> While they were in the house Dean Nelson said he had 2 or 3 people who said Inspector Anglesea had sexually abused them. He did not explain that any further and he never said who the others were, he only said that they had each signed affidavits and that he only needed one more person to say something similar so that he could make a case against Inspector Anglesea. It was obvious to me he was wanting me to be the third person because he said to me that someone had told him that I had been sexually abused by Inspector Anglesea, but as far as I was concerned that was not true. He wouldn't say who this person was.
>   Alison Taylor then said that when she worked in Bryn Estyn there was one occasion when I had been glue sniffing down by the bank when he came and I said that I had been buggered by Peter Howarth and that Inspector Anglesea was also involved. So far as I am concerned this is not true, as I was under the influence of glue at the time and cannot recall saying any such thing to her. At no time was I ever buggered by Peter Howarth. However, I was sexually abused by him and I described this in a previous statement I made to the police. I vaguely knew Inspector Anglesea, since he used to visit Bryn Estyn on occasions. I must have seen him about eight times during the time I spent at Bryn Estyn. This would be when he brought boys back from the attendance centre or attended Christmas dinners at the home. I personally have never spoken to Inspector Anglesea and have never had any-

thing to do with him. I knew him to be a policeman because the other boys at the home knew him and everybody used to refer to him as being a policeman and would describe him as having a very prominent birthmark on his neck, so each time I saw him, from the description, I was able to identify him. Dean Nelson told me the reason as to why he had visited me was because he put an article in the *Independent* newspaper about Inspector Anglesea concerning sexual abuse and that the police were threatening to turn over his computer files or something similar, to find where he had got the information from …[H]e also mentioned Inspector Anglesea's solicitors were threatening to sue him. I never spoke to Alison Taylor or Dean Nelson about anything else on this occasion (NWTT, pp. 9046–9).

361 Police statement, 17 December 1991
362 Police interview with Taylor, 11 February 1993
363 Police statement, 1 June 1993
364 The striking out of the words was raised when Nelson was cross-examined at the Tribunal. For a fuller account see NWTT, p. 24623.
365 Interestingly Taylor told the Tribunal that she had 'stayed in the car for a while actually, and then I went to the door' (NWTT, p. 16645). Nelson, however, told the police that if Taylor had joined them he would have asked Wynne's permission first. This implied that he would have fetched her and that she would not therefore have walked in when he was in mid-conversation (Nelson, police statement, 1 June 1993)
366 NWTT, p. 16645
367 NWTT, p. 16648
368 NWTT, pp. 24761–2
369 Tribunal statement, 9 January 1998, p. 9, paragraph 45
370 The *Observer*, 30 August 1992
371 From the contents of these two *Observer* articles it is clear that Brian Johnson-Thomas's main source had been Alison Taylor. During the Tribunal, Taylor confirmed that he had had access to her dossier and tried to suggest that this had been without her consent. She offered no explanation, however, of how such unauthorised access had come about, or of how it was that the *Observer* article had been able to quote accurately from the aide-memoire she had prepared for Harbour, whose text was not contained in her dossier; see NWTT, pp. 16541–2.
372 Telephone interview with David Rose, May 2003
373 *Observer*, 13 September 1992
374 HTV transcript of programme broadcast 17 September 1992.
375 NWTT, p. 16623
376 *Irish Independent*, 24 January 1980, cited in Chris Moore, *The Kincora*

Scandal: Political Cover-Up and Intrigue in Northern Ireland, Marino Books, Dublin, 1996, p. 147

376a Ian Paisley: the hardline anti-catholic leader of the Democratic Unionist Party (established by Paisley himself in the 1970s) and Moderator of the Free Presbyterian Church (which Paisley helped to found in 1951).

377 Moore, as above, p. 7

378 Nick Cohen, 'The Epistles of St Paul' *Observer,* 25 July 2004

379 Quoted from an article by Jane Ellison in the *Independent* in Adam Raphael, *My Learned Friends,* W. H. Allen, 1989, p. 196

380 same, p. 198

381 *Private Eye,* 27 January 1993

382 During the Tribunal D/Supt Ackerley was asked by Gerard Elias whether he had questioned Brian Johnson-Thomas about the *Observer* article in which this claim had originally been made, the 27 September story, which appeared under the headline 'Paedophile ring "includes 12 police"':

> ELIAS: On 27th September of 1992, Mr Ackerley, an article under the name of Brian Johnson Thomas appeared in the Observer newspaper?
> ACKERLEY: Yes, sir.
> ELIAS: And that dealt with allegations of a paedophile ring, allegedly including a number of policemen, is that right?
> ACKERLEY: That is correct, yes.
> ELIAS: Did you see Mr Brian Johnson-Thomas?
> ACKERLEY: I did, sir, yes.
> ELIAS: About the article that he had apparently written?
> ACKERLEY: That is correct.
> ELIAS: Was there any evidence forthcoming from him to substantiate the headline of the article or the content of the article that appeared in the Observer?
> ACKERLEY: Indeed not, no (NWTT, p.25511).

383 Police statement, Mon Williams, 29 October 1992

384 LiC, 52.62, p.787

385 Cooke never worked at Bryn Estyn, as Lee Steward once claimed, and as might have been inferred from the article. At some point between 1972 and 1974 he was employed for two weeks at Bersham Hall, but was then told by the officer-in-charge that his services were no longer required (NWTT, p. 15422; LiC, 52.41–3, pp. 782–3).

386 Viv Hector's words were quoted in a letter to the Press Complaints Commission from John Price, Deputy Editor of the *Observer,* 30 March 1995.

387 Gwen Hurst, interview, July 1998

388   NWTT, pp. 8084–5
389   NWTT, p. 871
390   NWTT, p. 925
391   NWTT, pp. 925–6
392   NWTT, p. 928
393   HTT, 5 July 1994, p. 4
394   HTT, 23 June 1994, pp. 39–40
395   HTT, 23 June 1994, p. 46
396   HTT, 6 July 1994 (Judge's summing-up), p. 98
397   As above
398   HTT, 6 July 1994 (Judge's summing-up), p. 102
399   As above, p. 93
400   HTT, 6 July 1994 (Judge's summing-up), p. 95
401   HTT, 27 June 1994, p. 40
402   HTT, 7 July 1994 (Judge's summing-up), pp. 51–2
403   As above, p. 45
404   As above, pp. 13–14
405   Interview with Paul Wilson, August 1996
406   HTT, 7 July 1994 (Judge's summing-up), p. 38
407   HTT, 5 July 1994 (Judge's summing-up), pp. 6–7
408   Interview with Isabel Williams, July 1996
409   Judicial Studies Board website, www.cix.co.uk/~jsb/specdir/evid.htm,
      October 2001
410   HTT, 7 July 1994 (Judge's summing-up), p. 29
411   HLP, medical notes.
412   HLP, photocopy of log book entry.
413   HTT, 5 July 1994 (Judge's summing-up), pp. 35–6
414   One useful gloss on corroboration is provided in the Australian case of
      Doney v The Queen: 'The essence of corroborative evidence is that it
      "confirms", "supports" or "strengthens" other evidence in the sense
      that it "renders [that] other evidence more probable" (*Reg v Kilbourne*,
      per Lord Simon of Glaisdale). It must do that by connecting or tend-
      ing to connect the accused with the crime charged in the sense that it
      "shows or tends to show that ... the story ... that the accused com-
      mitted the crime is true, not merely that the crime has been commit-
      ted, but that it was committed by the accused' (*R v Baskerville*). One
      extraordinary feature of the judge's ruling about the supposedly cor-
      roborative nature of the log book entry is that he himself offers a
      reasonable definition of corroboration as he actually gives the corrob-
      oration warning. This definition, already cited in the main text, is as
      follows: 'Corroboration means other evidence entirely independent of
      the complainant's evidence which confirms a relevant part of the com-
      plainant's account and tends to show that the offence alleged did hap-
      pen and that the defendant committed it.' It should be clear that the

log book entry does not show or tend to show either that the offence happened or that Howarth committed it.

415 As above, pp. 21–2

416 This phrase 'corroboration by volume' was used by Detective Super-intendent John Robbins, the head of Operation Care, when, during an interview I conducted with him at Upton Police Station on the Wirral in August 1996, I asked him how it was possible to tell whether any allegation trawled by the police was true or false.

417 HTT, 5 July 1994 (Judge's summing-up), p. 25

418 As above, pp. 25–6

419 As above, p. 17

420 As above, p. 27

421 As above, p. 28

422 HTT, 23 June 1994, pp. 20–1

423 HTT, 23 June 1994, p. 34

424 HTT, 6 July 1994 (Judge's summing-up), p. 121

425 On the appropriate judicial direction, see Judicial Studies Board web-site, www.cix.co.uk/~jsb/specdir/evid.htm, Similar Facts, 20.C.1, October 2001

426 HTT, 5 July 1994 (Judge's summing-up), p. 30

427 Sean Doran and John D. Jackson, 'Evidence', *All ER Annual Review 1995*, p. 224

428 AC 57, 65

429 *Sims*, p. 537

430 *R v Bailey*, KB, 1924, 301

431 The passage quoted here is cited by Colin Tapper in *Cross and Tapper on Evidence,* 9th edition, 1999, p. 355. More significantly still, it was cited by Mr Justice Eady in the course of his judgment in the Shieldfield libel case, *Christopher Lillie and Dawn Reed v Newcastle City Council and others,* [2002] EWHC 1600 (QB), paragraph 365

432 *R v Bailey*, KB, 1924, 305

433 same, p. 303

434 same, p. 307

435 Until 1861, there had been no offence of indecent assault at common law with the result that both women and girls were unprotected by the law against practically any form of sexual predation which fell short of rape. This gap in the law was filled when Section 52 of the 1861 Act made into a criminal offence 'any indecent assault upon any female'. The maximum penalty was two years' imprisonment.

Since an act is not generally an assault in law if done with the consent of the other party this meant that young girls were still in practice vulnerable to sexual seduction by men, who could claim that their victims had consented. There was widespread and understandable public concern when a defendant accused of indecently assaulting a six-year-old girl relied successfully for his defence on the claim that the child had consented. The Criminal Law Amendment Act of 1885, as well as raising the age of consent for girls to 16, provided that it would be no defence to a charge of indecent assault on a girl under the age of 13 to prove that she consented to the act of indecency. Sexual assaults on girls between 13 and 16 were defined as misdemeanours rather than crimes. The indecent assault provision was subsequently re-enacted in section 1 of the Criminal Law Amendment Act 1922 (which increased of the age to 16). It is the historical source of section 14(2) of the Sexual Offences Act 1956, which remains in force today.

436　Bailey, as above, p.301

437　*HM Advocate* v *AE,* 1937, JC 96. pp. 98–100

438　As above

439　cited in Jeffrey Weeks, *The Construction of Homosexuality,* www.torge. purespace.de/texte/weeks, first published as chapter 6 of Jeffrey Weeks, *Sex, Politics and Society: The Regulation of Sexuality since 1800,* London, Longman 1981

440　*Sunday Times* Obituary, www.muklaw.ac.ug/profiles/denning.html

441　As above

442　*R v Sims* (1946), 1 KB, p. 533

443　*Sims*, p. 535. Lord Goddard is perhaps now best remembered as the trial judge in the case of Derek Bentley, who was hanged for the murder of a policeman shot by his accomplice during a burglary.

444　*Sims,* p. 536

445　Cited in *Boardman*

446　J. R. S. Forbes, *Similar Facts,* The Law Book Company Ltd, Sydney, 1989, p. 102

447　*Sims*, p. 537; *Sims,* p. 540 *Criminal Law Review,* 1999, Commentary on 'Severance' by John C. Smith, p. 859

447　*Smith*, p. 233

447　*Sims,* p. 537

447　*Sims,* p. 540

448　Forbes, p. 103

449　As above, p. 103

450　*Boardman,* [photocopy p. 7a], phrasing given here as corrected by Lord Hailsham

451　As above, [p. 11 B]

452　*DPP v Boardman,* 1975 AC 457)

453　Kilbourne, pp. 748–749

454　*DPP v P,* 93 (1991) Cr App R, p. 271

455　As above

456　As above, p. 271

457　Colin Tapper, 'The Erosion of *Boardman v DPP*' (1995), *New Law Journal,* vol. 145, 1995, p. 1224

458 Tapper, *Erosion*, p. 1224

459 *P*, p. 270

460 NWTT, p. 194

461 Jean Bodin, *De la Démonomanie des Sorciers*, Paris, 1580. See Lynley Hood, *A City Possessed: The Christchurch Civic Creche Case* (Longacre Press, Dunedin, 2001), p. 72

462 Telephone interview with John Rayfield, 30 November 2004

463 Solicitor's memo, 22 July 1994, HLP

464 Alison Taylor, proof of evidence, 26 May 1994

465 NWTT, p.16663; Mrs Taylor replied by saying 'No, it isn't a fabrication. We are again in the same situation where I say one thing and you don't want me to.'

466 Quoted in NWTT, p. 5652

467 NWTT, p. 5657

468 The words are taken from an article by Ian Jack which appeared in the *Guardian* on 1 December 2001 under the title 'The playwright and the pop mogul'. Apparently written in response to the recent conviction of Jonathan King (whose fate had been compared to that of Oscar Wilde), the article also told, in outline, the story of the Anglesea libel trial. Whether by coincidence or design the article appeared on the tenth anniversary of the publication of Dean Nelson's original article in the *Independent on Sunday*.

469 *Guardian,* as above

470 For the description of Williams, see www.warrenevans.net

471 Anglesea libel trial, summing-up of Mr Justice Drake, pp. 36–7

472 As above, p. 41

473 As above, pp. 41–4

474 As above, p. 44

475 I am indebted for her observations on the demeanour of the witnesses and the conduct of the trial to Margaret Jervis, who attended the trial as a journalist.

476 As above, pp. 45–6

477 Margaret Jervis, unpublished article, 1996

478 *Guardian,* 1 December 2001. Jack refers in the article to an occasion when one of the witnesses was 'obviously drunk'. This appears to be a misremembered reference to Steward's drug-induced collapse.

479 As above, summing-up, p. 70

480 As above, pp. 73–4

481 Anglesea libel trial, closing address of Lord Williams, p. 22

482 As above, p.22

483 As above, p. 23

484 As above, p. 24

485 As above, pp. 28–30

486 As above, p. 25

487 As above, p.32

488 As above, pp. 35–36

489 As above, p. 51

490 Unusually the jury did not return a verdict on the level of damages to be awarded at the same time as they found in favour of Anglesea. The next day they spent several hours reaching such a decision. Just as they were about to return to the courtroom, lawyers acting for the opposing parties agreed a figure of £375,000. To this day nobody knows whether the jury, which was split 10–2 on the verdict, would have returned a higher or a lower figure.

491 Letter from Peter Watkins Jones to HTV's Director of Programmes, 8 January 1996

492 Interview with Peggy and Mandy Humphreys, July 1996; Margaret Jervis, unpublished article, 1996

493 *Observer*, 12 February 1995

494 These comments and the inquest were reported in the local press; see *Daily Post* and *Western Mail,* 15 June 1995

495 NWTT, p. 11147

496 The panel, having been commissioned in January 1994, carried out its investigation between March 1994 and December 1995, although its terms of reference were only finalised in late 1994. The panel was required to 'inquire into, consider and report to the County Council upon (1) what went wrong and (2) why did this happen and how this position could have continued undetected for so long' and they were asked to examine in particular such matters as recruitment and selection of staff, management and training, suspension, and complaints procedures.

497 Interview with John Jevons, November 13, 2003; John Jevons, personal communication, 21 December, 2003. Jevons's attitude appears to have shifted somewhat over the years. In an article in *Community Care* on 7 January 1993, he was quoted as saying he had 'created a new culture of openness in the [social services] department … and allowed a fresh wind to blow away the old conspiratorial atmosphere in which children's allegations were ignored.' On 13 January 1994 *Community Care* reported what it described as 'a public row' between residential care staff and senior management staff: 'Union members are angry at remarks made by Clwyd director John Jevons before Christmas. Addressing the social services committee, Jevons spoke of "a nagging concern that no one had taken what the children were saying seriously." Branding these comments "unhelpful", Unison went on to accuse Clwyd of failing to honour promises to support staff who say they are under pressure from the current atmosphere of allegations and counter-allegation. Unison members in social services say they have suffered in health, job prospects and from media harassment.'

498 In her report Nicola Davies recommended that there should be a detailed examination of the child care procedures and practices of both Gwynedd and Clwyd County Councils since 1991. Adrianne Jones, a former director of social services for Birmingham City Council was appointed to undertake this task. She presented her report to the secretary of state in May 1996.

499 John Jillings, telephone interview, May 1996

500 John Jevons, personal communication, 21 December 2003

501 Loveridge's verdict is noted in the Waterhouse report (LiC, 32.43). Waterhouse goes on to note that 'the form of the [Jillings] report was such that it contained a great deal of defamatory material based on hearsay and dealt with some matters that were not within the inquiry's terms of reference' (LiC, 32.58). It also refers to a letter written to Loveridge by the chief constable of North Wales on 12 March 1996 in which he 'made substantial criticisms of factual statements in the report and comments in it about the level of co-operation by the police with the Panel; and he referred also to potential liability for defamation. In the first of his concluding paragraphs he said: "I hope that the issues I have raised are sufficient in themselves to cause the County Council to reflect over the weight they place on some of the unsupported assertions made in the report, and to think very carefully over the potentially actionable consequences of publishing the report as it currently stands" '(LiC, 32.59).

502 NWTT, p. 375

503 Transcript of first preliminary meeting of the Tribunal, 10 September 1996, pp. 2–3

504 LiC, 6.02, p.55

505 Dermot P. J. Walsh, *Bloody Sunday and the Rule of Law in Northern Ireland*, p. 62 and passim.

506 Bob Woffinden and Margaret Jervis, *The Independent*, London, 8 October 1995. In June 1994 in Pembroke, west Wales, the largest trial for organised child sexual abuse ever to have taken place in Britain came to an end, with six men receiving prison sentences totalling 53 years. This was the first time in post-war Britain that conspiracy charges resulting out of allegations of organised ritual abuse had ever been sustained.

Convinced that they had uncovered a sinister conspiracy to abuse children, social workers in Pembrokeshire had elicited allegations from young children which implicated as many as 200 adults. On 8 December 1992 the arrests began. By the time they had finished, social workers had seized eighteen children from nine families and the police had arrested eleven men and two women. When he opened the prosecution in Swansea Crown Court in January 1994, Gerard Elias QC claimed that children had become the victims of 'the most depraved and revolting conduct imaginable ... [to] a degree of degradation that sometimes almost defies belief ... what is chillingly described as a paedophile ring grew up where acts of indecency, buggery and oral sex took place'. He went on to claim that adults had conspired to abuse both their own and others' children and that their crimes included sex orgies in homes, sheds, tunnels and seaside caves. Although most of the satanic allegations which had originally been elicited from the children were carefully excised from the prosecution's case, reference was made to the sacrifice of a goat and to a pit of snakes. The children, it was claimed, had been forced to participate from a very young age and the reason that none had spoken a word of all this until they were questioned by social workers was that they had been silenced by death threats.

When the jury convicted six men on the basis of the horrific allegations which had been presented to them so compellingly, defence lawyers immediately submitted an appeal. Even before this appeal was heard some of the parents who had had their children taken away by social workers had taken their case to the family courts, where Mr Justice Connell had criticised the conduct of the social workers in particularly severe terms:

> The children were praised when they confirmed a 'disclosure' or made a fresh one. It is very difficult for an adult to whom such information had been confided by a child to stand back and view it objectively. The understandable reaction of such an adult is invariably to believe what he or she has been told, so that when on a further occasion the child does not confirm what has been alleged earlier, the child is described as 'returning to denial' or as 'blocking'. An alternative solution, rarely considered, unhappily, is that the allegation may have been untrue or significantly exaggerated in the first place ... the impression left with the court is that those involved on behalf of the local authority were too ready to accept what the various children had to say, even some time after therapy had begun, without really testing its reliability or attempting to challenge or disconfirm it.

In 1995, prior to the hearing of the criminal appeal on the part of the six men who had been convicted, leave was sought to adduce the words of Mr Justice Connell as part of the evidence which would be offered on their behalf. Leave was duly granted and, in the view of many, the arguments now put forward on behalf of the six men demonstrated clearly that a terrible miscarriage of justice had taken place.

In spite of the strength of these arguments, however, the prosecuting barristers, led by Gerard Elias, maintained their original case with considerable force. On 3 November 1995, in *R v Davies, Jones, Evans, Evans, Cryer and Sealy*, the convictions of five of the six men were upheld by a panel of judges headed by Lord Justice Swinton Thomas and including Mr Justice Waterhouse, later to become Sir Ronald Waterhouse. Two of Byron Rogers's three *Sunday Telegraph* articles about the case, originally published in 1999, are reprinted in his collection of articles, *The Bank Manager and the Holy Grail*, Aurum, 2003, pp. 227–242.

507   NWTT, p. 237

508   Opening Statement, p. 140. (All page references to the opening statement are to the copy distributed to the press in January 1997. In accordance with the Tribunal's guidelines, however, quotations have been revised so that they correspond to the text as delivered.)

509   Brian Corby, Alan Doig and Vicki Roberts, *Public Inquiries into Abuse of Children in Residential Care*, Jessica Kingsley Publishers, 2001, p. 122

510   As above, p. 127

511   As above, p. 146

512   NWTT, p. 217, quoted from press copy

513   The question which is raised here is the one posed at the end of the previous chapter – whether the power or scale of a particular inquiry *is* the key to truth. For it is by no means self-evident that inquiries become more thorough in proportion to the number of people who are involved in them. Indeed, if we take an example from a slightly different field, the history of scientific investigation, it becomes reasonably clear that the opposite is sometimes the case. Significant scientific discoveries are very often made by individuals working on their own or in very small groups. Precisely because of their relative isolation such researchers find it much easier to challenge the powerful orthodoxies which frequently stand in the way of investigation.

What the example of scientific research suggests is that, if the true picture is actually quite different from the received view, then it might well be the case that the larger and more powerful a particular investigating body becomes, the less likely it is to uncover the truth. For such large groups tend almost inevitably to multiply the power of received views. They do so above all by the subtle and powerful psychological pressures which are brought to bear on any individual who appears to be out of step with the prevailing assumptions of the group. The process by which this happens has been described as 'groupthink'. The term was originally coined by the social psychologist Irving Janis. See his *Victims of Groupthink*, Boston, Houghton Mifflin, 1972. The process has been characterised well by the sociologist Jeffrey Victor:

The social process of groupthink is a collective response to conformity pressures ... Groupthink can be seen to operate in religious groups, therapy groups and even corporate bureaucracies, groups in which the need to maintain co-operative interaction between members creates social pressures to conform. These pressures, in turn, suppress critical analysis of, scepticism of, and dispute about prevailing beliefs. The desire of participants to preserve friendly relationships among themselves inhibits their expression of points of view that deviate from informally accepted group norms. Participants who attempt to bring up issues which might cause internal bickering and conflict are subtly ostracised or chastised for their disloyalty. The process works upon people's perception of reality. Members who might privately consider unacceptable beliefs, begin to doubt their own thinking and change their beliefs to fit in with the reality constructed by the group. As a result of groupthink, critical thinking and reality testing are repressed by the pressures for group solidarity. The process of groupthink is by no means unusual or rare. Many of us have been members of groups in which this process operates (Jeffrey S. Victor, *Satanic Panic: The Creation of a Contemporary Legend,* Chicago, Open Court, 1993, pp. 92–3).

514   *Guardian* 20 January 1997
515   NWTT, pp. 895–7
516   While the ruling may be understandable it is the Waterhouse report itself which suggests that it does not in fact rest on any solid legal foundation. Howarth's conviction is upheld in unequivocal terms in the report. What is perhaps more important than this, however, is the manner in which the members of the Tribunal describe the limits of their own jurisdiction, and particularly their powers in relation to convictions that have already been obtained. In the relevant passage in the report, they write:

> In respect of those individuals who have already been convicted of relevant offences against children in care ... our approach has been that, in the absence of a successful appeal, the convictions are evidence that the offences were committed and that it has not been within our jurisdiction to question the correctness of those convictions, *unless (possibly) fresh evidence were to be tendered going to the root of the convictions.*
>
> In the event no such fresh evidence has been submitted and none of the convicted persons referred to in Chapter 2 has appealed against conviction successfully (6.09–6.10) [italics added].

These words clearly imply that the Tribunal did not regard the decision of any court as sacrosanct and that, were they to have been supplied with significant new evidence, they were empowered, if not to overturn convictions, at least to question whether they were soundly based. In fact their criteria for doing so seemed, according to this statement, to correspond almost exactly to those applied by the Court of Appeal, which itself rarely overturns the decision of a jury unless there is 'fresh evidence ... going to the root of the conviction'.

This statement of the Tribunal's wide powers is in accord with the attitude they adopt towards the verdict of the jury in, for example, the Anglesea libel trial. For, although the Tribunal ends by upholding this verdict, it is clearly implied that this was not a preordained conclusion and that, had new evidence of sufficient quality been available (or even had a different view been taken of the original evidence), it was quite within their powers to question the outcome of the trial.

Yet, although the statement is consistent with the Tribunal's approach to the libel trial, it gives a misleading impression of the attitude adopted towards Peter Howarth's conviction during the Tribunal proceedings. From the very outset it was clearly implied by the Chairman that the Tribunal was *not* in a position to reconsider Howarth's conviction. The original application for Howarth to be separately represented at the Tribunal, made by the barrister Courtenay Griffiths, was accepted by the Chairman on this understanding:

> CHAIRMAN: The question I have to ask you is this: are you seeking to represent Howarth in order to question the correctness of his convictions?
> GRIFFITHS: This Tribunal is not – can't undertake that task, sir, and I appreciate that.
> CHAIRMAN: I am glad to hear you agree with that, because there is a mechanism – has he in fact appealed against the decision?
> GRIFFITHS: Those instructing me have recently been instructed by him to pursue an appeal on his behalf (NWTT p. 126).

Even if, in theory, it remained possible for Howarth's legal team to submit fresh evidence, no public indication was ever given, at any stage of the Tribunal's proceedings, that these convictions were open to question.

517 Technically the task of representing Howarth was actually passed to the Tribunal's own counsel, Gerard Elias QC. Given his onerous responsibilities, however, it would have been quite unreasonable to expect him to give the same attention to Howarth's case as his own counsel would have done. Howarth's counsel had never intended to be present throughout the Tribunal, some parts of which did not directly concern Bryn Estyn, but counsel would have been present – and active – during the cross-examination of a number of key witnesses, including

Gordon Anglesea, Alison Taylor, Councillors King and Parry and, perhaps most importantly of all, Dean Nelson.

518 NWTT, p. 28984
519 NWTT, p. 383
520 NWTT, pp. 394–7
521 NWTT, p. 430; Taylor's placement at Bryn Estyn was in 1982, not 1984
     as Moran suggests here.
522 NWTT, p. 29271
523 NWTT, pp. 29266–7
524 For a fuller account of the case of Terry Hoskin see below, pp. 483–9.
     See also my website, www.richardwebster.net/trawlingforcrimes.html
525 NWTT, p. 28881
526 *R v Brian Selwyn B*; Neutral Citation Number: [2003] EWCA Crim 319
     No. 2002/00540/Y4.
527 NWTT, p. 16–17
527a LiC, p. 870, paragraph 7; NWTT, p.27859
527b NWTT, pp.27862–3; the summary of the evidence given by the five
     witnesses is based on cross-referring to their evidence in the transcript
     from the names given by Mr Treverton-Jones.
528 LiC, 7.09, p. 67
529 NWTT, p. 10212
530 NWTT, p. 10167; LiC, 8.20, p. 78
531 See above, note 516
532 LiC, 8.22, p.79
533 This view was expressed to me by one of the press officers responsible
     for handling inquiries from journalists in the days following the pub-
     lication of the Waterhouse report.
534 LiC, 9.29, pp. 95–96. Elsewhere in the report the following comment is
     made about the course of the 1991–1993 police investigation: 'The
     waters had been muddied to *an uncertain and indeterminable extent* by the
     intervention of Nelson because he had returned to North Wales [in
     February 1992 and subsequently] to seek evidence against Anglesea …'
     (2.33, p. 20). No criticism is made at any point in the report of his orig-
     inal December 1991 article.
535 LiC, 34.28, p. 536
536 LiC, 33.96. p. 516
537 Although, in theory, this kind of evidence should have been covered
     anyway by counsel to the Tribunal, whose role was supposed to be
     inquisitorial, in practice the adversarial stance he had adopted made
     such an intervention unlikely.
538 In the *Mirror*, Tanner is quoted as saying about Tŷ'r Felin: 'The atmos-
     phere was one of constant fear. If the staff didn't believe you they gave
     you a double chester. Two would hold each of your arms and a third
     would fall on his knees on your chest' (p. 5). In the *Independent* on the

same day he is quoted as making a similar allegation not about Tŷ'r Felin, but about Bryn Estyn: 'At Bryn Estyn they had a special thing where two members of staff would each hold an arm so that your head was pushed forward. They would then take it in turn to kick you in the chest. I think I was 12 or 13 when that first happened to me' (p.3). The difference may, of course, be due to the reporters and not the source.

539 See website, www.childrenuk.co.uk/chukfeb/waterhouse.htm

540 See Alison Taylor's website, www.alisontaylor.net

541 An excellent resource in this respect has been provided by the Stead scholar, Owen Mulpetre, whose website, The W. T. Stead Resource Site, is a treasure-trove of contemporary documentation on Stead and Waugh, including the entire text of Stead's 'A Maiden Tribute to Modern Babylon' and much else besides (see www.attackingthedevil.co.uk).

542 The investigation was in Congleton, Cheshire, see J. S. La Fontaine, *Speak of the Devil: Tales of Satanic Abuse in Contemporary England*, Cambridge University Press, 1998, p. 11

543 When I interviewed him in prison in 1997, Langshaw accepted that he was guilty and did not complain about his conviction or his sentence. He said that many of the counts of indecent assault to which he had pleaded guilty were true. However, he also found himself facing a number of counts of buggery (including one from Keeley) which, he maintains, were not true. Indeed he says that, like many gay men, he never practised anal intercourse and had therefore never abused any of his victims in this manner. Given that at this stage Langshaw had no motive (other than attempting to minimise his offending) to misrepresent the facts, it seems to me entirely possible that his account of his own offending was accurate. What can be said with reasonable confidence is that any genuine offender in his position, investigated by the method of trawling, would almost inevitably find himself facing a significant number of *false* allegations. It would be implausible to suggest that all the counts to which he pleaded were in fact true. Interestingly Christian Wolmar, a writer who takes a starkly different view of care home investigations from the one presented here, and has been very critical of my work, accepts that true and false allegations can be mixed together. In his book *Forgotten Children: The Secret Abuse Scandal in Children's Homes*, Vision Paperbacks, 2000, he quotes from a letter written by a care worker who pleaded guilty to a number of charges against the advice of his lawyers because he did not want to force his genuine victims to go through the ordeal of giving evidence: 'The serious charges [those of buggery] were totally untrue ... two further accusers are totally lying ... distortion of events, facts, etc. are great but then in fairness it was a long time ago; exaggeration – some of the minor allegations were more honest and a couple of the 'middle'

charges/accusers also … The exaggeration was beyond comprehension …' (p. 162).

544   Wolmar, as above, pp. 9–10

545   *Panorama*, 'Hear No Evil', BBC Television, 10 March 1997

546   As above.

547   Terry Oates, 'The difficulties encountered when investigating abuse which has taken place in the past', in *Child Sexual Abuse: Providing for Victims, Coping with Offenders*, ed. Stephanie Hayman, The Institute for the Study and Treatment of Delinquency, King's College London, 1998, p. 69

548   As above

549   As above, p. 72

550   As above

551   As above

552   As above, p. 70

553   One question which arises from DI Oates's account of the prison 'exeat' scheme, is how it was decided that a particular prisoner was 'likely to disclose' and should therefore be a candidate for a visit to a police station. Since most prisoners are naturally wary of police officers, an initial visit by them might be self-defeating. One possible answer to this question is that the initial questioning of prisoners may sometimes have been conducted by social workers rather than police officers. One reason for saying this has been provided by Terry Hoskin, the former head of St Aidan's in Widnes in Cheshire, one of the community homes run by Nugent Care. Hoskin himself became an innocent victim of the Cheshire Police's trawling operation and spent several years in prison (see below, chapter 66). During his time in prison, he made an interesting observation about the conduct of the Cheshire investigation. While in the prison visiting room for a special legal visit he noticed that a fellow prisoner he knew slightly was also receiving a special visit from a woman and a man whose face he thought he recognised. Later that day he spoke to the prisoner and asked him about the special visit. He was told that the woman was a social worker and that the man was a victim support officer in Cheshire (whom Hoskin had met in the course of his work). They had come to ask him about his time in a community home and had explained that they were looking into the case of a care worker, whom they named, against whom allegations of abuse had been made. They explained that the man in question was still working with children and they had come to ask the prisoner whether he had anything to say about this man. They also said that he might at some later point receive a visit from the police. In the light of this evidence it would appear to be entirely possible that, on some occasions at least, the initial assessment of whether a prisoner was likely to disclose would be conducted

by social workers during the course of a visit similar to the one Hoskin describes.

554 Terry Oates, as above, p. 65

555 'Our Gulag', *Independent*, 9 June 1996

556 This is an extract from a contemporary letter, written in 1997

557 I take this figure from Wolmar, as above, p. 13

558 See Hansard, 19 June 2003: Claire-Curtis Thomas

559 David Rose and Gary Horne, *Observer*, 'Abuse witch-hunt traps innocent in a net of lies', 26 November 2000. Roy Shuttleworth's case was the subject of a moving *Panorama* documentary, 'In the name of the children', written and presented by David Rose, produced by Gary Horne and broadcast that evening. The documentary established, beyond reasonable doubt, that Roy Shuttleworth had not committed any of the crimes alleged against him. Shuttleworth was eventually released on parole in 2002. The solicitor Chris Saltrese, to whom I took Shuttleworth's case in 1996, has now submitted an application to the Criminal Cases Review Commission to refer the case back to the Court of Appeal.

560 The quotations here are taken from a contemporary newspaper report which appeared in 1996.

561 In 1996 I interviewed Adrian Coates in Walton Prison in Liverpool. He was deeply angry about what had happened and continued to protest his innocence.

562 Part of this chapter originally appeared in the *Guardian* Weekend magazine of 8 May 1998 in the article 'Abuse in the balance' which I wrote with Bob Woffinden. My thanks are due to him for allowing me to reproduce these sections here. For a longer version of this piece, see my website, www.richardwebster.net/trawlingforcrimes.html

563 Phillips's allegation first made its appearance on the day before he was due to appear in court at a critical moment in the troubled relationship he had with his wife, 'Carol'. In February 1992 he and his wife had separated and lived apart for thirteen months. In March 1993 they began to see each other again but, a few months later, in May or June, there was an argument, and Carol asked him to leave the house. He had been drinking and refused. The argument continued and he then slashed his wrists with a kitchen knife. At this point Carol called the police and he was taken into custody. Carol was later told that, while he was in the police station, he had attempted to hang himself in his cell. Phillips was then sent to a psychiatric hospital for three weeks. After he came out Carol agreed that he could come back and live with her.

At this point various prosecutions against Phillips were in progress. These involved one charge of assaulting a police officer, another charge of obstructing the police and another of shop-lifting. Because of these charges Phillips was regularly seeing a probation officer and at this stage it would appear that he had made no complaint about his time in care. On 1 July 1993, the day before he was due to appear in court on the charge of obstructing the police, he went to the probation office at a time when he knew his regular probation officer would not be present. He spoke to the duty officer and made to her an allegation of physical abuse which related to his time in care. He later outlined this allegation to his main probation officer and, with her help, he gradually pieced together, over the next three months a 'memory' of how he had been physically and sexually abused by the head of St Aidan's when he had been resident there – Terry Hoskin. She apparently accepted his allegations as a truthful account.

In September Phillips appeared in court on the charge of assaulting a police officer and a related charge of being drunk and disorderly. He then spent three months in prison. When he came out, towards the end of November, he contacted the police in relation to a complaint he was making against them. On 1 December 1993 a woman police officer returned his call. In the course of their conversation he said that a social worker had done 'something' to him while he had been at St Aidan's and she had the impression that he was referring to sexual abuse. As a result of this a police officer was sent to see him and on 8 December he made a carefully constructed statement detailing the prolonged abuse which he had supposedly suffered at the hands of Hoskin.

564   This description was actually adopted by journalist Angelique Chrisafis in an article in the Guardian which reported the Merseyside police's defence of trawling after the collapse of the David Jones trial: 'Trawling for abuse victims defended, *Guardian*, 7 December 2000.

565   Christian Wolmar, *Forgotten Children: The Secret Abuse Scandal in Children's Homes*, Vision Paperbacks, 2000, p. 15

566   *You told me you loved me*, Merseyside Police, Cheshire Constabulary, City of Liverpool Social Services Directorate and Cheshire Social Services, 1999, p. 3

567   As above, p. 5

568   Paul Foot, *London Review of Books*, 4 July 1996; my letter taking issue with Foot was published in the next edition of the *LRB*

569   David Rose and Gary Horne, *Observer*, 'Abuse witch-hunt traps innocent in a net of lies', 26 November 2000

570   This passage was cited in the report of the House of Commons Home Affairs Committee, *The Conduct of Investigations into Past Cases of Abuse in Children's Homes*, HMSO, 31 October, 2002, Volume 1, paragraph 436, pp. 62–3,

571   As above, Volume 1, 409, p. 60. A few moments later the chairman of the committee, Chris Mullin MP asked: 'Could I check that I heard

right. You said, not one person who is sitting in a prison cell who has been convicted in one of these cases is blameless. Did you just say that?' Garsden confirmed that this was what he believed: 'I do not believe that there are people sitting in prison cells who are wholly blameless. They may not be as blameful as they have been found by the courts to be, but I do not believe they are blameless.' After he had gone on to cite the statistics for St George's, talking of Operation Care's count of '89 alleged abusers and 125 victims', he said 'Those are staggering statistics, are they not?' He was reminded by Mullin that these figures referred to allegations and not to proved cases (412–16, p. 61).

572 David Rose and Gary Horne, as above

573 *Times Educational Supplement*, 29 January 1999

574 Christian Wolmar, *Forgotten Children: The Secret Abuse Scandal in Children's Homes*, Vision Paperbacks, 2000

575 This interview was conducted by Bob Woffinden in March 2003 for an article which was to appear in a national newspaper. The day scheduled for publication coincided with news of the final preparations for the American and British invasion of Iraq. The outbreak of war days later meant that the article was never published.

576 *Daily Mail*, March 2003

577 This evidence would eventually be given in 2003 during the appeal court hearing for Mike Lawson

578 *News of the World*, 10 December 2003, p. 7

579 *Daily Mail*, March 2003

580 I remain enormously grateful to John Jevons without whose helpful and extensive comments (often justly critical) on an earlier draft of this book, it would be a less accurate record than it is. Commenting on an earlier version of this paragraph he said: 'For the record, there was a significant difference about the South Wales case – there was at least one (possibly more) specific allegation. ... My overall view is that if people in positions of authority have reason to suspect that serious criminal acts might have been perpetrated, they have a duty to act by reporting those to the appropriate investigative authorities. The fact that the police sometimes make mistakes in investigating suspected crimes does not absolve that person from reporting the suspected crime.' The duty which Jevons invokes here is not in dispute. But there is a world of difference between passing on specific allegations to the police and relaying unfounded and alarmist speculation about paedophile rings. Perhaps more importantly, people in positions of authority have responsibilities to the public which may sometimes conflict with the duty invoked by Jevons. They have a duty to alert members of the public to injustices perpetrated by the authorities they are co-operating with. Jevons was ideally placed to observe the multiple injustices and the false allegations which resulted from the North Wales

inquiry. Any ordinarily perceptive observer at the centre of events, as Jevons was, would have been able to see that there was something very wrong, for example, with the case constructed against David Birch, and that police trawling operations posed huge dangers to innocent care workers. Yet Jevons says that at the time he did not see anything wrong with the investigation conducted by the North Wales police. When I asked him whether he now, with hindsight, had any regrets about his own role, he said that he did have regrets about the outcome of the police investigation in South Wales. But he went on to say (after having read this book in draft form): 'I have no regrets whatsoever in either North Wales or South Wales at referring those matters to the police – absolutely none – and if I were still a director of social services and similar sets of allegations came to light then I would consider doing the same again. I really would. Because I actually think that one has very little option about that. It would be quite wrong if serious allegations were made of that nature not to do anything with them.' When I reminded John Jevons that there weren't any allegations in North Wales, there was a pause. He then said 'There were allegations made by Alison Taylor'. This was an unexpected response in that Jevons had previously sought to minimise Taylor's role, writing to me that 'We only communicated to N W Police the concerns relating to Clwyd, matters on which Alison Taylor had been largely silent.' Eventually Jevons agreed that it had not so much been a question of passing on specific allegations but more a question of 'raising major suspicions' (telephone interview, 1 December 2004).

Of all the people who played major roles in the North Wales story, Jevons is among those whose attitude I find the most perplexing. He was certainly not guilty of any peculiar misjudgment, but it does seem to me that he was guilty of the kind of ordinary misjudgment which has been made throughout the current witch-hunt by national newspaper editors, journalists, senior police officers, politicians, lawyers, judges and many others who occupy positions of authority and influence. It is on such ordinary misjudgments, made by well-meaning, law-abiding citizens who are often anxious to be seen to be doing the right thing, that witch-hunts are, in part at least, built. What is perhaps most revealing is that, when I spoke to him almost fourteen years after the event, Jevons did not believe that his own actions in alerting the North Wales Police to a non-existent paedophile ring were a matter for regret at all.

581   Statement taken by a solicitor representing one of the defendants in the Headlands trial

582   Claire Curtis-Thomas MP, House of Commons Hansard Debates for 19 June 2003, (pt 18)

583   Kaufman Report, Nova Scotia Justice Department, 2002, Chapter 6

584 David Rose, ' "Abuser" was netted in police trawl. But is he innocent?', *Observer,* 6 January 2002

585 One honourable exception to this was the *New Statesman,* which, under the editorship of Peter Wilby (who had been deputy editor of the *Independent on Sunday,* at the time of Dean Nelson's original 1991 article, and editor in 1996 at the time of the post-Jillings campaign for a Tribunal) published a number of my articles on police trawling from February 1999 onwards. Another exception was the *Guardian,* which published an article of mine critical of trawling on the eve of the North Wales Tribunal in 1997 and who subsequently published, in the Weekend magazine on 8 May 1998, the long article about trawling investigations which I wrote with Bob Woffinden. However when I offered the *Guardian* another article on the same topic a year or so later, the section editor I spoke to declined it regretfully on the grounds that the previous two pieces had led to so many outraged letters that he was reluctant to risk the displeasure of his readers again.

586 (*Regina v John Maybery* [2003] EWCA Crim 782, No: 200204076 X3, before Lord Justice Latham, Mrs Justice Cox, Mr Justice Gross; John Maybery was represented by David Batcup.) The quotation from the judgment continues as follows: 'Those particular problems the courts, as we have already indicated, are familiar with and have developed techniques to deal with. The three sets of control mechanisms are: first, by way of controlling the number of allegations which can properly be included in an indictment – in other words, by exercising the power to sever; the second sanction, if there is nonetheless such unfairness that a fair trial cannot take place the court can, of course, stay the proceedings as an abuse of process; the third is by ensuring that the jury is directed adequately as to the way in which the defendant may be prejudiced generally, and how he may be prejudiced in relation to particular allegations, ensuring that the defendant's case in respect of individual complainants is adequately presented to the jury. This requires the judge to be scrupulous about putting the defendant's case in his summing-up.' It need scarcely be said that the impression conveyed here that the courts have developed adequate safety mechanisms to deal with the dangers of trawling comes close to being an inversion of the truth.

587 Montesquieu's words are used as the epigraph to *No Crueler Tyrannies: Accusation, False Witness and other Terrors of our Times* by Dorothy Rabinowitz, Free Press, 2003. Charles-Louis de Secondat, Baron de Montesquieu is generally recognised as one of the great political philosophers of the Enlightenment who argued that the best safeguard against despotic government lay in a system in which different bodies exercised legislative, executive and judicial power. He has been described (with John Locke) as 'the ideological co-founder of the

American constitution'.

588 Hansard, 16 Oct 2002 : Column 114WH

589 Barnaby Jones, *Spectator,* 3 August 2002

590 The investigative journalist Bob Woffinden and I spent some two years
piecing this particular case together and helping to bring the case to
the high court. Bob Woffinden deserves massive credit for developing
a style of investigative journalism which endeavours to work in parallel with the courts and in this respect and in others I will always be in
his debt. Without his experience of numerous other cases we would
never have been able to secure for Dawn Reed and Chris Lillie such
a decisive judgment. The judgment in question, all 250 pages of it, can
be read in full on the Court Service Website, links to which will be
found in the Shieldfield section of my website. The long article which
Bob and I wrote for the *Guardian,* 'Cleared' (G2, 31 July 2002 pp. 1–5),
can also be found there in an extended version.

591 Sydney Anglo, 'Evident Authority and Authoritative Evidence' in *The
Damned Art: Essays in the Literature of Witchcraft,* ed. Sydney Anglo,
Routledge and Kegan Paul, 1977. pp. 17–18

592 These rumours concerned several well known Conservative politicians. One reason I have not given much attention to them is that they
tended to be associated with the later Bryn Alyn allegations rather than
with the original Bryn Estyn story. Another reason is that they had a
limited circulation, being disseminated chiefly by the now-defunct
'satirical' magazine *Scallywag,* edited by the late Simon Regan. The
rumours did find their way, however, in a somewhat inchoate form,
into the account of the North Wales story given by Nick Davies in the
Guardian, see below, note 600.

593 On the recovered memory movement, see Mark Pendergrast, *Victims
of Memory: Incest Accusations and Shattered Lives,* HarperCollins, 1996,
passim. See also my 'Freud's False Memories: Psychoanalysis and the
Recovered Memory Movement' which forms the Afterword to my
Why Freud Was Wrong: Sin, Science and Psychoanalysis, Fontana Press,
1996; www.richardwebster.net/freudsfalsememories.html

594 Quoted by Daniel Lyons in 'God, Sex and Greed', *Forbes Magazine,* 6
September 2003

595 See the websites www.stopmormonsexualabuse.com and www.lamb-
sroar.org

596 *Sunday Times* (Ireland), 28 April 1996, citing the views of the surgeon,
J. B. Prendiville.

597 Mary Raftery and Eoin O'Sullivan, *Suffer the Little Children: The Inside
Story of Ireland's Industrial Schools,* New Island, Dublin, 1999, p. 16

598 As above, p. 3

599 *Irish Times,* 16 November 2004. The government estimate referred to
was made in the 2004 annual report of the Comptroller and Auditor

General. The same report notes that, although awards had been made to nearly 2,000 former residents, only 11 had been awarded more than €200,000, and only one had received the full payment of €300,000. It should be noted, though, that (as in any lottery) it is the theoretical availability of such high sums which tends to encourage false allegations. The average award was in any case €77,000 a figure which does not include legal costs.

600 Nick Davies wrote two long articles about North Wales which appeared in the G2 section of the *Guardian* in September and October 1997 while the Tribunal was still sitting. The first of these articles, 'Horror upon horror', was published on 24 September 1997. It began by making an implicit parallel between what had happened in North Wales children's homes and the Holocaust:

> No one is listening. For years the muffled sound of scandal has been leaking from the closed world of Britain's children's homes, sometimes through the trial of a care worker who has turned out to be a child rapist, sometimes in rumours about paedophile rings and cover-ups and connections in high places. Whispers of nightmares, never the whole story.
>
> Now, finally, for the first time, the truth is pouring out. In a former council chamber in a small village near Chester, dozens of men and women are stepping forward to speak in public. Some are the grown-up survivors – nearly 300 of them – recalling childhoods of unmitigated violence and exploitation ... Others are the men and women who are accused of tormenting them – 148 of them, skewered to the truth by ranks of lawyers. *It is a little Nuremberg* [italics added].

In fact the Tribunal heard evidence from only 264 people altogether, including many who were neither accusers nor accused, rather than the 450 plus claimed by Davies. Among the allegations he recounted as though they were proven facts was that of Brendan Randles:

> Another [man] described how he had arrived at Bryn Estyn to be greeted by Howarth who informed him immediately: 'I'm going to fuck you tonight.' In his first statement the man described how he managed to evade Howarth's frenzied lunges but he later agreed to make another statement in which he conceded that, in truth, Howarth had succeeded. More than that, he had invited a friend to join in, both of them raping him at the same time, one orally, the other anally. He said he never knew who the second man was.

At no point does Davies disclose that Randles made both his statements after he had been in touch with Ryan Tanner, that he only accused Howarth by name after Tanner had shown him a photograph of him, and that he only made the allegation of buggery after drinking and after being plied by Tanner with questions, to one of which he replied 'What do you want me to say, that he's fucked my arse?' (see above, pp. 246–53)

Elsewhere in his article Davies writes that Peter Howarth 'became deputy headmaster at the now notorious Bryn Estyn home where he teamed up with a housemaster named Stephen Norris for a paedophile orgy of huge self-indulgence'. In his article he offers no evidence to support this claim.

The second of Davies's articles, 'Abusers of power', dealt mainly with allegations about a paedophile ring:

> For more than 10 years a dark storm of scandal has been gathering over the children's homes of North Wales – a swirling mass of allegations not only of the routine rape and battering of children in care but of the existence of a paedophile ring, a conspiracy of abusers both in and outside the homes, who were nourished by each other's obsessions and protected by each other's power. Power is the key.
>
> Power is the fabric of a paedophile ring, essential first to subjugate the children, whose passivity is necessary for the adults' enjoyment; and second, where possible, to neutralise the authorities who might otherwise frustrate its activities (*Guardian*, 15 October 1997).

The article went on to relay many of the allegations made by Lee Steward, including the allegation against Gordon Anglesea, who was not named and was disguised as ' a powerful public official' who had previously been investigated and cleared.

601   *Time* (Europe), 'Better late than never' by Rod Usher, 2 June 2003

602   For the story of Francisco Pedro I am indebted to the Portuguese investigative journalist Jorge Van Krieken, telephone interview, April 2004. See www.reporterx.net for Van Krieken's coverage of the Casa Pia case.

603   This passage was cited by Lord Thomas of Gresford during the 2003 House of Lords debate on the Sexual Offences Bill then before the house, House of Lords Hansard, 2 June 2003 (230602-07), Column 1062. For a fuller citation, see the judgment in the House of Lords, *R v Lambert*, 5 July 2001, [2001] UKHL 37, paragraph 34

604   Quoted by Yasmin Alibhai-Brown, 'Irrational Responses', *Community Care*, 11 January 2001

605 Claire Curtis-Thomas MP. Statistics provided by the Association of Chief Police Officers (ACPO) in response to parliamentary questions

606 Victor Kravchenko, *I Chose Freedom*, Hale, 1947, p. 203

607 C. S. Lewis, *Mere Christianity*, Macmillan, 1952, pp. 50-51 (Book II, Chapter 2)

608 See D. P. Walker, *The Decline of Hell: Seventeenth-Century Discussions of Eternal Torment*, Routledge and Kegan Paul, 1964; Geoffrey Rowell, *Hell and the Victorians: A study of the nineteenth-century theological controversies concerning eternal punishment and the future life*, Clarendon Press, Oxford, 1974

609 S. G. F. Brandon, source untraced

610 John Updike, introduction to F. J. Sheed (ed.), *Soundings in Satanism*, Mowbrays, 1972, p. vii; see my *Why Freud Was Wrong: Sin, Science and Psychoanalysis*, HarperCollins, 1995, p. 6

611 'Charity's Child Cruelty Crusade', http://news.bbc.co.uk/1/hi/uk/1782106.stm, BBC News, 25 January 2002

612 On the content of the Criminal Law Amendment Act, see below, note 620. I am indebted to the Stead scholar, Owen Mulpetre, whose exceptional website, the W. T. Stead Resource Site (SRS), is a treasure-trove of contemporary documentation, including the entire text of 'The Maiden Tribute' and much else besides (see www.attackingthedevil.co.uk).

The title of Stead's series of articles, 'The Maiden Tribute of Modern Babylon' was derived from the Greek myth according to which Athens, after being defeated in a disastrous military campaign by King Minos of Crete, was compelled to send to its conqueror, once every nine years, a tribute of seven youths and seven maidens. These were flung into the labyrinth of Daedalus where they wandered blindly and without the possibility of escape until they were devoured by the Minotaur, 'a frightful monster, half man, half bull, the foul product of an unnatural lust' as Stead puts it. After despatching their tribute twice, the Athenians rebelled against their fate and Theseus insisted on being sent as part of the next tribute. With the help of Ariadne and a ball of thread, Theseus found his way to the centre of the labyrinth and, having slain the Minotaur, was able to retrace his steps and return in triumph to Athens. Stead uses the Greek myth to offer a harshly ironic perspective on the moral state of Victorian Britain:

> The fact that the Athenians should have taken so bitterly to heart the paltry maiden tribute that once in nine years they had to pay to the Minotaur seems incredible, almost inconceivable. This very night in London, and every night, year in and year out, not seven maidens only, but many times seven, selected almost as much by chance as those who in the Athenian market-place drew lots as to

which should be flung into the Cretan labyrinth, will be offered up as the Maiden Tribute of Modern Babylon. Maidens they were when this morning dawned, but tonight their ruin will be accomplished, and tomorrow they will find themselves within the portals of the maze of London brotheldom. Within that labyrinth wander, like lost souls, the vast host of London prostitutes, whose numbers no man can compute, but who are probably not much below 50,000 strong. Many, no doubt, who venture but a little way within the maze make their escape. But multitudes are swept irresistibly on and on to be destroyed in due season, to give place to others, who also will share their doom. The maw of the London Minotaur is insatiable, and none that go into the secret recesses of his lair return again. After some years' dolorous wandering in this palace of despair – for 'hope of rest to solace there is none, nor e'en of milder pang,' save the poisonous anodyne of drink – most of those ensnared tonight will perish, some of them in horrible torture. Yet, so far from this great city being convulsed with woe, London cares for none of these things, and the cultured man of the world, the heir of all the ages, the ultimate product of a long series of civilizations and religions, will shrug his shoulders in scorn at the folly of any one who ventures in public print to raise even the mildest protest against a horror a thousand times more horrible than that which, in the youth of the world, haunted like a nightmare the imagination of mankind. Nevertheless, I have not yet lost faith in the heart and conscience of the English folk, the sturdy innate chivalry and right thinking of our common people; and although I am no vain dreamer of Utopias peopled solely by Sir Galahads and vestal virgins, I am not without hope that there may be some check placed upon this vast tribute of maidens, unwitting or unwilling, which is nightly levied in London by the vices of the rich upon the necessities of the poor. London's lust annually uses up many thousands of women, who are literally killed and made away with – living sacrifices slain in the service of vice. That may be inevitable, and with that I have nothing to do. But I do ask that those doomed to the house of evil fame shall not be trapped into it unwillingly, and that none shall be beguiled into the chamber of death before they are of an age to read the inscription above the portal – 'All hope abandon ye who enter here.' If the daughters of the people must be served up as dainty morsels to minister to the passions of the rich, let them at least attain an age when they can understand the nature of the sacrifice which they are asked to make. And if we must cast maidens – not seven, but seven times seven – nightly into the jaws of vice, let us at least see to it that they assent to their own immolation, and are not unwilling sacrifices procured by force and fraud. That is surely not too much to ask from the dissolute rich (*Pall Mall Gazette*, 6 July 1885).

613 Frederick Whyte, *The Life of W. T. Stead* (2 volumes), Jonathan Cape, 1925; cited SRS

614 Cited in Owen Mulpetre, 'The Great Educator: A biography of W. T. Stead, SRS

615 *Pall Mall Gazette*, 4 July, 1885

616 *Pall Mall Gazette*, 6 July, 1885

617 Rev Benjamin Waugh, *William T. Stead: a Life for the People* (1885), SRS

618 As above

619 Quoted by Chris Lloyd in 'The Preacher's Son who Saved Prostitutes', SRS

620 The Criminal Law Amendment Act brought with it not only the raising of the age of consent to 16 but also a provision which had been energetically canvassed by Waugh on behalf of the SPCC. This removed from child witnesses the requirement that they must take an oath before giving evidence. Up to this time children under twelve had not generally been permitted to give evidence in court on the grounds that they were too young to understand the meaning of the oath. As a result the prosecution of the offence of child sexual abuse had been made much more difficult. The difficulty was particularly acute in a pre-forensic age when a child's testimony might be the only evidence available. Although the inclusion of this measure had at first been vigorously opposed by the home secretary and many other MPs, on the grounds that it might lead, by the admission of unreliable evidence, to miscarriages of justice, Stead had intervened once again. After a vote in favour of this proposal had been lost by 123 votes to 120, Stead published the names of all those MPs who opposed it in the *Pall Mall Gazette*, clearly implying that they were, or might be seen as, defenders of the molestation of children. Waugh then persuaded a member to re-introduce the clause and this time the vote was won.

621 Stead, 'The Maiden Tribute of Modern Babylon', Part 1, 6 July 1885, SRS

622 Transcripts of the trial can be consulted on the W. T. Stead Resource Site. At the end of the trial the jury of twelve men returned verdicts of guilty in relation both to Stead and Jarrett. but added their own plea that Stead should be treated with mercy. Mr Justice Lopes said that he would accept the jury's recommendation as far as he was able and that he would not punish Stead as he would a person 'who had been actuated by sordid and sinful motives'. He expressed his view, however, that 'an irreparable injury has been done to the parents of this child' and sentenced Stead to three months imprisonment without hard labour.

On Jarrett he was even more severe, sentencing her to six months' imprisonment. There were some observers who, having initially supported Stead, were disillusioned by the revelations made during the trial and heartily approved of the sentence. One of these was the young reviewer who was already working for the *Gazette* when Stead took over. More than thirty years later, in 1922, George Bernard Shaw set down his memories of his old editor:

> Stead was impossible as a colleague: he had to work single-handed because he was incapable of keeping faith when excited; and as his hyperaesthesia was chronic he generally *was* excited. Nobody ever trusted him after the discovery that the case of Eliza Armstrong in the Maiden Tribute was a put-up job, and that he himself had put it up. We all felt that if ever a man deserved six months' imprisonment [sic] Stead deserved it for such a betrayal of our confidence in him. And it was always like that, though the other cases were not police cases. He meant well: all his indignations did him credit; but he was so stupendously ignorant that he never played the game. ... He had, as far as I could see, no general knowledge of art or history, philosophy or science, with which to co-ordinate his journalistic discoveries; and it was consequently impossible for cultured minds to get into any sort of effective contact with his except on the crudest common ground. This is the explanation of his ineffectiveness for anything wider and deeper than a journalistic stunt (George Bernard Shaw, 1922. Quoted in Frederick Whyte, *The Life of W. T. Stead*, 2 Vols, London: Jonathan Cape, 1925, vol. I, pp. 304-6, SRS).

623   Bryan Appleyard, *Independent,* 29 August 1996
624   Trevor Fisher, 'Josephine Butler: Feminism's Neglected Pioneer', *History Today,* June 1996
625   The potency of this kind of secularised apocalyptic fantasy and the enduring appeal of such fantasies to the modern imagination is nowhere more clearly illustrated than in one of the most popular works of fiction to be written in recent years – Philip Pullman's *His Dark Materials* trilogy. Although Pullman, whose narrative genius is beyond question, presents his modern myth as an anti-Christian, anti-religious, or anti-clerical saga, its overall imaginative structure closely follows that of the traditional Christian apocalypse. One of the most interesting features of his saga is that the 'satanic' enemy is initially portrayed as a conspiratorial body of child abductors and abusers who are known as 'the Gobblers'. As one of the anxious mothers in the first part of the trilogy puts it: 'Lord Faa, we don't know what them Gobblers might've been doing to our children. We all heard rumours and

stories of fearful things. We hear about children with no heads, or about children cut in half and sewn together, or about things too awful to mention. I'm truly sorry to distress anyone, but we all heard this kind of thing, and I want to get it out in the open. Now in case you find anything of that awful kind, Lord Faa, I hope you're a-going to take powerful revenge. I hope you en't going to let thoughts of mercy and gentleness hold your hand back from striking and striking hard, and delivering a mighty blow to the heart of that infernal wickedness. And I'm sure I speak for any mother as has lost a child to the Gobblers' (Philip Pullman, *Northern Lights*, Scholastic Ltd, 1995, p. 138).

That one of the most widely read and highly prized works of fiction in the early part of the twenty-first century should have been inspired by a Puritan epic (Milton's *Paradise Lost*) and should take as its subject matter a cosmic battle between the forces of 'good', who set out to build a 'Republic of Heaven', and a conspiracy of child abductors who embody 'infernal wickedness', speaks volumes about our cultural history and our cultural psychology.

626 The kinship between the doctrines of psychoanalysis and the view of human nature favoured by radical Protestants is insufficiently understood. Writing in 1960, David McClelland, a Quaker descended from radical Protestants, who was also a Harvard psychologist, suggested that Freud's attitude towards human sinfulness is one of the reasons 'why psychoanalysis has had such a great appeal to American intellectuals': 'Its insistence on the evil in man's nature, and in particular on the sexual root of that evil, suited the New England temperament well which had been shaped by a similar Puritan emphasis. In fact, to hear Anna Freud speak of the criminal tendencies of the one and two-year-old is to be reminded inevitably of Calvinistic sermons on infant damnation.' See my *Why Freud Was Wrong: Sin, Science and Pychoanalysis*, Harper-Collins, revised edition 1996, p. 321

627 Susan Brownmiller, foreword to Florence Rush, *The Best Kept Secret: Sexual Abuse of Children*, 1980, p. ix. Rael Jean Isaac's account in *Women's Quarterly*, Summer 2001; www.findarticles.com/p/articles/ mi_m0IUK/is_2001_Summer/ai_78177292

628 Florence Rush, quoted in Louise Armstrong, *Kiss Daddy Goodnight*, New York: Pocket Books, 1978, p. 133

629 Cited in Rael Jean Isaac, see above. See also Christopher M. Finan, 'Catherine A. MacKinnon: The Rise of a Feminist Censor, 1983-1993', www.mediacoalition.org/reports/mackinnon.html

630 Rael Jean Isaac, see above

631 Feminists thus co-opted one of the most deeply and oppressively patriarchal of modern thinkers to their own cause, giving pride of place to an untested doctrine of repression according to which women (or children) could entirely repress or 'block' traumatic episodes of rape

or sexual abuse, and recover the memories only years later with the help of counselling or therapy.

Florence Rush herself was one of the pioneers in formulating the idea that the early Freud had accurately recognised the role of child sexual abuse in causing neurosis, but had backed away from his 'discovery' out of cowardice and deference to his male colleagues (Florence Rush, 'Freud and the Sexual Abuse of Children, *Chrysalis* 1, 1977). In adopting this view of Freud, a view which would subsequently be taken up by others, including Jeffrey Masson and Judith Herman, Rush was actually falling victim to Freud's own self-aggrandising misrepresentation of history. In reality, as Freud's own contemporary writings show quite clearly, there was never a time when women came to him bringing stories of how they had been sexually abused in childhood. This was a retrospective invention on Freud's part. In fact it was Freud who told his female patients that they had been sexually abused and they who resisted this patriarchal therapeutic bullying. For a discussion of Freud's 'seduction theory' and his significance in the new ideology of child sexual abuse, see my essay on the recovered memory movement, 'Freud's False Memories' in *Why Freud Was Wrong* (as above), pp. 511-28. See also the account of Freud's seduction theory given in the main body of the book, pp. 195-213.

632   We might note that, in March 1999, the NSPCC, with the support of the prime minister Tony Blair, and the sponsorship of the Microsoft Corporation, actually launched a campaign whose purpose was to end all child abuse, whether physical or sexual – the 'Full Stop Campaign'. In that it set out, quite literally, to banish the evil of child abuse for ever, this campaign resembled traditional apocalyptic fantasies even more closely than some other manifestations of the modern child protection movement.

633   *R v LPB* (1991) 91 Cr App R 359, cited in Margaret Jervis's memorandum, submitted on behalf of the British False Memory Society in *The Conduct of Investigations into Past Cases of Abuse in Children's Homes*, HMSO, 31 October 2002, Volume 2, pp. 25-6

634   *R v Telford Justices ex parte Badham* [1991] 2QB 78, 93 Cr App R 171; *Attorney General Ref. No 1 of 1990* [1992] QB 630, 95 Cr App, R 296

635   The next day, 24 November 2001, the *Independent* published a follow-up piece under the headline 'Alert over child abuse trials splits lawyers'. It reported Allan Levy QC who was described as 'an expert in such cases' as saying that 'in his experience most people who made allegations of child abuse were genuine. "Who would want to go through the ordeal of a criminal trial and put their credibility on the line?" he asked.' Malcolm Fowler, however, a senior member of the Law Society's criminal law committee was said to be in agreement with the sentiments of Lord Woolf. He reportedly took the view that

the circumstances of many convictions in child abuse cases were a source of concern: 'This is getting into Alice in Wonderland territory where we go through an expensive and elaborate quadrille just so we can convict the defendant. It's almost like having the sentence before the trial.'

636 *R v B*, Neutral Citation Number: [2003] EWCA Crim 319, para 27

637 'Free to do bad things', Brian Whitaker, the *Guardian*, 12 April 2003

638 Hans Sherrer, 'The Complicity of Judges in the Generation of Wrongful Convictions', *Northern Kentucky Law Review*, Vol, 30: 4, p. 557. The section headed 'The violence of judges' is particularly interesting and I am indebted to it in the argument presented here. See http://fore-justice.org/write/complicity_of_judges.pdf

639 *The Conduct of Investigations into Past Cases of Abuse in Children's Homes*, HMSO, 31 October 2002, Volume 1, pp. 30-1

640 Lord Wilberforce, *Boardman* 1975 AC 421, p. 456

641 Lord Cross, *Boardman* 1975 AC 421, p. 459

642 See High Court of Australia website, www.austlii.edu.au/au/cases/cth/high_ct/165clr292

643 As above

644 www.austlii.edu.au/cgi-bin/disp.pl/au/cases/nsw/NSWCCA/2000/404.html?query=title%28r+%20near+%20gd%29, paragraph 70.

645 One English appeal court case which is directly relevant to the argument here is that of *R v Ananthanarayanan* (1994) 98 Cr App R 1. This case relates to the role played by a social services department investigation in contaminating (and perhaps provoking) complaints of sexual misconduct which were subsequently placed before a criminal court.

In *Ananthanarayanan* the appellant, a consultant psychiatrist, was convicted of a number of indecent assaults against four nurses or care assistants with whom he worked at different hospitals or old people's homes. He had been accused variously of touching or rubbing their legs, of pressing his hands or legs against them, and of touching their breasts. At his trial the appellant denied all the offences, saying that although he was a tactile person and might well have touched the women innocently, he had not behaved indecently with any of them.

A formidable array of character witnesses were called to give evidence in support of him: seven consultants, a nursing manager, a matron in a private home, a professor of psychiatry, four nurses, two occupational therapists, a clinical psychologist and a senior probation officer. All said that he was a man of the highest integrity, that they had neither seen signs nor heard rumours of any such behaviour, and that they did not believe the allegations which had been made.

It emerged during the course of the trial that only one of the witnesses in the case had come forward of her own accord to make an allegation. The other three had made their complaints in response to an investigation which had been conducted by the Social Services Department. During this investigation the officers involved actively sought potential complainants who might make allegations of indecency against the appellant. None of the three women who subsequently made complaints had said anything at the time and the complaints they now made referred to events which had supposedly taken place up to two years previously.

Perhaps because it had been suggested by counsel for the defendant at the original trial that allegations made by these three witness had been prompted and even shaped by the social services investigation, the direction given by the judge to the jury on the question of contamination was unusually comprehensive:

'Go on to ask yourselves', the judge said, ' "are you sure that the evidence of all the women is free from ... contamination?" by which I mean that you are sure that they have not put their heads together to make false allegations or to exaggerate allegations or to put a sinister connotation on an incident which does not deserve a sinister connotation or they have been influenced by hearing of other people's allegations or they have been influenced by the suggestion by some third person such as a person carrying out the preliminary investigation in this case. You have to be satisfied that all these women are independent witnesses when they make these allegations.'

In commenting on this direction to the jury Lord Justice Steyn, Mr Justice Rougier and Mr Justice Laws held that, in its own terms, and if the initial issue of admissibility had been correctly decided, the judge's direction to the jury was proper:

'Had the judge only directed the jury that the possibility of contamination could be excluded if they were sure that the witnesses had not conspired to give false evidence, that, we think, would have been a misdirection. The reason is that for the evidence of one complainant to be admissible as corroborative of the evidence of another it is a necessary condition that each be truly independent of the other; and a witness's account may be infected by what another complainant has said without there being even a suspicion of a deliberate intention to tell a false story. One witness may be unconsciously influenced by what she had heard from another: she may adopt details of which she has been told as if they were details of what had happened to her, and may do it in all innocence, and so it is not enough to direct the jury that they must negative perjury or conspiracy to perjure. But the judge did not limit his direction in that way. He told the jury that they must also be sure that none of the women was ... "influenced by hearing of other people's allegations or ... by the suggestion of some third person". This was a proper direction ...'

The question which remained was whether the judge had in fact decided the initial question of admissibility correctly or not. This question was particularly important in view of the manner in which the jury had been instructed about the individual counts. Of the seven counts on the indictment, count 1 and count 7 both referred to touching the breasts. In respect of these counts the judge told the jury that there was no evidence capable of amounting to corroboration thus indicating that in his view the counts were not mutually admissible under the similar fact principle. The jury in fact went on to acquit the appellant on these counts. However, having been directed that there *was* evidence capable of amounting to corroboration in respect of counts 2 to 6, the jury returned a verdict of guilty on these counts. As was noted in the judgment of the appeal court: 'It seems reasonable to assume that the jury attached considerable importance to what they were told about corroboration (p.2).'

In considering this question the appeal court judges made their own assessment of the risks of contamination quite clear. They noted that in the original trial one of the four woman complainants 'told the court that in August 1991 the Social Services Department were looking for persons who might make an allegation against [the defendant]' and that another complainant said that she had made her statement because her superior had telephoned and asked her to do so.

The inference to be drawn was clear: 'In our judgment these circumstances give rise, at least, to a real possibility that the complaints which ultimately emerged, and which formed the basis of the prosecution case before the jury, were not truly independent one of another. The fact that some of them may have been prompted obviously suggests this. It is not necessary to speculate upon what precisely might have been said, for example, over the telephone to [two of the women who eventually made complaints] to conclude that there must at any rate have been a suggestion that there already existed a basis for suspecting the appellant of crimes of indecency which was sought to be bolstered by the active collection of further complaints (p. 6).'

The appeal court judges held that 'Given that the judge's direction as to what would constitute contamination of one witness's evidence by that of another cannot itself be impeached, the true question here is whether he should have left the possibility of mutual corroboration to the jury at all.' They noted that 'in a series of authorities it has been held that if there is a "real chance" that there has been collusion between the makers of two or more complaints one cannot be corroborative of the other. However, it was quite clear that what applied to collusion also applied to any form of contamination: 'There is no doubt that if there exists a "real risk" or "real possibility" that the evidence of one complainant may have been contaminated by that of another, there can be no mutual corroboration between them.'

'The question starkly raised in this case is whether it is for the judge or the jury to decide whether the risk exists. That being so, one can see at once that the answer depends upon a correct analysis of their respective roles. Elementarily it is always the judge's function to decide what evidence is admissible before the jury, and the jury's function to decide what facts to find on that evidence. In principle, therefore, where a question of admissibility depends upon the resolution of an issue of fact, it is for the judge to resolve it.'

The judgment went on to stress that, in order to rule the evidence inadmissible it was not necessary to prove that contamination had in fact taken place. It was merely necessary to establish that the circumstances in which the allegations had been made meant that there was a real possibility that it had: 'The value of potentially corroborative evidence of this kind critically depends upon its being independent of the complaint sought to be corroborated. If it is not independent it cannot qualify as corroboration, and the test of independence for this purpose is not whether contamination is proved but whether there is a real risk of contamination. It follows that where such a risk exists the evidence is not admissible as corroboration. It must, therefore, be the judge's task to decide whether the risk exists. In carrying out that task he is doing no more nor less than deciding a question of admissibility' (pp. 6–7).

Although there were precedents which appeared to go against this view of the judge's role (including *Johanssen* 1977 65 Cr App R 101, which was cited at some length) the judgment in *Ananthanarayanan* pointed out that in that case the issue was not that there was any evidence of the opportunity for collusion but that the defendant had merely alleged that this was a possibility. Where this point was raised on the basis merely of speculation it was maintained in this judgment that the evidence should go to the jury 'as capable of amounting to corroboration'. In the case under consideration, however, there was evidence of a 'real risk' of contamination. As had already been argued in *Hoch* (which itself relied on *Boardman* and many other authorities), this destroyed the probative power of the similar fact evidence, rendering it inadmissible.

The relevance of this case to that of Peter Howarth, and indeed to the entire subject of police trawling operations, should be clear. However, the judgment in *Ananthanarayanan* seems in some respects less faithful to the original similar fact principle than that in *Hoch*, which is why I have dealt with it in a note rather than in the main text. To this it should be added that the main reason why neither *Hoch* nor *Ananthanarayanan* carry the authority they once enjoyed in the Eng-

lish courts is that their sound legal reasoning was in practice super-
seded by the judgment of Lord Mackay in *R v H* in 1995.

646 One area where reform is clearly needed is indicated by Lord Woolf's
judgment in *R v B*. The fact that it is possible for a defendant to be
convicted in relation to crimes allegedly committed 30 years ago in the
absence of any direct evidence at all other than the complainant's own
testimony is one of the most striking features of English law. Other
jurisdictions in Europe and America do have statutory time limits
which serve to prevent late prosecutions. One objection which has
been made against such time limits is that they may prevent prosecution even when there is strong forensic or photographic evidence of a
crime having been committed by a particular person. The objection is
a reasonable one but it would seem to point in the direction of a more
discriminating approach to such matters rather than to ruling out time
limits completely. The cases which are the most dangerous are those
referred to above where there is no objective evidence at all and these
are disturbingly common. One alternative to a statutory time limit is
to reform the approach to abuse of process hearings. The Home Affairs
Committee report of 2002 recommended the reversal of the burden of
proof in such cases. 'The onus would then be on the prosecution to
prove that the proceedings were not an abuse of process, rather than
on the defendant to show that they were.' One problem with the
Committee's recommendation (which the government in any case
rejected) is that it suggested the reform would apply only in cases
where there was a gap of ten years between the crime alleged and the
prosecution *and* that the time should not begin to run until the complainant had reached the age of 21. Such a reform would therefore
have no effect at all on the hypothetical case of somebody who complains, 22 years after the alleged event, that they were indecently
assaulted at the age of eight. For this reason the recommendation
seems timorous, and constitutes an inadequate response to the very real
dangers delayed accusations pose to innocent people. See *The Conduct
of Investigations into Past Cases of Abuse in Children's Homes*, HMSO, 31
October 2002, Volume 1, pp. 28-29.

647 Some of the practicalities of these suggestions were considered by the
Home Affairs Committee of the House of Commons in their report
on police trawling (as above) Volume 1, pp. 34-38. The Committee
considered the possibility of withdrawing the public funding of civil
claims involving allegations of sexual abuse, but decided against rec-
ommending this course largely because of the fear of coming into
conflict with the European Convention on Human Rights. Such difficulties ought, I believe, to be overcome.

Index

Note: footnotes are indicated by the number of the page on which they occur, with *, as: 56*.

The endnotes on pages 619–89 are indicated by note (not page) number, in *italics*, as: *n16, 93, 206, 400*.

References in the index to 'Tribunal' are to the North Wales Tribunal of Inquiry into Child Abuse, 1997.

Abrantes, Manuel 547
abuse
  All Party Parliamentary Group for
    Abuse Investigations 524
  'historic' inquiries 592
    Historic Abuse Database 515
  see also allegations; child sexual
    abuse; organised abuse; ritual
    abuse; satanic abuse; sexual abuse
abuse of process 474, 519, 581, 583,
  n645
Ackerley, Peter, D/Supt. 100, 208, 225,
  226, 228, 232, 438
  interviews Taylor 193, 200
  in *Observer, 1992* 282
  visits Howarth in prison 373
  at Tribunal 199, 221, 223–4, *n190, 382*
Ackner, Lord 366
Adderley, Stephen *n108*
adolescent rebellion 131
affidavits, making *n343*
age of consent, girls' 559, 560, 564,
  n435, 620
Aherne, Bertie 545
Aitchison, Lord 351–2
Aitken, Jonathan 379
allegations
  abuse of process 474, 519, 581, 583,
    n645
  'carried' by police 223
  and counselling 226*
  cumulative 427–8
  delayed 229, 581–23
  false 4–8, 88, 125, 126, 225, 229, 342,
    450, 550, 587, 592
    by children 85–6
  conditions for making 469
  development 232
  motives for making 5, 8, 131–4,

213, 219, 222, 223–5, 228–9, 233,
  388, 404, 517, 518, 522–3, 526
  psychology of *n84*
  repeated 156
  statistics 550–1
  see also collusion and conspiracy
multiple 342, 348, 358, 363, 366, 368,
  369–70, 371, 491, 581, 588, 591
  safeguards against 532–3, 581
from prisoners 468
retrospective 310–11
of sexual abuse 234
  attitude to 83–4, 130, 225–8, 364,
    489
  'similar' 311, 315, 346–7, 350, 363,
    367–8, 588
  see also 'similar fact' evidence
  trawling for *see* trawling operations,
    police
  victims 550, 551
  see also corroboration and
    corroborative evidence; disclosure
    of abuse
Allen, Jani 379
Allen, John 407, *n11*
anal dilatation test 90, *n124*
Anglesea, Gordon 95, 142–3, 198–9,
  200, 202, 203
  appearance 253, 254
  career 382–3
  marriages 382
  letters to Sandra 381, 391, 395–8
  in *1979* 293–4
  visits to Bryn Estyn 27, 142–3, 251,
    271, 273, 382, 384, 390–1
    dates 273, 391
  and Howarth 384–5, 390
  resignation from police 18, 27–8,
    142, 143, 389–90

a mason, 288
in *Independent on Sunday* article
　18–19, 27, 383
　response to article 27, 250, 275
Nelson seeks evidence against 28,
　250–3, 258–64, 265–73, 275–80,
　281, 294, 439, *n360*, *n534*
allegations against 294, 343
　Holden's 296–8, 343, 389, 391–2
　Humphreys' 258, 259–63, 285–7,
　　285–7, 391–2, 393–4, *n343*
　Steward's 270–4, 284, 285–7, 288,
　　391–2, 395
　　Steward's earlier denial of
　　　abuse by 267–8, 273, 391,
　　　394–5
　　Taylor's 288, 306, 373, 374–5,
　　　439
　　that Dodd invoked him as
　　　threat 143, 198–200, 251
Wynne speaks of 276–7, *n360*
Observer articles on 283–5, 287, 288
HTV programme on 285–7
in *Private Eye* 292
sues *Private Eye* 294–5
CPS consider case of 307, 343
libel trial 343, 379, 384–99
　damages *n490*
and Tribunal 420, 454, 458
Anglesea, Sandra 287
　marriage to Gordon 382–3, 384
　at his libel trial 380–1, 384
　Gordon's letters to 381, 391, 395–8
Anglo, Sydney 539
animal sacrifice 230, *n506*
anti-semitism xv, 1, 2, *n1*, 556
apocalyptic fantasies, xv, 557–8, 572,
　573
　and Phillip Pullman *n625*
appeals 488, 520
　in Australia
　　Doney v The Queen n414
　　Hoch v the Queen 589–91
　　R v Jeffreys 359
　　*Makin v Attorney General for New
　　　South Wales* 345, 350, 356, 357,
　　　361, 364
　to Court of Appeal 425, *n506*, 516
　　Ananthanarayanan *n645*
　　R v B 583–4, 592

R v Bailey 348–50
　Burnett 450
　Howarth seeks leave to 372,
　　431–2
　Lawson and Williams-Rigby
　　533–4
　and legal aid 494
　Maybery 534–5, *n586*
　Moorov doctrine 351–2
　R v OGD 591
　R v P 364–5, 366–70
　Rutter seeks leave to *n144*
　R v Sims 356, 358–9, 588, 589
　to House of Lords 350, 359, 548, 549
　　Boardman v DPP 360–2, 363, 366,
　　　367, 368, 369, 533, 587, 588–9,
　　　591
　　DPP v P 311, 364, 366, 367, 368,
　　　369–70
Appleyard, Bryan
　'Return of the Angel' 567–8
approved schools
　become community homes 484
*Archbold's Criminal Pleading, Evidence
　and Practice* 348
Archer, Jeffrey 381
Argent, Michael CC 414, 438
Armstrong, Eliza 566, *n622*
Arnold, Matt 121
　at Axwell Park School 114, 173
　headmaster of Bryn Estyn 9, 33, 114,
　　167, 169, 173, 215, 327, 384, 430
　writes of Tanner 38–9
　and Howarth 114
　allegations against 236
　arrested 238
　and Tribunal 430–1
Ashton, Ann 46, *n67*
Association of Chief Police Officers
　550
Association of Child Abuse Lawyers
　(ACAL) 496–7
　1998 conference 497–8
Association of Community Homes
　483
Aubrey, David 510
Australia
　Doney v The Queen n414
　Hoch v the Queen 589–91
　Makin v Attorney General for New

South Wales 345, 350, 356, 357, 361, 364
R *v Jeffreys* 359
R *v OGD* 591
trawling operations 6, 542, 546
Axwell Park School 114, 173
Ayles, Penny 530

Bailey, Mr (headmaster)
   trial 348–51, 356, 422–3
Bangor, Gwynedd 79, 95, 193, 255, 275
Bangor and Anglesey News 58
Bangor Chronicle 60
Bangor Mail 57, 58, 91
Bangor police station 108–9, *n147*
Bangor University 577
Banham, John
   asked to conduct investigation into Bryn Estyn 98
   report 99, 100, *n133*
   suggests paedophile ring at Bryn Estyn 203, 464
Barlow, Mark 507
battered child syndrome 85, 463
Bays, Kevin 377
BBC
   and Holden 296, 389
   and Humphreys 256
   Law in Action 500
   Newsnight (TV programme) 448, 500
   Panorama 466, 467, 508–9, 511, *n559*
   PM 534
   Rough Justice 104
   The World at One 3, 415
Beck, Frank 15–16, 93, 94, 161, 201, 224, 234, 415, 531
'believe the children' precept 86–7, 125
Bentovim, Arnon 226–7
Bersham Hall, Wrexham 266, 269, *n385*
Bevan, Stephen *n147*
Bew, Connie
   allegations against 136–8, 140, 237
   arrested 140, 238
   at Tribunal 140
Bible 65, 556, 557
Birch, Claire 303, 304
   allegation 304
Birch, David
   at Bryn Estyn 210–11, 217–18, 578–9

allegations against 211, 235, 237, 340
   Wynne's 217–18, 308
   arrested 238, 239, 303
   awaiting trial 303–5, 309, 323
   and Howarth's trial 323
   trial and acquittal 237
   at Tribunal 420
   former resident asks after, after Tribunal 578–9
Birkett, Dea *n84*
Birley, Simon 54–5, 174, 182–3, 186, *n67*
   statements to police
      1986 54–5
      1991 183
      1992 190
   interviewed by Nelson 182, 183, 187–8, 191–2, *n255, 257*
   and Tanner 192–3, 315, 335
   allegations against Howarth 174, 183–4, 187–8, 190–2, 203, 309, 310, 316–17, 318
   and Wynne 189, 190, 192, 202
   in Taylor's statement 189–90
   in Nelson's article 202, 203, 204
   Nelson and Taylor fail to find 275, 280
   at Howarth's trial 315–16, 335, 340
   death 254, 404–5, 410
Blackstone, Sir William 352
Blair, Tony *n633*
Blakelock, Keith, PC 135
'blocking' *see* repression
Bloody Sunday Tribunals 419, 420*, 421, 424
Boardman v DPP 360–2, 363, 366, 367, 368, 369, 533, 587, 588–9, 591
Bodin, Jean 370–1
Booth, Bramwell 560, 568
Borrill, Rachel 201
Boswell, Tim, MP 532
Bott, Joanne, DC 41–2, 46, 48, 51, 53, 56
Bowskill, Eamon
   allegations by *n311*
Boys' Brigade, Congleton 475, 477, 480, 481
Brandon, S.G.F. 557
'brides in the bath' 346

Bridgewater, Carl 135
British Association of Social Workers
89, 91
British False Memory Society xvi, *n633*
Browne, James *see* Taylor, Geoffrey
Brownmiller, Susan 569
Bruck, Maggie 86
Brushett, Derek 119, 120, 121
    convicted 520–1
Bryanton, Steven 501, 506
Bryn Alyn home, Wrexham 294, 406,
    407, *n11*
Bryn Estyn, Wrexham xvi–xvii
    becomes community home 9
    pool and shower 323–4
    pyjamas 173–4, 310, 433–4
    smoking 110, 326–7
    survey, *1982* 36
    Taylor's placement at 17, 29, 35,
        36–9, 40, 79–80, 94, 161, 175–7,
        187
        entry in Bryn Estyn log book on
            leaving 37, 439, *n246*
    closed, *1984* 16
    Taylor's allegations against 98, 183,
        373–4, 375
    Taylor takes allegations to Dennis
        Parry 96–7
    Banham inquiry 98, 99, 100, 203,
        464, *n133*
    CCC investigates 100–3
    Nelson investigates 16, 22, 156,
        161–3, 164–5, 166–8, 171–2, 174,
        175–6, 178
    police called to investigate 16,
        102–3, 104, 315
    telephone helpline 208–9, 233, 263,
        301, 469, *n311*
    Independent on Sunday article on,
        1991 15–19, 27–8, 78, 183, 189,
        200, 201, 202, 203–4, 205–7, 234,
        264, 310, 390, 391–2
    reputation 301
        alleged paedophile ring 9, 16, 96,
            98, 99, 113, 137, 141, 161, 184,
            186, 198, 203, 208, 237, 238,
            376, 471, 514, 539, 540
    in *Observer, 1992* 284–5, 287–8
    portrayal at Howarth's trial 309–10,
        313–16, 320–5, 326–7

in *Observer* after Humphreys' death
    402–3
portrayal at Tribunal 9, 169–72, 428,
    430, 448, 451, 452, 453, 457, 578
Anglesea's visits to 27, 142–3, 251,
    271, 273, 382, 384, 390
STAFF
recruitment and qualifications
    326–7
    Arnold 9, 33, 114, 167, 169, 173,
        215, 327, 384, 430
    Connie Bew 136–7, 138, 140, 237
    D. Birch 210–11, 578–9
    Cheeseborough 168, 169, 170
    Dodd 18, 96, 168
    Liz Evans 169, 170, 181, 210–11,
        301, 577, 579
    Gillison 98
    Green 168
    Howarth 114–17, 118–22, 124,
        167, 172–4, 204–5, 245, 310,
        327, 374
    Gwen Hurst 170, 241, 301, 302
    John Ilton 168, 170
    Moira Jones 242
    Robert Jones 115, 116, 169, 578
    Leighton 168
    Massey 168
    Norris 16, 98, 136, 212–13
    Rutter 98, 104
    Soper 136–40
    Strich 168
    Isabel Williams 211, 242, 327
    Wilson 164–5, 167–74, 175,
        320–1, 328
    homes raided 235
    arrested and suspended 301–3
    RESIDENTS 235, 413
    Birley 154, 182–4, *n67*
    John Davis 578–9
    Duke 210–13
    John Evans 175–6, 177, 244, 327
    Hempnall 137–8
    Hinton 222–3
    Humphreys 254, 255, 256, 257–9,
        264, 386*
    Holden 106–7, 118–21
    Innes 115–16, 244, 327
    B. Jones 102
    Martell 168, 224, 305–6, 323, 444

Mead 240–1, 244, 309
Oliver 170
Purnell 243, 309
Randles 246, 248
Singer 118–27, 237
Steward 244–5, 273
Surtees 235–6, 309, 340
Tanner 38–9, 79–80, 106–7, 165, 214–15, 217–18, 220, 577–8, n538
Waite 241–2, 312–15, 337, 433–4
West 209–10, 213
Wynne 179–81, 184–8, 214–18, 219
Young 169
Bryn Estyn Support Group 302–3, 305, 322
Bulger, James 466–7
Burke, Claire 519
Burke, Tony 519, 520
Burnett, Roy 450
Butler, Josephine 568
Butler-Sloss, Dame Elizabeth 227
Butler-Sloss report, *1988* 90, 226, 227, 231, n124

Caldecott, Andrew, QC 250, 272–3
Anglesea libel trial 380–99
California 538, 556
Californian model of child protection 84, 85–7, 230, 231, 232, 463, n117
and Nelson 184
police and 91–2
Campaign for Freedom of Information
awards 439–40, 459
Campbell, Beatrix
Unofficial Secrets 90–1
Campbell-Savours, Dale 290
Canada 6–8, 542, n8
Anglican Church 6
Nova Scotia Department of Justice 7–8, n9, 10
Nova Scotia Residential Centre 6–7, 52–5
capital punishment 585, 586
CAPTA (Child Abuse Prevention and Treatment Act, US) 85
Cardiff 118, 119, 120–1, 516
prison 243–4

Cardiff Crown Court 519
care workers *see under* community homes
Caring for Children organisation 459
Carman, George, QC
Anglesea libel trial 379–82, 384, 387, 389–91, 397, 398
Carter, Sue 49–51
Cartrefle College, Wrexham 35, 40
Cartrefle community home 94, 97
Casa Pia children's homes, Portugal 547, 548
Castle Hill, Ludlow 83–4, 93, 103, 457, 468
Castle Hill Report 84
Catholic Children's Society 502
Catholic Church 542, 543
Ceci, Stephen 86
Cheeseborough, Dave 115, 168, 169, 170
Chenevix-Trench, Anthony 291
Cheshire
allegations in *Independent on Sunday* 414–15
supposed paedophile rings 414, 471, 476, 480
Cheshire County Council
'Coping with Sexual Abuse' leaflet 480
Cheshire Police 464, 465, 466, 479
training seminars 467–8
trawling operations 3–4, 414–15 485, 490
see also Operation Bugle; Operation Granite
Cheshire Social Services Department 464, 467, 479
You told me you loved me booklet 492–3
Chester Crown Court
Howarth trial 243, 309, 340, 370, 372
Hudson trial 480–1
Chevet Hey 210, 266, 304, 482
child prostitution 559, 560, 562, 564, 565, n612
child protection movement, culture and campaigns 84, 255, 463, 551–2. 556, 557–9, 567–72, 575
'Full Stop Campaign' n632
see also NSPCC

child protection workers 3, 86–7, 91
  guidelines for 89
  see also care workers *under*
    community homes; social workers
child sexual abuse 10–11, 87–91,
    226–7, 311, 537
  attitudes to 83, 352, 364, 371, 496,
    537–8, 567–75
  as supreme evil 87, 567–8
  in Californian nurseries, supposed
    87, 230
  child prostitution 559, 560, 562, 564,
    565, *n612*
  as *crimen exceptum* 370–1
  denial 227, 229, 231–2, 466, *n506*
  diagnosis, physical effects, signs and
    symptoms 89, 90, 91, 124–5, 159,
    227, 448–9, 569, *n124, 218*
  'disclosure' *see separate entry*
  McMartin case 88, 230–1
  medicalisation of 85
  and patriarchy 570–1
  in Pembrokeshire, alleged 88*
  prosecution, *19th cent. n620*
  satanic, supposed *see* satanic abuse
    and cults
  see also 'organised abuse';
    paedophiles
children
  'believe the children' 86–7, 125
  idealisation of 567
  making up stories 129, 130–1
  need for protection 1–3
  seized from families *n506*
  witnesses in court *n620*
  see also child sexual abuse
Children Act 89
'Children's Charter' 559
Children's Legal Centre 78–9, *n113*
Christian Brothers 544
Christianity 1, 2, 10, 556–60, 565
  revivalist 568
  see also churches
churches 542, 558, 564, 575
  Canadian 6
  Catholic 542, 543
CIA 143
Citizens Advice Bureau, Caernarfon
  59
Clark, Kenneth

Taylor's letter to 200
Clarke, Adrian 431–2
Clarke, Mr Justice 510
Clements, Leslie 21–2, 23, 24–5
Cleveland
  child abuse investigation xvi, 89–91,
    226, 227, 231
Clough, Margaret 416
Clwyd County Council (CCC) 16, 104,
    197, 206
  Taylor takes allegations to Parry
    95–7
  meeting to discuss allegations 97,
    100, 103, *n497*
  commissions police investigation
    102–3, 104
  in *Independent on Sunday* 19
  compensation claims against 19, 213,
    214
  Jillings inquiry panel 413, *n496*
    appointed 407
    inquiry 408–9
    report 409–10, 425, 427
Clwyd Social Services (CSS)
  suspected of covering up abuse 99,
    101, 102
  list of suspected workers supplied to
    police 102
  Bryn Estyn telephone helpline 209,
    233, 263, 301, 469, *n311*
  workers arrested 237–8
  workers suspended 301
  Jevons addresses *n497*
Coates, Adrian 476–7
Cohen, Nick 291
Cohn, Norman xv, *n1*
Colbert, Cath 181
collusion and conspiracy 334–8, 350,
    358, 361, 363, 364, 365, 369,
    588–91, *n645*
  concoction 588–91
  dismissed by Tribunal 494–50
  Duke and West, possible 210, 213,
    335, 336–7, 340, 357
Colwyn Bay, Clwyd
  CPS office *n108*
  NW Police HQ 208, 234, 505
Commission to Enquire into
  Childhood Abuse 545
Community Care 61, *n497*

Jevons writes in *n497*
Readers' Award 459
Taylor writes in 30
community homes 326
  approved schools become 484
  Association of Community Homes
    483
  care workers 574
    allegations against 4, 5, 289
    demonised 3, 6, 529, *n108*
    idealism 574
    pay and status 326, 574
    paedophile rings suspected in 3, 5,
      10, 29, 92, 93, 99, 144, 414,
      516, 538
      at Bryn Estyn *see under* Bryn
        Estyn
  residents 129–30, 131–2
  responsibility for 484
  see also names of homes
compensation and claims 4, 94, 240,
  242, 482, 578
  in Canada 6–8, *n5*
  Clwyd County Council 19, 206,
    213, 214
  in 'Coping With Sexual Abuse'
    leaflet 480
  funding of *n647*
  in Ireland 6, 545–6, *n599*
  as motive for false allegations 5, 8,
    133, 219, 222, 223–4, 233, 388,
    404, 517, 518, 522–3, 526, 583,
    593
    dismissed by Tribunal 449–50
  payment 593
  suggested by police 222, 223–4, 444,
    487–8, 583, *n287*
Compton, Edward 158, 159, 198, *n217*
concoction 588–91
Condra, Beryl 47, 57–8, 71, 72
Congleton, Cheshire 478
  satanic abuse investigation 87, 98,
    n542
Connell, Mr Justice *n506*
Connett, David 141, 201, 282–3, 284
Cook, Peter 381
Cooke, Gary 254–5, 266, 269, 284,
  n351, 385
  in *Private Eye* 294, 376
Cooke, T. J. W. 438

'Coping With Sexual Abuse' leaflet
  480
corporal punishment 484, 544, 546
corroboration and corroborative
  evidence 128, 333–4, 340, 346–7,
  351, 370, 428, 581–2, *n414, 645*
  'by volume' 334, 491, *n416*
  warning 333–4, 581, 587, 592–3, *n414*
  see also similar fact evidence
counselling 226, 232–3, 263–4, 315,
  546, *n631*
  telephone helpline 209, 233, 263,
    301, 469, *n311*
Court of Appeal *see* appeals
Court Service Website *n590*
cover-ups, alleged
  by police 16, 97, 99, 100, 193, 201–2,
    206–7, 214, 436
  by social services 41, 44, 45, 75, 99,
    101, 102
Cowie, Mark 479, 481
Crabtree, Jonathan, Judge 521–2
crimen exceptum 370–1
Criminal Cases Review Commission
  (CCRC) 488, 524, 532, 533, 559, 583
Criminal Injuries Compensation
  Authority (CICA) 133, 593
Criminal Injuries Compensation
  Board 480, 523, 583
Criminal Justice and Public Order Act
  333, 581
Criminal Law Amendment Act, *1885*
  559, 560–1, 564, *n435, 612, 620*
Cromwell, Oliver 559–60
Cronin, DI 228–9
Cross, Lord 360–2, 363, 368, 588–9
Crossley, Joseph 346
Crown Prosecution Service (CPS) 60,
  121, 125, 282, 513, 526, 584, *n329*
  Owen's reports on Gwynedd
    investigation to 56, 63
  decides against prosecution 56, 60
  Taylor writes to 76
  and proposed prosecution of
    Anglesea 307, 373, 438
  decision re Hadfield 526
  decision re Holden 121
  and Howarth's trial 306–7, *n329*
  in *Private Eye* 292–3
  decision re Singer 125

decision re St George's 513
crusaders, moral 64–7, 88, 220
Cruz, Carlos 547
'cultural physiology' of brain 558
Curran, Tony 181
Curtis, Nigel 221–2, 322–3, 327
Curtis-Thomas, Claire, MP 505, 506–7, 532, 550
Cutler, James 78–9, 83

Daily Express 456
Daily Mail
    1986 report on children's homes investigation 57, 58,
    after Tribunal of Inquiry 456, 457
    on David Jones 508, 510–11
Daily Mirror 456, *n538*
    'Pride of Britain' award 459
Daily Telegraph 457
Daly, Cathal, Cardinal 543
Dalyell, Tam, MP 290
Danesford community home, Congleton 475, 476–82
Davidson, Tara 143–4
Davies, Nick 546, *n592*, *600*
Davies, Nicola, QC 408, *n498*
Davis, John 577–9
death penalty 585, 586
delusions xv, 66, 88–9,
democracy 585–6, 587
demonisation 2–3, 10, 135, 311, 537–8, 546, 574, 575, 587, *n4*
    of Church 542
demonology 1–3, 10, 87, 537, 538, 539, 556–60, 565, 569
    see also satanic abuse and cults
Denham, John, MP 536
denial of sexual abuse 227, 229, 231–2, 466, *n506*
Denning, Lord 354–6, 357–9, 360, 361, 362, 364, 366, 589
Denver, Coloradi 85
Department of Health 89, 91
devil, the (Satan) 2, 496, 556–8, 568, 571
    in *His Dark Materials n625*
    see also demonisation; demonology; satanic abuse and cults
Devon and Cornwall Police 530
    Operation Lentisk 515, 530–1

Devon County Council 530
Dickens, Geoffrey 60
Director of Public Prosecutions
    Boardman v DPP 360–2, 363, 366, 367, 368, 369, 533, 587, 588–9, 591
    DPP v Kilbourne 360, 363, 388
    DPP v P 311, 364, 366, 367, 368, 369–70
    Taylor writes to 76, 77
'disclosure' of abuse 87–8, 92, 184, 190, 234, 257, 470, 517
    Bentovim on 226
    Butler-Sloss on 227
    DI Cronin on 228–9
    as crusade 231
    'disclosure work' 227
    'gradual disclosure model' 228–233, *n304*
    false allegations and 232
    Freudian origins of 230
    and McMartin case 230–1
    Marietta Higgs and 231
    Dr David Jones on 227
    leading questions and 230
    police seek 207, 288–9, 468
        from prisoners 468–9, *n553*
    prejudicial nature of term 229
    by young children *n506*
Dobson, Roger, articles by
    on homes in Cheshire 414–15, 470–1
    on Jillings report 410–11, 412–13
    on Tanner and Tribunal 458
Dodd, June 33, 45, 52, 67, 69, 147, 152
    allegations against 46–7, 49, 105, 109, 437
Dodd, Nefyn 27, 29
    career and reputation 33, 67
    at Bryn Estyn 18, 143, 161, 168, 198
    appointed to Tŷ Felin 33
    in charge at Tŷ'r Felin 29, 34–5, 38, 40, 54, 67–70, 96, 110–11, 154, 437–8, *n94*
        reports on Tanner 38, 110, *n43*
        relations with Taylor 33, 34–5, 38, 40, 43–4, *n67*
    and Ennis transfer 71, 72–5
    clears Harkness 74–5
    allegations against 47, *n94*
        Harbour's 48–52

P. Jones' *n205*
Steward's 244–5, 265, *n351*
Tanner's 18, 105–6, 107, 109,
    110–11
Taylor's 44, 45–6, 48, 77–9, 98,
    145, 146–52, 154, 161, 175,
    198–9, 206, 437, *n211*
  that he invoked Anglesea as
    threat 143, 198–9, 251
  that he beat Harper 18, 78,
    96, 145, 146
  that he had pornography
    161–4
  made to Nelson 146–9,
    157–60, 161–2
Hannah Thomas's 61–2
Wilson's 172, 174, 186, 320,
    321, *n240*
Owen interviews 56
Owen's report on 56, 70, *n92*
Nelson speaks of to Wilson 172, 174
in *Independent on Sunday* article 18,
    27, 202–3, 206
and Anglesea 143, 198–9, 251
and HTV programme 145
Millett's letter to 67–8
at Tribunal 74, 153
Tanner seeks allegations against 18,
    320, 321
Doherty, Sam 47
domestic abuse cases 581, 592–3
Doran, Sean, Prof. 344
Doughty, Barry 47, *n211*
DPP v Kilbourne 360, 363, 588
DPP v P case 311, 364, 366, 367, 368,
    369–70
Drake, Mr Justice
  Anglesea libel trial 377, 381, 386, 387
drug addiction 120, 206
drug dealing 216
Duke, John 209–13, 214, 234, 309, 323,
  at Howarth's trial 336–7, 340
  and Tribunal 212–13
  possible collusion with West 210,
    213, 335, 336–7, 340, 357
Dunlop, Jennifer 45–6, 437
Dyson House 494

Eady, Mr Justice *n431*
Edwards, Colin 438

Edwards, Gareth, Judge
  trial of Howarth 315, 326–38, 339,
    340, 342
  passing sentence 340–1
Edwards, Paul 487–8
Elias, Gerard, QC
  addresses ACAL conference 497
  Pembrokeshire satanic abuse trial
    n506
  at Tribunal 100, 223–4, 421, 425,
    443, *n150, 382, 517, 537*
  opening statement 370, 426,
    427–31, 445, 451, 458
Elliot, Christopher 415
Ellison, Jane 291
Ely, Brian 530–1
Embury, Nick 41–2
emotional attention, craving for 129
Ennis, Graham 57*, 71–4, 107, *n106,*
    108, 221
Eryl Wen community home 106, 109,
    n150
Evans, Dewi 68, *n87*
Evans, Gethin 40, 46, 163, *n51*
Evans, John Richard ('the black JE')
    244, 322
Evans, John Richard ('the white JE')
    106, 116–17, 175–6, 177, 181, 182,
    244, 374, 375, *n246*
  interviewed by police 221–2, 444
  Nelson interviews *n247*
  and Howarth's trial 322–3
  and Tribunal 222, 444, 456
Evans, Liz 169, 170, 181, 210, 215, 219,
    308
  suspended 301
  at Tribunal 220
  after Tribunal 577–9
Evans, PC 47, *n57*
Evans, R. E. 438
Evening Leader (Wrexham) 214
Everett, Tricia 158–60, *n221*
evidence
  admissibility 358–9, 361, 368–9,
    589–90, *n645*
    contaminated 93, 128, 591, 593,
    n645
  corroborative *see* corroboration and
    corroborative evidence
  disregarded 135

'forbidden reasoning' 344–5
'intra group' 588
prejudicial 583, 593
similar *see* 'similar fact' evidence
see also allegations; collusion;
　witnesses
evil 135, 311, 496, 529, 560, 567–8
　and Christianity 565
　　C. S. Lewis writes of 556–7
　crusade against 87–8, 131–2, 220
　fantasies of 1–3, 9, 10, 569–72
　　conspiracy of 144, 206–7, 237,
　　　464, 537–8, 539, 571–2
　psychoanalytic view of *n626*
　see also demonisation; demonology;
　　Devil, the; righteousness

FACT (False Allegations against Carers
　and Teachers) 505, 506–7
Fawcett, Roy 522
Fearns, Harry 505
Felton, David 146
feminists 3, 84, 86, 90–1, 592, *n631*
　US 569–71, 571*
Fennell, Mr Justice 84
Ferro Rodrigues, Eduardo 546–7
Fiddler, Phil 473, 475
First Tuesday (TV series) 78
Fitzgerald, Patrick 530
Fletcher, Stan 106–7
Flintshire County Council 419
Foley, Gail 256
Foot, Michael 290
Foot, Paul 290–1, 439, 546
　review of *The Kincora Scandal*
　　494–5, *n568*
Forbes, J. R. S.
　Similar Facts 356, 358
'forbidden reasoning' in court
　344–5
Forde Park school, Newton Abbot
　529–31
Formby, Merseyside 505, 506
Formby Times 505
Fowler, Malcolm *n633*
Fowler, Rebecca 457
freedom 585–6, 587
freemasons
　Anglesea a mason 288
　and North Wales Police, allegations

　143, 144, 200, 287–8, 289, 292,
　　438–9, 440
　in *Private Eye* 292, 440
　and Tribunal of Inquiry 454
Freud, Anna *n626*
Freud, Sigmund xvi, 226, 230, 569, *n1*,
　171, 305, 626, 631
Friends of Derek Brushett (FODB)
　520–1

Garnier, Edward, MP 532
Garsden, Peter 495, 496, 546, *n571*
Gatewen Hall School, Wrexham 179,
　529
Gillison, David 98, 182, 203, 403
girls 16, 198, 206
　age of consent 559, 560, 564, *n435,*
　　620
　alleged assaults on 142, 157–60
　child prostitution 559, 560, 562, 564,
　　565, *n612*
　law regarding offences against *n435*
　sexual assaults on *n435*
　taken into care 130*
Gladio, Operation 143, *n188*
Glasgow, David 465
glue-sniffing 179–80, 181, 183, 184,
　185, 186, 276
Goddard, Lord 355, *n443*
Godwin, David, xvi
Goffman, Erving 31
Golden Heart awards 302
Grain, Dennis 466, 472, 475
Grant, Linda 3
Great Ormond Street Hospital 226,
　408
Green, Brian 518
Green, Gladys 385–6
Green, Norman 115
Gregson, Roy, DI 41–2, 45
Greystone Heath community home,
　Warrington 464–6, 471–5, 495
Griffith-Williams, John 312, 319
Griffiths, Courtenay 432, *n516*
Griffiths, Roger 529
Groome, Richard 529
Groupthink 431, *n513*
Guardian 508, *n564, 585, 590, 592*
　on Cheshire investigation 415
　on Gladio *n188*

on Tribunal 432–3, 457
on paedophile rings 3, *n600*
Jack writes about libel trial in, *2001*
  379–80, *n468, 478*
Guardian Weekend 508, *n562, 585*
on Danesford investigation 481
Gwent Police 514–15
  Historic Abuse Database 515
Gwynedd County Council (GCC) 54,
  73, 75, 94, 158
  employs Taylor 40
  suspends Taylor 61
  dismisses Taylor 64
  employees 44
  Owen's reports on 56, 63, 70
  exonerates J. Harkness 72
  and North Wales Tribunal of
    Inquiry 458
Gwynedd Social Services 60, 64, 76,
  158
  complaint about sent to local
    officials 57
  investigation instigated 145

Hapgood, Terry, DCI 514–15
Hadfield, Paul 525–7, 529
  suicide letter 527–8
Hague, William 415
Hailsham, Lord 360, 363, 424
Hale, Eddie 115
Hall, Jenny 476–7
Hall, Mark 198
Hands, Christopher 219
Harbour, Peter 48–52, 55, 57, 107, 108,
  282, *n65, 71*
  Taylor prepares statement for 51–2
Harkness, Jane 71, 72, 73–4, 75, *n108*
Harper, Lewis 18, 78, 96, 145, 146–52,
  153, 157, 164, 192, 206, 440, *n205*
  hoax 999 call 150, 152
  Taylor visits in prison 151
Harris, Tony 61–2
Hart, Peter *n211*
Hatton, Jonathan 479–80, 481
Havers, Sir Michael 60
Headlands, South Wales 518
Heath, Edward 424
Hector, Viv 209, 263, 301, 404
Hempnall, Barry 136, 137–8
Hempnall, Liam 220

Herbert, Sean 54
Herman, Judith 570, *n631*
Herschell, Lord 345
Heseltine, R. 438
Hewart, Lord 348–9, 356, 422–3
Hicks, Oswald 262
'hidden' physical abuse 85
Higgs, Marietta, Dr 231
Hillrise Children's Centre 525
Hinchliff, Benjamin 278–9, 375
Hinton, Mark 222–3
Hislop, Ian 290, 292, 376–7, 404
  meeting with Steward 377
  Anglesea libel trial 379–80, 381,
    399
Historic Abuse Database 515
Hitler, Adolf 2
Hoch v the Queen 589–91
Holden, Carl 117, 118, 126–7, 128, 343
  in Bryn Estyn 106–7, 118–21
  allegations against Howarth 119–21,
    126–7, 296–7, 389
  police interview 119–22, 123
  BBC contact 296, 389
  records interview 296–7
  allegations against Anglesea 296–8,
    343, 389, 391–2
  as potential witness re Howarth
    307
  Anglesea libel trial 380, 388–9, 392
  at Tribunal 120
Home Office 484
  HOLMES computer 208
  Prison Liaison Section 468
homosexuality 54–5, 98, 116–17, 118
  attitudes to 352, 354, 359, 360, 364
  prejudicial 588–9
  as criminal behaviour 350, 352,
    360
  sodomy 357–9
  Wolfenden report 354, 359
Hood, Lynley *n115, 297, 461*
Hooper, Derek 530–1
Horne, Gary 509
Hoskin, Terry 483–9, 493, 521, *n553,
  563*
Houlden, Gerry 529–30
House of Commons 3
  All Party Group for Abuse
    Investigations 524

Criminal Law Amendment Act, *1885* 559, 560–1, 564, 582, *n435*, 612, 620
debates police trawling 536
Home Affairs Select Committee 496, 532, 535, *n570, 571, 575*, 647
House of Lords 359, 548, 549, 581
  appeal to 350
    Boardman v DPP 360–2, 363, 366, 367, 368, 369, 533, 587, 588–9, 591
    DPP v P 311, 364, 366, 367, 368, 369–70
    R v P 364–5, 366–70
  debate on Sexual Offences Bill *n603*
  debate on Wolfenden report 354
Howarth, Peter
  early career 114
  character 114
  at Bryn Estyn 114–17, 118–22, 124, 167, 172–4
  and Arnold 114
  and Innes 115–16
  dog owned by 209, 210, 212, 234
  'flat list' 172–4, 175, 204–5, 241, 245, 374, 579
    referred to at trial 310, 327
  and Anglesea 384–5, 390
  retirement from Bryn Estyn 316–17
  in Nelson's article 16–18, 27, 183–4, 203, 204–6, 209
  allegations against
    see separate sub-entry below
  arrested and interviewed by police 238, 239–40, 309
  Martell's letter to 303–6
  awaiting trial 305–6, 307, 308
  trial 102, 190, 236, 243, 244, 309–38, 339–41, 342–3, 344, 370, 371, 399, 509
    judge's summing-up 325, 326–38, 342
    verdicts 339–40
    sentence passed 340–1, 372
  in Walton Prison 372
  in Wakefield Prison 372, 384, 403, 434–5
    police interview in prison 343, 373

wish to appeal 372, 431–2
  in *Observer* after Humphreys' death 401–2
  in *Guardian 1996* 415
  Tribunal representation, 420, 431–5, 452–3, 456, *n516, 517*
  death 435
  ALLEGATIONS AGAINST 175, 222–3, 234, 239, 243, 338, 444, 579, *n311*
    similarities 356–7, 370
    Birley 174, 183–4, 187–8, 190–2, 203, 240, 309, 310, 316–17, 318
    Curtis 221–2
    Davis 579–80
    Duke 209–13, 357
    Evans 175, 176, 177, 244
    Holden 119–21, 126–7, 296–7, 389
    homosexuality 116–17
    Humphreys 257, 258, 262, 263, 343, *n343*
    Mead 240
    Purnell 243
    Randles 247, 248–9, 252, 253
    Singer 118–20, 122, 304, 317, 329, 330–3
      concerning vibrators 119, 223
      crowbar allegation 124–7, 317–318
      that Howarth made phone calls to him 126
    Soper 136
    Steward 245, 269
    Surtees 235–6
    Tanner 106–7
    Taylor 175–7, 180, 306, 374–5
    Waite 241
    West 209–10, 213, 357
    Wilson 171, 172–3, 174, 175, 320–1
    Wynne 185–8, 190–1, 203–4, 234, 276, 310, *n360*
Howe, Earl 532
HTV (Harlech Television)
  programme on Tŷ'r Felin, *1991* 28, 145, 149, 150, 151, 157, 208, 282, 285, 406
  programme on Anglesea, *1992* 285–7, 296, 297, 383, 384
  sued for libel 295

libel trial 379–99
Hudson, Brian 477–81
Hughes, Gwylim 214
Hughes, John 250, 287, 294, 383
Hughes, Lucille 41, 43, 50, 51, 59, 145, n46, 92
Hughes, Merfyn 314–15
Humphreys, Margaret 386*, 400–1, 404
Humphreys, Mark 253, 254–64, 265, 266, 267, 274
  early life 254–5
  and Cooke 254–5, 403
  in Bryn Estyn 254, 255, 256, 257–9, 264
  dates 257, 259, 264, 386*
  1991 police interview 254, 255
  marriage 255, 256–7, 400–1
  BBC contact 256
  interviewed by Nelson 256–62, 263, 265, 274, 385, 386, 392, 393–4, 403–4, n336, 337, 340, 342, 343, 344
  allegations against Anglesea 258, 259–63, 285–7, 285–7, 391–2, 393–4, n343
  allegations against Howarth 257, 258, 262, 263, 343, n343
  1992 police interviews 262–3, 264
  in *Observer* article 285
  on HTV 286, 287, 296, 297, 383
  Anglesea libel trial 380, 381, 385–6, 392, 402, 403–4
  subsequently 400–1
  and Jillings panel 409
  death 254, 401–2, 404–5, 410, 415
Humphreys, Wendy 255, 401
Hurd, Douglas
  Taylor writes to 76
Hurst, Gwen xvii, xviii, 115, 168, 170, 241, 321–2, 577
  career 301–2
  on suspension of Bryn Estyn staff 301, 302–3
  and Howarth 305, 372
  writes to Press Complaints Commission 403–4
  and Tribunal 301, 425, 453
Hurst, John, xviii

Ilton, John 168, 169, 170
incest 569, 570

DPP v P 311, 364, 366, 367, 368, 369–70
  therapeutic approach to allegations 85
Independent newspaper
  and *Independent on Sunday* xvi
  on Pindown 94, n15
  on Operation Gladio 143
  Dennis Parry contacts, 1991 141
  on Bryn Estyn xvii, 27–8, 146?
  on Tŷ Mawr 20–6, 78, 144
  Nelson faxes 3rd Wynne interview 251
  Tanner's allegations in 206, n538
  interview in solicitors' office 262
  libel writ 250, 275
  libel trial 379–99, 413
  articles following Jillings report, 1996 410–14, 415, 416, 567, 572
  Bryan Appleyard in 567–8
  on Cheshire investigation 414–15, 470–1
  and Tribunal 439
  following Tribunal 458
  on unsafe convictions, 2001 582–3, n633
Independent on Sunday
and *Independent* xvi
  on satanic abuse xvi, 88, n122
  on Tŷ Mawr 20–1
  commissions Nelson to write on Bryn Estyn, 146
  publishes his article 15–19, 27–8, 78, 183, 189, 200, 201, 202, 203–4, 205–7, 234, 264, 310, 390, 391–2
  reaction to and effects 27–8, 208, 209, 213, 214, 221, 235
  and libel trial 28, 373
  sends Nelson to investigate article 27–8, 156, 250
  declines to publish Nelson's article on Anglesea 281, 282–3
  on Jillings report 411, 414–15
  on Cheshire homes 414–15
Indictments Act 355
Ingrams, Richard 291–2
Innes, James 115, 244, 327
innocence, presumption of 85, 344, 352, 507, 548–9, 584–5

Intermediate Treatment 97
interviews, police 128, 221–6, 232–3,
    235, 486–7, 517
  and counselling 226*
  leading questions 5, 128
  prisoners 468–9, 487, n553
  seeking disclosure 207, 288–9, 468
  'therapeutic' 225–8
IRA Guildford bombings 135
Ireland, Republic of 543–6
  compensation and care homes 6,
    Goldenbridge 543
  Mary Raftery 544–5
  Redress Board 546–6, n599
  States of Fear, RTE 544
Irish Times n7, 599
Isaac, Rael Jean 570

Jack, Ian
  accepts Nelson's article for
    Independent on Sunday, 1991 15–19,
    20, 383, 404
  sends Nelson to investigate claim re
    Anglesea 27–8, 250
  declines to publish Nelson's *1992*
    article 281
  Anglesea libel trial 379–80, 387
    writes in *Guardian* about 379–80,
    n468, 478
Jackson, John, Prof. 344
Jarrett, Rebecca 565–6, n622
Jehovah's Witnesses 542
Jenkins, Philip n3
Jennings, Anthony, QC 432, 433–4, 435
Jervis, Margaret 582, n475, 633
Jevons, John xix, n133, 134, 497, 580
  director of social services, Clwyd
    97, 153, 228, 315, 540
  at meeting following Taylor's
    allegations about Bryn Estyn
    97–8, 99, 101, 102
  and police investigation 102–3,
    104
  after arrest of former Bryn Estyn
    staff 302
  and Jillings panel 407–8, 409
  in Cardiff 516
  writes in *Community Care* n497
Jews 2
  see also anti-semitism

Jillings, John 407–9
Jillings panel n496
  appointed 407
  inquiry 408–9
  report 409–10, 425, 427, n501
Johnson, Brian 523–4, 527
Johnson, Lorraine, DCI 225, 228, 229,
    232
Johnson, Paul Gwynfor 153–5
Johnson-Thomas, Brian 282, 288, 292,
    n371, 382
Johnston, Ian, CS 515
Joint Enquiry Team report
    (Nottingham) 90, n125
Jones, Adrianne n498
Jones, Ann 504, 508, 510, 512–13
Jones, Bill 512
Jones, Brendan 101–2
Jones, David, Dr 227, 229, n304
Jones, David (football manager) 500,
    508
  arrested 504, 507, 512–13
  trial of 5, 509–11, 512, 513, 519, 531
Jones, Eric, Acting D/Supt 145
Jones, G. (of NW Police) 438
Jones, Gwilym (of Welsh Office) 407
Jones, Haydn 32–3, 157
Jones, Helen 53–4, n67
Jones, Martyn, MP 283
Jones, Moira 242
Jones, Peter 147, 152, n205
Jones, Robert 115, 116, 168, 169, 578
Jones, Susan n67
Jonson, Ian 526–7
Jordon CJ 359
journalists 83, 91, 573
  see also names
Judge, Lord Justice 450, 581–2
judges 311, 474, 573, 585, 586–7, 590–1,
    593
  cautioning jury 522
  summing-up 326, 333
  see also names

Kahan, Barbara 497, n15
Kaufman, Fred 524–5
Keeley, Tim 465, 473
Kempe, C. Henry 85, 227, 463
Kenyon, Lord 284, 287–8
Kenyon, Thomas 284, 285, 287, 293

Killick, Barry 526
Kincora hostel, East Belfast 289–90,
    538, 547, 555
King, Jonathan *n468*
King, Larry 35, 45, 54, 72, 73
King, Malcolm 255–6, 410
    career 97
    chairman of social services, CCC
        at meeting following Taylor's
            allegations about Bryn Estyn
            97–100, 101–2, 141, 572
    David Rose contacts 283
    and Jillings inquiry 407–8, 414
    in *Observer* 285
    in *Independent on Sunday* 414
    and Tribunal 430
King, Timothy, QC 433
Kirby, Albert, D/Supt, 466–7, 470, 490
Knifton, David
    at Tribunal of Inquiry 108, 111, 138,
        148, 164, 169, 172, 220, 443, *n113*
Knight, Jill 58–9
Knight, Phillip 20, 23–4
Knights of Columbus 143, 543
Kokke, Tony 527
Kravchenko, Victor 550–1

La Fontaine, Jean 89, 201, 232
Laffoy, Mary 545
Lancet 231
Lane, Lord 365–6
Langshaw, Alan 464–6, 489, *n543*
Latham, Tony *n15*
Laverack, Keith 474
Lawson, Geraldine 507
Lawson, Mike 501–2, 505, 507
    appeal 533–4
    on BBC radio 534
lawyers 4–5
    solicitors 4, 305, 573
    trawling by 495–6, 542, 546–6
le Fleming, Morris 416
legal aid 494
legal cases
    R v Ananthanarayanan n645
    R v B 583–4, 592
    Boardman v DPP 360–2, 363, 366,
        367, 368, 369, 533, 587, 588–9, 591
    State v Coetzee 548–9
    Doney v The Queen n414

R v H 370, *n645*
R v Jefferies 359
DPP v Kilbourne 360, 363, 588
R v LPB 581–2
Makin v Attorney General for New
    South Wales 345, 350, 356, 357,
    361, 364
R v OGD 591
DPP v P 311, 364, 366, 367, 368,
    369–70
R v P 364–6, 367, 368–70
R v Sims 356, 358–9, 588, 589
R v Smith 346, 350, 357, 364, 367
Leicester Constabulary 224
Leicester Crown Court 161
Leicestershire Social Services 93
Lentin, Louis 543
Levy, Allan, QC 412, *n15, 633*
Lewis, C. S.
    Mere Christianity 556
libel
    in *Independent on Sunday* 27, 28
    writ issued by Anglesea's barrister
        250
    Steward threatens writ 295
    trials 400
        Anglesea 343, 379–99, 400, 402,
            403
        damages *n490*
        and Taylor 375
        Shieldfield xix, 538, *n431*
lies
    'lying for love' 129–30, 133, 525–6
    righteous deception 64–5
    told in court 329–30, 522
    told by women *n84*
    see also allegations / false
Lillie, Christopher xix, 538, *n431*, 590
Little Acton Assessment Centre,
    Wrexham 179
Liverpool City Police 501
Liverpool Crown Court 5, 505–6,
    509–11
Liverpool Crown Prosecution Service
    509
Livingstone, Ken 290
Llangollen, canoe trip near 124, 126,
    317
Lloyd, Chris 564
Lloyd, Margaret 346

London, Victorian 559, 561, 564, 568, *n612*
London Review of Books 494–5
Lopes, Mr Justice *n622*
Los Angeles 86
Lost in Care (report of North Wales Tribunal of Inquiry into Child Abuse; Waterhouse report) 8, 69, 448–59, 515, 579, *n150, 152, 516, 573*
    press coverage of 456–9
Louima, Abner 125
Loveridge, Andrew
    at meeting following Taylor's allegations about Bryn Estyn 97, 102, *n134*
    letter to NW Police 102, 104, *n133, 134, 141, 501*
    and Jillings panel 408, 410, *n501*
'Lucas direction' 329–30, 340

Mackay of Clashfern, Lord 366–7, 368, *n645*
MacKinnon, Catherine 570, 571*
Maidstone Prison 346
Mail on Sunday 512
Major, John 380, 415, 424
    Taylor writes to 76
Makin v Attorney General for New South Wales 345, 350, 356, 357, 361, 364
Malleus Maleficarum 539
Manchester 4
    Operation Cleopatra 515
Manchester Guardian 563–4
Mansfield, Michael, QC 135, 365
Marek, John, MP 283, 287, 288
Marshall, Keith 44–5, 54, 56, 58
Martell, Keith
    letter to Howarth 305–6
    and Howarth's trial 323
    letter to Saltrese 168, 169, 224, 444
Martin, Derek (at Tŷ'r Felin) 62
Martin, Michael 545
masculinity 91
    patriarchy 570–1, *n631*
Mason, John 40–2, 47, 49, 76, 107, *n46*
masonic lodges *see* freemasons
Massey, David 168
Masson, Jeffrey *n631*

Matthews, Mr (head of education at Bryn Estyn) 139
Maudling, Reginald 292
Maybery, John 530–1
    appeal 534–5, *n586*
Mayfield, Ian 136
McCann, John, Dr *n124*
McClelland, David *n626*
McCreadie, John 21, 22, 23–5
McGrath, William 289
McHenry, Brian 421
McMartin case of alleged child abuse 88, 230–1
Mead, Daniel 240–1, 244, 309, 339
memories 111, 112
    false 112, 133, 226*, 583
    repressed and recovered 112, 131, 187, 225–6, 228, 229, 230, 249, 483, 497, 542, 546, *n171, 563, 593, 631*
Merseyside 5
    Formby 505, 506
Merseyside Police 466–7
    and *Panorama* programme 509
    trawling operations 3–4, 464, 490
    see also Operation Care
    You told me you loved me booklet 492–3
Millett, Peter 67–8
Mills, Liz 505, 506
Milroy-Sloan, Nadine *n84*
Milton, John
    Paradise Lost n625
Minotaur *n612*
Mitchell, Austin, MP 532
Mold, Clywd
    County (Shire) Hall 97–8, 103, 572
Mold County Court 123
Mold police station 104, 108, 109, *n147*
Mondale, Walter 85
Monmouth assizes 348–51, 353, 422–3
Montesquieu 536, *n587*
Moore, Chris
    The Kincora Scandal 290, 494–5
Moore, Lee 497
Moorov doctrine 351–2
moral crusaders 64–7, 219
Moran, Andrew
    at Tribunal 144, 156, 176, 199, 223, 225–6, 228, 436–42, 456
Morgan, Rhodri 3

Mormon Church 542
Morris, Geoffrey 523
Morris, Lord 360, 362
Morris, Ralph (principal of Castle Hill home) 83–4
Morris, Shane 480
Mullin, Chris, MP 532, *n571*
Mulpetre, Owen *n612*
   W. T. Stead Resource Site www.attackingthedevil.co.uk *n612*
multiple allegations 342, 348, 358, 363, 366, 368, 369–70, 371, 491, 581, 588, 591
multiple charges 348–50, 355, 368, 592
Munday, Bessie 346
murder, ritual 2
Myers, Sir Philip 76

Nathan, Debbie 85, *n117*
National Children's Home (NCH) 475, 476, 478–9
National Society for the Prevention of Cruelty to Children (NSPCC) 264, 265, 463, *n632*
   origins 559
   telephone helpline 209, 233, 263, 301, 469, *n311*
National Union of Public Employees Taylor writes to 76
NAYPIC (National Association of Young People in Care) 21–2, 26
Neath Farm School 266
Nelson, Dean 98, 572
   early career 20
   interviews Clements 24–5
   article on Tŷ Mawr 20–1, 23, 201
   commissioned to write article on Bryn Estyn 146
   investigation of Bryn Estyn 16, 22, 156, 161–3, 164–5, 166–8, 171–2, 174, 175–6, 178
   article in *Independent on Sunday* 15–19, 27–8, 78, 146, 183–4, 189, 200, 201, 202, 203–4, 205–7, 234, 264, 310, 390, 391–2
   meets Denis Parry 141–4
   writes to Taylor 144–5, 150, 265
   cooperating with Taylor 29, 146–8, 149, 153, 156–60, 161–5, 175–6, 180, 199, 275–6, 280

   and Tanner 146, 191, 315, *n195*
   meets Wilson 164–5, 166–8, 171–4, 175, 205, 320
   and Birley 182, 183, 187, 191–2, *n255, 257*
   interviews Wynne
     15 Nov. *1991* 179, 181, 223
     16 Nov. 184–8, 192, 262, *n255*
   sent to seek evidence to substantiate article 27–8, 156, 178, 250
     Feb. *1992* 251–2, *n325*
     Sept., with Taylor 276–80, 439, 440–1, 456, *n360, 365*
   seeks allegations against Anglesea 28, 250–3, 258–64, 265–73, 275–80, 281, 294, 439, *n360, n534*
   interviews Humphreys 256–64, 265, 274, 385, 386, 392, 393–4, 403–4, *n336, 337, 340, 342, 343, 344*
   Steward complains of harrassment by 267–8
   interviews Steward 268, 269–71, 272, 273–4, 275, *n351*
   fails to find Birley 275
   interviews John Evans *n247*
   police statements, *1992 n336, 337, 338, 340*
   1992 story rejected by *Independent* 281, 282–3
   story accepted by *Observer* 282–4
   and libel trial 386, 392, 393, 394–5, 398–9
   testimony to Tribunal 146, 183, 201, 263, 279–80, 281, 453, 454, *n336, 343*
   on Humphreys' death 401–2
   joins *Observer* 410
   letter to *New Statesman n255*
New Labour government 549
New Statesman n585
   Nelson's letter to *n255*
   Taylor writes to 252, *n205, 326*
New York police station 125
New York Radical Feminists 569–70
New Zealand 6, 546
Newcastle 531, 538
Newcastle City Council
   Shieldfield libel case 538, *n431*
News of the World 512–13

Newsnight (TV programme) 448

Newton, Tony

    Taylor writes to 76, 77,-8 145, 146

Nice, Geoffrey, QC *n343*

Noakes, David 115

Nolan, Jim 168

Norbertine order 543

Norman, Gerry 49–51, 52, *n65*

Norris, Margaret 94, 180

Norris, Stephen 16, 94, 95, 96, 97–8,
      117, 136, 184, 186, 190, 203,
      212–13, 228, 235, 269, 407, 464,
      466

    arrested 238, 239

Norris, Steven, MP 440

North Wales Police

    Taylor complains to, *1984* 41–2, 44,
      76, 197

    1984 inquiry into care homes
      (Gregson) 39, 41–2, 64

    1986–7 investigation of care homes
      (Owen) 42, 44–7, 53–5, 76–7, 93,
      123, 149, 155, 163, 164, 197, 202–3

    requested by CCC to investigate
      abuse in Clywd 102–3

    Taylor complains about 76, 95, 96,
      97, 98, 100, 197–200, 288, 436, *n71*

    allegations against 95, 142, 143, 144,
      193, 202, 206, 436

      of cover-up 16, 97, 99, 100,
        201–2, 206–7

      by *Independent* 412

      of masonry 287–8, 292, 436

      alleged paedophiles in 288, 289,
        400, 412, 436, 539

    1991–2 inquiry 3, 16, 50–2, 62–3,
      104, 121–7, 128–31, 136, 141,
      183, 198, 206–7, 216, 217–18,
      220, 221–2, 227–8, 231–3, 234,
      239–43, 268–9, 406–7, 437, 463,
      467, 514

    inquiries into Clwyd and
      Gwynedd homes amalgamated,
      with HOLMES computer 208

    training/briefing meeting 221–6,
      233

    Bryn Estyn helpline 208–9, 233,
      263, 301, 469, *n311*

    raid homes of former Bryn Estyn
      staff 237–8

    and Waite 241–2, 314–15

    Steward complains of harrassment
      to 267–8

    in HTV programme 286

    in *Observer* 288

    in *Private Eye* 292–3

    view of Taylor 307, 436–7, 441–2

    file on Anglesea 395–6, 397

    recommend prosecution of Anglesea
      307, 343, 438

    interview Howarth in prison about
      Anglesea 343, 373

    and Anglesea libel trial 400

    and Jillings report 413–14

    and Tribunal 436–8, 454

    see also names of officers

North Wales Police Authority

    Taylor writes to 76

North Wales Tribunal of Inquiry into
      Child Abuse xviii, 8, 9, 419–26,
      427–31, 436–42, 443–7, 448, 463,
      536, 540, 573, *n11*

    Taylor and instigation 29, 95, 156

    set up 254, 415–16

    and Anglesea libel trial *n516*

    cost 420*

    powers *n516*

    terms of reference 422

    Guardian on 432–3

    Connie Bew at 140

    opening address 370, 426, 427–31,
      445, 451, 458, *n508*

    'the random 600' 451–2

    Pauffley's closing address 445–6,
      447

    Saltrese protests about trawling
      444–5

    report *see Lost in Care*

    witnesses

      Ackerley 199–200, 221, 223–4,
        226, 382, *n190*

      Doughty 47

      Duke 212–13

      Ennis 74, *n108*

      Dewi Evans 68

      John Evans 444, 456

      Liz Evans 220

      Hands 219

      Hinton 222–3

      Holden 120

Howarth representation 420,
431–5, 452–3, 456, *n516, 517*
Margaret Humphreys 404
Lorraine Johnson 225–6
Peter Jones *n205*
Larry King 35
Nelson 146, 183, 201, 263,
279–80, 281, 453, 454, *n336, 343*
Owen *n80, 92*
Dennis Parry 96, 100, 141, 144
Phelan 73
Singer 123
Soper 138–9
Steward 265, 272–3, 378, 381, 430,
449, 457
Tanner 108, 110, 166–7, 218, 430,
454–5, *n113, 147, 323*
Taylor and 62, 148–9, 162, 163,
176–8, 265, 278–9, 280, 436–7,
439–41, 453, 454, 455–6, *n31, 39,
46, 113, 129, 221, 246, 371, 465*
Waite 314–15, 433–4
Isabel Williams 211–12
Wilson 172, 174, 321, *n240*
Young 169–70
Northern Echo newspaper 560, 564
Northern Ireland 543
Kincora hostel, East Belfast 289–90,
538, 547, 556
NORWAS (North Wales Abuse
Survivors) 429
Norwich
12th-century anti-semitism 2
Nottingham
satanic abuse allegations xvi, 87, 88,
89–90, 93
Joint Enquiry Team report 90, *n125*
Nova Scotia Department of Justice
7–8, *n9, 10*
Nova Scotia Residential Centre 6–7,
52–5
NSPCC *see* National Society for the
Prevention of Cruelty to Children
Nugent Care Society 464–6, 483, 485,
488, 499

Oates, Terry, DI 467, 468, 469–70, *n547,
553*
O'Brien, Rory, xix
Observer

and Press Complaints Commission
263, 403–4
on child abuse inquiry, 30 August
1992 281–2, *n371*
on NW Police, 6 Sept. 282
on Anglesea, 13 Sept. *1992* 283–5,
287, 392
Anglesea's reaction 383
on Steward and Bryn Estyn, 20
Sept. 284–5, 287–8
on paedophile ring, 27 Sept. 288,
n382
libel writ issued 295
Anglesea libel trial 379–99, 400,
403–4
article on Humphreys' death 401–3
letters to Press Complaints
Commission 403–4
and Tribunal 439
on Ayles 530
OCEAN (Official Campaign for Ending
Abuse Nationwide) 429
Oliver, Derek 170
O'Neill, Jack 578
O'Neill Marques, Francisco 547
Onley Young Offenders' Institute 22
Operation Antelope 237–8
Operation Bugle (Cheshire) 475,
476–82
Operation Care (Merseyside) 415,
490–8, 499–507, 515, *n145, 416, 571*
Operation Cleopatra (Greater
Manchester) 515
Operation Flight (Gwent) 514–15
Operation Gladio 143, *n188*
Operation Goldfinch (South Wales)
515, 516–19, 520–1, 522–3
Operation Granite (Cheshire) 465–75,
476, 489
Operation Lentisk (Devon) 515, 530–1
Operation Middleton 516
Operation React (Bristol and Avon)
515
Operation Rose (Northumberland)
515, 531
Oppenheim, Robin 279–80
Opus Dei 543, 555–6
'organised abuse' 89, 92, 96–7, 98, 161,
464, 540, 555–6
institutionalised 83–4

Orkneys 87, 88
Orwell, George, 291
Owen, David, Chief Constable 413–14,
    438
Owen, Gwynne, DCS 438
  early career 44
  conducts investigation of care in
      Gywnedd 44–7, 48–9, 51–2, 53–5,
      62–3, 77, 93, 123, 155, 163, 164,
      437
  1986 report to CPS 56, 70
  1987 report to CPS 63
  view of Dodd 70
  view of Taylor 56, 63
  Taylor complains of 163, 164
  at Tribunal *n80, 92*
Owen, John Tecwyn 283, 438
Oxford 531

paedophile rings, supposed xix, 161,
    200, 207, 283, 412, 415, 567–8
  in care homes 3, 5, 10, 29, 92, 93, 99,
      144, 414, 516, 538
    at Bryn Estyn 9, 16, 96, 99, 113,
        141, 184, 186, 198, 203, 208,
        237, 238, 376, 471, 514, 539, 540,
        572
    Cheshire 414, 471, 476, 480
    Headlands 518
  in *Independent* 410
  Kincora 289–90
  in Loveridge's letter to NW Police
      102–3
  and masons 289
  and Tribunal of Inquiry 458
  in *Observer* 284, 288
  Pembrokeshire *n506*
  and police 288, 289, 400, 412, 436,
      539
  in Portugal 547
  in *Private Eye* 292, 293
paedophiles 89, 536, 537–8, 569, *n3,*
    600
  convictions 582–3
Paisley, Ian 289, *n376a*
Pall Mall Gazette 559, 560, 561–4, *n612,*
    620, 622
Panorama 466, 467, 508–9, 511, *n559*
Parfitt, Steven 154, 155
Park House, Prestatyn 179

Parry, David Alan (GSS deputy director)
    32, 33, 34, 157, 159, 163, *n217*
Parry, Dennis (leader of Clwyd
      County Council) 193, 197, 200
    237, 283
  Taylor takes allegations to 95–7, 116,
      145, 153, *n129*
  meeting following Taylor's
      allegations 97, 98–9, 100, 102–3
  and Jillings panel 407, 408
  interviewed by Nelson 141–4
  in *Independent on Sunday* 16, 202–3,
      206, 436
  at Tribunal 96, 100, 141, 144
Partington, Tracy 49
patriarchy 569–71, *n631*
Pauffley, Anna 169, 445–6, 447
Pedro, Francisco 347–8
Pedroso, Paulo 547
Pembrokeshire
  alleged satanic abuse 88*, 495, *n506*
Percival, Brian 474, 521*
Perkins, William 65
Phelan, Christopher 22–3, 72, 73, 74,
    n106
Phillips, Roy 484, *n563*
physical abuse and assault 8, 53, 80,
    161, 407, 531
  battered child syndrome 85, 463
  chastisement 53, *n94*
  'hidden' 85
  Wilson charged with 309, 407,
      n388a
'Pindown' regime *n15*, 201
  report on 20, 94
Poliakov, Léon *n1*
police
  arrest by 586
  Campbell's criticism of 90
  child protection ethos and concern
      91–2, 93, 130
  child protection units 91–2
  conduct of inquiries 128
  contaminated evidence 93, 128
  evidence-based ethos 91
  habits of mind 128
  homophobia 92
  interviews *see* interviews, police
  and masculinity 91
  New York 125

pressures on 135, 206–7, 208, 222, 225, 233, 235
scepticism about allegations 90, 130, 220, 228, 234
social workers, conflict with 93
statements 104, 486–7
   negative 235
stations 468–9
   see also names of stations
targeting by 135
traditional operations 128
trawling operations *see separate entry*
see also Cheshire Police; Merseyside Police; North Wales Police
Police and Criminal Evidence Act *n57*
Police Complaints Authority 283, 307
   Taylor writes to 76
Police Federation 294–5
pornography 93, 161–4, 206
   of righteousness 564
   snuff films 93
Portugal 6, 546–8, 556
Poulson, John 292
Pounders, Judge William 88
Powell, Colin 101, 256
power
   of accusation 131
   of moral crusader 64–6
Press Complaints Commission
   and *Observer* 263, 403–4, *n386*
presumption of innocence 85, 344, 352, 507, 548–9, 584–5
Price, John 403
prisoners 586
   interviewing 468–9, 487, *n553*
   parole *n144*
Private Eye 88
   editorship 290, 291–2
   Paul Foot in 290–1
   story on Anglesea 292–4, 383–4, 440, 539
   libel claims against 295
   Steward demands payment 375–8, 387
   libel trial 379–99, 400
   on Tribunal 62, 439–41
projection 1, 2, *n1*
'propensity evidence' 344–5
prosecution, court
   delayed 581–2

multiple charges 348–50, 355, 368, 592
'similar fact' evidence 311, 315
prostitution 561, 564, 566, *n612*
   child 559, 560, 562, 564, 565, *n612*
Protestants 557
   radical *n626*
psychiatrists 583
   convicted of indecent assaults *n645*
psychoanalysis 571, *n626*
   see also Freud, Sigmund
psychologists 85, 228, 231, 569
Public Inquiries into Abuse of Children in Residential Care 429, 430
Pullman, Philip
   His Dark Materials and apocalyptic fantasy *n625*
Puritanism 65–6, 559, 565, 569, 571, 585
Purnell, Nick 243, 309, 340

Queen's Park community home, Holyhead 71–5
Queen's Park Estate, Wrexham 97, 255, 276

R v Ananthanarayanan n645
R v B 583–4, 592
R v Bailey 348–51, 356, 422–3
R v H 370, *n645*
R v Howarth 309–341
R v Jefferies 359
R v LPB 581–2
R v OGD 591
R v P 364–6, 367, 368–70
R v Sims 354–6, 357, 358–9, 360, 361, 362, 364, 365, 588, 589
R v Smith 346, 350, 357, 364, 367
Rabbitte, Pat 543
Raftery, Mary 544–5
Randles, Brendan 246–9, 250, 251–3, 335, *n322*, 326
   in Bryn Estyn 246, 248
   allegations against Howarth 247, 248–9, 252, 253
   death 253, 254, 307, 410
'the random 600' 451–2
Rantzen, Esther 302, 459
rape, allegations of *n84*
Raphael, Adam 291, 292

rationalism 1, 558, 573
Rayfield, John xix, 322, *n39*
  and Howarth 339, 340, 372
  and Tribunal 425, 453
rebellion, adolescent 131–2
Reed, Dawn xix, 538, *n431*, *590*
Reeves, Robin 5, 531
Regan, Simon *n592*
religion 557–60, 568, 571
  see also Christianity; Puritanism
religious orders 544–5, 546
remand *n150*
repression ('blocking') 229, 230, *n305*,
  631
  see also memories / repressed and
  recovered
Residential Institutions Redress Board
  of Ireland 545–6, *n7*
Reynolds, Albert 543
Richards, Rod 410
righteousness 64–6, 75
  pornography of 564
Risley remand centre 266
Ritto, Jorge 547
ritual abuse 2, 85
  see also satanic abuse and cults
ritual murder 2
Robbins, John, D/Supt 490, 491–3,
  497–8, 499–501, *n416*
Roberts, Anthea 529
Roberts, Barbara 97
Roberts, Gillian 46–7, 437, *n56, 67*
Roberts, Graham 168
Roberts, John 152
  allegations against 145, 146–7, 148,
    150, 151, *n152, 211*
    Harbour's 48–9, 51, 52
    Mason's 41–2, 45
    Tanner's 105, 107, 109–10, 112,
    455, *n152*
Roberts, Wyn, MP
  Taylor writes to 76
Robinson, Henry *n46*
Robinson, Keith 496
Rochdale 87, 88
Rogers, Byron 425, *n506*
Rogers, Heather 379
Rogers, John, QC 191, 313, 318, 336,
  372
Roiphe, Katie 571*

Roman Catholic Church 542, 543
Rose, David xix, 282–3, 496, 532
  and Garsden 495
  and Shuttleworth 474, *n559*
  and trawling 508–9
  on Ayles 530
Rough Justice (TV programme) 104
Rowett, Arthur 519
Rowlands, DI 197, 267
Royal Courts of Justice, London 377,
  381
Royal Ulster Constabulary 289
RTE broadcasting station 543–5
Rumsfeld, Donald 585–6
Rush, Florence 569–70, 571, *n631*
Rutherford, Gill 531
Rutter, Fred 203
  arrested and released 98, 403
  further investigations 98, 102
  tried and sentenced, *1991* 104, *n132,*
    144
  released on parole *n144*
Ryan, Jim 473
Ryder, Ernest, QC 497, *n46, 221*

Sachs, Mr Justice 548–9
sacrifice 2, 230, *n506*
St Aidan's community home, Widnes
  483–7, *n563*
St George's community home,
  Formby 499–505, 510, 513, 534, *n571*
St Vincent's, Formby 464, 490
St Vincent's Industrial School,
  Goldenbridge 543–4
Salem 536
Salmon, Lord 360, 445
Salmon Commission 423, 445
Saltrese, Chris 500–1
  and Soper 137, 508*, *n559*
  Martell's letter to 168, 169, 224, 444
  and Tribunal of Inquiry 443–4
    complains re trawling 443–4, 511
  and Hoskin 485–8, 503
  speaks to FACT 507
  and Shuttleworth *n559*
Saltrese, Nick 443, 485, 500, 503–4, 506
Salvation Army 560, 564
Sankey, Lord 362
Saskatchewan Law Society *n8*
Satan *see* Devil, the

satanic abuse and cults, supposed 2,
   555, 567, *n122*
   in America 87, 88, 201, 538, 541,
      n117
   in Britain 88–90, 92, 464, 497, 537,
      541
   in Middle Ages 2, 537
   Lee Moore as victim of 497
   Newcastle 538
   Nottingham xvi, 87, 88, 89–90, 93
      Joint Enquiry Team report 90,
         n125
   Pembrokeshire 88*, 425, *n506*
   scepticism re 88–90, 130, *n122*
   South Wales 523
   see also 'organised abuse'
Saunders, Gail xix, 520
Scallywag (magazine) *n592*
Schiltz, Patrick 542
Scott, Richard 516–17
Scott, Sara *n122*
Scottish law 351–2
Seamark, Michael 508
Searle, Barrie
   at Tribunal 112, 139, 443
Selby, Michael 516–17
sexual abuse
   allegations of 4–5
      attitude towards 130, 489
      held as special category at
         Tribunal 449–50
      trawling for *see* trawling
         operations, police
   of children *see* child sexual abuse
   'Coping With Sexual Abuse' leaflet
      480
   County Council advice about 84
   see also denial; allegations / false;
      'organised abuse'; ritual abuse;
      satanic abuse and cults
sexual relationships, illicit, alleged 142
Shalders, Andy 508
Shaldon, James 106, 116, 117, 136
Shaw, George Bernard *n622*
Sheffield 30, 31
Shelburne Youth Centre, Nova Scotia
   6–7
Sherrer, Hans 586
Shieldfield nursery, Newcastle xix, 538,
   n431, 590

Shore, Bonnie 123
Shropshire County Council 84
Shuttleworth, Irene 473, 474
Shuttleworth, Roy 473–4, 509, 521,
   522–3, *n559*
Silcott, Winston 15
Silverbrook Treatment Centre,
   Pontypridd 158, 160, *n217*
Silvino, Carlos 547
similar allegations 311, 315, 346–7, 350,
   363, 367–8
similar fact evidence 311, 315, 334, 338,
   342-378, 581, 587–91, *n645*
   and admissibility 345, 350, 356, 358,
      361, 363, 368, 370-1, 589–90, *n645*
   and allegations, 350-2,
   and 'brides in the bath' 346, 350,
      357, 364, 367
   and buggery 357-8
   'a cause common to the witnesses'
      368, 587, 590
   and child sexual abuse 366-7, 370-1
   and collusion 334-7, 350, 589–90,
      363-5, 366, 368-9, *n* 645
      'indirect collusion'. 494
   and concoction 361, 588–91
      separate concoction, 590-1
   and contamination 334, 337-8, 350,
      361, 363-4, 371, 521, 590, 591,
      n645
      striking similarities 368-9
   and 'corroboration by volume'
      334
   and exclusionary principle 345
   and 'forbidden reasoning' 344-5
   'hallmark-of-vice' approach 365-6
   and homosexuality, 357-9, 360-2,
      588
   Home Affairs Committee
      recommendations 533
   and identity, 366-7
   and improbability 345, 589
   and incest 364-9
   Moorov doctrine 351-2
   and 'no-smoke-without-fire
      principle' 334
   and prejudice 311, 315, 342, 344, 348,
      352, 355, 357-9, 361-2, 364, 367,
      369, 511, 533, 549, 583, 587,
      588–90, 592,

similar fact evidence *cont.*
 and presumption of innocence 344,
  352, 359, 507, 531, 548–9
 and probative force 324, 344, 356–9,
  361–2, 367–70, 589–90, *n645*
 and propensity evidence 344, 355
 and Scottish courts 351–2
 'similar allegation' evidence 347,
  363, 587
similar fact principle 345–7, 581,
  587–93
  Denning and the destruction of
   354–9
  destruction of and police trawling
   371
  destruction of and witch-hunts
   370–1, 587
  child sexual abuse as *crimen*
   exceptum 370–1
  'striking similarities' 356–7, 360–2,
   365–70, 533, 588
  and copy-cat allegations 369
  and identity 366–7
  as safeguard against
   contamination 368–9
  Colin Tapper on 367, *n431*
  'The erosion of Boardman' 366*
  threshold of admissibility 350, 358,
   368
  CASES CHRONOLOGICALLY
   Makin 345, 350, 356, 357, 361, 364
   Smith (Brides in Bath) 346, 350,
    357, 364, 367
   Thompson 360
   Bailey 348–51, 356, 422–3
   Sims 354–6, 357, 358, 359, 360,
    361, 362, 364, 365
   Jefferies 359
   Kilbourne 363
   Boardman 360–2, 363, 366, 367,
    368, 369, 533, 587, 588–9, 591
   Hoch 589–91
   DPP v P 311, 364, 366, 367, 368,
    369–70
   Ananthanarayanan n645
   R v H 370, *n645*
   OGD 591
similar offences, charges of 355–6
Sims, George, trial and appeal of
 354–6, 357, 358, 359, 360, 361, 362,
  364, 365
sinfulness *n626*
Singer, Andrew 116–17
 Tanner names as victim of Howarth
  106
 Taylor names as victim 175–6
 Wynne names as victim 181
 possible collusion with Tanner 127
 police statements 118–20, 122,
  123–6, 128–9, 223
 allegations against Birch 237
 allegations against Howarth 118–20,
  122, 304, 317, 329, 330–3
  concerning vibrators 119, 223
  that Howarth made phone calls
   to him 126
 claim re Bonnie Shore 122
 conviction for attempting to pervert
  the course of justice 123, 320
 sentence for child abuse 122–3, 320
 and Howarth / Wilson trial 309,
  317–20, 328–9, 330–4, 339
  court verdicts on 339, 340
 testimony to Tribunal 123
Sisters of Charity 544
Sisters of Mercy 544
Smith, Alice 346
Smith, Danny 477, 478–80, 481
Smith, George Joseph 346, 356, 357,
 361, 364
Smith, Gerrilyn 408
Smith, Sean 61
Smith, Simon 519
Smith's, W. H. 564
Smyth, Brendan
Snedeker, Michael 85, *n117*
snuff films 93
social services departments 484
 allegations against 203, 227–8
  of cover-ups 41, 44, 45, 75, 99,
   101, 102
 trawling by *n645*
 see also Clwyd Social Services;
  community homes; Gwynedd
  Social Services
social workers 3, 83, 84, 89, 90–1, 92,
 94, 95, 228, 231, 529, 567, 569,
 573
 'believe the children' precept 86–7,
  125

and allegations *v* care workers 94
police, conflict with 93
prejudice against 522
press 96
    see also Community Care
revivalist culture 91
seize children from families *n506*
in trawling operations 469–70, 472,
    479
Society for Prevention of Cruelty to
    Children (SPCC) 559, *n620*
solicitors 4, 305, 573
Sons of Glyndwr 144
Soothill, Keith *n84*
Soper, Justin 136–40, 237
South Africa 548
South Wales Police Force 515, 516–19,
    520
    Operation Goldfinch 515, 516–19,
    520–1, 522–3
Soviet Union 550–1
Stacey, Debbie 296
Stafford Crown Court 364
Staffordshire
    Pindown regime 15, 94, 201, *n15*
Stalin 551
Stalker, John 102
State v Coetzee 548–9
States of Fear (RTE broadcast) 544
statistics 550–1
Stead, W. T. 463, 559–66, 567, 568, 569,
    571, *n541, 620*
    'The Maiden Tribute of Modern
    Babylon' 559, 562–4, 565, *n612*
    tried for child abduction 566, *n622*
    W. T. Stead Resource Site
    www.attackingthedevil.co.uk *n612*
Steward, Jane 266, 268, 449
Steward, Lee 253, 265–74, 343
    early life 265–6
    at Bryn Estyn 244–5, 273
        dates 273
    and Cooke 266, 284–5, 376
    allegation against Kenyon 287–8
    marriage 266
    Nelson approaches 266–7
    complains of harrassment by Nelson
    267–8, 395
    denies having been abused by
        Anglesea 267–8, 273, 391, 394–5

Nelson interviews 268, 269–71, 272,
    273–4, 275, *n351*
makes allegations against Anglesea
    270–4, 284, 285–7, 288, 391–2, 395
statements to police, *1992*
    March 244–5, 265, 269, 387–8,
        394–5
    April 269
    Sept. 271–2
    Nov. 272
allegation against 'Claire' 304
swears affidavit 281
in *Observer* 284–5, 287–8
in HTV programme 286–7, 296,
    297–8, 383
in *Private Eye* 293, 294
demands payment from *Private Eye*
    295, 375–8, 387
as potential witness 307
Anglesea libel trial 380, 381, 383,
    385, 386–8, 392, 394–5, 398
and Tribunal 265, 272–3, 378, 381,
    430, 449, 457
Storr, Anthony, xv
Strettle, Barry 507
Stritch, Len 168
'striking similarities' 356–7, 360–2,
    365–70, 533, 588
Strudwick, Linda 530
suicide, publicity re 24–5, 548
Summit, Roland 86
Sumner, Lord 357–8, 360
Sun newspaper 457
Sunday Sport 392
Sunday Telegraph n506
Surtees, Ian 235, 309, 340
Sussams, Robert 45, 53–4, *n67*
Swansea Crown Court 5, *n506*
Swansea Prison 20, 23–4, 335, 336, 337

Tanner, Ryan 133, 136
    early life 37–8, *n150*
    character 216, 577–8
        zeal and crusading spirit 107,
        219–20
    at Tŷ'r Felin 18, *n150*
        makes allegations against *n538*
    in Bryn Estyn 38–9, 79–80, 106–7,
        215–16, 217–18, 220, 577–8
    and funeral for baby jay 215–16

Tanner, Ryan *cont.*
  Arnold writes of 38–9
  Dodd's reports on 38, 110, *n43*
  after leaving Bryn Estyn 216, 218,
      245
  in Y Gwyngyll 106, 107, 216, *n43*
  to TV researchers 111, 145, *n113*
  contacted by Taylor and Yorkshire
      TV 79–80
  statement to police, *1991* 104–13,
      116, 117, 119, 127, 128–9, 140
    attempt to make statement at
        Bangor 108–9, *n147*
  allegations against Roberts 105, 107,
      109, 110, 112, 455, *n152*
  and Nelson 146, 191, 315, *n195*
  approaches Wilson 165–7, 320, 321
  Wilson speaks of 174
  contacts Birley 191–2, 315, 335
  in Nelson's *1991* article 206, *n538*
  in Wrexham press 214
  compensation claim 214, 219, 222,
      n287
  and Howarth 106–7, 239
  and Randles 246–9
  relations with Wynne 215–20, 251–2
    at Bryn Estyn 215–16, 217
    Wynne attacks with bayonet 216
  at Howarth's trial 335
  and Tribunal 108, 110, 166–7, 218,
      430, 454–5, *n113, 147, 323*
  in press after Tribunal 456, 457
  in *2004* 577
Tapper, Colin, Prof. 366*, 367, *n431*
Taylor, Alan 101
Taylor, Alison 28, 63, 540–1
  early life 29–30
  character, motives and sense of
      mission 64, 112–13
  deputy / acting officer-in-charge,
      Tŷ'r Felin 18, 29, 31, 32–5, 69,
      77–8, 158, 199
    complaints about her 60–1, *n67*
  at College to obtain CQSW 35, 40,
      69
  placement at Bryn Estyn 17, 29, 35,
      36–9, 40, 79–80, 94, 161, 175–7,
      187
    entry in Bryn Estyn log book on
        leaving 37, 439, *n246*

  'Perceptions of Care' *n39*
  officer-in-charge at Tŷ Newydd
      40–1, 51, 59, 154–5
    complaints about her 43–4, 53,
        60–1
  relations with Dodd 33, 34–5, 38,
      40, 43–4, *n67*
  given disciplinary warning 43
  complains to police, *1984* 41–2, 44,
      76, 197
  Gregson writes of 42
  approaches Cllr Marshall 44–5
  statement and letter to police, *1986*
      45–7, 48, *n71*
  DCS Owen's view of 56, 63
  and statement sent to Gwynedd
      officials 57
  and Hannah Thomas 62–3
  suspended by GCC 61
  dismissed by GCC 64, 202, 206, 282
  writes letters to politicians 76, 77–8
    to DPP 77, *n111*
  and Yorkshire TV 79
  takes allegations to Dennis Parry
      95–7, 99–100, 116, 145, 153, *n129*
  complains about NW Police 76, 95,
      96, 97, 98, 100, 163, 164, 197–200,
      288, 436, *n71*
  NW Police view of 42, 63, 307,
      436–7, 441–2
  and Tanner's statement 107–9, *n147*
  Nelson writes to 144–5, 150
  on HTV 28, 145
  cooperates with Nelson 29, 146–8,
      149, 153, 156–60, 161–5, 175–6,
      178, 180, 181, 182, 192, 199, 265,
      282, 275–6
  writes to home secretary 200
  in Nelson's *1991* article 17, 202, 204
  statement re Birley 189–90
  in contact with Birley 192
  searches for Birley 275, 280
  D/Supt Ackerley visits and cautions
      193
  Ackerley interviews 200
  writes to *New Statesman* 252, *n205,*
      329
  with Nelson interviewing Wynne,
      1992 276–80, 439, 440–1, 456,
      n360, 365

Taylor, Alison *cont.*
  interviewed by police under caution
    277, 441
  in *Observer, 1992* 282
  correspondence with CPS about
    Howarth's trial 306–7
  awards 439–40, 459
  and Tribunal 62, 148–9, 162, 163,
    176–8, 265, 278–9, 280, 436–7,
    439–41, 453, 454, 455–6, *n31, 39,
    46, 113, 129, 221, 246, 371, 465*
  in media following Tribunal of
  Inquiry 457, 458, 459, 540
  novels by 28–9
  ALLEGATIONS MADE OR RELAYED BY
    28, 29, 39, 44–7, 48, 49, 53–5,
    70, 75, 76–80, 83, 94, 108, 140,
    141, 142, 145, 149–50, 155, 156–
    60, 161, 175–8, 181, 197, 436–7
    of assault on boy by Tŷ'r Felin
      teacher 40–1
    against Anglesea 288, 306, 373,
      374–5, 439
    about Bryn Estyn 98, 183, 373–4,
      375
    against Dodd 18, 44, 45–6, 48, 77,
      96, 98, 145, 146–52, 154, 161,
      175, 206, 437, *n211*
    that he invoked Anglesea as
      threat 143, 198–200, 251
    that he kept pornography
      161–3
    'Gwynedd County Council
      Analysis' (dossier) 98, 153–5,
      156, 163, 164, 175, 179, 180, 192,
      200, 251, *n147*
    against Howarth 175–7, 180, 306,
      374–5
    concerning Wynne 179–80, 184,
      185–6, 189, 204, 276–80
Taylor, Barton 295
  Anglesea libel trial 380
Taylor, Geoffrey 43, 77
  marriage to Alison 30–1
  letters to press as 'James Browne'
    58–9, 87
Templeton, Harry 95, 142, 182
Thatcher, Margaret
  Taylor's letter to 76, 77, 78, 150
'therapeutic' interviews 225–8

therapists 85, 89, 230, 231, 269
Thomas, Hannah 61–3, 67
Thomas, Michael 46–7, 437
Thomas of Gresford, Lord *n603*
Thorpe, Jeremy 292
Times Educational Supplement 497
trauma, unrecognised 85
trawling operations, police 3–4, 5, 128,
    133–4, 135–6, 220, 225, 311, 342,
    370, 371, 443, 463–4, 466, 491–3,
    517, 521–2, 531, 550, 552, 573,
    n580 , 645
  appeal court comments on 534–5,
    n586
  become national 513–16, 540
  costs 4, 592, *n5*
  dangers 130–1
  FACT oppose 506–7
  House of Commons debates 536
  'mushrooming effect' 493, 494, 514
  'mushrooming technique' 493–4,
    501
  public criticism of 508–9, 510–11,
    531–5
  safeguards recommended 532–3
  Saltrese expresses concern about at
    Tribunal 443–5
  and similar fact principle 591–2
  statistics 550–1
  You told me you loved me booklet
    492–3
  NAMES OR SUBJECTS
    Antelope 237–8
    Bugle (Cheshire) 475, 476–82
    Care (Merseyside) 415, 490–8,
      499–507, 515, *n145, 416, 571*
    Castle Hill 83
    Cheshire 443
      Granite 465–75, 476, 489
    Cleopatra (Greater Manchester)
      515
    Flight (Gwent) 514–15
    Gladio 143, *n188*
    Goldfinch (South Wales) 515,
      516–19, 520–1, 522–3
    Hadfield 525–8
    Hoskin 484–9, 493, *n553, 563*
    Hudson 479–82
    David Jones 504, 507, 508,
      509–10, 511, 512–13

Kincora 289
Lentisk (Devon) 515, 530–1
Middleton 516
Pembrokeshire 88*, 495, n506
React (Bristol and Avon) 515
Rose (Northumberland) 515, 531
Rutter 98
Traynor, Des 494
Treasury Solicitor's Department 421
Treverton-Jones, Mr (junior counsel to
North Wales Tribunal of Inquiry)
451
Tribunals of Inquiry 416, 419, 423–5,
429, n513
see also Bloody Sunday Tribunals;
North Wales Tribunal of Inquiry
into Child Abuse
truth 129
see also lies
Tunstill, Jane 407–8
Turton, Ed 136
Tŷ Mawr children's home,
Abergavenny 22
suicide and 24–5
Independent story on, *1991* 20–1, 201
photograph published 20, 26
riot 21, 26
inquiry into 21–6, 27, 380
Ennis sent to 71–3
1998 investigation 514–15
Tŷ Newydd, Bangor 48, 56
Taylor officer-in-charge at 40–1, 51,
59, 154–5
staff complain about 60–1
Tŷ'r Felin Assessment Centre, Bangor
31–2, 57–8, 60, 67–70, 71
Taylor deputy / acting officer-in-
charge at 18, 29, 31, 32–5, 69,
77–8, 157–60, 199
complaints about Taylor 60–1, n67
under Dodd 33, 34–5, 38, 40, 54,
67–70, 96, 105–6, 110–11, 154,
437–834–5, 198–9
Taylor's allegations against 40–2,
45–7, 48–9, 51–2, 77–9, 145,
146–50, 436, 437, 454
that girls were abused there
157–60
Tanner at 18, 37, 38, 105–6, 109–11,
n150

Tanner's allegations against 105,
107, 109, 110, 112, 455, n538
Hannah Thomas's allegations
against 61–2
Daily Mail on 57
Yorkshire TV investigates 78–9
HTV programme on, *1991* 28, 145,
149, 150, 151, 157, 208, 282, 285,
406
Independent on Sunday allegations
against 18, 78
inquiry into 41–2, 48–51, 208,
436–7, n205
and Tribunal 42, 436–7, 454, 455

Unison n497
United States of America 6, 84–7, 88,
90, 91, 92, 226, 229–30, 542, 556,
n124
New York police station 125
New York Radical Feminists 569–
70
University of East Anglia, xv
Updike, John 557
Urry, Alan 466
Utting, Sir William 549

Varley, Jenny 525, 527
Venture, The, Wrexham youth club 97,
101, 102, 255–6
Verkaik, Robert
in *Independent* 582–3
vice rings *see* paedophile rings
'victims' 584
Victor, Geoffrey 431, n513
violence, state 585–7

Waite, Gary 309
police statement 241–2, 314–15
at Howarth's trial 312–14, 315
at Tribunal 314–15, 433–4
Wakefield prison 343, 359, 372–3
Walmer, Mark 525–6, 527
Walton Prison, Liverpool 486
Coates in n561
Hoskin in 488
Howarth in 372
Hudson in 480
Singer in 122
Walzer, Michael 65

Warrington police station 476
Waterhouse, Sir Ronald 432
  in appeal court 425, *n506*
  Chairman of Tribunal 8, 148–9, 416,
      419–22, 424, 433–4, 442, 446–7,
      448, 451, 454, *n516*
    and Saltrese 443–4
Waterhouse, Rosie xvi, 16, 88, 448,
    n122
Waterhouse report *see Lost in Care*
Waugh, Benjamin 463, 559, 563–4,
    568, 569, *n541, 620*
Webster, Alistair, QC
  at North Wales Tribunal of Inquiry
      443, *n326*
Webster, Sir Richard, QC 566
Welsh Assembly 410
Welsh floods, *1990* 302
Welsh Office 408
West, Martin 214, 309, 339
  police visit in prison 209
  possible collusion with Duke 210,
      213, 335, 336–7, 340, 357
White, James 472
Whitehead, David 467
Whitman, Howard *n3*
Widgery, Lord 424
Wilberforce, Lord 360, 363, 367, 368,
    588–9
Wilby, Peter 19, *n585*
Williams, David 145, 285, 404
Williams, Florence 62
Williams, G. R. 438
Williams, Gareth, QC (later Lord
    Williams of Mostyn) 509
  investigates Tŷ Mawr 21–2, 23–5, 514
  Anglesea libel trial 296, 380–2, 385,
      387–9, 391–8
Williams, Isabel 211, 242, 327
  at Tribunal 211–12
  Waite speaks of 241–2, 313
  Wynne speaks of 217
Williams-Rigby, Basil 502–3, 504–5,
    506
  appeal 533–4
  on *BBC* radio 534
Wilson, Paul
  career and character 167
  criminal record 167
  comes to Bryn Estyn 167

  allegations made against 119, 124,
      125–6, 157, 167, 170, 176–7,
      235, 237, 240
    by Martell 168–9
  and Tanner 166–7, 320, 321
  and Nelson 164–5, 166–8, 171–3,
      174, 175, 186, 205
  allegations against Howarth and
      Bryn Estyn 171, 172–3, 174, 175,
      320–1
  allegations against Dodd 172, 174,
      186, 320, 321, *n240*
  arrested 171, 238, 239
  trial (with Howarth) 309–41
    comes to believe Howarth
        innocent 321–2
    in judge's summing-up 328–38
    verdicts 339–40
  charged with physical assaults 309,
      407, *n388a*
  at Tribunal 172, 321, 420, *n241*
witch-hunts xv, 1, 2, 9–10, 370–1,
    536–7, 539–40, 541, 552, 556, 573–4,
    556, 573–4, *n1*
witnesses 135–6
  child *n620*
  'coaching' 193
  corroborative 351
  experts in fabrication 129–30
  management of 193, 262, 263
  plausibility 449–50
  suggestibility 130, 225
  unavailable 582
  see also interviews, police
Woffinden, Bob xix, 502, 508, 532,
    n562, 575, 590
Wolmar, Christian 466, 472, 492
  chairs ACAL conference 497
  Forgotten Children 492, *n543*
Woodcock, Frank 58
Woodlands unit, Danesford 477–9
Woods, David 473
Woolf, Lord 450, 582–5, 587, 592
*Working Together Under the Children Act
    1989* 89, 91, *n123*
World at One (BBC) 3
Worrall, Mrs 49–50
Wragg, Mandy 79, 151, *n205*
Wrexham, Clwyd 193, 216, 250–1, 255,
    259, 268, 275–6, 302, 464, 577

newspaper 214
see also Bryn Estyn Community
    Home; Gatewen Hall School;
    Queen's Park estate; Venture, The
Wrexham attendance centre 273
Wrexham College, Cartrefle branch
    35, 40
Wrexham golf course 296, 297, 316,
    317
Wrexham police station 303
Wyatt, Geoffrey, Dr 231
Wymott Prison 151
Wynne, Peter
    early life 179
    in Bryn Estyn 179–80, 181, 184–8,
        214–18, 219
        loss of budgerigar 215
    relations with Tanner 215–20, 251–2
        at Bryn Estyn 215–16, 217
        attacks Tanner with bayonet 216
    career after Bryn Estyn 216
    Taylor speaks of to Nelson 180,
        189
    Taylor's allegations concerning
        179–80, 184, 185–6, 189, 191, 204,
        276–80
    and Birley 189, 190, 192, 202
    speaks of Anglesea 276–7, 439, *n360*
    Nelson interviews
        15 Nov. *1991* 179, 181, 223
        16 Nov. 184–8, 192, 262, *n255*
        Feb. *1992* 251–2, *n325*

Sept., with Taylor 276–80, 439,
    440–1, 456, *n360, 365*
statements to police
    1991 180–1, 217, 219, 223
    1992 189, 191, 217–18, 219, 234
    1993 n360
allegations against Birch 217–18,
    308
allegations against Howarth 185–8,
    190–1, 203–4, 234, 276, 310, *n360*
in Nelson's *1991* article 203
in Wrexham press, *1991* 214
compensation claim 214, 219
marriage 307–8
death 254, 308, 335, 404–5, 410
Wyre, Ray 468

Xavieria, Sister 544

Y Gwyngyll, Llanfairpwll, Anglesey
    48, 49–51, 52, 197–8
    Tanner in 106, 107, 216, *n43*
York Crown Court 521
Yorkshire Television 95, 145, 151
    investigates Tŷ'r Felin 78–9
    on Castle Hill 83, 103
    and Peter Jones *n205*
    and Tanner 110, *n113*
You told me you loved me booklet 492–3
Young, Norman 169–70

Zeitlin, Harry, Dr 231

Cold light on the childr

Britain's biggest abuse inquiry begins: 650 cases, up to 80 staf

Witnesses tell of child abuse at Welsh home

By Roger Dobson

The first witnesses in the North Wales child abuse inquiry told yesterday how they were physically abused at a children's home when they were teenagers and how difficult it was to explain.

...sent to th... now-closed ...cord...

...ing evidence about ab... about c... cases ...ey ...placed there because ... suffered sexual, or ... abuse within their fam...

But many of them we... difficult to handle bec... their experiences, and the... cusations were not believ...

DI Oates said: "The ...ubt that in that period ... dents ... was at its height.

Pédophilie : la Grande-Bretagne découvre à son tour l'horreur.

Derrière les portes de Bryn Estyn, le cauchemar de l'enfance

S/...

...the officers int... ...abuse and assaults when police were asked by council staff to 'help discipline' unruly children in care.

The disclosure comes amid mounting evidence that the abuse had been covered up for years. A former North Wales police authority chairman yesterday claimed that attempts to ...nch a full inquiry six years ...ad been stifled deliberately ...rials.

...uncillors and execu...

...ed victims of the scandal, which *The Observer* has seen, give a terrifying litany of beatings and sexual abuse. The statements, taken independently over many months, suggest the existence of a culture of violence in which abuse had become an accepted norm.

A boy, 14, described beating by a policeman at a home near Bangor: 'He was called in by th... teacher to make me ... con... downstairs although I had be... told I could stay in m... room. Because ... dragge... alo...

Report of the Tribunal of Inquiry into the abuse of children in care in the former county council areas of Gwynedd and Clwyd since 1974

Lost in Care

Summary of Report with Conclusions and Recommendations in full

---

24 YEARS ON
..THE BROKEN VICTIMS

12 people have died over this and they deserve justice..

...s. I was ...an office... ...d com... ...t was a... ...uddle. ...

...h a win... ...be picke... ...aken b... ...rs what ... ...d that it ...

...ne disrup... ...r and lour... When he ... ...e had beco... ...e was bein... ...tyn.

...e joking ...e Coldit... ...hat. I ra... ...l me.'

BRITAIN'S WORST
BRITAIN'S WORST
HOMES

By ADRIAN SHAW, STEPHEN WHITE and PAUL BYRNE

THEY were meant to protect the most vulnerable — instead they raped, beat, bullied and abused.

Hidden among the 480,000 words of the ...Waterhouse report into ...care scandal are the ...man who over...

PETER HOWARTH, 65, deputy head of Bryn Estyn children's home in Clwyd, now Flintshire. He took his favourites home four times a week for sex for up ... caught. He was ...lf years and ...sc...

The child entered the system bewildered, a... left it brutalised, sexually damaged, abandon...

men at ce... ...h of ab...

The 'Colditz of care': The former Bryn Estyn children's home in North Wales

...within days ...ally assaulted by ...e later lived in Wrex-

Howarth at the age o... rapes continued until he le... home as a 16-year-old alcoholic. In adult life, he suffered from drunken

...ing petrol ...and trying to ignite it. In 1995, he hanged himself.

in 1994 at the age ... ROBERT CHA... death from a railw...

In my dreams, I hear the screa...

Why did it take 14 years, asks whistleb...

WITH ...